THE GREGG

REFERENCE MANUAL

Sixth Canadian Edition

William A. Sabin

Wilma K. Millar
Southern Alberta Institute of Technology

Sharon L. Sine
Southern Alberta Institute of Technology

G. Wendy Strashok
Southern Alberta Institute of Technology

 **McGraw-Hill Ryerson**

Toronto Montréal Boston Burr Ridge, IL Dubuque, IA Madison, WI
New York San Francisco St. Louis Bangkok Bogotá Caracas
Kuala Lumpur Lisbon London Madrid Mexico City Milan
New Delhi Santiago Seoul Singapore Sydney Taipei

McGraw-Hill
Ryerson Limited

*A Subsidiary of The **McGraw·Hill** Companies*

The Gregg Reference Manual
Sixth Canadian Edition

ISBN: 0-07-089166-4

1 2 3 4 5 6 7 8 9 10   TCP   0 9 8 7 6 5 4 3

Printed and bound in Canada.

Care has been taken to trace ownership of copyright material contained in this text; however, the publisher will welcome any information that enables them to rectify any reference or credit for subsequent editions.

Vice President and Editorial Director: Patrick Ferrier
Sponsoring Editor: James Buchanan
Developmental Editor: Darren Hick
Marketing Manager: Sharon Loeb
Copy Editor: Wayne Herrington
Production Coordinator: Madeleine Harrington
Page Layout: Bookman Typesetting Co.
Cover Design: Greg Devitt
Cover Image Credit: © Artville
Printer: Transcontinental Printing

National Library of Canada Cataloguing in Publication
Gregg reference manual / William A. Sabin . . . [et al.]. — 6th Canadian ed.
Includes index.
ISBN 0-07-089166-4
1. English language—Business English.   2. English language—Grammar.
3. Commercial correspondence.   I. Sabin, William A.

PE1116.S6G3 2002   808'.06665   C2002-901685-1

CONTENTS

PREFACE

The Gregg Reference Manual with its accompanying *Workbook* has been updated to reflect the impact of computer technology and the World Wide Web. The manual offers more concise examples and computer-generated illustrations to help you find solutions to the various problems faced in everyday communications—from e-mail messages to formal reports.

The Canadian edition of *The Gregg Reference Manual* has been published specifically for use in English-speaking Canada. For different rules applied to usage in French-speaking Canada, we recommend you refer to *Le Français au Bureau Office de la Française Langue*, 5e édition, Les Publications du Québec, 2000.

Organization and Features of the New Edition. This sixth Canadian edition, adapted from William A. Sabin's ninth U.S. edition of *The Gregg Reference Manual*, consists of twenty sections divided into three parts.

Part One (Sections 1–11) presents basic rules and the fine points of grammar, usage, punctuation, capitalization, numbers, abbreviations, plurals, possessives, spelling, compound words, and word division. New features include:

- Increased number of Canadian examples with words, phrases, acronyms, and initialisms that are continually appearing in our language.
- Stylistic issues from spacing for punctuation marks, to the use of various dashes, quotation marks, italics, underscores, bullets, and other symbols that are affected by desktop publishing standards.

Part Two (Sections 12–17) addresses the formatting style of letters, memos, reports, manuscripts, tables, agendas, minutes, itineraries, fax cover sheets, e-mails, outlines, and résumés. While the use of templates (in this edition those of Microsoft Word) to produce expedient documents is often convenient, the preset defaults are not always suitable for all occasions. To help you cope with this situation, new features include:

- Guidelines to modify templates or to create your own formats to produce letters, reports, and memos that are more effective and acceptable.
- Step-by-step illustrations and explanations showing how a table created with the table feature of Microsoft Word can be progressively modified to achieve results that are more readable and attractive.
- Online source material for constructing footnotes, endnotes, and bibliographic entries that are necessary to include in report writing today.

v

- Web site (URLs) and e-mail addresses that are described and decoded for easier understanding. Word division for these addresses is also included.
- Format guidelines for preparing traditional and scannable résumés, as well as one-page résumés that are suitable for young people entering the work force.

Part Three (Sections 18–20) provides a listing of model forms of address, a glossary of grammatical terms, and an updated glossary of computer terms.

Workbook. The *Workbook and Answer Key* (ISBN 007-089167-2) to accompany *The Gregg Reference Manual* promotes the learning particularly of the key rules in Sections 1–11 of the manual. This self-study workbook provides answers and solutions to the survey tests and worksheets. For students and office professionals alike, there is no better way to learn the content and apply the rules of *The Gregg Reference Manual.*

Acknowledgments. We would like to acknowledge the able assistance and encouragement of the staff at McGraw-Hill Ryerson Limited—Marianne Minaker, Lesley Mann, Darren Hick, Kelly Dickson, Nicla Dattolico, Jeff Snook, James Buchanan, Greg Devitt, Kim Brewster, Pat Ferrier, and freelance editor Wayne Herrington.

We wish to acknowledge and extend our thanks to Peggy Noble of the Southern Alberta Institute of Technology for her contribution in helping to update the content of Sections 13–17 and Section 20.

Our warm thanks as well to our reviewers and colleagues who corrected our copy, offered helpful suggestions and constructive criticism, and authenticated the content of this edition: Joan Parson, Academy Canada; Alberta Smith, Algonquin College; Diane Blaney, Capilano College; Louise Winterstein, Centennial College; Cynthia Nolan, College of the North Atlantic; Vivian Lee, Durham College; Nancy Barry, Georgian College; Pati Russell, Grant MacEwan College; Veronica Weir, Mohawk College; Laurie Schmit, SIAST; Peggy Pepper, Sprott-Shaw Community College; Sandra B. Rose, Toronto School of Business.

Wilma Millar
Sharon Sine
Wendy Strashok

HOW TO LOOK THINGS UP

Suppose you were writing to someone in another department:

> May I please get an advance copy of your confidential report [You hesitate. Should this sentence end with a period or a question mark?]

A common problem in written communication is finding an answer quickly. In this manual there are several ways to proceed.

Using the Index. At the back of this manual is a detailed index. Any of the following entries will solve the problem sentence above:

Periods, **101–109**	Question Marks, **110–118**	Request, punctuation of, **103**
. . .	. . .	
at end of requests, **103**	at end of requests, **103, 113**	

In each entry, the **boldface number** refers to the proper rule, ¶**103**. (If you look up ¶103, you will find that a question mark is the right punctuation for the sentence in question.)

Most index entries show specific rule numbers. In a few cases, however, references may be to page numbers, and these are shown in lightface type. Suppose you were confronted with this problem:

> If you compare the performance records of Catano, Harris, and Williams, you won't find much difference *(between/among)* them.

The index will show the following entries:

> *among-between,* 288   **OR**   *between-among,* 288

(The rule on page 288 indicates that *between* is correct in this situation.)

Using a Fast-Skim Approach. If you have little patience with detailed indexes and would rather skim through pages to find what you are looking for, then several features of this manual may be helpful:

* The table of contents indicates each major subject.
* At the start of each section except the glossaries, you will find a detailed list of all the topics covered in that section. This list will help you quickly focus on the rule or rules that pertain to your problem. Suppose the following problem came up:

> The point is that new *Federal* [or is it *federal*?] legislation is needed.

The table of contents shows that Section 3 is about capitalization. Skimming the list of topics reveals *Names of Government Bodies* (¶¶325–330). Within that set of rules ¶328 states that *federal* is the proper form.

Cross-references, which could prove helpful, have also been provided throughout the manual. Some take this form: *See* ¶324; others may read *See also* ¶324. The form *See* ¶324 indicates that ¶324 contains significant information that adds to or qualifies the rule you are currently reading; the word *See* suggests that you really ought to pursue the cross-reference before making a decision. The form *See also* ¶324 carries a good deal less urgency. It indicates that you will find some additional examples in ¶324 and perhaps a restatement of the rule. It suggests that you don't have to pursue the cross-reference if you don't want to—but it couldn't hurt.

Playing the Numbers. There is still a third way to find the answer to a specific problem. You will observe from the rule numbers that they all carry a section number as a prefix. Section 3 (on capitalization) has a "300" series of rules; Section 4 (on number style) has a "400" series; and so on. Once you become familiar with the section numbers and the section titles, you can find your way around quite easily.

A familiarity with the section numbers and section titles can also save you time when you are using the index. If your index entry lists several different paragraph numbers, you can often anticipate what the paragraphs will deal with. For example, if you want to know whether to write *5 kg* or *5 kgs* on a purchase order, you might encounter the following entry in the index:

> Weights, 429–430, 535–538, 620

If you know that Section 6 deals with plurals, you will try ¶620 first. (The answer you are looking for is *5 kg.*)

Looking Up Specific Words. Many of the problems that arise deal with specific words. For this reason the index provides as many entries for such words as space will permit. For example, in the following sentence, should *therefore* be set off by commas or not?

> It is(,) *therefore*(,) essential that operations be curtailed.

A check of the index will show the following entry:

> *therefore*, **122**, **138–142**

(The rules in ¶141 will indicate that no commas should be used in this sentence.)

If you ask the same question about another specific word and do not find it listed as a separate entry in the index, you should check the index under "Comma" and investigate the most promising references or make a direct scan of the comma rules in Section 1 until you find the answer you are looking for.

If you are having difficulty with words that look alike and sound alike—*gibe* and *jibe* or *advice* and *advise*—turn directly to ¶719. For other troublesome words and phrases, consult Section 11.

P A R T

ONE

Grammar, Usage, and Style

SECTION ONE

Punctuation: Major Marks

THE PERIOD (¶¶101–109)
At the End of a Statement or Command (¶¶101–102)
At the End of a Polite Request or Command (¶103)
At the End of an Indirect Question (¶104)
With Decimals (¶105)
In Outlines and Displayed Lists (¶¶106–107)
With Headings (¶108)
A Few Don'ts (¶109)

THE QUESTION MARK (¶¶110–118)
To Indicate Direct Questions (¶¶110–113)
To Indicate Questions Within Sentences (¶¶114–117)
To Express Doubt (¶118)

THE EXCLAMATION POINT (¶¶119–121)
To Express Strong Feeling (¶¶119–120)
With *Oh* and *O* (¶121)

THE COMMA (¶¶122–175)
Basic Rules for Commas That Set Off (¶122)
Basic Rules for Commas That Separate (¶¶123–125)
With Clauses in Compound Sentences (¶¶126–129)
With Clauses in Complex Sentences (¶¶130–132)
   Introductory Dependent Clauses (¶130)
   Dependent Clauses Elsewhere in the Sentence (¶¶131–132)
With Clauses in Compound-Complex Sentences (¶¶133–134)
With Participial, Infinitive, and Prepositional Phrases (¶¶135–137)
   Introductory Phrases (¶135)
   Phrases at the Beginning of a Clause (¶136)
   Phrases Elsewhere in the Sentence (¶137)
With Transitional Expressions and Independent Comments (¶¶138–143)
   At the Beginning of a Sentence (¶139)
   At the End of a Sentence (¶140)
   Within the Sentence (¶141)
   At the Beginning of a Clause (¶142)
   With the Adverb *Too* (¶143)

THE SEMICOLON (¶¶176–186)

THE COLON (¶¶187–199)

Punctuation marks are the mechanical means for making the meaning of a sentence easily understood. They indicate the proper relationships between words, phrases, and clauses when word order alone is not sufficient to make these relationships clear.

One important caution about punctuation. If you find it particularly hard to determine the appropriate punctuation for a sentence you have written, the chances are that the sentence is improperly constructed. To be on the safe side, recast your thought in a form you can handle with confidence. Do not try to save a badly constructed sentence by means of punctuation.

Section 1 deals with the three marks of terminal punctuation (the period, the question mark, and the exclamation point) plus the three major marks of internal punctuation (the comma, the semicolon, and the colon). All other marks of punctuation are covered in Section 2.

For the number of spaces to leave either before or after a punctuation mark, refer to the chart in ¶298.

THE PERIOD
At the End of a Statement or Command

101 Use a period to mark the end of a sentence that makes a statement or expresses a command.

> Nunavut was established as a new Canadian territory in 1999.
>
> I question the need to cut advertising and promotion expenses at this time.
>
> All monthly expense reports must be in by the 10th of the following month.
>
> Make sure that Kate gets to the airport by 10 a.m. (The period that marks the end of the abbreviation also serves to mark the end of the sentence.)

102 Use a period to mark the end of an *elliptical* (condensed) expression that represents a complete statement or command. Elliptical expressions often occur as answers to questions or as transitional phrases.

> Yes.   No.   Of course.   Indeed.   By all means.
> Enough on that subject.   Now, to proceed to your next point.

NOTE: Do not confuse elliptical expressions with sentence fragments. An elliptical expression represents a complete sentence. A sentence fragment is a word, phrase, or clause that is incorrectly treated as a separate sentence when it ought to be incorporated with adjacent words to make up a complete sentence.

> Great news! The laser printer arrived yesterday. After we had waited for six weeks. (*Great news* is an elliptical expression; it represents a complete sentence, *I have great news. After we had waited for six weeks* is a sentence fragment, incorrectly treated as a sentence in its own right; this dependent clause should be linked with the main clause that precedes it.)
>
> **REVISED:** Great news! The laser printer arrived yesterday, after we had waited for six weeks.

At the End of a Polite Request or Command

103 **a.** Requests, suggestions, and commands are often phrased as questions out of politeness. Use a period to end this kind of sentence if you expect your reader to respond *by acting* rather than by giving you a yes-or-no answer.

> Will you please call us at once if we can be of further help.
>
> Would you please send all bills to my bank for payment while I'm away.
>
> May I suggest that you put your request in writing and send it to Mr. Ludwar.
>
> If you can't attend the meeting, could you please send someone else.

NOTE: Use a period only when you are sure that your reader is not likely to consider your request presumptuous.

b. If you are asking a favour or making a request that your reader may be unable or unwilling to grant, use a question mark at the end of the sentence. The question mark offers your reader a chance to say no to your request and helps to preserve the politeness of the situation.

May I ask a favour of you? Could you spare fifteen minutes to tell my son about career opportunities in your company?

Will you be able to have someone in your department help me on the Hibernia project?

Will you please handle the production reports for me on Monday?

c. If you are not sure whether to use a question mark or a period, reword the sentence so that it is clearly a question or a statement; then punctuate accordingly. For example, the sentence directly above could be revised as follows:

Would you be willing to handle the production reports for me on Monday?

I would appreciate your handling the production reports for me on Monday.

d.. When you are addressing a request to someone who reports to you, you expect that person to comply. Therefore, a period can properly be used to punctuate such requests. However, since most people prefer to be *asked* to do something rather than be *told* to do it, a question mark establishes a nicer tone and often gets better results. Consider using a question mark when your request to a subordinate involves something beyond the routine aspects of the job.

Will you please let me know what your vacation plans are for the month of August. (Routine request to a subordinate.)

May I ask that you avoid scheduling any vacation time during August this year? I will need your help in preparing next year's forecasts and budgets. (Special request to a subordinate. The question mark suggests that the writer is sensitive to the problems this request could cause.)

NOTE: If you are unwilling to give your subordinate the impression that your request allows for a yes-or-no answer, simply drop the attempt at politeness and issue a straightforward command.

I must ask that you not schedule any vacation time during August this year. I will need your help in preparing next year's forecasts and budgets.

At the End of an Indirect Question

104 Use a period to mark the end of an indirect question. (See also ¶¶115–116.)

Jean Le Blanc has asked whether an exception can be made for him.

The only question she asked was when the report had to be on your desk.

Why Janet Murray left the company so quickly has never been explained.

I would like to question if migraines are linked to diabetes.

With Decimals

105 Use a period (without space before or after it) to separate a whole number from a decimal fraction; for example, *$5.50, 33.33 percent.*

In Outlines and Displayed Lists

106 Use periods after numbers or letters that enumerate items in an outline or a displayed list—unless the numbers or letters are enclosed in parentheses. Set a tab 0.25" to 0.5" to give an adequate visual break between the numbers or letters and the items that follow on the same line. (See also ¶¶107, 199c, 223, 1357d, 1425e, 1722, 1723 for examples.)

107 **a.** Use periods after independent clauses, dependent clauses, or long phrases that are displayed on separate lines in a list. Also use periods after short phrases that are essential to the grammatical completeness of the statement introducing the list. (In the following example, the three listed items are all objects of the preposition *on* in the introductory statement.)

Please get me year-end figures *on*:   **OR**   Please get me year-end figures *on*:

a. Domestic sales revenues.   • Domestic sales revenues.
b. Total operating costs.   • Total operating costs.
c. Net operating income.   • Net operating income.

NOTE: Avoid the following treatment of displayed lists, which uses semicolons and the words *and* or *or*.

You will profit from inquiries through: You will profit from inquiries through:

1. An 800 number;   • An 800 number;
2. A reader service card; and   • A reader service card; or
3. A fax-on-demand service.   • A fax-on-demand service.

b. No periods are needed after short phrases in a list if the introductory statement is grammatically complete (as in the first example below) or if the items are like those on an inventory sheet or a shopping list.

The computers in this price range offer the following features:

• 64-MB SDRAM
• 15-GB hard drive
• Ethernet Adapter

When you come to take the qualifying examination, please bring:

2 HB pencils
1 ballpoint pen

☞ *See ¶1425f for formatting enumerated items in a list.*
See ¶301e for the capitalization of items displayed in a list or an outline.

With Headings

108 **a.** Use a period after a *paragraph* heading (one that begins a paragraph and is immediately followed by text matter on the same line) unless some other mark of punctuation, such as a question mark, is required.

> **Insuring Your Car.** Automobile insurance is actually a package of six different types of coverage. . . .

> **How Much Will It Cost?** How much automobile insurance will cost you depends on your driving record, your age, and how much shopping around you do. . . .

b. Omit the period if the heading is *freestanding* (displayed on a line by itself). However, retain a question mark or an exclamation point with a freestanding head if the wording requires it.

DEBT INVESTMENTS

Traded Debt Investments

> **Advantages and Limitations.** Traded debt investments can be purchased for a variety of fixed-term periods depending upon the specific investment. This allows you to . . .

> **Are They Risky?** These investments are generally fully liquid because you can sell them to another investor . . .

NOTE: A period follows a run-in expression like *Table 6*, even though the heading as a whole is freestanding.

Table 6. SALARY RANGES   Figure 2–4. DEPARTMENTAL STAFF

☞ *For the treatment of headings in reports and manuscripts, see ¶1426.*
For the treatment of headings in tables, see ¶¶1619–1622.
For spacing with periods, see ¶298.

A Few Don'ts

109 Don't use a period:

a. After letters used to designate persons or things (for example, *Manager A, Class B, Grade C, Brand X*). **EXCEPTION:** Use a period when the letter is the initial of a person's last name (for example, *Mr. A.* for *Mr. Adams*).

b. After contractions (for example, *cont'd;* see ¶505).

c. After ordinals expressed in figures (*1st, 2nd, 3rd, 4th*).

d. After Roman numerals (for example, *Volume I, Elizabeth II*).

EXCEPTION: Periods follow Roman numerals in an outline. (See ¶¶223, 1722–1723.)

☞ *Periods with abbreviations: see ¶¶506–513, 515.*
Periods with brackets: see ¶296.
Periods with dashes: see ¶¶213, 214a, 215a.
Periods with parentheses: see ¶¶224c, 225a, 225c, 226c.
Periods with quotation marks: see ¶¶247, 252, 253, 257, 258, 259.

Three spaced periods (ellipsis marks): see ¶¶274–280, 292.
Spacing with periods: see ¶298.

THE QUESTION MARK
To Indicate Direct Questions

110　**a.** Use a question mark at the end of a direct question. (For guidelines on spacing, see ¶298.)

Will you be able to meet with us after 5 p.m.?

Either way, how can we lose?

NOTE: Be sure to place the question mark at the *end* of the question.

How do you account for this entry: "Paid to E. M. Johnson, $300"?
(**NOT:** How do you account for this entry? "Paid to E. M. Johnson, $300.")

☞　*For the punctuation of indirect questions, see ¶¶104, 115, 116.*
For the punctuation of questions with quotations, see ¶249.

b. Use a question mark (or, for special emphasis, an exclamation point) after a *rhetorical question*, a question to which no reply is expected. (See also ¶119b.)

Who wouldn't snap up an opportunity like that?

Wouldn't you rather be stuck in the sands of Florida this winter than in the snowdrifts of Manitoba?

Isn't it incredible that people could fall for a scheme like that? (**OR** !)

NOTE: If the first clause of a compound sentence is a rhetorical question and the second clause is a statement, use a period to end the sentence.

Why don't you look at the attached list of tasks, and then let's discuss which ones you would like to take on.

111　**a.** Use a question mark at the end of an *elliptical* (condensed) *question*, that is, a word or phrase that represents a complete question.

Marion tells me that you are coming to the Okanagan. When? (The complete question is, "When are you coming?")

NOTE: When a single word like *how*, *when*, or *why* is woven into the flow of a sentence, capitalization and special punctuation are not usually required.

The questions we need to address at our next board meeting are not *why* or *whether* but *how* and *when*.

b. Punctuate complete and elliptical questions separately, according to your meaning.

When will the job be finished? In a week or two?
(**NOT:** When will the job be finished in a week or two?)

Where shall we meet? At the airport? (With this punctuation, the writer allows for the possibility of meeting elsewhere.)

(Continued on page 10.)

1

> Where shall we meet at the airport? (With this punctuation, the writer simply wants to pinpoint a more precise location within the airport.)

112 Use a question mark at the end of a sentence that is phrased like a statement but spoken with the rising intonation of a question.

> You expect me to believe this story?   He still intends to proceed?

113 A request, suggestion, or command phrased as a question out of politeness may not require a question mark. (See ¶103.)

To Indicate Questions Within Sentences

114 When a short direct question falls *within a sentence*, set the question off with commas and put a question mark at the end of the sentence. However, when a short direct question falls *at the end of a sentence*, use a comma before it and a question mark after.

> I can alter the terms of my will, *can't I,* whenever I wish?
>
> We aren't obligated to attend the meeting, *are we?*

NOTE: Short questions falling within a sentence may also be set off with dashes or parentheses in place of commas. (See ¶¶214b, 224d.)

115 When a longer direct question comes *at the end of a sentence*, it starts with a capital letter and is preceded by a comma or a colon. The question mark that ends the question also serves to mark the end of the sentence.

> **NOTE:** In the examples below and in ¶116 notice how a simple shift in word order converts a direct question to an indirect question. When the verb precedes the subject (*shall we, can we*), the question is direct. When the verb follows the subject (*we shall, we can*), the question is indirect.

> The key question is, Whom *shall we* nominate for next year's election?
>
> This is the key question: Whom *shall we* nominate for next year's election? (Use a colon if the introductory material is an independent clause.)
>
> **BUT:** We now come to the key question of whom *we shall* nominate for next year's election. (An indirect question requires no special punctuation or capitalization.)
>
> **OR:** We now come to the key question of whom to nominate for next year's election.

116 When a longer direct question comes *at the beginning of a sentence*, it should be followed by a question mark (for emphasis) or simply a comma.

> How *can we* achieve these goals? is the next question. (Leave one space after a question mark within a sentence.)
>
> **OR:** How *can we* achieve these goals, is the next question.
>
> **BUT:** How *we can* achieve these goals is the next question. (Indirect question; no special punctuation is needed. See ¶115, note.)

117 **a.** A series of brief questions at the end of a sentence may be separated by commas or (for emphasis) by question marks. Do not capitalize the individual questions.

Who will be responsible for drafting the proposal, obtaining comments from all the interested parties, preparing the final version, and co-ordinating the distribution of copies? (As punctuated, this sentence implies that one person may be asked to perform all these tasks.)

OR: Who will be responsible for drafting the proposal? obtaining comments from all the interested parties? preparing the final version? co-ordinating the distribution of copies? (As punctuated, this sentence implies that a number of people may be asked to perform one or more of these tasks.)

☞ *See ¶298 for spacing after a question mark within a sentence.*

b. The brief questions in ¶117a are all related to the same subject and predicate (*Who will be responsible for*). Do not confuse this type of sentence pattern with a series of independent questions. Each independent question starts with a capital letter and ends with a question mark.

Before you accept the job offer, think about the following: Will this job give you experience relevant to your real career goal? Will it permit you to keep abreast of the latest technology? Will it pay what you need?

c. Independent questions in a series are often elliptical (condensed) expressions. (See ¶111.)

Has Walter's loan been approved? *When? By whom? For what amount?* (In other words: *When* was the loan approved? *By whom* was the loan approved? *For what amount* was the loan approved?)

(**NOT:** Has Walter's loan been approved, when, by whom, and for what amount?)

To Express Doubt

118 A question mark enclosed in parentheses may be used to express doubt or uncertainty about a word or phrase within a sentence. (See ¶298 for the spacing guidelines of parentheses.)

He joined the firm after his graduation in 2001 (?) from Osgoode Hall.

NOTE: When dates are already enclosed within parentheses, question marks may be inserted as necessary to indicate doubt.

the explorer John Cabot (1455?–1498?)

☞ *Question marks with dashes: see ¶¶214b, 215a.*
Question marks with parentheses: see ¶¶224d, 225a, 225d, 226c.
Question marks with quotation marks: see ¶¶249, 252, 254, 257, 258, 259, 261b–c.
Spacing with question marks: see ¶¶298, 1433c.

THE EXCLAMATION POINT

The exclamation point is an emotional mark of punctuation that is most often found in sales and advertising copy. Like the word *very*, it loses its force when overused, so avoid it wherever possible.

1

To Express Strong Feeling

119 **a.** Use an exclamation point at the end of a sentence (or an elliptical expression that stands for a sentence) to indicate enthusiasm, surprise, disbelief, urgency, or strong feeling. (Refer to ¶298 and ¶1433c for guidelines on spacing after an exclamation point.)

> Yes! We're selling our entire inventory below cost! Doors open at 9 a.m.!
>
> No! I don't believe it!   What a fantastic achievement!   Incredible!

b. An exclamation point may be used in place of a question mark to express strong feeling. (See also ¶110b.)

> How could you do it! What made you think I'd welcome a call at 2:30 a.m.!

c. The exclamation point may be enclosed in parentheses and placed directly after a word that the writer wants to emphasize.

> We won exclusive(!) distribution rights in the Western Hemisphere.

120 **a.** A single word may be followed by an exclamation point to express intense feeling. The sentence that follows it is punctuated as usual.

> Congratulations! Your summation at the trial was superb.

b. When such words are repeated for emphasis, an exclamation point follows each repetition.

> Going! Going! Our bargains are almost gone!

c. When exclamations are mild, a comma or a period is sufficient.

> Well, well, things could be worse.   No. I won't accept those conditions.

With *Oh* and *O*

121 The exclamation *oh* may be followed by either an exclamation point or a comma, depending on the emphasis desired. It is capitalized only when it starts a sentence. The capitalized *O*, the sign of direct address, is not usually followed by any punctuation.

> Oh! I didn't expect that!   Oh, what's the use?   O Lord, help me!

☞ *Exclamation point with dashes: see ¶¶214b, 215a.*
Exclamation point with parentheses: see ¶¶224d, 225a, 225d, 226c.
Exclamation point with quotation marks: see ¶¶249, 252, 254, 257, 258, 259, 261.
Spacing with exclamation points: see ¶¶298, 1433c.

THE COMMA

The comma has two primary functions: it *sets off* non-essential expressions that interrupt the flow of thought from subject to verb to object or complement, and it *separates* elements within a sentence to clarify their relationship to one another. **Two commas** are typically needed **to set off**, but only a **single comma** is needed **to separate**.

The following paragraphs (¶¶122–125) present an overview of the rules governing the use of the comma. For a more detailed treatment of the specific rules, see ¶¶126–175.

Basic Rules for Commas That Set Off

122 Use commas to set off *non-essential expressions*—words, phrases, and clauses that are not necessary for the meaning or the structural completeness of the sentence.

> **IMPORTANT NOTE:** In many sentences you can tell whether an expression is non-essential or essential by trying to omit the expression. If you can leave it out without affecting the meaning or the structural completeness of the sentence, the expression is non-essential and should be set off by commas.

> **NON-ESSENTIAL:** Let's get the advice of Tony Bocale, *who has in-depth experience with all types of personal computers.*
> **ESSENTIAL:** Let's get the advice of someone *who has in-depth experience with all types of personal computers.* (Without the *who* clause, the meaning of the sentence would be incomplete.)

> **NON-ESSENTIAL:** There is, *no doubt,* a reasonable explanation for his behaviour at the board meeting.
> **ESSENTIAL:** There is *no doubt* about her honesty. (Without *no doubt*, the structure of the sentence would be incomplete.)

However, in other sentences the only way you can tell whether an expression is non-essential or essential is by the way you would say it aloud. If your voice tends to *drop* as you utter the expression, it is non-essential; if your voice tends to *rise*, the expression is essential.

> **NON-ESSENTIAL:** Finch and Chan would prefer, *therefore,* to limit the term of the agreement to two years.
> **ESSENTIAL:** Finch and Chan would *therefore* prefer to limit the term of the agreement to two years.

☞ *For additional examples, see ¶141, note.*

a. **Interrupting Elements.** Use commas to set off words, phrases, and clauses when they break the flow of a sentence from subject to verb to object or complement. (See also ¶¶144–147.)

> We can deliver the car on your husband's birthday or, *if you wish,* on the Saturday before. (When this sentence is read aloud, notice how the voice drops on the non-essential expression *if you wish.*)

> They have sufficient assets, *don't they,* to cover these losses?

> Let's take advantage of the special price and order, *say,* 200 reams this quarter instead of our usual quantity of 75.

> Maria LaPierre, *rather than Guy desRosiers,* has been appointed head of the Longueuil office.

> **BUT:** Maria LaPierre has been appointed head of the Longueuil office *rather than Guy desRosiers.* (This phrase is not set off when it does not interrupt.)

b. **Afterthoughts.** Use commas to set off words, phrases, or clauses loosely added onto the end of a sentence. (See also ¶144.)

(Continued on page 14.)

1

Send us your cheque as soon as you can, *please.*

Grant promised to share expenses with us, *if I remember correctly.*

It is not too late to place an order, *is it?*

c. **Transitional Expressions and Independent Comments.** Use commas to set off transitional expressions (like *however, therefore, on the other hand*) and independent comments (like *obviously, in my opinion, of course*) when they interrupt the flow of the sentence. Do not set these elements off, however, when they are used to emphasize the meaning; the voice goes up in such cases. In the examples that follow, consider how the voice drops when the expression is non-essential and how it rises when the expression is essential. (See also ¶¶138–143.)

NON-ESSENTIAL: We are determined, *nevertheless,* to finish on schedule.
ESSENTIAL: We are *nevertheless* determined to finish on schedule.

NON-ESSENTIAL: It is, *of course,* your prerogative to change your mind. (Here the voice rises on *is* and drops on *of course.*)
ESSENTIAL: It is *of course* your prerogative to change your mind. (Here the voice rises on *of course.*)

d. **Descriptive Expressions.** When descriptive expressions *follow* the words they refer to and provide additional but non-essential information, use commas to set them off. (See also ¶¶148–153.)

NON-ESSENTIAL: His most recent article, "How to Make a Profit With High-Tech Investments," appeared in the June 1 issue of *Forbes.* (*His most recent* indicates which article is meant; the title gives additional but non-essential information.)
ESSENTIAL: The article "How to Make a Profit With High-Tech Investments" appeared in the June 1 issue of *Forbes.* (Here the title is needed to indicate which article is meant.)

NON-ESSENTIAL: Thank you for your letter of April 12, in which you questioned our discount terms. (The date indicates which letter; the *in which* clause gives additional information. See also ¶152.)
ESSENTIAL: Thank you for your letter in which you questioned our discount terms. (Here the *in which* clause is needed to indicate which letter is meant.)

e. **Dates.** Use commas to set off the year in complete dates (for example, Sunday, May 1, 2004, . . .). (See also ¶¶154–155.)

f. **Names.** Use commas to set off abbreviations that follow a person's name (Julie Merkin, *CPS,* announces the opening . . .) and to set off names of provinces or countries following city names (Hull, *Quebec,* will host . . .). In personal and company names, the trend is not to set off elements like *Jr., Sr., III, Inc.,* or *Ltd.* (for example, *Guy Tracy Jr.* and *ATCO Ltd.*); however, individual preferences should be respected when known. (See also ¶¶156–161.)

Basic Rules for Commas That Separate

123   Use a single comma:

a. To separate the two main clauses in a compound sentence when they are joined by *and, but, or,* or *nor,* and occasionally *for, so,* or *yet.* (See also ¶¶126–129.)

We can't accept the marketing restrictions you proposed, *yet* we think there is some basis for a mutually acceptable understanding.

b. To separate three or more items in a series—unless all the items are joined by *and* or *or*. (See also ¶¶162–167.)

It takes time, effort, *and* a good deal of money.

BUT: It takes time *and* effort *and* a good deal of money.

c. To separate two or more adjectives that both modify the same noun. (See also ¶¶168–171.)

We need to mount an *exciting, hard-hitting* ad campaign.

d. To separate the digits of numbers into groups of thousands where the readability of numbers in documents is required. (See Section 14.)

Sales projections for the Southern Region next year range between $900,000 and $1,000,000.

e. To indicate the omission of key words or to clarify meaning when the word order is unusual. (See also ¶¶172–175.)

Half the purchase price is due on delivery of the goods; the balance, in three months. (The comma here signifies the omission of *is due*.)

What will happen, we don't know. (The comma here helps the reader cope with the unusual word order; it separates the object, *What will happen*, from the subject, *we*, which follows.)

124 Use a single comma after *introductory elements*—items that begin a sentence and come before the subject and verb of the main clause.

Yes, we can deliver your new printer by Wednesday. (Introductory word.)

Taking all the arguments into consideration, we have decided to modernize these facilities rather than close them down. (Introductory participial phrase.)

To determine the proper mix of ingredients for a particular situation, see the table on page 141. (Introductory infinitive phrase.)

Before we can make a final decision, we will need to run another cost-profit analysis. (Introductory dependent clause.)

a. Use a comma after an *introductory request or command*.

Look, we've been through tougher situations before.

You see, the previous campaigns never did pan out.

Please remember, all expense reports must be on my desk by Friday.

BUT: *Please remember that* all . . . (When *that* is added, *please remember* becomes the main verb and is no longer an introductory element.)

b. Commas are not needed after *ordinary introductory adverbs* or *introductory prepositional phrases* that answer such questions as:

WHEN:	tomorrow, yesterday, recently, early next week, in the morning, soon, in five years, in 2001
HOW OFTEN:	occasionally, often, frequently, once in a while
WHERE:	here, in this case, at the meeting

(Continued on page 16.)

WHY: for that reason, because of this situation

In the morning things may look better. (Short prepositional phrase telling *when*; no comma needed.)

Recently we had a request for school enrolment trends. (Introductory adverb telling *when*; no comma needed.)

NOTE: Many writers use commas after *all* introductory elements to avoid having to analyse each situation.

c. Commas are used after introductory elements and phrases:

(1) When they function as *transitional expressions* (such as *well, therefore, however, for example, in the first place*), which provide a transition in meaning from the previous sentence.

(2) When they function as *independent comments* (such as *in my opinion, by all means, obviously, of course*), which express the writer's attitude toward the meaning of the sentence. (See also ¶¶138–143.)

In the first place, they don't have sufficient capital. (Transitional expression; followed by comma.)

In my opinion, we ought to look for another candidate. (Independent comment; followed by comma.)

Consequently, we will have to cancel the agreement. (Transitional expression; followed by comma.)

Obviously, the request will have to be referred elsewhere. (Independent comment; followed by comma.)

125 Separating commas are often improperly used in sentences. In the following examples, the diagonal marks indicate points at which single commas *should not* be used.

a. Do not separate a subject and its verb.

The person she plans to hire for the job/ is Peter Crotty.

BUT: The person she plans to hire for the job, *I believe,* is Peter Crotty. (Use *two* commas to set off an interrupting expression.)

Whether profits can be improved this year/ depends on several key variables. (Noun clause as subject.)

BUT: *Anyone who contributes, contributes* to a most worthy cause. (In special cases like this, a comma may be required for clarity. See also ¶175b.)

b. Do not separate a verb and its object or complement.

The test mailing *has not produced/ the results* we were hoping for. (Verb and object.)

Mrs. Palmer *will be/ the company's new director of marketing.* (Verb and complement.)

The equipment *is/ easy to operate, inexpensive to maintain, and built to give reliable service for many years.* (Verb and complement.)

Rebecca Hingham *said/ that the research data would be on your desk by Monday morning.* (Noun clause as object.)

1

BUT: Rebecca Hingham *said, "The research data will be on your desk by Monday morning."* (A comma ordinarily follows a verb when the object is a direct quotation. See also ¶256.)

OR: The question we really need to address *is, Do we have a better solution to propose?* (A comma also follows a verb when the object or complement is a direct question. See also ¶115.)

c. Do not separate an adjective from a noun that follows it.

The project requires a highly motivated, research-oriented, cost-conscious/manager.

d. Do not separate a noun and a prepositional phrase that follows.

The board of directors/ of the La Flamme Corporation will announce its decision this Friday.

BUT: The board of directors, *of necessity,* must turn down the merger at this time. (Use *two* commas to set off an interrupting expression.)

e. Do not separate a co-ordinating conjunction (*and, but, or,* or *nor,* and occasionally *for, so,* or *yet*) and the following word.

You can read the draft of the division's medium-range plan now *or/ when* you get home tonight.

BUT: You can read the draft of the division's medium-range plan now or, *if you prefer,* when you get home tonight. (Use *two* commas to set off an interrupting expression.)

f. Do not separate *two* words or phrases that are joined by a co-ordinating conjunction.

The letters on the Gray case/ and *those concerning Mr. Pendleton* should be shown to Mrs. Almquist. (Two subjects.)

I *have read Ms. Popov's capital spending proposal/* and *find it well done.* (Two predicates. See also ¶127.)

We hope *that you will visit our store soon/* and *that you will find the styles you like.* (Two noun clauses serving as objects of the verb *hope.*)

The CEO plans *to visit the Western Region/* and *call personally on the large accounts that have stopped doing business with us.* (Two infinitive phrases serving as objects of the verb *plans.*)

He may go on to graduate school at *McGill/* or *Dalhousie.* (Two objects of the preposition *at.*)

BUT: *Frank Albano will handle the tickets,* and *Edna Hahn will be responsible for publicity.* (A comma separates two independent clauses joined by a co-ordinating conjunction. See ¶126.)

The following rules (¶¶126–137) deal with the punctuation of clauses and phrases in sentences.

With Clauses in Compound Sentences

126 a. When a compound sentence consists of *two* independent clauses joined by a co-ordinating conjunction (*and, but, or,* or *nor,* and sometimes *for, so,* or *yet*), place a separating comma before the conjunction. (See ¶129.)

(Continued on page 18.)

1

Mrs. Fenster noticed a small discrepancy in the figures, *and* on that basis she began to reanalyse the data.

BUT: Mrs. Fenster noticed a small discrepancy in the figures *and* on that basis began to reanalyse the data. (See ¶127a–b.)

Show this proposal to Mr. Florio, *and* ask him for his reaction. (See ¶127c.)

Either we step up our promotion efforts, *or* we must be content with our existing share of the market.

Not only were we the developers of this process, *but* we were the first to apply it to the field of pollution control.

b. For special effect the comma before the co-ordinating conjunction can be replaced by a period, a question mark, or an exclamation point. The co-ordinating conjunction is then capitalized, and the second independent clause is treated as a separate sentence. However, this treatment, if overused, quickly loses its effectiveness. (See Section 11 for a usage note on *and*.)

Is it self-confidence that makes you successful? Or is it success that makes you self-confident?

I told Callahan that we would not reorder from his company unless he cuts his prices by 20 percent. And he did.

NOTE: Do not insert a comma directly after the co-ordinating conjunction unless a parenthetical element begins at that point.

I told Callahan that we would not reorder from his company unless he cut his prices by 20 percent. And, to my total amazement, he did.

c. When a compound sentence consists of *three* or more independent clauses, punctuate this series like any other series. (See also ¶162.)

Bob can deal with the caterer, Nora can handle publicity, and Bev and I can take care of the rest.

127 Do not confuse a *compound sentence* with a simple sentence containing a *compound predicate*.

a. A *compound sentence* contains at least two independent clauses, and each clause contains a subject and a predicate.

Barbara *just got her master's,* and *she is now looking for a job in sales.*

b. A sentence may contain one subject with a *compound predicate*, that is, two predicates connected by a co-ordinating conjunction. In such sentences no comma separates the two predicates.

Barbara *just got her master's* and *is now looking for a job in sales.* (When *she* is omitted from the example in *a* above, the sentence becomes a simple sentence with a compound predicate.)

Ogilvey not only *wants a higher discount* but also *demands faster turnarounds on his orders.* (Compound predicate; no comma before *but*.)

BUT: Ogilvey not only *wants a higher discount,* but he also *demands faster turnarounds on his orders.* (Compound sentence; comma before *but*.)

c. When one or both verbs are in the imperative and the subject is not expressed, treat the sentence as a compound sentence and use a comma between the clauses.

Please look at the brochure I have enclosed, and then *get* back to me if you have additional questions.

You may not be able to get away right now, but *do plan* to stay with us whenever you find the time.

Call Ellen Chen sometime next week, and *ask* her whether she will speak at our conference next fall.

BUT: *Call* Ellen Chen and *ask* her whether she will speak at our conference next fall. (Omit the comma if the first clause is short. See ¶129.)

d. When non-essential elements precede the second part of a *compound predicate,* they are treated as interrupting expressions and are set off by two commas. When these same expressions precede the second clause of a *compound sentence,* they are treated as introductory expressions and are followed by one comma.

We can bill you on our customary terms or, *if you prefer,* offer you our new deferred payment plan. (Interrupting expression requires two commas.)

We can bill you on our customary terms or *if you prefer,* we can offer you our new deferred payment plan. (Introductory expression requires one comma.)

Frank Harrison went into the boardroom and, *without consulting his notes,* proceeded to give the directors precise details about our financial situation. (Interrupting expression.)

Frank Harrrison went into the boardroom, and *without consulting his notes,* he proceeded to give the directors precise details about our financial situation. (Introductory expression.)

☞ *See also* ¶¶*131c, 136a, 142.*

128 Do not use a comma between two independent clauses that are not joined by a co-ordinating conjunction (*and, but, or,* or *nor,* and occasionally *for, so,* or *yet*). This error of punctuation is known as a *comma splice* and produces a *run-on sentence.* Use a semicolon, a colon, or a dash (whichever is appropriate), or start a new sentence. (See ¶¶176, 187, 204–205.)

WRONG: Please review these spreadsheets quickly, I need them back tomorrow.

RIGHT: Please review these spreadsheets quickly; I need them back tomorrow.

OR: Please review these spreadsheets quickly. I need them back tomorrow.

129 If either clause of a compound sentence is short, the comma may be omitted before the conjunction.

Their prices are low and *their service is efficient.*

Please initial these forms and *return them by Monday.*

Consider leasing and see whether it costs less in the long run than buying.

Consider whether leasing costs more than buying and *then decide.*

(Continued on page 20.)

1

NOTE: Make sure that the omission of a comma does not lead to confusion.

CLEAR: *Please don't litter,* and *recycle whenever possible.*

CONFUSING: *Please don't litter* and *recycle whenever possible.* (Without a comma after *litter,* the sentence could seem to be saying, ". . . and please don't recycle whenever possible.")

With Clauses in Complex Sentences

A complex sentence contains one independent clause and one or more dependent clauses. *After, although, as, because, before, if, since, unless, when,* and *while* are among the words most frequently used to introduce dependent clauses. (See ¶132 for a longer list.)

130 INTRODUCTORY DEPENDENT CLAUSES

a. When a dependent clause *precedes* the independent clause, separate the clauses with a comma.

Before we can make a decision, we must have all the facts.

When you read the Cameron study, look at Appendix 2 first.

If they had invested more carefully, they could have avoided bankruptcy.

After we have studied all aspects of the complaint, <u>we will make</u> a recommendation.

BUT: *Only after we have studied all aspects of the complaint* <u>will we make</u> a recommendation. (No comma follows the introductory clause when the word order in the main clause is abnormal. Compare the abnormal *will we make* here with the normal *we will make* in the preceding example.)

b. Be sure you can recognize an introductory dependent clause, even if some of the essential words are omitted from the clause. (Such constructions are known as *elliptical clauses.*)

Whenever possible, he leaves his office by six. (*Whenever it is* possible, . . .)

If so, I will call you tomorrow. (*If that is* so, . . .)

Should you be late, just call to let me know. (*If you should be late,* . . .)

c. Use a comma after an introductory clause when it serves as the *object* of a sentence (but not when it serves as the *subject*).

Whomever you nominate, I will support. (Introductory clause as object.)

Whomever you nominate will have my support. (Introductory clause as subject.)

That the department must be reorganized, I no longer question. (Introductory clause as object.)

That the department must be reorganized is no longer questioned. (Introductory clause as subject.)

d. Sentences like those illustrated in ¶130a–c are often introduced by an expression such as *he said that, she believes that,* or *they know that.* In such cases use the same punctuation as prescribed in *a–c.*

Liz believes that *before we can make a decision,* we must have all the facts. (A separating comma follows the dependent clause, just as if the sentence began with the word *Before*. No comma precedes the dependent clause because it is considered introductory, not interrupting.)

I think that *when you read the Nagano study*, you will gain a new perspective on the situation.

Harry says that *whenever possible*, he leaves his office by six.

Everyone knows that *whomever you nominate* will have my support in the next election.

BUT: He said that, *as you may already know*, he was planning to take early retirement. (Two commas are needed to set off an interrupting dependent clause. See also ¶131c.)

131 DEPENDENT CLAUSES ELSEWHERE IN THE SENTENCE

When a dependent clause follows the main clause or falls within the main clause, commas are used or omitted depending on whether the dependent clause is essential (restrictive) or non-essential (non-restrictive).

a. An *essential* clause is necessary to the meaning of the sentence. Because it *cannot be omitted*, it should not be set off by commas.

The person *who used to be Nova's operations manager* is now doing the same job for Gucci Brothers. (Tells which person.)

The Pennington bid arrived *after we had made our decision*. (Tells when.)

Damato's suggestion *that we submit the issue to arbitration* may be the only sensible alternative. (Tells which of Damato's suggestions is meant.)

Mrs. Foy said *that she would send us an advance program*. (Tells what was said.)

b. A non-essential clause provides additional descriptive or explanatory detail. Because it *can be omitted* without changing the meaning of the sentence, it should be set off by commas.

George Pedersen, *who used to be Nova's operations manager*, is now doing the same job for Gucci Brothers. (The name indicates which person; the *who* clause simply gives additional information.)

The Pennington bid arrived on Tuesday, *after we had made our decision*. (*Tuesday* tells when; the *after* clause simply adds information.)

Damato's latest suggestion, *that we submit the issue to arbitration*, may be the only sensible alternative. (*Latest* tells which suggestion is meant; the *that* clause is not essential.)

c. A dependent clause occurring within a sentence must always be set off by commas when it *interrupts* the flow of the sentence.

We can review the wording of the announcement over lunch or, *if your time is short*, over the telephone.

Please tell us when you plan to be in town and, *if possible*, where you will be staying. (The complete dependent clause is *if it is possible*.)

Senator Jones, *when offered the chance to refute his opponent's charges*, said he would respond at a time of his own choosing.

(Continued on page 22.)

1

Mrs. Kourakis is the type of person who, *when you need help badly*, will be the first to volunteer.

If, *when you have weighed the alternatives*, you choose one of the models that cost over $500, we can arrange special credit terms for you.

BUT: He said that *if we choose one of the models that cost over $500*, his firm can arrange special credit terms for us. (See ¶130d for dependent clauses following *he said that, she knows that,* and similar expressions.)

132 The following list presents the words and phrases most commonly used to introduce dependent clauses. For most of these expressions, two sentences are given: one containing an essential clause and one a non-essential clause. In a few cases, only one type of clause is possible. If you cannot decide whether a clause is essential or non-essential (and therefore whether commas are required or not), compare it with the related sentences that follow.

After. ESSENTIAL: His faxed response came *after you left last evening.* (Tells when.)
NON-ESSENTIAL: His faxed response came this morning, *after the decision had been made.* (The phrase *this morning* clearly tells when; the *after* clause provides additional but non-essential information.)

All of which. ALWAYS NON-ESSENTIAL: The rumours, *all of which were unfounded,* brought about his defeat in the last election.

Although, even though, and **though.** ALWAYS NON-ESSENTIAL: She has typed her letter of resignation, *although I do not believe she will submit it.*

As. ESSENTIAL: The results of the mailing are *as you predicted they would be.*
NON-ESSENTIAL: The results of the mailing are disappointing, *as you predicted they would be.* (See Section 11 for a usage note on *as.*)

As . . . as. ALWAYS ESSENTIAL: He talked *as* persuasively at the meeting *as* he did over the telephone. (See Section 11 for a usage note on *as . . . as.*)

As if and **as though.** ESSENTIAL: She drove *as if* (or *as though*) *the road were a minefield.* (The *as if* clause tells how she drove.)
NON-ESSENTIAL: She drove cautiously, *as if* (or *as though*) *the road were a minefield.* (The adverb *cautiously* tells how she drove; the *as if* clause provides additional but non-essential information.)

As soon as. ESSENTIAL: We will fill your order *as soon as we receive new stock.*
NON-ESSENTIAL: We will fill your order next week, *as soon as we receive new stock.*

At, by, for, in, and **to which.** ESSENTIAL: I went to the floor *to which I had been directed.*
NON-ESSENTIAL: I went to the tenth floor, *to which I had been directed.*

Because. *Essential* or *non-essential,* depending on closeness of relation.
ESSENTIAL: She left *because she had another appointment.* (Here the reason expressed by the *because* clause is essential to complete the meaning.)
NON-ESSENTIAL: I need to have two copies of the final report by 5:30 tomorrow, *because I am leaving for Chicago on a 7:30 flight.* (Here the meaning of the main clause is complete; the reason expressed in the *because* clause offers additional but non-essential information.)

NOTE: See how the use or omission of a comma in the following sentences affects the meaning: I'm not taking that course of action,

1

because I distrust Harry's recommendations. **BUT:** I'm not taking that course of action *because I distrust Harry's recommendations.* I based my decision on another reason altogether.

Before. ESSENTIAL: The shipment was sent *before your letter was received.* NON-ESSENTIAL: The shipment was sent on Tuesday, *before your letter was received.* (*Tuesday* tells when the shipment was sent; the *before* clause provides additional but non-essential information.)

Even though. See *Although.*

For. ALWAYS NON-ESSENTIAL: Jim needs to raise money quickly, *for his tuition bill has to be paid by next Friday.* (A comma should always precede *for* as a conjunction to prevent misreading *for* as a preposition.)

If. ESSENTIAL: Let us hear from you *if you are interested.* NON-ESSENTIAL: She promised to write from Toronto, *if I remember correctly.* (Clause added loosely.)

In order that. *Essential* or *non-essential*, depending on closeness of relation. ESSENTIAL: Please notify your instructor promptly *in order that a make-up examination may be scheduled.* NON-ESSENTIAL: Please notify your instructor if you will be unable to attend the examination on Friday, *in order that a make-up examination may be scheduled.*

No matter what (why, how, etc.). ALWAYS NON-ESSENTIAL: The order cannot be ready by Monday, *no matter what the store manager says.*

None of which. ALWAYS NON-ESSENTIAL: We received five boxes of samples, *none of which are in good condition.*

None of whom. ALWAYS NON-ESSENTIAL: We have interviewed ten applicants, *none of whom were satisfactory.*

Not so . . . as. ALWAYS ESSENTIAL: The second copy was *not so* clear *as* the first one. (See Section 11 for a usage note on *not so . . . as.*)

Since. ESSENTIAL: We have taken no applications *since we received your memo.* NON-ESSENTIAL: We are taking no more applications, *since our lists are now closed.* (Clause of reason.)

So that. *Essential* or *non-essential*, depending on closeness of relation. ESSENTIAL: Examine all shipments *so that any damage may be detected promptly.* NON-ESSENTIAL: Examine all shipments as soon as they arrive, *so that any damage may be detected promptly.*

So . . . that. ALWAYS ESSENTIAL: The costs ran *so* high *that we could not make a profit.*

Some of whom. ALWAYS NON-ESSENTIAL: The agency has sent us five applicants, *some of whom seem promising.*

Than. ALWAYS ESSENTIAL: The employees seem to be more disturbed by the rumour *than they care to admit.*

That. When used as a relative pronoun, *that* refers to things; it also refers to persons when a class or type is meant. ALWAYS ESSENTIAL: Here is a picture of the plane *that I own.* She is the candidate *that I prefer.* (See also ¶1062.)

(Continued on page 24.)

When used as a subordinating conjunction, *that* links the dependent clause it introduces with the main clause.

ALWAYS ESSENTIAL: We know *that we will have to make concessions in the upcoming talks.* (See Section 11 for a usage note on *that.*)

Though. See *Although.*

Unless. ESSENTIAL: This product line will be discontinued *unless customers begin to show an interest in it.*

NON-ESSENTIAL: I plan to work on the Delta proposal all though the weekend, *unless Cindy comes into town.* (Clause added loosely as an afterthought.)

Until. ALWAYS ESSENTIAL: I will continue to work *until my children are out of school.*

When. ESSENTIAL: The changeover will be made *when Mr. Ruiz returns from his vacation.*

NON-ESSENTIAL: The changeover will be made next Monday, *when Mr. Ruiz returns from his vacation.* (*Monday* tells when; the *when* clause provides additional but non-essential information.)

Where. ESSENTIAL: I plan to visit the town *where I used to live.*

NON-ESSENTIAL: I plan to stop off in London, *where I used to live.*

Whereas. ALWAYS NON-ESSENTIAL: The figures for last year cover urban areas only, *whereas those for this year include rural areas as well.* (Clause of contrast.)

Which. Use *which* (rather than *who*) when referring to animals, things, and ideas. Always use *which* (instead of *that*) to introduce non-essential clauses: The revised report, *which was done by Mark,* is very impressive. *Which* may also be used to introduce essential clauses. (See ¶1062b, note.)

While. ESSENTIAL: The union has decided not to strike *while negotiations are still going on.* (Here *while* means "during the time that.")

NON-ESSENTIAL: The workers at the Apex Company have struck, *while those at the Powers Company are still at work.* (Here *while* means "whereas.")

Who. ESSENTIAL: All students *who are members of the Backpackers Club* will be leaving for Banff on Friday.

NON-ESSENTIAL: John Behnke, *who is a member of the Backpackers Club,* will be leading a group on a weekend trip to Banff.

Whom. ESSENTIAL: This package is for the friend *whom I am visiting.*

NON-ESSENTIAL: This package is for my cousin Amy, *whom I am visiting.*

Whose. ESSENTIAL: The prize was awarded to the employee *whose suggestion yielded the greatest cost savings.*

NON-ESSENTIAL: The prize was awarded to Joyce Bruno, *whose suggestion yielded the greatest cost savings.*

With Clauses in Compound-Complex Sentences

133 A compound-complex sentence typically consists of two independent clauses (joined by *and, but, or,* or *nor,* and sometimes *for, so,* or *yet*) and one or more dependent clauses. To punctuate a sentence of this kind, first place a separating comma before the conjunction that joins the two main parts. Then consider each half of the sentence alone and provide additional punctuation as necessary.

> The computer terminals were not delivered until June 12, five weeks after the promised delivery date, and *when I wrote to complain to your sales manager*, it took another three weeks simply for him to acknowledge my letter. (No comma precedes *when* because the *when* clause is considered an introductory expression, not an interrupting expression. See also ¶127d.)

> Jeff Adler, the CEO of Marshfield & Duxbury, is eager to discuss a joint venture with my boss, *who is off on a six-week trip to the Far East*, but the earliest date I see open for such a meeting is Wednesday, October 30.

NOTE: If a misreading is likely or a stronger break is desired, use a semicolon rather than a comma to separate the two main clauses. (See ¶177.)

134 When a sentence starts with a dependent clause that applies to both independent clauses that follow, do not use a comma to separate the independent clauses. (A comma would make the introductory dependent clause seem to apply only to the first independent clause.)

> Before you start to look for new capital, you need to prepare an analysis of the market *and* you must make a detailed set of financial projections. (The *before* clause applies equally to the two independent clauses that follow; hence no comma before *and*.)

> **BUT:** Before you start to look for new capital, you need to prepare an analysis of the market, *but* don't think that's all there is to it. (The *before* clause applies only to the first independent clause; hence a comma is used before *but*.)

With Participial, Infinitive, and Prepositional Phrases*

135 INTRODUCTORY PHRASES

a. Use a comma after an *introductory participial phrase.*

> *Seizing the opportunity,* I presented an overview of our medium-range plans.

> *Established* in 1905, our company takes great pride in its reputation for high-quality products and excellent service.

> *Having checked the statements myself,* I feel confident that they are accurate.

> **NOTE:** Watch out for phrases that look like introductory participial phrases but actually serve as the subject of the sentence or part of the predicate. Do not put a comma after these elements.

> *Looking for examples of good acknowledgment letters in our files* has taken me longer than I had hoped. (Gerund phrase as subject.)

> **BUT:** *Looking for examples of good acknowledgment letters in our files,* I found four that you can use. (Participial phrase used as an introductory element; the subject is *I*.)

> *Following Mrs. Forest's speech* was a presentation by Ms. Paley. (With normal word order, the sentence would read, "A presentation by Ms. Paley was *following Mrs. Forest's speech*." The introductory phrase is actually part of the predicate; the subject is *a presentation by Ms. Paley*.)

> **BUT:** *Following Mrs. Forest's speech,* Ms. Paley made her presentation. (Participial phrase used as an introductory element; the subject is *Ms. Paley*.)

(Continued on page 26.)

* See Section 19 for definitions of grammatical terms.

1

b. Use a comma after an *introductory infinitive phrase* unless the phrase is the subject of the sentence. (Infinitive phrases are introduced by *to*.)

To get the best results from your dishwasher, follow the printed directions. (The subject *you* is understood.)

To have displayed the goods more effectively, he should have consulted a lighting specialist. (The subject is *he*.)

BUT: *To have displayed the goods more effectively* would have required a lighting specialist. (Infinitive phrase used as subject.)

c. As a general rule, use a comma after all *introductory prepositional phrases.* A comma may be omitted after a *short* prepositional phrase if (1) the phrase does not contain a verb form, (2) the phrase is not a transitional expression or an independent comment, or (3) there is no sacrifice in clarity or desired emphasis. (Many writers use a comma after all introductory prepositional phrases to avoid analysing each situation.)

In response to the many requests of our customers, we are opening a branch in Hanover Square. (Comma required after a long phrase.)

In 2001 our entire inventory was destroyed by fire. (No comma required after a short phrase.)

BUT: *In 2001,* 384 cases of potential lung infections were reported. (Comma required to separate two numbers. See ¶456.)

In preparing your report, be sure to include last year's figures. (Comma required after a short phrase containing a verb form.)

In addition, an 8 percent sales tax must be imposed. (Comma required after a short phrase used as a transitional expression. See ¶¶138a, 139.)

In my opinion, your ads are misleading as they now appear. (Comma required after short phrase used as an independent comment. See ¶¶138b, 139.)

In legal documents, amounts of money are often expressed both in words and in figures. (Comma used to give desired emphasis to the introductory phrase.)

CONFUSING: After all you have gone through a great deal.

CLEAR: *After all,* you have gone through a great deal. (Comma required after a short phrase to prevent misreading.)

NOTE: Omit the comma after an introductory prepositional phrase if the word order in the rest of the sentence is inverted.

Out of an initial investment of $5 000 came a stake that is worth over $2 500 000. (Normal word order: A stake that is worth over $2 500 000 came out of an initial investment of $5 000.)

In an article I read in <u>Time</u> was an account of his trip. (Omit the comma after the introductory phrase when the verb in the main clause immediately follows.)

BUT: *In an article I read in* <u>Time</u>, there was an account . . .

d. When a compound sentence starts with a phrase that applies to both independent clauses, do not use a comma to separate the two clauses if doing so would make the introductory phrase seem to apply only to the first clause. (See also ¶134.)

In response to the many requests of our customers, we are opening a branch in Hanover Square and we are extending our evening hours in all our stores.

136 PHRASES AT THE BEGINNING OF A CLAUSE

a. When a participial, infinitive, or prepositional phrase occurs *at the beginning of a clause within the sentence*, insert or omit the comma following, just as if the phrase were an introductory element at the beginning of the sentence. (See ¶135.)

I was invited to attend the monthly planning meeting last week, and *seizing the opportunity,* I presented an overview of our medium-range plans. (A separating comma follows the participial phrase just as if the sentence began with the word *Seizing.* No comma precedes the phrase because the phrase is considered introductory, not interrupting. See also ¶127d.)

The salesclerk explained that *to get the best results from your dishwasher,* you should follow the printed directions.

We would like to announce that *in response to the many requests of our customers,* we are opening a branch in the Bayview Centre.

Last year we had a number of thefts, and *in 2001* our entire inventory was destroyed by fire. (No comma is needed after a short introductory prepositional phrase.)

b. If the phrase interrupts the flow of the sentence, set it off with two commas.

Pamela is the type of person who, *in the midst of disaster,* will always find something to laugh about.

If, *in the attempt to push matters to a resolution,* you offer that group new terms, they will simply dig in their heels and refuse to bargain.

137 PHRASES ELSEWHERE IN THE SENTENCE

When a participial, infinitive, or prepositional phrase occurs *at some point other than the beginning of a sentence* (see ¶135) *or the beginning of a clause* (see ¶136), commas are omitted or used depending on whether the phrase is essential or non-essential.

a. An *essential* participial, infinitive, or prepositional phrase is necessary to the meaning of the sentence and cannot be omitted. Therefore, do not use commas to set it off.

The catalogue *scheduled for release in November* will have to be delayed until January. (Participial).

The decision *to expand our export activities* has proved sound. (Infinitive.)

The search *for a new general manager* is still going on. (Prepositional.)

b. A non-essential participial, infinitive, or prepositional phrase provides additional information but is not needed to complete the meaning of the sentence. Set off such phrases with commas.

(Continued on page 28.)

1

This new collection of essays, *written in the last two years before his death,* represents his most distinguished work. (Participial.)

I'd rather not attend her reception, *to be frank about it.* (Infinitive.)

Morale appears to be much better, *on the whole.* (Prepositional.)

c. A phrase occurring within a sentence must always be set off by commas when it *interrupts* the flow of the sentence.

The commission, *after hearing arguments on the proposed new tax rate structure,* will consider amendments to the tax law.

The company, *in its attempt to place more women in high-level management positions,* is undertaking a special recruitment program.

The following rules (¶¶138–161) deal with the various uses of commas to set off non-essential expressions. See also ¶¶201–202 and ¶¶218–219 for the use of dashes and parentheses to set off these expressions.

With Transitional Expressions and Independent Comments

138 **a.** Use commas to set off *transitional expressions.* These non-essential words and phrases are called *transitional* because they help the reader mentally relate the preceding thought to the idea now being introduced. They express such notions as:

ADDITION:	additionally (see Section 11), also, besides, furthermore, in addition, moreover, too (see ¶143), what is more
CONSEQUENCE:	accordingly, as a result, consequently, hence (see ¶139b), otherwise, so (see ¶179), then (see ¶139b), therefore, thus (see ¶139b)
SUMMARIZING:	after all, all in all, all things considered, briefly, by and large, in any case, in any event, in brief, in conclusion, in short, in summary, in the final analysis, in the long run, on balance, on the whole, to sum up
GENERALIZING:	as a rule, as usual, for the most part, generally, generally speaking, in general, ordinarily, usually
RESTATEMENT:	in essence, in other words, namely, that is, that is to say
CONTRAST AND COMPARISON:	by contrast, by the same token, conversely, instead, likewise, on one hand, on the contrary, on the other hand, rather, similarly, yet (see ¶179)
CONCESSION:	anyway, at any rate, be that as it may, even so, however, in any case, in any event, nevertheless, still, this fact notwithstanding
SEQUENCE:	afterward, at first, at the same time, finally, first, first of all, for now, for the time being, in conclusion, in the first place, in time, in turn, later on, meanwhile, next, second, then (see ¶139b), to begin with
DIVERSION:	by the by, by the way, incidentally
ILLUSTRATION:	for example, for instance, for one thing

NOTE: The co-ordinating conjunctions *and, but, or,* or *nor* are sometimes used as transitional expressions at the beginning of a sentence. See ¶126b.

☞ *See ¶¶139–142 for the punctuation of transitional expressions depending on where they occur in a sentence.*

b. Use commas to set off *independent comments*, that is, non-essential words or phrases that express writers' attitudes toward the meaning of the sentence. By means of these independent comments, writers indicate that what they are about to say carries their whole-hearted endorsement (*indeed, by all means*) or deserves only their lukewarm support (*apparently, presumably*) or hardly requires saying (*as you already know, clearly, obviously*) or represents only their personal views (*in my opinion, personally*) or arouses some emotion in them (*unfortunately, happily*) or presents their honest position (*frankly, actually, to tell the truth*). Such terms modify the meaning of the sentence as a whole rather than a particular word within the sentence.

AFFIRMATION:	by all means, indeed, of course, yes
DENIAL:	no
REGRET:	alas, unfortunately, regrettably
PLEASURE:	fortunately, happily
QUALIFICATION:	ideally, if necessary, if possible, literally, strictly speaking, theoretically, hopefully (see Section 11)
PERSONAL VIEWPOINT:	according to her, as I see it, in my opinion, personally
ASSERTION OF CANDOUR:	actually, frankly, in reality, to be honest, to say the least, to tell the truth
ASSERTION OF FACT:	as a matter of fact, as it happens, as you know, believe it or not, certainly, clearly, doubtless, in fact, naturally, needless to say, obviously, without doubt
WEAK ASSERTION:	apparently, perhaps, presumably, well

☞ *See ¶¶139–142 for the punctuation of independent comments depending on where they occur in a sentence.*

139 AT THE BEGINNING OF A SENTENCE

a. When the words and phrases listed in ¶138a–b appear at the beginning of a sentence, they should be followed by a comma unless they are used as essential elements.

NON-ESSENTIAL: *After all*, you have done more for him than he had any right to expect.
ESSENTIAL: *After all* you have done for him, he has no right to expect more.

NON-ESSENTIAL: *However*, you look at the letter yourself to see whether you interpret it as I do.
ESSENTIAL: *However* you look at the letter, there is only one interpretation.

NON-ESSENTIAL: *Obviously*, the guest of honour was quite moved by the welcome she received. (Here *obviously* modifies the meaning of the sentence as a whole.)

ESSENTIAL: *Obviously* moved by the welcome she received, the guest of honour spoke with an emotion-choked voice. (Here *obviously* modifies *moved*. In the preceding sentence, *obviously* modifies the meaning of the sentence as a whole.)

(Continued on page 30.)

1

b. When *hence, then,* or *thus* occurs at the beginning of a sentence, the comma following is omitted unless the connective requires special emphasis or a non-essential element occurs at that point.

> *Thus* they thought it wise to get an outside consultant's opinion.
>
> *Then* they decided to go back to their original plan.
>
> **BUT:** *Then,* after they rejected the consultant's recommendation, they decided to go back to their original plan.

☞ *See also ¶142a, note.*

c. When an introductory transitional expression or independent comment is incorporated into the flow of the sentence without any intervening pause, the comma may be omitted.

> *Of course* I can handle it.   *Perhaps* she was joking.
> *No doubt* he meant well.   *Indeed* she was not.

140   AT THE END OF A SENTENCE

Use one comma to set off a transitional expression or an independent comment at the end of a sentence. However, be sure to distinguish between non-essential and essential elements.

> **NON-ESSENTIAL:** Philip goes to every employee reception, *of course.*
> **ESSENTIAL:** Philip goes to every employee reception as a matter *of course.*
>
> **NON-ESSENTIAL:** The deal is going to fall through, *in my opinion.*
> **ESSENTIAL:** It doesn't rank very high *in my opinion.*

141   WITHIN THE SENTENCE

Use two commas to set off a transitional expression or an independent comment when it occurs as a non-essential element within the sentence.

> I, *too,* was not expecting a six-month convalescence.
>
> The doctors tell me, *however,* that I will regain full use of my left leg.

If, however, the expression is used as an essential element, leave the commas out.

> **NON-ESSENTIAL:** Let me say, *to begin with,* that I have always thought highly of him.
> **ESSENTIAL:** If you want to improve your English, you ought *to begin with* a good review of grammar.

NOTE: In many sentences the only way you can tell whether an expression is non-essential or essential is by the way you say it. If your voice tends to *drop* as you utter the expression, it is non-essential and should be set off by commas.

> We concluded, *nevertheless,* that their offer was not serious.
>
> Millie understands, *certainly,* that the reassignment is only temporary.
>
> It is critical, *therefore,* that we rework all these cost estimates.

If your voice tends to *rise* as you utter the expression, it is essential and should not be set off by commas.

> We *nevertheless* concluded that their offer was not serious.

Millie *certainly* understands that the reassignment is only temporary.

It is *therefore* critical that we rework all these cost estimates.

If commas are inserted in the last example above, the entire reading of the sentence will be changed. The voice will rise on the word *is* and drop on *therefore*. (If this is the inflection intended, then commas around *therefore* are appropriate.)

It is, *therefore*, critical that we rework all these cost estimates.

142   AT THE BEGINNING OF A CLAUSE

a. When a transitional expression or independent comment occurs *at the beginning of the second independent clause* in a compound sentence and is *preceded by a semicolon*, use one comma following the expression.

I would love to work in a side trip to Bali; *however*, I don't think I can pull it off.

My boss just approved the purchase order; *therefore*, let's confirm a delivery date.

In sentences like the two above, a period may be used in place of a semicolon. The words *however* and *therefore* would then be capitalized to mark the start of a new sentence, and they would be followed by a comma.

NOTE: When *hence, then,* or *thus* appears at the beginning of an independent clause, the comma following is omitted unless the connective requires special emphasis or a non-essential element occurs at that point. (See also ¶139b.)

Melt the butter over high heat; *then* add the egg.

BUT: Melt the butter over high heat; *then*, when the foam begins to subside, add the egg.

☞ *For the use of a semicolon before a transitional expression, see ¶¶178–180.*

b. When the expression occurs *at the beginning of the second independent clause* in a compound sentence and is *preceded by a comma and a co-ordinating conjunction*, use one comma following the expression. (See also ¶127d.)

The location of the plant was not easy to reach, and *to be honest about it*, I wasn't very taken with the people who interviewed me.

The job seemed to have no future, and *to tell the truth*, the salary was pretty low.

In the first place, I think the budget for the project is unrealistic, and *in the second place*, the deadlines are almost impossible to meet.

NOTE: If the expression is a simple adverb like *therefore*, the comma following the expression is usually omitted. (See also ¶180.)

The matter must be resolved by Friday, and *therefore* our preliminary conference must be held no later than Thursday.

All the general managers have been summoned to a three-day meeting at the home office, and *consequently* I have had to reschedule all my meetings.

(Continued on page 32.)

1

c. If the expression occurs *at the beginning of a dependent clause,* either treat the expression as non-essential (and set it off with two commas) or treat it as essential (and omit the commas).

If, *moreover,* they do not meet the deadline, we can cancel the contract.

If *indeed* they want to settle the dispute, why don't they agree to arbitration?

He is a man who, *in my opinion,* will make a fine marketing director.

She is a woman who *no doubt* knows how to run a department smoothly and effectively.

The situation is so serious that, *strictly speaking,* bankruptcy is the only solution.

The situation is so serious that *perhaps* bankruptcy may be the only solution.

143 WITH THE ADVERB *TOO*

a. When the adverb *too* (in the sense of "also") occurs at the end of a clause or a sentence, the comma preceding is omitted.

If you feel that way *too,* why don't we just drop all further negotiation?

They are after a bigger share of the market *too.*

b. When *too* (in the sense of "also") occurs elsewhere in the sentence, particularly between subject and verb, set it off with two commas.

You, *too,* could be in the Caribbean right now.

Then, *too,* there are the additional taxes to be considered.

c. When *too* is used as an adverb meaning "excessively," it is never set off with commas.

The news is almost *too* good to be believed.

With Interruptions and Afterthoughts

144 Use commas to set off words, phrases, or clauses that interrupt the flow of a sentence or that are loosely added at the end as an afterthought.

Pam is being pursued, *so I've been told,* by three headhunters.

Bob spoke on state-of-the-art financial software, *if I remember correctly.*

Our order processing service, *you must admit,* leaves much to be desired.

His research work has been outstanding, *particularly in the field of ergonomics.*

☞ *See also ¶¶131c, 136b, 137c.*

CAUTION: When enclosing an interrupting expression with two commas, be sure the commas are inserted accurately.

WRONG: That is the best, *though not the cheapest way,* to proceed.
RIGHT: That is the best, *though not the cheapest,* way to proceed.

WRONG: This is better written, *though less exciting than,* her last book.
RIGHT: This book is better written, *though less exciting,* than her last book.

WRONG: Her work is as good, *if not better than,* that of the man she replaced.
RIGHT: Her work is as good as, *if not better than,* that of the man she replaced.

WRONG: Glen has a deep interest in, *as well as a great fondness*, for jazz.
RIGHT: Glen has a deep interest in, *as well as a great fondness for,* jazz.

With Direct Address

145 Names and titles used in direct address must be set off by commas.

We agree, *Mrs. Connolly,* that your order was badly handled.

No, *sir,* that is privileged information.

I count on your support, *Bob.*

With Additional Considerations

146 **a.** When a phrase introduced by *as well as, in addition to, besides, along with, including, accompanied by, together with, plus,* or a similar expression falls between the subject and the verb, it is ordinarily set off by commas. Commas may be omitted, however, if the phrase fits smoothly into the flow of the sentence or is essential to the meaning.

Everyone, *including the top corporate managers,* will be required to attend the in-house seminars on the ethical dimensions of business.

The business plan *including strategies for the new market segments we hope to enter* is better than the other plans I have reviewed. (The *including* phrase is needed to distinguish this plan from the others; hence no commas.)

One *plus one* doesn't always equal two, as we have seen in the Parker-Jackel merger. (The *plus* phrase is essential to the meaning; hence no commas.)

Stephanie *as well as George* should be asked to attend the convention in Vancouver. (The *as well as* phrase flows smoothly in the sentence.)

☞ *For the effect these phrases have on the choice of a singular or a plural verb, see ¶1007. For a usage note on* as well as, *see Section 11.*

b. When the phrase occurs elsewhere in the sentence, commas may be omitted if the phrase is closely related to the preceding words.

The refinancing terms have been approved by the trustees *as well as the creditors.*

BUT: I attended the international monetary conference in Bermuda, *together with five associates from our Montreal office.*

With Contrasting Expressions

147 Use commas to set off contrasting expressions. (Such expressions often begin with *but, not,* or *rather than.*)

The Sanchezes are willing to sell, *but only on their terms.*

He had changed his methods, *not his objectives,* we noticed.

Paula, *rather than Al,* has been chosen for the job.

The CEO and not the president will make that decision. (See ¶1006b.)

NOTE: When such phrases fit smoothly into the flow of the sentence, no commas are required.

(Continued on page 34.)

1

It was a busy *but enjoyable* trip.   They have chosen Paula *rather than Al.*

☞ *For the punctuation of balancing expressions, see ¶172c.*

The following rules (¶¶148–153) deal with descriptive expressions that immediately follow the words to which they refer. When non-essential, these expressions are set off by commas.

With Identifying, Appositive, or Explanatory Expressions

148 Use commas to set off expressions that provide additional but non-essential information about a noun or pronoun immediately preceding. Such expressions serve to further identify or explain the word they refer to.

> Harriet McManus, *an independent real estate agent for the past ten years,* will be joining our agency on Tuesday, *October 1.* (Phrases such as those following *Harriet McManus* and *Tuesday* are appositives.)
>
> Acrophobia, *that is, the fear of great heights,* can now be successfully treated. (See also ¶¶181–183 for other punctuation with *that is, namely,* and *for example.*)
>
> His first book, *written while he was still in graduate school,* launched a successful writing career.
>
> Our first thought, *to run to the nearest exit,* would have resulted in panic.
>
> Ms. Ballantine, *who has been a copywriter for six years,* will be our new copy chief.
>
> Everyone in our family likes outdoor sports, *such as tennis and swimming.* (See ¶149, note.)

NOTE: In some cases other punctuation may be preferable in place of commas.

> CONFUSING: Mr. Newcombe, *my boss,* and I will discuss this problem next week. (Does *my boss* refer to Mr. Newcombe, or are there three people involved?)
>
> CLEAR: Mr. Newcombe (my boss) and I will be discussing this problem next week. (Use parentheses or dashes instead of commas when an appositive expression could be misread as a separate item in a series.)
>
> There are two factors to be considered, *sales and collections.* (A colon or a dash could be used in place of the comma. See ¶¶189, 201.)
>
> BUT: There are three factors to be considered: sales, collections, and inventories. (When the explanatory expression consists of a series of *three* or more items and comes at the end of the sentence, use a colon or dash. See ¶¶189, 201.)
>
> OR: These three factors—sales, collections, and inventories—should be considered. (When the explanatory series comes within the sentence, set it off with dashes or parentheses. See ¶¶183, 202, 219.)

149 When the expression is *essential* to the completeness of the sentence, do not set it off. (In the following examples, the expression is needed to identify which particular item is meant. If the expression were omitted, the sentence would be incomplete.)

> The year *2005* marks the one hundredth anniversary of our company.
>
> The word *liaison* is often misspelled.
>
> The poet *Al Purdy* gave a reading last week from a work in progress.
>
> The statement *"I don't remember"* was frequently heard in court yesterday.

The impulse *to get away from it all* is very common.

The notes *in green ink* were made by Mrs. Long.

The person *who takes over as general manager* will need everyone's support.

NOTE: Compare the following sets of examples:

Her article *"Colour and Design"* was published in June. (The title is essential; it identifies *which* article.)

Her latest article, *"Colour and Design,"* was published in June. (Non-essential; the word *latest* already indicates which article.)

Her latest article *on colour and design* was published in June. (Without commas, this means she had earlier articles on the same subject.)

Her latest article, *on colour and design*, was published in June. (With commas, this means her earlier articles were on other subjects.)

Everyone in our family likes such outdoor sports *as tennis and swimming*. (The phrase *as tennis and swimming* is essential; without it, the reader would not know which outdoor sports were meant.)

Everyone in our family likes outdoor sports, *such as tennis and swimming*. (The main clause, *Everyone in our family likes outdoor sports*, expresses a complete thought; the phrase *such as tennis and swimming* gives additional but non-essential information. Hence a comma is needed before *such as*.)

Words *such as peak, peek, and pique* can be readily confused. (The *such as* phrase indicates which words are meant.)

A number of Fortune 500 companies, *such as GE, TRW, and Du Pont*, have introduced new programs to motivate their middle managers. (The *such as* phrase provides additional but non-essential information.)

150   A number of expressions are treated as essential simply because of a very close relationship with the preceding words. (If read aloud, the combined phrase sounds like one unit, without any intervening pause.)

After a while Gladys *herself* became disenchanted with the Vancouver scene.

We *legislators* must provide funds for retraining unemployed workers.

My wife Patricia has begun her own consulting business. (Strictly speaking, *Patricia* should be set off by commas, since the name is not needed to indicate *which* wife. However, commas are omitted in expressions like these because they are read as a unit.)

My brother Paul may join us as well.
BUT: My brother, *Paul Strand*, may join us.

The composer *Stephen Sondheim* has many broadway hits to his credit.
BUT: My favourite composer, *Stephen Sondheim*, has many Broadway hits . . .

The Story of English by Robert McCrum, William Cran, and Robert MacNeil has been made into a highly praised television series. (Unless there is another book with the same title, the *by* phrase identifying the authors is not essential and should be set off by commas. However, since a book title and a *by* phrase are typically read as a unit, commas are usually omitted.)

151   When *or* introduces a word or a phrase that identifies or explains the preceding word, set off the explanatory expression with commas.

(Continued on page 36.)

1

Determine whether the clauses are co-ordinate, *or of equal rank.* (The non-essential *or* phrase may also be set off by parentheses.)

However, if *or* introduces an alternative thought, the expression is essential and should not be set off by commas.

Determine whether the clauses are co-ordinate *or not co-ordinate.*

152 When a business letter or some other document is referred to by date, any related phrases or clauses that follow are usually non-essential.

Thank you for your letter of February 27, *in which you questioned the balance on your account.* (The date is sufficient to identify which letter is meant; the *in which* clause simply provides additional but non-essential information.) Of course, if one received more than one letter with the same date from the same person, the *in which* clause would be essential and the comma would be omitted.

However, no comma is needed after the date if the following phrase is short and closely related.

Thank you for your letter of February 27 *about the balance on your account.*

NOTE: Under certain circumstances—for example, around the end of the year—it is better to provide the full date rather than the month and day alone. (See ¶409.)

Thank you for your letter of December 27, 2003, in which . . .

With Residence and Business Connections

153 Use commas to set off a *long phrase* denoting a person's residence or business connections.

Ken Gary, *of Hartco Enterprises in Anjou, Quebec,* will be visiting us next week.

Ken Gary *of Anjou, Quebec,* will be visiting us next week. (Omit the comma before *of* to avoid too many breaks in a short phrase. The provincial name must be set off by commas when it follows a city name. See also ¶160.)

Ken Gary *of Hartco Enterprises* will be visiting us next week. (Short phrase; no commas.)

Ken Gary *of Anjou* will be visiting us next week. (Short phrase; no commas.)

The following rules (¶¶154–161) deal with the "non-essential" treatment of certain elements in dates, personal names, company names, and addresses. However, the established tradition of setting them off with commas has in many cases begun to change.

In Dates

154 **a.** Use two commas to set off the year when it follows the month and day.

On July 1, *2006,* I plan to retire and open a bookshop in Moncton.

The August 28, *2003,* issue of *Legend* forecasted that telecommunication carriers will continue to spend more in the critical area of bandwidth expansion and optical systems.

b. When the month, day, and year are used as a non-essential expression, be sure to set the entire phrase off with commas.

The conference scheduled to begin on Monday, *November 27, 2003,* has now been rescheduled to start on February 6, 2004.

Payment of estimated income taxes for the fourth quarter of 2003 will be due no later than Wednesday, *January 15, 2004.*

155 Omit the commas when only the month and year are given.

In *August 2001* Glen and I dissolved our partnership and went our independent ways.

Isn't it about time for *Consumer Reports* to update the evaluation of cordless telephones that appeared in the *November 2000* issue?

☞ *For additional examples involving dates, see ¶410.*

With *Jr., Sr.,* Etc.

156 Do not use commas to set off *Jr., Sr.,* or Roman or Arabic numerals following a person's name unless you know that the person in question prefers to do so.

Kelsey R. Patterson Jr.	Benjamin Hart 2nd
Christopher M. Gorman Sr.	Anthony Jung III

John Bond Jr.'s resignation will be announced tomorrow.

NOTE: When a person prefers to use commas in his or her name, observe the following style:

Peter Passaro, Jr. (Use one comma when the name is displayed on a line by itself.)

Peter Passaro, Jr., director of . . . (Use two commas when other copy follows.)

Peter Passaro, Jr.'s promotion . . . (Drop the second comma when a possessive ending is attached.)

157 Abbreviations like *Esq.* and those that stand for academic degrees or religious orders are set off by two commas when they follow a person's name.

Address the letter to Martin E. Prest, *Esq.,* in Winnipeg.

Roger Farrier, *LL.D.,* will address the Elizabethan Club on Wednesday.

The Reverend James Hanley, *S.J.,* will serve as moderator of the panel.

158 When a personal name is given in inverted order, set off the inverted portion with commas.

McCaughan, James W., Jr.

With *Inc.* and *Ltd.*

159 Do not use commas to set off *Inc., Ltd.,* and similar expressions in a company name unless you know that a particular company prefers to do so. (See also ¶¶1328–1329.)

Time Inc.   Field Hats, Ltd.

Time *Inc.* has expanded its operations beyond magazine publishing.

Field Hats, *Ltd.,* should be notified about this mistake.

(Continued on page 38.)

1

NOTE: When commas are to be used in a company name, follow this style:

McGraw-Hill, Inc. (Use one comma when the name is displayed on a line by itself.)

McGraw-Hill, Inc., announces the publication of . . . (Use two commas when other copy follows.)

McGraw-Hill, Inc.'s annual statement . . . (Drop the second comma after a possessive ending.)

☞ *For the use of commas with other parts of a company name, see ¶163.*

In Geographic References and Addresses

160 Use two commas to set off the name of a province, country, or the equivalent when it directly follows the name of a city or a county.

Four years ago I was transferred from Calgary, *Alberta*, to Nairobi, *Kenya*.

Could Parkview County, *Alberta*, become a haven for retired teachers?

Our LaSalle, *Quebec*, office is the one nearest to you.
OR: Our LaSalle (Quebec) office is the one nearest to you. (Parentheses are clearer than commas when a city-province expression serves as an adjective.)

Victoria, *B.C.'s* transportation system has improved greatly since I was last there. (Omit the second comma after a possessive ending.)

NOTE: In sentences that mention one or more cities, omit the province or country names if the cities are well known and are clearly linked with only one province or country.

We'll be holding meetings in Montreal, Toronto, and Vancouver.

My agent has arranged for me to address conference delegates in Rome, Paris, and London.

161 When expressing complete addresses, follow this style:

IN SENTENCES: During the month of August, you can send all documents directly to me at 402 Woodbury Road, Toronto, ON M3X 4B4, or you can ask my assistant to forward it. (Note that a comma follows the postal code but does not precede it.)

IN DISPLAYED BLOCKS: 402 Woodbury Road
Toronto, ON M3X 4B4

The following rules (¶¶162–175) deal with various uses of separating commas: to separate items in a series, to separate adjectives that precede a noun, and to clarify meaning in sentences with unusual word order or omitted words.

In a Series

162 When three or more items are listed in a series and the last item is preceded by *and*, *or*, or *nor*, place a comma before the conjunction as well as between the other items. (See also ¶126c.)

Study the rules for the use of the comma, the semicolon, *and* the colon.

The consensus is that your report is well written, that your facts are accurate, *and* that your conclusions are sound.

The show will appeal equally to women and men, adults and children, *and* sophisticates and innocents. (See Section 11 for a usage note on *and*.)

NOTE: If a non-essential element follows the conjunction (*and, or,* or *nor*) in a series, omit the comma before the conjunction to avoid excessive punctuation.

We invited Ben's business associates, his friends and, of course, his parents.

(**RATHER THAN:** . . . his friends, and, of course, his parents.)

163 For a series in an organization's name, always follow the style preferred by that organization.

Merrill Lynch, Pierce, Fenner & Smith, Inc.	Fraser Milner Casgrain
Smith Barney, Harris Upham & Co.	Rauscher Pierce Refnes, Inc.

If you do not have the company's letterhead or some other reliable resource at hand, follow the standard rule on commas in a series (see ¶162).

Our primary supplier is *Ames, Koslow, Milke, and Company.*

NOTE: Do not use a comma before an ampersand (&) in an organization's name unless you know that a particular organization prefers to do so.

Fric, Lowenstein & Co.

164 When an expression such as *and so on* or *etc.* closes a series, use a comma before and after the expression (unless the expression falls at the end of a sentence).

Our sale of suits, coats, hats, *and so on,* starts tomorrow.

Tomorrow morning we will start our sale of suits, coats, hats, *etc.*

☞ *For a usage note on* etc., *see Section 11.*

165 Do not insert a comma after the last item in a series unless the sentence structure demands a comma at that point.

May 8, June 11, and July 14 are the dates for the next three hearings.

May 8, June 11, and July 14, *2006,* are the dates for the next three hearings.

(The comma after *2006* is one of a pair that sets off the year. See ¶154.)

166 When *and, or,* or *nor* is used to connect all the items in a series, do not separate the items by commas. (See also ¶123b.)

Send copies to our employees *and* stockholders *and* major customers.

167 If a series consists of only two items, do not separate the items with a comma. (See also ¶125f.)

We can send the samples to you *by regular mail* or *by one of the express services.*

NOTE: Use a comma, however, to separate two independent clauses joined by *and, but, or,* or *nor.* (See ¶¶123a, 126a.)

☞ *For the use of the semicolon in a series, see ¶¶184–185.*

1

With Adjectives

168 When two consecutive adjectives modify the same noun, separate the adjectives with a comma.

> Jean is a *generous, outgoing* person. (A person who is *generous and outgoing.*)

NOTE: Do *not* use a comma between the adjectives if they are connected by *and*, *or*, or *nor*.

> Jean is a *generous and outgoing* person.

169 When two adjectives precede a noun, the first adjective may modify the combined idea of the second adjective plus the noun. In such cases do not separate the adjectives by a comma.

> The estate is surrounded by an *old stone* wall. (A *stone* wall that is *old.*)

> Here is the *annual financial* statement. (A *financial* statement that is *annual.*)

TEST: To decide whether consecutive adjectives should be separated by a comma or not, try using them in a relative clause *after* the noun, with *and* inserted between them. If they read smoothly and sensibly in that position, they should be separated by a comma in their actual position.

> We need an *intelligent, enterprising* person for the job. (One can speak of "a person who is *intelligent* and *enterprising,*" so a comma is correct.)

> Throw out your *old winter* coat. (One cannot speak of "a coat that is *old* and *winter,*" so no comma should be used in the actual sentence.)

> You can purchase any of these printers with a *low down* payment. (In this case the adjective *low* modifies a compound noun, *down payment.*)

> To put it gently but plainly, I think Jason is a *low-down* scoundrel. (In this case *low-down* is a compound adjective and requires a hyphen to connect *low* and *down*. See ¶¶813–832 for a discussion of compound adjectives.)

170 When more than two adjectives precede a noun, insert a comma only between those adjectives where *and* could have been used.

> a *relaxed, unruffled, confident* manner (a relaxed *and* unruffled *and* confident manner)

> an *experienced, efficient* legal secretary (an experienced *and* efficient legal secretary)

> the established Canadian political system (*and* cannot be inserted between these three adjectives)

171 Do not use a comma between the final adjective in a series and the following noun.

> I put in a long, hard, *demanding day* on Monday.

> (**NOT:** I put in a long, hard, *demanding, day* on Monday.)

To Indicate Omitted Words

172 **a. Omission of Repetitive Wording.** Use a comma to indicate the omission of repetitive wording in a compound sentence. (This use of the comma usually occurs when clauses are separated by semicolons.)

> Employees aged 55 and over are eligible for a complete physical examination every year; those between 50 and 54, every two years; and those under 50, every three years.

NOTE: If the omitted words are clearly understood from the context, simpler punctuation may be used.

Employees aged 55 and over are eligible for a complete physical examination every year, those between 50 and 54 every two years, and those under 50 every three years.

b. Omission of *That*. In some sentences the omission of the conjunction *that* creates a definite break in the flow of the sentence. In such cases insert a comma to mark the break.

Remember, this offer is good only through May 31.

The problem is, not all of these assumptions may be correct.

The fact is, things are not working out as we had hoped.

Chances are, the deal will never come off.

NOTE: In sentences that are introduced by expressions such as *he said*, *she thinks*, *we feel*, or *they know*, the conjunction *that* is often omitted following the introductory expression. In such cases no comma is necessary because there is no break in the flow of the sentence.

We know you can do it.	She said she would handle everything.
They think our price is too high.	We believe we offer the best service.

c. Balancing Expressions. Use a comma to separate the two parts of a balancing expression from which many words have been omitted.

First come, first served.	The more we give, the more they take.
First in, last out.	Here a comma, there a comma.
Here today, gone tomorrow.	The less I see of him, the better I like it.

NOTE: The phrase *The sooner the better* usually appears without a separating comma.

To Indicate Unusual Word Order

173 In some colloquial sentences, clauses or phrases occur out of normal order and connective words may be omitted. Use a comma to mark the resulting break in the flow of the sentence.

You must not miss the play, it was that good.

(**NORMAL ORDER:** The play was so good that you must not miss it.)

Why he took the money, I'll never understand.

That the shipment would be late, we were prepared to accept; that you would ship the wrong goods, we did not expect.

NOTE: In formal writing, these sentences should be recast in normal word order.

☞ *See also ¶135c, note.*

For Special Emphasis

174 Individual words may be set off by commas for special emphasis.

I have tried, *sincerely*, to understand your problems.

(Continued on page 42.)

1

They contend, *unrealistically*, that we can cut back on staff and still generate the same amount of output.

NOTE: The use of commas in the examples above forces the reader to dwell momentarily on the word that has been set off in each case. Without this treatment *sincerely* and *unrealistically* would not receive this emphasis.

For Clarity

175 **a.** Use a comma to prevent misreading.

As you know, nothing came of the meeting.

(**NOT:** As you know nothing came of the meeting.)

To a skydiver like Marc, Garneau seems to be out in space.

Soon after, the committee disbanded without accomplishing its goal.

b. Sometimes, for clarity, it is necessary to separate two verbs.

All any insurance policy is, is a contract for services.

c. Use a comma to separate repeated words.

It was a *long, long* time ago.

That was a *very, very* old argument.

Well, well, we'll find a way.

Now, now, you don't expect me to believe that!

☞ *Commas with dashes: see ¶¶213, 215b.*
Commas in numbers: see ¶¶413b, 461–463.
Commas with questions within sentences: see ¶¶114–117.
Commas with parentheses: see ¶224a.
Commas inside closing quotation marks: see ¶247.
Commas at the end of quotations: see ¶¶253–255.
Commas preceding quotations: see ¶256.
Commas with quotations within a sentence: see ¶¶259–261.
Commas to set off interruptions in quoted matter: see ¶¶262–263.
Spacing with commas: see ¶298.

THE SEMICOLON
Between Independent Clauses—*And, But, Or,* or *Nor* Omitted

176 **a.** When a co-ordinating conjunction (*and, but, or,* or *nor,* and sometimes *for, so,* or *yet*) is omitted between two independent clauses, use a semicolon—not a comma—to separate the clauses. If you prefer, you can treat the second clause as a separate sentence. (See ¶187.)

Most of the stockholders favoured the sale; management did not.
OR: Most of the stockholders favoured the sale. Management did not.
NOT: Most of the stockholders favoured the sale, management did not.

Bob is going for his M.B.A.; Janet already has hers.

Subnotebooks aren't just smaller; they're cheaper.

NOT: Subnotebooks aren't just smaller, they're cheaper.

b. If the clauses are not closely related, treat them as separate sentences.

WEAK: Thank you for your letter of September 8; your question has already been passed on to the manager of mail-order sales, and you should be hearing from Ms. Livonia within three days.

BETTER: Thank you for your letter of September 8. Your question has already been passed on to the manager of mail-order sales, and you should be . . .

c. The omission of *but* between two independent clauses requires, strictly speaking, the use of a semicolon between the two clauses. However, when the clauses are short, a comma is commonly used to preserve the flow of the sentence.

Not only was the food bad, the portions were minuscule.

Between Independent Clauses—
And, But, Or, or *Nor* Included

177 A comma is normally used to separate two independent clauses joined by a co-ordinating conjunction. However, under certain circumstances a semicolon is appropriate before the co-ordinating conjunction.

a. Use a semicolon in order to achieve a stronger break between clauses than a comma provides.

NORMAL BREAK: Many people are convinced that they could personally solve the problem if given the authority to do so, but no one will come forward with a clear-cut plan that we can evaluate in advance.

STRONG BREAK: Many people are convinced that they could personally solve the problem if given the authority to do so; but no one will come forward with a clear-cut plan that we can evaluate in advance.

b. Use a semicolon when one or both clauses have internal commas, and a misreading might occur if a comma also separated the clauses.

CONFUSING: I sent you an order for copier paper, computer paper, and No. 10 envelopes, and shipping tags, cardboard cartons, stapler wire, and binding tape were sent to me instead.

CLEAR: I sent you an order for copier paper, computer paper, and No. 10 envelopes; and shipping tags, cardboard cartons, stapler wire, and binding tape were sent to me instead.

NOTE: To prevent misreading, you will usually find it better to reword the sentence than rely on stronger punctuation.

BETTER: I sent you an order for copier paper, computer paper, and No. 10 envelopes, and you sent me shipping tags, cardboard cartons, stapler wire, and binding tape instead. (The shift in the verb from passive to active eliminates any confusion and produces a stronger sentence as well.)

(Continued on page 44.)

1

On June 8, 2003, I discussed this problem with your customer service manager, Betty Dugan; but your company has taken no further action.

All in all, we are satisfied with the job Chen Associates did; and in view of the tight deadlines they had to meet, we are pleased that they came through as well as they did.

☞ *For additional examples, see ¶133.*

With Transitional Expressions

178 When independent clauses are linked by transitional expressions (see a partial list below), use a semicolon between the clauses. (If the second clause is long or requires special emphasis, treat it as a separate sentence.)

accordingly	however	so (see ¶179)
besides	moreover	that is (see ¶181)
consequently	namely (see ¶181)	then
for example (see ¶181)	nevertheless	therefore
furthermore	on the contrary	thus
hence	otherwise	yet (see ¶179)

They have given us an oral okay to proceed; *however,* we are still waiting for written confirmation.

Our costs have started to level off; our sales, *moreover,* have continued to grow.

Let's give them another month; *then* we can pin them down on their progress.

NOTE: Use a comma after the transitional expression when it occurs at the start of the second clause. (See the first example above.) However, no comma is needed after *hence, then, thus, so,* and *yet* unless a pause is wanted at that point. (See the third example above.)

☞ *For the use of commas with transitional expressions, see ¶¶138–143.*

REMEMBER: A semicolon is needed to separate independent clauses, not so much because a transitional expression is present but because a co-ordinating conjunction is absent.

179 An independent clause introduced by *so* (in the sense of "therefore") or *yet* may be preceded by a comma or a semicolon. Use a comma if the two clauses are closely related and there is a smooth flow from the first clause to the second. Use a semicolon or period if the clauses are long and complicated or if the transition between clauses calls for a long pause or a strong break.

Sales have been good, *yet* profits are low.

This report explains why production has slowed down; *yet* it does not indicate how to avoid future glitches.

These sale-priced attaché cases are going fast, *so* don't delay if you want one.

We have been getting an excessive number of complaints during the last few months about our service; *so* I would like each of you to review the operations in your department and indicate what corrective measures you think ought to be taken. (**OR:** . . . about our service. So I would like . . .)

180 If both a co-ordinating conjunction and a transitional expression occur at the start of the second clause, use a comma before the conjunction.

The site has a number of disadvantages, *and furthermore* the asking price is quite high. (See ¶142b and note.)

With *For Example, Namely, That Is,* Etc.

181 BEFORE AN INDEPENDENT CLAUSE

a. In general, when two independent clauses are linked by a transitional expression such as *for example (e.g.), namely,* or *that is (i.e.),* use a semicolon before the expression and a comma afterward.

She is qualified for the job; *for example,* she has had ten years' experience.

NOTE: You can replace the semicolon with a period and treat the second clause as a separate sentence.

She is qualified for the job. *For example,* she has had . . .

b. If the first clause serves to anticipate the second clause and the full emphasis is to fall on the second clause, use a colon before the transitional expression.

Your proposal covers all but one point: *namely,* who is going to foot the bill?

c. For a stronger but less formal break between clauses, the semicolon or the colon may be replaced by a dash.

Hampton says he will help—*that is,* he will help if you ask him to.

NOTE: Use the abbreviated forms *e.g.* and *i.e.* only in informal, technical, or expedient documents (such as business forms, catalogues, and routine memos, e-mails, and letters between business offices). (See ¶502.)

182 AT THE END OF A SENTENCE
When *for example, namely,* or *that is* introduces words, phrases, or a series of clauses *at the end of a sentence,* the punctuation preceding the expression may vary as follows:

a. If the first part of the sentence expresses the complete thought and the explanation that follows seems to be added on as an afterthought, use a semicolon before the transitional expression.

Always use figures with abbreviations; *for example,* 6 m, 9 cm^2, 4 p.m. (Here the earlier part of the sentence carries the main thought; the examples are a welcome but non-essential addition.)

NOTE: The use of a semicolon before *for example* with a series of phrases is an exception to the general rule that a semicolon is always followed by an independent clause.

b. If the first part of the sentence suggests that an important explanation or illustration will follow, use a colon before the transitional expression to throw emphasis on what *follows.*

(Continued on page 46.)

1

My assistant has three important duties: *namely*, attending all meetings, writing the minutes, and sending out notices. (The word *three* anticipates the enumeration following *namely*. The colon suggests that what follows is the main thought of the sentence.)

NOTE: Use a comma before the transitional expression to throw emphasis on what *precedes*.

I checked these figures with three people, *namely, Joan, Andy, and Jim.* (This punctuation emphasizes *three people* rather than the specific names.)

  c. If the expression introduces an appositive that explains a word or phrase immediately preceding, a comma should precede the transitional expression.

Most of the committee voted to reject the plan, *that is, several of the more influential members.* (Here again, a comma is used because what precedes the transitional expression is more important than what follows.)

  d. The semicolon, the colon, and the comma in the examples in ¶182a–c may be replaced by a dash or by parentheses. The dash provides a stronger but less formal break; the parentheses serve to subordinate the explanatory element. (See also ¶¶201–205, 219.)

183 WITHIN A SENTENCE
When *for example, namely,* or *that is* introduces words, phrases, or clauses *within a sentence*, treat the entire construction as non-essential and set it off with commas, dashes, or parentheses. Dashes will give emphasis to the interrupting construction; parentheses will make the construction appear less important than the rest of the words in the sentence.

Many of the components, *for example, the motor,* are manufactured in Barrie.

Many of the components—*for example, the motor*—are manufactured in Barrie.

Many of the components (*for example, the motor*) are manufactured in Barrie.

NOTE: Commas can be used to set off the non-essential element so long as it contains no internal punctuation (other than the comma after the introductory expression). If the non-essential element is internally punctuated with several commas, set it off with either dashes or parentheses.

Many of the components—*for example, the motor, the batteries, and the cooling unit*—are manufactured . . . (Use dashes for emphasis.)

OR: Many of the components (*for example, the motor, the batteries, and the cooling unit*) are manufactured . . . (Use parentheses for subordination.)

In a Series
184 Use a semicolon to separate items in a series if any of the items already contain commas.

The company will be represented on the Yorkton Environmental Council by May Janowski, director of public affairs; Harris Madsen, vice-president of manufacturing; and Daniel St. Clair, director of environmental systems.

NOTE: As an alternative, use parentheses to enclose the title following each name. Then use commas to separate the items in the series.

The company will be represented on the Yorkton Environmental Council by May Janowski (director of public affairs), Harris Madsen (vice-president of manufacturing), and Daniel St. Clair (director of environmental systems).

185 Avoid starting a sentence with a series punctuated with semicolons. Try to recast the sentence so that the series comes at the end.

AWKWARD: New offices in Whitby, Ontario; Brandon, Manitoba; Red Deer, Alberta; and Laval, Quebec, will be opened next year.

IMPROVED: Next year we will open new offices in Whitby, Ontario; Brandon, Manitoba; Red Deer, Alberta; and Laval, Quebec.

With Dependent Clauses

186 Use semicolons to separate a series of parallel dependent clauses if they are long or contain internal commas.

They promised that they would review the specifications, costs, and estimates; that they would analyse Mark's alternative figures; and that they would prepare a comparison of the two proposals and submit their recommendations.

If you have tried special clearance sales but have not raised the necessary cash; if you have tried to borrow the money and have not been able to find a lender; if you have offered to sell part of the business but have not been able to find a partner, then your only course of action is to go out of business. (See ¶185.)

NOTE: A simple series of dependent clauses requires only commas, just like any other kind of series. (See also ¶162.)

Mrs. Mah said that all the budgets had to be redone by Monday, that she could not provide us with any extra help, and that we'd better cancel any weekend plans.

☞ *Semicolons with dashes: see ¶¶213, 215c.*
Semicolons with parentheses: see ¶224a.
Semicolons with quotation marks: see ¶248.
Spacing with semicolons: see ¶298.

THE COLON
Between Independent Clauses

187 **a.** Use a colon between two independent clauses when the second clause explains or illustrates the first clause and there is no co-ordinating conjunction or transitional expression linking the two clauses.

I have a special fondness for the Nova Scotia coast: it reminds me of the many happy summers we spent there before our children went off to college.

I have two major hurdles to clear before I get my Ph.D.: pass the oral exam and write a dissertation.

NOTE: The second clause that explains or illustrates the first clause may itself consist of more than one independent clause.

It has been said that a successful project goes through three stages: it won't work, it costs too much, and I always knew it was a good idea.

(Continued on page 48.)

1

b. Compare the use of the colon and the semicolon in the following sentences.

The job you have described sounds very attractive: the salary, the benefits, and the opportunities for training and advancement seem excellent. (Use a colon when the second clause explains the first.)

The job you have described sounds very attractive; it is the kind of job I have been looking for. (Use a semicolon when the second clause does not explain the first.)

The job you have described sounds very attractive; for example, the salary and the benefits are good, and the opportunities for advancement seem excellent. (Ordinarily, use a semicolon when a transitional expression links the clauses. However, see ¶188.)

c. If you aren't sure whether to use a semicolon or a colon between two independent clauses, you can always treat each clause as a separate sentence and use a period at the end of each.

The job you have described sounds very attractive. For example, the salary and the benefits are good, and the opportunities for advancement seem excellent.

Before Lists and Enumerations

188 Place a colon before such expressions as *for example, namely,* and *that is* when they introduce words, phrases, or a series of clauses anticipated earlier in the sentence. (See ¶¶181–182.)

The company provides a number of benefits not commonly offered in this area: for example, free dental insurance, low-cost term insurance, and personal financial counselling services.

189 When a clause contains an anticipatory expression (such as *the following, as follows, thus,* and *these*) and directs attention to a series of explanatory words, phrases, or clauses, use a colon between the clause and the series.

These are some of the new features in this year's models: a fuel economy indicator, a new rear suspension, and a three-year limited warranty.

The following staff members have been selected to attend the national sales conference in Quebec City:

Frances Beaulieu
Bayda Grewal
Kelly Chow

190 Use a colon even if the anticipatory expression is only implied and not stated.

The house has attractive features: cross ventilation in every room, a two-storey living room, and two terraces.

Scientists have devised a most appropriate name for a physical property opposed to gravity: levity. (The colon may be used even when what follows is only a single word. See also ¶210.)

191 Do not use a colon in the following cases:

a. If the anticipatory expression occurs near the beginning of a long sentence.

We have set *the following* restrictions on the return of merchandise, so please be aware of this new policy when dealing with customers. Goods cannot be returned after five days, and price tags must not be removed.

BUT: We have set *the following* restrictions on the return of merchandise: goods cannot be returned . . .

b. If the sentence containing the anticipatory expression is followed by another sentence.

Campers will find that *the following* small items will add much to their enjoyment of the summer. These articles may be purchased from a store near the camp.

Flashlight	Hot-cold food bag
Camera	Fishing gear

c. If an explanatory series follows an introductory clause that does not express a complete thought. (In such cases the introductory element often ends with a verb or a preposition.)

WRONG: Some of the questions that this book answers are: How can you reduce your insurance expenses without sacrificing protection? How can you avoid being over- or underinsured? How can you file a claim correctly the first time around? (Here the introductory clause is incomplete. It has a subject, *Some*, and a verb, *are*, but it lacks a complement.)

RIGHT: Some of the questions that this book answers are these: How can you . . . ? (Here the introductory clause is complete; hence a colon is acceptable.)

RIGHT: Here are some of the questions that this book answers: How can you . . . ? (Here again the introductory clause is complete; hence a colon is acceptable.)

WRONG: The panel consists of: Ms. Seidel, Mrs. Kitay, and Mr. Haddad.

RIGHT: The panel consists of Ms. Seidel, Mrs. Kitay, and Mr. Haddad.

RIGHT: The panel consists of the following people: Ms. Seidel, Mrs. Kitay, and Mr. Haddad.

WRONG: This set of china includes: 12 dinner plates, 12 salad plates, and 12 cups and saucers.

RIGHT: This set of china includes 12 dinner plates, 12 salad plates, and 12 cups and saucers.

RIGHT: This set of china includes the following items: 12 dinner plates, 12 salad plates, and 12 cups and saucers.

EXCEPTION: A colon may be used after a preposition or a verb if the items in the series are enumerated or listed on separate lines.

This set of china includes:	The panel consists of:
12 dinner plates	Ms. Seidel
12 salad plates	Mrs. Kitay
12 cups and saucers	Mr. Haddad

In Expressions of Time and Proportions

192 When hours and minutes are expressed in figures, separate them with a colon, as in the expression *8:25*. (No space precedes or follows this colon. See also ¶¶298, 1625b.)

193 A colon is used to represent the word *to* in proportions, as in the ratio *2:1*. (No space precedes or follows this colon. See also ¶298.)

1

In Business Documents

194 a. If punctuation is to follow the salutation in business letters, use a colon (see also ¶1346). In social-business letters, use a comma. (See also ¶1397b.)

b. In business letters, a colon is often used with such elements as reference notations (see ¶1316), attention and subject lines (see ¶¶1344–1353), and closing notations required after the signature line (see ¶¶1370–1381).

c. In memos and other business documents, use a colon after displayed guide words. (See ¶1395d.)

TO: FROM: DATE: SHIP TO: BILL TO: *Distribution:*

In References to Books or Publications

195 a. Use a colon to separate the title and the subtitle of a book.

W.F. Garrett-Petts, in *Writing About Literature: A Guide for Students,* has provided practical advice for writing essays.

b. A colon may be used to separate volume number and page number in footnotes and similar references. (Leave no space before or after the colon. See also ¶298.)

8:763–766 (meaning *Volume 8, pages 763–766;* see also ¶1512, note)

NOTE: A reference to chapter and verse in the Bible is handled the same way:

Is. 55:10 (meaning *Chapter 55, verse 10* in the Book of Isaiah)

Capitalizing After a Colon

196 Do not capitalize after a colon if the material that follows cannot stand alone as a sentence.

All cash advances must be countersigned by me, with one exception: when the amount is less than $50. (Dependent clause following a colon.)

Two courses are required: algebra and English. (Words following a colon.)

EXCEPTION: Capitalize the first word after the colon if it is a proper noun, a proper adjective, or the pronoun *I*.

Two courses are required: English and algebra.

197 Do not capitalize the first word of an independent clause after a colon if the clause explains, illustrates, or amplifies the thought expressed in the first part of the sentence. (See ¶196, exception.)

Essential and non-essential elements require altogether different punctuation: the latter should be set off by commas; the former should not.

198 Capitalize the first word of an independent clause after a colon if it requires special emphasis or is presented as a formal rule. (In such cases the independent clause expresses the main thought; the first part of the sentence usually functions only as an introduction.)

Let me say this: If the company is to recover from its present difficulties, we must immediately devise an entirely new marketing strategy.

Here is the key principle: Non-essential elements must be set off by commas; essential elements should not.

199 Capitalize the first word after a colon under these circumstances:

a. When the material following the colon consists of two or more sentences.

There are several drawbacks to this proposal: First, it will tie up a good deal of capital for the next five years. Second, the likelihood of a significant return on the investment has not been shown.

b. When the material following the colon is a quoted sentence.

Frederick Raine responded in this way: "We expect to win our case once all the facts are brought out in the trial." (See ¶256 for the use of a colon before a quoted sentence.)

c. When the material following the colon starts on a new line (for example, the body of a letter following the salutation or the individual items displayed on separate lines in a list).

Dear John:

I have read your latest draft, and I find it much improved. However, on page 4 I wish you would redo . . .

Capitalize the first word of:

a. Every sentence.
b. Direct quotations.
c. Salutations in letters.

d. When the material *preceding* the colon is a short introductory word such as *Note, Caution,* or *Wanted*.

Note: All expense reports must be submitted no later than Friday.

Remember: All equipment must be turned off before you leave.

e. When the material *preceding* the colon is the name of a speaker in the transcription of court testimony or in a script for a play. (See also ¶270.)

THOMAS: Why commit robbery here?

VAILLANCOURT: I came to Toronto because the banks have more money in them.

☞ *Colons with dashes: see ¶¶213, 215c.*

Colons with parentheses: see ¶224a.

Colons with quotation marks: see ¶¶248, 256.

Spacing with colons: see ¶298.

 See the Online Learning Centre at www.mcgrawhill.ca/college/gregg for related weblinks.

SECTION TWO

Punctuation: Other Marks

ITALICS AND UNDERLINING (¶¶285–290)

OTHER MARKS OF PUNCTUATION (¶¶291–297)

SPACING: WITH PUNCTUATION MARKS (¶298)

THE DASH

Although the dash has a few specific functions of its own, it most often serves in place of the comma, the semicolon, the colon, or parentheses. When used as an alternative to these other marks, it creates a much more emphatic separation of words within a sentence. Because of its versatility, some writers are tempted to use a dash to punctuate almost any break within a sentence. However, this indiscriminate use of dashes destroys the special forcefulness that a dash can convey. So use it sparingly— and then only for deliberate effect.

The dash used in ¶201 up to and including ¶215 is known as the **em dash** and has the same width as a capital M. The remaining kinds of dashes are discussed and illustrated in ¶216.

In Place of Commas

201   Use dashes in place of commas to set off a non-essential element that requires special emphasis. (See ¶216 for the construction of a dash.)

(Continued on page 54.)

At this year's annual banquet, the speakers—and the food—were superb.

Of all the colour samples you sent me, there was only one I liked—taupe.

202 If a non-essential element already contains internal commas, use dashes in place of commas to set the element off. (If dashes provide too emphatic a break, use parentheses instead. See ¶¶183, 219.)

Our entire inventory of Oriental rugs—including a fine selection of Sarouks, Kashans, and Bokharas—will be offered for sale at a 40 percent discount.

203 To give special emphasis to the second independent clause in a compound sentence, use a dash rather than a comma before the co-ordinating conjunction.

The information I sent you is true—and you know it!

In Place of a Semicolon

204 For a stronger but less formal break, use a dash in place of a semicolon between closely related independent clauses. (See ¶¶176, 178.)

I do the work—he gets the credit!

The job needs to be done—moreover, it needs to be done well.

Wilson is totally unqualified for a promotion—for example, he still does not grasp the basic principles of good management.

In Place of a Colon

205 For a stronger but less formal break, use a dash in place of a colon to introduce explanatory words, phrases, or clauses. (See ¶¶187–189.)

I need only a few items for my meeting with Kaster—namely, a copy of his letter of May 18, a copy of the contract under dispute, and a bottle of aspirin.

My arrangement with Gina is a simple one—she handles sales and I take care of production.

In Place of Parentheses

206 Use dashes instead of parentheses when you want to give the non-essential element strong emphasis. (See ¶¶183, 219.)

Call Mike Habib—he's with Jax Electronics—and get his opinion.

To Indicate an Abrupt Break or an Afterthought

207 Use a dash to show an abrupt break in thought or to separate an afterthought from the main part of a sentence. When a sentence breaks off after a dash, leave a space or two before the next sentence. (See ¶208.)

I wish you would— Is there any point in telling you what I wish for you?

We offer the best service in town—and the fastest!

Geoff Parry's plane will be landing at Dorval—or did he say Mirabel?

208 If a *question* or an *exclamation* breaks off abruptly before it has been completed, use a dash followed by a question mark or an exclamation point as appropriate. If the sentence is a *statement*, however, use a dash alone.

> Do you want to tell him or—? Suppose I wait to hear from you.

> If only— Yet there's no point in talking about what might have been.
> (NOT: If only—. Yet there's no point in talking about what might have been.)

☞ *For the use of ellipsis marks to indicate a break in thought, see ¶292a.*

To Show Hesitation

209 Use a dash to indicate hesitation, faltering speech, or stammering.

> The work on the Patterson project was begun—oh, I should say—well, about May 1—certainly no later than May 15.

To Emphasize Single Words

210 Use dashes to set off single words that require special emphasis.

> Jogging—that's what he lives for.

> There is, of course, a secret ingredient in my pasta sauce—fennel.

With Repetitions, Restatements, and Summarizing Words

211 **a.** Use dashes to set off and emphasize words that repeat or restate a previous thought.

> Next week—on Thursday at 10 a.m.—we will be making an important announcement at a press conference.

> Don't miss this opportunity—the opportunity of a lifetime!

b. Use a dash before such words as *these, they*, and *all* when these words stand as subjects summarizing a preceding list of details.

> Network television, magazines, and newspapers—*these* will be the big gainers in advertising revenues next year.

> India, Korea, and Australia—*all* are important new markets for us.

> BUT: India, Korea, and Australia are all important new markets for us. (No dash is used when the summarizing word is not the subject.)

Before Attributions

212 When providing an attribution for a displayed quotation—that is, when identifying the author or the source of the quotation—use a dash before the name of the author or the title of the work.

> My idea of luck is that it is opportunity seized.
> —Roy Thomson

NOTE: The attribution typically appears on a separate line, aligned at the right with the longest line in the displayed quotation above. For additional examples, see ¶284b.

Punctuation Preceding an Opening Dash

213   Do not use a comma, a semicolon, or a colon before an opening dash. Moreover, do not use a period before an opening dash (except a period following an abbreviation).

> Quality circles boost productivity—and they pay off in higher profits too.
> (**NOT:** Quality circles boost productivity,—and they pay off in higher profits too.)

> The catalogue proofs arrived before 11 a.m.—just as you promised.

Punctuation Preceding a Closing Dash

214   **a.** When a *statement* or a *command* is set off by dashes within a sentence, do not use a period before the closing dash (except a period following an abbreviation).

> Ernie Korolchuk—he used to have his own consulting firm—has gone back to his old job at Marker's.
> (**NOT:** Ernie Korolchuk—He used to have his own consulting firm.—has gone back to his old job at Marker's.)

> Your proposal was not delivered until 6:15 p.m.—more than two hours after the deadline.

b. When a *question* or an *exclamation* is set off by dashes within a sentence, use a question mark or an exclamation point before the closing dash.

> The representative of the Hitchcock Company—do you know her?—has called again for an appointment.

> The new sketches—I can't wait to show them to you!—should be ready by Monday.

NOTE: When a complete sentence is set off by dashes, do not capitalize the first word unless it is a proper noun, a proper adjective, the pronoun *I*, or the first word of a quoted sentence.

Punctuation Following a Closing Dash

215   When the sentence construction requires some mark of punctuation following a closing dash, either retain the dash or use the sentence punctuation—but do not use both marks together.

a. When a closing dash falls at the end of a sentence, it should be replaced by the punctuation needed to end the sentence—a period, a question mark, or an exclamation point. (See ¶208 for exceptions.)

> Wheeler's Transport delivers the goods—on time!

> (**NOT:** Wheeler's Transport delivers the goods—on time—!)

b. When a closing dash occurs at a point where the sentence requires a comma, retain the closing dash and omit the comma.

> The situation has become critical—indeed dangerous—but no one seems to care.
> (Here the closing dash is retained, and the comma before the co-ordinating conjunction is omitted.)

If you feel you are qualified for the job—and you may very well be—you ought to take the employment test. (Here the closing dash is retained, and the comma that separates a dependent clause from an independent clause is omitted.)

Brophy said—and you can check with him yourself—"This office must be vacated by Friday." (Here the closing dash is retained, and the comma before the quotation is omitted.)

NOTE: Do not put a phrase in dashes if the closing dash occurs at a point where a comma is needed after an item in a series. Put the phrase in parentheses instead.

CONFUSING: I plan to ask Spalding, Crawford—Betty, not Harold—Higgins, and Martin to investigate why sales have fallen off so sharply.

CLEAR: I plan to ask Spalding, Crawford (Betty, not Harold), Higgins, and Martin to investigate why sales have fallen off so sharply.

   c. If a closing dash occurs at a point where the sentence requires a semicolon, a colon, or a closing parenthesis, drop the closing dash and use the required sentence punctuation.

Please try to get your sales projections to us by Wednesday—certainly by Friday at the latest; otherwise, they will be of no use to us in planning next year's budget.

Here is what Marsha had to say—or at least the gist of it: look for new opportunities in niche marketing, and move quickly to capitalize on them.

You need a volunteer (for example, someone like Louis Morales—he's always co-operative) to play the part of the customer.

Constructing Dashes

216   **a.** Most word processing packages have access to several dash characters, and by default, the em dash may easily be constructed by striking the hyphen key twice. There are no spaces before, between, or after an em dash.

Don't believe him—ever!   **NOT:** Don't believe him — ever!

☞ *For spacing after a dash when a statement breaks off abruptly, see ¶¶207, 208, and 298.*

   b. A two-em dash is used to indicate that letters are missing from a word. Type four consecutive hyphens (with no space between) if you do not have access to a two-em dash. If the letters are missing from *within* a word, leave no space before or after. If the letters are missing *at the end* of a word, leave no space before but leave one space after unless a mark of punctuation is required at that point.

Mr. T——n was the one who lied.   **OR:** Mr. T----n was the one . . .

Mrs. J—— asked not to be identified.   **OR:** Mrs. J---- asked not to be identified.

   c. A three-em dash is used to indicate that an entire word has been left out or needs to be provided. If you do not have access to the three-em dash, key

(Continued on page 58.)

six consecutive hyphens; leave one space before and after unless a mark of punctuation is required at this point.

Our sales will reach ——— by March 31.   **OR:** reach ------ by March 31.

NOTE: A three-em dash is also used in bibliographies to represent an author's name in subsequent entries, after the first entry in which the author's name is given in full. See ¶1543 and the illustration on page 450.

d. Use an en dash—half the length of an em dash but longer than a hyphen—to connect numbers in a range. (If you do not have access to an en dash, use a hyphen.) The en dash means "up to and including" in expressions like these:

open 10 a.m.–6 p.m., Monday–Friday   see Chapters 2–3, pages 86–116
planned for the week of March 2–8   during the years 2002–2005
a loan of $50 000–$75 000 for 5–10 years   plans for employees aged 55–62

☞ *For the use of an en dash in certain compound adjectives, see ¶819b, note, and ¶821b. For other examples showing the use of an en dash, see ¶¶459–460.*

e. In preparing a manuscript for publication, special proofreaders' marks are used to distinguish en dashes from em dashes and hyphens. See ¶1205 for proofreaders' coding for the length of dashes.

217 Type a dash at the end of a line (rather than at the start of a new line).

He lives in the Gatineaux—   **NOT:** He lives in the Gatineaux
in Wakefield, I believe.   —in Wakefield, I believe.

PARENTHESES

Parentheses and dashes serve many of the same functions, but they differ in one significant respect: parentheses can set off only non-essential elements, whereas dashes can set of essential and non-essential elements.

REMEMBER: In setting off elements, dashes emphasize; parentheses de-emphasize.

With Explanatory Matter

218 Use parentheses to enclose explanatory material that is independent of the main thought of the sentence. The material within parentheses may be a single word, a phrase, a sentence, a number, or an abbreviation.

Canada's official national games are lacrosse (summer) and hockey (winter). (Single words.)

By Friday (and sooner if possible) I will have an answer for you. (A phrase.)

Our competitors (we underprice them) can't understand how we do it. (A sentence.)

This note for Five Thousand Dollars ($5000) is payable within ninety (90) days. (Numbers. See ¶¶420a, 436, note.)

Many corporations have created a new top-level job: chief information officer (CIO). (Abbreviations. See ¶504, note.)

NOTE: Be sure that the parentheses enclose only what is truly parenthetical.

WRONG: I merely said I was averse (not violently opposed *to*) your suggestion.

RIGHT: I merely said I was averse (not violently opposed) *to* your suggestion.

219 Use parentheses to set off a non-essential element when dashes would be too emphatic and commas might create confusion.

a. Parentheses are clearer than commas when a city-province expression occurs as an adjective.

Sales are down in our Moncton (New Brunswick) office.

BETTER THAN: Sales are down in our Moncton, New Brunswick, office.

b. Parentheses are clearer than commas when the non-essential element already contains commas. (See ¶¶183, 202.)

In three of our factories (Oshawa, Hull, and Chicoutimi) output is up.

With References

220 Use parentheses to set off references and directions.

When I last wrote to you (see my letter of July 8 attached), I enclosed photocopies of cheques that you had endorsed and deposited.

When a reference falls *at the end of a sentence*, it may be treated as part of the sentence or as a separate sentence. (See also ¶225, note.)

This point is discussed at greater length in Chapter 7 (see pages 90–101).

OR: This point is discussed at greater length in Chapter 7. (See pages 90–101.)

☞ *For the use of parentheses in footnotes, endnotes, and textnotes, see Section 15.*

With Dates

221 Use parentheses to enclose dates that accompany a person's name, a publication, or an event.

He claims that he can trace his family back to Charlemagne (742–814).

The "Sin On" Bible (1716) got its name from an extraordinary typographical error: instead of counselling readers to "sin no more," it urged them to "sin on more."

With Enumerated Items

222 **a.** **Within a Sentence.** Use parentheses to enclose numbers or letters that accompany enumerated items within a sentence.

We need the following information to complete our record of Ms. Pavlick's experience: (1) the number of years she worked for your company, (2) a description of her duties, and (3) the number of promotions she received.

NOT: . . . our record of Ms. Pavlick's experience: 1) the number of years she worked for your company, 2) a description of her duties, and 3) the number of promotions she received. (The only acceptable use of a single closing parenthesis is in an outline. See ¶223.)

(Continued on page 60.)

NOTE: Letters are used to enumerate items within a sentence when the sentence itself is part of a *numbered* sequence.

3. Please include these items on your expense report: (a) the cost of your hotel room, (b) the cost of meals, and (c) the amount spent on travel.

b. In a Displayed List. If the enumerated items appear on separate lines, the letters or numbers are usually followed only by periods. (See ¶107.)

223 Subdivisions in outlines are often enclosed in parentheses. It is sometimes necessary to use a single closing parenthesis to provide another level of subdivision.

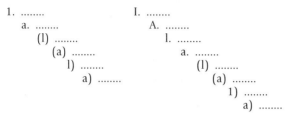

NOTE: At every level of an outline, there should be at least two items. If an item is labelled *A*, there must be at least one more item (labelled *B*) at the same level.

☞ *For guidelines on formatting outlines, see ¶¶1719–1723.*

Parenthetical Items Within Sentences

224 If the item in parentheses falls *within a sentence*:

a. Make sure that any punctuation that comes after the item (such as a comma, a semicolon, a colon, or a dash) falls *outside* the closing parenthesis.

Unless I hear from you within five working days (by May 3), I will turn this matter over to my lawyer.

I tried to reach you last Monday (I called just before noon); however, no one in your office knew where you were.

For Jane there is only one goal right now (and you know it): getting that M.B.A.

I saw your picture in a newspaper last week (in the *Sun,* I think)—and how I laughed when I saw who was standing next to you!

NOTE: Do not insert a comma, a semicolon, a colon, or a dash *before* an opening parenthesis.

b. Do not capitalize the first word of the item in parentheses, even if the item is a complete sentence. **EXCEPTIONS:** Proper nouns, proper adjectives, the pronoun *I*, and the first word of a quoted sentence. (See examples in *c* and *d*.)

c. Do not use a period before the closing parenthesis except with an abbreviation.

Plan to stay with us (we are only fifteen minutes from the airport) whenever you come to Victoria.

NOT: Plan to stay with us (We are only fifteen minutes from the airport.) whenever you come to Victoria.

Paul Melnick (Bascomb's new sales manager) wants to take you to lunch.

At last week's hearing (I had to leave at 4 p.m.), was the relocation proposal presented?

d. Do not use a question mark or an exclamation point before the closing parenthesis unless it applies solely to the parenthetical item *and* the sentence ends with a different mark of punctuation.

At the coming meeting (will you be able to make it on the 19th?), let's plan to discuss next year's budget. (Question mark used in parentheses because the sentence ends with a period.)

May I still get tickets to the show (and may I bring a friend), or is it too late? (Question mark omitted in parentheses because the sentence ends with a question mark.)

NOT: May I still get tickets to the show (and may I bring a friend?), or is it too late?

Parenthetical Items at the End of Sentences

225 If the item in parentheses is to be incorporated *at the end of a sentence:*

a. Place the punctuation needed to end the sentence *outside* the closing parenthesis.

Please return the payroll review sheets by Monday (October 8).

How can I reach Jan Weidner (she spoke at yesterday's seminar)?

What a prima donna I work with (you know the one I mean)!

b. Do not capitalize the first word of the item in parentheses, even if the item is a complete sentence. (See ¶224b for exceptions. Note examples in *c* and *d* below.)

c. Do not use a period before the closing parenthesis except with an abbreviation.

Our office is open late on Thursdays (until 9 p.m.).

Our office is open late on Thursdays (we're here until nine).

NOT: Our office is open late on Thursdays (We're here until nine.).

d. Do not use a question mark or an exclamation point before the closing parenthesis unless it applies solely to the parenthetical element *and* the sentence ends with a different mark of punctuation.

My new assistant is Arjun Singh (didn't you meet him once before?).

Be sure to send the letter to London, England (not London, Ontario!).

Then he walked out and slammed the door (can you believe it?)!

Do you know Ellen Smyth (or is it Smythe)?

NOT: Do you know Ellen Smyth (or is it Smythe?)?

I am through with the job (and I mean it)!

NOT: I am through with the job (and I mean it!)!

(Continued on page 62.)

NOTE: When a complete sentence occurs within parentheses at the end of another sentence, it may be incorporated into the sentence if it is short and closely related, as shown in the examples above; otherwise, treat it as a separate sentence (see ¶226).

Parenthetical Items as Separate Sentences

226 If the item in parentheses is to be treated as a *separate sentence:*

a. The preceding sentence should close with a punctuation mark of its own.

b. The item in parentheses should begin with a capital letter.

c. A period, a question mark, or an exclamation point (whichever is appropriate) should be placed *before* the closing parenthesis.

d. No other punctuation mark should follow the closing parenthesis. (See ¶298 for additional guidelines on spacing.)

Then Steven Pelletier made a motion to replace the existing board of directors. (He does this at every stockholders' meeting.) However, this year . . .

I was most impressed with the speech given by Helena Verdi. (Didn't you used to work with her?) She knew her subject and she knew her audience.

☞ *Parentheses around question marks: see ¶118.*
Parentheses around exclamation points: see ¶119c.
Parentheses around confirming figures: see ¶420.
Parentheses around area codes in telephone numbers: see ¶454.
Parenthetical elements within parenthetical elements: see ¶297.
Plural endings in parentheses, see ¶626.

QUOTATION MARKS

Quotation marks have three main functions: to indicate the use of someone else's exact words (see ¶¶227–234), to set off words and phrases for special emphasis (see ¶¶235–241), and to display the titles of literary and artistic works (see ¶¶242–244).

For guidance on how to position punctuation marks in relation to the closing quotation mark—*inside* or *outside*—see ¶¶247–251.

For more specific guidance on when to use punctuation with quoted matter and which punctuation to use, refer to the following paragraphs:

☞ *Quotations standing alone: see ¶252.*
Quotations at the beginning of a sentence: see ¶¶253–255.
Quotations at the end of a sentence: see ¶¶256–258.
Quotations within a sentence: see ¶¶259–261.
Quotations with interrupting expressions: see ¶¶262–263.
Quotations within quotations: see ¶¶245–246.
Long quotations: see ¶264–265.

Quoted letters: see ¶266.

Quoted poetry: see ¶¶267–268.

Quoted dialogues and conversations: see ¶¶269–270.

Quotation marks as a symbol for inches: see ¶543.

With Direct Quotations

227 Use quotation marks to enclose a *direct quotation*, that is, the exact words of a speaker or a writer.

> When the final gavel sounded, Ferguson merely said, "Let's get out of here before someone reconsiders the verdict."

> When I asked Diana whether she liked the new format of the magazine, all she said was "No." (See ¶¶233, 256a.)

228 **a.** Do not use quotation marks for an *indirect quotation*, that is, a restatement or rearrangement of a person's exact words. (An indirect quotation is often introduced by *that* or *whether* and usually differs from a direct quotation in person, verb tense, or word order.)

> **DIRECT QUOTATION:** Mrs. Knudsen asked her supervisor, "Am I still being considered for the transfer?"
> **INDIRECT QUOTATION:** Mrs. Knudsen asked her supervisor whether she was still being considered for the transfer.

> **DIRECT QUOTATION:** Her supervisor said, "You're still in the running, but don't expect a quick decision."
> **INDIRECT QUOTATION:** Her supervisor said that she was still in the running but that she should not expect a quick decision.

> **NOTE:** Sometimes *direct* quotations are introduced by *that*. See ¶¶256f and 272, note.

b. In some cases a person's exact words may be treated as either a direct or an indirect quotation, depending on the kind of emphasis desired.

> The chairman himself said, "The staff should be told at once that the rumours about a new building have no foundation." (The use of quotation marks emphasizes that these are the chairman's exact words.)

> The chairman himself said the staff should be told at once that the rumours about a new building have no foundation. (Without quotation marks, the emphasis falls on the message itself. The fact that the chairman used these exact words is not important.)

229 Do not use quotation marks to set off a *direct question* at the end of a sentence unless it is also a *direct quotation* of someone's exact words.

> **DIRECT QUESTION:** The question is, Who will pay for restoring the landmark?

> **DIRECT QUOTATION:** Mrs. Burchall then asked, "Who will pay for restoring the landmark?" (See ¶¶247–249 for the sequencing of punctuation marks.)

> **DIRECT QUOTATION:** Mrs. Burchall then replied, "The question is, Who will pay for restoring the landmark?" (See also ¶115.)

2

230 Quotation marks are not needed to set off interior thoughts or imagined dialogue. Treat this kind of material like a *direct question* (as shown in ¶229).

> After I left Joe's office, I thought, He has no business telling me what to do. I should have said, I can handle this situation—thank you very much!—without your help.

NOTE: In special cases quotation marks may help to preserve clarity or maintain stylistic consistency (for example, when imaginary dialogue is interspersed with actual dialogue).

231 a. When only a word or phrase is quoted from another source, be sure to place the quotation marks only around the words extracted from the original source and not around any rearrangement of those words.

> Tanya said she would need "more help" in order to finish your report by this Friday. (Tanya's exact words were, "How can he expect me to finish his report by this Friday without more help?")

b. When a quoted word or phrase comes at the end of a sentence, the period goes *inside* the closing quotation mark.

> Barbara described the plain white shift she wore to the masquerade party as a "Freudian slip." (See also ¶247a, particularly examples 2–4.)

c. Be particularly sure not to include such words as *a* and *the* at the beginning of the quotation or *etc.* at the end unless these words were actually part of the original material.

> Ben thought you did a "super" job on the packaging design. (Ben's exact words were, "Tell Bonnie I thought the job she did on the packaging design was super.")

> Explain the decision any way you want, but tell George I said, "I'm truly sorry about the way things turned out," etc., etc.

232 When quoting a series of words or phrases in the exact sequence in which they originally appeared, use quotation marks before and after the complete series. However, if the series of quoted words or phrases did not appear in this sequence in the original, use quotation marks around each word or phrase.

> According to Selma, the latest issue of the magazine looked "fresh, crisp, and appealing." (Selma's actual words were, "I think the new issue looks especially fresh, crisp, and appealing.")

> **BUT:** Selma thinks the magazine looks "fresh" and "crisp."
> (**NOT:** Selma thinks the magazine looks "fresh and crisp.")

233 Do not quote the words *yes* and *no* unless you wish to emphasize that these were (or will be) the exact words spoken.

> Please answer the question yes or no.

> Don't say no until you have heard all the terms of the proposal.

> Once the firm's board of directors says yes, we can draft the contract.

> When asked if he would accept a reassignment, Nick thought for a moment; then, without any trace of emotion, he said "Yes." (The quotation marks imply that Nick said precisely this much and no more. See ¶256a, note, for the use or omission of a comma after *he said*.)

NOTE: When quoting these words, capitalize them if they represent a complete sentence.

> All she said was "No."

> I would have to answer that question by saying "Yes and no."

> **BUT:** That question requires something more than a yes-or-no answer.

234 Do not use quotation marks with well-known proverbs and sayings. They are not direct quotations.

> Sidney really believes that an apple a day keeps the doctor away.

For Special Emphasis

235 When using technical terms, business jargon, or coined words not likely to be familiar to your reader, enclose them in quotation marks when they are first used.

> Some software users become confused when directed to press any key. They complain that they cannot find the "any" key.

> Will you agree to a "desktop" approach for approving the trustee's accounts?

236 **a.** Words used humorously or ironically may be enclosed in quotation marks. However, unless you are convinced your reader will otherwise miss the humour or the irony, omit the quotation marks.

> I was totally underwhelmed by Joe's proposal to centralize all purchasing. (**RATHER THAN:** I was totally "underwhelmed" by Joe's proposal . . .)

> HDL cholesterol is the good kind; it's LDL that's the bad kind. (**RATHER THAN:** . . . the "good" kind . . . the "bad" kind . . .)

> Nothing would please me more than looking at the slides of Mike's tour of Egypt. (One might reasonably conclude that the writer takes unalloyed pleasure at the prospect.)

> **BUT:** "Nothing" would please me more than looking at the slides of Mike's tour of Egypt. (When *Nothing* is enclosed in quotation marks, the writer makes it clear that doing nothing would be preferable to looking at Mike's slides.)

b. A slang expression, the use of poor grammar, or a deliberate misspelling is enclosed in quotation marks to indicate that such usage is not part of the writer's normal way of speaking or writing.

> Now that his kids have run off to Europe with the college tuition money, Bob has stopped boasting about his close-knit "nucular" family. (The writer is mimicking Bob's habitual mispronunciation of *nuclear*.)

> As far as I'm concerned, Polly Harrington's version of what happened "ain't necessarily so."

c. Quotation marks are not needed for colloquial expressions.

> She cares less about the salary than she does about the perks—you know, chauffeured limousine, stock options, and all the rest of it. (*Perks* is short for perquisites, meaning "special privileges.")

> Pam is planning to temp until she's sure about staying in Sherbrooke. (*To temp* means "to do temporary work.")

2

237 a. Use quotation marks to enclose words and phrases that have been made to play an abnormal role in a sentence—for example, verb phrases made to function as adjectives.

> We were all impressed by her "can do" attitude. (*Can do* is a verb phrase used here as an adjective modifying *attitude*.)
>
> **OR:** We were all impressed by her can-do attitude. (A hyphen may also be used to hold together a phrase used as an adjective before a noun. See ¶828.)
>
> **BUT NOT:** We were all impressed by her "can-do" attitude. (Do not use both quotation marks and a hyphen for the same purpose.)
>
> I'm selling my car on an "as is" (**OR** as-is) basis.
>
> **NOTE:** When a verb like *must* or a preposition-adverb like *in* becomes established as a noun or an adjective (as indicated in the dictionary), use quotation marks only in those constructions where confusion could otherwise result.
>
> You have to read that book; it's a must.
>
> **BUT:** You have to get that book; it's "must" reading.
>
> Frank must have an in with their purchasing department.
>
> **BUT:** I guess she thinks it's still the "in" thing to do.

b. Do not use quotation marks to enclose phrases that are taken from other parts of speech and are now well established as nouns; for example, *haves and have-nots, pros and cons, ins and outs*. (See also ¶625.)

> a helpful list of dos and don'ts.
>
> all the whys and wherefores.
>
> a lot of ifs, ands, or buts. (See also ¶285.)

238 When a word or an expression is formally defined, the word to be defined is usually italicized or underlined and the definition is usually quoted so that the two elements may be easily distinguished. (See ¶286.)

> ☞ *For guidelines on italics and underlining, see ¶290.*

239 A word referred to as a word may be enclosed in quotation marks but is now more commonly italicized or underlined. (See ¶285.)

240 a. Words and phrases introduced by such expressions as *marked, labelled, signed, titled,* and *entitled* are enclosed in quotation marks.

> The carton was marked "Fragile."
>
> He received a message signed "A Friend."
>
> The article entitled "Write Your Chairman" was in that issue. (See ¶260.)
>
> **NOTE:** Titles of complete published works following the expression *entitled* or *titled* require italics or underlining rather than quotation marks. (See ¶289 for titles to be italicized or underlined; ¶¶242–244 for titles to be quoted.)

b. Words and phrases introduced by *so-called* do not require quotation marks, italics, or underlining. The expression *so-called* is sufficient to give special emphasis to the term that follows.

> The so-called orientation session struck me as an exercise in brainwashing.

241 The translation of a foreign expression is enclosed in quotation marks; the foreign word itself is italicized or underlined. (See ¶287.)

With Titles of Literary and Artistic Works

242 Use quotation marks around the titles that represent only *part* of a complete published work—for example, the titles of chapters, lessons, topics, sections, and parts within a book; the titles of articles and feature columns in newspapers and magazines; and the titles of essays, short poems, lectures, sermons, and conference themes. (Italicize or underline titles of *complete* published works. See ¶289.)

> The heart of her argument can be found in Chapter 3, "The Failure of Traditional Therapy." You will especially want to read the section entitled "Does Father Know Best?"
>
> An exciting article—"Can Cancer Now Be Cured?"—appears in the magazine I'm enclosing. (See ¶¶260–261 for the use of commas, dashes, and parentheses with quoted titles.)
>
> The theme of next month's workshop is "Imperatives for the Twenty-First Century—From the Ragged Edge to the Cutting Edge."
>
> The title of my speech for next month's luncheon will be "Reforming Our Sales Tax Policy."
>
> **BUT:** At next month's luncheon, I will be talking about reforming our sales tax policy. (Do not enclose the words with quotation marks when they describe the topic rather than signify the exact title.)

NOTE: The titles *Preface, Contents, Appendix,* and *Index* are not quoted, even though they represent parts within a book. They are often capitalized, however, for special emphasis.

> All the supporting data is given in the Appendix. (Often capitalized when referring to another section within the same work.)
>
> **BUT:** You'll find that the most interesting part of his book is contained in the appendix. (Capitalization is not required when reference is made to a section within another work.)

243 Use quotation marks around the titles of *complete but unpublished* works, such as manuscripts, dissertations, and reports.

> I would like to get a copy of Sandor's study, "Criteria for Evaluating Staff Efficiency."
>
> Thank you for giving us the chance to review "Working out of Your Home." I have given your manuscript to an editor with a good deal of personal experience in this field.

244 Use quotation marks around the titles of songs and other short musical compositions and around the titles of individual segments or programs that are part of a larger television or radio series. (Series titles are italicized or underlined.)

(Continued on page 68.)

Just once I would like to get through a company party without having to hear Reggie sing "Danny Boy."

I understand that our company was briefly mentioned on the *Sunday Report* program entitled "Ottawa, Inc.," which was shown last Sunday night.

Quotations Within Quotations

245 A quotation within another quotation is enclosed in single quotation marks. Use the apostrophe for a single quotation mark.

Fowler then said, "We were all impressed by her 'can do' attitude."

246 If a quotation appears within the single-quoted material, revert to double quotation marks for the inner portion.

Mrs. DeVries then remarked, "I thought it a bit strange when Mr. Fowler said, 'Put these cheques in an envelope marked "Personal Funds," and set them aside for me.'" (When single and double quotation marks occur together, insert extra space between the two marks to keep them distinct.)

NOTE: For the positioning of punctuation in relation to a single quotation mark, see the following paragraphs:

☞ *For placement of periods and commas, see ¶247b.*

For placement of semicolons and colons, see ¶248b.

For placement of question marks and exclamation points, see ¶249d.

For placement of dashes, see ¶250b.

The following rules (¶¶247–251) indicate how to position punctuation marks in relation to the closing quotation mark—inside *or* outside.

With Periods and Commas

247 **a.** Periods and commas always go *inside* the closing quotation mark. This is the preferred North American style. (Some writers, however, follow the British style: Place the period *outside* when it punctuates the whole sentence, *inside* when it punctuates only the quoted matter. Place the comma *outside*, since it always punctuates the sentence, not the quoted matter.)

Before the conference began, Mr. Karras made a point of saying, "Let me do the talking."

He wants to change "on or about May 1" to read "no later than May 1."

The price tag on the leather sofa was clearly marked "Sold."

Sign your name wherever you see an "X."

"Let's go over the details again," she said.

"The date stamp indicates that my copy arrived at 10:50 a.m.," he said.

Their latest article, "Scanning the Future," will appear in next month's issue of *Equinox* magazine.

"Witty," "clever," "amusing," and "hilarious" are only a few of the adjectives that are being applied to her new book.

The package was labelled "Fragile," but that meant nothing to your delivery crew.

b. Periods and commas also go *inside* the single closing quotation mark.

Mr. Poston said, "Please let me see all the orders marked 'Rush.'"

"All he would say was 'I don't remember,'" answered the witness.

NOTE: Do not confuse a single quotation mark with an apostrophe used to show possession. When a sentence requires the use of a comma or a period at the same point as an apostrophe showing possession, the comma or period *follows* the apostrophe.

I recently took over the management of the Murrays', the Boyarskys', and the Cabots' investment portfolios.

With Semicolons and Colons

248 a. Semicolons and colons always go *outside* the closing quotation mark.

Last Tuesday you said, "I will mail a cheque today"; it has not yet arrived.

When the announcement of the changeover was made, my reaction was "Why?"; John's only reaction was "When?"

Please send me the following items from the file labelled "In Process": the latest draft of the Berryman agreement and CJS Statement 33.

The memo I sent you yesterday said that the new workstations would cost "a nominal egg"; it should have said "an arm and a leg."

b. Semicolons and colons also go *outside* the single quotation mark.

Alice Arroyo called in from her country place to say, "Please send me the following items from the file labelled 'In Process': the latest draft of the Berryman agreement and CJS Statement 33."

With Question Marks and Exclamation Points

249 a. A question mark or an exclamation point goes *inside* the closing quotation mark when it applies only to the quoted material.

His first question was, "How long have you worked here?" (Quoted question at the end of a statement.)

Garland still ends every sales meeting by shouting, "Go get 'em!" (Quoted exclamation at the end of a statement.)

b. A question mark or an exclamation point goes *outside* the closing quotation mark when it applies to the entire sentence.

When will she say, for a change, "You did a nice job on that"? (Quoted statement at the end of a question.)

Stop saying "Don't worry"! (Quoted statement at the end of an exclamation.)

c. If the quoted material and the entire sentence each require the same mark of punctuation, use only one mark—the one that comes first. (See also ¶¶257–258.)

Have you seen the advertisement that starts, "Why pay more?" (Quoted question at the end of a question.)

(Continued on page 70.)

Let's not panic and yell "Fire!" (Quoted exclamation at the end of an exclamation.)

d. These same principles govern the placement of a question mark or an exclamation point in relation to a single quotation mark.

What prompted her to say, "Be careful in handling documents marked 'Confidential' "? (Quoted phrase within a quoted statement within a question.)

Dr. Marks asked, "Was the cheque marked 'Insufficient Funds'?" (Quoted phrase within a quoted question within a statement.)

Miss Parsons then said, "How did you answer him when he asked you, 'How do you know?' " (Quoted question within a quoted question within a statement.)

With Dashes

250 **a.** A dash goes *inside* the closing quotation mark to indicate that the speaker's or writer's words have broken off abruptly.

It was tragic to hear Tom say, "If he had only listened—"

b. A dash goes *outside* the closing quotation mark when the sentence breaks off abruptly *after* the quotation.

If I hear one more word about "boosting productivity"—

BUT: Mrs. Halliday said, "If I hear one more word from the general manager about 'boosting productivity'—"

c. A closing dash goes *outside* the closing quotation mark when the quotation itself is part of a non-essential element being set off by a pair of dashes.

Get the latest draft—it's the one with the notation "Let's go with this"—and take it to Gladys Pomeroy for her approval.

With Parentheses

251 **a.** The closing parenthesis goes *inside* the closing quotation mark when the parenthetical element is part of the quotation.

Fox agreed to settle his account "by Friday (July 28)" when he last wrote us.

b. The closing parenthesis goes *outside* the closing quotation mark when the quotation is part of the parenthetical element.

Joe Elliott (the one everyone calls "Harper's gofer") will probably get the job.

The following rules (¶¶252–270) indicate what punctuation to use with various kinds of quoted matter.

Punctuating Quotations That Stand Alone

252 When a quoted sentence stands alone, put the appropriate mark of terminal punctuation—a period, a question mark, or an exclamation point—*inside* the closing quotation mark.

"I think we should switch suppliers at once."

"Can you send us your comments within two weeks?"

"I won't accept that kind of response!"

Punctuating Quotations That Begin a Sentence

253 **a.** When a quoted *statement* occurs at the beginning of a sentence, omit the period before the closing quotation mark and use a comma instead.

"I think we should switch suppliers at once," he said.
(**NOT:** . . . at once.," he said.)

EXCEPTION: Retain the period if it accompanies an abbreviation.

"I'm still planning to go on for an LL.B.," she said.

b. Omit the comma after a quoted statement if it is smoothly woven into the flow of the sentence.

"He hasn't a clue" is all Bert says when you ask how Joe is doing.
(**NOT:** "He hasn't a clue," is all Bert says . . .)

254 When a quoted *question* or *exclamation* occurs at the beginning of a sentence, retain the question mark or the exclamation point before the closing quotation mark and do *not* insert a comma.

"Can you send us your comments within two weeks?" she asked.
(**NOT:** . . . within two weeks?," she asked.)

"I won't accept that kind of response!" I told him.
(**NOT:** . . . that kind of response!," I told him.)

255 When a quoted *word* or *phrase* occurs at the beginning of a sentence, no punctuation should accompany the closing quotation mark unless required by the overall construction of the sentence.

"An utter bore" was the general reaction to yesterday's speaker.

"Managing Your Portfolio," the second chapter in the Klingenstein book, sets forth some guidelines I have never seen anywhere else. (The comma that follows the chapter title is the first of a pair needed to set off a non-essential expression.)

Punctuating Quotations That End a Sentence

256 **a.** When a quoted *statement, question,* or *exclamation* comes at the end of a sentence and is introduced by an expression such as *he said* or *she said*, a comma usually precedes the opening quotation mark.

Mr. Kelley said, "We'll close early on Friday."

In her letter Diana said, "I plan to arrive on Thursday at 6 p.m."

NOTE: If the quotation is quite short or is woven into the flow of the sentence, omit the comma.

All she said was "No." **OR:** All she said was, "No." (The comma creates a slight pause and throws greater emphasis on the quotation.)

Why does he keep saying "It won't work"?

b. Use a colon in place of a comma if the introductory expression is an independent clause.

Jerry would say only this: "I'll send you my new address once I'm settled."

(Continued on page 72.)

Here is the key statement in his letter: "If my loan is approved, the deal is on."

c. Use a colon in place of a comma if the quotation contains more than one sentence.

Mr. Bowles then said: "If the legislation is passed by Parliament, we have an excellent chance to compete effectively in international markets. However, if the legislation is held up in committee, our competitive position will worsen."

d. Use a colon in place of a comma if the quotation is set off on separate lines as an extract. (See also ¶265.)

Sheila's letter said in part:

> I have greatly valued your assistance. You have always
> acted as if you were actually part of our staff, with our best
> interests in mind.

e. Do not use either a comma or a colon before an indirect quotation.

Sheila said that she had always valued Bob's assistance on various projects.

f. Do not use either a comma or a colon when a direct quotation is introduced by *that* or is otherwise woven into the flow of the sentence.

In a previous letter to you, I noted that "you have always acted as if you were actually part of our staff, with our best interests in mind."

NOTE: The first word of the quotation is not capitalized in this case, even though it was capitalized in the original. Compare *you* here with *You* in the example in *d* above. (See ¶272 for the rule on capitalizing the first word of a quoted sentence.)

257 When a quoted *sentence* (a statement, a question, or an exclamation) falls at the end of a larger sentence, do not use double punctuation—that is, one mark to end the quotation and another to end the sentence. Choose the stronger mark. (**REMEMBER:** *A question mark is stronger than a period; an exclamation point is stronger than a period or a question mark.*) If the same mark of punctuation is required for both the quotation and the sentence as a whole, use the first mark that occurs—the one within quotation marks.

Quoted Sentences at the End of a Statement

Bob said, "I can't wait to get back to work." (**NOT** .".)

Mrs. Fahey asked, "How long have you been away?" (**NOT** ?".)

Mr. Auden shouted, "We can't operate a business this way!" (**NOT** !".)

Quoted Sentences at the End of a Question

Did you say, "I'll help out"? (**NOT** .".?)

Why did Mary ask, "Will Joe be there?" (**NOT** ?"?)

Who yelled "Watch out!" (**NOT** !"?)

Quoted Sentences at the End of an Exclamation

How could you forget to follow up when you were specifically told, "Give this order special attention"! (**NOT** .".!)

Stop saying "How should I know"! (**NOT** ?"!)

How I'd like to walk into his office and say, "I quit!" (**NOT** !"!)

NOTE: When a quoted sentence ends with an abbreviation, retain the abbreviation period, even though a question mark or an exclamation point follows as the terminal mark of punctuation.

The reporter asked, "When did you first hear about the board's decision to sell Modem Inc.?"

Didn't Larry tell Meg, "I'll help you with the tuition for your M.D."?

However, if a period is required as the terminal mark of punctuation, use only one period to mark the end of the abbreviation and the end of the sentence.

Gloria said, "You can call as early as 6:30 a.m." (**NOT** ".")

☞ For placement of periods, see ¶247.

For placement of question marks and exclamation points, see ¶249.

258 When a quoted *word* or *phrase* occurs at the end of a sentence, punctuate according to the appropriate pattern in the following examples. (**NOTE:** If the quoted word or phrase represents a complete sentence, follow the patterns shown in ¶257.)

Quoted Words and Phrases at the End of a Statement

He says he is willing to meet "at your convenience." (**NOT** ".)

I thought her letter said she would arrive "at 10 p.m." (**NOT** ".)

I've been meaning to read "Who Pays the Bill?" (**NOT** ?".)

Critics have praised his latest article, "Freedom Now!" (**NOT** !".)

Quoted Words and Phrases at the End of a Question

Why is he so concerned about my "convenience"?

Didn't she clearly state she would arrive "at 10 p.m."?

Have you had a chance to read "Who Pays the Bill?" (**NOT** ?"?)

What did you think of the article "Freedom Now!"?

Quoted Words and Phrases at the End of an Exclamation

He couldn't care less about my "convenience"!

You are quite mistaken—she clearly said "at 10 a.m."!

Don't waste your time reading "Who Pays the Bill?"!

What a reaction he got with his article "Freedom Now!" (**NOT** !"!)

Punctuating Quotations Within a Sentence

259 Do not use a comma before or after a quotation when it is woven into the flow of the sentence.

Don't say "I can't do it" without trying.

No considerate person would say "Why should I care?" under such desperate circumstances.

(Continued on page 74.)

The audience shouted "Bravo!" and "Encore!" at the end of Ben Heppner's recital last night.

NOTE: In such cases do not use a period at the end of a quoted statement, but retain the question mark or the exclamation point at the end of a quoted question or exclamation (as illustrated in the examples above).

260 Do not use commas to set off a quotation that occurs within a sentence as an *essential* expression. (See ¶149.)

The luxurious practice of booking passage between England and India on the basis of "Port Outward, Starboard Homeward" (so as to get a cabin on the cooler side of the ship) is said to be the origin of the word *posh*.

The chapter entitled "Locating Sources of Venture Capital" will give you specific leads you can pursue.

261 **a.** When a quotation occurs within a sentence as a non-essential expression, use a comma before the opening quotation mark and before the closing quotation mark.

His parting words, "I hardly know how to thank you," were sufficient.

The next chapter, "The Role of Government," further clarifies the answer.

b. If the non-essential quoted matter requires a question mark or an exclamation point before the closing quotation mark, use a pair of dashes or parentheses (rather than commas) to set off the quoted matter.

Your last question—"How can we improve communications between departments?"—can best be answered by you.

RATHER THAN: Your last question, "How can we improve communications between departments?," can best be answered by you.

NOTE: When some or all of the quoted items in a series end with a question mark or an exclamation point, display them in a list to avoid the awkwardness of inserting commas before the quotation marks.

Next month's issue will feature the following articles:

"What Is Your Investor Personality?"

"Tax Law Changes—Again!"

"Is It the Bay Connection?"

RATHER THAN: Next month's issue will feature the following articles: "What Is Your Investor Personality?," "Tax Law Changes—Again!," and "Is It the Bay Connection?"

c. If *essential* quoted matter ends with a question mark or an exclamation point and occurs within a sentence where a comma would ordinarily follow (for example, at the end of an introductory clause or phrase), omit the comma.

Although we were all asked last week to read an article entitled "Can Our Manufacturers Prosper in Today's World Markets?" the topic was totally ignored in this week's seminar.

RATHER THAN: . . . an article entitled "Can Our Manufacturers Prosper in Today's World Markets?," the topic was . . .

NOTE: If the omission of a comma at this point could lead to confusion, reword the sentence to avoid the problem.

We were all asked last week to read an article entitled "Can Our Manufacturers Prosper in Today's World Markets?" Yet the topic was . . .

OR: We were all asked last week to read an article entitled "Can Our Manufacturers Prosper in Today's World Markets?"; yet the topic was . . .

Punctuating Quoted Sentences With Interrupting Expressions

262   When a quoted sentence is *interrupted* by an expression such as *he asked* or *she said*, use a comma and a closing quotation mark before the interrupting expression and another comma after it. Then resume the quotation with an opening quotation mark. Put the first word in lower case letters unless it is a proper noun, a proper adjective, or the pronoun *I*.

"During the past month," the memo said in part, "we have received some welcome news from our overseas branches."

263   If the interrupting expression ends the sentence and the quotation continues in a new sentence, put a period after the interrupting expression and start the new sentence with an opening quotation mark and a capital letter.

"Perhaps we should decline the invitation," he said. "It would be better not to go than to arrive late."

Punctuating Long Quotations

264   If a quotation consists of more than one sentence without any interrupting elements, use quotation marks only at the beginning and at the end of the quotation. Do not put quotation marks around each sentence within the quotation.

Here is the full text of the release he gave to the media: "I have decided to withdraw from the upcoming election. I wish to thank my supporters for their enormous help. I am sorry to disappoint them."

265   A long quotation that will make four or more lines may be handled in one of the following ways:

a.   The preferred style for displaying the quoted matter is to treat it as a single-spaced extract. Indent the extract one-half inch from each side margin, and leave one blank line above and below the extract. Do not enclose the quoted matter in quotation marks; the indention replaces the quotation marks. If any quoted material appears within the extract, retain the quotation marks around this material. If the extract consists of more than one paragraph, leave a blank line between paragraphs. (See page 338 for an illustration of an extract in the body of a letter.)

NOTE: Ordinarily, start the quoted material flush left on the shorter line length; however, if a paragraph indention was called for in the original, tab the first line 0.25" to 0.5". Tab the first line of any additional para-

(Continued on page 76.)

graphs 0.25" to 0.5" also, but do not leave a blank line between indented paragraphs.

b. Use the same line length and spacing for the quoted matter as for other text material on the page.

(1) If the quoted matter consists of one paragraph only, place quotation marks at the beginning and end of the paragraph. Use the normal paragraph indention of one-half inch.

(2) If the quoted matter consists of two or more paragraphs, place a quotation mark *at the start* of each paragraph but at the end of only one paragraph—the last one.

(3) Change double quotation marks within the quoted matter to single quotation marks, and vice versa. (See ¶¶245–246.)

> "When you are writing a letter that grants a request, you can follow this pattern:
>
> "First, express appreciation for the writer's interest in the company's product or service.
>
> "Next, give the exact information requested and, if possible, additional information that may be of interest.
>
> "Finally, express willingness to 'be of further help.'"

Quoting Business Documents

266 For documents and letters that are to be quoted in entirety, make a printout, a photocopy, or a scanner copy of the material. No quotation marks are required. (See ¶1437 regarding copyright laws.)

Quoting Poetry

267 When quoting a complete poem (or an extended portion of one) in a letter or a report, key it line for line, single-spaced (except for stanza breaks). If the line length is shorter than that of the text above and below the poem, no quotation marks are needed; the poem will stand out sufficiently. If, however, quotation marks are needed to indicate the special nature of the poem, place a quotation mark at the beginning of each stanza and at the end of only the last stanza. (See also ¶284b.)

NOTE: As a rule, follow the poet's layout of the poem. If the poet uses an irregular pattern of indention (instead of the customary practice of aligning all lines at the left), try to reproduce this layout.

268 A short extract from a poem is sometimes woven right into a sentence or a paragraph. In such cases use quotation marks at the beginning and end of the extract, and use a diagonal line (with one space before and after) to indicate where each line breaks in the actual poem.

> As Pauline Johnson mused, "Crown of her, young Vancouver; crest of her, old Quebec; / Atlantic and far Pacific sweeping her, keel to deck. / North of her, ice and arctics; southward a rival's stealth; / Aloft her Empire's pennant; below a nation's wealth."

Quoting Dialogues and Conversations

269 When quoting dialogues and conversations, start the remarks of each speaker as a new paragraph, no matter how brief.

> "They come from the North," she said.
>
> "Why north?"
>
> "In Canada everything that's not American comes from the North."
>
> —Don Delillo

270 In plays, court testimony, and transcripts of conversations, where the name of the speaker is indicated, quotation marks are not needed.

> CECILY: Uncle Jack is sending you to Australia.
>
> ALGER: Australia! I'd sooner die.
>
> CECILY: Well, he said at dinner on Wednesday night that you would have to choose between this world, the next world, and Australia.
>
> ALGER: Oh, well! The accounts I have received of Australia and the next world are not particularly encouraging. This world is good enough for me, cousin Cecily.
>
> —Oscar Wilde

The following rules (¶¶271–284) cover a number of stylistic matters, such as how to style quoted material (¶271), how to capitalize in quoted material (¶¶272–273), how to handle omissions in quoted material (¶¶274–280), how to handle insertions in quoted material (¶¶281–283), and how to align quotation marks (¶284).

Style in Quoted Matter

271 In copying quoted matter, follow the style of the extract exactly in punctuation, spelling, hyphenation, and number style. (See ¶283 for the use of [*sic*] to indicate errors in the original.)

Capitalization in Quoted Matter

272 Ordinarily, capitalize the first word of every complete sentence in quotation marks.

> I overheard Chow mutter, "Only a fool would make such a claim."
>
> Here is the key sentence in her memo: "Despite the understaffing in the department, everyone is expected to meet the goals established for the coming year."

NOTE: If the quoted sentence is preceded by *that* or is otherwise incorporated into the flow of a larger sentence, do not capitalize the first word (unless it is a proper noun, a proper adjective, or the pronoun *I*).

> I overheard Chow mutter that "only a fool would make such a claim."
>
> In essence, she says that "despite the understaffing in the department, everyone is expected to meet the goals established for the coming year."

273 When quoting a word or phrase, do not capitalize the first word unless it meets *one* of these conditions:

    a. The first word is a proper noun, a proper adjective, or the pronoun *I*.

        No one is terribly impressed by his "Irish temper."

    b. The first word was capitalized in its original use.

        I watched her scrawl "Approved" and sign her name at the bottom of the proposal.

    c. The quoted word or phrase occurs at the beginning of a sentence.

        "Outrageous" was the publisher's reaction to Maxon's attempt to duck the questions of the reporters. (Even if the expression was not capitalized in the original material, it is capitalized here to mark the start of the sentence.)

    d. The first word represents a complete sentence.

        The Crawleys said "Perhaps"; the Calnans said "No way."

    ☞ *See ¶¶277–278 on capitalizing the first word of a quoted sentence fragment.*

Omissions in Quoted Matter

274 If one or more words are omitted *within a quoted sentence*, use ellipsis marks (three spaced periods, with one space before and after each period) to indicate the omission.

    "During the past fifty years . . . we have been witnessing a change in buying habits, particularly with respect to food."

NOTE: Omit any marks of internal punctuation (a comma, a semicolon, a colon, or a dash) on either side of the ellipsis marks unless they are required for the sake of clarity.

    ORIGINAL VERSION: "The objectives of the proposed bill are admirable, I will cheerfully concede; the tactics being used to gain support for the bill are not."

    CONDENSED VERSION: "The objectives of the proposed bill are admirable . . . ; the tactics being used to gain support for the bill are not." (The comma preceding the omitted phrase is not needed; however, the semicolon following the omitted phrase must be retained for clarity.)

275 If one or more words are omitted *at the end of a quoted sentence*, use three spaced periods followed by the necessary terminal punctuation for the sentence as a whole.

    "Can anyone explain why . . . ?" (The original question read, "Can anyone explain why this was so?")

    "During the past fifty years, starting in the late 1950s, we have been witnessing a change in buying habits . . . . Consumers have become more concerned with what's in the package rather than with the package itself." (The first three periods represent the omitted words "particularly with respect to food"; the fourth period marks the end of the sentence. Two spaces follow before the next sentence.)

NOTE: If the quotation is intended to trail off, use only three spaced periods at the end of the sentence. (See also ¶291b.)

His reaction was, "If I had only known . . ."

276 If one or more sentences are omitted *between other sentences* within a long quotation, use three spaced periods *after* the terminal punctuation of the preceding sentence.

> "During the past fifty years, starting in the late 1950s, we have been witnessing a change in buying habits, particularly with respect to food. . . . How far this pattern of change will extend cannot be estimated."

NOTE: There is no space between *food* and the first period because that period marks the end of a sentence. The remaining three periods signify the omission of one or more complete sentences. Two spaces follow before the next sentence.

277 If only a fragment of a sentence is quoted within another sentence, it is not necessary to use ellipsis marks to signify that words before or after the fragment have been omitted.

> According to Robertson's report, there has been "a change in buying habits" during the past fifty years.

Moreover, if the fragment as given can be read as a complete sentence, capitalize the first word in the quoted fragment, even though this word was not capitalized in the original. (Compare *We* in the following example with *we* in the example in ¶276.)

> According to Robertson's report, "We have been witnessing a change in buying habits, particularly with respect to food."

278 If a displayed quotation starts in the middle of a sentence, use three spaced periods at the beginning of the quotation.

> According to Robertson's report, there has been
>
> . . . a change in buying habits, particularly with respect to food. . . . How far this pattern of change will extend cannot be estimated.

If the fragment, however, can be read as a complete sentence, capitalize the first word of the fragment and omit the ellipsis marks. (Compare *Starting* in the following example with *starting* in the example in ¶276.)

> According to Robertson's report:
>
> Starting in the late 1950s, we have been witnessing a change in buying habits, particularly with respect to food.

279 When a long quotation starts with a complete sentence and ends with a complete sentence, do not use three spaced periods at the beginning or the end of the quotation unless you need to emphasize that the quotation has been extracted from a larger body of material.

280 If one or more paragraphs are omitted within a long quotation, indicate the omission by adding three spaced periods *after* the terminal punctuation that concludes the preceding paragraph.

Insertions in Quoted Matter

281   For clarity, it is sometimes necessary to insert explanatory words or phrases within quoted matter. Enclose such insertions in brackets. (See also ¶¶296–297.)

> Miss Rawlings added, "At the time of the first lawsuit [2001], there was clear-cut evidence of an intent to defraud."

282   For special emphasis, you may wish to italicize words that were not so treated in the original. In such cases insert a phrase like *emphasis added* in brackets at the end of the quotation or immediately after the italicized words.

> In the course of testifying, she stated, "I never met Mr. Norman in my life, *to the best of my recollection.* [Emphasis added.]"

283   When the original wording contains a misspelling, a grammatical error, or a confusing expression of thought, insert the term *sic* (meaning "so" or "this is the way it was") in brackets to indicate that the error existed in the original material.

> As he wrote in his letter, "I would sooner go to jail then [*sic*] have to pay your bill."

NOTE: Italicize the word *sic* when it is used in this way. If you do not have access to an italic font, do not underline *sic*.

☞   *For simple interruptions such as* he said *or* she said, *see* ¶¶262–263.

Aligning Quotation Marks

284   **a.**   In a list, any opening quotation mark should align with the first letter of the other items.

> I urge you to read the following materials (which I am sending to you by courier tomorrow):
>
>   *Leading the Revolution* by Gary Hamel
>
>   "The Bay Connection" by Bruce Thorson
>
>   *The Money Machine* by Daniel Stoffman

   b.   In a poem, the opening quotation mark at the beginning of each stanza should clear the left margin so that the first letter of each line will align. (See also ¶267.)

> "The lonely sunsets flare forlorn
> Down valleys dreadly desolate;
> The lordly mountains soar in scorn
> As still as death, as stern as fate . . ."
> —Robert W. Service

ITALICS AND UNDERLINING

Italic type (the counterpart of underlining or underscoring) is now widely available and is the preferred means of giving special emphasis to words and phrases and to the titles of literary and artistic works.

For Special Emphasis

285 A word referred to as a word is usually italicized or underlined. (Some writers prefer to enclose the word in quotation marks instead.) A word referred to as a word is often introduced by the expression *the term* or *the word*.

> The term *muffin-choker* refers to a bizarre item in the morning newspaper that you read as you eat your breakfast.
>
> We use the word *eh?* too often, but it is only to include others in our conversation.
>
> If you used fewer compound sentences, you wouldn't have so many *and*s (**OR** *and*s) in your writing. (Only the root word is italicized or underlined, not the *s*.
>
> **BUT:** She refused to sign the contract because she said it had too many ifs, ands, or buts. (Neither italics nor underlining is required for the phrase *ifs, ands, or buts* because the writer is not referring literally to these words as words. (The phrase means "too many conditions and qualifications.")

NOTE: Letters referred to as letters are often italicized or underlined if they are not capitalized. In such cases underlining may be preferable since an italic letter may not look sufficiently different to stand out.

dotting your i's (**OR** *i*'s)	the three Rs
solving for x when y = 3 (**OR** for *x* when *y*)	three Bs and one C
minding your p's and q's (**OR** *p*'s and *q*'s)	**BUT:** to the nth degree

☞ *For the plurals of letters such as i's and Rs, see* ¶¶622–623.

286 In a formal definition, the word to be defined is usually italicized or underlined and the definition quoted. In this way the two elements may be easily distinguished.

> The verb *prevaricate* (a polite way of saying "to lie") comes from the Latin word *praevaricari*, which means "to go zigzag, to walk crookedly."

NOTE: An informal definition does not require any special punctuation.

> Voyageurs were canoemen employed by the early fur trading companies.
>
> A bowler hat was a prize won by a cricketer who took three wickets on three successive balls. Hence, the term *hat trick* now refers to three hockey goals scored in one game by a single player. (Because the definition is informal, it does not have to be set off in quotation marks. However, *hat trick* is italicized or underlined, as indicated in ¶285, because the words are referred to as words.)

287 Italicize or underline foreign expressions that are not considered part of the English language. (Use quotation marks to set off translations of foreign expressions.)

> It's true, *n'est-ce pas?* (Meaning "isn't that so?")

NOTE: Once an expression of foreign origin becomes part of the English language, italics or underlining is no longer necessary. (Most dictionaries offer guidance on this point.) Here are some frequently used expressions that do not need italics or any other special display:

(Continued on page 82.)

à la carte	de jure	lang syne	quid pro quo
à la mode	déjà vu	maven	raison d'être
a priori	en masse	modus operandi	rendezvous
ad hoc	en route	modus vivendi	repertoire
ad infinitum	esprit de corps	non sequitur	résumé
ad nauseam	et al.	ombudsman	savoir faire
alfresco	etc.	par excellence	sic (see ¶283)
alma mater	ex officio	per annum	sine qua non
alter ego	fait accompli	per capita	status quo
bona fide	habeas corpus	per diem	summa cum laude
carte blanche	ibid. (see ¶1532)	prima facie	tête-à-tête
caveat emptor	in absentia	prix fixe	vis-à-vis
chimo	in toto	pro forma	vive
cul-de-sac	joie de vivre	pro rata	voilà
de facto	laissez-faire	pro tem	voir dire

☞ *For the use of accents and other diacritical marks with foreign words, see ¶718.*

288 *Individual* names of ships, trains, airplanes, and spacecraft may be italicized or underlined for special display or written simply with initial caps.

The *St. Roch* braved the Northwest Passage route.   **OR:** The St. Roch . . .

BUT: I flew to Paris on a Concorde and came back on a DC-10. (No special display is needed for the names *Concorde* and *DC-10* because they identify classes of aircraft but are not the individual names of planes.)

With Titles of Literary and Artistic Works

289 **a.** Italicize or underline titles of *complete* works that are published as separate items—for example, books, pamphlets, long poems, magazines, and newspapers. Also italicize or underline titles of movies, plays, musicals, operas, television and radio series, long musical pieces, paintings, and works of sculpture.

Our ads in *The Globe and Mail* have produced excellent results.

(**OR**) Our ads in The Globe and Mail have produced excellent results.

You will particularly enjoy a book entitled *The Best of Bridge.*

Next Friday we will hear Der Rosenkavalier (**OR** . . . *Der Rosenkavalier).*

The painting popularly referred to as *Whistler's Mother* is actually entitled *Arrangement in Gray and Black No. 1.*

NOTE: Do not italicize, underline, or quote the titles of musical pieces that are identified by form (for example, *symphony, concerto, sonata*) or by key (for example, *A Major, B Flat Minor*). However, if a descriptive phrase accompanies this type of title, italicize or underline this phrase if the work is long; quote this phrase if the work is short.

Beethoven's Sonata No. 18 in E Flat Minor, Op. 31, No. 3

Tchaikovsky's Symphony No. 6 in B Flat minor (the *Pathétique*)

Chopin's Etude No. 12 (the "Revolutionary" Etude)

  b. Titles of complete works may be keyed in all capitals as an alternative to italics or underlining.

Every executive will find RIGHT ON TIME! a valuable guide.

NOTE: The use of all capitals is acceptable when titles occur frequently (as in the correspondence of a publishing house) or when the use of all-capital letters is intended to have an eye-catching effect. In other circumstances use italics or underlining.

c. In material that is being prepared for publication, titles of complete works must be italicized or underlined. This special display indicates that the title must appear in italics in the final version.

Every executive will find *Right on Time!* a valuable guide.

d. In titles of magazines, do not italicize, underline, or capitalize the word *magazine* unless it is part of the actual title.

Chatelaine magazine　　**BUT:** *The National Magazine*

e. In some cases the name of the publishing company is the same as the name of the publication. Italicize or underline the name when it refers to *the publication* but not when it refers to *the company.*

I saw her column in *Maclean's.*

BUT: I wrote to Maclean's about a job.

Joe used to be *Fortune's* management editor; now he works as a management consultant to half a dozen Fortune 500 companies.

f. Italicize or underline a subtitle (but not an edition number) that accompanies the main title of a book.

If you're looking for a good overview of the subject, get hold of Kinnear and Taylor's *Marketing Research: An Applied Approach*, Fourth Edition.

g. Italicize or underline the titles of books, newspapers, and magazines that are published in electronic form.

Britannica Online (the electronic version of the *Encyclopaedia Britannica*)

Globeandmail.com (the electronic version of *The Globe and Mail*)

Slate and *Feed* (electronic magazines, referred to as *e-zines* or *Web zines*)

☞ *For the use of quotation marks with titles of literary and artistic works, see* ¶¶242–244. *For the treatment of titles of sacred works, see* ¶350.

Guidelines for Italics and Underlining

290 Italicize or underline as a unit whatever should be grasped as a unit—individual words, titles, phrases, or even whole sentences.

a. Use **italics** when you want to give special emphasis to a unit consisting of two or more words. Be sure to italicize the entire unit, including space between words and any punctuation that is part of the unit.

Ipso facto, sine qua non, and *pro forma:* these are the kinds of expressions you must be able to define. (**NOT:** *and pro forma:*)

(Continued on page 84.)

b. When using **underlining** to give special emphasis to words or phrases in a series, underline only the terms themselves and not any punctuation that intervenes or follows.

Ipso facto, sine qua non, and pro forma: these are the kinds of expressions . . .

Have you ever read Moby Dick or War and Peace?

EXCEPTION: This week the Confederation Theatre is presenting Oklahoma!, next week Where's Charley?, and the following week My Fair Lady. (The exclamation point and the question mark are underlined in this sentence because they are an integral part of the material to be emphasized; however, the commas and the sentence-ending period are not.)

c. Do not underline a possessive or plural ending that is added on to a word being emphasized.

the Times-Picayune's editorial   too many ands

d. Parentheses are italicized when the words they enclose begin *and* end with italicized words.

Use a comma to separate independent clauses joined by a co-ordinating conjunction *(and, but, or,* or *nor).*

Use commas to set off transitional expressions (like *however* and *therefore*). (Note that the first word is not italicized; therefore the parentheses are not italicized.)

(*What we need* is the subject of that sentence.) (In this case the last word is not italicized.)

e. Brackets are not usually italicized.

OTHER MARKS OF PUNCTUATION

The Apostrophe (')

291 The use of the apostrophe is covered in the following paragraphs. (The font you select will determine the style of apostrophe to be used. If you wish, you can switch from the default style to an alternative one by accessing an extended character set. See ¶227.)

☞ *As a single quotation mark, see ¶¶245–246, 247b, 248b, 249d, 250b, 265b.*
To indicate the omission of figures in dates, see ¶¶412, 439a.
As a symbol for feet, see ¶¶432, 543.
To form contractions, see ¶505.
To form plurals of figures, letters, etc., see ¶¶622–625.
To form possessives, see ¶¶247b, 627–651.
To form expressions derived from all-capital abbreviations, see ¶522d.

Ellipsis Marks (. . .)

292 Ellipsis marks are three spaced periods, with one space before and after each period.

a. As a general rule, do not use ellipsis marks in place of a period at the end of a sentence. However, ellipses may be used to indicate that a sentence trails off before the end. The three spaced periods create an effect of uncertainty or suggest an abrupt suspension of thought. (No terminal punctuation is used with ellipsis marks in this kind of construction.)

He could easily have saved the situation by . . . But why talk about it?

b. Ellipsis marks are often used in advertising to display individual items or to connect a series of loosely related phrases.

Where can you match these services?

. . . Free ticket delivery

. . . Flight insurance

. . . On-time departures

The Inn at the End of the Road . . . where you may enjoy the epicure's choicest offerings . . . by reservation only . . . closed Tuesdays.

☞ *For the use of ellipsis marks to indicate omissions in quoted matter, see ¶¶274–280.*

The Asterisk (*)

293 The asterisk may be used to refer the reader to a footnote or to an unprintable word. (See ¶¶1502f, 1634c.)

a. When the asterisk and some other mark of punctuation occur together within a sentence, the asterisk *follows* the punctuation mark, with no intervening space.

b. In the footnote itself, leave no space after the asterisk.

c. Asterisks are used to replace words that are considered unprintable.

If the TV cameras had been present when Finney called Schultz a ***** (and about 50 other names as well), tonight's newscast would have contained the longest bleep in television history.

The Diagonal (/)

294 The diagonal occurs (without space before or after) in certain abbreviations and expressions of time.

B/L	bill of lading	m/s	metres per second
w/	with	n/30	net amount due in 30 days
c/o	care of	/S/	signed (used before a copied signature)

The copy deadline for the fall '03/winter '04 catalogue is April 15.

Please check the figures for fiscal year 2003/04.

I'm concerned about their P/E ratio. (Referring to the price/earnings ratio of a company's stock.)

295 a. The diagonal is used to express alternatives.

a go/no-go decision	read/write files
input/output systems	meet on Monday and/or Tuesday
an AM/FM tuner	on/off switch

(Continued on page 86.)

b. The diagonal may be used to indicate that a person has two functions or a thing has two components.

the owner/member	zoned for commercial/industrial activities
a client/server network	planning to elect a secretary/treasurer

NOTE: A hyphen may also be used in such expressions. (See ¶806.)

c. The diagonal is also used in writing fractions (4/5), code and serial numbers (2S/394), and Web site addresses (www.canoe.ca/macleans).

☞ *For the use of the diagonal when quoting poetry, see ¶268.*
For the use of the diagonal in telephone numbers, see ¶454.

Brackets ([ ])

296 A correction or an insertion in a quoted extract should be enclosed in brackets. (See also ¶¶281–283.)

His final request was this: "Please keep me appraised [*sic*] of any new developments." (See ¶283, note.)

The transcript of his testimony contains this incredible statement: "I did not approach Commissioner Lali *at any time* [emphasis added] while my petition was being considered."

"If we all pull together, we can bring a new level of political leadership to this province. [Extended applause.] Please give me your support in this campaign." (Note the capitalization of *Extended* and the use of a period before the closing bracket when the bracketed element is treated as a separate sentence. See also ¶¶226, 282.)

297 When a parenthetical element falls within another parenthetical element, enclose the smaller element in brackets and enclose the larger element in parentheses.

Sihota said on television yesterday that prices would begin to fall sharply. (However, in an article published in the *Star* [May 12, 2003], he was quoted as saying that prices would remain steady for the foreseeable future.)

SPACING: WITH PUNCTUATION MARKS

298 The following chart gives the *traditional* spacing required before and after punctuation marks and the asterisk symbol. Although it is generally accepted today that one space is sufficient after ending punctuation marks, there are some who still prefer the visual break that two spaces provide, especially when proportional fonts are used. However, if the justification feature is used to achieve even right margins, then one space only is necessary to avoid large areas of white space within a line of text.

Traditional Spacing

Punctuation Symbol	Spacing *Before*	Spacing *After*
Period (.)	none	one or two after the end of a sentence
		two after the period following an enumeration number or bullet [Software features will include an automatic tab which may be adjusted 0.25" to 0.5".]
		one after an abbreviation (See also ¶511.)
		none after a decimal point
		none when another punctuation mark follows (e.g., a closing quotation mark, parenthesis, dash; a comma, a semi-colon, or a colon following an "abbreviation" period)
Question Mark (?) *or* **Exclamation Mark (!)**	none	one or two after the end of a sentence
		one if a question mark is within a sentence (See ¶¶116–117.)
		none if another punctuation mark follows (e.g., a closing quotation mark, parenthesis, or dash)
Comma (,)	none	one
		none if followed by closing quotation mark
		none if comma is within a number (e.g., 92,539)
Semicolon (;)	none	one
Colon (:)	none	two if it is within a sentence
	none *before* **or** *after* in expressions of time (8:20 p.m.) or in proportions (2:1)	
En Dash (–) **Em Dash (—)**	none	none **EXCEPT** if the dash ends a statement that breaks off abruptly (See ¶¶207–208.)
Hyphen (-)	none	none
	one before *and* after if used in an address as follows: (e.g., 10964 - 125 Street, but *not* 10964 - Centre Street)	
Apostrophe (')	none	one if at the **end** of a word within a sentence
Asterisk (*)	none	one or two if at the end of a sentence
		one if within a sentence
		none if in a footnote (See ¶293.)
Diagonal (/)	none before *or* after (See ¶268 for exception in poetry.)	

(Continued on page 88.)

Punctuation Symbol	Spacing *Before*	Spacing *After*
Opening Parenthesis [(] or Bracket ([)	one if text is within a sentence two if text follows a sentence and is itself a separate sentence	none
Closing Parenthesis [)] or Bracket (])	none	one if text is within a sentence two if text is a complete sentence followed by another sentence (See ¶226.) none if another punctuation mark follows
Opening Quotation Mark (")	two if quoted text starts a new sentence or follows a colon none if a dash or opening parenthesis precedes one in all other cases	none
Closing Quotation Mark (")	none	two when quoted matter ends the sentence none when another mark of punctuation immediately follows (e.g., semicolon or colon) one in all other cases
Single Quotation Mark (')	Extra space between single and double quotation marks when they occur together (See ¶246.)	
Ellipsis Marks (. . .) or (. . . .) includes the period at the end of a sentence	one space before and after each of the three periods within a sentence (See ¶¶274–275.)	
	none when preceded by a quotation mark	none when followed by a quotation mark (See last example in ¶275.) two after ellipses marks that follow a period, question mark, or exclamation point at the end of a sentence (See ¶276.)

☞ *See ¶543 for spacing required before and after symbols such as @, &, and =.*

  See the Online Learning Centre at www.mcgrawhill.ca/college/gregg for related weblinks.

SECTION THREE

Capitalization

BASIC RULES (¶¶301–310)

First Words (¶¶301–302)
Proper Nouns (¶¶303–306)
Common Nouns (¶¶307–310)

SPECIAL RULES (¶¶311–365)

Personal Names (¶311)
Titles With Personal Names (¶¶312–317)
Family Titles (¶¶318–319)
Names of Organizations (¶¶320–324)
Names of Government Bodies (¶¶325–330)
Names of Places (¶¶331–337)
Points of the Compass (¶¶338–341)
Days of the Week, Months, Holidays, Seasons, Events, Periods (¶¶342–345)
Acts, Laws, Bills, Treaties (¶346)
Programs, Movements, Concepts (¶347)
Races, Peoples, Languages (¶348)
Religious References (¶¶349–350)
Celestial Bodies (¶351)
Course Titles, Subjects, Academic Degrees (¶¶352–354)
Commercial Products (¶¶355–356)
Advertising Material (¶357)
Legal Documents (¶358)
Nouns With Numbers or Letters (¶359)
Titles of Literary and Artistic Works; Headings (¶¶360–362)
Hyphenated Words (¶363)
Awards and Medals (¶364)
Computer Terminology (¶365)
Intercaps (¶366)

The function of capitalization is to give distinction, importance, and emphasis to words. Thus the first word of a sentence is capitalized to indicate distinctively and emphatically that a new sentence has begun. Moreover, proper nouns like *George, Toronto, Dun & Bradstreet, the Parthenon, January,* and *Friday* are capitalized to signify the special importance of these words as the official names of particular persons, places, and things. A number of words, however, may function either as proper nouns or as common nouns—for example, terms like *the board of directors* or *the company*. For words like these, capitalization practices vary widely, but the variation merely reflects the relative importance each writer assigns to the word in question.

Despite disagreements among authorities on specific rules, there is a growing consensus against overusing capitalization in business writing. When too many words stand out, none stand out. The current trend, then, is to use capitalization more sparingly—to give importance, distinction, or emphasis only when and where it is warranted.

The following rules of capitalization are written with ordinary situations in mind. If you work in a specialized field, you may find it necessary to follow a different style.

BASIC RULES
First Words

301 Capitalize the first word of:

a. Every sentence. (See ¶302 for exceptions.)

> Try to limit each of your e-mail messages to one screen.
> Will you be able to pull everything together by then?
> The deadline we have been given is absolutely impossible!

b. An expression used as a sentence. (See also ¶¶102, 111, 119–120.)

So much for that.	Really?	No!
Enough said.	How come?	Congratulations!

c. A quoted sentence. (See also ¶¶272–273.)

> Mrs. Eckstein herself said, "We surely have not heard the complete story."

d. An independent question within a sentence. (See also ¶¶115–117.)

> The question is, Whose version of the argument shall we believe?
>
> **BUT:** Have you approved the divisional sales forecasts? the expense projections? the requests for staff expansion? (See ¶117.)

e. Each item displayed in a list or an outline. (See also ¶¶107, 199c, 1357c, 1425e, 1723d.)

> Here is a powerful problem-solving tool that will help you:
> - Become an effective leader.
> - Improve your relations with subordinates, peers, and superiors.
> - Cope with stressful situations on the job.

f. Each line in a poem. (Always follow the style of the poem, however.)

> From wrong to wrong the exasperated spirit
> Proceeds, unless restored by that refining fire
> Where you must move in measure, like a dancer.
>
> —T. S. Eliot

g. The salutation and the complimentary closing of a letter. (See also ¶¶1348, 1359.)

Dear Mrs. Pancetta   Sincerely yours

302 **a.** When a sentence is set off by *dashes* or *parentheses* within another sentence, do not capitalize the first word following the opening dash or parenthesis unless it is a proper noun, a proper adjective, the pronoun *I*, or the first word of a quoted sentence. (See ¶¶214, 224–225 for examples.)

b. Do not capitalize the first word of a sentence following a colon except under certain circumstances. (See ¶¶196–199.)

Proper Nouns

303 Capitalize every *proper noun*, that is, the official name of a particular person, place, or thing. Also capitalize the pronoun *I*.

Cirque du Soleil	Roy Thomson Hall
Meech Lake Accord	Monday, January 30
Dalhousie University	Whitby, Ontario
the 2002 Winter Olympics	War of 1812
Political Science 321	Zamboni
Commonwealth of Nations	the Memorial Cup
the Internet (**OR**) the Net	*Maclean's*

NOTE: Prepositions (like *of*, *for*, and *in*) are not capitalized unless they have four or more letters (like *with* and *from*). (See also ¶¶360–361.) The articles *a* and *an* are not capitalized; the article *the* is capitalized only under special circumstances. (See ¶324.) Conjunctions (like *and* and *or*) are also not capitalized. However, follow the capitalization style used by the owner of the name; for example, *3-In-One oil, One-A-Day vitamins, Book-Of-The-Month Club, Fruit of the Loom.*

304 Capitalize adjectives derived from proper nouns.

America (n.), American (adj.)	Machiavelli (n.), Machiavellian (adj.)
Canada (n.), Canadian (adj.)	Halifax (n.), Haligonian (adj.)

EXCEPTIONS: Parliament, parliamentary; Senate, senatorial; Constitution, constitutional. (See also ¶306.)

305 Capitalize imaginative names and nicknames that designate particular persons, places, or things. (See ¶¶333–335 for imaginative place names; ¶344 for imaginative names of historical periods.)

the Famous Five	the Milky Way
Herring Chockers	Upper House
the Bluenosers	Generation Y
Fathers of Confederation	Big Mac
Jack Frost	Ogopogo
the Middle Ages	Bonhomme

306 Some expressions that originally contained or consisted of proper nouns or adjectives are now considered common nouns and should not be capitalized. (See ¶309b.)

(Continued on page 92.)

blue jeans	boycott	watt	fanny pack
manila envelope	diesel	joule	roman print

NOTE: Check an up-to-date dictionary to determine capitalization for words of this type.

Common Nouns

307 A *common noun* names a class of things (for example, *books*), or it may refer indefinitely to one or more things within that class (*a book, several books*). Nouns used in this way are considered general terms of classification and are often modified by indefinite words such as *a, any, every,* or *some.* Do not capitalize nouns used as general terms of classification.

a company	every board of directors
any corporation	some lawyers

308 A common noun may also be used to name a *particular* person, place, or thing. Nouns used in this way are often modified (a) by *the, this, these, that,* or *those* or (b) by possessive words such as *my, your, his, her, our,* or *their.* Do not capitalize a general term of classification, even though it refers to a particular person, place, or thing.

COMMON NOUN:	our doctor	the hotel	the river
PROPER NOUN:	Dr. Tsai	Empress Hotel	the Churchill River

309 **a.** Capitalize a common noun when it is part of a proper name but not when it is used alone in place of the full name. (For exceptions, see ¶310.)

Professor Perry	**BUT:** the professor
Cameco Corporation	the corporation
Confederation Bridge	the bridge
ESL Cultural Program	the program
Victoria Park	the park

NOTE: Also capitalize the plural form of a common noun in expressions such as *the Micmac and the Antigonish Malls, Main and Tenth Streets,* the *Peace and Hay Rivers,* and *the Atlantic and Pacific Oceans.*

b. In a number of compound nouns, the first element is a proper noun or a proper adjective and the second element is a common noun. In such cases capitalize only the first element, since the compound as a whole is a common noun.

a Scottish terrier	a Ferris wheel	Chinese checkers	Brussels sprouts
a Dutch oven	Danish pastry	French doors	Texas gate

NOTE: Check an up-to-date dictionary for words of this type. After extensive usage the proper noun or adjective may become a common noun and no longer require capitalization. (See ¶306.)

310 Some *short forms* (common-noun elements replacing the complete proper name) are capitalized when they are intended to carry the full significance of the complete proper name. It is in this area, however, that the danger of over-capitalizing most often occurs. Therefore, do not capitalize a short form unless it clearly warrants the importance, distinction, or emphasis that capitalization conveys. The following kinds of short forms are commonly capitalized:

PERSONAL TITLES: Capitalize titles replacing names of high-ranking international, national, and provincial officials (but not generally local officials or company officers). (See ¶313.)

ORGANIZATIONAL NAMES: Do not capitalize short forms of company names except in formal or legal writing. (See ¶321.)

GOVERNMENTAL NAMES: Capitalize short forms of names of international and national bodies (but not usually provincial or local bodies). (See ¶¶326–327, 334–335.)

PLACE NAMES: Capitalize only well-established short forms. (See ¶¶332, 335.)

NOTE: Do not use a short form to replace a full name unless the full name has been mentioned earlier or will be understood from the context.

SPECIAL RULES
Personal Names

311 **a.** Treat a person's name—in terms of capitalization, spelling, punctuation, and spacing—exactly as the person does.

Alice Mayer	Charles Burden Wilson
Rita Naser	L. Westcott Quinn
Steven J. Dougherty, Jr.	H. M. Nakagawa
Stephen J. Dockerty Jr.	Peter B. J. Hallman

☞ *For the treatment of initials, see ¶516.*
For the use or omission of commas with terms such as Jr., see ¶156.

  b. Respect individual preferences in the spelling of personal names.

Ann Marie, Anne Marie, Anna Marie, Annemarie, Annamarie, Anne-Marie, AnnMarie

Macmillan, MacMillan, Mac Millan, Macmillen, MacMillen, MacMillin, McMillan, Mc Millan, McMillen, McMillin, McMillon

  c. In names containing the prefix *O'*, always capitalize the *O* and the letter following the apostrophe; for example, *O'Brian* or *O'Brien*.

  d. Watch for differences in capitalization and spacing in names containing prefixes like *d', da, de, del, della, di, du, l', la, le, van,* and *von.*

D'Amelio, d'Amelio, Damelio	deLaCruz, DeLacruz, Dela Cruz, DelaCruz
LaCoste, Lacoste, La Coste	VanDeVelde, Van DeVelde, vandeVelde

  e. When a surname with an uncapitalized prefix stands alone (that is, without a first name, a title, or initials preceding it), capitalize the prefix to prevent a misreading.

Paul de Luca   Mr. de Luca   P. de Luca   **BUT:** Is De Luca leaving?

  f. When names that contain prefixes are to be keyed in all-capital letters, follow these principles: If there is no space after the prefix, capitalize only the initial letter of the prefix. If space follows the prefix, capitalize the entire prefix.

(Continued on page 94.)

NORMAL FORM:	MacDonald	Mac Donald
ALL-CAPITAL FORM:	MacDONALD	MAC DONALD

g. When a nickname or a descriptive expression precedes or replaces a person's first name, simply capitalize it. However, if the nickname or descriptive expression falls between a person's first and last names, enclose it either in quotation marks or in parentheses.

Rocket Richard	BUT:	Maurice "Rocket" Richard
	OR:	Maurice (Rocket) Richard

☞ *For the plurals of personal names, see ¶¶615–616.*

For the plurals of possessives of personal names, see ¶¶630–633.

Titles With Personal Names

312 a. Capitalize all official titles of honour and respect when they *precede* personal names.

PERSONAL TITLES:
Mrs. Norma Washburn (see ¶517)   Miss Yamulky
Ms. Terry Fiske   Mr. Benedict

EXECUTIVE TITLES:
President Julia McLeod   Vice-President Saulnier

PROFESSIONAL TITLES:
Professor Henry Pelligrino   Dr. Khalil (see ¶517)

CIVIC TITLES:
Councillor Samuel O. Bolling   Ambassador Staedler
Mayor-elect Louis K. Uhl (see ¶317)   ex-Senator Hayes (see ¶317)

MILITARY TITLES:
Colonel Perry L. Forrester   Captain Comerford

RELIGIOUS TITLES:
the Reverend William F. Dowd   Rabbi Gelfand

b. Do not capitalize such titles when the personal name that follows is in apposition and is set off by commas.

Yesterday the *president*, Julia McLeod, revealed her plans to retire next June.

BUT: Yesterday *President* Julia McLeod revealed her plans to retire next June.

c. Do not capitalize occupational titles (such as *author, surgeon, publisher,* and *lawyer*) preceding a name.

The reviews of *drama critic* Simon Ritchey have lost their bite.
(**NOT:** The reviews of *Drama Critic* Simon Ritchey have lost their bite.)

NOTE: Occupational titles can be distinguished from official titles in that only official titles can be used with a last name alone. Since one would not address a person as "Author Berton" or "Publisher Ward," these are not official titles and should not be capitalized.

d. Do not confuse a true title preceding a name (such as *Judge*) with a generic expression (such as *federal judge*).

Judge Ann Bly **OR** federal judge Ann Bly (**BUT NOT:** federal Judge Ann Bly)

President Julia McLeod **OR** company president Julia McLeod
(**BUT NOT:** company President Julia McLeod)

313 a. In general, do not capitalize titles of honour and respect when they *follow* a personal name or are used *in place of* a personal name.

Julia McLeod, *president* of McLeod Inc., has revealed her plans to retire next June. During her sixteen years as *president*, the company grew . . .

However, exceptions are made for important officials and dignitaries, as indicated in the following paragraphs.

b. Retain capitalization in titles of high-ranking national, provincial, and international officials when they *follow* or *replace* a specific personal name. Below are examples of titles that remain capitalized.

NATIONAL OFFICIALS: the *Prime Minister*, Cabinet members (such as the *Secretary of State*, the *Speaker of the House of Commons*, and the *Attorney General*), the heads of government agencies and bureaus (such as the *Deputy Minister*, or the *Commissioner*), the *Chief Justice*, the *Ambassador*, the *Member of Parliament*.

PROVINCIAL OFFICIALS: the *Premier*, the *Lieutenant-Governor*.

ROYAL DIGNITARIES: the *Queen*, the *Duke*, the *Prince of Wales*.

INTERNATIONAL FIGURES: the *Pope*, the *Secretary General of the United Nations*, the *President*.

c. Titles of local governmental officials and those of lesser federal and provincial officials are not usually capitalized when they follow or replace a personal name. However, these titles are sometimes capitalized in writing intended for a limited readership (for example, in a local newspaper, in internal communications within an organization, or in correspondence coming from or directed to the official's office), where the intended reader would consider the official to be of high rank.

The *Mayor* promised only last fall to hold the property tax at its present level. (Excerpt from an editorial in a local newspaper.)

BUT: Francis Fahey, *mayor* of Peterborough, Ontario, was interviewed at City Hall earlier today. The *mayor* spoke forcefully about the need to maintain aid to . . . (Excerpt from a national news service release.)

I would like to request an appointment with the *Solicitor General*. (In a letter sent to the provincial solicitor general's office.)

BUT: I have written for an appointment with the *solicitor general* and expect to hear from his office soon.

d. Titles of *company officials* (for example, the *president*, the *general manager*) should not be capitalized when they follow or replace a personal name. Exceptions are made in formal minutes of meetings (see page 488) and in rules and by-laws.

The *president* will visit thirteen countries in a tour of company installations abroad. (Normal style.)

The *Secretary's* minutes were read and approved. (In formal minutes.)

(Continued on page 96.)

3

NOTE: Some companies choose to capitalize these titles in all their communications because of the great respect the officials command within the company. However, this practice confers excessive importance on people who are neither public officials nor eminent dignitaries, and it should be avoided.

e. In general, do not capitalize job titles when they stand alone. However, in procedures manuals and in company memos and announcements, job titles are sometimes capitalized for special emphasis.

Marion Conroy has been promoted to the position of *senior accountant* (**OR** *Senior Accountant*).

f. Titles *following* a personal name or *standing alone* are sometimes capitalized in formal citations and acknowledgments.

314 Do not capitalize titles used as general terms of classification. (See ¶307.)

a Canadian senator   every king
a provincial premier   any ambassador

EXCEPTION: Because of the special regard for the office of the Prime Minister of Canada, this title is capitalized even when used as a general term of classification (for example, a *Prime Minister*, every *Prime Minister*).

315 Capitalize any title (even if not of high rank) when it is used in *direct address* (that is, quoted or unquoted speech made directly to another person).

DIRECT ADDRESS: Please tell me, *Doctor*, what risks are involved in this treatment.

INDIRECT ADDRESS: I asked the *doctor* what risks are involved in this treatment.

NOTE: In direct address, do not capitalize a term like *madam, miss,* or *sir* if it stands alone without a proper name following.

Isn't it true, *sir*, that the defendant offered you money for trade secrets?

316 In the *inside address* of a letter and in the *writer's name and title*, capitalize all titles whether they precede or follow the name. (See ¶¶1321–1325 and 1362–1369.)

317 Do not capitalize *former, late, ex-,* or *-elect* when used with titles. (See ¶363 for the style in headings.)

the late Premier Bennett   ex-Chairman Richards   mayor-elect Drever

Family Titles

318 Capitalize words such as *mother, father, aunt,* and *uncle* when they stand alone or are followed by a personal name.

Let me ask *Mother* and *Dad* if that date is open for them.

We'll be glad to put up *Aunt Peg* and *Uncle Fred* when they come to visit.

I hear that *Brother Bobby* has gone mountain climbing.

Do you think *Grandmother Veinot* will be pleased when she hears the news?

319 Do not capitalize family titles when they are preceded by possessives (such as *my, your, his, her, our,* and *their*) and simply describe a family relationship.

> Let me ask my *mother* and *dad* if that date is open for them.

> Do you think your *brother* Bobby would like to meet my *sister* Fern?

NOTE: If the words *uncle, aunt,* or *cousin* form a unit when used together with a first name, capitalize these titles, even when they are preceded by a possessive.

> Frank wants us to meet his *Uncle John*. (Here *Uncle John* is a unit.)

> **BUT:** Frank wants us to meet his *uncle*, John Cunningham. (Here *uncle* simply describes a family relationship.)

> I hope you can meet my *Cousin May*. (The writer thinks of her as *Cousin May*.)

> **BUT:** I hope you can meet my *cousin* May. (Here the writer thinks of her as *May*; the word *cousin* merely indicates relationship.)

Names of Organizations

320 a. Capitalize the names of companies, unions, associations, societies, independent committees and boards, schools, political parties, conventions, foundations, fraternities, sororities, clubs, and religious bodies.

Sun Life of Canada	Niagara Chamber of Commerce
Bank of Montreal	Progressive Conservative Party
Canadian Cancer Society	Victorian Order of Nurses
the Canadian Wheat Board	Canadian Automobile Association
Telesat Canada	Beta Sigma Phi Sorority
Rideau Ski Club	Saskatchewan Roughriders
St. Peter's Anglican Church	the University of Winnipeg

NOTE: Try to follow the style established by the organization itself, as shown in the letterhead or some other written communication from the organization.

Talbots (Canada) Inc.	Wal-Mart	RE/MAX
Sears Canada Inc.	!ndigo	Apple Computer Inc.

b. Also capitalize imaginative names used to refer to specific organizations. (See also ¶333b.)

Big Blue (IBM)   Ma Bell (Bell Canada)

☞ *For the treatment of articles (like* the*), prepositions (like* of *or* for*), and conjunctions (like* and*), see ¶303, note.*

For the capitalization of abbreviations and acronyms used as organizational names, see ¶¶520, 522.

321 When the common-noun element is used in place of the full name (for example, *the company* in place of *the Andersen Hardware Company*), do not capitalize the short form unless special emphasis or distinction is required (as in legal documents, minutes of meetings, by-laws, and other formal communications,

(Continued on page 98.)

3

where the short form is intended to invoke the full authority of the organization). In most cases, however, capitalization is unnecessary because the short form is used only as a general term of classification. (See ¶¶307–308.)

> The *company* has always made a conscientious effort to involve itself in community affairs. However, our *company* policy specifically prohibits our underwriting any activity in support of a candidate for public office. (As used here, *company* is a term of general classification.)
>
> **BUT:** On behalf of the *Company*, I am authorized to accept your bid. (Here the full authority of the company is implied; hence *Company* is spelled with a capital *C*.)
>
> Mr. Weinstock has just returned from a visit to Hillcrest College. He reports that the *college* is planning a new fund-raising campaign to finance the construction of the new media centre.
>
> **BUT:** The *College* hopes to raise an additional $10 million this year to finance the construction of the new media resource centre. (Announcement in the alumni bulletin.)

NOTE: Do not capitalize the short form if it is modified by a word other than *the*. In constructions such as *our company, this company,* and *every company,* the noun is clearly a general term of classification. (See also ¶308.)

322 Capitalize organizational terms within the writer's organization; for example, *advertising department, manufacturing division, finance committee,* and *board of directors.* These terms are not capitalized when they refer to an outside organization unless the writer has reason to give these terms special importance or distinction.

> The *Board of Directors* will meet next Thursday at 2:30. (From a company memo.)
>
> **BUT:** Julia Perez, senior vice-president of the Mulholland Bancorp, has been elected to the *board of directors* of the Kensington Trade Corporation. (From a news release intended for a general audience.)
>
> The *Finance Committee* will meet all week to review next year's budget. (Style used by insiders.)
>
> **BUT:** Gilligan says his company can give us no encouragement about the sponsorship of a new art centre until its *finance committee* has reviewed our proposal. (Style normally used by outsiders.)
>
> The *Advertising Department* will unveil the fall campaign this Friday. (Style used by insiders.)
>
> **BUT:** The *advertising department* of Black & London will unveil its fall campaign this Friday. (Style used by outsiders.)

NOTE: Constructions such as *this credit department, their credit department, every credit department,* and *your credit department* are terms of general classification and should not be capitalized. (See also ¶321, note.)

> Black & London always seems to have a great deal of turnover in *its advertising department.*
>
> We don't have as much turnover in *our advertising department* as you may think. (Some insiders prefer to write "our Advertising Department" because of the special importance they attach to their own organizational structure.)
>
> I would like to apply for the position of copywriter that is currently open in *your advertising department.* (Some outsiders might write "your Advertising Department"

if they wanted to flatter the reader by giving special importance to the reader's organizational structure.)

IMPORTANT: Companies' policies regarding capitalization of their organizational structures may vary from one business to another. Whatever style is dictated, it is important to maintain *consistency*.

323 Capitalize such nouns as *marketing, advertising,* or *promotion* when they are used alone to designate a department within an organization.

> Paul Havlicek in *Corporate Communications* is the person to talk with.
>
> I want to get a reaction from our people in *Marketing* first.
>
> **BUT:** I want to talk to our *marketing* people first. (Here *marketing* is simply a descriptive adjective.)

324 Capitalize the word *the* preceding the name of an organization only when it is part of the legal name of the organization.

> The Canadian Press   The House Doctor
> The Insurance Group   **BUT:** the Bay

a. Even when part of the organizational name, *the* is often uncapitalized except in legal or formal contexts where it is important to give the full legal name.

b. Do not capitalize *the* when the name is used as a modifier or is given in the form of an abbreviation.

> the Canadian Press report   the CP   works for the Post

Names of Government Bodies

325 Capitalize the names of countries and international organizations as well as national, provincial, county, and city bodies and their subdivisions.

> the Commonwealth Secretariat   the Manitoba Land Titles Office
> the World Trade Organization   the New Brunswick Legislature
> the Republic of Korea   the Barrie Board of Education
> the European Community   the Alberta Securities Commission
> the Chrétien Government   the Bruce County Heritage Board
> the Privy Council   the Northwest Territories Housing
> the Prime Minister's Office   Corporation
> the Penticton Police Service   Thirty-eighth Parliament (see ¶363)
>
> **BUT:** the feds (referring to the federal government regulators)

☞ *For city and provincial names, see ¶¶334–335.*

326 Capitalize short forms of names of international and national bodies and their major divisions.

> the Commons or the House (referring to the House of Commons)
>
> the Agency (referring to the Canada Customs and Revenue Agency, Parks Canada Agency, Atlantic Canada Opportunities Agency, etc.)
>
> the Department (referring to the Department of National Defence, the Department of Foreign Affairs and International Trade, Justice Canada, Industry Canada, etc.)

(Continued on page 100.)

the Court (referring to the Supreme Court of Canada, the International Court of Justice, etc.)

As a rule, do not capitalize short forms of names of provincial or local governmental groups except when special circumstances warrant emphasis or distinction. (See ¶327.)

327 Common terms such as *police service, board of education,* and *provincial court* need not be capitalized (even when referring to a specific body), since they are terms of general classification. However, such terms should be capitalized when the writer intends to refer to the organization in all of its official dignity.

> The *Police Service* has announced the promotion of Robert Boyarsky to the rank of sergeant. (The short form is capitalized here because it is intended to have the full force of the complete name, the *Cornwall Police Service*.)

> **BUT:** The *Cornwall police service* sponsors a youth athletic program that we could well copy. (No capitalization is used here because the writer is referring to the service in general terms and not by its official name.)

NOTE: Do not capitalize the short form if it is not actually derived from the complete name. For example, do not capitalize the short form *police service* if the full name is *Department of Public Safety.*

328 Capitalize *federal* only when it is part of the official name of a federal agency, a federal act, or some other proper noun.

> the *Federal* Court of Canada   the *Federal*-Provincial Relations Office

> **BUT:** . . . subject to federal, provincial, and local laws.

329 The terms *federal government* and *government* (referring specifically to the Canadian government) are now commonly written in small letters because they are considered terms of general classification. In government documents, however, and in other types of communications where these terms are intended to have the force of an official name, they are capitalized.

> The *federal government* is questioning its corporate welfare policy—that is, *federal* subsidies to large corporations.

> If you can't fight City Hall, what makes you think it's any easier to fight the *Federal Government?* (Here the writer wants to emphasize the full power of the national government as an adversary.)

330 Capitalize such words as *union, commonwealth, republic,* and *kingdom* when they refer to a country or countries.

Commonwealth of Nations	the Commonwealth	Kingdom of Spain	the Kingdom
People's Republic of China	the Republic	Union of Myanmar	the Union

Names of Places

331 Capitalize the names of places, such as streets, buildings, parks, monuments, rivers, oceans, and mountains. Do not capitalize short forms used in place of the full name. (See ¶332 for a few exceptions.)

Wellington Street	**BUT:** the street
Montmorency Falls	the falls
CN Tower	the tower
Butchart Gardens	the gardens
Victoria Park	the park
Annapolis River	the river
Lions Gate Bridge	the bridge
Lake Memphremagog	the lake
Banff Springs Hotel	the hotel
Whistler Mountain	the mountain
Mirabel Airport	the airport
the National Art Gallery	the gallery

☞ *For plural expressions like* the Atlantic and Pacific Oceans, *see ¶309a, note.*

For the treatment of prepositions and conjunctions in proper names, see ¶303, note.

332 A few short forms are capitalized because of clear association with one place

the Coast (the West Coast)   the Hill (Parliament Hill)
the Continent (Europe)   the Island (Prince Edward Island
the Channel (English Channel)   **OR** Vancouver Island)

333 **a.** Capitalize imaginative names that designate specific places or areas.

the Golden Horseshoe   Gateway to the North
  (southern Ontario)   (Edmonton)
Gastown (Vancouver)   the Pacific Rim
Hogtown (Toronto)   the Breadbasket of Canada
the Big Nickel   (the Prairies)
  (Sudbury)   the Rock (Newfoundland)
Wild Rose Country   the Cradle of Confederation
  (Alberta)   (Charlottetown)
Gateway to the West   Land of the Midnight Sun
  (Winnipeg)   (the Far North)

b. Some place names are used imaginatively to refer to types of businesses or institutions.

Wall Street (the U.S.   Bay Street (brokerage firms
  financial industry)   in Toronto)

334 **a.** Capitalize the word *city* only when it is part of the corporate name of the city or part of an imaginative name.

Quebec City   the Stampede City (Calgary)
BUT: the city of Montreal the Queen City (Regina)

335 **a.** Capitalize *province* only when it follows the name of a province or is part of an imaginative name.

Known as the Island, Prince Edward Island is the smallest *province*.

In 1949 the tenth *province*, Newfoundland, entered Confederation.

Victoria is the capital of the *province* of British Columbia.

(Continued on page 102.)

New Brunswick is known as the Picture *Province*.

Next year we plan to visit the *States*. (Meaning the United States.)

b. Do not capitalize *province* when used in place of the actual name.

He is an employee of the *province*. (People working for provincial governments, however, might write *Province*.)

336 According to Canadian dictionaries, the terms used to refer to the residents of provinces and territories are formed as follows:

A Resident of	Is Called a/an
Newfoundland and Labrador	Newfoundlander, Labradorian
Prince Edward Island	Prince Edward Islander
Nova Scotia	Nova Scotian
New Brunswick	New Brunswicker
Quebec	Quebecker or Québécois (m); Québécoise (f)
Ontario	Ontarian
Manitoba	Manitoban
Saskatchewan	Saskatchewanian or Saskatchewanite (Informal)
Alberta	Albertan
British Columbia	British Columbian
Yukon	Yukoner
Nunavut	Nunavummiut
Northwest Territories	(None indicated)

337 a. Capitalize *the* only when it is part of the official name of a place.

The Pas	**BUT:** the Maritimes
The Hague	the Netherlands

b. Capitalize the words *upper* and *lower* only when they are part of an actual place name or a well-established imaginative name.

Upper Canada	Lower Canada
Upper Chamber	Lower Town
Upper Lakes	Lower House

Points of the Compass

338 a. Capitalize *north, south, east, west*, and derivative words when they designate definite regions or are an integral part of a proper name.

in the North	the Far North	the North Pole
down South	the Deep South	the South Shore
out West	the Middle West	the West Coast
back East	the Near East	the Eastern Townships

b. Do not capitalize these words when they merely indicate direction or general location.

Many factories have relocated from the *Northeast* to the *South*. (Region.)

BUT: They maintain a villa in the *south* of France. (General location.)

OR: Go *north* on Highway 3 and then *east* on the Coquihalla. (Direction.)

John is coming back *East* after three years on the *West Coast.* (Region.)

BUT: The *west coast* of Canada borders on the Pacific. (Referring only to the shoreline, not the region.)

Most of our customers live in the *Far North.* (Definite locality.)

BUT: Most of our customers live on the *north side* of town. (General location.)

339   Capitalize such words as *Northerner, Southerner,* and *Westerner.*

340   Capitalize such words as *northern, southern, eastern,* and *western* when they refer to the people in a region or to their political, social, or cultural activities. Do not capitalize these words when they merely indicate general location or refer to the geography or climate of the region.

Eastern bankers	**BUT:** the eastern half of Ontario
Southern hospitality	southern temperatures
Western civilization	westerly winds
the Northern vote	a northern winter

The *Western* provinces did not vote as they were expected to. (Political activities.)

BUT: The drought is expected to continue in the *western* provinces. (Climate.)

My sales territory takes in most of the *eastern* provinces. (General location.)

NOTE: When terms like *western region* and *southern district* are used to name organizational units within a company, capitalize them.

The *Western Region* (referring to a part of the national sales staff) reports that sales are 12 percent over budget for the first six months this year.

341   When words like *northern, southern, eastern,* and *western* precede a place name, they are not ordinarily capitalized because they merely indicate general location within a region. However, when these words are actually part of the place name, they must be capitalized. (Check an atlas or the geographic listings in a dictionary when in doubt.)

Preceding a Place Name	Part of a Place Name
northern Alberta	**BUT:** Northern Ireland
western Ontario	Western Australia

NOTE: Within certain regions it is not uncommon for many who live there to capitalize the adjective because of the special importance they attach to the regional designation. Thus people who live in southern Ontario may prefer to write *Southern Ontario.*

Days of the Week, Months, Holidays, Seasons, Events, Periods

342   Capitalize names of days, months, holidays, and religious days.

Tuesday	Mother's Day	Good Friday
February	Remembrance Day	All Saints' Day
New Year's Eve	Victoria Day	Rosh Hashanah
April Fools' Day	Oktoberfest	Yom Kippur
Canada Day	Ramadan	**BUT:** polling day

☞ *For the use of apostrophes in names of holidays, see ¶650.*

343 Do not capitalize the names of the seasons unless they are personified.

> We hold our regional sales conferences during the *fall* and *winter*, but our national conference always takes place early in the *spring*.

> We do not plan to announce our new line of software applications until our fall '03/winter '04 catalogue.

> **BUT:** The Winter speeds his fairies forth and mocks
> Poor bitten men with laughter icy cold.
>
> —Archibald Lampman

344 **a.** Capitalize the names of historical events and imaginative names given to historical periods.

the French Revolution	the Renaissance
World War II	the Counter-Reformation
the Holocaust	Confederation
Fire Prevention Week	the Great Depression

b. References to cultural *ages* are usually capitalized. However, contemporary references are not usually capitalized unless they appear together with a capitalized reference.

the Bronze Age	**BUT:** the space age
the Dark Ages	the atomic age
the Middle Ages	the nuclear age

The course spans the development of civilization from the *Stone Age* to the *Space Age*.

c. References to cultural *eras* are usually capitalized, but references to cultural periods are usually not.

the Christian Era	**BUT:** the romantic period
the Victorian Era	the colonial period

d. Capitalize the names of sporting events.

the Brier	the Commonwealth Games
the Grey Cup Game	the Queen's Plate
the Canadian Open	the Ironman Triathalon

345 Do not capitalize the names of decades and centuries.

during the fifties	in the twenty-first century
in the nineteen-nineties	during the nineteen hundreds

NOTE: Decades are capitalized, however, in special expressions.

the Networked Nineties	the Roaring Twenties

Acts, Laws, Bills, Treaties

346 **a.** Capitalize formal titles of acts, laws, bills, and treaties, but do not capitalize common-noun elements that stand alone in place of the full name.

the Income Tax Act	the act

Public Law 480	the law
the Treaty of Versailles	the treaty
the Canadian Constitution	**BUT:** the Constitution (see ¶304)

b. Do not capitalize generic or informal references to existing or pending legislation except for proper nouns and adjectives.

environmental protection laws   the Liberal tax proposals

c. "Laws" that make humorous or satirical observations about human and organizational behaviour are capitalized to suggest that they carry the same authority as an actual piece of legislation.

Parkinson's Law states that work expands to fill the time that has been allotted for its completion.

Murphy's Law holds that if something can go wrong, it will.

The *Peter Principle* maintains that people in an organization tend to be promoted until they reach their level of incompetence.

d. In the names of authentic scientific laws, capitalize only proper nouns and adjectives.

| Gresham's law | Newton's first law of motion |
| Mendel's law | the first law of thermodynamics |

Programs, Movements, Concepts

347 **a.** Do not capitalize the names of programs, movements, or concepts when used as general terms.

employment insurance benefits	the labour movement
BUT: the Employment Insurance Act	**BUT:** the Labour Program
equal opportunities	paternalism
BUT: Equal Opportunities Program	existentialism and rationalism

b. Capitalize proper nouns and adjectives that are part of such terms.

| the Socratic method | Newtonian physics |
| Keynesian economics | Marxist-Leninist theories |

c. Capitalize imaginative names given to programs and movements.

| the New Deal | the New Frontier |
| the Just Society | the War on Poverty |

d. Capitalize terms like *liberal, socialist,* and *communist* when they signify formal membership in a political party but not when they merely signify belief in a certain philosophy.

a lifelong *Conservative* (refers to a person who consistently votes for candidates of the Conservative Party)	a lifelong *conservative* (refers to a person who believes in the principles of conservatism)
independent voters	leftists
the right wing	separatists

Races, Peoples, Languages

348   **a.** Capitalize the names of races, peoples, bands, and languages.

Caucasians	Canadians	Native Americans	the Blacks
East Indians	Hispanics	Mandarin Chinese	Aboriginals
Anglophones	Francophones	First Nations	the Bloods

NOTE: The majority of people who live in the North are called *Inuit*, meaning "the people." Therefore, they should never be referred to as *the* Inuit. The singular form of Inuit is *Inuk* and the language spoken by most inhabitants is *Inuktituk*.

b. Do not hyphenate terms like *African Americans* or *French Canadians* when they are used as nouns, because the first word in each case modifies the second. However, hyphenate such terms when they are used as adjectives; for example, *African-American enterprises, French-Canadian voters.* Moreover, hyphenate such terms when the first element is a prefix; for example, *an Afro-American style, the Anglo-Saxons, the Indo-Chinese.*

Religious References

349   **a.** Capitalize all references to a supreme being.

God	the Supreme Being	Allah
the Lord	the Messiah	Yahweh
the Holy Spirit	the Almighty	Jehovah

NOTE: The word *God* is capitalized in such compound expressions as *God-given* and *Godspeed* but not in such terms as *godforsaken* and *godless*.

b. Capitalize personal pronouns referring to a supreme being when they stand alone, without an antecedent nearby.

Offer thanks unto *Him*.   **BUT:** Ask the Lord for *his* blessing.

NOTE: Some writers capitalize these personal pronouns under all circumstances.

c. Capitalize references to persons revered as holy.

the Prince of Peace	Buddha	John the Baptist
the Good Shepherd	the Prophet	Saint Peter (see ¶518e)
the Blessed Virgin	the Apostles	Luke the Evangelist

d. Capitalize the names of religions, their members, and their buildings.

Reform Judaism	Mormons	Saint Mark's Anglican Church
Zen Buddhism	Methodists	Temple Beth Sholom

the Roman Catholic *Church* (meaning the institution as a whole)

BUT: the Roman Catholic *church* on Waverly Avenue (referring to a specific building)

e. Capitalize references to religious events. (See also ¶342.)

the Creation	the Exodus	the Crucifixion
the Flood	the Second Coming	the Resurrection

f. In general, do not capitalize references to specific religious observances and services. However, if you are writing from the perspective of a particular religion, follow the capitalization style of that religion.

bar mitzvah	baptism	**BUT:** the Eucharist
seder	christening	the Mass

350 Capitalize (but do not quote, underscore, or italicize) references to works regarded as sacred.

the King James Bible	the Koran	the Ten Commandments
BUT: biblical sources	the Talmud	the Sermon on the Mount
the Revised Standard	the Torah	Psalms 23 and 24
Version	the Our Father	Kaddish
the Old Testament	the Lord's Prayer	Hail Mary
the Book of Genesis	Hebrews 13:8	the Apostles' Creed

NOTE: Do not capitalize *bible* when the work it refers to is not sacred.

Celestial Bodies

351 Capitalize the names of planets (*Jupiter, Mars*), stars (*Polaris, the North Star*), and constellations (*the Big Dipper, the Milky Way*). However, do not capitalize the words *sun, moon,* and *earth* unless they are used in connection with the capitalized names of other planets or stars.

With the weather we've been having, we haven't seen much of the *sun*.

I have gone to the ends of the *earth* to assemble this collection of jewellery.

Compare the orbits of *Mars, Venus,* and *Earth*.

Course Titles, Subjects, Academic Degrees

352 Capitalize the names of specific course titles. However, do not capitalize names of subjects or areas of study (except for any proper nouns or adjectives in such names).

Canadian History 201 meets on Tuesdays and Thursdays. (Course title.)

Harriet has decided to major in *Canadian history*. (Area of study.)

353 Do not capitalize academic degrees used as general terms of classification. However, capitalize a degree used after a person's name.

a bachelor of arts degree	received his bachelor's
a master of science degree	working for a master's
a doctor of laws degree	will soon receive her doctorate

BUT: Claire Hurwitz, Doctor of Philosophy

354 In references to academic years, do not capitalize the words *freshman* (or *first-year students*), *sophomore, junior,* and *senior*. In references to grade levels, capitalize the word *grade* when a number follows but not when a number precedes.

All *first-year students* must register by August 30.

Harriet spent her *senior* year in Germany.

Our oldest child is in *Grade 6;* our second child is in the *third grade*.

Commercial Products

355 Capitalize trademarks, brand names, proprietary names, names of commercial products, and market grades. The common noun following the name of a product should not ordinarily be capitalized; however, manufacturers and advertisers often capitalize such words in the names of their own products to give them special emphasis.

> Elmer's glue **BUT:** Krazy Glue

NOTE: Be alert to the correct spelling of proper nouns.

> Macintosh computers **BUT:** McIntosh apples

☞ *For the capitalization of short words in the names of products, see ¶303, note. For the use of intercaps, see ¶366.*

356 Capitalize all trademarks except those that have become clearly established as common nouns. To be safe, check an up-to-date dictionary or consult Fraser's Canadian Trade Directory; the Canadian Intellectual Property Office (CIPO); Industry Canada, 50 Victoria Street, Place du Portage I, Hull, QC K1A 0C9; or visit CIPO on the Web at http://www.cipo.gc.ca.

> Scotch tape, Post-it notes, Magic Marker, Jiffy bag
> Acrilan, Dacron, Lycra, Orlon, Ultrasuede; **BUT:** nylon, spandex
> Levi's, Guess, Loafers, Topsiders Reebok, Birkenstock sandals
> Monopoly, Scrabble, Trivial Pursuit, Hula Hoop
> Bauer, Graft, Daoust, CCM skates
> Teflon, Velcro, Ziploc, Baggies
>
> Band-Aid, Ace Bandage, Q-Tip
> Tylenol, Novocain, Demerol
> Kool-Aid, 7UP, Gatorade, Brita, Dry Ice, Canada Dry
> Jell-O, Tabasco sauce, Popsicle
> Crockpot, Pyrex, Corningware
> Dictaphone
> Frigidaire, Disposall, Jacuzzi, Laundromat, Rubbermaid
> Frisbee, Ping-Pong, Rollerblades

Advertising Material

357 Words ordinarily written in small letters may be capitalized in advertising copy for special emphasis. (This style is inappropriate in all other kinds of written communication.)

> Save money now during our *Year-End Clearance Sale.*

> It's the event *Luxury Lovers* have been waiting for . . . from Whitehall's!

Legal Documents

358 In legal documents many words that ordinarily would be written in small letters are written with initial capitals or all capitals—for example, references to parties, the name of the document, special provisions, and sometimes spelled-out amounts of money (see ¶420b).

> THIS AGREEMENT, made this 31st day of January, 2003

> . . . hereinafter called the SELLER . . .

> WHEREAS the Seller has this day agreed . . .

> WITNESS the signatures . . .

Nouns With Numbers or Letters

359 Capitalize a noun followed by a number or a letter that indicates sequence. **EXCEPTIONS:** Do not capitalize the nouns *line, note, page, paragraph, size, step,* and *verse.*

Account 66160	Cheque 181	Invoice 270487	Platform 3
Act 1	Class 4	Item 9859D	Policy 394857
Appendix A	Column 1	Lesson 20	Room 501
Article 2	Diagram 4	line 4	Rule 7
Book III	Exercise 8	Model B671-4	Section 1
Building 4	Exhibit A	note 1	size 10
Bulletin T-119	Extension 2174	Order J2462	step 3
Car 8171	Figure 9	page 158	Table 7
Channel 36	Flight 626	paragraph 2a	Unit 2
Chapter V	Highway 2	Part Three	verse 3
Chart 3	Illustration 19	Plate XV	Volume II

NOTE: It is often unnecessary to use *No.* before the number. (See ¶455.)

Purchase Order 4713 (**RATHER THAN:** Purchase Order *No.* 4713)

Titles of Literary and Artistic Works; Headings

360 In titles of literary and artistic works and in displayed headings, capitalize all words with *four or more* letters. Also capitalize words with fewer than four letters except:

ARTICLES: *the, a, an*

SHORT CONJUNCTIONS: *and, as, but, if, or, nor*

SHORT PREPOSITIONS: *at, by, for, in, of, off, on, out, to, up*

How to Succeed in Business Without Really Trying

NOTE: Be sure to capitalize short verb forms like *Is* and *Be.* However, do not capitalize *to* when it is part of an infinitive.

"Redevelopment Proposal Is Not Expected to Be Approved"

361 Even articles, short conjunctions, and short prepositions should be capitalized under the following circumstances:

a. Capitalize the first and last word of a title.

"A Home to Be Proud *Of*"

CAUTION: Do not capitalize *the* at the beginning of a title unless it is actually part of the title.

For further details check *the Encyclopaedia Britannica.*
This clipping is from *The Globe and Mail.*

b. Capitalize the first word following a dash or colon in a title.

Sharing the Good Times—A History of Women's Fun and Frivolity
Turmoil and Triumph: The Controversial Railway to Hudson Bay

(Continued on page 110.)

c. Capitalize short words like *in, out, off,* and *up* in titles when they serve as adverbs rather than as prepositions. (These words may occur as adverbs in verb phrases or in hyphenated compounds derived from verb phrases. See ¶¶803, 1070.)

"AT&T Chalks *Up* Record Earnings for the Year"

"LeClaire Is Runner-*Up* in Election" (see also ¶363)

BUT: "Sailing *up* the St. Lawrence"

The Spy Who Came In From the Cold

"Foxworth Is Considered a Shoo-*In* for Premier"

BUT: "Pollster Project an Easy Win for Foxworth *in* Heavy Voter Turnout"

d. Capitalize short prepositions like *in* and *up* when used together with prepositions having four or more letters.

"Sailing *Up* and *Down* the St. Lawrence"

"Happenings *In* and *Around* Town"

"Mall Opening *On* or *About* May 1"

e. When a title or column heading is displayed on more than one line, do not capitalize the first word of any turnover line unless it needs to be capitalized on the basis of the preceding guidelines.

Should You Invest for the Long Pull	Millions	Income
or Should You Trade Continually?	*of* Dollars	*per* Capita

☞ *For the capitalization of* Preface, Contents, Appendix, *and* Index, *see* ¶242, *note. For the use of all capitals with titles, see* ¶289b.

362 Do not capitalize a book title when it is incorporated into a sentence as a descriptive phrase.

In his book on *economics*, Samuelson points out that . . .

BUT: In his book *Economics*, Samuelson points out that . . .

Hyphenated Words

363 *Within a sentence*, capitalize only those elements of a hyphenated word that are proper nouns or proper adjectives. *At the beginning of a sentence*, capitalize the first element in the hyphenated word but no other elements unless they are proper nouns or adjectives. *In a heading or title*, capitalize all the elements except articles, short prepositions, and short conjunctions. (See ¶360.)

Within Sentences	Beginning Sentences	In Headings
up-to-date	Up-to-date	Up-to-Date
French-Canadian	French-Canadian	French-Canadian
English-speaking	English-speaking	English-Speaking
mid-September	Mid-September	Mid-September
ex-Premier Davies	Ex-Premier Davies	Ex-Premier Davies
Mayor-elect Smith	Mayor-elect Smith	Mayor-Elect Smith
self-confidence	Self-confidence	Self-Confidence
de-emphasize	De-emphasize	De-Emphasize
follow-up	Follow-up	Follow-Up (see ¶361c)

Forty-ninth Regiment	Forty-ninth Regiment	Forty-Ninth Regiment
e-mail	E-mail	E-Mail
one-sixth	One-sixth	One-Sixth
post-World War II	Post-World War II	Post-World War II

Awards and Medals

364 Capitalize the names of awards and medals.

the Order of Canada	the Rutherford Medal in Physics
the Juno Awards	the Distinguished Conduct Medal
the Victoria Cross	Governor General's Literary Award

Computer Terminology

365 **a.** Use all-capital letters for the names of many programming languages. (See also ¶544.)

BASIC	FORTRAN	**BUT:**	Java
COBOL	APL		Ada

b. Use all-capital letters for the names of many operating systems.

MS-DOS	UNIX	**BUT:**	MacOS X
PC-DOS	OS/2		Microsoft Windows

c. Capitalize the names of Internet search engines (*Excite, Yahoo!*), Internet service providers (*UUNet*), and commercial online services (*America Online, Cadvision*), Web sites (*HotWired*), online communities (*Usenet*), and online databases (*Lexis, Dialog*).

☞ *For the capitalization of words or phrases beginning with* Web, *see ¶847a.*

Intercaps

366 The names of many organizations and products follow a special capitalization style known as *intercaps* or *Bicaps*. Follow the organization's style in each case.

a. The names of computer organizations and products commonly reflect an intercap style. For example:

AltaVista	TrueType	NetNanny
PageMaker	PowerPoint	VirusScan
WebCrawler	WordPerfect	CorelDRAW
VisiCalc	InterNIC	RealTIME Media

b. The use of intercaps appears in other areas of business as well. For example:

NordicTrack	NutraSweet	CreataCard greeting cards
PlaySkool toys	DieHard batteries	MasterCard purchases
ReaLemon juice	AstroTurf	TraveLodge motels

☞ *Capitalization of questions within sentences: see ¶¶115, 117.*
Capitalization after a colon: see ¶¶196–199.

(Continued on page 112.)

Capitalization after an opening bracket: see ¶296.
Capitalization after an opening dash: see ¶214, note.
Capitalization with parenthetical items: see ¶¶224–226.
Capitalization after an opening quotation mark: see ¶¶272–273.
Capitalization of abbreviations: see ¶514.

See the Online Learning Centre at www.mcgrawhill.ca/college/gregg for related weblinks.

SECTION **FOUR**

Numbers

There is a significant difference between using figures and using words to express numbers. Figures are big (like capital letters) and compact and informal (like abbreviations); when used in a sentence, they stand out clearly from the surrounding words. By contrast, numbers expressed in words are unemphatic and formal; they do not stand out in a sentence. It is this functional difference between figures and words that underlies all aspects of number style.

BASIC RULES

The rules for expressing numbers would be quite simple if writers would all agree to express numbers entirely in figures or entirely in words. However, in actual practice the exclusive use of figures is considered appropriate only in tables and statistical matter, whereas the exclusive use of words to express numbers is found only in formal documents (such as proclamations and social invitations). In writing that is neither ultraformal nor ultratechnical, most style manuals call for the use of both figures and words in varying proportions. Although authorities do not agree on details, there are two sets of basic rules in wide use: the *figure style* (which uses figures for most numbers above 10) and the *word style* (which uses figures for most numbers above 100). Unless you deal with a very limited type of business correspondence, you should be familiar with both styles and be prepared to use each appropriately as the situation demands.

In countries like Canada, which follow the metric (SI) style, spaces are used to separate numbers. There is a trend, however, to return to the use of the comma. The main reason for this is to ensure readability of numbers, especially when smaller fonts are used. This is particularly true in legal and financial documents.

Figure Style

The figure style is most commonly used in ordinary business correspondence (dealing with sales, production, finance, advertising, and other routine commercial matters). It is also used in journalistic and technical material and in academic work of a technical or statistical nature. In writing of this kind, most numbers represent significant quantities or measurements that should stand out for emphasis or quick comprehension.

401 **a.** Spell out numbers from 1 through 10; use figures for numbers above 10. This rule applies to both exact and approximate numbers.

I would like *ten* copies of this article, but I need only *two* or *three* right away.

We expect about *30* to *35* employees to sign up for the graphic arts course.

The advertising is deliberately pitched at the *40-plus* age group.

My letter in last Sunday's paper apparently provoked over *25* letters and some *60-odd* phone calls.

There has been a *sixfold* increase in the number of incidents. (See ¶817a.)
BUT: There has been a *20-fold* increase in the number of incidents.

One bookstore chain has already ordered *2500* copies. (See ¶461b on the omission of spaces.)

We send out about *200 000* catalogues every month, but our year-end holiday catalogue is mailed to over *1 000 000* households. (See ¶403b.)

b. Use all figures—even for the numbers 1 through 10 (as in this sentence)—when they have technical significance or need to stand out for quick comprehension. This all-figure style is used in tables, in statistical matter, and in expressions of dates *(May 3)*, money *($6)*, clock time *(4 p.m.)*, proportions and ratios *(a 5-to-1 shot)*, sports scores *(3 to 1)*, academic grades *(95)*, and percentages *(8 percent)*. This style is also used with abbreviations and symbols *(12 cm, 8°C)*, with numbers referred to as numbers *(think of a number from 1 to 10)*, with highway designations *(Highway 16, 401)*, and with technical or emphatic references to age *(a clinical study of 5-year-olds)*, periods of time *(a 6-month loan)*, measurements *(parcels over 2 kg)*, and page numbers *(page 2)*.

c. In isolated cases spell out a number above 10 in order to de-emphasize the number or make it seem indefinite.

Sanjay may give you *a thousand and one* reasons why he cannot go.

Thanks *a million* for all your help on the deposition.

I have *a hundred* things to do today. (In this context *100 things* would seem too precise, too exact.)

d. Use words for numbers at the beginning of a sentence, for most ordinals *(our twenty-fifth anniversary)*, for fractions *(one-third of our sales)*, and for non-technical or non-emphatic references to age *(my son just turned twelve)*, periods of time *(twenty years ago)*, and measurements *(I need to lose another thirty pounds)*.

☞ *For rules on how to express numbers in figures, see ¶¶461–464.*

For rules on how to express numbers in words, see ¶¶465–467.

402 Use the same style to express *related* numbers above and below 10. If any of the numbers are above 10, put them all in figures.

We used to have *two* dogs, *one* cat, and *one* rabbit.

BUT: We now have *5* dogs, *11* cats, and *1* rabbit.

Our *four* sons consumed a total of *18* hamburgers, *5* large bottles of diet Coke, *12* Mars Bars, and about *2000* cookies—all at *one* sitting. (Figures are used for all the related items of food; the other numbers—*four* and *one*—are spelled out, since they are not related and are not over 10.)

NOTE: In the names of companies and products, follow the organization's style.

a 7-Eleven store	3-In-One oil	9-Lives cat food
a can of 7UP	3M office products	V8 juice

403 **a.** For fast comprehension, numbers in the *millions* or higher may be expressed as follows:

21 million (in place of 21 000 000)

3 billion (in place of 3 000 000 000)

$14\frac{1}{2}$ million (in place of 14 500 000)

(Continued on page 116.)

2.4 billion (in place of 2 400 000 000)

Bindel & Boggs is placing an order for *2.4 million* barrels of oil.

BUT: Bindel & Boggs is placing a *2.4-million-barrel* order. (See ¶817.)

NOTE: This style may be used only when the amount consists of a whole number with nothing more than a simple fraction or decimal following. A number such as 4 832 067 must be written all in figures. (However, if rounding numbers is permitted, this number could be rewritten as *4.8 million*.)

b. Treat related numbers alike.

Last year we sold *21 557 000* items; this year, nearly *23 000 000*.

(**NOT:** 21 557 000 . . . 23 million.)

☞ *For examples involving money, see ¶416.*

To prevent line-ending difficulties with larger numbers, see ¶919b.

Word Style

The word style of numbers is used in high-level executive correspondence (see ¶¶1395–1396) and in non-technical material, where the writing is of a more formal or literary nature and the use of figures would give numbers an undesired emphasis and obstructiveness. Here are the basic rules for the word style.

404 Spell out all numbers, whether exact or approximate, that can be expressed in one or two words. (A hyphenated compound number like *twenty-one* or *twenty-nine* counts as one word.) In effect, spell out all numbers from 1 through 100 and all round numbers above 100 that require no more than two words (such as *sixty-two thousand* or *forty-five million*).

Mr. Ryan received *twenty-five* letters praising his talk last Wednesday at the Rotary Club.

Last year more than *twelve million* people attended the art exhibition our company sponsored.

Some *sixty-odd* people have called to volunteer their services.

Over *two hundred* people attended the reception for Helen and Frank Russo.

BUT: Over *250* people attended the reception. (Use figures when more than two words are required.)

NOTE: In writing of a very formal nature—proclamations, social invitations, and many legal documents—even a number that requires more than two words is spelled out. However, as a matter of practicality the word style ordinarily uses figures when more than two words are required.

☞ *For rules on how to express numbers in words, see ¶¶465–467.*

405 Express related numbers the same way, even though some are above 100 and some below. If any must be in figures, put all in figures.

We sent out *three hundred* invitations and have already received over *one hundred* acceptances.

BUT: We sent out *300 invitations and have already received 125* acceptances. (**NOT:** three hundred . . . 125.)

406 Numbers in the millions or higher *that require more than two words when spelled out* may be expressed as follows:

> 231 million (in place of 231 000 000)
> $9\frac{3}{4}$ billion (in place of 9 750 000 000)
> 671.4 million (in place of 671 400 000)

Even a two-word number such as *sixty-two million* should be expressed as *62 million* when it is related to a number such as *231 million* (which cannot be spelled in two words). Moreover, it should be expressed as *62 000 000* when it is related to a number such as *231 163 520*.

SPECIAL RULES

The preceding rules on figures style (¶¶401–403) and word style (¶¶404–406) are basic guidelines that govern in the absence of more specific principles. The following rules cover those situations that require special handling (for example, expressions of dates and money). In a number of cases where either figures or words are acceptable, your choice will depend on whether you are striving for emphasis or formality.

Dates

These rules apply to dates in sentences. See ¶1314 for date lines in business correspondence.

407 When the day *precedes* the month or *stands alone*, express it either in ordinal figures (*1st, 2nd, 3rd, 4th,* etc.) or in ordinal words (the *first,* the *twelfth,* the *twenty-eighth*).

> **FOR EMPHASIS:** This year's international sales conference runs from Monday, the *2nd* of August, through Thursday, the *5th.*

> **FOR FORMALITY:** We leave for Europe on the *third* of June and do not return until the *twenty-fifth.*

NOTE: When the year is added to the day and month, the following forms should be avoided: the *sixth of March, 2005; 6th of March, 2005.*

408 When the day *follows* the month, use a cardinal figure (*1, 2, 3,* etc.).

> on March 6 (**NOT:** March *6th* **OR** March *sixth*)

> **NOTE:** Do not use the form *March 6th, 2005,* or *March sixth, 2005,* even though these versions reflect how the date would sound when spoken aloud.

409 **a.** Express complete dates in month-day-year sequence.

> March 6, 2005

> **NOTE:** In military correspondence and in letters from foreign countries, the complete date is expressed in day-month-year sequence.

> 6 March 2005

(Continued on page 118.)

b. The form *3/6/05* or *03/06/05* indicating a *month*-day-year sequence is acceptable **only** on business forms and when instructed; but avoid this form if your reader could misinterpret it as a *day*-month-year sequence.

c. Descending order of magnitude in metric numeric dating expresses dates with 8 digits. March 8, 2005, is written as:

2005 03 08	2005-03-08	20050308

410 Note the use of commas and other punctuation with expressions of dates.

On *August 13, 2004,* my husband and I received the bank loan that permitted us to start our own restaurant. (Two commas set off the year following the month and day.)

We set a formal opening date of *November 15, 2004;* we actually opened on *March 18, 2005* (because of the flash fire that virtually destroyed the restaurant and forced us to start from scratch). (Note that the second comma is omitted *after* *2004* and *2005* because in each case some other punctuation mark—a semicolon or an opening parenthesis—is required at that point.)

Sales for *February 2005* hit an all-time low. (Omit commas around the year when it follows the month alone.)

BUT: Once we introduced our new product line in *September 2005,* it was clear that we were finally on the road to a strong recovery. (The comma following *2005* is needed to separate an introductory dependent clause from the rest of the sentence, not because of the date.)

The *May 2004* issue of *Maclean's* carries an excerpt from Brenda's forthcoming book. (No commas are used when the month-year expression serves as an adjective.)

BUT: The *May 4, 2004,* issue of *Newsweek* broke the story. (Use two commas to set off the year when a complete date serves as an adjective. See ¶154.)

In *2004* we opened six branch offices in . . . (No comma follows the year in a short introductory phrase unless a non-essential element follows immediately.)

On *February 28* we will decide . . . (No comma follows the month and day in a short introductory phrase unless a non-essential element follows immediately.)

BUT: On *February 28,* the date of the next board meeting, we will decide . . . (Insert a comma when a non-essential element follows immediately.)

On *February 28,* 27 managers from the Oshawa plant will . . . (Insert a comma when another figure follows immediately. See ¶456.)

Yesterday, *April 3,* I spoke to a group of exporters in Calgary. On Tuesday, *April 11,* I will be speaking at an international trade fair in Singapore. (Set off a month-day expression when it serves as an appositive. See ¶148.)

☞ *For the use or omission of a comma when a date is followed by a related phrase or clause, see ¶152.*

411 In formal legal documents, formal invitations, and proclamations, spell out the day and the year. A number of styles may be used:

May twenty-first	two thousand and five
the twenty-first of May	in the year of our Lord two thousand
this twenty-first day of May	and five

412 a. Class graduation years and well-known years in history may appear in abbreviated form.

the class of '06   the winter of '03   the market crash of '29

b. Years also appear in abbreviated form in certain business expressions. (See also ¶294.)

fiscal year 2004/05 **OR** FY 2004/05   the fall '05/06 catalogue

☞ *For the expression of centuries and decades, see ¶¶438–439.*
For dates in a sequence, see ¶¶458–460.

Money

413 a. Use figures to express exact or approximate amounts of money.

$7	about $1500	a $50 bill
$13.50	nearly $50 000	$350 worth

b. When amounts of money from different countries are referred to in the same context, the unit of currency usually appears as an abbreviation or symbol (or both) directly preceding the numeral amount. (The use of commas rather than spaces is still preferred by many banking and legal institutions to prevent the addition of "bogus" figures.)

US$10 000   (refers to 10 000 U.S. dollars)

Mex$10 000   (refers to 10 000 Mexican pesos)

DM10 000   (refers to 10 000 German deutsche marks)

£10 000   (refers to 10 000 British pounds)

¥10 000   (refers to 10 000 Japanese yen)

€10 000   (refers to 10 000 euros)

Can$10 000   (refers to 10 000 Canadian dollars)

NOTE: Special character sets will print monetary symbols.

c. An isolated, non-emphatic reference to money may be spelled out.

two hundred dollars	half a million dollars
a twenty-dollar bill	five thousand dollars' worth (note
a million-dollar beach house	the apostrophe with *dollars*)

414 Spell out indefinite amounts of money.

a few million dollars   many thousands of dollars

415 It is not necessary to add a decimal point or zeros to a *whole* dollar amount when it occurs in a sentence.

I am enclosing a cheque for *$125*.

This model costs $12.50; that one costs *$10*.

(Continued on page 120.)

In a column, however, if any amount contains cents, add a decimal point and two zeros to all *whole* dollar amounts to maintain a uniform appearance. (See also ¶1624.)

$$\begin{array}{r} \$150.50 \\ 25.00 \\ \underline{8.05} \\ \$183.55 \end{array}$$

416 **a.** Money in round amounts of a million or more may be expressed partially in words. (The style given in the first column is preferred.)

$12 million	**OR**	12 million dollars		
$10½ million	**OR**	10½ million dollars		
$10.5 million	**OR**	10.5 million dollars		
$6¼ billion	**OR**	6¼ billion dollars	**OR**	$6250 million
$6.25 billion	**OR**	6.25 billion dollars	**OR**	6250 million dollars

b. This style may be used only when the amount consists of a whole number with nothing more than a simple fraction or decimal following:

10.5 million dollars   **BUT:** $10 235 000

c. Express related amounts the same way.

from $500 000 to $1 000 000 (**NOT:** from $500 000 to $1 million)

d. Repeat the word *million* (*billion*, etc.) with each figure to avoid misunderstanding.

$5 million to $10 million (**NOT:** $5 to $10 million)

417 Fractional expressions of large amounts of money should be either completely spelled out or converted to an all-figure style.

one-quarter of a million dollars **OR** $250 000
(**BUT NOT:** ¼ of a million dollars **OR** $¼ million)

a half-billion dollars **OR** $500 000 000
(**BUT NOT:** ½ billion dollars **OR** $½ billion)

418 **a.** For amounts under a dollar, ordinarily use figures and the word *cents*.

I am sure that customers will not pay more than *50 cents* for this item.

This machine can be fixed with *80 cents'* worth of parts. (Note the apostrophe with *cents*.)

These *25-cent* tokens can be used at all tollbooths.

NOTE: An isolated, non-emphatic reference to cents may be spelled out.

I wouldn't give *two cents* for that car.

b. Do not use the style *$.75* in sentences except when related amounts require a dollar sign.

It will cost you *$4.84* a copy to do the company manual: *$.86* for the paper, *$1.54* for the printing, and *$2.44* for the special binder.

c. The cent sign (¢) may be used in technical and statistical matter.

The price of lead, *34.5¢* a kilogram in 2000, is now *82¢* a kilogram; zinc, averaging *28¢* a kilogram in 2000, now sells for *98¢* a kilogram.

NOTE: The cent sign (¢) on a computer must be accessed through special character symbols.

419 **a.** When using the dollar sign or the cent sign with a price range or a series of amounts, use the sign with each amount.

$5 000 to $10 000	$10 million to $20 million
10¢ to 20¢	(**BUT NOT:** $10 to $20 million)

These three properties are valued at $832 900, $954 500, and $1 087 000 respectively.

b. If the term *dollars* or *cents* is to be spelled out, use it only with the final amount.

10 to 20 cents   10 million to 20 million dollars (see ¶416c)

420 **a.** In legal documents, amounts of money are often expressed first in words and then, within parentheses, in figures.

One Hundred Dollars ($100)   **OR**   One Hundred (100) Dollars
(**BUT NOT:** One Hundred ($100) Dollars)

Three Thousand One Hundred and 50/100 Dollars ($3100.50)

b. When spelling out amounts of money, omit the *and* between hundreds and tens of dollars if *and* is used before the fraction representing cents.

Six Hundred Thirty-two and 75/100 Dollars
(**NOT:** Six Hundred *and* Thirty-two and 75/100 Dollars)

NOTE: In whole dollar amounts, the use of *and* between hundreds and tens of dollars is optional.

Six Hundred Thirty-two Dollars   **OR**   Six Hundred and Thirty-two Dollars

c. The capitalization of spelled-out amounts may vary. Sometimes the first letter of each main word is capitalized (as in the examples in ¶420a); sometimes only the first letter of the first word is capitalized (as on cheques); sometimes the entire amount is in all capital letters.

The following rules (¶¶421–428) cover situations in which numbers are usually spelled out: at the beginning of sentences and in expressions using indefinite numbers, ordinal numbers, and fractions.

At the Beginning of a Sentence

421 Spell out a number that begins a sentence, as well as any related numbers.

Thirty-four former students of Dr. Helen VanVleck came from all parts of the country to honour their professor on the occasion of her retirement.

Eight hundred people have already signed the recall petition.

(Continued on page 122.)

Forty to *fifty* percent of the people polled on different occasions expressed disapproval of the mayor's performance in office.
(**NOT:** *Forty* to *50* percent . . .)

422 If the number requires more than two words when spelled out or if figures are preferable for emphasis or quick reference, reword the sentence.

You ought to consider a minimum of *456 MHz* if you want to boost your productivity.
(**NOT:** *456 MHz* are worth considering . . .)

The company sent out *298* copies of its consumer guidelines last month.
(**NOT:** *Two hundred and ninety-eight* copies of its consumer guidelines were sent out by the company last month.)

We had a good year in *2003*.
(**NOT:** *Two thousand three* [**OR** *2003*] was a good year for us.)

Our mines provide *60* to *70* percent of our revenues.
(**NOT:** *Sixty* to *seventy* percent of our revenues come from our mines.)

Indefinite Numbers and Amounts

423 Spell out indefinite numbers and amounts.

several hundred investors	thousands of readers
a few hundred kilometres	many millions of dollars
a man in his late forties	a roll of fifties and twenties

☞ *For approximate numbers, see ¶401 (figure style) and ¶404 (word style).*

Ordinal Numbers

424 In general, spell out all ordinal numbers (*first, second, third*, etc.) that can be expressed in one or two words. (A hyphenated number like *twenty-first* counts as one word.)

twentieth-century art	the firm's one hundredth anniversary
(see ¶817)	(**BUT:** the firm's 125th anniversary)
on the forty-eighth floor	the Thirty-eighth Parliament (in text)
my fifty-fifth birthday	the Thirty-Eighth Parliament (in
the Fourteenth Ward	headings and titles; see ¶363)
the two millionth visitor	the Forty-Ninth Regiment

NOTE: When a hyphenated term like *twenty-first* is the first element in a compound adjective (as in *twenty-first-century art*), the second hyphen may be changed to an en dash (*twenty-first–century art*).

☞ *For the rule on how to express ordinal numbers in words, see ¶465.*
For the distinction between ordinals and fractions, see ¶427d.

425 Use figures for ordinals in certain expressions of dates (see ¶407), in numbered street names above 10 (see ¶1333), and in situations calling for special emphasis.

In Advertising Copy

Come to our *25th* Anniversary Sale! (Figures for emphasis.)

Come to our *Twenty-fifth* Anniversary Sale! (Words for formality.)

In Ordinary Correspondence

Watkins & Glenn is having a *twenty-fifth* anniversary sale.

NOTE: Ordinal figures are expressed as follows: *1st, 2nd, 3rd, 4th, 5th, 6th,* etc. Do not use an "abbreviation" period following an ordinal figure.

426 Ordinals that follow a person's name may be expressed in Arabic or Roman numerals. As a rule, use Arabic numerals unless you know that the person in question prefers Roman numerals.

James A. Wilson 3rd   **OR** James A. Wilson III
C. Roy Post 4th   C. Roy Post IV

☞ *For the use or omission of commas with numerals that follow a person's name, see ¶156.*

Fractions

427 FRACTIONS STANDING ALONE

a. Ordinarily, spell out a fraction that stands alone (that is, without a whole number preceding). Use figures, however, if the spelled-out form is long and awkward or if the fraction is used in some type of computation.

one-half the audience (see ¶427c)   three-fourths of the profits
a two-thirds majority   nine-tenths of a mile away
multiply by 2/5   a quarter box of pasta

He came back *a half hour* later (**OR** *half an hour* later).

NOTE: Hyphenate *half dozen* or *half a dozen* when this phrase is used as a compound modifier before a noun. (See ¶817.)

I'll take *a half-dozen* eggs (**OR** *half-a-dozen* eggs).

BUT: I'll take *a half dozen* (**OR** *half a dozen*).

NOTE: In the metric system, numeric expressions in measurements show decimals in preference to mixed fractions. The decimal marker is placed as a point on the line.

73.6 kg   3.21 mm   7.5 m/s

b. When a fraction is spelled out, the numerator and the denominator should be connected by a hyphen unless either element already contains a hyphen.

five-eighths   thirteen thirty-seconds   twenty-seven sixty-fourths

c. In constructions involving the balanced phrases *one half . . . the other half,* do not hyphenate *one half.*

One half of the shipment was damaged beyond use; *the other half* was salvageable.

d. Distinguish between large spelled-out fractions (which are hyphenated) and large spelled-out ordinals (which are not).

The difference is less than *one-hundredth* of 1 percent. (Hyphenated fraction meaning *1/100.*)

(Continued on page 124.)

BUT: This year the company will be celebrating the *one hundredth* anniversary of its founding. (Unhyphenated ordinal meaning *100th*.)

e. Fractions expressed in figures should not be followed by endings like *sts, nds, rds,* or *ths* or by an *of* phrase.

3/200 (**NOT:** 3/200ths)   9/64 (**NOT:** 9/64ths)

When an *of* phrase follows the fraction, spell the fraction out.

three-quarters of an hour (**NOT:** 3/4 of an hour)

428 FRACTIONS IN MIXED NUMBERS

a. Ordinarily use figures to express a mixed number (a whole number plus a fraction); for example, $3\frac{1}{4}$. Spell out a mixed number at the beginning of a sentence.

Our sales are not $4\frac{1}{2}$ times what they were in 2002.

Two and a quarter (**OR** *Two and one-quarter*) percent is too low. (Note the use of *and* between the whole number and the fraction.)

b. When constructing fractions that do not appear on the keyboard or in a special character set with word processing software, use the diagonal (/). Separate a whole number from a fraction by means of a space (not with a hyphen).

I can remember when an 8 5/8 percent mortgage seemed high.

(**NOT:** . . . an 8-5/8 percent mortgage.)

c. In the same sentence, do not mix ready-made fractions ($\frac{1}{2}$, $\frac{1}{4}$) with those that you construct yourself (7/8, 5/16). It may be necessary to disengage the automatic convert option of your computer to ensure that the style of all fractions is the same.

The rate on prime commercial paper has dropped from 11 1/2 percent a year ago to 8 3/4 percent today.

(**NOT:** $11\frac{1}{2}$ . . . 8 3/4.)

NOTE: To simplify keying, convert constructed fractions (and simpler ones used in the same context) to a decimal form whenever feasible.

The rate on prime commercial paper has dropped from 11.5 percent a year ago to 8.75 percent today.

The following rules (¶¶429–442) deal with measurements and with expressions of age and time (elements that often function as measurements). When these elements have technical or statistical significance, they are expressed in figures; otherwise, they are expressed in words.

Measurements

429 Most measurements have a technical significance and should be expressed in figures (even from 1 through 10) for emphasis or quick comprehension. However, spell out an isolated measurement that lacks technical significance.

A higher rate is charged on parcels over *2 kg*.
BUT: He weighed *two kilograms* too much for his weight class.

There is no charge for delivery within a *40-km* distance of Whitby.
BUT: It's only a *forty-kilometre* drive to our summer place.

NOTE: Dimensions, sizes, and actual temperature readings are always expressed in figures.

I'm looking for a *2- by 3-metre* Oriental rug for my reception room. (See also ¶432.)

Please send me a half-dozen blue oxford shirts, size *17½/33*.

The thermometer now stands at *22°C*, a drop of five degrees in the past two hours.

BUT: The temperature has been in the low *twenties* (**OR** *20s*) all week. (An indefinite reference to the temperature may be spelled out or expressed in figures.)

430 When an imperial measurement consists of several elements, do not use commas to separate the elements. They are considered a single unit.

Hal is *6 feet 8 inches* tall in his stocking feet.

NOTE: If this type of measurement is used as a compound modifier before a noun, use hyphens to connect all elements as a single unit. (See ¶817.)

a *6-foot-8-inch* man

431 In using a metric prefix, select the numerical value that lies between 0.1 and 1000; but when similar measurements are compared, it is better to use the same prefix for all items even though some values may fall outside that range.

12 000 g is better shown as *12 kg*; **BUT:** 321 mm is better than *0.003 21 m*.

The distance from Ottawa to Toronto is *400 km*; and from the North Pole to the Equator, it is *10 000 km*.

☞ *For the style of abbreviations for units of measure, see* ¶¶535–538.
For the use of figures with abbreviations and symbols, see ¶453.

432 Dimensions may be expressed as follows:

GENERAL USAGE:	a room 5 by 10 metres	a 5- by 10-metre room
TECHNICAL USAGE:	a room 5 m × 10 m	a 5-m × 10-m room
GENERAL USAGE:	15 feet 6 inches by 30 feet 9 inches	
TECHNICAL USAGE:	15 ft 6 in × 30 ft 9 in **OR**	15' 6" × 30' 9"

Ages and Anniversaries

433 Express ages in figures (including 1 through 10) when they are used as significant statistics or as technical measurements.

Ethel Kassarian, *38*, has been promoted to director of marketing services.

The attached printout projects the amount of the monthly retirement benefit payable *at the age of 65*. (See the entry for *Age—aged—at the age of* in Section 11.)

(Continued on page 126.)

A computer literacy program is being offered in the schools to all *8- and 9-year-olds*. (See ¶832.)

This insurance policy is specially tailored for people in the *50-plus* age group.

You cannot disregard the job application of a person *aged 58*. (**NOT:** age 58.)

NOTE: When age is expressed in years, months, and days, do not use commas to separate the elements; they make up a single unit.

On January 1 she will be *19 years 4 months and 17 days old*. (The *and* linking months and days may be omitted.)

434 Spell out ages in non-technical references and in formal writing.

My son is *three years old,* and my daughter is *two*.

Shirley is in her early *forties;* her husband is in his *mid-sixties*.

Have you ever tried keeping a group of *five-year-olds* happy?

435 Spell out ordinals in references to birthdays and anniversaries except where special emphasis or more than two words are required. (See also ¶¶424–425.)

on my thirtieth birthday	her forty-first class reunion
our twenty-fifth anniversary	the company's 135th anniversary

Periods of Time

436 Use figures (even from 1 through 10) to express periods of time when they are used as technical measurements or significant statistics (as in discounts, interest rates, and credit terms).

a 35-hour workweek 1 30-year mortgage a note due in 6 months

NOTE: In legal documents, periods of time are often expressed twice: first in words and then in figures (enclosed in parentheses).

Payable in ninety (90) days **NOT:** payable in ninety (90 days)

437 Spell out non-technical references to periods of time unless the number requires more than two words.

a twenty-minute wait	in twenty-four months	three hundred years ago
eight hours later	in the last thirty years	**BUT:** 350 years ago
twelve days from now	forty-odd years ago	two thousand years ago

438 Centuries may be expressed as follows:

the 1900s **OR** the nineteen hundreds **OR** the twentieth century
the twenty-first century   twenty-first–century literature

439 **a.** Decades may be expressed as follows:

the 1990s **OR** the nineteen-nineties **OR** the nineties **OR** the '90s

the mid-1960s **OR** the mid-sixties **OR** the mid-'60s

in the 1980s and 1990s   **OR** in the '80s and '90s
NOT: in the 1980s and '90s   **OR** in the '80s and nineties

during the years 1995–2005 **OR** from 1995 to 2005 (see ¶459)

NOTE: Our present decade is best referred to as *the first decade of the twenty-first century.*

b. Decades are not capitalized except in special expressions such as *the Networked Nineties, the Roaring Twenties.*

Clock Time

440 WITH *A.M., P.M., NOON,* AND *MIDNIGHT*

a. Always use figures with *a.m.* or *p.m.*

We take off at *8:45 a.m.*   The bus is due at *2 p.m.*

By *8 p.m.*, CST, the first election returns should be in.

OR: By *8 p.m.* (CST) the first election returns should be in.

☞ *For abbreviations of time zones, see* ¶534.

b. In printed material, *a.m.* and *p.m.* usually appear in small capitals without internal space (A.M., P.M.). In other material, *a.m.* and *p.m.* typically appear in small letters without internal space; however, you can use small capitals if you have that option. Avoid the use of all-capital letters.

c. For time "on the hour," zeros are not needed to denote minutes.

Our store is open from 9:30 a.m. to *6 p.m.* (**NOT:** 6:00 p.m.)

BUT: Our store is always open until 6:00. (See ¶442 for the use of zeros when *a.m.* or *p.m.* is omitted.)

We always close from *12 noon* to 1:30 p.m.

You can buy your tickets between *9* and *10 a.m.*

In tables, however, when some entries are given in hours and minutes, add a colon (no space before or after) and two zeros to exact hours to maintain a uniform appearance. (For more complex illustrations showing the alignment of clock times in columns, see ¶1625b.)

Arr.	Dep.
8:45	9:10
9:00	9:25
9:50	10:00

d. Do not use *a.m.* or *p.m.* unless figures are used.

this morning   tomorrow afternoon
(**NOT:** this a.m.)   (**NOT:** tomorrow p.m.)

e. Do not use *a.m.* or *p.m.* with *o'clock* or with the expressions *in the morning, in the afternoon, in the evening,* or *at night.* (See ¶441b.)

10 o'clock   **OR**   10 a.m.   **OR**   at ten in the morning
NOT: 10 a.m. o'clock   **NOT:** at 10 a.m. in the morning

NOTE: The expression *o'clock* is more formal than *a.m.* or *p.m.*

f. The times *noon* and *midnight* may be expressed in words alone. However, use the forms *12 noon* and *12 midnight* when these times are given with other times expressed in figures.

(Continued on page 128.)

> Dinner is served in the main dining room until *midnight.*
>
> **BUT:** Dinner is served from *6 p.m.* until *12 midnight.*

441 WITH *O'CLOCK*

a. With *o'clock*, use figures for emphasis or words for formality.

3 o'clock (for emphasis)   three o'clock (for formality)

b. Expressions of time containing *o'clock* may be reinforced by such phrases as *in the morning* and *in the afternoon.*

10 o'clock at night   seven o'clock in the morning

For quick comprehension, the forms *10 p.m.* and *7 a.m.* are preferable.

442 WITHOUT *A.M.*, *P.M.*, OR *O'CLOCK*

When expressing time without *a.m.*, *p.m.*, or *o'clock*, either spell the time out (for quick comprehension) or convert the expression to an all-figure style. The 24-hour clock can also be used by adding 12 hours to the customary afternoon times.

arrive at eight	**OR**	8:00	**OR**	08 00	(**NOT:** at 8)
five after six	**OR**	6:05	**OR**	06 05	(18 05, if past noon)
a quarter past midnight	**OR**	12:15	**OR**	00 15	
half past nine	**OR**	9:30	**OR**	09 30	(21 30, if past noon)
ten forty-two	**OR**	10:42	**OR**	10 42	(22 42, if past noon)

NOTE: A hyphen is used between hours and minutes (*seven-thirty*) but not if the minutes must be hyphenated (*seven thirty-five*).

The following rules (¶¶443–455) deal with situations in which numbers are always expressed in figures.

Decimals

443 Always write decimals in figures.

165.318 436 8   58 919.237 85

☞ *For the metric style of writing decimal figures, see ¶461a.*

444 When a decimal stands alone (without a whole number preceding the decimal point), insert a zero before the decimal point. (Reason: The zero keeps the reader from overlooking the decimal point and prevents a misreading of *0.5 percent* as the amount *5 percent.*

0.55   0.09

445 Ordinarily, drop the zero at the end of a decimal (for example, write *2.78* rather than *2.780*). However, retain the zero (*a*) if you wish to emphasize that the decimal is an exact number or (*b*) if the decimal has been rounded off from a longer figure. In a column of figures, add zeros to the end of a decimal in order to make the number as long as other numbers in the column. (For illustrations, see ¶¶1625, 1627, 1629.)

446 Do not begin a sentence with a decimal figure.

> The temperature was 23.7. (**NOT:** 23.7 was the temperature.)

Percentages

447 Express percentages in figures, and spell out the word *percent*. (See ¶¶421–422 for percentages at the beginning of a sentence.)

> When your mortgage rate goes from *6 percent* to *6.6 percent*, it may have increased by less than 1 percentage point, but you'll pay *10 percent* more in interest.
>
> My client expected a *25 percent* discount. (**NOT:** a 25-percent discount. See ¶817.)
>
> Our terms are *2 percent* 10 days, net 30 days. (These credit terms may be abbreviated as *2/10, n/30* on invoices and other business forms.)

> **NOTE:** The % symbol may be used in tables, on business forms, and in statistical or technical matter.

448 **a.** Fractional percentages *under 1 percent* may be expressed as follows:

> one half of 1 percent **OR** 0.5 percent (See ¶444.)
>
> Workers were offered a *zero percent* wage package.

> **NOTE:** To avoid misreading, use *zero percent* unless it is shown with other percentages.

> Workers were offered a *0%, 0.5%,* and a *1%* increase.

    b. Fractional percentages *over 1 percent* should be expressed in figures.

> $7\frac{1}{2}$ percent **OR** 7.5 percent $9\frac{1}{4}$ percent **OR** 9.25 percent

449 In a range or series of percentages, the word *percent* follows the last figure only. If the symbol % is used (see ¶447, note), it must follow each figure.

> Price reductions range from *20 to 50 percent.* (**OR:** from 20% to 50%.)
>
> We give discounts of *10, 20, and 30 percent.* (**OR:** 10%, 20%, and 30%.)

> ☞ *For the use of % in a column of figures, see ¶1628; for the use of* percent *and* percentage, *see Section 11.*

Ratios and Proportions

450 As a rule, write ratios and proportions in figures.

> a proportion of 5 to 1 **OR** a 5-to-1 ratio **OR** a 5:1 ratio
> the odds are 100 to 1 **OR** a 100-to-1 shot

> **NOTE:** A non-technical reference may be spelled out.

> a *fifty-fifty* chance of success **OR** a *50-50* chance of success

Scores and Voting Results

451 Use figures (even for 1 through 10) to express scores and voting results.

> a score of 85 on the test   a vote of 17 to 6
> Montreal 8, Toronto 6   **BUT:** a 17-16 vote

Numbers Referred to as Numbers

452 Always use figures to express numbers referred to as numbers.

pick a number from 1 to 10   divide by 16
the number 7 is considered lucky   multiply by $\frac{7}{8}$

Figures With Abbreviations and Symbols

453 **a.** Always use figures with abbreviations and symbols.

$50	10:15 a.m.	43%	2 in **OR** 2"	FY2003 (see ¶1615c)
65¢	6 p.m.	No. 631	I-95	200 km (see ¶537)

b. If a symbol is used in a range of numbers, it should be repeated with each number. A full word or an abbreviation used in place of the symbol is given only with the last number.

20°–30°C	**BUT:** 20 to 30 degrees Celsius (see ¶538c)
$8\frac{1}{2}" \times 11"$	$8\frac{1}{2}$ by 11 inches or $8\frac{1}{2} \times 11$ in
5 m × 8 m	5 by 8 metres
30%–40%	30 to 40 percent
50¢–60¢	50 to 60 cents
$70–$80	seventy to eighty dollars

NOTE: A symbol should be used with each number in a series.

discounts of 5%, 10%, and 15%   **BUT:** discounts of 5, 10, and 15 percent

Telephone Numbers

454 **a.** For a local telephone number of 7 digits, it is usual to insert a hyphen after the first three digits; for example, *123-4567*. If a company chooses to express its number partially or entirely in words, follow the company's style; for example, *345-GIFT, 4-ANGIES, JOB-HUNT, CASH-NOW, GOFEDEX, PICK-UPS.*

b. Area codes were once needed for long-distance calls only. However, the increasing number of cellular phones and faxes in use today together with a greater demand for telephones has necessitated the inclusion of area codes as part of local telephone numbers. (For example, in Toronto and surrounding region, area codes 416 and 905 must be included when dialling all local calls simply because available 7-digit numbers ran out.) To record a telephone number with an area code, use hyphens, a diagonal, spaces, parentheses, periods, or a combination of these. When using hyphens, the diagonal, or periods, leave no space on either side of the elements. If using spaces, separate each element with one space only.

604-555-3998	604/555-3998	604.555.3998
604 555 3998	(604) 555-3998	

A style commonly seen is the area code placed inside parentheses. However, in text material when the area code and the telephone number as a unit have to be enclosed in parentheses, use one of the other four styles (as shown above). Using periods to separate the elements is relatively new to North

Americans. This style is growing in popularity because these periods resemble dots in e-mail addresses.

You can always reach me by telephone (613-555-6939) between 8:30 and 11:30 a.m.

OR: . . . by telephone (613/555-6939) between 8:30 and 11:30 a.m.

BUT NOT: . . . by telephone ((613) 555-6939) between 8:30 and 11:30 a.m.

c. When an access code precedes the area code and the telephone number, use hyphens (or periods) to connect all the elements.

Use our toll-free telephone number: 1-800-555-6400 (1.800.555.6400)

NOTE: International telephone numbers typically contain a series of special access codes. Hyphens (or periods) are used to connect all the elements.

011-64-9-555-1523
   └ international access code from Canada
     └ country access code
       └ routing code

d. When providing a telephone extension along with the main number, use the following form: *244-4890, Ext. 6041.* (In formal correspondence, spell out *Extension.*)

No. or # With Figures

455 **a.** If the term *number* precedes a figure, express it as an abbreviation (singular: *No.;* plural: *Nos.*). At the beginning of a sentence, however, spell out *Number* to prevent misreading.

Our cheque covers the following invoices: *Nos.* 8592, 8653, and 8654.

Number 82175 has been assigned to your new policy. (**NOT:** No. 82175 . . .)

b. If an identifying noun precedes the figure (such as *Invoice, Cheque, Room, Box,* or the like), the abbreviation *No.* is usually unnecessary.

Our cheque covers *Invoices* 8592, 8653, and 8654.

EXCEPTIONS: Licence No. HLM 744; Social Insurance No. 604 356 289; Patent No. 953-461.

c. The symbol # may be used on business forms (such as invoices) and in technical matter.

☞ *For the capitalization of nouns preceding figures, see ¶359.*

The following rules (¶¶456–471) deal with two technical aspects of style: treating numbers that are adjacent or in a sequence and expressing numbers in figures, words, or Roman numerals.

Adjacent Numbers

456 When two numbers come together in a sentence and both are in figures or both are in words, separate them with a comma.

(Continued on page 132.)

In *2004, 78* percent of our field representatives exceeded their sales goal.

Although the meeting was scheduled for *two, ten* of the participants did not show up until two-thirty.

On Account *53512, $125.40* is the balance outstanding.

NOTE: No comma is necessary when one number is in figures and the other is in words.

On May *9 seven* customers called to complain.

457 In compound adjectives

  a. Numbers one to ten should be written in words; numbers above ten should be written in figures. (See ¶817.)

two-way street	20-year mortgage
three-cornered hat	15-page report

  b. When two numbers come together and one is part of a compound modifier, express one of the numbers in figures and the other in words. As a rule, spell the first number unless the second number would make a significantly shorter word. (See ¶817.)

two 8-room houses	**BUT:** 500 four-page leaflets
sixty $5 bills	150 five-dollar bills

Numbers in a Sequence

458 Use commas to separate numbers that do not represent a continuous sequence.

    on pages 18, 20, and 28   the years 1992, 1994, and 1997

459 **a.** Use an en dash to link two figures that represent a continuous sequence. The en dash means "up to and including" in the following expressions:

on pages 18–28	in Articles I–III
during the week of May 15–21	during the years 1990–2000

NOTE: Do not leave any space before or after the en dash or hyphen. (See ¶216.)

  b. Do not use the en dash (or hyphen) if the sequence is introduced by the word *from* or *between*.

from 1998 to 2002	between 2001 and 2010
(**NOT:** from 1998–2002)	(**NOT:** between 2001–2010)

460 **a.** In a continuous sequence of figures connected by an en dash or a hyphen, the second figure may be expressed in abbreviated form. This style is used for sequences of page numbers or years when they occur quite frequently. (In isolated cases, do not abbreviate.)

1990–99 (**OR** 1990–1999)	pages 110–12 (**OR** pages 110–112)
2003–4 (**OR** 2003–2004)	pages 101–2 (**OR** pages 101–102)

b. Do not abbreviate the second number when the first number ends in two zeros.

2000–2004 (**NOT:** 2000–04)   pages 100–101 (**NOT:** pages 100–1)

c. Do not abbreviate the second number when it starts with different digits.

1996–2005 (**NOT:** 1996–05)   pages 999–1004 (**NOT:** pages 999–04)

d. Do not abbreviate the second number when it is under 100.

46–48 A.D. (See Section 11.)   pages 46–48

Expressing Numbers in Figures

461   **a.** When numbers run to five or more figures, spaces (not commas) are left between groups of three figures to the left and right of the decimal marker.

12 375 $411 275 478   4 300 000 000   0.594 31   70 670.372 48

  b. When numbers run to four figures to the left or right of the decimal, the space is unnecessary unless these numbers occur together with larger numbers that require spaces.

5181 **OR** 5 181   0.3725 **OR** 0.372 5

☞ *For the use of commas with numbers, see ¶413b.*

462   Do not use commas in house or building numbers, postal or ZIP Code numbers, telephone numbers, page numbers, heat or temperature units, or years.

351 Woodglen Drive   Ottawa, ON K1Y OZ2
New York, New York   100221   1-800-435-4321
page 1246   2006

463   Serial numbers (for example, invoice, style, model, lot, licence, or card numbers) are usually written without commas. However, some serial numbers are written with hyphens, spaces, or other devices. In all cases follow the style of the source.

Invoice 38162   Social Insurance No. 699 999 999
Model G-43348   City Licence No. SO14.785.053
Style SKU 39822047   Card No. 3510 9999 6422 9999

☞ *For the capitalization of nouns before numbers, see ¶359.*
    For the use of No., *see ¶455.*

464   To form the plurals of figures, omit apostrophes and add *s* only. (See ¶624.)

in the 1990s   '90s (decades)   in the 30s (temperature)

Expressing Numbers in Words

465   **a.** When expressing numbers in words, hyphenate all compound numbers between *21* and *99* (or *21st* and *99th*), whether they stand alone or are part of a number over 100.

(Continued on page 134.)

twenty-one
twenty-first

twenty-one hundred
twenty-one hundredth

seven hundred and twenty-five (*and* may be omitted)

five thousand seven hundred and twenty-five (no commas)

b. Do not hyphenate other words in a spelled-out number over 100.

one hundred
two thousand
four million

nineteen hundred
three hundred thousand
fifty-eight trillion

c. When a spelled-out number appears in a place name, follow the style shown in the *Postal Code Directory* or an authoritative atlas.

Three Hills, AB
Trois-Rivières, QC

Seven Mile Lake, NB
BUT: 100 Mile House, BC

☞ *For the capitalization of hyphenated numbers, see ¶363.*
For expressing numbers in street addresses, see ¶471.

466 When there are two ways to express a number in words, choose the simpler form. For example, use the form *fifteen hundred* rather than *one thousand five hundred*. (The longer form is rarely used except in formal expressions of dates. See ¶411 for examples.)

467 To form the plurals of spelled-out numbers, add *s* or *es*. (For numbers ending in *y*, change the *y* to *i* before *es*.)

ones
thirds

twos
sixths

threes
eighths

sixes
twenties

twenty-fives
thirty-seconds

☞ *For spelled-out dates, see ¶411.*
For spelled-out amounts of money, see ¶¶413c, 414, 417, 418, 420.
For spelled-out fractions, see ¶¶427–428.

Expressing Numbers in Roman Numerals

468 **a.** Roman numerals are used chiefly for the important divisions of literary and legislative material, for main topics in outlines, for dates, and in proper names.

Chapter IX
Pentium III

World Wars I and II
King George VI

MCMXCIX (1999)
MMIV (2004)

NOTE: Pages in the front section of a book or a formal report (such as the preface and table of contents) are usually numbered in small Roman numerals: *iii, iv, v,* etc. Other pages are numbered in Arabic numerals: *1, 2, 3,* etc. (See ¶¶1429, 1634, 1723.)

b. To form Roman numerals, consult the table below. (A bar appearing over any Roman numeral indicates that the original value of the numeral is to be multiplied by 1000.)

1	I	13	XIII	60	LX	1100	MC
2	II	14	XIV	70	LXX	1400	MCD
3	III	15	XV	80	LXXX	1500	MD
4	IV	19	XIX	90	XC	1600	MDC
5	V	20	XX	100	C	1900	MCM
6	VI	21	XXI	200	CC	2000	MM
7	VII	24	XXIV	400	CD	5000	V̄
8	VIII	25	XXV	500	D	10 000	X̄
9	IX	29	XXIX	600	DC	50 000	L̄
10	X	30	XXX	800	DCCC	100 000	C̄
11	XI	40	XL	900	CM	500 000	D̄
12	XII	50	L	1000	M	1 000 000	M̄

Expressing Large Numbers in Abbreviated Form

469   In technical and informal contexts and in material where space is tight (for example, newspaper headlines and classified advertisements), numbers in the thousands, millions, or greater may be expressed as follows:

ROMAN STYLE: 38M (38 000); 6.3M̄ (6 300 000)

METRIC STYLE: 31K (31 000); K stands for *kilo*, signifying thousands
5.2M (5 200 000); M stands for *mega*, signifying millions
8.76G (8 760 000 000); G stands for *giga*, signifying billions
2.9T (2 900 000 000 000); T stands for *tera*, signifying trillions

☞   *For division of larger numbers at the end of a line: see ¶915.*
For house, street, and postal code numbers: see ¶¶1332–1333, 1339.

Expressing Numbers in Street Addresses

470   Use figures for house and building numbers. **EXCEPTION:** For clarity, use the word *One* instead of the figure *1* in a house or building number. (See ¶1332.)

One Tulip Street   One Centre Avenue

471   Numbers used as street names are written as designated by the municipality. (See ¶1333.)

209 Fifth Avenue   186 5th Street NW

   See the Online Learning Centre at www.mcgrawhill.ca/college/gregg for related weblinks.

SECTION **FIVE**

Abbreviations

BASIC RULES
When to Use Abbreviations

501 **a.** An abbreviation is a shortened form of a word or phrase used primarily to save space. Abbreviations occur most frequently in technical writing, statistical matter, tables, and notes.

b. Abbreviations that are pronounced letter by letter—for example, *RCMP, B.Sc., p.m.*—may be referred to as *initialisms*. Abbreviations that are pronounced as words—for example, *NATO, AIDS, modem*—are called *acronyms* (see ¶522).

c. When using an abbreviation, do not follow it with a word that is part of the abbreviation (see ¶522f).

Marie has an enormous collection of *CD*s (**NOT**: CD discs).

502 In business writing, abbreviations are appropriate in expedient documents (such as business forms, catalogues, and routine memos and letters between business offices), where the emphasis is on communicating data in the briefest form. In other kinds of writing, where a more formal style is appropriate, use abbreviations sparingly. When in doubt, spell it out.

a. Some abbreviations are always acceptable, even in the most formal contexts: those that precede or follow personal names (such as *Mr., Ms., Mrs., Jr., Sr., Esq., Ph.D., S.J.*); those that are part of an organization's legal name (such as *Co., Inc., Ltd.*); those used in expressions of time (such as *a.m., p.m., CST, EDT*); and a few miscellaneous expressions (such as *A.D.* and *B.C.*).

b. Organizations with long names are now commonly identified by their initials in all but the most formal writing (for example, *YMCA, CDIC, IBM, CLC*).

c. Days of the week, names of the months, geographic names, and units of measure should be abbreviated only on business forms, in expedient correspondence, and in tables, lists, and narrow columns of text (for example, in a newsletter or brochure) where space is tight.

d. When an abbreviation is only one or two keystrokes shorter than the full word (for example, *Pt.* for *Part*), do not bother to abbreviate except to achieve consistency in a context where similar terms are being abbreviated. (See also ¶532 for abbreviations of months.)

503 Consult a dictionary or an authoritative reference work for the acceptable forms of abbreviations. When a term may be abbreviated in several ways, choose the form that is shortest without sacrifice of clarity.

continued:	Use *cont.* rather than *contd.*
especially:	Use *esp.* rather than *espec.*
Enclosures 2:	Use *Enc. 2* rather than *Encs. 2* or *Encl. 2.*
24 hours:	Use *24 h* rather than *24 hrs.*
megabyte, kilobyte	Use *MB, KB* for clarity rather than *M, K.*

(Continued on page 138.)

NOTE: The *Gage Canadian Dictionary* (published by Gage Education Publishing Company) is the authority used for all spellings and abbreviations in this manual. Whenever two abbreviations are presented, the first form is the one given here. For specific abbreviations not shown in this manual, you will need to consult another up-to-date dictionary. The forms shown here reflect the spellings found in the *Gage Canadian Dictionary*, but the punctuation is based on observations of actual practice and is consistent with the style recommended by other authorities.

504 Be consistent within the same material: do not abbreviate a term in some sentences and spell it out in other sentences. Moreover, having selected one form of an abbreviation (say, *c.o.d.*), do not use a different style (*COD*) elsewhere in the same material. (See ¶542.)

NOTE: When using an abbreviation that may not be familiar to the reader, spell out the full term along with the abbreviation when it is first used.

> At the end of *fiscal year (FY) 2003*, we showed a profit of $1.2 million; at the end of *FY2004*, however, we showed a loss of $1.8 million.
>
> OR: At the end of *FY2004 (fiscal year 2004)* . . .

505 a. Given a choice between an abbreviation and a contraction, choose the abbreviation. It not only looks better but is easier to key and to read.

acct. (RATHER THAN: acc't)	govt. (RATHER THAN: gov't)
dept. (RATHER THAN: dep't)	mfg. (RATHER THAN: m'f'g)

b. When a word or phrase is shortened by contraction, an apostrophe is inserted at the exact point where letters are omitted and no period follows the contraction except at the end of a sentence.

let's	doesn't	you're
ma'am	o'clock	I'm

NOTE: Respect a company's preference when it uses a contraction in its corporate name or in the name of a product.

Magic 'N Miracles	Family 'N' Friends	Pins'n Things
Shake 'n Bake	Cap'n Crunch	Winkin' Owl
Will O' The Woods	His N Hers	Free Wheelin'

c. As a rule, contractions are used only in informal writing or in tables where space is limited. However, contractions of verb phrases (such as *can't* for *cannot*) are commonly used in business letters where the writer is striving for an easy, conversational tone. In formal writing, contractions are not used (except for *o'clock*, which is considered a more formal way to express time than *a.m.* or *p.m.*).

d. Be sure to distinguish certain contractions from possessive pronouns that sound the same but do not use an apostrophe.

> Ron has been pushing the Kirschner proposal for all *it's* worth. (In other words, for all *it is* worth.)

Let's get an outside consultant to analyse the Kirschner proposal and assess *its* worth. (Here *its* is a possessive pronoun; no apostrophe should be used.)

☞ *See ¶1056e for further examples and a test on how to determine the correct form.*

e. Note that certain contractions can have more than one meaning; for instance, the apostrophe plus *s* can represent *is, does, has, was,* or *us.*

What's her name? (What *is* her name?)

What's he do for a living? (What *does* he do for a living?)

What's been happening? (What *has* been happening?)

When's the last time you saw her? (When *was* the last time you saw her?)

Let's find out. (Let *us* find out.)

Punctuation and Spacing With Abbreviations

506 The abbreviation of a single word requires a period at the end.

Mrs.	Jr.	Corp.	pp.	Wed.
misc.	Esq.	Inc.	Nos.	Oct.

NOTE: Units of measurement are now commonly written without periods. (See ¶¶535a, 538a.)

507 Almost all lower-case abbreviations made up of single initials require a period after each initial but no space after each internal period.

a.m.	i.e.	f.o.b.	c.o.d.	**BUT:** rpm
p.m.	e.g.	e.o.m.	c.i.f.	km/h

☞ *For the omission of periods with abbreviations of units of measure, see ¶535a.*
For the definition of business abbreviations like f.o.b. *and* e.o.m., *see ¶541.*

508 All-capital abbreviations made up of single initials normally require no periods and no internal space.

IBM	CAA	CNIB	CBC	TLC
UIC	CMA	NHL	UN	CN

EXCEPTIONS: Retain the periods in abbreviations of geographic names (such as U.S.A.), academic degrees (B.A., M.Sc.), expressions (A.D., B.C.E., V.P.), and in the names of organizations and products (C.C.M. skates, S.O.S soap pads). (See ¶¶526–529.)

509 If an abbreviation stands for two or more words and consists of more than single initials, insert a period and a space after each element in the abbreviation.

at. no.	Lt. Col.	Rt. Rev.	loc. cit.	Co. Ltd.

EXCEPTIONS: Academic abbreviations, such as *Ph.D., B.Ed., LL.B.,* and *Litt.D.,* are written with periods but no spaces. Units of measurement such as *sq ft* and *cu cm* are written with spaces but no periods.

510 A number of shortened forms of words are not abbreviations and should not be followed by a period.

caps	exam	limo	prefab	specs
cell phone	expo	logo	prep	stereo
condo	fax	memo	promo	sync
co-op	high-tech	micros	repro	temp
deli	hype	perks	sales rep	typo
demo	lab	photo	sci-fi	before the 2nd

When you check the *repros* for *typos*, please watch out for the problems we had with *caps* in our last *promo* piece, and make sure our *logo* is not left off this time.

Also check everything against the original *specs*, and then *fax* me a copy.

511 *One space* should follow an abbreviation within a sentence unless another mark of punctuation follows immediately.

You ought to talk to your CMA about that problem.

Dr. Watts works in Nanaimo, B.C., but his home is in Sidney. (See Note ¶526.)

Please call tomorrow afternoon (before 5:30 p.m.).

When Jonas asked, "When do you expect to finish your Ph.D.?" Fred looked embarrassed. (See ¶261c regarding the omission of a comma after an introductory dependent clause.)

I'm waiting for some word on Harrison, Inc.'s stock repurchase plan. (See ¶¶638–639 for possessive forms of abbreviations.)

512 If the abbreviation ends with a period, that period also serves to mark the end of the sentence. However, if the abbreviation at the end of a sentence ends without a period, insert a period to mark the end of the sentence.

Helen will be returning to the office at 10 a.m. (Here the period applies to the end of the statement *and* the abbreviation.)

The correct postal abbreviation for the *Yukon Territory* is *YT*. (Here the period applies only to the end of the sentence.)

513 *No space* should follow an abbreviation at the end of a question or an exclamation. The question mark or the exclamation point should come directly after the abbreviation.

Did you see Celine Dion being interviewed last night on CBC?

Because of bad weather our flight didn't get in until 4 a.m.!

Capitalization

514 Most abbreviations use the same capitalization as the full words for which they stand.

Mon.	Monday	e-mail	electronic mail
Btu	British thermal unit	CFB	Canadian Forces Base
EXCEPTIONS: kW	kilowatt	A.D.	anno Domini

The following rules (¶¶515–549) offer guidance on how to treat specific types of abbreviations.

SPECIAL RULES
Personal Names and Initials

515 Use periods with abbreviations of first or middle names but not with nicknames.

Thos.	Jos.	Robt.	Benj.	Jas.	Wm.	Theo.	Edw.
Tom	Joe	Bob	Ben	Jim	Bill	Ted	Ed

NOTE: Do not abbreviate first and middle names unless (1) you are preparing a list or table where space is tight or (2) a person uses such abbreviations in his or her legal name. (See also ¶1321a.)

516 **a.** Each initial in a person's name should be followed by a period and one space.

John T. Noonan   Mr. L. Bradford Anders
J. T. Noonan & Co.   L. B. Anders Inc. (See also ¶159.)

NOTE: Respect the preference of the individual or of the company that uses a person's initials in its corporate name.

Lester B. Pearson   k.d. lang
BFGoodrich   J.D. Edwards Canada Ltd.

b. When personal initials stand alone, it is preferable to key them without periods. If periods are used, omit the internal space.

JTN   **OR**   J.T.N.

c. For names with prefixes, initials are formed as follows:

JDM (for John D. MacDonald)   FGO (for Frances G. O'Brien)

NOTE: If you know that an individual prefers some other form (for example, *FGO'B* rather than *FGO*), respect that preference.

d. Do not use a period when the initial is only a letter used in place of a real name. (See also ¶109a.)

I have selected three case studies involving a Ms. A, a Mr. B, and a Miss C. (Here the letters are used in place of real names, but they are not abbreviations of those names.)

BUT: Call Mrs. G. when you get a chance. (Here G. is an initial representing an actual name like *Galanos*.)

Abbreviations With Personal Names

517 **a.** Always abbreviate the following titles when they are used with personal names.

SINGULAR: { Mrs. (for Mistress)   Ms.   Mr.   Dr.
              { Mme. (for Madame)

(Continued on page 142.)

| PLURAL: | Mmes. | **OR** | Mesdames | Mses. | **OR** | Mss. | Messrs. | Drs. |

Mr. and *Mrs.* Pollo both speak highly of *Dr.* Fry.

Ms. Harriet Porter will serve as a consultant to the Finance Committee.

NOTE: *Ms.* (**OR** *Ms*) is an imitation of an abbreviation made up to parallel *Mr.* or *Mrs.* It is used (1) when a woman has indicated that she prefers this title, (2) when a woman's marital status is unknown, or (3) when a woman's marital status is considered not relevant to the situation. Always respect the individual woman's preference. If her preference is unknown, use the title *Ms.* or omit the title altogether. (See also ¶¶618, 1322b, 1366a.)

☞ *For the proper use of the singular and plural forms of these titles, see ¶618.*
For the use of Dr. *with degrees, see ¶519c.*

b. The titles *Miss* and *Misses* are not abbreviations and should not be followed by periods.

c. In general, spell out all other titles used with personal names.

Vice-President Howard Morse	Professor Zhang
Mayor Wilma Washington	Father Hennelly
Chairman William Rain	Dean Castaneda

d. Long military, religious, and honourable titles are spelled out in formal situations but may be abbreviated in informal situations as long as the surname is accompanied by a first name or initials.

Formal	Informal
Brigadier-General George Cook	Brig-Gen G. Cook
Lieutenant-Governor Marion Reid	Lt. Gov. Marion Reid

(**BUT NOT:** Brig-Gen Cook, Lt. Gov. Reid)

NOTE: Do not abbreviate *Reverend* or *Honourable* when these words are preceded by *the.*

Formal	Informal
the Reverend William R. Bullock	Rev. W. R. Bullock
the Honourable Sarah T. McCormack	Hon. Sarah T. McCormack

☞ *For the treatment of titles in addresses, see ¶¶1321–1325.*
For the treatment of titles in salutations, see ¶¶1347–1350.

518 a. Always abbreviate *Jr., Sr.,* and *Esq.* when these terms follow personal names.

b. The forms *Jr.* and *Sr.* should be used only with a full name or initials but not with a surname alone. A title like *Mr.* or *Dr.* may precede the name.

Mr. Henry J. Boardman Jr.

OR: Mr. H. J. Boardman Jr.

(**BUT NOT:** Mr. Boardman Jr.)

☞ *For the use or omission of commas with* Jr. *and* Sr., *see ¶156.*

c. The form *Esq.* should also be used only with a full name or initials, but no title should precede the name. (See ¶157.)

George W. LaBarr, *Esq.*

NOT: Mr. George W. LaBarr, Esq.

NOTE: The form *Esq.*, used rarely in official and professional circles, is used primarily by lawyers. While the title once applied strictly to males, it is now used by some women lawyers to show a professional designation.

d. The terms *2nd* or *II* and *3rd* or *III* following personal names are not abbreviations and should not be used with periods.

e. When the word *Saint* is part of a person's name, follow that person's preference for abbreviating or spelling out the word.

Yves Saint-Laurent   Ruth St. Denis
Buffy Sainte-Marie   St. John Perse

NOTE: When used with the name of a person revered as holy, the word *Saint* is usually spelled out, but it may be abbreviated in informal contexts and in lists and tables where space is tight.

Saint Martin   Saint Thérèse
Saint Francis   Saint Catherine

☞ *For the treatment of* Saint *in place names, see* ¶529b.

Academic Degrees, Religious Orders, and Professional Designations

519   **a.** Abbreviations of academic degrees and religious orders require a period after each element in the abbreviation but no internal space.

B.Sc.	Ph.D.	D.D.S.	M.D.	S.J.
M.B.A.	LL.B.	B.Arch.	R.N.	O.S.A.

NOTE: The term *ABD* (without periods) is often used to identify a graduate student who has completed all the requirements for a doctorate except the dissertation. (The initials stand for *all but dissertation.*)

So far we have received résumés from two *Ph.D.s* and seven *ABDs.* (See ¶622a for guidelines on forming the plurals of these abbreviations.)

b. The term *M.B.A.* is now commonly written without periods when it is used to signify an executive with a certain type of training rather than the degree itself.

We have just hired two *MBAs* from Western and one from McGill.

BUT: After I get my *M.B.A.*, I plan to get a second degree in law.

c. When academic degrees follow a person's name, do not use such titles as *Dr., Mr., Ms., Miss,* or *Mrs.* before the name.

Dr. Helen Wadhera   **OR**   Helen Wadhera, M.D.

(**BUT NOT:** Dr. Helen Wadhera, M.D.)

(Continued on page 144.)

However, other titles may precede the name as long as they do not convey the same meaning as the degree that follows.

Professor Rex Ford, Ph.D.	the Reverend John Day, D.D.
President Jean Dill, M.Com.	**OR:** the Reverend Dr. John Day
Dean May Ito, Mus.D.	(**BUT NOT:** the Reverend Dr. John Day, D.D.)

☞ *See also ¶¶1324c, 1364a.*

d. Academic degrees standing alone may be abbreviated except in very formal writing.

I am now completing my *Ph.D.* thesis.

She received her *M.A.* degree last year.

OR . . . her *master of arts* degree last year. (See also ¶353.)

e. Professional designations such as *CMA* (certified management accountant), *CPS* (certified professional secretary), *CFP* (certified financial planner), *CLU* (chartered life underwriter), and *FRCS* (fellow of the Royal College of Surgeons) are commonly written *without* periods when they are used alone but with periods when they are used *with* academic degrees.

Anthony Filippo, CMA	**BUT:** Anthony Filippo, B.Sc., M.B.A., C.M.A.
Ruth L. Morris, CLU	Ruth L. Morris, B.A., C.L.U.

NOTE: List professional designations after a person's name (for example, in the signature line in a letter) only in situations where one's professional qualifications are relevant to the topic under discussion.

Names of Organizations

520 Names of well-known business organizations, labour unions, societies, associations (trade, professional, charitable, and fraternal), and government agencies are often abbreviated except in the most formal writing. When these abbreviations consist of all-capital initials, they are keyed without periods or spaces.

CNIB	Canadian National Institute for the Blind
TSE	Toronto Stock Exchange
SPCA	Society for the Prevention of Cruelty to Animals
RCMP	Royal Canadian Mounted Police
YMCA	Young Men's Christian Association
IOOF	Independent Order of Odd Fellows
CIBC	Canadian Imperial Bank of Commerce
CUPW	Canadian Union of Postal Workers

521 The following terms are often abbreviated in the names of business organizations. However, follow the individual company's preference for abbreviating or spelling out.

Mfg.	Manufacturing	Co.	Company	Inc.	Incorporated
Mfrs.	Manufacturers	Corp.	Corporation	Ltd.	Limited

Acronyms

522 a. Acronyms, pronounced like words, are written in all capitals and without periods. Because they have been deliberately coined to replace the longer expressions they represent, acronyms are appropriate in most informal, expedient correspondence.

AIDS	acquired immune deficiency syndrome
CIDA	Canadian International Development Agency
CLEAR	Canadian Loss Experience Automobile Rating
DART	Disaster Assistance Response Team
GATT	General Agreement on Tariffs and Trade
OPEC	Organization of Petroleum Exporting Countries
NIMBY	not in my backyard (as in a *NIMBY* protest)
NAFTA	North American Free Trade Agreement

b. In a few cases acronyms derived from initial letters are written entirely in small letters without periods.

scuba	self-contained underwater breathing apparatus
laser	light amplification by stimulated emission of radiation
yuppies	young urban professionals
gorp	good old raisins and peanuts

c. Some coined names use more than the first letters of the words they represent. Such names are usually written with only the first letter capitalized.

modem	modulator and demodulator
canola (oil)	Canada, oil low acid
pixel	picture element
BUT: StatsCan	Statistics Canada
INTELPOST	International Electronic Postal Service
IMAX	I (eye) + Maximum (the most the eye can see)

d. In a few cases all-capital abbreviations such as *MC* (for *master of ceremonies*) or *DJ* (for *disc jockey*) may also be spelled out in an uncapitalized form (*emcee* and *deejay*). The spelled-out forms are preferable when such abbreviations are used as verbs.

Fran Zangwill *emceed* (**RATHER THAN:** MC'd) the fund-raiser kickoff dinner.

Who has been *okaying* (**RATHER THAN:** OK'ing) these bills? (See ¶548.)

e. Very long acronyms (with six or more letters) are sometimes written with only the initial letter capitalized to avoid the distracting appearance of too many capital letters.

UNESCO **OR** Unesco (the United Nations Educational, Scientific, and Cultural Organization)

INSTRAW **OR** Instraw (the International Research and Training Institute for the Advancement of Women)

f. Do not follow an acronym with a word that is part of that acronym. See the examples below using *PIN* (personal identification number) and *ATM* (automated teller machine).

(Continued on page 146.)

There are just too many PINs (**NOT** PIN numbers) to remember these days.

That ATM (**NOT** that ATM machine) has swallowed my card again.

Names of Broadcasting Stations and Systems

523 The names of radio and television broadcasting stations and the abbreviated names of broadcasting systems are written in capitals without periods and without spaces.

CBRT-FM	CFQR-FM	YTV	WTN
CIGV-FM	CKSO-TV	CBC	BVO

According to the *CBC* news reports, the fire blazed for two hours.

Names of Government and International Agencies

524 The names of well-known government and international agencies are often abbreviated. They are written without periods or spaces.

CMHC	Canada Mortgage and Housing Corporation
DND	Department of National Defence
EU	European Union
IOC	International Olympic Committee
NFB	National Film Board
CSA	Canadian Space Agency
WTO	World Trade Organization

525 The name *United States* is usually abbreviated when it is part of the name of a government agency. When used as an adjective, the name is often abbreviated, though not in formal usage. When used as a noun, the name is spelled out.

U.S. Air Force	**OR** USAF
the United States government	the U.S. government
United States foreign policy	U.S. foreign policy

throughout the United States (**NOT:** throughout the U.S.)

Geographic Names

526 Do not abbreviate geographic names except in tables, business forms, expedient documents (see ¶502), and when space is a factor in accommodating lengthy names. Use internal periods with no spaces for these abbreviations.

INFORMAL CONTEXT: Joe Mahal has been transferred from the P.E.I. office to our branch in B.C.

FORMAL CONTEXT: Joe Mahal has been transferred from the Prince Edward Island office to our branch in British Columbia.

527 When abbreviating the names of provinces and territories in addresses, use the following two-letter postal abbreviations, which are written without periods. (Additional postal abbreviations for street types are shown on the last page of the book.) These abbreviations are also used on many expedient business forms.

POSTAL ABBREVIATIONS FOR CANADA

Alberta	AB	Nova Scotia	NS
British Columbia	BC	Nunavut	NU
Manitoba	MB	Ontario	ON
New Brunswick	NB	Prince Edward	
Newfoundland and		Island	PE
Labrador	NF	Quebec	QC
Northwest		Saskatchewan	SK
Territories	NT	Yukon Territory	YT

☞ *For the two-letter postal abbreviations of American state names, see ¶1341.*

528 Geographic abbreviations made up of single initials require a period after each initial but **no space** after each internal period.

B.W.I.	British West Indies	U.K.	United Kingdom
N.A.	North America	C.I.S.	Commonwealth of Independent
S.A.	South Africa		States (formerly the U.S.S.R.)

529 **a.** In place names, do not abbreviate *Fort, Mount, Point,* or *Port* except in tables and lists where space is tight.

Fort Garry	Mount Logan	Pointe Claire	Port Elgin
Fort Henry	Mount Robson	Point McKay	Port Hardy

b. For place names involving *Saint,* follow the style shown in an authoritative dictionary or atlas.

St. Catharines, Ontario	Ste-Foy, Quebec
St. John's, Newfoundland	Sault Ste. Marie, Ontario
St. Lawrence River	Saint John, New Brunswick

☞ *For the abbreviation or the spelling out of names of streets, cities, and provinces, see the last page of the book and ¶¶1334–1337, 1340–1341.*

Compass Points

530 **a.** Spell out compass points used as ordinary nouns and adjectives.

The company has large landholdings in the *Southwest.*

We purchased a lot at the *southwest* corner of Green and Union Streets.

☞ *For the capitalization of compass points, see ¶¶338–341.*

b. Spell out compass points included in street names except in lists and tables where space is tight. (See also ¶1334.)

143 South Mountain Avenue   1232 East Franklin Street

531 **a.** Abbreviate compass points without periods when they are used *following* a street name to indicate the section of the city.

1330 South Bay Boulevard SW   15 Varscona Drive NW

NOTE: Since postal regulations require no punctuation of any kind, compass points are not preceded by a comma. (See also ¶1335.)

(Continued on page 148.)

b. In technical material (especially pertaining to real estate and legal or nautical matters), abbreviate compass points without periods.

N north   NE northeast   NNE north-northeast

Days and Months

532 Do not abbreviate names of days of the week and months of the year except in tables or lists where space is limited. In such cases the following abbreviations may be used:

Sun.	Thurs., Thu.	Jan.	May	Sep.
Mon.	Fri.	Feb.	Jun.	Oct.
Tues., Tue.	Sat.	Mar.	Jul.	Nov.
Wed.		Apr.	Aug.	Dec.

NOTE: When space is very tight, as in the column headings of some computer reports, the following one- and two-letter abbreviations may be used.

| Su | M | Tu | W | Th/R | F | Sa | | | | |
| Ja | F | Mr | Ap | My | Je | Jl | Au | S | O | N | D |

Time and Time Zones

533 Use the abbreviations *a.m.* and *p.m.* in expressions of time. These abbreviations most commonly appear in small letters, but you may use small capitals (A.M., P.M.) too. (See ¶440.) For more formal expressions of time, use o'clock. (See ¶441.)

534 a. The time zones in Canada are abbreviated as follows:

Time Zones	Standard Time	Daylight Time	Alternate Abbrev.
Newfoundland	NST	NDT	NT
Atlantic	AST	ADT	AT
Eastern	EST	EDT	ET
Central	CST	CDT	CT
Mountain	MST	MDT	MT
Pacific	PST	PDT	PT

b. If it is 12 noon Pacific Standard Time, it is 1 p.m. Mountain Standard; 2 p.m. Central Standard; 3 p.m. Eastern Standard; 4 p.m. Atlantic Standard; but 4:30 p.m. Newfoundland Standard Time.

☞ *See ¶440a for examples.*

Imperial Measurements

535 Abbreviate imperial units of measure when they occur frequently on invoices, other business forms, and in tables.

a. Units of measure are now commonly abbreviated without periods. The abbreviations are the same for the singular and the plural.

yd (yard, yards)	oz (ounce, ounces)	rpm (revolutions per minute)
ft (foot, feet)	gal (gallon, gallons)	cpi (characters per inch)
mi (mile, miles)	lb (pound, pounds)	mph (miles per hour)

NOTE: The abbreviation *in* (for *inch* or *inches*) may be written without a period if it is not likely to be confused with the preposition *in*.

8 in OR 8 in.   BUT: 8 sq in   8 ft 2 in

b. In a set of simple dimensions or a range of numbers, use an abbreviation only with the last number. Repeat a symbol with each number.

a room 10 × 15 ft   BUT: a room 10' × 15' (See ¶543b.)

35° to 45°F   OR: 35°–45°F (See ¶¶538c, 543b.)

NOTE: In a set of complex dimensions, where more than one unit of measure is involved, repeat the abbreviations with each number. (See ¶432.)

a room 10 ft 6 in × 19 ft 10 in OR: a room 10' 6" × 19' 10"

536 In non-technical writing, spell out units of measure.

a 20-gallon container $8\frac{1}{2}$ by 11 inches
a 150-acre estate   an $8\frac{1}{2}$- by 11-inch book (See ¶817.)

Metric Measurements

537 The rules of style followed in this manual are found in the *Metric Style Guide* prepared by the Council of Ministers of Education, Canada, 252 Bloor Street West, Toronto, Ontario M5S 1V5.

a. The most common metric units of measurement and their symbols are shown below.

Quantity	Unit	Symbol
Length	metre	m
Volume	litre	ℓ OR l OR L
Mass	gram	g
Time	second	s
Temperature	degree Celsius	°C

NOTE: There are two international symbols for the litre. Since the upward *l* may be confused with the number one (1), the cursive ℓ or the word *litre* should be used. To accommodate equipment and clarity, the capital letter *L* is sometimes used.

1 litre OR 1 ℓ OR 1 L NOT: 1 l

b. Prefixes, based on a decimal structure, are attached to units to give metric names.

kilo (k)	one thousand (1000)	deci (d)	one tenth
hecto (h)	one hundred (100)	centi (c)	one hundredth
deca (da)	ten (10)	milli (m)	one thousandth

NOTE: Units higher than a *kilo* are capitalized.

mega (M) one million (1 000 000)   giga (G) one billion (1 000 000 000)

The familiar everyday prefixes, *kilo, centi,* and *milli,* are used with metric units to form the following relationships:

(Continued on page 150.)

1 km = 1000 m	(One kilometre equals one thousand metres.)
1 kg = 1000 g	(One kilogram equals one thousand grams.)
1 m = 100 cm	(One metre equals one hundred centimetres.)
1 ℓ = 100 cℓ	(One litre equals one hundred centilitres.)
1 cm = 10 mm	(One centimetre equals ten millimetres.)

538 The symbols for metric units of measurement are always used with numbers and should not be used to start a sentence.

a. Abbreviations of metric units of measurement are written without periods, except at the end of a sentence.

35-mm film	weighs 100 kg	a 100-km trip
an office 5 × 3 m	a 30-cm width	50 to 75 kg

NOTE: In abbreviations of expressions like *kilometres per hour*, a solidus (forward slash or diagonal) is used to express *per*.

an 80 km/h speed limit   an average run of 7 m/s

b. Metric abbreviations are the same for the singular and the plural.

1 kg (1 kilogram)   5 kg (5 kilograms)

c. When expressing temperatures, leave no space between the number and the degree symbol or between the degree symbol and the abbreviation for Celsius.

Water freezes at 0°C (**NOT** 0° C), and boils at 100°C.

d. Measurements for area and volume are expressed with superscripts or raised numbers.

m^2 square metre cm^3 cubic centimetre

If the equipment you are using makes it difficult or awkward to create raised numbers, use the following forms:

sq m   square metre   cu cm   cubic centimetre

Chemical and Mathematical Expressions

539 Do not use a period after the symbols that represent chemical elements and formulas.

K (potassium)   NaCl (sodium chloride—table salt)

The chemical notations H_2O and CO_2 stand for "dihydrogen oxide" (namely, water) and "carbon dioxide."

540 Do not use a period after such mathematical abbreviations as *log* (for *logarithm*) and *tan* (for *tangent*).

Business Expressions

541 A number of terms are commonly abbreviated on business forms, in tables, and in routine business correspondence. (See also ¶¶544–546.)

acct.	account	COLA	cost of living
ack.	acknowledge		adjustment
addl.	additional	cont.	continued
agt.	agent	COO	chief operating officer
AI	artificial intelligence	Corp.	Corporation
a.k.a.	also known as	CPI	consumer price index
amt.	amount	CPM	cost per thousand
anon.	anonymous	CPS	certified professional
AP	accounts payable		secretary
approx.	approximately	cr.	credit
APR	annual percentage rate	ctn.	carton
AR	accounts receivable	d	day
ASAP	as soon as possible	dept.	department
Assn.	Association	dist.	district
assoc.	associate(s)	distr.	distributor, distribution,
asst.	assistant		distributed
att.	attachment	div.	division
Attn.	Attention	DJIA	Dow Jones industrial
avg.	average		average
bal.	balance	doz.	dozen
bbl	barrel(s)	dr.	debit
bf	boldface type	dstn.	destination
bl	bale(s)	dtd.	dated
B/L **OR**	bill of lading	ea.	each
BL		enc.	enclosed (see ¶1373)
bldg.	building	e.o.m.	end of month (see ¶542)
BO	back order	Esq.	Esquire
B/S **OR**	bill of sale	ETA	estimated time of arrival
BS		ETD	estimated time of
bu	bushel(s)		departure
c	copy	exec.	executive
C	100; Celsius (see ¶538c)	F	Fahrenheit
CA	chartered accountant		(temperature)
	(see ¶519e)	f.a.s.	free alongside ship
cc	circulated copy,		(see ¶542)
	computer copy	f.b.o.	for the benefit of (see
CEO	chief executive officer		¶542)
CFO	chief financial officer	FIFO	first in, first out
cg	centigram	f.o.b.	free on board (see ¶542)
CGA	certified general	ft	foot, feet
	accountant (see	fwd.	forward
	¶519e)	FY	fiscal year (see ¶504)
chg.	charge	FYI	for your information
c.i.f. **OR**	cost, insurance, and	g	gram(s) (see ¶537)
CIF	freight (see ¶542)	GAAP	generally accepted
cL	centilitre		accounting principles
cm	centimetre(s)	gal	gallon(s)
CMA	certified management	GL	general ledger
	accountant (see ¶519e)	GM	general manager
Co.	Company	gr.	gross
c/o	care of	gr. wt.	gross weight
c.o.d.	Cash (or collect) on	GST	goods and services
	delivery (see ¶542)		tax

5

(Continued on page 152.)

h	hour(s)
hdlg.	handling
ht.	height
HO	head office
HP **or** hp	horsepower
HQ	headquarters
HS	high school
Hz	hertz (unit of frequency)
in **or** in.	inch(es)
	(see ¶535a, note)
Inc.	incorporated
incl.	including, include
ins.	insurance
intl.	international
inv.	invoice, investment
IPO	initial public offering (of company shares)
kg	kilogram(s)
kL	kilolitre(s)
km	kilometre(s)
km/h	kilometres per hour
km/L	kilometres per litre
ℓ, l, **or** L	litre(s) (see ¶537a, note)
l., ll.	line, lines
lb	pound(s)
LBO	leveraged buy out
l.c.l.	less-than-carload lot (see ¶542)
LIFO	last in, first out
Ltd.	Limited
m	metre(s) (see ¶537)
M	thousand (Roman); mega (metric) (see ¶469)
M&A	mergers and acquisitions
max.	maximum
mdse.	merchandise
mfg.	manufacturing
mfr.	manufacturer
mg	milligram(s)
mgr.	manager
mgt. **or** mgmt.	management
MHz	megahertz
min	minute(s)
min.	minimum
misc.	miscellaneous
mL	millilitre(s)
mm	millimetre(s)
mo	month(s)
MO	mail order, money order
m/s	metres per second
msg.	message

mtg.	mortgage
n/30	net in 30 days
NA	not applicable, not available
n.d.	no date
No., Nos	number(s) (see ¶455)
nt. wt.	net weight
NV	no value
OAG	*Official Airline Guide*
OJT	on-the-job training
opt.	optional
OS	out of stock
OTC	over the counter
oz	ounce(s)
p., pp.	page, pages
P&H	postage and handling
P&L **or** P/L	profit and loss (statement)
pc	photocopy
PC	personal computer, politically correct
P.C.	professional corporation
pd.	paid
P/E	price/earnings ratio
PERT	program evaluation and review technique
pkg.	package
PO	post office, purchase order
p.o.e.	port of entry (see ¶542)
pop	population
POP	point of purchase
POS	point of sale
PP	parcel post
ppd.	postpaid, prepaid
pr.	pair(s)
PS, P.S.	postscript
pt	pint(s)
pt.	part, point(s), port
qr	quire(s)
qt	quart(s)
qtr.	quarter, quarterly
qty.	quantity
®	registered trademark
recd.	received
reg.	registered, regular
ret.	retired
rev.	revised
rm	ream(s)
ROA	return on assets
ROE	return on equity
ROI	return on investment
rpm	revolutions per minute
s	second(s)

/S/	signed (before a copied signature)	treas.	treasurer
S&H	shipping and handling	UPC	Universal Product Code
SASE	self-addressed, stamped envelope	VAT	value-added tax
		V.P.	Vice-President
shtg.	shortage	w/	with
SO	shipping order	whsle.	wholesale
std.	standard	w/o	without, week of
stge.	storage	wt.	weight
stmt.	statement	yd	yard(s)
TD	term deposit	YOB	year of birth
TM	trademark	yr	year(s)
		YTD	year to date

542 A few common business abbreviations listed in ¶541 are frequently keyed in lower case (with periods) when they occur within sentences but are capitalized (without periods) when they appear on business forms.

c.i.f. **OR** CIF   e.o.m. **OR** EOM   l.c.l. **OR** LCL

c.o.d. **OR** COD   f.o.b. **OR** FOB   p.o.e. **OR** POE

Symbols

543 A number of symbols are commonly used on business forms, in tables and statistical matter, and in informal business communications.

@	at	°	degree(s)	"	inches, ditto, second
&	and	=	equals	¶	paragraph
%	percent	#	number (before a figure)	§	section
$	dollar(s)	*	asterisk	×	by, multiplied by
¢	cent(s)	'	feet, minute		

a. Leave one space before and after the following symbols:

@ order 200 @ $49.95   = if $a = 7$ and $b = 9$

& Kaye & Elman Inc.   × a room 4×6 m

NOTE: As a rule, do not leave a space before and after an ampersand (&) in all-capital abbreviations.

AT&T pursues a wide range of R&D activities. (See ¶546.)

At the next shareholders' meeting, we need to anticipate some queries during the Q&A session about our M&A [merger and acquisition] plans.

b. Do not leave a space between a figure and any of the following symbols:

% a 65% sales increase   ° reduce heat to 180°C

¢ about 30¢ a litre   " an $8\frac{1}{2}$" × 11" page

c. Do not leave a space after these symbols when they are followed by a figure:

$ in the $250–$500 range   ¶¶ as explained in ¶¶1218–1220

reorder #4659 and #4691   § will be covered in §14.26

Computer Abbreviations and Acronyms

544   The following list presents some of the abbreviations and acronyms commonly used in references to computers and office automation.

ASCII	American Standard Code for Information Interchange (pronounced *as-kee*)
BIOS	basic input/output system
bit	binary digit
bps	bits per second
CAD	computer-aided design
CAI	computer-aided instruction
CD-ROM	compact disc–read-only memory
CGA	colour graphics adapter
CPU	central processing unit
DBMS	database management system
DOS	disk operating system
dpi	dot per inch
DTP	desktop publishing
e-mail	electronic mail
EOF	end of file
FAQ	frequently asked questions (pronounced *fak*)
GUI	graphical user interface (pronounced *goo-ee*)
I-Way	Information Superhighway
IC	integrated circuit
I/O	input/output
ISP	Internet service provider
K **OR** Kb	kilobyte
KISS	keep it short and simple
LAN	local area network
LCD	liquid crystal display
M **OR** Mb	megabyte
MICR	magnetic ink character reader
NC	network computer
NIC	network interface card
OCR	optical character recognition **OR** reader
OS	operating system
PC	personal computer
PPP	point-to-point protocol
RAM	random-access memory
ROM	read-only memory
SET	Secure Electronic Transactions
TCP/IP	transmission control protocol/Internet protocol
UCE	unsolicited commercial e-mail (also called *spam*)
VM	voice mail
W3C	World Wide Web Consortium
WAN	wide area network
WWW	World Wide Web
XGA	extended graphics array

☞ *For a glossary of computer terms, see Section 20.*

For the capitalization of computer terms, see ¶365, 366.

Foreign Expressions

545 Many foreign expressions contain or consist of short words, some of which are abbreviations and some of which are not. Use periods only with abbreviations.

A.D.	(*anno Domini*, meaning "in the year of our Lord")
ad hoc	(meaning "for a particular purpose")
ad val.	(*ad valorem*, meaning "according to the value")
c. **OR** ca	(*circa*, meaning "approximately")
cf.	(*confer*, meaning "compare")
Cie. **OR** cie.	(*Compagnie*, meaning "Company")
C.V.	(*curriculum vitae*, meaning "course of one's life"; a résumé)
e.g.	(*exempli gratia*, meaning "for example")
et al.	(*et alii*, meaning "and other people")
etc.	(*et cetera*, meaning "and other things," "and so forth")
ibid.	(*ibidem*, meaning "in the same place")
idem	(meaning "the same")
i.e.	(*id est*, meaning "that is")
infra	(meaning "below")
inst.	(*instans*, meaning "the current month")
loc. cit.	(*loco citato*, meaning "in the place cited")
M.O.	(*modus operandi*, meaning "the way in which something is done")
N.B.	(*nota bene*, meaning "note well")
nol. pros.	(*nolle prosequi*, meaning "to be unwilling to prosecute")
non seq.	(*non sequitur*, meaning "it does not follow")
op. cit.	(*opere citato*, meaning "in the work cited")
p.a. **OR** PA	(*per annum*, meaning "for each year")
p.d. **OR** PD	(*per diem*, meaning "for each day")
pro tem.	(*pro tempore*, meaning "for the time being")
Q.E.D.	(*quod erat demonstrandum*, meaning "which was to be demonstrated")
q.v.	(*quod vide*, meaning "which see")
re **OR** in re	(meaning "in the matter of," "concerning")
R.S.V.P. **OR** r.s.v.p.	(*Répondez s'il vous plaît*, meaning "please reply")
supra	(meaning "above")
ult.	(*ultimo*, meaning "in the last month")
via	(way, meaning "by a route that passes through or along")
viz.	(*videlicet*, meaning "namely")
vo.	(*verso folio*, meaning "the left hand page or the reverse side of a sheet of paper")
vs.	(*versus*, meaning "against")

5

Miscellaneous Expressions

546 The following list presents common abbreviations acceptable in general usage.

A1	first-rate	PA	public address
ATM	automated teller machine	PR	public relations
AV	audiovisual	Q&A	questions and answers
B.C.	before Christ	QC	Queen's Counsel
B.C.E.	before the Christian (or Common) Era	R&D	research and development
CB	citizens band	R&M	repairs and maintenance
CD	compact disc	R&R	rest and relaxation
DAT	digital audio tape	RSP	retirement savings plan
DVD	digital videodisc	SOP	standard operating procedure
ESP	extrasensory perception		
GIC	guaranteed investment certificate	SRO	standing room only
		SUV	sports utility vehicle
GNP	gross national product	TBA	to be announced (See ¶542.)
ID	identification data		
IOU	I owe you	TLC	tender, loving care
IQ	intelligent quotient	VCR	videocassette recorder
JIT	just in time	VIP	very important person

547 Do not use periods with letters that are not abbreviations. (See also ¶109a.)

A-frame	B rating	T-bill	T-shirt	V-chip
Brand X	S-Curve	T-bone	Type A	X ray*

548 The abbreviation *OK* is written without periods. In sentences, the forms *okay, okayed,* and *okaying* look better than *OK, OK'd,* and *OK'ing,* but the latter forms may be used.

549 Some dictionaries recognize *x* as a verb; however, *cross out, crossed out,* and *crossing out* look better than *x out, x-ed out,* and *x-ing out.*

☞ *Plurals of abbreviations: see ¶¶619–624.*

Possessives of abbreviations: see ¶¶638–639.

 See the Online Learning Centre at www.mcgrawhill.ca/college/gregg for related weblinks.

---

*In the Gage dictionary, the term *X ray* (which is two words when used as a noun) is hyphenated when used as a verb or an adjective and may be keyed as *x-ray.*

SECTION SIX

Plurals and Possessives

FORMING PLURALS (¶¶601–626)

FORMING POSSESSIVES (¶¶627–652)

FORMING PLURALS

When you are uncertain about the plural form of a word, consult a dictionary. The *Gage Canadian Dictionary* is the reference used for all words in this manual. If no plural is shown, form the plural according to the rules in ¶¶601–626.

Basic Rule

601   Plurals are regularly formed by adding *s* to the singular form.

suburb	suburbs	quota	quotas
fabric	fabrics	idea	ideas
yield	yields	committee	committees
length	lengths	alibi	alibis
cheque	cheques	taxi	taxis
rhythm	rhythms	menu	menus

NOTE: A few words have the same form in the plural as in the singular. (See ¶¶603, 1014, 1016, 1017.)

Nouns Ending in *S, X, CH, SH,* or *Z*

602   When the singular form ends in *s, x, ch, sh,* or *z,* the plural is formed by adding *es* to the singular.

bias	biases	sketch	sketches
summons	summonses	wish	wishes
virus	viruses	waltz	waltzes
fax	faxes	**BUT:** quiz	quizzes

NOTE: When *ch* at the end of a singular word has the sound of *k,* form the plural by simply adding *s.*

epoch	epochs	monarch	monarchs

603   Singular nouns ending in silent *s* do not change their forms in the plural. (However, the *s* ending is pronounced when the plural form is used.)

one corps	two corps	a faux pas several faux pas

Nouns Ending in *Y*

604   When a singular noun ends in *y* preceded by a *consonant*, the plural is formed by changing the *y* to *i* and adding *es* to the singular.

copy	copies	liability	liabilities
policy	policies	proxy	proxies

605   When a singular noun ends in *y* preceded by a *vowel*, the plural is formed by adding *s* to the singular.

delay	delays	guy	guys
survey	surveys	**BUT:** soliloquy	soliloquies
boy	boys	colloquy	colloquies

NOTE: The regular plural of *money* is *moneys*. The plural form *monies* does not follow the rule, but it often appears in legal documents.

Nouns Ending in O

606 Singular nouns ending in *o* preceded by a *vowel* form their plurals by adding *s* to the singular.

ratio	ratios	shampoo	shampoos
portfolio	portfolios	tattoo	tattoos
scenario	scenarios	duo	duos

607 Singular nouns ending in *o* preceded by a *consonant* form their plurals in different ways.

a. Some nouns in this category simply add *s*.

ego	egos	memo	memos
photo	photos	logo	logos
typo	typos	two	twos
macro	macros	ghetto	ghettos

b. Some add *es*.

potato	potatoes	hero	heroes
tomato	tomatoes	embargo	embargoes
echo	echoes	innuendo	innuendoes

c. Some have two plural forms. The preferred form is given first.

cargo	cargoes, cargos	proviso	provisos, provisoes
motto	mottoes, mottos	tuxedo	tuxedos, tuxedoes
fiasco	fiascoes, fiascos	zero	zeros, zeroes
banjo	banjos, banjoes	placebo	placebos, placeboes

d. Most singular musical terms ending in *o* form their plurals by simply adding *s*.

soprano	sopranos	piano	pianos
alto	altos	cello	cellos
basso	bassos	vibrato	vibratos

☞ *For foreign nouns ending in o, see ¶614.*

Nouns Ending in F, FE, or FF

608 **a.** Most singular nouns that end in *f, fe,* or *ff* form their plurals by adding *s* to the singular form.

belief	beliefs	safe	safes
proof	proofs	tariff	tariffs

b. Some commonly used nouns in this category form their plurals by changing the *f* or *fe* to *ve* and adding *s*.

half	halves	self	selves
wife	wives	shelf	shelves
leaf	leaves	knife	knives
thief	thieves	life	lives

(Continued on page 160.)

c. A few of these nouns have two plural forms. (The preferred form is given first.)

scarf	scarves, scarfs	dwarf	dwarfs, dwarves

Nouns With Irregular Plurals

609 The plurals of some nouns are formed by a change of letters within.

wo<u>ma</u>n	wo<u>me</u>n	foot	feet
m<u>ouse</u>	m<u>ice</u>*	goose	geese

610 A few plurals end in *en* or *ren*.

ox	oxen	child	children
brother	brethren (*an alternative plural to* brothers)		

Compound Nouns

611 When a compound noun is a *solid* word, pluralize the final element in the compound as if it stood alone.

print*out*	print*outs*	birth*day*	birth*days*
flash*back*	flash*backs*	photo*copy*	photo*copies*
wine*glass*	wine*glasses*	grand*child*	grand*children*
hat*box*	hat*boxes*	foot*hold*	foot*holds*
eye*lash*	eye*lashes*	fore*foot*	fore*feet*
straw*berry*	straw*berries*	tooth*brush*	tooth*brushes*
book*shelf*	book*shelves*	mouse*trap*	mouse*traps*
BUT: *passer*by	*passers*by	work*man*	work*men*
stand*by*	stand*bys*	**BUT:** talis*man*	talismans
	(**NOT:** standbies)		(**NOT:** talismen)

612 **a.** The plurals of *hyphenated* or *spaced* compounds are formed by pluralizing the chief element of the compound.

sister-in-law	*sisters*-in-law	*letter* of credit	*letters* of credit
court-martial	*courts*-martial	*leave* of absence	*leaves* of absence
runner-up	*runners*-up	*account* payable	*accounts* payable
notary public	*notaries* public	*chief* of staff	*chiefs* of staff
editor-in-chief	*editors*-in-chief	*coat* of arms	*coats* of arms
major-general	*major*-generals	*work* of art	*works* of art
BUT: time-*out*	time-*outs*	**BUT:** chaise *longue*	chaise *longues*

☞ See ¶614 for the plurals of foreign compound words.

b. When a hyphenated compound does not contain a noun as one of its elements, simply pluralize the final element.

go-*between*	go-*betweens*	two-by-*four*	two-by-*fours*
get-*together*	get-*togethers*	has-*been*	has-*beens*
hand-me-*down*	hand-me-*downs*	have-*not*	have-*nots*
tie-*in*	tie-*ins*	know-it-*all*	know-it-*alls*
fade-*out*	fade-*outs*	so-and-*so*	so-and-*sos*
show-*off*	show-*offs*	higher-*up*	higher-*ups*

*Mice refers to computer devices as well as to rodents.

c. Some of these compounds have two recognized plural forms. (The first plural form shown below is preferred because it adds the plural sign to the chief element of the compound.)

auditor general	*auditors* general, auditor *generals*
attorney general	*attorneys* general, attorney *generals*

d. When the first element of a compound is a *possessive*, simply pluralize the final element.

traveller's cheque	traveller's cheques
rabbit's foot	rabbit's feet
proofreaders' mark	proofreaders' marks
rogues' gallery	rogues' galleries
finder's fee	finder's fees

NOTE: Do not convert a singular possessive form into a plural unless the context clearly requires it.

We issued 15 percent more *driver's licences* last year.

BUT: Over 200 *drivers' licences* have been revoked in the past four weeks.

☞ *See also* ¶651.

613 The plurals of compounds ending in *ful* are formed by adding *s*.

armful	armfuls	handful	handfuls
cupful	cupfuls	teaspoonful	teaspoonfuls

Compare the difference in meaning in these phrases:

six *cupfuls* of sugar (a quantity of sugar that would fill one cup six times)

six *cups full* of sugar (six separate cups, each filled with sugar)

Foreign Nouns

614 Many nouns of foreign origin retain their foreign plurals, others have been given English plurals, and still others have two plurals—an English and a foreign one. When two plural forms exist, one may be preferred to the other or there may be differences in meaning that govern the use of each. Consult your dictionary to be sure of the plural forms and the meanings attached to them.

☞ *For agreement of foreign-plural subjects with verbs, see* ¶1018.

WORDS ENDING IN *US*

Singular	English Plural	Foreign Plural
alumnus		alumni
apparatus	apparatuses	apparatus*
cactus	cactuses*	cacti
corpus		corpora
focus	focuses*	foci

*Preferred form.

(Continued on page 162.)

genus	genuses	genera*
nucleus	nucleuses	nuclei*
opus	opuses*	opera
radius	radiuses	radii*
stimulus		stimuli
syllabus	syllabuses*	syllabi
terminus	terminuses*	termini
BUT: census	census	
prospectus	prospectus	
status	status	

NOTE: The term *alumni* (the plural of *alumnus*) may be used to refer either to a group of male graduates or to a mixed group of male and female graduates. The term *alumnae* (the plural of *alumna*) is used to refer only to a group of female graduates.

WORDS ENDING IN *A*

Singular	**English Plural**	**Foreign Plural**
agenda	agendas	
alumna		alumnae
antenna	antennas (of radios)	antennae (of insects)
formula	formulas*	formulae
minutia		minutiae
schema		schemata
stigma	stigmas*	stigmata
vertebra	vertebras	vertebrae*

WORDS ENDING IN *UM*

Singular	**English Plural**	**Foreign Plural**
addendum		addenda
auditorium	auditoriums*	auditoria
bacterium		bacteria
consortium		consortia
cranium	craniums*	crania
curriculum	curriculums*	curricula
datum		data* (see ¶1018)
erratum		errata
gymnasium	gymnasiums*	gymnasia
maximum	maximums*	maxima
medium	mediums (spiritualists or sizes)	media (advertising and communication)
memorandum	memorandums*	memoranda
millennium	millenniums*	millennia
minimum	minimums*	minima
momentum	momentums*	momenta
optimum	optimums	optima*
referendum	referendums*	referenda
stadium	stadiums*	stadia

*Preferred form.

stratum	stratums	strata*
symposium	symposiums*	symposia
ultimatum	ultimatums*	ultimata

WORDS ENDING IN O

Singular	English Plural	Foreign Plural
concerto	concertos*	concerti
graffito		graffiti
paparazzo		paparazzi
tempo	tempos*	tempi (in music)
virtuoso	virtuosos*	virtuosi

WORDS ENDING IN ON

Singular	English Plural	Foreign Plural
automaton		automata
criterion	criterions	criteria*
phenomenon	phenomenons	phenomena*

WORDS ENDING IN X

Singular	English Plural	Foreign Plural
apex	apexes*	apices
appendix	appendixes*	appendices
codex		codices
crux	cruxes*	cruces
index	indexes*	indices
larynx	larynxes	larynges*
matrix	matrixes	matrices*
vertex	vertexes*	vertices
vortex	vortexes*	vortices

WORDS ENDING IN IS

Singular	English Plural	Foreign Plural
analysis		analyses
axis		axes
basis		bases
crisis		crises
diagnosis		diagnoses
ellipsis		ellipses
emphasis		emphases
hypothesis		hypotheses
parenthesis		parentheses
synopsis		synopses
synthesis		syntheses
thesis		theses

WORDS ENDING IN EAU

Singular	English Plural	Foreign Plural
beau	beaus*	beaux

*Preferred form.

(Continued on page 164.)

bureau	bureaus*	bureaux
chateau		chateaux
plateau	plateaus*	plateaux
trousseau	trousseaus	trousseaux*

NOTE: The *x* ending for these foreign plurals is pronounced like *z*.

COMPOUND WORDS

Singular	English Plural	Foreign Plural
charge d'affaires		charges d'affaires
coup d'état		coups d'état
hors d'oeuvre		hors d'oeuvres
maître d'hôtel		maîtres d'hôtel
nouveau riche		nouveaux riches
table d'hote		tables d'hote

Proper Names

615   **a.** Most *surnames* are pluralized by the addition of *s*.

Mrs. and Mrs. Brinton	the Brintons
Mr. and Mrs. Romano	the Romanos
Mr. and Mrs. Yu	the Yus

b. When a surname ends in *s*, *x*, *ch*, *sh*, or *z*, add *es* to form the plural.

Mr. and Mrs. Banks	the Bankses
Mr. and Mrs. Van Ness	the Van Nesses
Mr. and Mrs. Maddox	the Maddoxes
Mr. and Mrs. March	the Marches
Mr. and Mrs. Welsh	the Welshes
Mr. and Mrs. Katz	the Katzes
Mr. and Mrs. Jones	the Joneses
Mr. and Mrs. James	the Jameses

NOTE: Omit the *es* ending if it makes the plural surname awkward to pronounce.

the Hodges (**NOT:** Hodgeses)	the Hastings (**NOT:** Hastingses)

c. Never change the original spelling of a surname when forming the plural. Simply add *s* or *es*, according to ¶615*a* and *b*.

Mr. and Mrs. McCarthy	the McCarthys (**NOT:** McCarthies)
Mr. and Mrs. Wolf	the Wolfs (**NOT:** Wolves)
Mr. and Mrs. Martino	the Martinos (**NOT:** Martinoes)
Mr. and Mrs. Goodman	the Goodmans (**NOT:** Goodmen)
Mr. and Mrs. Lightfoot	the Lightfoots (**NOT:** Lightfeet)

d. When a surname is followed by *Jr.*, *Sr.*, or a number like *2nd* or *II*, the plural can be formed two ways:

ORDINARY USAGE: the Roy Van Allen *Jrs.*	the Ellsworth Hadley *3rds*
FORMAL USAGE: the Roy Van *Allens* Jr.	the Ellsworth *Hadleys* 3rd

616 To form the plurals of *first names*, add *s* or *es* but do not change the original spellings.

Marie	Maries	Douglas	Douglases	Timothy	Timothys
Ralph	Ralphs	Dolores	Doloreses	Beatrix	Beatrixes
Waldo	Waldos	Gladys	Gladyses	Fritz	Fritzes

617 To form the plural of other proper names, add *s* or *es* but do not change the original spelling.

three Albertans	two Christmases ago
the Haligonians (natives of Halifax)	checked our Rolodexes
Februarys	Marches (*es* after *ch* sound)
the two Kansas Citys (**NOT:** Cities)	Czechs (*s* after *k* sound)

EXCEPTIONS:

the Gatineaux (for Gatineau Hills)	the Rockies (for Rocky Mountains)

Personal Titles

618 a. The plural of *Mr.* is *Messrs.*; the plural of *Ms.* is *Mses.* or *Mss.*; *the plural of Mrs.* or *Mme.* is *Mmes.* (for *Mesdames*); the plural of *Miss* is *Misses* (no period follows). However, the use of plural titles normally occurs only in formal situations. In ordinary usage, simply retain the singular form and repeat it with each name. (*Ms.* imitates *Mr.* and *Mrs.* as an abbreviation, thus the period. See ¶517.)

Formal Usage	Ordinary Usage
Messrs. Rae and Tate	Mr. Rae and Mr. Tate
Mmes. (**OR** Mesdames) Byrd and Clyde	Mrs. Byrd and Mrs. Clyde
Misses Russo and Dupree	Miss Russo and Miss Dupree
Mses. (**OR** Mss.) Lai and Cohen	Ms. Lai and Ms. Cohen

b. When personal titles apply to two or more people with the same surname, the plural may be formed in two ways: (1) pluralize only the title (formal usage); (2) pluralize only the surname (ordinary usage).

Formal Usage	Ordinary Usage
the Messrs. Steele	the Mr. Steeles
the Mmes. (**OR** Mesdames) Bergeret	the Mrs. Bergerets
the Misses Conroy	the Miss Conroys
the Mses. (**OR** Mss.) Purdy	the Ms. Purdys

Abbreviations, Letters, Numbers, and Words

619 Form the plurals of most abbreviations by adding *s* to the singular.

bldg.	bldgs.	par.	pars.	No.	Nos.	Co.	Cos.
vol.	vols.	apt.	apts.	Dr.	Drs.	tsp.	tsps.

620 a. The abbreviations of many imperial units of weight and measure, however, are the same in both the singular and plural.

(Continued on page 166.)

oz (ounce **OR** ounces)   ft (foot **OR** feet)
deg (degree **OR** degrees)   in (inch **OR** inches)
bbl (barrel **OR** barrels)   mi (mile **OR** miles)

NOTE: For a number of these abbreviations, two plural forms have been widely used: for example, *lb* or *lbs* (meaning "pounds"), *yd* or *yds* (meaning "yards"), *qt* or *qts* (meaning "quarts"). However, the trend is toward using *lb*, *yd*, and *qt* to signify the plural.

b. The abbreviations of metric units of weight and measure are the same in both the singular and plural. (See also ¶¶537–538.)

km (kilometre **OR** kilometres)   cg (centigram **OR** centigrams)
mL (millilitre **OR** millilitres)   dam (dekametre **OR** dekametres)

☞ *For the omission of periods with abbreviations of measurements, see ¶¶535a, 538a. For the abbreviations of litre, see ¶537a.*

621   **a.** The plurals of a few single-letter abbreviations (such as *p.* for *page* and *c.* for *copy*) consist of the same letter doubled.

p. 64 (page 64)   l. 23 (line 23)
pp. 64–72 (pages 64 through 72)   ll. 23–24 (lines 23 through 24)
pp. 9 f. (page 9 and the following page)   n. 3 (note 3)
pp. 9 ff. (page 9 and the following pages)   nn. 3–4 (notes 3 and 4)

b. Plurals of certain symbols consist of the same symbol doubled.

¶ paragraph   ¶¶ paragraphs   § section   §§ sections

622   **a.** Capital letters and abbreviations ending with capital letters are pluralized by adding *s* alone.

three Rs   CEOs   VPs   M.D.s
four Cs   IQs   CPUs   LL.B.s
five VIPs   PTAs   MPs   Ph.D.s

b. Some authorities will sanction the use of an apostrophe before the *s* (for example, *four C's, PTA's*). However, the apostrophe is functionally unnecessary except where confusion might otherwise result.

three A's   too many I's   two U's   too many M's

BUT: His report card showed three As, two Bs, and one C. (When the context is clear, no apostrophes are necessary.)

623   For the sake of clarity, uncapitalized letters and uncapitalized abbreviations are pluralized by adding an apostrophe plus *s*. (See ¶285.)

dotting the *i's*   *p's* and *q's*   four *c.o.d.'s*   wearing *pj's*

NOTE: When initials are spelled out in letters, the plurals are formed normally.

emcees   dejays   okays   Jaycees

624   Numbers expressed in figures are pluralized by the addition of *s* alone. (See, however, ¶622b.)

| in the 1920s | sort the W2s | Catch-22s | file the T4s |

Numbers expressed in words are pluralized by the addition of *s* or *es*.

| ones | twos | threes | sixes | twenties | twenty-fives |

625 **a.** When words taken from other parts of speech are used as nouns, they are usually pluralized by the addition of *s* or *es*.

ifs, ands, or buts	the ins and outs	pros and cons	whereabouts
dos and don'ts	ups and downs	the haves and	whys and
yeses and noes	yeas and nays	have-nots	wherefores

b. If the pluralized form is unfamiliar or is likely to be misread, use an apostrophe plus *s* to form the plural.

which's and that's   or's and nor's

c. If the singular form already contains an apostrophe, simply add *s* to form the plural.

| ain'ts | mustn'ts | don'ts | ma'ams |

☞ *For the use of italics or underlining with words referred to as words, see ¶¶285, 290c.*

Plural Endings in Parentheses

626 When referring to an item that could be either singular or plural, enclose the plural ending in parentheses.

Please send the appropriate form(s) to the appropriate *agency(ies)*.

FORMING POSSESSIVES
Possession Versus Description

627 A noun ending in the sound of *s* is usually in the possessive form if it is followed immediately by another noun. An apostrophe alone or an apostrophe plus *s* is the sign of the possessive. (See ¶¶630–640.) Note in the examples below that the possessive form expresses different relationships, only one of which refers to ownership.

the *company's* profits (meaning the profits *of the company*)

Hodgkins' product line (meaning the product line *of the Hodgkins Company*)

McTavish's property (meaning the property *belonging to McTavish*)

my *boss's* approval (meaning the approval of *my boss*)

Joe's nickname (meaning the nickname *given to* or *used by Joe*)

Atwood's novels (meaning the novels *written by Atwood*)

a two *weeks'* vacation (meaning a vacation *for* or *lasting two weeks*)

BUT: a *two-week* vacation (See Note ¶817a.)

NOTE: To be sure that the possessive form should be used, try substituting an *of* phrase or making a similar substitution as in the examples above. If the substitution works, the possessive form is correct.

628 Do not mistake a descriptive form ending in *s* for a possessive form.

sales effort (*sales* describes the kind of effort)

savings account (*savings* describes the kind of account)

news release (*news* describes the type of press release)

earnings record (*earnings* describes the type of record)

NOTE: Some cases can be difficult to distinguish. Is it *the girls basketball team* or *the girls' basketball team?* Try substituting an irregular plural like *women*. You wouldn't say *the women basketball team;* you would say *the women's basketball team.* By analogy, *the girls' basketball team* is correct.

☞ *For descriptive and possessive forms in organizational names, see ¶640.*

629 In a number of cases, only a slight difference in wording distinguishes a descriptive phrase from a possessive phrase.

Descriptive	Possessive
a six-month leave of absence	a six months' leave of absence
the Manitoba climate	Manitoba's climate
the Burgess account	Burgess's account
the Crosby children	the Crosbys' children
	OR: Mr. and Mrs. Crosby's children

Singular Nouns

630 **a.** To form the possessive of a singular noun *not* ending in an *s* sound, add an apostrophe plus *s* to the noun.

my lawyer's advice	Alberta's mountains
Gloria's career	Brantford's mayor
Mr. and Mrs. Goodwin's party	a child's game

b. When a singular noun ends in a silent *s*, add an apostrophe plus *s*.

The Pas's mayor	Trois-Rivières's historical sites
Sept-Îles's fort	Ville St-Georges's beach

631 To form the possessive of a singular noun that ends in an *s* sound, be guided by the way you pronounce the word.

a. If a new syllable is formed in the pronunciation of the possessive, add an apostrophe plus *s*.

your boss's approval	Hotel Ajax's lobby
the witness's reply	Mr. and Mrs. Morris's plane tickets
Rose's intention	Halifax's waterfront
Dundas's business district	Ms. Lopez's application

b. If the addition of an extra syllable would make a word ending in an *s* hard to pronounce, add the apostrophe only.

Mrs. Phillips' request	the Hayes' farm
Mr. Hastings' proposal	Delores' flight to Ottawa
the Burroughs' condominium	for goodness' sake (see ¶646)
the Laurentians' ski slopes	Achilles' heel
	BUT: Achilles tendon

NOTE: Individual differences in pronunciation will affect the way some of these possessives are written. For example, if you pronounce the possessive form of *Perkins* as two syllables, you will write *Mr. Perkins' kindness*; if you pronounce the possessive of *Perkins* as three syllables, you will write *Mr. Perkins's kindness*. The important thing is to listen to your own pronunciation. When you hear yourself pronounce the possessive of *boss* as two syllables (*boss's*) and the possessive of *witness* as *witness's*, you will not be tempted to write *your boss' approval* or *the witness' reply*. Naturally, tradition should take precedence over your ear. For example, High Commissioners to Great Britain are appointed to the *Court of St. James's* (not, as you might expect, *Court of St. James*).

c. When forming the possessive of any noun ending in *s* (for example, *Mr. Hodges*), always place the apostrophe at the end of the original word, never within it.

Mr. Hodges' message (**NOT:** Mr. Hodge's message)

Plural Nouns

632 a. For a *regular* plural noun (one that ends in *s* or *es*), add only an apostrophe to form the plural possessive. (See ¶¶639–640 for the use of the apostrophe in organizational names.)

investors' objectives	lawyers' fees
the witnesses' contradiction	the agencies' conflicting rules
the United States' policy	the Gaineses' legal residence

b. Since the singular and plural possessives for the same word usually sound exactly alike, pay particularly close attention to the meaning in order to determine whether the noun in question is singular or plural. To help determine whether the possessive is singular or plural (since they sound alike), you can isolate the phrase, turn it around, and look at the possessive to see if it ends in *s* or not.

I especially want to hear the last witness's testimony.
I especially want to hear the testimony of the last witness. (Singular)

I especially want to hear the last two witnesses' testimony.
I especially want to hear the testimony of the last two witnesses. (Plural)

NOTE: In some cases only a dictionary can help you determine whether the possessive form should be singular or plural. For example, a plural possessive is used in *Legionnaires' disease*, but a singular possessive is used in *Hodgkin's disease* since the discoverer's name was Dr. Hodgkin (and not, as you might have expected, the more common name Hodgkins).

633 For an *irregular* plural noun (one that does not end in *s*), add an apostrophe plus *s* to form the plural possessive.

women's blouses	men's shirts	the alumni's reunion
children's toys	**BUT:** menswear	the alumnae's contribution
	(originally, men's wear)	

(Continued on page 170.)

IMPORTANT NOTE: To avoid mistakes in forming the possessive of plural nouns, form the plural first; then apply the rule in ¶632 or ¶633, whichever fits.

Singular	Plural	Plural Possessive
boy	boys (regular)	boys'
boss	bosses (regular)	bosses'
hero	heroes (regular)	heroes'
Mr. and Mrs. Fox	the Foxes (regular)	the Foxes'
child	children (irregular)	children's
mother-in-law	mothers-in-law (irregular)	mothers-in-law's
alumnus	alumni (irregular)	alumni's
alumna	alumnae (irregular)	alumnae's

Compound Nouns

634 To form the *singular* possessive of a compound noun (whether solid, spaced, or hyphenated), add an apostrophe plus *s* to the last element of the compound.

my son-in-law's job prospects	my stockbroker's advice
the secretary-treasurer's report	the notary public's seal
the owner-manager's policies	an eyewitness's account

635 To form the *plural* possessive of a compound noun, first form the plural.

a. If the plural form ends in *s*, add only an apostrophe.

Singular	Plural	Plural Possessive
stockholder	stockholders	stockholders'
vice-president	vice-presidents	vice-presidents'
do-it-yourselfer	do-it-yourselfers	do-it-yourselfers'
salesclerk	salesclerks	salesclerks'

b. If the plural form does not end in *s*, add an apostrophe plus *s*.

Singular	Plural	Plural Possessive
editor-in-chief	editors-in-chief	editors-in-chief's
brother-in-law	brothers-in-law	brothers-in-law's

NOTE: To avoid the awkwardness of a plural possessive such as *editors-in-chief's* or *brothers-in-law's*, rephrase the sentence.

AWKWARD: We may have to invite my three *sisters-in-law's* parents too.
BETTER: We may have to invite the parents of my three *sisters-in-law* too.

AWKWARD: Mr. Ahmed's statement agrees with both *attorneys general's* views.
BETTER: Mr. Ahmed's statement agrees with the views of both *attorneys general*.

Pronouns

636 The possessive forms of *personal pronouns* and of the relative pronoun *who* do not require the apostrophe. These pronouns have their own possessive forms.

I: my, mine	she: her, hers	they: their, theirs
you: your, yours	it: its	who: whose
he: his	we: our, ours	

My copy of the letter arrived last week, so she should have received *hers* by now. (**NOT:** her's.)

Each unit comes carefully packed in *its* own carton. (**NOT:** it's.)

The two products look so much alike that it's (it is) hard to tell *ours* from *theirs*. (**NOT:** our's from their's.)

CAUTION: Do not confuse personal possessive pronouns with similarly spelled contractions. (See ¶1056e for examples.)

637 Some *indefinite pronouns* have regular possessive forms.

one's choice	the other's claim	anybody's guess
anyone else's job	the others' claim	no one's responsibility
one another's time	each other's claim	someone's chance

For those indefinite pronouns that do not have possessive forms, use an *of* phrase.

Although the children in this group seem very much alike, the needs *of each* are different. (**NOT:** each's needs.)

Abbreviations

638 To form the singular possessive of an abbreviation, add an apostrophe plus *s*. To form the plural possessive, add an *s* plus an apostrophe to the singular form. (See also ¶639.)

Singular	Plural
Mr. C.'s opinion	the M.D.s' diagnoses
CBC's programming	the Ph.D.s' theses
the CA's audit	the CGAs' meeting

6

Personal, Organizational, and Product Names

639 To form the possessive of a personal or organizational name that ends with an abbreviation, a number, a mark of punctuation, or a prepositional phrase, add an apostrophe plus *s* at the end of the complete name.

the Winger Co.'s new plant	McGraw-Hill, Inc.'s dividends
Yahoo!'s Web site	Queen Elizabeth II's reign
Bank of Nova Scotia's loan rates	the G-7's proposal

NOTE: If *no* extra *s* sound is created when you pronounce the possessive form, add only an apostrophe.

the Gerald Curry Jrs.' yacht

☞ *For the treatment of possessive forms when terms like* Jr. *and* Inc. *are set off by commas, see* ¶¶156 *and* 159.

640 Many organizational names and products contain words that could be considered as either possessive or descriptive terms.

a. As a rule, use an apostrophe if the term is a singular possessive noun or an irregular plural noun.

(Continued on page 172.)

| Wendy's | Fanny's Fabrics | Woman's Show | Children's Hospital |
| McDonald's | Levi's jeans | Don Cherry's | Reese's Pieces |

b. Do not use an apostrophe if the term is a regular plural.

Canadian Securities Institute	Hamilton Singles Society
Professional Marketers Association	Bankers Hall Club
Retail Merchants Association	Investors Group Inc.

c. In all cases follow the organization's preference or style as given.

Life Underwriters' Association	Ranchmen's Club
Consumer's Association of Canada	*Reader's Digest*
Grandma Lee's Bakery	Robin's Donuts
Western Stock Grower's Association	Fry's cocoa
Hudson's Bay Company	Planters peanuts
Campbell's soups	Tim Horton Donuts

d. When adding the sign of the possessive to a phrase that must be italicized or underlined, do not italicize or underline the possessive ending. (See also ¶290c.)

| *Jake and the Kid*'s story | *Remember*'s author | *Survivor*'s success |

Nouns in Apposition

641 Sometimes a noun that ordinarily would be in the possessive is followed by an *appositive*, a closely linked explanatory word or phrase. In such cases add the sign of the possessive to the appositive.

Peggy's Cove, *Nova Scotia's* attraction for artists goes back many decades. (Note that the comma that normally follows an appositive is omitted after a possessive ending.)

You will faint when you see Paul *the plumber's* bill. (If the noun and the appositive are closely linked as a unit, even the first comma is omitted. See also ¶150.)

NOTE: To avoid an awkward construction, use an *of* phrase instead.

You will need to get the signature *of Mr. Bartel*, the executor.

(**BETTER THAN:** You will need to get Mr. Bartel, *the executor's* signature.)

Separate and Joint Possession

642 **a.** To indicate separate possession, add the sign of the possessive to the name of each individual.

the buyer's and the seller's signatures   the Joneses' and the Browns' houses

NOTE: Repeating *the* with each name emphasizes that ownership is separate.

b. If one or both of the individuals' names are replaced by a possessive pronoun, watch out for awkwardness and reword if necessary.

AWKWARD: my and the seller's signatures
BETTER: the seller's and my signatures

OR: the seller's signature and mine

AWKWARD: their and our houses
BETTER: their house and ours

AWKWARD: your and your husband's passports
BETTER: the passports for you and your husband

643 **a.** To indicate joint (or common) ownership, add the sign of the possessive to the *final* name alone.

the Barneses and Terrys' property line

NOTE: In organizational names, follow the company's preference.

Ben & Jerry's ice cream   Kroch's & Brentano's bookstores

b. If one of the owners is identified by a pronoun, make each name and pronoun possessive.

Karen's and my ski lodge   BUT: Karen and Brian's ski lodge

Possessives Standing Alone

644 Sometimes the noun that the possessive modifies is not expressed but merely understood.

Fred is getting a *master's* [degree] in international economics.

Ask for it at you *grocer's* [store].

Wear your oldest shirt and *Levi's* [jeans]. (The trademark *Levi's* is a singular possessive form.)

We have been invited to dinner at the *Furnesses'* [house].

BUT: We always enjoy an evening with the *Furnesses*. (The people themselves are referred to; hence no possessive.)

NOTE: The possessive form must be used in the following construction in order to keep the comparison parallel.

This year's product line is pulling better than *last year's* [product line].

NOT: This year's product line is pulling better than *last year*. (Incorrectly compares *product line* with *last year*.)

Inanimate Possessives

645 As a rule, nouns referring to inanimate things should not be in the possessive. Use an *of* phrase instead.

the bottom of the barrel (NOT: the barrel's bottom)

the wording of the agreement (NOT: the agreement's wording)

the lower level of the terminal (NOT: the terminal's lower level)

646 In many common expressions that refer to time and measurements, however, and in phrases implying personification, the possessive form has come to be accepted usage. (See also ¶817a.)

one day's notice	a dollar's worth	a stone's throw
a nine days' wonder	several dollars' worth	in today's world
an hour's work	two cents' worth	for conscience' sake
two years' progress	at arm's length	(see ¶631b)
the company's assets	New Year's resolutions	the earth's atmosphere
the computer's memory	this morning's news	the next world's fair

NOTE: Be sure to distinguish possessive expressions like those above from similar wording where no possessive relation is involved.

two weeks' salary   **BUT:** two weeks ago, two weeks later, two weeks overdue

I bought *five dollars' worth* of chocolate truffles.

BUT: I found *five dollars lying* on the sidewalk.

Possessives Preceding Verbal Nouns

647 **a.** When a noun or a pronoun modifies a *gerund* (the *ing* form of a verb used as a noun), the noun or pronoun should be in the possessive.

What was the point of *our* asking any further questions? (**NOT:** of us asking.)

NOTE: The use of a possessive form before a gerund can produce a sentence that is grammatically correct but awkward nonetheless. In such cases reword the sentence.

AWKWARD: He wanted to be reassured about his *children's* being given a ride home.

BETTER: He wanted to be reassured that his children would be given a ride home.

b. Not every noun or pronoun preceding the *ing* form of a verb should be in the possessive form. Compare the following pairs of examples:

I heard *you* singing at the party. (Here the emphasis is on *you*, the object of *heard*; *singing* is a participle that modifies *you*.)

I liked *your* singing at the party. (Here the emphasis is on *singing*, a gerund that is the object of *liked*; the pronoun *your* is in the possessive form because it modifies *singing*.)

Our success in this venture depends on *Allen* acting as the co-ordinator. (This suggests that the success depends on Allen himself rather than on the role he is playing. Even if Allen's role should change, success seems likely as long as he is associated with the project in some way.)

Our success in this venture depends on *Allen's* acting as the co-ordinator. (This puts the emphasis squarely on Allen's acting in a certain role. If he ceases to function as the co-ordinator, the venture may not succeed.)

Possessives in *Of* Phrases

648 **a.** The object of the preposition *of* should not ordinarily be in the possessive form, since the *of* phrase as a whole expresses possession. However, possessives are used in a few idiomatic expressions.

Tony and Fiona are good friends of *ours* as well as our *children's*.

Did you know that Polly and Fred are neighbours of the *Joneses'*?

Bobby Busoni is a business associate of *Gordon's*.

b. Note the difference in meaning in the following phrases:

a statue of Rodin (a statue showing the likeness of the sculptor Rodin)
a statue of Rodin's (a statue created by Rodin)

a controversial view of the Premier (a view held by someone else)
a controversial view of the Premier's (a view held by the Premier)

c. Attaching the sign of the possessive to an *of* phrase can sometimes create humorous confusion in addition to awkwardness.

CONFUSING: Negotiate the purchase price with the owner of the horse's wife.

CLEAR: Negotiate the purchase price of the horse with the owner's wife.

Possessives Modifying Possessives

649 Avoid attaching a possessive form to another possessive. Change the wording if possible.

AWKWARD: I have not yet seen the *utility company's lawyer's* petition.

BETTER: I have not yet seen the petition of the *utility company's lawyer*.

Possessives in Holidays

650 Possessives in names of holidays are usually singular.

New Year's Eve	Valentine's Day	**BUT:** Robbie Burns' Day
Queen's Birthday	Saint Patrick's Day	April Fools' Day
Mother's Day	Orangeman's Day	All Saints' Day

NOTE: Some holiday names contain a plural form rather than a plural possessive; for example: *United Nations Day*.

Possessives in Place Names

651 Place names that contain a possessive form typically do not use an apostrophe.

Baxters Corner, New Brunswick	Rogers Pass, British Columbia
Clarkes Beach, Nova Scotia	Smiths Falls, Ontario

Miscellaneous Expressions

652 A number of common expressions contain possessive forms. Most of these involve singular possessives.

driver's licence	journey's end
collector's item	visitor's permit
seller's market	lovers' lane
workers' compensation	writer's cramp
witches' brew	citizen's arrest

(Continued on page 176.)

women's rights   teacher's pet
dog's life   monkey's uncle

 For the plural forms of expressions like these, see ¶612d.

See the Online Learning Centre at www.mcgrawhill.ca/college/gregg for related weblinks.

6

SECTION SEVEN

Spelling

SPELLING GUIDES (¶¶701–718)

When a Final Consonant Is Doubled (¶¶701–702)
When a Final Consonant Is Not Doubled (¶¶703–706)
Final Silent *E* (¶¶707–709)
When Final *Y* Is Changed to *I* (¶¶710–711)
EI and *IE* Words (¶712)
Words Ending in *ABLE* and *IBLE* (¶713)
Words Ending in *ANT, ANCE, ENT,* and *ENCE* (¶714)
Words Ending in *IZE, ISE,* and *YSE* (¶715)
Words Ending in *CEDE, CEED,* and *SEDE* (¶716)
Words Ending in *C* (¶717)
Words With Diacritical Marks (¶718)

WORDS THAT SOUND ALIKE OR LOOK ALIKE (¶719)

TROUBLESOME WORDS (¶720)

COLOUR OR COLOR? (¶721)

Section 7 offers three kinds of assistance: ¶¶701–718 present the basic guidelines for correct spelling; ¶719 provides a list of look-alike and sound-alike words for review and fast reference; ¶720 presents a list of troublesome words. Also added is ¶721, which compares British, American, and Canadian spellings.

Throughout this manual the *Gage Canadian Dictionary*, published by Gage Educational Publishing Company, has been followed. Whenever two spellings are presented in the dictionary, only the first form is given.

NOTE: The dictionaries and spell checkers that are built into word processing software do not always agree with the dictionaries that serve as the authority for spelling in this manual. A spell checker will flag any word not listed in its own dictionary or in one you create, even if the word is spelled correctly. Reduce the number of "false alarms" by expanding your dictionary to include frequently used terms and names. In addition, always proofread carefully since no spell checker will flag words spelled correctly but used incorrectly. (See ¶1203d.) For example, if you write "Summer is our peek season for swimwear," the spell checker will not question *peek* because it is spelled correctly. You will have to find the error yourself or suffer the embarrassing consequences.

SPELLING GUIDES
When a Final Consonant Is Doubled

701 When a word of one syllable ends in a single consonant (ba*g*) preceded by a single vowel (b*a*g), double the final consonant before a suffix beginning with a vowel (bagg*age*) or before the suffix *y* (bagg*y*). (See ¶703.)

rub	rub*b*ed	swim	swim*m*er	slip	slip*p*age
glad	glad*d*en	skin	skin*n*y	star	star*r*ing
beg	beg*g*ar	clan	clan*n*ish	bet	bet*t*or

EXCEPTIONS:

yes	yeses	dew	dewy	fix	fixed
bus	buses	bow	bowed	tax	taxing

NOTE: When a one-syllable word ends in *y* preceded by a single vowel, do not double the *y* before a suffix beginning with a vowel. (See ¶711.)

pay	payee	joy	joyous	toy	toying
key	keyed	boy	boyish	buy	buyer

702 When a word of more than one syllable ends in a single consonant (refe*r*) preceded by a single vowel (ref*e*r) and the accent falls on the last syllable of the root word (re*fer*), double the final consonant before a suffix beginning with a vowel (referr*ed*). (See ¶704.)

forbid	forbid*d*en	begin	begin*n*ing	infer	infer*r*ed
unclog	unclog*g*ed	unzip	unzip*p*ed	occur	occur*r*ing
control	control*l*er	concur	concur*r*ent	regret	regret*t*able

EXCEPTIONS (see ¶711):

display	displaying	obey	obeyed	enjoy	enjoyable

NOTE: When a suffix beginning with a vowel is added, do not double the final consonant if the accent *shifts* from the second syllable.

refer	refer*r*ed	prefer	prefer*r*ed	transfer	transfer*r*ed
BUT: ref*e*rence		BUT: pref*e*rable		BUT: transfer*ee*

When a Final Consonant Is Not Doubled

703 When a word of one syllable ends in a single consonant (ba*d*) preceded by a single vowel (b*a*d), *do not* double the final consonant before a suffix beginning with a *consonant* (bad*ly*).

glad	glad*ness*	star	star*dom*	play	play*ful*
ten	ten*fold*	wit	wit*less*	joy	joy*fully*
ship	ship*ment*	flag	flag*ship*	boy	boy*hood*

704 When a word of more than one syllable ends in a single consonant (benefi*t*) preceded by a single vowel (benef*i*t) and the accent *does not* fall on the last syllable of the root word (*bene*fit), *do not* double the final consonant before a suffix beginning with a vowel (benefit*ed*).

benefit	benefited, benefiting	
borrow	borrowed, borrowing	differ	differed, different
credit	credited, creditor	index	indexed, indexing
		profit	profited, profiting

EXCEPTIONS:

cancel	cancelled, cancelling	program	programmed, programmer
format	formatted, formatting	total	totalled, totalling
handicap	handicapped, handicapping	travel	travelled, traveller

705   When a word of one or more syllables ends in a single consonant (clou*d*, repea*t*) preceded by more than one vowel (cl*ou*d, rep*ea*t), *do not* double the final consonant before any suffix, whether it begins with a consonant (cloud*less*) or a vowel (repeat*ing*).

gain	gain*ful*	bias	bias*ed*	boil	boil*ed*
haul	haul*ing*	chief	chief*ly*	brief	brief*ly*
dream	dream*y*	riot	riot*ous*	loud	loud*ness*
cheer	cheer*y*	broad	broad*ly*	shout	shout*ing*
deceit	deceit*ful*	poet	poet*ic*	oil	oil*y*
feud	feud*al*	toil	toil*some*	buoy	buoy*ant*

EXCEPTIONS:

equip	equipped, equipping (**BUT:** equipment)	quit	quitting
quiz	quizzed, quizzing, quizzical	squat	squatter
equal	equalled, equalling	wool	woollen, woolly

706   When a word of one or more syllables ends with more than one consonant (wor*k*, deta*ch*), *do not* double the final consonant before any suffix (work*day*, detach*ed*).

comb	comb*ing*	back	back*ward*	shirr	shirr*ing*
hand	hand*y*	curl	curl*y*	mass	mass*ive*
self	self*ish*	warm	warm*ly*	slant	slant*wise*
swing	swing*ing*	return	return*ed*	jinx	jinx*ed*
wish	wish*ful*	harp	harp*ing*	blitz	blitz*ing*

NOTE: Words ending in *ll* usually retain both consonants before a suffix. However, when adding the suffix *ly*, drop one *l* from the root word. When adding the suffix *less* or *like*, insert a hyphen between the root and the suffix to avoid three *l*'s in a row.

full	fully	shell	shelly	hull	hull-less
skill	skilled	install	installed	bell	bell-like
(**BUT:** skilful)		(**BUT:** instalment)			

Final Silent *E*

707   **a.** Words ending in silent *e* usually *drop* the *e* before a suffix beginning with a vowel.

sale	sal*able*	sense	sens*ible*	propose	propos*ition*
move	mov*able*	argue	argu*ing*	execute	execut*ive*
store	stor*age*	issue	issu*ing*	sincere	sincer*ity*
arrive	arriv*al*	blue	blu*ish*	desire	desir*ous*
accuse	accus*ation*	true	tru*ism*	use	us*ual*

EXCEPTIONS:

agree	agreeing	mile	mileage	dye	dyeing
see	seeing	acre	acreage	hoe	hoeing

(Continued on page 180.)

b. Words ending in silent *e* usually *drop* the *e* before the suffix *y*.

ease	easy	ice	icy	edge	edgy
chance	chancy	bounce	bouncy	range	rangy

EXCEPTIONS:

cage	cagey	dice	dicey	price	pricey

c. Words ending in *ce* or *ge* usually *retain* the *e* before a suffix beginning with *a* or *o* so as to preserve the soft sound of the *c* and *g*.

enforce	enforce*able*	courage	courage*ous*
notice	notice*able*	outrage	outrage*ous*
trace	trace*able*	change	change*able*
replace	replace*able*	knowledge	knowledge*able*
service	service*able*	manage	manage*able*
advantage	advantage*ous*	marriage	marriage*able*

EXCEPTIONS:

mortgage	mortgagor

NOTE: Before suffixes beginning with *i*, the *e* is usually dropped.

force	forc*ible*	college	colleg*ial*	rage	rag*ing*
reduce	reduc*ible*	finance	finan*cial*	enforce	enforc*ing*

EXCEPTIONS:

singe	singeing	tinge	tingeing	age	ageing

708 Words ending in silent *e* usually *retain* the *e* before a suffix beginning with a consonant.

hope	hope*ful*	flame	flame*proof*
care	care*less*	trouble	trouble*some*
sincere	sincere*ly*	nine	nine*ty*
manage	manage*ment*	subtle	subtle*ty*
like	like*ness*	edge	edge*wise*

EXCEPTIONS:

wise	wisdom	judge	judgment
awe	awful	acknowledge	acknowledgment
true	truly	subtle	subtly
due	duly	nine	ninth
argue	argument	whole	wholly

709 Words ending in *ie* change the *ie* to *y* before *ing*.

die	dying	tie	tying	lie	lying

When Final Y Is Changed to I

710 Words ending in *y* preceded by a consonant change the *y* to *i* before any suffix except one beginning with *i*.

vary	vari*able*	accompany	accompani*ment*
custody	custod*ial*	happy	happi*ness*
Italy	Ital*ian*	fallacy	fallac*ious*
defy	defi*ant*	try	try*ing*

carry	carried	thirty	thirtyish
fly	flier	lobby	lobbyist
easy	easier	fancy	fanciful
heavy	heaviest	likely	likelihood
fifty	fiftieth	ordinary	ordinarily

BUT: sky skyward   shy shyly   country countryside
dry dryly   academy academic   economy economist

711 Words ending in *y* preceded by a vowel usually retain the *y* before any suffix.

okay	okayed	convey	conveyance	employ	employable
clay	clayey	obey	obeying	joy	joyful
display	displaying	survey	surveyor	buy	buyer

EXCEPTIONS:

| pay | paid | day | daily | gay | gaily |
| lay | laid | say | said | slay | slain |

EI and IE Words

712 According to the old rhyme:
Put *i* before *e*
Except after *c*
Or when sounded like *a*
As in *neighbour* and *weigh*.

I Before E

believe	brief	field	niece	**BUT:** either	height
relieve	chief	wield	piece	neither	leisure
belief	thief	yield	anxiety	seize	deign
relief	friend	view	variety	weird	their

After C

| deceive | receive | conceive | perceive | **BUT:** ancient | species |
| deceit | receipt | conceit | ceiling | science | financier |

Sounded Like A

| freight | neigh | eight | vein | beige | deign |
| weight | heir | sleigh | skein | reign | their |

Words Ending in ABLE and IBLE

713 **a.** The ending *able* is more commonly used.

admirable	dependable	likable	probable	saleable
advisable	doable	movable	reasonable	transferable
changeable	knowledgeable	payable	receivable	valuable

☞ *See ¶707 on dropping or retaining silent e before the ending.*

b. However, a number of frequently used words end in *ible*.

compatible	eligible	irrepressible	possible	susceptible
convertible	feasible	irresistible	responsible	terrible
credible	flexible	legible	sensible	visible

Words Ending in *ANT, ANCE, ENT,* and *ENCE*

714 Words ending in *ant, ance, ent,* and *ence* follow no clear-cut pattern. Therefore, consult a dictionary when in doubt.

assist*ant*	exist*ent*	assur*ance*	defi*ance*	occurr*ence*
defend*ant*	immin*ent*	attend*ance*	inherit*ance*	persist*ence*
descend*ant*	insist*ent*	continu*ance*	intellig*ence*	prud*ence*

Words Ending in *IZE, ISE,* and *YSE*

715 **a.** Most words end in *ize.*

apologize	criticize	minimize	realize	summarize
authorize	economize	organize	recognize	vandalize
characterize	emphasize	prize	specialize	visualize

b. A number of common words end in *ise.*

advertise	compromise	enterprise	improvise	supervise
advise	devise	exercise	merchandise	surprise
arise	disguise	franchise	revise	televise

c. Only a few words end with *yse.*

analyse	paralyse	catalyse

Words Ending in *CEDE, CEED,* and *SEDE*

716 **a.** Only *one* word ends in *sede: supersede.*

b. Only *three* words end in *ceed: exceed, proceed, succeed.*

NOTE: Derivatives of these three words are spelled with only one *e:*

excess	process	success
excessive	procedure	succession

c. All other words ending with the sound of "seed" are spelled *cede: accede, concede, intercede, precede, recede, secede.*

Words Ending in *C*

717 Words ending in *c* usually take the letter *k* before a suffix so as to preserve the hard sound of the *c.*

mimic	mimicked, mimicking (BUT: mimicry)
panic	panicked, panicking, panicky
picnic	picnicked, picnicking, picnicker
shellac	shellacked, shellacking
traffic	trafficked, trafficking, trafficker
BUT: arc	arced, arcing

Words With Diacritical Marks

718 Many French words are now considered part of the English language and therefore do not require italics or underlines. (See ¶287.) Nevertheless, some of these words retain diacritical marks from their original French form that can be accessed from special character sets.

a. Acute Accent. An acute accent (´) over the letter *e* (*é*) signifies that the letter is to be pronounced "ay" (as in *may*). Moreover, it signifies that at the end of a word the letter *é* is to be pronounced as a separate syllable.

attaché	crudités	glacé	purée
blasé	détente	habitué	risqué
café	éclair	ingénue	roué
canapé	éclat	macramé	sauté
chassé	élan	matinée	soirée
cliché	exposé	née	soufflé
communiqué	financé (m)	outré	touché
consommé	financée (f)	passé	toupée

A few words call for two acute accents:

protégé	Québécois	résumé	négligé

b. Grave Accent. A few expressions taken from the French retain a grave accent (`).

à la carte	crème de la crème	pied-à-terre	vis-à-vis
à la mode	derrière	tourtière	voilà

c. The Circumflex. A few phrases derived from the French still retain a circumflex (^).

tête-à-tête	crêpe suzette	papier-mâché	maître d'hôtel
château	raison d'être	pâté	table d'hôte

WORDS THAT SOUND ALIKE OR LOOK ALIKE

719 The following list contains two types of words: (a) words that are pronounced *exactly alike* though spelled differently; and (b) words that look and sound *somewhat alike*. Try reading aloud the words in this list and watch your pronunciation. (See Section 11 for more words that are frequently confused.)

accede to comply with; to give consent
exceed to surpass

accent stress in speech or writing
ascent act of rising
assent consent

accept to take; to receive
except (v.) to exclude; (prep.) excluding (see Section 11)

access admittance
excess surplus

ad short for *advertisement*
add to join

adapt to adjust
adept proficient
adopt to choose

addenda additional items
agenda list of things to be done

addition something added
edition one version of a printed work

adherence attachment
adherents followers

adverse hostile: unfavourable
averse disinclined

advice (n.) information; recommendation
advise (v.) to recommend; to give counsel

affect to influence; to change; to assume (see Section 11)
effect (n.) result; impression; (v.) to bring about

(Continued on page 184.)

aid (n.) a form of help; (v.) to help
aide an assistant

ail to be in ill health
ale a drink much like beer

air atmosphere
err to make a mistake
heir one who inherits

aisle passage between rows
isle island

allot to assign or distribute a share of something (see Section 11)
a lot a great deal; **NOT:** alot

allowed permitted
aloud audibly

allusion an indirect reference
illusion an unreal vision; misapprehension
delusion a false belief
elusion adroit escape

altar part of a church
alter to change

alternate (n.) substitute; (v.) to take turns
alternative (n.) one of several things from which to choose

annual yearly
annul to cancel

ante- a prefix meaning "before"
anti- a prefix meaning "against"

antecedence priority
antecedents preceding things; ancestors

apportion to allot
portion a part
proportion a ratio of parts

appraise to set a value on
apprise to inform

arc something arched or curved
ark a ship; a place of protection and safety

area surface; extent
aria a melody
arrears that which is due but unpaid

arrange to put in order
arraign to call into court

ascent (see *accent*)

assay to test, as an ore or a chemical
essay (n.) a treatise; (v.) to attempt

assistance help
assistants those who help

attain to gain; to achieve
attend to be present at

attendance presence
attendants escorts; followers; companions; associates

aught anything; all
ought should
naught nothing; zero

bail (n.) security; the handle of a pail; (v.) to dip water
bale a bundle

baited past tense of *bait*
bated restrained (as in *bated breath*)

baloney nonsense
bologne smoked sausage

bare (adj.) naked; empty; (v.) to expose
bear (n.) an animal; (v.) to carry; to endure; to produce

base (n.) foundation; (adj.) mean
bass a fish (rhymes with *mass*); lower notes in music (pronounced *base*)

bases plural of *base* and of *basis*
basis foundation

bazaar a place for selling goods
bizarre fantastic; extravagantly odd

beat (n.) throb; tempo; (v.) to strike
beet a vegetable

berry a fruit
bury to submerge; to cover over

berth a bed
birth being born

better (adj.) greater than, more effective; (adv.) to a greater degree
bettor one who bets

bibliography list of writings pertaining to a given subject or author
biography written history of a person's life

billed charged
build to construct

blew past tense of *blow*
blue a colour

block (n.) a solid piece of material; (v.) to obstruct
bloc an interest group pursuing certain political or economic goals

board a piece of wood; an organized group; meals
bored penetrated; wearied

boarder one who pays for meals and often for lodging as well
border edge

bolder more daring
boulder a large rock

born brought into life
borne carried; endured

boy a male child
buoy a float

brake (n.) a retarding device; (v.) to retard
break (n.) an opening; a fracture; (v.) to shatter; to divide

bread food
bred brought up

breath respiration
breathe (v.) to inhale and exhale
breadth width

bridal concerning the bride or the wedding

bridle (n.) means of controlling a horse; (v.) to take offence

broach to open; to introduce
brooch ornamental clasp

bullion uncoined gold or silver
bouillon broth

cache a hiding place
cash ready money

calendar a record of time
calender a machine used in finishing paper and cloth
colander a strainer

callous (adj.) hardened
callus (n.) a hardened surface

cannot usual form (meaning "to be unable")
can not two words in the phrase *can not only* (where *can* means "to be able")

canvas (n.) a coarse cloth
canvass (v.) to solicit

capital (n.) city serving as the seat of government; a principal sum of money; a large-sized letter; (adj.) chief; foremost; punishable by death
capitol building in which a U.S. state legislative body meets

Capitol the building in which the U.S. Congress meets

caret a wedge-shaped mark (^)
carat a unit of weight for precious stones
karat a unit of quality for gold

carton a pasteboard box
cartoon a caricature

casual incidental
causal causing

cease to stop
seize to grasp

cede to grant; to give up
seed that from which anything is grown

ceiling top of a room; any overhanging area
sealing closing

cell a small compartment
sell to transfer for a price
cellar an underground room
seller one who sells

census statistics of population
senses mental faculties

cent penny
scent odour
sense meaning
sent did send

cereal any grain food
serial arranged in a series

(Continued on page 186.)

cession a yielding up
session the sitting of
a court or other
body

choose to select
chose did choose
(past tense of
choose)
chews masticates

chord combination of
musical tones
cord string or rope

chute a slide
shoot to fire

cite (v.) to quote; to
summon
sight a view; vision
site a place

click a slight, sharp
noise
clique an exclusive
group
cliché a trite phrase

climatic referring to
climate
climactic referring to a
climax

clothes garments
cloths fabrics
close (n.) the end; (v.)
to shut

coarse rough; common
course direction;
action; a way; part
of a meal

collision a clashing
collusion a scheme to
defraud

colonel military rank
below general
kernel seed; essential
part

coma an unconscious
state
comma a mark of
punctuation

command (n.) an
order; (v.) to
order
commend to praise; to
entrust

commence (v.) to begin
comments (n.) remarks

complement some-
thing that
completes
compliment (n.) a
flattering remark;
(v.) to praise

comprehensible
understandable
comprehensive
extensive

comptroller a man-
ager of financial
affairs
controller a person
who directs, con-
trols, or regulates

confidant a friend; an
adviser (feminine
form: *confidante*)
confident sure;
positive

confidently certainty;
positively
confidentially
privately

conscience (n.) the
sense of right or
wrong
conscious (adj.) cog-
nizant; sensible;
aware

conservation preserva-
tion
conversation a talk

consul a foreign representative
council an assembly

counsel (n.) a lawyer,
advice; (v.) to
advise

consular (adj.) of a
consul
councillor a member
of a council
counsellor one who
advises

continual occurring
steadily but with
occasional breaks
continuous uninter-
rupted; unbroken

co-operation working
together
corporation a form
of business
organization

core the central part;
the heart
corps a group of
persons with a
common activity

correspondence letters
correspondents those
who write letters;
journalists
corespondents certain
parties in divorce
suits

costume dress
custom habit

courtesy a favour;
politeness
curtesy a husband's
life interest in
the lands of his
deceased wife
curtsy a gesture of
respect

credible believable
creditable meritorious;
deserving of praise
credulous ready to
believe

critic one who makes judgments

criticize to judge negatively

critique (n.) a critical assessment; (v.) to judge; to criticize

cue a hint
queue a line of people

currant a berry
current (adj.) present time; (n.) a flow of water or electricity

curser one who curses
cursor a computer symbol used as a pointer

dairy source of milk products
diary daily record

deceased dead
diseased sick

decent proper; right
descent going down
dissent disagreement

decree a law
degree a grade; a step

deduce to infer
deduct to subtract

defer to put off
differ to disagree

deference respect; regard for another's wishes
difference dissimilarity; controversy

definite distinct, certain, unquestionable
definitive authoritative; providing a final answer

defuse to make less harmful; to make less tense
diffuse wordy, badly organized

delusion (see *allusion*)

dependant (n.) one who relies on another
dependent (adj.) relying on another for help

deposition a formal written statement
disposition temper; disposal

depraved morally debased
deprived taken away from

deprecate to disapprove
depreciate to lessen in estimated value

desert (n.) barren land; (plural) a deserved reward; (v.) abandon
dessert the last course of a meal

desolate lonely; sad
dissolute loose in morals

detract to take away from
distract to divert the attention of

device (n.) a contrivance
devise (v.) to plan; to convey real estate by will

dew moisture
do to perform
due owing

die (n.) mould; (v.) to cease living
dye (n.) colouring matter; (v.) to become coloured; to change the colour of

disapprove to withhold approval
disprove to prove the falsity of

disassemble to take apart
dissemble to disguise; to feign

disburse to pay out
disperse to scatter

disc a flat surface; used with *laser, compact, optical*
disk a storage device; used with *drive, floppy, directory*

discreet prudent
discrete distinct; separate

disinterested unbiased; impartial
uninterested bored; unconcerned

divers (adj.) various or sundry; (n.) plural of *diver*
diverse different

done finished
dun to demand payment

dose a measured quantity
doze to sleep lightly

dual double
duel a combat

ducked avoided

(Continued on page 188.)

duct pipe or tube (as in *duct tape*)

dying near death
dyeing changing the colour of

edition (see *addition*)

effect (see *affect*)

elapse to pass
lapse to become void
relapse to slip back into a former condition

elicit to draw forth
illicit unlawful

eligible qualified
illegible unreadable

elusion (see *allusion*)

elusive baffling; hard to catch
illusive misleading; unreal

emanate to originate from; to come out of
eminent well known; prominent
immanent inherent; residing within
imminent threatening; impending

emerge to rise out of
immerge to plunge into

emigrate to go away from a country
immigrate to come into a country

en route (see *root*)

envelop (v.) to cover; to wrap
envelope (n.) a wrapper for a letter

equable even; tranquil
equitable just; right

erasable capable of being erased
irascible quick-tempered

especially to an exceptional degree
specially particularly, as opposed to generally

essay (see *assay*)

exalt to glorify
exult to be joyful

exceed (see *accede*)

excess (see *access*)

expand to increase in size
expend to spend

expansive capable of being extended
expensive costly

expatiate to enlarge on
expiate to atone for

explicit easily understood
implicit unquestioning

extant still existing
extent measure

facet aspect
faucet a tap

facetious witty
factitious artificial
fictitious imaginary

facilitate to make easy
felicitate to congratulate

facility ease
felicity joy

faint (adj.) dim; weak; (v.) to pass out
feint a trick; a deceptive move

fair (adj.) favourable; just; (n.) an exhibit
fare (n.) cost of travel; food; (v.) to go forth

faze to disturb
phase a stage in development

feet plural of *foot*
feat an act of skill or strength

finale the end
finally at the end
finely in a fine manner

fineness delicacy
finesse tact

fir a tree
fur skin of an animal

fiscal financial
physical of the body

flack (n.) one who provides publicity; (v.) to provide publicity
flak criticism

flair aptitude
flare a light; a signal

flaunt to display showily
flout to treat with contempt

flew did fly
flue a chimney
flu short for *influenza*

flounder to move clumsily
founder to collapse; to sink; one who establishes something

flour ground meal
flower blossom

for a preposition

fore first; preceding; the front
four numeral

forbear to bear with
forebear an ancestor

forgo to relinquish; to let pass
forego to go before

formally in a formal manner
formerly before

fort a fortified place
forte (n.) area where one excels; (adv.) loud (musical direction)

forth away; forward
fourth next after third

forward ahead
foreword preface

foul unfavourable; unclean
fowl a bird

gaff hook, ordeal, rough treatment
gaffe blunder

gage pledge, token of defiance
gauge measuring device

genius talent
genus a classification in botany or zoology

gibe (n.) a sarcastic remark; (v.) to scoff at
jibe to agree

gourmet a connoisseur of food and drink
gourmand a person who eats and drinks to excess

grate (n.) a frame of bars (as in a fireplace); (v.) to scrape; to irritate
great large; magnificent

guarantee an assurance of some kind
guaranty a promise to answer for another's debt

guessed past tense of *guess*
guest visitor

hail (n.) a shower of icy pellets; (v.) to call out to
hale (adj.) healthy (v.) to compel to go

hall a corridor
haul to drag

hangar a building relating to aircraft
hanger a device for hanging something

heal to cure
heel part of a foot or a shoe

hear to perceive by ear
here in this place

heard past tense of *hear*
herd a group of animals

heir (see *air*)

higher at a greater height
hire to employ; to use someone's services

hoard (n.) a hidden supply; (v) to hide a supply
horde a crowd or throng

hoarse harsh or rough in sound
horse a large animal

holy sacred
holey full of holes
wholly entirely
holly a tree

hour sixty minutes
our belonging to us

human pertaining to humanity
humane kindly

hypercritical overcritical
hypocritical pretending virtue

ideal a standard of perfection
idle unoccupied; without worth
idol object of worship
idyll a description of rural life

illegible (see *eligible*)

illicit (see *elicit*)

illusion (see *allusion*)

illusive (see *elusive*)

imitate to resemble; to mimic
intimate (adj.) innermost; familiar; (v.) to hint; to make known

immerge (see *emerge*)

immigrate (see *emigrate*)

imminent (see *eminent*)

implicit (see *explicit*)

inane senseless
insane of unsound mind

(*Continued on page 190.*)

incidence range of occurrence
incidents occurrences; happenings

incinerate to burn
insinuate to imply

incite (v.) to arouse
insight (n.) understanding

indict to charge with a crime
indite to compose; to write

indigenous native
indigent needy
indignant angry

inequity unfairness
iniquity wickedness; sin

ingenious clever
ingenuous naive

insoluble incapable of being dissolved
insolvable not explainable
insolvent unable to pay debts

instants short periods of time
instance an example

intelligent possessed of understanding
intelligible understandable

intense acute; strong
intents aims

intermural between schools, colleges
intramural within one school or college

irascible (see erasable)

isle (see aisle)

jibe (see gibe)

key a means of gaining entrance or understanding
quay a wharf (also pronounced key)

knew understood
new fresh; novel

know to understand
no not any

lapse (see elapse)

lath a strip of wood
lathe a wood-turning machine

lead (n.) heavy metal (pronounced like led); (v.) to guide (pronounced leed)
led guided (past tense of to lead)

lean (adj.) thin; (v.) to incline
lien a legal claim

leased rented
least smallest

legislator a lawmaker
legislature a body of lawmakers

lend to allow the use of temporarily
loan (n.) something lent; (v.) to lend
lone solitary

lessee a tenant
lesser of smaller size
lessor one who gives a lease

lessen (v.) to make smaller
lesson (n.) an exercise assigned for study

levee embankment of a river

levy (n.) money raised by; authority; (v.) order to be paid

liable responsible
libel defamatory statement

licence (n.) card, plate, etc.; permission granted by law
license (v.) to authorize

lightening making lighter
lightning accompaniment of thunder
lighting illumination

load a burden to be carried
lode a mineral deposit; an abundant supply

loath (adj.) reluctant
loathe (v.) to detest

local (adj.) pertaining to a particular place
locale (n.) a particular place

loose (adj.) not bound; (v.) to release
lose (v.) to suffer the loss of; to part with unintentionally
loss something lost

made constructed
maid a servant

magnificent grand, stately
munificent unusually generous

mail correspondence
male masculine

main (adj.) chief; (n.) a conduit

mane long hair on the neck of certain animals

manner a way of acting
manor an estate

marital pertaining to marriage
martial military
marshal (n.) an official; (v.) to arrange

mean (adj.) unpleasant; (n.) the midpoint; (v.) to intend
mien appearance

meat flesh of animals
meet (v.) to join; (adj.) proper
mete to measure

medal badge of honour
meddle to interfere
metal a mineral
mettle courage; spirit

miner a worker in a mine
minor (adj.) lesser, as in size, extent, or importance; (n.) a person who is under legal age

missal a book of prayers
missile a rocket; a projectile

mist haze
missed failed to do

mite a tiny particle
might (n.) force; (v.) past tense of *may*

monogram a set of initials

monograph a short book; a pamphlet

mood disposition
mode fashion; method

moot debatable; disputed
mute unable to speak

moral virtuous
morale spirit

morality virtue
mortality death rate

morning before noon
mourning grief

naught (see *aught*)

new (see *knew*)

no (see *know*)

oculist an ophthalmologist or an optometrist
ophthalmologist a doctor who treats eyes
optician one who makes or sells eyeglasses
optometrist one who measures vision

official authorized
officious overbold in offering services

one a single thing
won did win

ordinance a local law
ordnance arms; munitions

ought (see *aught*)

our (see *hour*)

overdo to do too much
overdue past due

packed crowded

pact an agreement

pail a bucket
pale (adj.) light-coloured; (n.) an enclosure

pain suffering
pane window glass

pair two of a kind
pare to peel
pear a fruit

palate roof of the mouth; the sense of taste
palette an artist's board; a range of colours
pallet a bed; a mattress; a portable platform for stacking materials

parameter a quantity with an assigned value; a constant
perimeter the outer boundary

partition division
petition prayer; a formal written request

partly in part
partially to some degree

past (n.) time gone by; (adj., adv., or prep.) gone by
passed moved along; transferred (past tense of *pass*)

patience composure; endurance
patients sick persons

peace calmness
piece a portion

peak the top

(Continued on page 192.)

peek to look slyly at
pique (n.) resentment; (v.) to offend; to arouse
piqué cotton fabric

peal to ring out
peel (n.) the rind; (v.) to strip off

pedal (adj.) pertaining to the foot; (n.) a treadle
peddle to hawk; to sell

peer (n.) one of equal rank or age; (v.) to look steadily
pier a wharf

perfect without fault
prefect an official

perpetrate to be guilty of
perpetuate to make perpetual

perquisite privilege
prerequisite a preliminary requirement

persecute to oppress
prosecute to sue

personal private
personnel the staff

perspective a view in correct proportion
prospective anticipated

peruse to read
pursue to chase

phase (see *faze*)

physic a medicine
physics science dealing with matter and energy
psychic (adj.) of the soul or mind; (n.) a medium
physical (see *fiscal*)
psychical mental

plain (adj.) undecorated; (n.) prairie land
plane (n.) a level surface, an airplane; (v.) to make level

plaintiff party in a lawsuit
plaintive mournful

pleas plural of *plea*
please to be agreeable

pole a long, slender piece of wood or metal
poll (n.) a voting; survey; (v.) to register votes

poor (adj.) inadequate; (n.) the needy
pore to study intently; skin opening
pour to flow

populace the common people; the masses
populous thickly settled

portion (see *apportion*)
proportion (see *apportion*)

practicable workable; feasible
practical useful

practice (n.) exercise; custom; following a profession
practise (v.) do again and again; do as a rule

pray to beseech
prey a captured victim

precede to go before
proceed to advance

precedence priority

precedents established rules

preposition a part of speech
proposition an offer

prescribe to designate
proscribe to outlaw

presence bearing; being present
presents gifts

presentiment a foreboding
presentment a proposal

pretend to make believe
portend to foreshadow

principal (adj.) chief; main; (n.) main sum of money; chief official of a school
principle a general truth; a rule

profit gain
prophet one who forecasts

prophecy a prediction
prophesy to foretell

propose to suggest
purpose intention

quay (see *key*)

queue (see *cue*)

quiet calm; not noisy
quite entirely; wholly
quit to stop

rain falling water
rein part of a bridle; a curb
reign (n.) the term of a ruler's power; (v.) to rule

raze to destroy
rays beams

rap to knock
wrap (n.) a garment; (v.) to enclose

rapt engrossed
wrapped past tense of *wrap*

read to perform the act of reading
reed a plant; a musical instrument
red a colour

real actual
reel (n.) a spool; a dance; (v.) to whirl

reality actuality
realty real estate

rebut to argue in opposition
refute to prove wrong

receipt an acknowledgment of a thing received
recipe a formula for mixing ingredients

recent (adj.) relating to a time not long past
resent (v.) to feel hurt by

reference that which refers to something
reverence profound respect

relapse (see *elapse*)

residence a house
residents persons who reside in a place

respectably in a manner worthy of respect
respectfully in a courteous manner
respectively in the order indicated

right (adj.) correct; (n.) a privilege
rite a ceremony
wright a worker; a maker (used as a combining form, as in *playwright*)
write to inscribe

role a part in a play
roll (n.) a list; a type of bread; (v.) to revolve

root (n.) underground part of a plant; (v.) to implant firmly
route (n.) an established course of travel; (v.) to send by a certain route
en route on or along the way
rout (n.) confused flight; (v.) to defeat

rote repetition
wrote did write

rye a grain to make bread; whiskey
wry ironically humorous

sail (n.) part of a ship's rigging; (v.) to travel by water
sale the act of selling

scene a setting; an exhibition of strong feeling
seen past participle of *to see*

scent (see *cent*)

sealing (see *ceiling*)

seam a line of junction
seem to appear

seed (see *cede*)

seize (see *cease*)

sell (see *cell*)

seller (see *cellar*)

sense, sent (see *cent*)

senses (see *census*)

serge a kind of cloth
surge (n.) a billow; (v.) to rise suddenly

serial (see *cereal*)

session (see *cession*)

sew to stitch
so therefore
sow to scatter seed

shear to cut; to trim
sheer transparent; steep; utter

shoot (see *chute*)

shown displayed; revealed; past participle of *show*
shone gave off light

sight, site (see *cite*)

simple uncomplicated
simplistic oversimplified

sleight dexterity, as in "sleight of hand"

(Continued on page 194.)

slight (adj.) slender; scanty; (v.) to make light of

soar (see *sore*)

soared did fly
sword weapon

sole one and only
soul the immortal spirit

soluble having the ability to dissolve in a liquid
solvable capable of being solved or explained

some a part of
sum a total

son male child
sun the earth's source of light and heat

sore painful
soar to fly

spacious having ample room
specious outwardly correct but inwardly false

specially (see *especially*)

staid grave; sedate
stayed past tense and past participle of *to stay*

stair a step
stare to look at

stake (n.) a pointed stick; the prize in a contest; (v.) to wager
steak a slice of meat or fish

stanch to stop the flow of something

staunch faithful, steadfast

stationary fixed
stationery writing materials

statue a carved figure
stature height
statute a law

steal to take unlawfully
steel a form of iron

storey a level or floor of a building
story a tale; account

straight not crooked; directly
strait a water passageway; (plural) a distressing situation

succor (n.) something that provides relief; (v.) to relieve

sucker someone easily cheated

suit (n.) a legal action; clothing; (v.) to please
suite a group of things forming a unit
sweet having an agreeable taste; pleasing

superintendence management
superintendents supervisors

tack (n.) direction; (v.) to change direction
tact considerate way of behaving so as to avoid offending others

tail the end
tale a story

tare allowance for weight
tear (n.) a rent or rip (pronounced like *tare*); a secretion from the eye (pronounced like *tier*); (v.) to rip
tier a row or layer

taught did teach
taut tight; tense

team a group
teem to abound

tenant one who rents property
tenet a principle

their belonging to them (see ¶1056e)
there in that place
they're contraction of *they are*

theirs possessive form of *they*, used without a following noun (see ¶1056e)
there's contraction of *there is* or *there has*

therefor for that thing
therefore consequently

throes a painful struggle
throws hurls; flings

through by means of; from beginning to end; because of
threw did throw
thorough carried through to completion

to (prep.) toward
too (adv.) more than enough; also

two one plus one

tortuous winding; twisty; devious
torturous cruelly painful

track a trail
tract a treatise; a piece of land

trial examination; an experiment; hardship
trail a path

undo to open; to render ineffective
undue improper; excessive

uninterested (see *disinterested*)

urban pertaining to the city
urbane polished; suave

vain proud; conceited; futile
vane a weathercock
vein a blood vessel; a bed of mineral materials

vale a valley
veil a concealing cover or coth

vendee purchaser
vendor seller

veracious truthful
voracious greedy

veracity truthfulness
voracity ravenousness; greediness

vial a small flask for liquids
vile disgusting, despicable

vice wickedness; a prefix used with nouns to designate titles of office (see ¶808c)
vise a clamp

waist part of the body
waste (n.) needless destruction; useless consumption; (v.) to expend uselessly

wait to stay
weight heaviness

waive (v.) to give up
wave (n.) a billow; a gesture; (v.) to swing back and forth

waiver the giving up of a claim
waver to hesitate

want (n.) a need; (v.) to lack; to desire
wont a custom (pronounced like *want*)
won't contraction of *will not*

ware goods
wear to have on
were form of *to be*
where at the place in which

way direction; distance; manner
weigh to find the weight of

weak not strong
week period of seven days

weather (n.) state of the atmosphere; (v.) to come through safely
whether if (see Section 11)

weight (see *wait*)

wet (v.) to moisten
whet (v.) to sharpen

wholly (see *holy*)

whose possessive of *who*
who's contraction of *who is* (see ¶1063)

wilfully in a determined manner
willingly cheerfully; happily; with one's free will

won (see *one*)

wood lumber
would an auxiliary verb form (as in *they would like some*)

wrap (see *rap*)

wright, write (see *right*)

wrote (see *rote*)

yoke a crosspiece that holds two things together; an oppressive constraint
yolk the yellow part of an egg

you second-person pronoun
yew an evergreen tree or bush

yore of time long past
your belonging to *you* (see ¶1056e)
you're contraction of *you are*

TROUBLESOME WORDS

720 The following is a list of words that writers often misspell or puzzle over. In some cases the difficulty is the inability to apply an established rule; for such words, references are given. In other instances, however, errors result from the peculiar spelling of the words themselves; in these cases the only remedy is to master the correct spelling on an individual basis.

NOTE: For troublesome words that sound alike or look alike, see ¶719. For troublesome compound words, see Section 8. For alternative spellings such as *colour* or *color*, *centre* or *center*, *analyse* or *analyze*, see ¶721. For alternative words that have the same meaning, consult a thesaurus. Synonyms help create variety in your writing style.

abscess	architect	cemetery
absence	argument (see ¶708)	census
absorption	assistance (see ¶714)	changeable
accessory	asterisk	Charlottetown
accidentally	asthma	chronological
accommodate	attendance	circuit
accompanying	attorney	clientele
accumulate	auditor	coincidence
achievement	autumn	collateral
acknowledgment	auxiliary	collectable
acquaintance	bachelor	colonel
acquire	bankruptcy	colossal
acquisition	basically	column
acquittal	behaviour (see ¶721)	comparative
adjacent	believe (see ¶712)	competitor
advantageous (see ¶707)	beneficiary	concede (see ¶716)
adviser	benefited (see ¶704)	conceive
advisory	benign	condemn
aegis	biased (see ¶705)	connoisseur
affidavit	boundary	conscience
affiliated	Brampton	conscientious
aggressive	Brantford	conscious
ageing	brilliant	consensus
alignment	brochure	convenience
aluminum	buoyant	convertible (see ¶713b)
amateur	bureau	corduroy
amortize	calendar	correctable
analogous	calibre (see ¶721)	correspondent
analysis	campaign	corroborate
anomalous	cancelled (see ¶704)	courtesy
antecedent	candour (see ¶721)	debt, debtor
appall	Caribbean	deductible
apparatus	carriage	de-emphasize
apparent	catalogue	defence
appropriate	category	defendant (see ¶714)

deficit
definitely
dependant (noun)
dependent (adj.)
descendant (see ¶714)
description
desirable
desperately
detrimental
development
dilemma
disastrous
disbursement
discrepancy
dissatisfied
dissimilar
dissipate
dossier
ecstasy
eighth
eligible (see ¶713b)
eliminate
embarrass
emphasize
endorsement
entrepreneur
enumerate
envelop (verb)
environment
erroneous
escrow
exaggerate
exceed (see ¶716)
excellent
exhaustible
exhibition
exhilarate
exonerate
exorbitant
extension
extraordinary
facsimile
fallacy
familiar
fascinating
fatigue
February
financier

flexible (see ¶713b)
fluctuation
fluorescent
foreign (see ¶712)
foresee
forfeit
forty
fourth
Fredericton (NB)
freight
fulfil (see ¶721)
gauge
gesture
glamour
government
grammar
grateful
gratuity
grievance
gruesome
guarantee
guardian
Guelph
harass
height (see ¶712)
hemorrhage
heterogeneous
hindrance
homogeneous
honourable
hors d'oeuvre
humorous
hygiene
hypocrisy
idiosyncrasy
illegible
impasse
impostor
inasmuch as
incidentally
indict
indispensable
innocuous
innuendo
inoculate
insistent
instalment (see ¶721)
interim

intermediary
irrelevant
itinerary
jeopardy
jewellery
judgment (see ¶708)
judicial
knowledgeable
labelled
laboratory
leisure
liable
liaison
library
licence (noun)
license (verb)
lien
lieutenant
likable (see ¶713a)
liquefy
maintenance
manoeuvre
marshal (see ¶721)
martyr
medieval
mediocre
memento
mileage
milieu
millennium
millionaire
miniature
minuscule
miscellaneous
mischievous
misspell
mnemonic
mortgage
necessary
negligence
negotiable
neighbour (see ¶721)
newsstand
nickel
niece (see ¶712)
ninety
ninth
noticeable (see ¶¶707c)

(Continued on page 198.)

nuclear
obsolescent
occurrence (see ¶714)
offence
omission
oscillate
pamphlet
panicky (see ¶717)
paradigm
parallel
paralyse (see ¶715c)
parliament
part-time
pastime
patience
peaceable
permissible (see ¶713b)
perseverance
persistent
personnel
persuade
Peterborough
phase
phenomenal
Philippines
phony
physician
picnicking (see ¶717)
plagiarism
plausible (see ¶713b)
poinsettia
practice (noun)
practise (verb)
prairie
preceding (see ¶716c)
preferable (see ¶702)
preferred
prerogative
presumptuous
pretence (see ¶721)
privilege
procedure (see ¶716b)
proceed (see ¶716b)
programmed (see ¶704)
pronunciation
protégé

psalm
pseudonym
psychiatric
psychological
publicly
pursue
questionnaire
queue
rarefy
rarity
realize (see ¶715a)
receipt
receive (see ¶712)
recommend
reconnaissance
reinforce
relevant (see ¶714)
rendezvous
renowned
rescind
resistance
restaurant
rhetorical
rhyme
rhythm
sacrilegious
Saint John (NB)
Saskatchewan
satellite
Sault Ste. Marie
schedule
scissors
separate
sergeant
siege (see ¶712)
similar
simultaneous
sincerely (see ¶708)
skeptic
skilful
souvenir
specimen
sponsor
St. Catharines (ON)
St. John's (NF)
stratagem

strength
subpoena
subtlety
subtly
summary
superintendent
supersede (see ¶716a)
surgeon
surreptitious
surveillance
tangible
tariff
taxiing
technique
temperament
thoroughly
threshold
totalled (see ¶721)
tragedy
tranquillizer
truly (see ¶708)
unanimous
unctuous
unique
unmanageable
   (see ¶707c)
unwieldy (see ¶712)
usage (see ¶707a)
vaccinate
vacillate
vacuum
Vancouver
vicious
vinyl
warrant
Wednesday
weird (see ¶712)
Westminster
wherever
Winnipeg
withhold
woeful
woollen (see ¶705)
worshipped (see ¶721)
yield (see ¶712)

COLOUR OR COLOR?

721 In spelling, as in pronunciation and vocabulary, Canadian usage is neither American nor British, although there is much in common with both. When British and American practices differ, Canadian usage is far from uniform in the selection of a "correct" spelling; indeed, it sometimes varies from one province to another. While Canadians may be accustomed to word variants as shown in dictionaries, the choice made should remain consistent in all writing.

The following lists compare word variants according to *The Oxford Concise Dictionary* (published by Clarendon Press, Oxford, England), the *Gage Canadian Dictionary* (published by Gage Educational Publishing Company, Toronto, Ontario), and *Webster's New World Dictionary* (published by Simon and Shuster, New York, U.S.A.). In all cases, the first word entered in a dictionary is the preferred usage. Canadianize your spell checker by setting the language to English (Canadian) or by adding the words in the middle column to the default dictionary.

	Oxford	Gage	Webster

a. A single or double consonant when adding a suffix.

	Oxford	Gage	Webster
cancel	cancelled	cancelled	canceled
council	councillor	councillor	councilor
counsel	counselling	counselling	counseling
diagram	diagrammed	diagrammed	diagramed
duel	duelled	duelled	dueled
enrol (U.S. enroll)	enrolled	enrolled	enrolled
	enrolment	enrolment	enrollment
equal	equalled	equalled	equaled
fulfil (U.S. fulfill)	fulfilled	fulfilled	fulfilled
	fulfilment	fulfilment	fulfillment
install	installed	installed	installed
	instalment	instalment	installment
jewel	jewelled	jewelled	jeweled
	jewellery	jewellery	jewelry
label	labelled	labelled	labeled
marshal	marshalled	marshalled	marshaled
program	programmed	programmed	programed
total	totalled	totalled	totaled
tranquil	tranquillity	tranquillity	tranquility
travel	travelled	travelled	traveled
wool	woollen	woollen	woolen
worship	worshipped	worshipped	worshiped

b. Suffixes added to words ending in a silent *e*.

	Oxford	Gage	Webster
acknowledge	acknowledgement	acknowledgment	acknowledgment
judge	judgement	judgment	judgment
like	likeable	likable	likable
live	liveable	livable	livable
sale	saleable	saleable	salable

(*Continued on page 200.*)

	Oxford	Gage	Webster

c. Words ending in *yse* or *yze*.

	Oxford	Gage	Webster
	analyse	analyse	analyze
	catalyse	catalyse	catalyze
	paralyse	paralyse	paralyze

d. Words ending in *or* or *our*.

	Oxford	Gage	Webster
	behaviour	behaviour	behavior
	candour	candour	candor
	colour	colour	color
	endeavour	endeavour	endeavor
	favourite	favourite	favorite
	flavour	flavour	flavor
	glamour	glamour	glamour
	BUT: glamorous	glamorous	glamorous
	harbour	harbour	harbor
	honour	honour	honor
	humour	humour	humor
	BUT: humorous	humorous	humorous
	labour	labour	labor
	neighbour	neighbour	neighbor
	odour	odour	odor
	BUT: odorous	odorous	odorous
	parlour	parlour	parlor
	rumour	rumour	rumor
	savour	savour	savor
	saviour	saviour	savior

e. Words ending in *er* or *re*.

	Oxford	Gage	Webster
	calibre	calibre	caliber
	centre	centre	center
	litre	litre	liter
	lustre	lustre	luster
	manoeuvre	manoeuvre	maneuver
	metre	metre	meter
	sabre	sabre	saber
	theatre	theatre	theater

f. Words ending in *ence* or *ense*.

	Oxford	Gage	Webster
	defence	defence	defense
	licence (noun)	licence (noun)	license
	license (verb)	license (verb)	
	offence	offence	offense
	pretence	pretence	pretense

Oxford	Gage	Webster

g. Other variants.

catalogue	catalogue	catalog
cheque	cheque	check
collectible	**BUT:** collectable	collectible
dependant (noun)	dependant (noun)	dependent
dependent (adj.)	dependent (adj.)	
practice (noun)	practice (noun)	practice
practise (verb)	practise (verb)	

 See the Online Learning Centre at www.mcgrawhill.ca/college/gregg for related weblinks.

SECTION **EIGHT**

Compound Words

COMPOUND NOUNS (¶¶801–810)

COMPOUND VERBS (¶¶811–812)

COMPOUND ADJECTIVES (¶¶813–832)
Basic Rules (¶¶813–815)
Adjective + **Noun** (*as in* short-**term** *note:* ¶816)
Compound With Number or Letter (*as in* **40-hour** *week:* ¶817)
Compound With Noun (*as in* **high school** *graduate:* ¶818)
Proper Name (*as in* **Younge Street** *agencies:* ¶819)
Noun + **Adjective** (*as in* tax-**free** *imports:* ¶820)
Noun + **Participle** (*as in* time-**consuming** *details:* ¶821)
Adjective + **Participle** (*as in* nice-**looking** *layout:* ¶822)
Adjective + **Noun + ED** (*as in* quick-**witted** *assistant:* ¶823)
Adverb + **Participle** (*as in* privately **owned** *stock* and *as in* well-**known** *facts:* ¶824)
Adverb + **Adjective** (*as in* very **exciting** *test results:* ¶825)
Participle + **Adverb** (*as in* warmed-**over** *ideas:* ¶826)
Adjective + **Adjective** (*as in* black **leather** *notebook:* ¶827)
Verb + **Verb** (*as in* stop-and-**go** *traffic:* ¶828)
Verb + **Adverb** (*as in* read-**only** *memory:* ¶829)
Verb + **Noun** (*as in* take-**home** *pay:* ¶830)
Phrasal Compound (*as in* **up-to-date** *accounts:* ¶831)
Suspending Hyphen (¶832)

PREFIXES AND SUFFIXES (¶¶833–846)

COMPOUND COMPUTER TERMS (¶847)

**SOMETIMES ONE WORD,
SOMETIMES TWO WORDS (¶848)**

Some compound words are written as solid words, some are written as separate words, and some are hyphenated. As in other areas of style, authorities do not agree on the rules. Moreover, style is continually changing: many words that used to be hyphenated are now written solid or as separate words. The only complete guide is an up-to-date dictionary. However, a careful reading of the following rules will save you many a trip to the dictionary.

NOTE: The spellings in this section agree with those in the *Gage Canadian Dictionary* (published by Gage Educational Publishing Company, Toronto, Ontario) unless otherwise indicated.

COMPOUND NOUNS

801 Compound nouns follow no regular pattern. Some are written solid, some are spaced, and some are hyphenated.

a.

court order	courtroom	court-martial
cross section	crossroad	cross-reference
eye shadow	eyewitness	eye-opener
free trade	freelance	free-for-all
half size	halfback	half-hour
light bulb	lightweight	light-year
show bill	showroom	show-off
trade name	trademark	trade-in
voice mail	voiceprint	voice-over
water power	waterproof	water-skiing

b. To be sure of the spelling of a compound noun, check a dictionary. If the noun is not listed, the traditional guideline is to treat the elements of the compound as separate words. As an alternative, you may treat the noun the same way that similar compounds appear in the dictionary.

c. For the spelling of compounds in company names, check letterheads for possible variations. (Compare, for example, *North West Life Assurance Company*, *Northwest Airlines*, and *North-West Inspections Ltd.*)

802 Some solid and hyphenated compound nouns closely resemble verb phrases. Be sure, however, to treat the elements in a verb phrase as separate words.

Nouns	Verb Phrases
protect data with regular *backups*	always *back up* the data in the file
a *breakdown* in communications	when communications *break down*
devise another plan as a *fallback*	we can always *fall back* on Plan B
a thorough *follow-up* of the report	to *follow up* on your recommendation
when they give us the *go-ahead*	we can *go ahead* with the project
they have the *know-how*	they *know how* to handle it
after you complete the *logon*	after you *log on* to the program
the *roundup* of local news	be sure to *round up* the crew
let's have a *run-through*	let's *run through* the plan
I was a *standby* on Flight 940	we can't *stand by* and do nothing
need to reduce staff *turnover*	need to *turn over* a new leaf

803 **a.** *Up* **Words.** Compound nouns ending in *up* are either solid or hyphenated. For example:

blowup	break-up	hang-up	smash-up
brushup	call-up	line-up	stick-up
buildup	clean-up	mock-up	tie-up
checkup	close-up	paste-up	toss-up
holdup	cover-up	pile-up	tune-up
hookup	crack-up	punch-up	walk-up
letup	cut-up	set-up	warm-up
lockup	flare-up	shake-up	wind-up
markup	foul-up	shape-up	wrap-up
pickup	freeze-up	slip-up	write-up

b. *Down* **Words.** Most compound nouns ending in *down* are solid. For example:

breakdown	meltdown	shakedown	**BUT:** dressing-down
comedown	rubdown	slowdown	knock-down
countdown	rundown	splashdown	put-down
letdown	showdown	touchdown	
lowdown	shutdown	turndown	

c. *In* **Words.** Compound nouns ending in *in* are typically hyphenated. For example:

break-in	fill-in	shut-in	trade-in
cut-in	lead-in	sit-in	tuck-in
drive-in	run-in	stand-in	walk-in
fade-in	shoo-in	step-in	write-in

d. *Out* **Words.** Compound nouns ending in *out* are either solid or hyphenated. For example:

blackout	hangout	takeout	drop-out
blowout	holdout	tryout	fade-out
breakout	knockout	turnout	fall-out
burnout	layout	walkout	hide-out
buyout	lockout	washout	pay-out
checkout	lookout	whiteout	sell-out
cutout	phaseout	workout	shut-out
farmout	printout	call-out	stand-out
foldout	putout	carry-out	time-out

e. *On* **Words.** Compound nouns ending in *on* are typically hyphenated. For example:

add-on	clip-on	hangers-on	run-on
carry-on	come-on	lookers-on	slip-on
carryings-on	goings-on	put-on	turn-on

f. *Off* **Words.** Compound nouns ending in *off* are either solid or hyphenated. For example:

brushoff	layoff	face-off	show-off
castoff	liftoff	jump-off	shut-off

checkoff	payoff	rip-off	stand-off
cutoff	playoff	run-off	trade-off
kickoff	spinoff	set-off	write-off

g. *Over* **Words.** Compound nouns ending in *over* are either solid or hyphenated. For example:

crossover	leftover	switchover	change-over
flashover	popover	takeover	going-over
hangover	pullover	turnover	once-over
holdover	spillover	walkover	push-over
layover	stopover	carry-over	voice-over

h. *Back* **Words.** Compound nouns ending in *back* are typically solid. For example:

buyback	drawback	hatchback	playback
comeback	feedback	kickback	setback
cutback	flashback	piggyback	throwback

i. *Away* **Words.** These compounds are typically solid. For example:

breakaway	getaway	layaway	stowaway
castaway	giveaway	rollaway	straightaway
cutaway	hideaway	runaway	throwaway

j. **Compounds Ending in** *About,* *Around,* **and** *By.* These compounds are typically solid. For example:

knockabout	roundabout	runaround	passerby
layabout	turnabout	turnaround	standby

804 **a.** Hyphenate a compound noun that lacks a noun as one of its elements.

a free-for-all	a know-it-all	two-by-fours
no get-up-and-go	a lean-to	the well-to-do
give-and-take	a look-alike	a has-been
a go-getter	make-believe	**BUT:** show and tell
a good-for-nothing	merry-go-round	wear and tear

b. Words coined from repeated or rhyming syllables are typically hyphenated. Other coined words may be hyphenated, solid, or written as separate words.

fuddy-duddy	hurry-scurry	**BUT:** eager beaver
goody-goody	namby-pamby	hodgepodge
hocus-pocus	walkie-talkie	mumbo jumbo
hurly-burly	yo-yo	whodunit

c. Some compound nouns that end with a prepositional phrase are hyphenated.

aide-de-camp	joie-de-vivre	**BUT:** bill of lading
ambassador-at-large	lady-in-waiting	line of credit
son-in-law	stick-in-the-mud	play on words
editor-in-chief	stay-at-home	stock in trade

8

805 Treat a compound noun like *problem solving* as two words unless your dictionary specifically shows it as solid or hyphenated. (Most words of this pattern are not shown in a dictionary. However, the solid and hyphenated examples below have been taken from the *Gage Canadian Dictionary*, published by Gage Educational Publishing Company.)

bean counting	cheerleading	troubleshooting
data processing	housewarming	cross-checking
decision making	peacekeeping	feather-bedding
number crunching	skateboarding	loan-sharking
profit sharing	skydiving	name-dropping
programmed learning	storytelling	soul-searching

☞ *For words like* air conditioning, *which are derived from hyphenated infinitives like* air-condition, *see* ¶*812.*

806 Hyphenate two nouns when they signify that one person or one thing has two functions. (See also ¶295b.)

actor-director	dinner-dance	secretary-treasurer
editor-publisher	owner-manager	photocopier-printer

807 Compound nouns that have a single letter as their first element are either hyphenated or written as two words.

A-frame	f-stop	I-beam	U-turn
D-Day	G-suit	T-bar	V neck

NOTE: The term *X ray* (which is two words when used as a noun) is hyphenated when used as a verb or an adjective. (See also ¶815a.)

808 **a.** Do not hyphenate civil titles of two or more words.

the chief of police	High Commissioner	Governor General
a general manager	consul general	**BUT:** lieutenant-governor

b. Hyphenate military commissioned ranks in the Land and Air Command. With one exception, *Rear-Admiral*, Maritime Command ranks are not hyphenated.

Lieutenant-Colonel	Major-General	**BUT:** 2nd Lieutenant
Brigadier-General	Commander-in-Chief	Vice Admiral

c. Hyphenate compound titles containing *vice, ex,* and *elect.*

Vice-President	ex-Mayor White	Chairman-elect Lai
Vice-Chancellor	ex-President Mohtadi	Premier-elect Harris

NOTE: Also use a hyphen when *ex* is attached to a noun (for example, *ex-wife, ex-convict*), but omit the hyphen in Latin phrases (for example, *ex officio, ex cathedra, ex libris*).

☞ *For the capitalization of titles with* ex *and* elect, *see* ¶¶*317 and 363.*
 For the correct usage of ex, *see the entry for* Ex-Former *in Section 11.*

809 **a.** The generic use of such compound nouns as *businessmen, manpower, man-hours, alderman, etc.,* is now considered unacceptable to many people who feel that the masculine bias of these terms makes them unsuitable. Therefore, they should be avoided whenever possible. The following list suggests appropriate alternatives.

In Place of the Generic Term	Use
layman	layperson
businessmen	business owners, business executives, business managers, business people
alderman	city councillor, ward representative
mankind	people, humanity, the human race, human beings
man-hours	worker-hours
manpower	work force, human resources, staff
salesmen	salespeople, sales representatives, salespersons, salesclerks, sales staff, sales force, sales associates
foremen	supervisors
policemen	police officers
mailmen	mail carriers
workmen	workers

b. Whenever possible, replace a word like *salesmanship* with an alternative expression (for example, *selling skills*). However, words such as *craftsmanship, workmanship, sportsmanship, horsemanship, brinkmanship,* and *one-upmanship* are still widely used because of the difficulty in devising alternative expressions.

c. When naming a job or role, avoid the use of compound terms ending in *man* or *woman* unless the term refers to a specific person whose gender is known.

There are ten candidates seeking election to the City *Council.* (**NOT:** . . . seeking election as *aldermen.*)

BUT: I was very impressed by *Councilwoman* Schroeder of Ward IV.

Who will be appointed as *head* of the committee? **OR** Who will be appointed to *chair* the committee? (**NOT:** . . . appointed *chairman* of the committee?)

BUT: Robert Haas has been appointed *chairman* of the committee.

NOTE: Words like *chairperson* and *spokesperson* have been coined as a means of avoiding the generic use of masculine compound nouns. Personal taste or institutional policy will dictate whether to use these terms or not.

☞ *See ¶840 for alternatives to words ending with feminine suffixes.*

810 Terms like *doctor, lawyer,* and *nurse* are generic—that is, they apply equally to women and men. Therefore, do not use compound nouns like *woman lawyer* and *male nurse* unless there is a legitimate reason for making a distinction according to gender.

Next Wednesday there will be a seminar on the special problems facing *women lawyers* in the courtroom.

(Continued on page 208.)

☞ *For capitalization of hyphenated compound nouns: see ¶363.*
For plurals of compound nouns: see ¶¶611–613.
For possessives of compound nouns: see ¶¶634–635.

COMPOUND VERBS

811 a. Compound verbs are usually hyphenated or solid.

to baby-sit	to ghost-write	to backpack	to moonlight
to back-order	to off-load	to buttonhole	to pinpoint
to colour-code	to second-guess	to download	to proofread
to double-check	to short-change	to downsize	to sidetrack
to double-click	to soft-pedal	to highlight	to spotlight
to fine-tune	to window-shop	to mastermind	to troubleshoot

NOTE: If you try to check the spelling of a compound verb in a dictionary and do not find the verb listed, *hyphenate the components.*

b. Do not hyphenate verb phrase combinations such as *make up, slow down, tie in.* (See ¶802 for examples.)

812 a. If the infinitive form of a compound verb has a hyphen, retain the hyphen in the other forms of the verb. (See ¶812b for one type of exception.)

Would you like to *air-condition* your entire house?
The theatre was not *air-conditioned.*
We need an *air-conditioning* expert to advise us.

You need to *double-space* all these reports.
Please *double-space* this letter.
This material should not be *double-spaced.*
BUT: Leave a *double space* between paragraphs. (No hyphen in *double space* as a compound noun.)

b. The gerund derived from a hyphenated compound verb requires no hyphen unless it is followed by an object. (See ¶135a.)

Dry cleaning is the best way to treat this garment.
BUT: *Dry-cleaning* this *sweater* will not remove the spot.

Air conditioning is no longer as expensive as it used to be.
BUT: In *air-conditioning* an *office,* you must take more than space into account.

Spot checking is all we have time for.
BUT: In *spot-checking* the *data,* I found some disturbing errors.

COMPOUND ADJECTIVES

No aspect of style causes greater difficulty than compound adjectives. When such adjectives are shown hyphenated in the dictionary, you can assume only that the expressions are hyphenated when they occur directly *before* nouns. When the same combinations of words fall elsewhere in sentences, the uses or omissions of hyphens depend on how the words are used.

For the basic rules, see ¶¶813–815. For detailed comments, see the following paragraphs:

Adjective + **Noun** (*as in* short-**term** *note:* ¶816)
Compound With Number or Letter (*as in* **40-hour** *week:* ¶817)
Compound With Noun (*as in* **high school** *graduate:* ¶818)
Proper Name (*as in* **Yonge Street** *agencies:* ¶819)
Noun + **Adjective** (*as in* tax-**free** *imports:* ¶820)
Noun + **Participle** (*as in* time-**consuming** *details:* ¶821)
Adjective + **Participle** (*as in* nice-**looking** *layout:* ¶822)
Adjective + **Noun** + **ED** (*as in* quick-**witted** *assistant:* ¶823)
Adverb + **Participle** (*as in* privately **owned** *stock* and *as in* well-**known** *facts:* ¶824)
Adverb + **Adjective** (*as in* very **exciting** *test results:* ¶825)
Participle + **Adverb** (*as in* warmed-**over** *ideas:* ¶826)
Adjective + **Adjective** (*as in* black **leather** *notebook:* ¶827)
Verb + **Verb** (*as in* stop-and-**go** *traffic:* ¶828)
Verb + **Adverb** (*as in* read-**only** *memory:* ¶829)
Verb + **Noun** (*as in* take-**home** *pay:* ¶830)
Phrasal Compound (*as in* **up-to-date** *accounts:* ¶831)
Suspending Hyphen (¶832)

NOTE: If you try to check the spelling of a compound adjective in a dictionary and do not find it listed, match up the components with one of the patterns shown above and follow the standard style for that pattern.

Basic Rules

813 A compound adjective consists of two or more words that function as a unit and express a single thought. These one-thought modifiers are derived from (and take the place of) adjective phrases and clauses. In the following examples, the left column shows the original phrase or clause; the right column shows the compound adjective.

Adjective Phrase or Clause	Compound Adjective
Terminals *installed at the point of sale*	*point-of-sale* terminals
a career *moving along a fast track*	a *fast-track* career
a woman *who speaks quietly*	a *quiet-spoken* woman
an actor *who is well known*	a *well-known* actor
a conference *held at a high level*	a *high-level* conference
a building *ten storeys high*	a *ten-storey* building
a report *that is up to date*	an *up-to-date* report
an article *that is as long as a book*	a *book-length* article
an environment *where people work under high pressure*	a *high-pressure* environment
a guarantee *to give you your money back*	a *money-back* guarantee
a PC *that delivers a high level of performance, carries a low cost, and is easy to use*	a *high-performance, low-cost, easy-to-use* PC

NOTE: In the process of becoming compound adjectives, the adjective phrases and clauses are usually reduced to a few essential words. In addition, these words frequently undergo a change in form (for example, *ten*

(*Continued on page 210.*)

storeys high becomes *ten-storey*); sometimes they are put in inverted order (for example, *free of duty* becomes *duty-free*); sometimes they are simply extracted from the phrase or clause without any change in form (for example, *well-known*, *high-level*).

814 Hyphenate the elements of a compound adjective that occurs *before* a noun. (**REASON:** The words that make up the compound adjective are not in their normal order or a normal form and require hyphens to hold them together.)

> *high-tech* equipment (equipment *that reflects a high level of technology*)
>
> a *worst-case* scenario (a scenario *based on the worst case that could occur*)
>
> a *$40 000-a-year* salary (a salary *of $40 000 a year*)
>
> *long-range* plans (plans *projected over a long range of time*)
>
> *machine-readable* copy (copy *readable by a machine*)
>
> an *eye-catching* display (a display *that catches the eye*)
>
> a *high-ranking* official (an official *who ranks high in the organization*)
>
> *same-day* service (service *completed the same day you bring the item in*)
>
> *bottom-line* results (the results *shown on the bottom line of a financial statement*)

EXCEPTIONS: A number of compounds like *real estate* and *high school* do not need hyphens when used as adjectives before a noun. (See ¶818.)

815 a. When these expressions occur *elsewhere in the sentence*, drop the hyphen if the individual words occur in a normal order and in a normal form. (In such cases the expression no longer functions as a compound adjective.)

Before the Noun	Elsewhere in Sentence
an *X-ray* treatment	This condition can be treated by *X ray*. (Object of preposition.)
an *up-to-date* report	Please bring the report *up to date*. (Prepositional phrase.)
a *follow-up* letter	Let's *follow up* at once with a letter. (Verb + adverb.)
a *high-level* decision	The decision must be made at a *high level*. (Object of preposition.)
a *never-to-be-forgotten book*	Your latest book is *never to be forgotten*. (Adverb + infinitive phrase.)
an *off-the-record* comment	The next comment is *off the record*. (Prepositional phrase.)
a *no-nonsense* attitude	Marion will tolerate *no nonsense* from you. (Object of verb.)
a *thank-you* note	We *thank you* for your contribution. (Object of verb.)
a *low-key* sales approach	Christopher pitches his sales approach in a *low key*. (Object of preposition.)
a *cause-and-effect* relationship	Is there a relationship of *cause and effect* in this case? (Object of preposition.)

b. When these expressions occur elsewhere in the sentence *but are in an inverted word order or an altered form,* retain the hyphen.

Before the Noun	Elsewhere in Sentence
a *tax-exempt* purchase	The purchase was *tax-exempt.*
	BUT: The purchase was *exempt from taxes.*
government-owned lands	These lands are *government-owned.*
	BUT: These lands are *owned by the government.*
a *friendly-looking* salesclerk	That salesclerk is *friendly-looking.*
	BUT: The salesclerk *looks friendly.*

NOTE: The following kinds of compound adjectives almost always need to be hyphenated:

☞ *Noun + adjective (for example,* tax-exempt*): see ¶820.*

Noun + participle (for example, government-owned*): see ¶821.*

Adjective + participle (for example, friendly-looking*): see ¶822.*

Adjective + noun + ed (for example, high-priced*): see ¶823.*

Adjective + Noun (see also ¶¶817–819)

816 a. Hyphenate an adjective and a noun when these elements serve as a compound modifier *before* a noun. Do not hyphenate these elements when they play a normal role *elsewhere in the sentence* (for example, as the object of a preposition or of a verb). However, if the expression continues to function as a compound adjective, retain the hyphen.

Before the Noun	Elsewhere in Sentence
high-speed printers	These printers run at *high speed.* (Object of preposition.)
a *plain-paper* fax	Please be sure to order a fax that uses *plain paper.* (Object of verb)
red-carpet treatment	They plan to roll out the *red carpet.* (Object of infinitive.)
a *closed-door* discussion	The discussion was held behind *closed doors.* (Object of preposition.)
an *all-day* seminar	The seminar will last *all day.* (Normal adverbial phrase.)
a *long-term* investment in bonds	This investment in bonds runs for a *long term.* (Object of preposition.)
	BUT: This investment in bonds is *long-term.* (Compound adjective.)
a *part-time* job	This job is *part-time.* (Compound adjective.)
	I work *part-time.* (Compound adverb.)
	I travel *part of the time.* (Normal adverbial phrase.)

NOTE: Combinations involving comparative or superlative adjectives plus nouns follow the same pattern.

(Continued on page 212.)

Before the Noun	Elsewhere in Sentence
a *larger-size* shirt	He wears a *larger size*. (Object of verb.)
the *finest-quality* goods	These goods are of the *finest quality*. (Object of preposition.)

b. A few compound adjectives in this category are now written solid—for example, *a commonplace event, a freshwater pond, a widespread belief*.

Compound With Number or Letter

817 a. When a number and a noun form a one-thought modifier *before* a noun (as in *six-storey building*), make the noun singular and hyphenate the expression. When the expression has a normal form and a normal function *elsewhere in the sentence*, do not hyphenate it.

Before the Noun	Elsewhere in Sentence
a *one-way* street	a street that runs only *one way*
a *first-person* account	an account written in the *first person*
a *two-piece* suit	a suit consisting of *two pieces*
a *four-colour* illustration	an illustration printed in *four colours*
a *5-litre* container	a container that holds *5 litres*
an *8-foot* ceiling	a ceiling *8 feet* above the floor
a *20-year* mortgage	a mortgage running for *20 years*
an *$85-a-month* charge	a charge of *$85 a month*
a *100-metre* sprint	a sprint of *100 metres*
an $8\frac{1}{2}$- *by 11-inch* book (see ¶832)	a book $8\frac{1}{2}$ *by 11 inches*
an *80-kilometre-an-hour* speed limit	a speed limit of *80 kilometres an hour*
a *5-centimetre-thick* panel	a panel *5 centimetres thick*
24-hour-a-day service	service *24 hours a day*
600-dpi graphics	graphics composed of *600 dpi* (dots per inch)

EXCEPTIONS: a *15 percent* decline, a *$4 million* profit, a *twofold* increase (**BUT:** a *12-fold* increase).

☞ *For the hyphenation of fractional expressions serving as compound adjectives (like half-dozen or 1/4-inch), see* ¶427a.

NOTE: A hyphenated compound adjective and an unhyphenated possessive expression often provide *alternative* ways of expressing the same thought. Do not use both styles together.

a *one-year* extension	a *two-week* vacation
OR: a *one year's* extension	**OR:** a *two weeks'* vacation
(**BUT NOT:** a one-year's extension)	(**BUT NOT:** a two-weeks' vacation)

b. Hyphenate compound adjectives involving a number and *odd* or *plus*.

The embezzlement occurred some *twenty-odd* years ago.

I now give my age simply as *forty-plus*.

c. Compound adjectives involving two numbers (as in ratios and scores) are expressed as follows:

a *50-50* (**OR** *fifty-fifty*) chance a *1000-to-1* possibility
20/20 (**OR** *twenty-twenty*) vision a *3-to-1* ratio **OR** a *3:1* ratio
an *18-7* victory over the Lions **BUT:** a ratio of *3 to 1*

☞ *See also ¶¶450–451.*

d. Other compound expressions involving a number or letter are expressed as follows:

the Title IX heading in *A-one (A1)* condition
the cost of *Class A* materials a call for blood group *AB*
my grade of *B plus (B+)* **BUT:** a *B-plus (B+)* student
a *number-one (No. 1)* priority **BUT:** our goal is to be *number one*

Compound With Noun

818 **a.** A number of adjective-noun combinations (such as *real estate* or *social studies*) and noun-noun combinations (such as *life insurance* or *money market*) are actually well-established compound nouns serving as adjectives. Unlike *short-term*, *low-risk*, and the examples in ¶816, these expressions refer to well-known concepts or institutions. Because they are easily grasped as a unit, they *do not* require a hyphen.

accounts payable records *life insurance* policy *public relations* adviser
branch office reports *mass production* techniques *real estate* agent
high school diploma *money market* funds *social studies* text
income tax return *nuclear energy* plant *word processing* centre

EXCEPTION: a *mail-order* business

NOTE: When dictionaries and style manuals do not provide guidance on a specific adjective-noun combination, consider whether the expression is more like a well-known compound such as *income tax* or whether it is more like *short-term*. Then space the combination or hyphenate it accordingly.

b. When a noun-noun combination involves two words of relatively equal rank, hyphenate the combination. (See also ¶¶295, 806.)

input-output device the *space-time* continuum an *air-sea* search
cost-benefit analyses *labour-management* relations a *sand-gravel* mixture

c. As a general rule, when a compound noun is used as a compound adjective, the decision to hyphenate or not will depend on how familiar you think your reader is with the term in question. Thus a term like *small business owner* would not be hyphenated if you feel your reader is familiar with the concept of *small business*.

d. A compound noun like *French Canadian* is hyphenated when used as an adjective. (See ¶348, note.)

Proper Name

819 **a.** Do not hyphenate the elements in a proper name used as an adjective.

a *Supreme Court* decision a *Lakeside Drive* location
Sears Eighth Avenue store *Mickey Mouse* procedures

b. When two or more distinct proper names are combined to form a one-thought modifier, use a hyphen to connect the elements.

a *German-Canadian* restaurant the cuisine is *German-Canadian*
the *Thunder Bay-Montreal-Quebec City* flight (no hyphens within *Thunder Bay* and *Quebec City*) **BUT:** the flight to *Thunder Bay, Montreal,* and *Quebec City*
the *Borden-Carleton* span of the Confederation Bridge

NOTE: If one of the elements already contains a hyphen, use an en dash to connect the two proper names.

the *Toronto–Ottawa-Hull* bus trip the *Banff-Jasper–Golden* area

Noun + Adjective

820 **a.** When a compound adjective consists of a noun plus an adjective, hyphenate this combination whether it appears before or after the noun. (See ¶815b.)

brand-new	knee-deep	scot-free	user-friendly
bone-dry	paper-thin	sky-high	wafer-thin
capital-intensive	pitch-dark	tax-exempt	weather-bound
class-conscious	power-hungry	tone-deaf	world-weary
fuel-efficient	rock-bottom	top-heavy	year-round

Your suggestion is ingenious but not *cost-effective.*

You are trying to solve an *age-old* problem.

She wants everything to be *letter-perfect.*

We import these *water-repellent* fabrics *duty-free.*

I want a computer that is *IBM-compatible.*

NOTE: Retain the hyphen in a noun + adjective combination when the expression functions as an adverb rather than as an adjective.

ADJECTIVE: Please call me on my *toll-free* number.
ADVERB: You can always call me *toll-free.*

ADJECTIVE: The information is encoded on *paper-thin* wafers.
ADVERB: The wafers have to be sliced *paper-thin.*

b. A few words in this category are now written solid. For example:

-wide: citywide, nationwide, storewide, worldwide **BUT:** country-wide

-proof: bombproof, bulletproof, burglarproof, childproof, fireproof, rainproof, shatterproof, shockproof, waterproof, weatherproof

-worthy: airworthy, blameworthy, newsworthy, noteworthy, praiseworthy, roadworthy, seaworthy, trustworthy

-long: agelong, daylong, lifelong, nightlong, yearlong

8

Noun + Participle

821 **a.** When a compound adjective consists of a noun plus a participle, hyphenate this combination whether it appears before or after the noun. (See ¶815b.)

attention-getting	interest-bearing	mind-boggling	tailor-made
coin-operated	law-abiding	money-making	tax-sheltered
eye-catching	machine-oriented	panic-stricken	time-consuming
face-saving	market-tested	snow-covered	Windows-based

The *number-crunching* software uses *eye-popping* graphics.

Computer-aided design was one of the great breakthroughs of the 1980s.

Buying *custom-tailored* suits can easily become habit-forming.

b. When an open compound noun is combined with a participle to form a one-thought modifier, insert a hyphen only before the participle.

provincial *government-owned* site	a *Pulitzer Prize-winning* play
a *Labour Department-sponsored* conference	*health care-related* expenditures
a *London, Ontario-based* consortium	*solar energy-oriented* research

c. A few words in this category are now written solid. For example:

hand-: handmade, handwoven, handwritten **BUT:** hand-picked

heart-: heartbreaking, heartbroken, heartfelt
BUT: heart-rending, heart-stricken

home-: homebound, homebred, homemade, homespun
BUT: home-grown

Adjective + Participle (see also ¶824b)

822 **a.** When a compound adjective consists of an adjective plus a participle, hyphenate this combination whether it appears before or after the noun. (See ¶815b.)

clean-cut	high-ranking	ready-made
friendly-looking (see ¶824a)	long-standing	rough-hewn
hard-hitting	odd-sounding	sweet-smelling

EXCEPTIONS: *easygoing, hardworking*

I'm *half-tempted* to apply for the Singapore opening myself.

He is a *smooth-talking* operator who never delivers what he promises.

Betty was anything but *soft-spoken* in arguing against the new procedures.

b. Retain the hyphen even when a comparative or superlative adjective is combined with a participle—for example, *nicer-looking, best-looking, oddest-sounding, better-tasting.*

As the *highest-ranking* official present, Mrs. Egan took charge of the meeting.

This year's brochure is *better-looking* than last year's.

Why can't we attract *better-qualified* people to our company?

Adjective + Noun + *ED*

823 a. When a compound adjective consists of an adjective plus a noun plus *ed*, hyphenate this combination whether it appears before or after the noun. (See ¶815b.)

broad-based	hard-wired	open-ended
clear-eyed	heavy-armed	public-spirited
coarse-grained	high-priced	quick-tempered
deep-seated	light-fingered	right-angled
double-breasted	like-minded	short-staffed
empty-handed	long-winded	snow-capped
fair-minded	loose-jointed	two-faced
full-bodied	low-pitched	**BUT:** bareheaded
good-natured	one-sided	farsighted

I'm too *old-fashioned* to be that *broad-minded*.

He's too *big-hearted* to be that *small-minded*.

His interview was seen on *closed-captioned* television last Saturday.

b. Retain the hyphen in comparative or superlative forms—for example, *smaller-sized, highest-priced, best-natured.*

Our *higher-priced* articles sold well this year.

These goods are *higher-priced* than the samples you showed me.

Fred is the *longest-winded* speaker I ever heard.

Fred's speech was the *longest-winded* I ever heard.

c. Compound adjectives ending in *sized* (such as *pint-sized, pocket-sized, life-sized,* and *king-sized*) may also be written without the final *d*.

It was a *full-size (full-sized)* TV screen.

A *king-size (king-sized)* bed is about 200 cm long.

Adverb + Participle (see also ¶825)

824 a. Do not hyphenate an adverb-participle combination if the adverb ends in *ly*.

a *poorly constructed* house	a *wholly owned* corporation
a *highly valued* employee	a *newly formed* division
a *clearly defined* set of terms	an *extremely tiring* trip

NOTE: Hyphenate adjectives ending in *ly* when they are used with participles. (See ¶822.)

a *friendly-sounding* voice	a *motherly-looking* woman

☞ *To distinguish between adjectives and adverbs ending in* ly, *see* ¶1069.

b. Other adverb-participle compounds are hyphenated *before* the noun. When these same combinations occur in the predicate, drop the hyphen if the participle is part of the verb.

Before the Noun	Elsewhere in Sentence
a *well-known* consultant	This consultant *is* well *known*.
much-needed reforms	These reforms *were* much *needed*.
the *above-mentioned* facts	These facts *were mentioned* above.
a *long-remembered* tribute	Today's tribute *will be* long *remembered*.

However, if the participle does not become part of the verb and continues to function with the adverb as a one-thought modifier in the predicate, retain the hyphen.

Before the Noun	Elsewhere in Sentence
a *well-behaved* child	The child is *well-behaved*.
a *clear-cut* position	Their position was *clear-cut*.
a *well-intentioned* proposal	The proposal was *well-intentioned*.

NOTE: You couldn't say, "The child is behaved" or "Their position was cut" or "The proposal was intentioned." Since the participle is not part of the verb, it must be treated as part of a compound adjective. Compare the use of *fast-moving* in the following examples.

Before the Noun	Elsewhere in Sentence
a *fast-moving* narrative	The narrative is *fast-moving*.
	BUT: The narrative *is* fast *moving* toward a climax.

c. Hyphenated adverb-participle combinations like those in *b* retain the hyphen even when the adverb is in the comparative or superlative.

a *better-known* brand	the *hardest-working* assistant
the *best-behaved* child	a *faster-moving* stock clerk

Adverb + Adjective

825 a. A number of adverb-adjective combinations closely resemble the adverb-participle combinations described in ¶824. However, since an adverb normally modifies an adjective, do not use a hyphen to connect these words.

a *not too interesting* report	a *very moving* experience
a *rather irritating* delay	a *quite trying* day

NOTE: In these examples you can omit the adverb and speak of an *interesting* report, a *moving* experience, and a *trying* day; hence no hyphen is needed. However, in the second set of examples in ¶824b, you cannot speak of a *behaved* child or an *intentioned* proposal; for that reason, the adverb preceding *behaved* and *intentioned* must be linked by a hyphen.

b. Do not hyphenate comparative and superlative forms where the adverbs *more*, *most*, *less*, and *least* are combined with an adjective.

a *more determined* person	a *less complicated* transaction
the *most exciting* event	the *least interesting* lecture

Participle + Adverb

826 Hyphenate a participle-adverb combination *before* the noun but not when it occurs elsewhere in the sentence.

Before the Noun	Elsewhere in Sentence
worn-out equipment	The equipment was *worn out*.
a *scaled-down* proposal	The proposal must be *scaled down*.
baked-on enamel	This enamel has been *baked on*.
a *cooling-off* period	Don't negotiate without *cooling off* first.
unheard-of bargains	These bargains were *unheard of*.
warmed-over ideas	His ideas were *warmed over* for the occasion.

☞ *See also the examples in ¶831.*

Adjective + Adjective

827 **a.** Do not hyphenate independent adjectives preceding a noun.

> a *long* and *tiring* trip (*long* and *tiring* each modify *trip*)

> a *warm, enthusiastic* reception (*warm* and *enthusiastic* each modify *reception;* a comma marks the omission of *and*)

> a *distinguished public* orator (*public* modifies *orator; distinguished* modifies *public orator*)

☞ *For the use of commas with adjectives, see ¶¶168–171.*

b. In a few special cases, two adjectives joined by *and* are hyphenated because they function as one-thought modifiers. These, however, are rare exceptions to the rule stated in *a.*

a *cut-and-dried* presentation	an *out-and-out* lie
a *hard-and-fast* rule	an *up-and-coming* lawyer
a *high-and-mighty* attitude	a *rough-and-tumble* environment
an *open-and-shut* case	a *sweet-and-sour* sauce

> Henry views the matter in *black-and-white* terms. (A one-thought modifier.)

> **BUT:** Why not pack your *black and white* dress? (Two independent adjectives.)

c. Hyphenate two adjectives that express the dual nature of the thing that they refer to. (See also ¶¶295b, 806.)

> a *true-false* test   a *compound-complex* sentence
> **BUT:** a *bittersweet* ending

d. Hyphenate expressions such as *blue-black, green-grey, snow-white,* and *red-hot* before and after a noun. However, do not hyphenate expressions such as *bluish green, dark grey,* or *bright red* (where the first word clearly modifies the second).

> Sales have been *red-hot* this quarter.   Her dress was *bluish green*.

8

Verb + Verb

828 a. Hyphenate a compound adjective consisting of two verbs (sometimes joined by *and* or *or*) when the adjective appears *before* the noun.

a *hit-or-miss* marketing strategy   the *cut-and-paste* procedure
a *make-or-break* financial decision   *point-and-click* navigating

b. Do not hyphenate these elements when they play a normal function *elsewhere in the sentence*. However, retain the hyphen if these expressions continue to function as a compound adjective.

They're never sure whether they'll *hit or miss* their marketing targets.
BUT: Their marketing strategy can best be described as *hit-or-miss*.

Verb + Adverb

829 a. Hyphenate a compound adjective consisting of a verb plus an adverb when the adjective appears *before* the noun.

our *break-even* point   a *pop-up* menu
a *read-only* memory   a *zip-out* lining
a *get-well* card   a *tow-away* zone
a *drive-through* window   *run-on* sentences
a *twist-off* cap   a *mail-in* rebate

b. Do not hyphenate these elements when they play a normal function *elsewhere in the sentence*.

At what point will we *break even*?   Does this lining *zip out*?

Verb + Noun

830 a. Hyphenate a compound adjective consisting of a verb plus a noun (or pronoun) when the adjective appears *before* the noun.

take-home pay   a *show-me* kind of attitude
a *take-charge* kind of person   **BUT:** a *turnkey* computer system
a *thank-you* note   a *lacklustre* approach

b. Do not hyphenate these elements when they play a normal function *elsewhere in the sentence*.

In terms of salary it's not so much what you gross as it is what you *take home*.
Betsy is inclined to *take charge* of any situation in which she finds herself.

Phrasal Compound

831 a. Hyphenate phrases used as compound adjectives *before* a noun. Do not hyphenate such phrases when they occur normally elsewhere in the sentence.

(Continued on page 220.)

Before the Noun	Elsewhere in Sentence
down-to-earth projections	These projections appear to be *down to earth*.
on-the-job training	I got my training *on the job*.
a *well-thought-out* plan	Our plan was *well thought out*.
an *in-depth* analysis	Carpentier has analysed the subject *in depth*.
an *out-of-the-way* location	Why is the shopping mall so far *out of the way*?
over-the-counter stocks	These stocks are sold only *over the counter*.
an *above-average* rating	Our unit's performance was rated *above average*.
below-the-line charges	These charges will show up *below the line*.
middle-of-the-road view	His view is not far from the *middle of the road*.
before-tax earnings	What were our earnings *before taxes*?
after-dinner speeches	Speeches *after dinner* ought to be prohibited.
around-the-clock service	We provide order service *around the clock*.
across-the-board cuts	The CEO wants budget cuts *across the board*.
behind-the-scenes talks	Contract talks are going on *behind the scenes*.
a *state-of-the-art* model	This model reflects the current *state of the art*.
a *change-of-address* form	Please show your *change of address*.
a *matter-of-fact* approach	Jan accepted the situation as a *matter of fact*.
made-to-order wall units	These wall units were *made to order*.
a *pay-as-you-go* tax plan	The new tax plan requires you to *pay as you go*.
a *would-be* expert	Roy hoped he *would be* accepted as an expert.
bumper-to-bumper traffic	The traffic stood *bumper to bumper*.
a *case-by-case* analysis	We must resolve these problems *case by case*.
a *by-invitation-only* seminar	Attendance at the seminar is *by invitation only*.
a *$150 000-a-year* fee	Our legal fees run about *$150 000 a year*.
a *nine-year-old* girl	Michelle is only *nine years old*.
BUT: a *9½-year-old* girl	Michelle is only *9½ years old*. (See ¶428a.)

(**NOT:** a nine-and-a-half-year-old girl)

b. When two nouns joined by *and* are used as a compound adjective before a noun, hyphenate the phrase.

a *town-and-gown* conflict	a *trial-and-error* approach
a *chicken-and-egg* situation	a *mom-and-pop* operation
a *life-and-death* matter	a *cause-and-effect* hypothesis
bread-and-butter issues	a *cloak-and-dagger* operation

c. As a rule, do not hyphenate foreign phrases used as adjectives before a noun. (See also ¶287.)

an *ad hoc* committee	an *ex officio* member
an *à la carte* menu	a *pro rata* assessment
a *bona fide* transaction	a *per diem* fee

EXCEPTIONS: an *ad-lib* speech, a *laissez-faire* economic policy

d. When a compound modifier consists of two or more hyphenated phrases, separate the phrases with a comma.

an *all-out, no-holds-barred* strategy

the *first-in, first-out* method of accounting

a *first-come, first-served* policy of seating

a *chin-up, back-straight, stomach-in* posture

an *on-again, off-again* wedding

e. Hyphenate repeated or rhyming words used before a noun.

a *go-go* attitude   a *teeny-weeny* salary increase

a *hush-hush* plan   a *topsy-turvy* world

Suspending Hyphen

832 **a.** When a series of hyphenated adjectives has a common basic element and it is shown only with the last term, insert a suspending hyphen after each of the incomplete adjectives to indicate a relationship with the last term.

long- and short-term securities $8\frac{1}{2}$- *by 11-inch* paper

private- and public-sector partnerships   *10- and 20-year* bonds

single-, double-, or triple-spaced copy   *a three- or four-colour* cover

ice- and snow-packed roads   *open- and closed-door* sessions

b. Use one space after each suspending hyphen unless a comma is required at that point.

a *six- to eight-week* delay   *3-, 5-, and 8-litre* buckets

a *10- to 12-hour* trip   *6-, 12-, and 24-month* terms

c. When two or more solid compound adjectives with a common element are used together (for example, *lightweight* and *heavyweight*) and the common element is shown only with the last term, use a suspending hyphen with the incomplete forms to indicate a relationship with the common element.

This product is available in *light-* and *heavyweight* versions.

Please provide *day-* and *nighttime* phone numbers.

NOTE: Repeat the common element with each word if the use of the suspending hyphen looks odd or confusing; for example, *boyfriend or girlfriend* (rather than *boy- or girlfriend*).

☞ *See ¶833d–e for the use of a suspending hyphen with prefixes or suffixes.*

PREFIXES AND SUFFIXES

833 **a.** In general, do not use a hyphen to set off a prefix at the beginning of a word or a suffix at the end of a word. (See ¶808c for two exceptions: *ex-* and *-elect*.)

*after*taste	*out*run	*backward*
*ambi*dextrous	*over*confident	*booklet*

(*Continued on page 222.*)

*ante*date	*para*medical	censor*ship*
*anti*trust (see ¶834)	*poly*syllabic	change*able*
*circum*location	*post*graduate	child*like*
*counter*balance	*pre*requisite	convert*ible*
*de*centralize	*pro*active	edge*wise*
*dis*appear	*re*organize	fifty*ish*
*extra*marital	*retro*active	fire*proof*
*fore*front	*sub*division	free*dom*
*hyper*sensitive	*super*natural	friend*ly*
*il*legal	*supra*national	hand*some*
*im*material	*trans*continental	happi*ness*
*in*defensible	*ultra*conservative	home*stead*
*infra*structure	*un*accustomed	induce*ment*
*inter*provincial	*under*current	meaning*ful*
*intro*version	*up*shot	misspell*ing*
*micro*processor	**BUT:** *audio*-visual	mono*gram*
*mid*stream	*by*-line	patron*age*
*mini*bike	*co*-author (see ¶835)	photo*graph*
*mis*spell	*de*-icer	thank*less*
*mono*syllable	*non*-essential	trust*worthy*
*multi*processing	*post*-operative	upper*most*
*off*beat	*semi*-annual	world*wide*

b. Whenever necessary, use a hyphen to prevent one word from being mistaken for another. (See ¶837.)

lock the *coop*	*multiply* by 12	a *unionized* factory
join a *co-op*	a *multi-ply* fabric	an *un-ionized* substance

c. As a rule, when adding a prefix to a hyphenated or spaced compound word, use a hyphen after the prefix.

pre-high school texts	*non*-interest-bearing notes
post-bread-winning years	*non*-computer-literate adults
ex-attorney general	*non*-civil service position

EXCEPTIONS: unair-conditioned, unself-conscious

d. When two or more prefixes have a common element and this element is shown only with the final prefix, insert a suspending hyphen after each of the unattached prefixes to indicate a relationship with the common element.

pre- and *post*natal care	*maxi-*, *midi-*, and *mini*skirts
up- and *down*hill slopes	*inter-* and *intra*office networks
pro- and *anti*nuclear issues	*over-* and *under*qualified job applicants

e. When two or more suffixes have a common element, it is possible to leave one of the suffixes unattached and insert a suspending hyphen to indicate the relationship with the common element. To avoid confusion or awkwardness, it is usually better to repeat the common element with each suffix.

AWKWARD: I thought Nancy's reaction was more *thoughtless* than *-ful.*
BETTER: I thought Nancy's reaction was more *thoughtless* than *thoughtful.*

8

AWKWARD: I would characterize his behaviour as *childlike* rather than *-ish*.
BETTER: I would characterize his behaviour as *childlike* rather than *childish*.

834 When the prefix ends with *a* or *i* and the base word begins with a vowel, use a hyphen after the prefix to prevent misreading.

anti-aircraft	intra-abdominal	semi-annual
anti-inflationary	ultra-ambitious	semi-independent

835 **a.** When the prefix ends with *e* and the base word begins with *e*, the hyphen is usually added.

de-emphasize	pre-empt	re-educate	re-entry
de-escalate	pre-engineered	re-elect	re-establish
pre-eminent	pre-existing	re-enact	re-examine

b. In most cases a hyphen follows co.

co-author	co-executor	co-partner	**BUT:** coefficient
co-chair	co-exist	co-pilot	cohabit
co-education	co-ordinate	co-worker	cosignatory

836 **a.** Use a hyphen after *self* when it serves as a prefix.

self-addressed	self-evident	self-paced	self-supporting
self-confidence	self-help	self-serving	self-taught
self-educated	self-image	self-starter	self-worth

b. Omit the hyphen when *self* serves as the base word and is followed by a suffix.

selfish	selfhood	selfless	selfsame

837 As a rule, the prefix *re* (meaning "again") should not be followed by a hyphen. A few words require the hyphen so that they can be distinguished from other words with the same spelling but a different meaning.

to *re-collect* the slips	to *recollect* the mistake
to *re-cover* a chair	to *recover* from an illness
to *re-form* the class	to *reform* a sinner
she *re-marked* the ticket	as he *remarked* to me
to *re-press* the jacket	to *repress* one's emotions
to *re-sort* the cards	to *resort* to persuasion
to *re-sign* the contracts	to *resign* the position
to *re-treat* the cloth	to *retreat* to safer ground
a *re-creation* of the original sketches	a *recreation* program for employees

838 When a prefix is added to a word that begins with a capital, use a hyphen after the prefix.

anti-American	mid-January	non-Windows application
non-Asiatic	trans-Canadian	post-World War II period

BUT: transatlantic, transpacific, the Midwest

839 Always hyphenate family terms involving the prefix *great* or the suffix *in-law*, but treat terms involving *step* and *grand* solid.

(Continued on page 224.)

my great-grandfather	my grandmother	your brother-in-law
their great-aunt	his grandchild	my stepdaughter

840 Avoid feminine suffixes like *ess, ette,* and *trix.*

> She has an established reputation as an *author* and a *poet.* (**NOT:** *authoress* and *poetess.*)

> If you have any questions, ask your *flight attendant.* (**NOT:** *steward* or *stewardess.*)

NOTE: A few terms with feminine suffixes are still widely used; for example, *hostess, heroine, waitress,* and *fiancée.* In legal documents, the terms *executrix* and *testatrix* are increasingly being replaced by *executor* and *testator.*

841 Use a hyphen after *quasi* when an adjective follows.

quasi-judicial	quasi-public
quasi-legislative	**BUT:** quasi corporation

842 When *after* is used as a prefix, do not use a hyphen to set if off from the root word; but when *after* is used as a preposition in a compound adjective, insert a hyphen.

aftereffect	aftershock	**BUT:** an after-dinner speech
aftershave	afterthought	my after-tax income

843 When *in* is used as a prefix meaning "not," do not use a hyphen to set if off from the root word; but when used as a preposition in a compound adjective, insert a hyphen.

inactive	insensitive	**BUT:** an in-depth analysis
indecisive	intolerable	an in-house program

844 A hyphen normally follows *mid* in expressions involving numbers (see ¶439a) or capitalized words (see ¶838). When *mid* is used as a prefix, a hyphen is not ordinarily used.

the mid-'60s	mid-sixties	at midnight
mid-Atlantic	mid-June	a midway point

845 Words beginning with the prefix *off* are written solid or hyphenated.

offhand	offshore	off-key
offline	offspring	off-season

846 If the addition of the suffix *less* or *like* causes three *l*'s to occur in succession, insert a hyphen before the suffix. (See also ¶706, note.)

shell-less	bell-like	wall-like

COMPOUND COMPUTER TERMS

847 The escalation of computer technology with its related compound terms means that dictionaries are not able to keep pace with the changes taking place in the field. It is impossible, therefore, to establish a style that will last. At any given time a particular word may appear as hyphenated, spaced, or solid. The general tendency is for hyphenated forms to give way to either spaced or solid forms and for the spaced forms to eventually give way to solid forms.

When your dictionary does not show an updated version of a word, the best places to look are the magazines, manuals, and style guides devoted to computer and Internet technology. Depending on the computer literacy level of your readers, you must decide if they would prefer to see the following term written as *filename* or the more conservative style, *file name*.

The following terms show a conservative form first and the emerging style second.

voice mail	**OR**	voicemail	spell checker	**OR**	spellchecker
log off, log-off	**OR**	logoff	word wrap	**OR**	wordwrap
e-mail	**OR**	email	Web site	**OR**	Website

NOTE: The term *Web site* and a few other *Web* compounds are now losing their initial capital letters *(website)*.

SOMETIMES ONE WORD, SOMETIMES TWO WORDS

848 A number of common words may be written either as one solid word or as two separate words, depending on the meaning. See individual entries listed alphabetically in Section 11 (unless otherwise indicated) for the following words:

Almost—all most
Already—all ready
Altogether—all together
Always—all ways
Anyone—any one (see ¶1010, note)
Anytime—any time
Anyway—any way
Awhile—a while
Everyday—every day
Everyone—every one (see ¶1010, note)
Indifferent—in different
Indirect—in direct

Into—in to (see *In*)
Maybe—may be
Nobody—no body
None—no one (see ¶1013)
Onto—on to (see *On*)
Someday—some day
Someone—some one (see ¶1010, note)
Sometime—sometimes—some time
Upon—up on (see *On*)
Whoever—who ever

☞ *Hyphens in spelled-out numbers: see ¶465.*
   Hyphens in spelled-out dates: see ¶411.
   Hyphens in spelled-out amounts of money: see ¶420.
   Hyphens in spelled-out fractions: see ¶427.
   Hyphens in numbers representing a continuous sequence: see ¶¶459–460.

See the Online Learning Centre at www.mcgrawhill.ca/college/gregg for related weblinks.

SECTION **NINE**

Word Division

BASIC RULES (¶¶901–906)

PREFERRED PRACTICES (¶¶907–918)

BREAKS WITHIN WORD GROUPS (¶¶919–920)

GUIDES TO CORRECT SYLLABICATION (¶¶921–922)

Automated hyphenation, a feature of many word processing programs, is best used after editing a document. Since this feature may disagree with the authority of the word division rules shown in this manual (the 1997 printing of the *Gage Canadian Dictionary*), you may wish to review and adjust hyphenation as necessary.

For an expression that must include a hyphen, the use of a regular hyphen will ensure its inclusion in text material whether it appears within a line or at the end of a line. For an expression that *must* always stay together on the same line (such as a telephone number), use a hard (non-breaking) hyphen.

Whenever possible, avoid dividing a word. Word divisions are unattractive and they may sometimes confuse a reader. However, an extremely ragged right margin is also unattractive. When word division is unavoidable, try to divide at the point that is least likely to disrupt the reader's grasp of the word. The following word division rules include (1) those that must never be broken (¶¶901–906) and (2) those that should be followed whenever space permits a choice (¶¶907–920).

NOTE: Professional typesetters often take liberties with rules of word division in order to fit copy within a limited amount of space.

BASIC RULES

901 Divide words only between syllables. Whenever you are unsure of the syllabi-cation of a word, consult a dictionary. (See also ¶¶921–922 for some guides to correct syllabication.)

> ex- traordinary **OR** extraor- dinary **OR** extraordi- nary   **NOT:** extra- ordinary

NOTE: Some syllable breaks shown in the dictionary are not acceptable as points of word division.

902 Do not divide one-syllable words. Even when *ed* is added to some words, they still remain one-syllable words and cannot be divided.

stressed	through	spring	strength
planned	thoughts	straight	breathe

903 Do not divide five-letter words. When dividing words of six letters or more, there must be a minimum of three characters, including the hyphen, at the beginning or at the end of a line.

ad- here	de- pend	un- even	in- cise
do- cile	re- turn	set- up,	happi- ly.

904 When keying a word like *e-business* or *e-commerce*, use a hard (non-breaking) hyphen to ensure that the word will remain as a single unit.

905 Do not divide abbreviations or acronyms.

> assoc.   Introd.   INSTRAW   UNICEF

NOTE: An abbreviation like *AFL-CIO* may be divided after the hyphen.

906 Do not divide contractions.

> haven't   shouldn't   mustn't   doesn't

PREFERRED PRACTICES

It is often better to divide words at some points than at others in order to obtain a more intelligible grouping of syllables. The following rules indicate preferred practices when-ever you have sufficient space left in the line to permit a choice.

907 Divide a solid compound word between the elements of the compound.

> eye- witness   time- saving   photo- copy   trust- worthy

908 Divide a hyphenated compound word at the point of the hyphen.

> self- confidence   father- in-law   cross- reference   mayor- elect

909 Divide a word *after* a prefix (rather than within the prefix).

> circum- stances (**RATHER THAN:** cir- cumstances)
> intro- duce (**RATHER THAN:** in- troduce)
> inter- national (**RATHER THAN:** in- ternational)
> super- sonic (**RATHER THAN:** su- personic)

(Continued on page 228.)

9

Use divisions such as the following:

> am- bitious (**RATHER THAN:** ambi- tious)
> co- incide (**RATHER THAN:** coin- cide)
> ex- traneous (**RATHER THAN:** extra- neous)
> hy- perbole (**RATHER THAN:** hyper- bole)

910 Divide a word *before* a suffix (rather than within the suffix).

> appli- cable (**RATHER THAN:** applica- ble)
> comprehen- sible (**RATHER THAN:** comprehensi- ble)

911 When a word has both a prefix and a suffix or a suffix added to a suffix, choose the division point that groups the syllables more intelligibly and produces a better grouping.

> replace- ment (**RATHER THAN:** re- placement)
> helpless- ness (**RATHER THAN:** help- lessness)

912 Whenever you have a choice, divide after a prefix or before a suffix (rather than within the root word).

> over- active (**RATHER THAN:** overac- tive)
> success- ful (**RATHER THAN:** suc- cessful)
> co- defendant (**RATHER THAN:** code- fendant)
> re- ality (**RATHER THAN:** real- ity)
> re- arrange (**RATHER THAN:** rear- range)
> re- instate (**RATHER THAN:** rein- state)

913 When a one-letter syllable occurs within the root of a word, divide *after* it (rather than before it).

> apolo- gize   congratu- late   impera- tive   reme- dies

914 When two separately sounded vowels come together in a word, divide between them.

> cha- otic   courte- ous   patri- otic   influ- ential
> recre- ation   medi- ation   po- etry   ingenu- ity
> spontane- ity   experi- ence   situ- ated   continu- ous

NOTE: Do not divide between two or more vowels when they are used together to represent one sound.

> main- tained   treas- urer   en- croaching   pa- tience
> ac- quaint   es- teemed   amoe- ba   lieu- tenant
> guess- ing   per- ceive   ap- point   con- scious
> acquit- tal   sur- geon   ty- coon   opin- ion
> mis- quoted   neu- tral   pro- nounce   ma- noeuvre

915 *When absolutely necessary*, an extremely long number could be divided after a space or comma; for example, *24 358- 692 000.* Try to leave at least four digits on the line above and at least six digits on the line below, but always divide after a space or comma.

9

916 Try not to end more than two consecutive lines in hyphens.

917 Try not to divide at the end of the first line or at the end of the last full line in a paragraph.

918 Do not divide the last word on a page.

BREAKS WITHIN WORD GROUPS

919 **a.** Try to keep together certain kinds of word groups that need to be read together—for example, page and number, month and day, month and year, title and first name or surname, surname and abbreviation (or number), number and abbreviation, or number and unit of measure.

page 203	September 2005	Paula Schein, J.D.	10:30 a.m.
April 29	Mrs. Connolly	Adam Hagerty Jr.	465 km

b. For elements of a word group that should not be broken at the end of a line, insert a **hard (non-breaking) space** or hyphen, whichever suits the situation. This will force the entire word group to move to the next line.

> . . . . when
> Mrs. Jean Yuen arrives . . . .

> **NOT:** . . . . when Mrs.
> Jean Yuen arrives . . . .

> . . . . Purchase Order
> 259-6693 . . . .

> **NOT:** . . . . Purchase Order 259-
> 6693 . . . .

920 When necessary, longer word groups may be broken as follows:

a. *Dates* may be broken between the day and year.

> . . . . November 14,
> 2005 . . . .

> **NOT:** . . . . November
> 14, 2005 . . . .

b. *Street addresses* may be broken between the name of the street and *Street, Avenue,* or the like. If the street name consists of two or more words, the break may come between words in the street name.

> . . . . 1024 Westmount
> Boulevard . . . .

> **NOT:** 1024
> Westmount Boulevard . . . .

> . . . . 617 North
> Fullerton Street . . . .

> **NOT:** 617
> North Fullerton Street . . . .

c. *Names of places in text* may be broken between the city and the province or between the province and the postal code. If either name consists of two or more words, the break may come between these words.

> . . . . Kingston,
> Ontario K7L 4T5 . . . .

> **OR:** . . . . Kingston, Ontario
> K7L 4T5 . . . .

> . . . . Sault Ste.
> Marie, Ontario P6C 1Y3 . . . .

> **OR:** . . . . Summerside, Prince
> Edward Island C1N 4S3 . . . .

d. *Names of persons* may be broken between the given name (including middle initial if given) and surname.

(Continued on page 230.)

| . . . . Mildred R. Palumbo . . . . | **NOT:** . . . . Mildred R. Palumbo . . . . |

NOTE: If it is absolutely necessary, a person's name may be divided. Follow the same principles given for dividing ordinary words.

Diefen- baker   Spil- lane (See ¶922b.)   Kach- marski

e. *Names preceded by long titles* may be broken between the title and the name (preferably) or between words in the title.

| . . . . Assistant Commissioner Roy N. Frawley . . . . | **OR:** . . . . Assistant Commissioner Roy N. Frawley . . |

f. A *numbered or lettered enumeration* may be broken before (but not directly after) any number or letter.

| . . . . these points: (1) All cards should . . . . | **NOT:** . . . . these points: (1) All cards should . . . . |

g. A *sentence with a dash in it* may be broken after the dash.

| . . . . Early next year— say, in March—let's . . . . | **NOT:** . . . . Early next year —say, in March—let's . . . . |

h. A *sentence with ellipsis marks in it* may be broken after the ellipsis marks.

| Tennis . . . health spa . . . golf . . . and more . . . make this a world-class resort. | **NOT:** Tennis . . . health spa . . . golf . . . and more . . . make this a world-class resort. |

GUIDES TO CORRECT SYLLABICATION

921 Syllabication is generally based on pronunciation rather than on roots and derivations. Careful pronunciation will often aid you in determining the correct syllabication of a word.

knowl- edge (**NOT:** know- ledge)   prod- uct (**NOT:** pro- duct)
chil- dren (**NOT:** child- ren)   ser- vice (**NOT:** serv- ice)

Note how syllabication changes as pronunciation changes.

Verbs	Nouns
pre- sent (to make a gift)	pres- ent (a gift)
re- cord (to make an official copy)	rec- ord (an official copy)
pro- ject (to throw forward)	proj- ect (an undertaking)

922 The following paragraphs offer some guides to syllabication when double letters occur in words.

a. If a final consonant of the base word is doubled *because* a suffix is added, you can safely divide *between* the double consonants (so long as the suffix creates an extra syllable).

ship- ping   omit- ted   begin- ner   drum- ming
BUT: shipped, drummed (remain as one-syllable words; see ¶902)

b. When double consonants appear elsewhere *within* the base word (but not as the final consonants), you can safely divide between them.

bub- bling	strug- gle	recom- mend	cur- rent
suc- cess	mil- lion	sup- pose	neces- sary

See the Online Learning Centre at www.mcgrawhill.ca/college/gregg for related weblinks.

SECTION **TEN**

Grammar

PRONOUNS (¶¶1049–1064)

Agreement With Antecedents: Basic Rules (¶1049)
Agreement With Common-Gender Antecedents (¶¶1050–1052)
Agreement With Indefinite-Pronoun Antecedents (¶1053)
Personal Pronouns (¶¶1054–1059)
   Nominative Forms of Personal Pronouns (¶1054)
   Objective Forms of Personal Pronouns (¶1055)
   Possessive Forms of Personal Pronouns (¶1056)
Compound Personal Pronouns (¶1060)
Interrogative and Relative Pronouns (¶¶1061–1063)
   Who and *Whom; Whoever* and *Whomever* (¶1061)
   Who, Which, and *That* (¶1062)
   Whose and *Who's* (¶1063)
Pronouns With *To Be* (¶1064)
Troublesome Pronouns

ADJECTIVES AND ADVERBS (¶¶1065–1073)

Troublesome Adjectives and Adverbs

NEGATIVES (¶¶1074–1076)

PREPOSITIONS (¶¶1077–1080)

Words Requiring Certain Prepositions (¶1077)
Superfluous Prepositions (¶1078)
Necessary Prepositions (¶1079)
Prepositions at the End of Sentences (¶1080)
Troublesome Prepositions

SENTENCE STRUCTURE (¶¶1081–1086)

Parallel Structure (¶1081)
Dangling Constructions (¶¶1082–1085)
Misplaced Modifiers (¶1086)

    ☞ *For definitions of grammatical terms, see the appropriate entries (such as* number *and* person*) in Section 19.*

SUBJECTS AND VERBS
Basic Rule of Agreement

1001 a. A verb must agree with its subject in number and person.

   I am eager to get back to work. (First person singular subject *I* with first person singular verb *am*.)

   It seems odd that *Farmer has not followed up* on our report. (Third person singular subjects *it* and *Farmer* with third person singular verbs *seems* and *has not followed up*.)

(Continued on page 234.)

10

He is coming to stay with us for a week. (Third person singular subject *he* with third person singular verb *is coming*.)

She does intend to call you this week. (Third person singular subject *she* with third person singular verb *does intend*.)

We were delighted to read about your promotion. (First person plural subject *we* with first person plural verb *were*.)

They are convinced that the *Foys are* worth millions. (Third person plural subjects *they* and *Foys* with third person plural verbs *are convinced* and *are*.)

Your *order* for six laptop computers *was shipped* last Friday. (Third person singular subject *order* with third person singular verb *was shipped*.)

Our *efforts* to save the business *have been* unsuccessful. (Third person plural subject *efforts* with third person plural verb *have been*.)

NOTE: A plural verb is always required after *you*, even when *you* is singular, referring to only one person.

You alone *have understood* the full dimensions of the problem. (Second person singular subject *you* with second person plural verb *have understood*.)

You both *have been* a great help to us. (Second person plural subject *you* with second person plural verb *have been*.)

b. Although *s* or *es* added to a *noun* indicates the plural form, *s* or *es* added to a verb indicates the third person singular. (See ¶1035.)

Singular	Plural
The price *seems* reasonable.	The prices *seem* reasonable.
The tax *applies* to everyone.	The taxes *apply* to everyone.

Subjects Joined by *And*

1002 a. If the subject consists of two or more words that are connected by *and* or by *both . . . and*, the subject is plural and requires a plural verb.

Ms. Rizzo and *Mr. Huynh have received* promotions.

Both the *collection* and the *delivery* of mail *are* to be curtailed as of July 1. (The repetition of *the* with the second subject emphasizes that two different items are meant.)

The *general managers* and the *controllers are attending* a seminar today.

The *director of marketing* and the *product managers are reviewing* their budgets.

b. Use a singular verb when two or more subjects connected by *and* refer to the same person or thing. (See also ¶1028a, fourth example.)

Our *secretary and treasurer is* Frances Kernaghan. (One person.)

Corned beef and cabbage was his favourite dish. (One dish.)

Wear and tear has to be expected when you are renting. (One type of damage.)

c. Use a singular verb when two or more subjects connected by *and* are preceded by *each, every, many a,* or *many an.* (See also ¶1009b.)

Every computer, printer, and fax machine *is marked* for reduction.

Many a woman and man *has responded* to our plea for contributions.

10

Subjects Joined by *Or* or Similar Connectives

1003 If the subject consists of two or more *singular* words that are connected by *or, either . . . or, neither . . . nor,* or *not only . . . but also,* the subject is singular and requires a singular verb.

> Either *July* or *August is* a good time for the sales conference.
>
> Neither the *Credit Department* nor the *Accounting Department has* the file.
>
> Not only a cost-profit *analysis* but also a marketing *plan needs* to be developed.

1004 If the subject consists of two or more *plural* words that are connected by *or, either . . . or, neither . . . nor,* or *not only . . . but also,* the subject is plural and requires a plural verb.

> Neither the regional *managers* nor the *salesclerks have* the data you want.
>
> Not only the *dealers* but also the *retailers are* unhappy about our new policy.

1005 If the subject is made up of both singular and plural words connected by *or, either . . . or, neither . . . nor,* or *not only . . . but also,* the verb agrees with the nearer part of the subject. Since sentences with singular and plural subjects usually sound better with plural verbs, try to locate the plural subject close to the verb whenever this can be done without sacrificing the emphasis desired.

> Either *Miss Huva* or her *assistants have* copies of the new catalogue. (The verb *have* agrees with the nearer subject, *assistants.*)
>
> Neither the *buyers* nor the *sales manager is* in favour of the system. (The verb *is* agrees with the nearer subject, *sales manager.*)
>
> **BETTER:** Neither the *sales manager* nor the *buyers are* in favour of the system. (The sentence reads better with the plural verb *are.* The subjects *sales manager* and *buyers* have been rearranged without changing the emphasis.)
>
> Not only the *teachers* but also the *superintendent is* in favour of the plan. (The verb *is* agrees with the nearer subject, *superintendent.* With the use of *not only . . . but also,* the emphasis falls on the subject following *but also.*)
>
> Not only the *superintendent* but also the *teachers are* in favour of the plan. (When the sentence is rearranged, the nearer subject, *teachers,* requires the plural verb *are.* However, the emphasis has now changed.)
>
> Not only my *colleagues* but I *am* in favour of the plan. (The first person verb *am* agrees with the nearer subject, *I.* Rearranging this sentence will change the emphasis.)

NOTE: When the subjects reflect different grammatical persons (first, second, or third), the verb should agree in person as well as number with the nearer subject. If the result seems awkward, reword as necessary.

> **ACCEPTABLE:** Neither you nor I *am* in a position to pay Ben's legal fees.
> **BETTER:** Neither *one* of us *is* in a position to pay Ben's legal fees. (See ¶1009a.)
>
> **ACCEPTABLE:** Neither you nor *she has* the time to take on the Fuller case.
> **ACCEPTABLE:** Neither she nor *you have* the time to take on the Fuller case.
> **BETTER:** *You are* both too busy to take on the Fuller case.
>
> **AWKWARD:** If you or Gary *is coming* to the convention, please visit our booth.
> **BETTER:** If Gary or you *are coming* to the convention, please visit our booth.

(Continued on page 236.)

☞ *For* neither . . . nor *constructions following* there is, there are, there were, *or* there was, *see the last four examples in* ¶1028a.

For examples of subject-verb-pronoun agreement in these constructions, see ¶1049c.

Intervening Phrases and Clauses

1006 a. When establishing agreement between subject and verb, disregard intervening phrases, clauses, and appositives. (See ¶148.)

The *purchase order* for new diskettes *has not been found.* (Disregard *for new diskettes. Purchase order* is the subject and takes the singular verb *has not been found.*)

The *prices* shown in our catalogue *do not include* sales tax.

Only *one* of the items that *I* ordered *has been delivered.* (See also ¶1008.)

Her *experience* with banks and brokerage houses *gives* her excellent qualifications.

A key *factor*, the company's assets, *is not being given* sufficient weight.

BUT: The company's *assets*, a key factor, *are not being given* sufficient weight.

NOTE: When certain indefinite pronouns *(all, none, any, some, more, most)* and certain fractional expressions (for example, *one-half of, a part of, a percentage of*) are used as subjects, you may have to look at an intervening phrase or clause to determine whether the verb should be singular or plural. (See ¶¶1013, 1025 for examples.)

b. When a sentence has both a positive and a negative subject, make the verb agree with the positive subject. Set off the negative subject with commas unless it is preceded by *and* or *but.*

Profit and not sales *is* the thing to keep your eye on. (The verb *is* agrees with the positive subject *profit.*)

The *design* of the container, not the contents, *determines* what the consumer's initial reaction to the product will be.

The *members* of the Executive Committee and not the president *wield* the real power in the corporation.

It is not the president but the *members* of the Executive Committee who *wield* the real power in the corporation. (In the main clause, the verb *is* agrees with the subject *it*; the verb *wield* in the *who* clause is plural to agree with the antecedent of *who*, the positive subject *members.* See ¶1062c.)

BUT: It is the *president* and not the members of the Executive Committee who *wields* the real power in the corporation. (In this sentence the positive subject is *president*, a singular noun; therefore, the verb *wields* in the *who* clause must also be singular.)

10

1007 The number of the verb is not affected by the insertion between subject and verb of phrases with such expressions as:

along with	as well as	plus	except
together with	in addition to	besides	rather than
and not (see ¶1006b)	accompanied by	including	not even

If the subject is singular, use a singular verb; if the subject is plural, use a plural verb.

Mrs. Swenson, together with her husband and daughter, *is going* to Quebec.

This *study*, along with many earlier reports, *shows* that the disease can be arrested.

No one, not even the vice-president, *knows* when the CEO plans to resign. (See ¶1010.)

The *divisional controllers*, not the director of finance, *are authorized* to approve unbudgeted expenditures over $500. (See ¶1006b.)

NOTE: When the construction of a sentence like those above requires a singular verb but a plural verb would sound more natural, reword the sentence to create a plural subject.

CORRECT: The national sales *report*, as well as the regional breakdowns you requested plus the individual printouts, *was sent* to you last week.

BETTER: The national sales *report*, the regional *breakdowns* you requested, and the individual *printouts were sent* to you last week. (The three subjects joined by *and*—*report*, *breakdowns*, and *printouts*—call for a plural verb.)

One of . . .

1008 a. Use a singular verb after a phrase beginning with *one of* or *one of the*; the singular verb agrees with the subject *one*. (Disregard any plural that follows *of* or *of the*.)

One of my backup disks *has been lost*.

One of the reasons for so many absences *is* poor motivation.

One of us *has* to take over the responsibility for in-service training.

One of you *is* to be nominated for the office.

b. The phrases *one of those who* and *one of the things that* are followed by plural verbs because the verbs refer to *those* or *things* (rather than to *one*).

She is one of *those* who *favour* increasing the staff. (In other words, of *those* who *favour* increasing the staff, she is one. Favour is plural to agree with *those*.)

He is one of our *employees* who *are* never late. (Of our *employees* who *are* never late, he is one.)

I ordered one of the new *copiers* that *were advertised* in Monday's paper. (Of the new *copiers* that *were advertised* in Monday's paper, I ordered one.)

You are one of *those* rare individuals who *are* always honest with *themselves*. (Of those rare *individuals* who *are* always honest with *themselves*, you are one.)

EXCEPTION: When the words *the only* precede such phrases, the meaning is singular and a singular verb is required. Note that both words, *the* and *only*, are required to produce a singular meaning.

John is *the only one* of the staff members who *is going* to be transferred. (Of the staff members, John is *the only one* who *is going* to be transferred. Here the singular verb *is going* is required to agree with *one*.)

BUT: John is only one of the *staff members* who *are going* to be transferred. (Of the *staff members* who *are going* to be transferred, John is only one.)

10

Indefinite Pronouns Always Singular

1009 a. The words *each, every, either, neither, one, another,* and *much* are always singular. When they are used as subjects or as adjectives modifying subjects, a singular verb is required.

Neither one of the applicants *is* eligible.　　**OR**　　Neither applicant *is* eligible.

Much work *remains* to be done.　　**OR**　　Much *remains* to be done.

Each has a clear-cut set of responsibilities.

Each employee is responsible for maintaining an orderly work station.

One shipment *has* already gone out; *another is* to leave the warehouse tomorrow.

☞ *For the use of* either . . . or *and* neither . . . nor, *see ¶¶1003–1005.*

b. When *each, every, many a,* or *many an* precedes two or more subjects joined by *and,* the verb should be singular.

Every customer *and* supplier *has been notified.*

☞ *See ¶1002c for other examples.*

c. When *each* follows a plural subject, keep the verb plural. In that position, *each* has no effect on the number of the verb. To test the correctness of such sentences, mentally omit *each.*

The *members* each *feel* their responsibility.

They each *have* high expectations.

1010 The following compound pronouns are always singular and require a singular verb:

anybody	everybody	somebody	nobody
anything	everything	something	nothing
anyone	everyone	someone	no one
OR any one	**OR** every one	**OR** some one	

Everyone is required to register in order to vote.

Something tells me I'm wrong.

NOTE: Spell *anyone, everyone,* and *someone* as two words when these pronouns are followed by an *of* phrase or are used to mean "one of a number of things."

Every one of us (each person in the group) *likes* to be appreciated.

BUT: *Everyone* (everybody) *likes* to be appreciated.

1011 Use a singular verb when two compound pronouns joined by *and* are used as subjects.

Any and *everyone is entitled* to a fair hearing.

Nobody and *nothing is going* to stop me.

Indefinite Pronouns Always Plural

1012 The words *both, few, many, others,* and *several* are always plural. When they are used as subjects or as adjectives modifying subjects, a plural verb is required.

Several members *were invited;* the *others were overlooked.*

Both books *are* out of print.

Many were asked, but *few were* able to answer.

Indefinite Pronouns Singular or Plural

1013 a. *All, none, any, some, more,* and *most* may be singular or plural, depending on the noun they refer to. (The noun often occurs in an *of* phrase that follows.)

All the manuscript *has been printed.*	*All* the books *have been printed.*
Is there *any* (money) left?	*Are* there *any* (bills) to be paid?
Most of the stock *has been sold.*	*More* of these stands *are* due.
Some of the software *was* acceptable.	*Some* of the tapes *were* acceptable.

Some was acceptable. (Meaning some of the software.)
Some were acceptable. (Meaning some of the tapes.)

Do any of you *know* Mas Fukumoto well? (*Any* is plural because it refers to the plural *you;* hence the plural verb *do know.*)
Does any one of you *know* Mas Fukumoto well? (*Any* is singular because it refers to the singular *one;* hence the singular verb *does know.*)

More than one customer *has complained* about that item. (*More* refers to the singular noun *customer;* hence the singular verb *has complained.*)
More than five customers *have complained* . . . (*More* refers to the plural noun *customers;* hence the plural verb *have complained.*)

b. In formal usage, *none* is still considered a singular pronoun. In general usage, however, *none* is considered singular or plural, depending on the number of the noun to which it refers. *No one* or *not one* is often used in place of *none* to stress the singular idea.

None of the merchandise *was stolen.*

None of the packages *were* properly *wrapped.*

None were injured. (Meaning none of the passengers.)

Not one of the associates *has* a good word to say about the managing partner.

NOTE: The relative pronouns *who, which,* and *that* (like the indefinite pronouns discussed in *a* above) may be singular or plural, depending on the noun they refer to. (See ¶1062c.)

Nouns Ending in *S*

1014 Some nouns appear to be plural but are actually singular. When used as subjects, these nouns require singular verbs.

news *(no plural)*	measles *(no plural)*
lens *(plural:* lenses)	summons *(plural:* summonses)
The *news* from overseas *is* discouraging.	The *lens has* to be reground.

1015 A number of nouns are always considered plural, even though they each refer to a single thing. As subjects, they require plural verbs.

(Continued on page 240.)

assets	dues	grounds	proceeds	savings
belongings	earnings	odds	quarters	thanks
credentials	goods	premises	riches	winnings

The *premises are* available for viewing.   My *savings have* not increased.

NOTE: The following nouns are considered plural unless preceded by the term *a pair of.*

glasses	slacks	jeans	pants	trousers

The *scissors need* sharpening. (**BUT:** A *pair* of scissors *has been taken.*)

1016 A few nouns (not all of which end in *s*) have the same form in the plural as in the singular. When used as subjects, these nouns take singular or plural verbs according to the meaning.

series	means	chassis	headquarters	deer
species	gross	corps	sheep	moose

The *series* of concerts planned for the spring *looks* very exciting. (One series.)
Three *series* of tickets *are going* to be issued. (Three series.)

One *means* of breaking the impasse *is* to offer more money.
Other *means* of solving the problem *have* not *come* to mind.

Headquarters is not pleased with the performance of the Eastern Region. (Referring to top management or central authority.)
Their *headquarters are located* at the corner of Seventh Street and Seventh Avenue. (Referring to the offices of top management.)

Nouns Ending in *ICS*

1017 Many nouns ending in *ics* (such as *acoustics, economics, ethics, politics,* and *statistics*) take singular or plural verbs, depending on how they are used. When they refer to a body of knowledge or a course of study, they are *singular*. When they refer to qualities or activities, they are *plural*.

Economics (a course of study) *is* a prerequisite for advanced business courses.
The *economics* (the economic aspects) of his plan *are* not very sound.

Statistics is the one course in which I needed my wife's help.
The *statistics indicate* that the market for this product line is shrinking.

Acoustics is not *listed* in next year's course offerings.
The *acoustics* in the new concert hall *are* remarkably good.

Nouns With Foreign Plurals

1018 Watch for nouns with foreign-plural endings. (See ¶614.) Such plural nouns, when used as subjects, require plural verbs.

No *criteria have been established.*   **BUT:** No *criterion has been established.*

Parentheses set off expressions.   **BUT:** The closing *parenthesis was omitted.*

The *media* used for clients *are* magazines, television, and radio.
BUT: The *medium* we find most effective *is* television.

NOTE: The noun *data,* which is plural in form, is commonly followed by a plural verb in technical and scientific usage. In general usage *data* in the sense of "information" is followed by a singular verb; in the sense of "distinct bits of information," it is followed by a plural verb.

The *data* obtained after two months of experimentation *is* now *being analysed.* (Here *data* means "information.")

BUT: The *data* assembled by six researchers *are* now *being compared.* (Here *data* refers to several distinct bits of information.)

Collective Nouns

1019 The following rules govern the form of verb to be used when the subject is a collective noun. (A *collective noun* is a word that is singular in form but represents a group of persons, animals, or things; for example, *army, audience, board, cabinet, class, committee, company, corporation, council, department, faculty, firm, group, jury, majority, minority, public, school, society, staff.*)

a. If the group is acting as a unit, use the singular form of the verb.

The *Board of Directors meets* Friday. The *firm is* one of the oldest in the city.

The *committee has agreed* to submit *its* report on Monday. (The pronoun *its* is also singular to agree with *committee.*)

b. If the members of the group are acting separately, use a plural verb.

A *group* of researchers *are coming* from all over the world for the symposium next month. (The members of the group are acting separately in the process of coming together from all over the world.)

BUT: A *group* of researchers *is meeting* in Geneva next month. (The members of the group are acting as a unit in the process of meeting.)

NOTE: The use of a collective noun with a plural verb often produces an awkward sentence. Whenever possible, recast the sentence by inserting a phrase like *the members of* before the collective noun.

AWKWARD: The *Committee are* not in agreement on the action *they* should take. (The verb *are* and the pronoun *they* are plural to agree with the plural *committee.*)

BETTER: The *members* of the committee *are* not in agreement . . .

c. In a number of constructions, the choice of a singular or plural verb often depends on whether you wish to emphasize the group as a unit or as a collection of individuals. However, once the choice has been made, treat the collective noun consistently within the same context. If the resulting sentence sounds awkward, recast it as necessary.

I hope your *family is* well. (Emphasizes the family as a whole.)
OR: I hope your *family are* all well. (Emphasizes the individuals in the family.)

SMOOTHER: I hope all the *members* of your family *are* well.
OR: I hope *everyone* in your family *is* well.

The *couple was* married (**OR** *were married*) last Saturday.
OR: *Bob and Pauline were* married last Saturday.

The *couple have moved* into *their* new house. (More idiomatic than: "The *couple has moved into its* new house.")
OR: The *Goodwins have moved* into *their* new house.

(Continued on page 242.)

10

NOTE: The expression *a couple of* is usually plural in meaning.

A *couple of* customers *have already reported* the error in our ad.

A *couple of* orders *have been shipped* to the wrong address.

BUT: A *couple of days is* all I need to complete the report. (When the phrase refers to a period of time, an amount of money, or a quantity that represents a total amount, treat the phrase as singular. See also ¶1024.)

Organizational Names

1020 Organizational names may be treated as either singular or plural. Ordinarily, treat the name as singular unless you wish to emphasize the individuals who make up the organization; in that case, use the plural. Once a choice has been made, use the singular or plural form consistently within the same context.

Brooks & Rice *has lost its* lease. *It is* now *looking* for a new location.

OR: Brooks & Rice *have lost their* lease. *They are* now *looking* for . . .

(BUT NOT: Brooks & Rice *has lost its* lease. *They are* now *looking* for . . .)

NOTE: If the organization is referred to as *they* or *who*, use a plural verb with the company name. If the organization is referred to as *it* or *which*, use a singular verb. (See ¶1049a.)

Geographic Names

1021 Geographic names that are plural in form are treated as *singular* if they refer to only one thing.

The *Netherlands is* the first stop on my itinerary.

The *Queen Charlotte Islands consists* of two large islands (Graham and Moresby) and several smaller islands.

The *United States has undertaken* a new foreign aid program.

BUT: All the *United States are bound* together by a common heritage.

Names of Publications and Products

1022 The name of a publication or product is considered singular, even though it may be plural in form.

Physicians & Computers is the one magazine you should consider.

Libby's baked beans *is* a good source of fibre.

Canadian Gardens is offering new subscribers a special rate for a limited time.

The Number; A Number

1023 The expression *the number* has a singular meaning and requires a singular verb; *a number* has a plural meaning and requires a plural verb.

The number of branch offices *has increased* in each of the last five years.

A number of our branch offices *are* now *located* in suburban malls.

10

Expressions of Time, Money, and Quantity

1024 When subjects expressing periods of time, amounts of money, or quantities represent *a total amount*, use singular verbs. When these subjects represent *a number of individual units*, use plural verbs.

> *Three months is* too long a time to wait.
> **BUT:** *Three months have passed* since our last exchange of letters.

> *That $10 000 was* an inheritance from my uncle.
> **BUT:** *Thousands* of dollars *have* already *been spent* on the project.

> *Ten hectares is considered* a small piece of property in this area.
> **BUT:** *Ten hectares were plowed* last spring.

> A first-grader knows that *2 plus 2 is 4.*
> **BUT:** Every teacher knows that *2 and 2 are 4.*

Fractional Expressions

1025 When the subject is an expression such as *one-half of, two-thirds of, a part of, a majority of, a percentage of, a portion of,* or *the rest of:*

a. Use a *singular verb* if a singular noun follows *of* or is implied.

> *Three-fourths* of the *mailing list has been checked.*

> *Part* of our Windsor *operation is being closed down.*

> A *majority of 2000 signifies* a landslide in this town. (The noun *2000* is considered singular because it is a total amount. See ¶1024.)

> A large *percentage has* to be rekeyed. (Referring to a manuscript.)

b. Use a *plural verb* when a *plural noun* follows *of* or is implied.

> *One-third* of our *clients live* downtown.   *Part* of the *walls are* to be papered.

> A *majority* of our *employees have contributed* to the United Way fund drive.

> A large *percentage work* part-time. (Referring to the students at a college.)

> **NOTE:** When used as a subject, the word *percentage* preceded by *the* requires a singular verb.

> *The percentage* of students who work part-time *is* quite large. (*The percentage* takes a singular verb, even though it is followed by a plural noun, *students.*)

c. Consider the word *half* as a condensed version of *one-half of.*

> *Half* the *staff have signed up* for benefits. (A collective noun such as *staff*, though singular in form, takes a plural verb when it is plural in meaning. See ¶1019b.)

Phrases and Clauses as Subjects

1026 When a phrase or clause serves as the subject, the verb should be singular.

> *Reading e-mail is* the first item on my morning agenda.

> *Whatever sales brochure they mail me goes* directly into the circular file.

> *Whether the decision was right or not is* no longer important.

> *That they will accept the offer is* far from certain.

(Continued on page 244.)

10

EXCEPTION: Clauses beginning with *what* may be singular or plural according to the meaning.

What we need *is* a new *statement* of policy. (The *what* clause refers to *statement*; hence the verb is singular.)

What we need *are* some *guidelines* on personal time off. (Here the *what* clause refers to *guidelines*; hence the verb is plural.)

Subjects in Inverted Sentences

1027 Whenever the verb precedes the subject, make sure they agree.

Attached are two *copies* of the January mailing piece.

What *were* your *reasons* for resigning?

Where *is* (**OR** Where's) this *strategy going* to take us?

Where *are* the *reviews* of the Kelly book?
NOT: Where *is* (**OR** Where's) the *reviews* of the Kelly book?

What *is* missing from the report *is* the *rationale* for the decision.

What *appear* to be problems *are* often *opportunities*.

Should a position become available, we will let you know. (In this case, the helping verb *should* precedes the subject. If written in normal word order, this sentence would read: If a *position should become* available . . .)

1028 a. In a sentence beginning with *there is, there are, here is, here are,* or similar constructions, the real subject follows the verb. Use *is* when the real subject is singular, *are* when it is plural.

There *is* a vast *difference* between the two plans.
There *are* a great many *angles* to this problem.

Here *are* two catalogues and an *order blank*. (See ¶¶1002a, 1028b.)
Here *is* an old *friend* and former *partner* of mine. (The subject, *friend and partner*, is singular because only one person is referred to. See ¶1002b.)

There *is* many an *investor* who regrets not having bought bonds. (See ¶1002c.)

There *is* a *branch office* or an *agency* representing us in every major city. (See ¶1003.)

There *is* not only *GST* but *provincial tax* as well. (See ¶1003.)

There *is* the *cost* of your own time in addition to the substantial outlay for materials that must be figured in the total. (See ¶1007.)

There's (There *is*) *more* than one *way* to solve the problem. (See ¶1013a.)

There *are more* than five *candidates* running for mayor.
(**NOT:** There's more than five candidates running for mayor.)

There *are a number* of problems to be resolved. (See also ¶1023.)
Here *is the number* of orders received since Monday.

Here *is $10* as a contribution. (See also ¶¶413, 1024.)
Here *are ten loonies* for your collection.

There *is* neither a *hospital* nor a *clinic* on the island. (See ¶1003 for two singular subjects joined by *neither . . . nor.*)

There *are* neither *motel rooms* nor *condominiums* available for rent this late in the season. (See ¶1004 for two plural subjects joined by *neither . . . nor.*)

There *were* neither *tennis courts* nor a *swimming pool* in the hotel where we finally found a room. (*Were* agrees with the nearer subject, *tennis courts*. See also ¶1005 for singular and plural subjects joined by *neither . . . nor.*)

There *was* neither central *air conditioning* nor *fans* for any of the rooms in the hotel. (*Was* agrees with the nearer subject, *air conditioning*. See also ¶1005.)

b. When the subject consists of a series of singular nouns—or a series of nouns, the first of which is singular—*there is* or *here is* usually sounds more idiomatic (despite the fact that the subject is plural) than *there are* or *here are*. If you do not feel comfortable with this idiomatic construction, change the wording as necessary.

In the higher-priced model there *is* a more powerful *processor*, a 19-inch *colour display*, and a 40-GB *hard drive*. (In this construction, *there is* is understood to be repeated before the second and third subjects.)

OR: In the higher-priced model there *are* the following features: a more powerful *processor*, a 19-inch *colour display*, and a 40-GB *hard drive*. (In this version, *are* agrees with the plural subject *features;* the three subjects in this sentence are now simply appositives modifying *features*.)

Within a kilometre of the airport, there *is* a full-service *hotel* and three *motels*.

OR: Within a kilometre of the airport, there *is* a full-service hotel *plus* (**OR** *in addition to* **OR** *as well as*) three motels. (By changing the connective from *and* to *plus* or something similar, you are left with a singular subject, *hotel*, that calls for the singular verb *is*.)

OR: Within a kilometre of the airport, there *are* three *motels* and a full-service *hotel*. (When the first subject in the series is plural, the verb *are* not only is grammatically correct but also sounds natural.)

Subjects and Predicate Complements

1029 Sentences containing a linking verb (such as *become* or some form of *to be*) sometimes have a plural subject and a singular complement or a singular subject and a plural complement. In such cases make sure that the verb agrees with the *subject* (and not with the complement).

Bicycles are the only product we make.   The key *issue is* higher wages.

One of the things we have to keep track of *is* entertainment expenses. (Use *is* to agree with *one*, the subject.)

It is they who are at fault. (Use *is* to agree with *it*, the subject.)

NOTE: Do not confuse the last two examples with the *inverted* sentences shown in ¶1028. In a sentence beginning with *here is* or *there is*, the subject *follows* the linking verb. In a sentence beginning with *it is* or *one . . . is*, the subject *precedes* the linking verb.

VERBS

This section deals with the correct use of verb tenses and other verb forms. For the rules on agreement of verbs with subjects, see ¶¶1001–1029.

Principal Parts

1030 The principal parts of a verb are the four simple forms upon which all tenses and other modifications of the verb are based.

a. For most verbs, the past and the past participle are formed simply by adding *d* or *ed* to the present form; the present participle is formed by adding *ing* to the present. (Some verbs require a minor change in the ending of the present form before *ed* or *ing* is added.)

Present	Past	Past Participle	Present Participle	
argue	argued	argued	arguing	(see ¶707)
die	died	died	dying	(see ¶709)
drop	dropped	dropped	dropping	(see ¶701)
fill	filled	filled	filling	(see ¶706)
need	needed	needed	needing	(see ¶705)
obey	obeyed	obeyed	obeying	(see ¶711)
occur	occurred	occurred	occurring	(see ¶702)
offer	offered	offered	offering	(see ¶704)
panic	panicked	panicked	panicking	(see ¶717)
try	tried	tried	trying	(see ¶710)
taxi	taxied	taxied	taxiing	(see ¶720)

b. Many frequently used verbs, however, have principal parts that are irregularly formed.

Present	Past	Past Participle	Present Participle
choose	chose	chosen	choosing
do	did	done	doing
fly	flew	flown	flying
get	got	gotten or got	getting
give	gave	given	giving
go	went	gone	going
grow	grew	grown	growing
know	knew	known	knowing
lay (place)	laid	laid	laying
lie (recline)	lay	lain	lying
pay	paid	paid	paying
raise	raised	raised	raising
ring	rang	rung	ringing
rise	rose	risen	rising
say	said	said	saying
set	set	set	setting
sit	sat	sat	sitting
speak	spoke	spoken	speaking
take	took	taken	taking
wear	wore	worn	wearing
write	wrote	written	writing

10

NOTE: Dictionaries typically show the principal parts for all *irregular* verbs. If you are in doubt about any form, consult your dictionary. If the principal parts are not shown, the verb is regular. (See ¶1030a.)

c. The past participle and the present participle, if used as a part of a verb phrase, must *always* be used with one or more helping (auxiliary) verbs. The most common helping verbs are:

is	was	can	do	has	have	might	shall	will
are	were	could	did	had	may	must	should	would

Verb Tenses

1031 The first principal part of the verb (the *present tense*) is used:

a. To express *present time.*

We *fill* all orders promptly.   She *does* what is expected of her.

b. To make a statement that is *true at all times.*

There *is* an exception to every rule (including this one).

c. With *shall* or *will* to express *future time.*

We *will order* (**OR** *shall order*) new stock next week. (For the use of the helping verbs *shall* and *will* in the future tense, see Section 11.)

☞ *For the third person singular form of the present tense, see ¶1035.*

1032 a. The second principal part of the verb (the *past tense*) is used to express *past time.* No helping verb is used with this form.

We *filled* the order yesterday.   She *did* what was expected of her.

b. Do not use a past participle form to express the past tense.

He *drank* his coffee. (**NOT:** He *drunk* his coffee.)

I *saw* it. (**NOT:** I *seen* it.)

They *began* it together. (**NOT:** They *begun* it together.)

He was the one who *did* it. (**NOT:** He was the one who *done* it.)

I can't believe this sweater *shrank*. (**NOT:** . . . this sweater *shrunk*.)

Jill *brought* me up to date on the Cox project. (**NOT:** Jill *brung* me . . .)

Someone *sneaked* into my office last night. (**NOT:** Someone *snuck* . . .)

1033 The third principal part of the verb (the *past participle*) is used:

a. To form the *present perfect tense.* This tense indicates action that was started in the past and has recently been completed or is continuing up to the present time. It consists of the verb *have* or *has* plus the past participle.

We *have filled* the orders. (**NOT:** We *have filled* the orders yesterday.)

She *has* always *done* what we expect of her.

Consumers *have become* an articulate force in today's business world.

(Continued on page 250.)

10

CONJUGATION OF THE VERBS *TO SEE, TO BE, TO HAVE*

PRESENT, PAST, AND FUTURE TENSES (¶¶1031–1032)

INFINITIVE	TO SEE		TO BE		TO HAVE	
PRESENT TENSE	I	see	I	*am*	I	have
First Principal Part	you	see	you	are	you	have
	he or she	*sees*	he or she	*is*	he or she	*has*
	we	see	we	are	we	have
	you	see	you	are	you	have
	they	see	they	are	they	have
PAST TENSE	I	saw	I	*was*	I	had
Second Principal Part	you	saw	you	were	you	had
	he or she	saw	he or she	*was*	he or she	had
	we	saw	we	were	we	had
	you	saw	you	were	you	had
	they	saw	they	were	they	had
FUTURE TENSE	I *shall*	see	I *shall*	be	I *shall*	have
Helping Verb (*shall* OR *will*)	you will	see	you will	be	you will	have
+	he or she will	see	he or she will	be	he or she will	have
Main Verb (first principal part)	we *shall*	see	we *shall*	be	we *shall*	have
	you will	see	you will	be	you will	have
	they will	see	they will	be	they will	have

PASSIVE TENSES (¶1036)

INFINITIVE	TO SEE	
PRESENT PASSIVE TENSE	I *am*	seen
Helping Verb (present tense of *be*)	you are	seen
+	he or she *is*	seen
Main Verb (past participle)	we are	seen
	you are	seen
	they are	seen
PAST PASSIVE TENSE	I *was*	seen
Helping Verb (past tense of *be*)	you were	seen
+	he or she *was*	seen
Main Verb (past participle)	we were	seen
	you were	seen
	they were	seen
FUTURE PASSIVE TENSE	I *shall* be	seen
Helping Verb (future tense of *be*)	you will be	seen
+	he or she will be	seen
Main Verb (past participle)	we *shall* be	seen
	you will be	seen
	they will be	seen

PROGRESSIVE TENSES (¶1034)

INFINITIVE	TO SEE	
PRESENT PROGRESSIVE TENSE	I *am*	seeing
Helping Verb (present tense of *be*)	you are	seeing
+	he or she *is*	seeing
Main Verb (present participle)	we are	seeing
	you are	seeing
	they are	seeing
PAST PROGRESSIVE TENSE	I *was*	seeing
Helping Verb (past tense of *be*)	you were	seeing
+	he or she *was*	seeing
Main Verb (present participle)	we were	seeing
	you were	seeing
	they were	seeing
FUTURE PROGRESSIVE TENSE	I *shall* be	seeing
Helping Verb (future tense of *be*)	you will be	seeing
+	he or she will be	seeing
Main Verb (present participle)	we *shall* be	seeing
	you will be	seeing
	they will be	seeing

10

PERFECT TENSES (¶1033)

INFINITIVE	TO SEE		TO BE	
PRESENT PERFECT TENSE	I have	seen	I have	been
Helping Verb (present tense of *have*)	you have	seen	you have	been
+	he or she *has*	seen	he or she *has*	been
Main Verb (past participle)	we have	seen	we have	been
	you have	seen	you have	been
	they have	seen	they have	been
PAST PERFECT TENSE	I had	seen	I had	been
Helping Verb (past tense of *have*)	you had	seen	you had	been
+	he or she had	seen	he or she had	been
Main Verb (past participle)	we had	seen	we had	been
	you had	seen	you had	been
	they had	seen	they had	been
FUTURE PERFECT TENSE	I *shall* have	seen	I *shall* have	been
Helping Verb (future tense of *have*)	you will have	seen	you will have	been
+	he or she will have	seen	he or she will have	been
Main Verb (past participle)	we *shall* have	seen	we *shall* have	been
	you will have	seen	you will have	been
	they will have	seen	they will have	been

PERFECT PASSIVE TENSES (¶1036)

INFINITIVE	TO SEE	
PRESENT PERFECT PASSIVE TENSE	I have been	seen
Helping Verb (present perfect tense of *be*)	you have been	seen
+	he or she *has* been	seen
Main Verb (past participle)	we have been	seen
	you have been	seen
	they have been	seen
PAST PERFECT PASSIVE TENSE	I had been	seen
Helping Verb (past perfect tense of *be*)	you had been	seen
+	he or she had been	seen
Main Verb (past participle)	we had been	seen
	you had been	seen
	they had been	seen
FUTURE PERFECT PASSIVE TENSE	I *shall* have been	seen
Helping Verb (future perfect tense of *be*)	you will have been	seen
+	he or she will have been	seen
Main Verb (past participle)	we *shall* have been	seen
	you will have been	seen
	they will have been	seen

PERFECT PROGRESSIVE TENSES (¶1034)

INFINITIVE	TO SEE	
PRESENT PERFECT PROGRESSIVE TENSE	I have been	seeing
Helping Verb (present perfect tense of *be*)	you have been	seeing
+	he or she *has* been	seeing
Main Verb (present participle)	we have been	seeing
	you have been	seeing
	they have been	seeing
PAST PERFECT PROGRESSIVE TENSE	I had been	seeing
Helping Verb (past perfect tense of *be*)	you had been	seeing
+	he or she had been	seeing
Main Verb (present participle)	we had been	seeing
	you had been	seeing
	they had been	seeing
FUTURE PERFECT PROGRESSIVE TENSE	I *shall* have been	seeing
Helping Verb (future perfect tense of *be*)	you will have been	seeing
+	he or she will have been	seeing
Main Verb (present participle)	we *shall* have been	seeing
	you will have been	seeing
	they will have been	seeing

10

b. To form the *past perfect tense*. This tense indicates action that was completed *before another past action*. It consists of the verb *had* plus the past participle.

We *had filled* the orders before we saw your letter.

She *had finished* the job before we arrived.

c. To form the *future perfect tense*. This tense indicates action that will be completed *before a certain time in the future*. It consists of the verb *shall have* or *will have* plus the past participle.

We *will have filled* the orders by that time. (See Section 11 for the use of *shall* and *will*.)

She *will have finished* the job by next Friday.

NOTE: Be careful not to use a past tense form (the second principal part) in place of a past participle.

I have *broken* the racket. (**NOT:** I have *broke* the racket.)

The dress has *shrunk*. (**NOT:** The dress has *shrank*.)

Prices have *risen* again. (**NOT:** Prices have *rose* again.)

He has *worn* his shoes out. (**NOT:** He has *wore* his shoes out.)

1034 The fourth principal part of the verb (the *present participle*) is used:

a. To form the *present progressive tense*. This tense indicates action still in progress. It consists of the verb *am, is,* or *are* plus the present participle.

We *are filling* all orders as fast as we can.

She *is doing* all that can be expected of her.

b. To form the *past progressive tense*. This tense indicates action in progress some-time in the past. It consists of the verb *was* or *were* plus the present participle.

We *were waiting* for new stock at the time your order came in.

She *was doing* a good job when I last checked her work.

c. To form the *future progressive tense*. This tense indicates action that will be in progress in the future. It consists of the verb *shall be* or *will be* plus the present participle.

We *will be working* overtime for the next two weeks. (See Section 11 for the use of *shall* and *will*.)

They *will be receiving* additional stock throughout the next two weeks.

d. To form the *present perfect progressive*, the *past perfect progressive*, and the *future perfect progressive tenses*. These tenses convey the same meaning as the simple perfect tenses except that the progressive element adds the sense of continuous action. (See ¶1033.) These tenses consist of the verbs *has been, have been, had been, shall have been,* and *will have been* plus the present participle. Compare the following examples with those in ¶1033.

We *have been filling* these orders with Model 212A instead of 212. (Present perfect progressive.)

10

We *had been filling* these orders with Model 212A until we saw your directive. (Past perfect progressive.)

By next Friday we *will have been working* overtime for two straight weeks. (Future perfect progressive.)

1035 The first principal part of the verb undergoes a change in form to express the third person singular in the present tense.

a. Most verbs simply add *s* in the third person singular.

he feels	**BUT:** I feel, you feel, we feel, they feel
she thinks	I think, you think, we think, they think
it looks	I look, you look, we look, they look

b. Verbs ending in *s, x, z, sh, ch,* or *o* add *es.*

he misses	it buzzes	she watches
she fixes	he wishes	it goes

c. Verbs ending in a vowel plus *y* add *s*; those ending in a consonant plus *y* change *y* to *i* and add *es.*

say: he says	employ: she employs	try: it tries
convey: she conveys	buy: he buys	apply: she applies

d. Verbs ending in *i* simply add *s.*

taxi: he taxis	ski: she skis

e. The verb *to be* is irregular since *be*, the first principal part, is not used in the present tense.

I am	he, she, it is	you are
you are	we are	they are

f. The present and past tenses of a few verbs remain unchanged in the third person singular.

he may	she can	it will
he might	she could	it would

☞ *See the entry for* Don't *in Section 11.*

Passive Forms

1036 The passive forms of a verb consist of some part of the helping verb *to be* plus the past participle of the main verb.

it is intended (present passive of *intend*)

we were expected (past passive of *expect*)

they will be audited (future passive of *audit*)

she has been notified (present perfect passive of *notify*)

you had been told (past perfect passive of *tell*)

he will have been given (future perfect passive of *give*)

1037 A *passive* verb directs the action toward the subject. An *active* verb directs the action toward an object.

> ACTIVE: Melanie *(subject)* will lead *(verb)* the discussion *(object)*.
>
> PASSIVE: The discussion *(subject)* will be led *(verb)* by Melanie.

☞ *For additional examples, see the entry for* Voice *in Section 19.*

a. The passive form of a verb is appropriate (1) when you want to emphasize the *receiver* of the action (by making it the subject) or (2) when the *doer* of the action is not important or is deliberately not mentioned.

> I was seriously injured as a result of your negligence. (Emphasizes *I*, the receiver of the action. RATHER THAN: Your negligence seriously injured me.)

> This proposal is based on a careful analysis of all available research studies. (Emphasizes the basis for the proposal; the person who drafted the proposal is not important.)

> Unfortunately, the decision was made without consulting any of the board members. (Emphasizes how the decision was made and deliberately omits the name of the person responsible.)

b. In all other cases use active verb forms to achieve a simpler and more vigorous style. Except in those circumstances cited in ¶1037a, passive verb forms typically produce awkward or stilted sentences.

> WEAK PASSIVES: It *has been decided* by the Human Resources Committee that full pay *should be given* to you for the period of your hospitalization.

> STRONG ACTIVES: The Human Resources Committee *has decided* that you *should receive* full pay for the period of your hospitalization.

c. Watch out for passive constructions that unintentionally point to the wrong *doer* of the action.

> CONFUSING: Two computer terminals were reported stolen over the weekend by the head of corporate security.
> CLEAR: The head of corporate security reported that two computer terminals were stolen over the weekend.

> CONFUSING: One of our second-shift workers was found injured by a Good Samaritan outside the parking lot entrance last night.
> CLEAR: Last night one of our second-shift workers was injured outside the parking lot entrance and was found there by a Good Samaritan.

10 Verbs Following Clauses of Necessity, Demand, Etc.

1038 Sentences that express *necessity, demand, strong request, urging,* or *resolution* in the main clause require a *subjunctive* verb in the dependent clause that follows.

a. If the verb in the dependent clause requires the use of the verb *to be,* use the form *be* with all three persons (not *am, is,* or *are*).

> NECESSITY: It is necessary (OR important OR essential) that these questions *be answered* at once. (NOT: are answered.)

> DEMAND: I insist that I *be allowed* to present a minority report at the next board meeting. (NOT: am allowed.)

REQUEST: They have asked that you *be notified* at once if matters do not proceed according to plan. (NOT: are notified.)

URGING: We urged (OR suggested) that he *be given* a second chance to prove himself in the job. (NOT: is given.)

RESOLUTION: The committee has resolved (OR decided OR ruled) that the decision *be deferred* until the next meeting. (NOT: is deferred.)

b. If the verb in the dependent clause is a verb other than *be*, use the ordinary *present tense* form for all three persons. However, do not add *s* (or otherwise change the form) for the third person singular.

NECESSITY: It is essential that he *arrive* on time. (NOT: arrives.)

DEMAND: They insist that he *do* the work over. (NOT: does.)

REQUEST: They have asked that she *remain* on the committee until the end of the year. (NOT: remains.)

URGING: I suggested that she *triple-space* the material to allow room for some very heavy editing. (NOT: triple-spaces.)

RESOLUTION: They have resolved that Fred *represent* them. (NOT: represents.)

☞ *See the entry for* Mood, subjunctive *in Section 19.*

Verbs Following *Wish* Clauses

1039 Sentences that start with *I wish, she wishes,* and so on, require a subjunctive verb in the dependent clause that follows.

a. To express *present* time in the dependent clause, put the verb in the *past tense.*

I wish I *knew* how to proceed.

I wish I *could attend.*

NOTE: If the verb is *to be*, use *were* for all three persons.

I wish I *were going* to the reception. (NOT: was going.)

I wish he *were going* with me.

b. To express *past* time in the dependent clause, put the verb in the *past perfect tense.*

I wish that she *had invited* me.

I wish that I *had been* there.

I wish that I *could have attended.*

c. To express *future* time in the dependent clause, use the helping verb *would* instead of *will.*

I wish he *would arrive* on time.

I wish she *would make* more of an effort.

Verbs in *If* Clauses

1040 When an *if* clause states a condition that is *highly improbable, doubtful,* or *contrary to fact,* the verb in the *if* clause requires special treatment, like that described in ¶1039; *to express present time, use the past tense; to express past time,*

(Continued on page 254.)

10

use the past perfect tense. (In the following examples note the relationship of tenses between the dependent clause and the main clause.)

> If I *knew* the answer (but I don't), I *would* not *ask* you.
> If I *had known* the answer (but I didn't), I *would* not *have asked* you.

> If I *were* you (but I am not), I *would take* the job.
> If I *had been* in your shoes (but I wasn't), I *would have taken* the job.

> If he *were invited* (but he isn't), he *would be* glad to go.
> If he *had been invited* (but he wasn't), he *would have been* glad to go.

NOTE: Do not use *would have* for *had* in an *if* clause. See Section 11 for a usage note on *would have*.

1041 When an *if* clause states a condition that is *possible* or *likely*, the verb in the *if* clause requires no special treatment. *To express present time, use the present tense; to express past time, use the past tense.* Compare the following pairs of examples. Those labelled "Probable" reflect the verb forms described here in ¶1041. Those labelled "Improbable" reflect the verb forms described in ¶1040.

> **PROBABLE:** If I *leave* this job (and I may do so), I *will take* a full-time teaching position.
> **IMPROBABLE:** If I *left* this job (but I probably won't), I *would take* a full-time teaching position.

> **PROBABLE:** If I *go* to Fredericton (and I may), I *will want* you to go with me.
> **IMPROBABLE:** If I *were going* to Fredericton (but I probably won't), I *would want* you to go with me.

> **PROBABLE:** If she *was* in yesterday (and she may have been), I *did* not *see* her.
> **IMPROBABLE:** If she *had been* in yesterday (but she wasn't), I *would have seen* her.

Verbs in *As If* or *As Though* Clauses

1042 When an *as if* or *as though* clause expresses a condition *contrary to fact*, the verb in the clause requires special treatment, like that described in ¶1040.

> She acts as if she *were* the only person who mattered. (But she isn't.)

> He talks as if he *knew* the facts of the situation. (But he doesn't.)

> You act as though you *hadn't* a care in the world. (But you have.)

1043 *As if* or *as though* clauses are now often used to express a condition that is *highly probable.* In such cases do not give the verb special treatment. *Use the present tense to express present time, the future tense to express future time, and the past tense to express past time.*

> It looks as if it *will* rain. (**OR:** It looks as if it *is going* to rain.)

> She acted as if she *planned* to look for another job.

Infinitives

1044 An infinitive is the form of the verb preceded by *to* (for example, *to write, to do, to be*). When two or more infinitives are used in a parallel construction, the word *to* may be omitted after the first infinitive unless special emphasis is desired.

> Ask Ruth Gregoire *to sign* both copies of the contract, *return* the original to us, and *keep* the other copy. (*Return* and *keep* are infinitives without *to*.)

I would like you *to explain* the job to Harry, *to give* him help if he needs it, and *to see* that the job is done properly. (For emphasis, *to* is used with all three infinitives—*explain, give,* and *see.*)

NOTE: The word *to* is usually dropped when the infinitive follows such verbs as *see, hear, feel, let, help,* and *need.*

Will you please help me *copy* the disk? (**RATHER THAN:** help me *to copy* . . .)

You need not *return* the clipping. (**OR:** You do not need *to return* the clipping.)

1045 a. Infinitives have two main tense forms: present and perfect.

(1) The perfect infinitive is used to express action that has been completed before the time of the main verb.

I *am sorry to have caused* you so much trouble last week. (The act of causing trouble was completed before the act of expressing regret; therefore, the perfect infinitive is used.)

(2) The present infinitive is used in all other cases.

I planned *to leave* early. (**NOT:** *to have left.* The act of leaving could not have been completed before the act of planning; therefore, the present infinitive is used.)

b. The passive form of the present infinitive consists of *to be* plus the past participle. Do not omit *to be* in such constructions. (See ¶1036.)

This office needs *to be repainted.* (**NOT:** This office needs *repainted.*)

1046 *Splitting an infinitive* (that is, inserting an adverb between *to* and the verb) should be avoided because (a) it typically produces an awkward construction and (b) the adverb usually functions more effectively in another location.

WEAK: It was impossible to *even* see a foot ahead.
BETTER: It was impossible to see *even* a foot ahead.

WEAK: He always tries to *carefully* do the work.
BETTER: He always tries to do the work *carefully.*

However, split the infinitive when alternative locations of the adverb produce an awkward or weakly constructed sentence.

a. Before splitting an infinitive, first try to place the adverb *after the object* of the infinitive. In many instances the adverb functions most effectively in that location.

You ought *to review* these plans *thoroughly.*
(**BETTER THAN:** You ought to thoroughly review these plans.)

I need *to make* the decision *quickly.*
(**BETTER THAN:** I need to quickly make the decision.)

b. If step *a* does not produce an effective sentence, try to locate the adverb directly *before* or directly *after* the infinitive. In some cases the adverb functions effectively in this position; in other cases the resulting sentence is awkward.

(Continued on page 256.)

CONFUSING: I want you *to supervise* the work that is to be done *personally*. (When the object of the infinitive is long or involved, it is difficult to place the adverb after the object without creating confusion. Here *personally* seems to modify *to be done* when in fact it should modify *to supervise*.)

AWKWARD: I want you to supervise *personally* the work that is to be done.

GOOD: I want you *personally* to supervise the work that is to be done.

c. If steps *a* and *b* fail to produce an effective sentence, try splitting the infinitive. If a good sentence results, keep it; if not, try rewording the sentence.

CONFUSING: I want you *to consider* Jenkins' proposal to handle all our deliveries *carefully*. (When *carefully* is located after the complete object, it no longer clearly refers to *to consider*.)

AWKWARD: I want you *carefully* to consider Jenkins' proposal to handle all our deliveries.

AWKWARD: I want you to consider *carefully* Jenkins' proposal to handle all our deliveries.

GOOD: I want you to *carefully* consider Jenkins' proposal . . .

d. When an infinitive consists of *to be* plus a past or present participle of another verb, inserting an adverb before the participle is not considered splitting an infinitive. Nevertheless, in many such sentences it may be possible to locate the adverb to better advantage elsewhere in the sentence.

These plans need to be *thoroughly* reviewed.

Claude appears to be *continually* turning up with last-minute objections to any decision I make.

NOTE: By the same token, it is perfectly acceptable to position an adverb between a helping verb and a past or present participle. It is even acceptable to position an adverb *within* the elements of a helping verb.

This new technology has *already* been *effectively* applied in many industries.

I hear that Martha has been *seriously* considering early retirement.

☞ *For dangling infinitive phrases, see also ¶1082b.*

Sequence of Tenses

1047 When the verb in the main clause is in the past tense, the verb in a dependent *that* clause should also express past time. Consider the tenses in the following pairs of examples:

She *says* (present) that she *is* now *working* (present) for CBC.
She *said* (past) that she *was* now *working* (past) for CBC.

He *says* (present) that he *has seen* (present perfect) your résumé.
He *said* (past) that he *had seen* (past perfect) your résumé.

I *think* (present) that he *will see* (future) you tomorrow.
I *thought* (past) that he *would see* (past form of *will see*) you tomorrow.

EXCEPTION: The verb in the dependent clause should remain in the present tense if it expresses a general truth.

Our legal adviser *pointed out* (past) that all persons under 18 *are* (present) legally considered minors. (General truth.)

Omitting Parts of Verbs

1048 When compound verbs in the same sentence share a common element, that element does not need to be repeated.

> We *have* received your letter and forwarded it to our office. (The helping verb *have* shared by the two main verbs, *received* and *forwarded*.)

> We can and will *achieve* these goals. (The main verb *achieve* is shared by the two helping verbs *can* and *will*.)

However, do not omit any element when different parts of the main verb are required.

> **WRONG:** I never have and I never will forget what you have done for me.
> **RIGHT:** I never have *forgotten* and I never will *forget* . . .

> **WRONG:** We have and still are asking for an accounting of the assets.
> **RIGHT:** We have *asked* and still are *asking* for . . .

Troublesome Verbs

☞ *See individual entries listed alphabetically in Section 11 for the following verbs:*

Affect—Effect	Ensure—Insure—Assure	Of—Have
Appreciate	Enthused Over	Raise—Rise
Being that	Graduated—Was Graduated	Serve—Service
Bring—Take	Help	Set—Sit
Cannot help but	Imply—Infer	Shall—Will
Come—Go	Lay—Lie	Should—Would
Come and	Learn—Teach	Supposed to
Comprise—Compose	Leave—Let	Try and
Done	May—Can (Might—Could)	Used to
Don't	Maybe—May Be	Would Have

PRONOUNS

Agreement With Antecedents: Basic Rules

1049 a. A pronoun must agree with its *antecedent* (the word for which the pronoun stands) in number, gender, and person.

> *I* must stand by *my* client, just as *you* must stand by *yours.*

> *Frank* said that *he* could do the job alone.

> *Alice* wants to know whether *her* proposal has been approved.

> The *company* has not decided whether to change *its* policy on vacations. (See ¶¶1019–1020.)

> *We* plan to explain *our* shift in corporate strategy at the next shareholders' meeting.

> The company's *auditors* will issue *their* report tomorrow.

> The *Vanderveers* are giving a party at *their* house.

> The *committee* has completed *its* investigation. (See ¶1019 for collective nouns.)

(Continued on page 258.)

Why not have *each witness* write *his* or *her* version of the accident? (See ¶1053 for indefinite pronouns as antecedents.)

It is *I* who *am* at fault. (*Who* agrees in person and number with the antecedent *I;* the verb *am* also agrees with *I.*)

It is *she* who *is* willing to compromise.   It is *they* who *are* not.

It is *we*, the individual taxpayers, who *have* to make up for the loss of commercial property taxes.

It is *they* who *are* behind schedule.

It is *you* who *are* to blame. (*Who* refers to *you;* hence the verb *are* is plural to agree with *you.* (See also Note ¶1001a.)

BUT: You are the *person* who *is* to blame. (Here *who* refers to *person;* hence the verb *is* is singular to agree with *person.*)

b. Use a plural pronoun when the antecedent consists of two nouns or pronouns joined by *and.*

Can *Mary* and *you* give us *your* decision by Monday?

Sonia and *Dave* say *they* will attend.

The *Montaignes* and the *Reillys* have sent *their* regrets.

Are *you* and *I* prepared to say that *we* can handle the assignment?

c. Use a singular pronoun when the antecedent consists of two *singular* nouns joined by *or* or *nor.* Use a plural pronoun when the antecedent consists of two *plural* nouns joined by *or* or *nor.* (See also ¶¶1003–1005.)

Either *Will* or *Ed* will have to give up *his* office. (**NOT:** their.)

Neither *Joan* nor *Helen* wants to do *her* share. (**NOT:** their.)

Either the *Kopecks* or the *Henleys* will bring *their* videocassette recorder.

NOTE: When *or* or *nor* joins a singular noun and a plural noun, a pronoun that refers to this construction should agree in number with the nearer noun. However, a strict application of this rule can lead to problems in sentence structure and meaning. Therefore, always try to make this kind of construction plural by locating the plural subject nearer the verb.

Neither Mr. Wing nor his *employees have* reached *their* goal. (The plural pronoun *their* is used to agree with the nearer noun, *employees;* the verb *have* is also in the plural.)

NOT: Neither the employees nor Mr. Wing *has* reached *his* goal. (The sentence follows the rule—*his* agrees with Mr. Wing, the nearer noun, and the verb *has* is singular; however, the meaning of the sentence has been distorted.)

d. Make sure that the pronouns you use agree in gender with their antecedents. To avoid confusion, reword as necessary.

The entire *staff* wishes to express *its* gratitude. (Third person singular.)

We (**OR** *All of us*) wish to express *our* gratitude. (First person plural).

BUT NOT: The entire *staff* wishes to express *our* gratitude. (Do not use a first person pronoun to refer to a third person antecedent.)

10

Unrealistic deadlines, excessive pressures, and unsafe working conditions can be very damaging to your employees. You must do everything you can to eliminate these destructive conditions.

BUT NOT: Unrealistic deadlines, excessive pressures, and unsafe working conditions can be very damaging to your employees. You must do everything you can to eliminate them. (The employees or the destructive conditions?)

Agreement With Common-Gender Antecedents

1050 Nouns that apply both to males and females have a *common* gender.

parent	doctor	assistant	writer
child	lawyer	supervisor	speaker
customer	professor	employee	listener
manager	instructor	student	consultant

When a singular noun of common gender serves as a *definite* antecedent (one that names a specific person whose gender is known), use the pronoun *he* or *she* as appropriate.

My *employer* (previously identified as Robert Hayes) prefers to open *his* own mail.

Ask your *doctor* (known to be a woman) to sign *her* name on the attached form.

1051 When a singular noun of common gender serves as an *indefinite* antecedent (*a doctor, any doctor, every doctor*) or as a *generic* antecedent (*the doctor,* meaning "doctors in general"), the traditional practice has been to use *he* as a generic pronoun applying equally to males and females.

The *writer* should include a table of contents with *his* manuscript.

When an indefinite or generic antecedent names an occupation or a role in which women predominate (for example, *the dietitian, the secretary, the nurse*), the traditional practice has been to use *she* as a generic pronoun.

An *executive assistant* needs to organize *her* work and set priorities each day.

1052 There are some people who feel that the masculine bias in the word *he* makes it unsuitable as a pronoun that applies equally to women and men. Moreover, they feel that the generic use of *she* serves to reinforce stereotyped notions about women's occupations or roles. Consider the following alternatives to the generic use of *he* or *she.*

a. Use *he or she, his or her,* or *him or her.* This works well in isolated cases but can be clumsy if repeated frequently in the same context. (In any case, avoid the use of *he/she, s/he,* and similar constructions.)

An *instructor* should offer *his or her* students challenging projects.

(**RATHER THAN:** An instructor should offer *his* students . . .)

b. Change the wording from singular to plural.

Parents of teenagers often *wonder* where *they* went wrong.

(**RATHER THAN:** The *parent* of a teenager often *wonders* where *he or she* went wrong.)

(Continued on page 260.)

c. Reword to avoid the generic pronoun.

When a customer calls, be sure to ask for a phone number.

(**RATHER THAN:** When a customer calls, ask *him or her* to leave *his or her* phone number.)

An assistant tries to anticipate the needs of the employer.

(**RATHER THAN:** An assistant tries to anticipate the needs of *his or her* employer.)

d. If the application of these various alternatives produces wordiness or an unacceptable shift in meaning or emphasis, then as a last resort use the generic *he* or the generic *she* as described in ¶1051. However, try to avoid doing so whenever possible.

Agreement With Indefinite-Pronoun Antecedents

1053 a. Use a singular pronoun when the antecedent is a singular indefinite pronoun. The following indefinite pronouns are always singular:

anyone	everyone	someone	no one
anybody	everybody	somebody	nobody
anything	everything	something	nothing
each	every	either	one
each one	many a	neither	another

Every company has *its* own vacation policy. (**NOT:** their.)

Neither one of the campaigns did as well as *it* was supposed to. (**NOT:** they were.)

NOTE: These singular indefinite pronouns often call for the generic use of *he* or *she*. (See ¶¶1051–1052.) In the following sentences, alternative wording is shown to suggest how the generic *he* or *she* can be avoided.

Everyone should submit *his* expense report by Friday.
BETTER: All staff *members* should submit *their* expense reports by Friday.

If *anyone* should ask for me, tell *him* that I won't return until Monday.
BETTER: If anyone should ask for me, say that I won't return . . .

Does *every assistant* know how *she* is to handle *her employer's* calls?
BETTER: Do *all the assistants* know how *they* are to handle *their employers'* calls?

☞ *For agreement of these indefinite pronouns with verbs, see ¶¶1009–1011.*

For possessive forms of these pronouns, see ¶637.

b. Use a plural pronoun when the antecedent is a plural indefinite pronoun. The following indefinite pronouns are always plural:

many	few	several	others	both

Many customers prefer to help *themselves; others* usually like to have someone wait on *them*.

A *few* of the directors have not yet taken *their* vacations.

Several sales representatives made *their* annual goals in nine months.

Both managers have said that *they* want to be considered for Mr. Hall's job.

☞ *For agreement of these indefinite pronouns with verbs, see ¶1012.*

c. The following indefinite pronouns may be singular or plural, depending on the noun they refer to.

all	none	any	some	more	most

When these words are used as antecedents, determine whether they are singular or plural. Then make the pronouns that refer to them agree in number.

Some employees have not yet had *their* annual physical checkup. (*Some* refers to *employees* and is plural; *some* is the antecedent of *their*.)

Some of the manuscript has been keyed, but *it* has not been proofread. (*Some* refers to *manuscript* and is singular; *some* is the antecedent of *it* in the second clause.)

☞ *For agreement of these indefinite pronouns with verbs, see ¶1013.*

d. Since indefinite pronouns express the third person, pronouns referring to these antecedents should also be in the third person *(he, she, it, they)*.

If *anyone* wants a vacation pay advance, *he* or *she* should apply for it in writing.

(**NOT:** If *anyone* wants a vacation pay advance, *you* should apply for it . . .)

If the indefinite pronoun is modified so that it strongly expresses the first or second person, the personal pronoun must also agree in number. Compare the following examples:

Most parents want *their* children to go to college. (Third person.)
Most of *us* want *our* children to go to college. (First person.)

A *few* have missed *their* deadlines. (Third person.)
A *few* of *you* have missed *your* deadlines. (Second person.)

Each employee knows how much *he* or *she* ought to contribute to the United Way fund drive. (Third person.)
BUT: *Each* of us knows how much *he* or *she* ought to contribute to the United Way fund drive. (Third person. In this sentence, *of us* does not shift the meaning to the first person; the emphasis is on what the individual contributes, not on what *we* contribute.)

IMPORTANT NOTE: Pronouns take different forms, not only to indicate a difference in person *(I, you, he)*, number *(he, they)*, and gender *(he, she)*, but also to indicate a difference in case *(nominative, possessive, objective)*. Although a pronoun must agree with its antecedent in person, number, and gender, it does *not* necessarily agree with its antecedent in case. The case of a pronoun depends on its own relation to the other words in the sentence. The rules in ¶¶1054–1064 indicate how to choose the right case for pronouns.

Personal Pronouns
1054 NOMINATIVE FORMS OF PERSONAL PRONOUNS

Use *I, we, you, he, she, it, they:*

a. When the pronoun is the subject of a verb.

(Continued on page 262.)

I wrote to Gemma Petrini, but *she* hasn't answered.

Debbie and *I* can handle the job ourselves.
(**NOT:** Debbie and me **OR:** me and Debbie.)

Either *he* or *I* can work late tonight. (**NOT:** him or me.)

NOTE: In sentences like the last two above, try each subject alone with the verb. You would not say "Me can handle the job" or "Him can work late tonight." Therefore, *I* and *he* must be used.

b. When the pronoun appears in the predicate after some form of the verb *to be* (*am, is, are, was, were*) or after a verb phrase containing some form of *to be* (see the list below). Pronouns that follow these verb forms should be in the nominative.

shall (**OR** will) be	have (**OR** has) been
should (**OR** would) be	had been
shall (**OR** will) have been	may (**OR** might) be
should (**OR** would) have been	may (**OR** might) have been
can (**OR** could) be	must (**OR** ought to) be
could have been	must have (**OR** ought to have) been

It could have been *they*.   Was it *he* or *she* who phoned?
It is *I*.   This is *she*.

NOTE: A sentence like *It could have been they*, while grammatically correct, would sound better if reworded in idiomatic English: *They could have been the ones.* Moreover, a sentence like *It's me* is acceptable in colloquial speech but not in writing. When you hear a telephone caller ask for you by name, do not respond by saying *This is him* or *This is her*. If you wish to respond correctly (and somewhat pompously), say *This is he* or *This is she*. If you wish to respond correctly (and sound more natural), say *This is . . .* and then give your name.

☞ *For special rules governing pronouns with the infinitive* to be, *see* ¶1064.

1055 OBJECTIVE FORMS OF PERSONAL PRONOUNS

Use *me, us, you, him, her, it, them*:

a. When the pronoun is the direct or indirect object of a verb.

Larry gave Maris and *us* tickets for the opening.

They invited my husband and *me* for the weekend.

NOTE: When *my husband and* is mentally omitted, the objective form *me* is clearly the correct pronoun ("They invited *me* for the weekend").

b. When the pronoun is the object of a preposition.

This is for *you* and *her*.

No one knows except *you* and *me*. (**NOT:** except you and I.)

Between *you* and *me*, that decision is unfair. (**NOT:** between you and I.)

EXCEPTION: He is a friend of *mine* (*yours, his, hers, ours, theirs*). (See ¶648.)

c. When the pronoun is the subject or object of an infinitive. (See ¶1064.)

The department head asked *him* to resign. (*Him* is the subject of *to resign*.)

Did you ask Janet to call *me*? (*Me* is the object of *to call*.)

1056 POSSESSIVE FORMS OF PERSONAL PRONOUNS

a. Most personal pronouns have two possessive forms:

my	your	his	her	its	our	their
mine	yours	. . .	hers	. . .	ours	theirs

b. Use *my, your, his, her, its, our,* or *their* when the possessive pronoun immediately precedes the noun it modifies.

That is *my* book.   It was *their* choice.   George is *her* neighbour.

c. Use *mine, yours, his, hers, its, ours,* or *theirs* when the possessive pronoun stands apart from the noun it refers to.

That book is *mine*.   The choice was *theirs*.   George is a neighbour of *hers*.

NOTE: Do not insert an apostrophe before the final *s* in possessive pronouns.

yours (**NOT:** your's)   ours (**NOT:** our's)

hers (**NOT:** her's)   theirs (**NOT:** their's)

d. A pronoun that modifies a *gerund* (a verbal noun ending in *ing*) should be in the possessive. (See ¶647.)

I appreciate *your shipping* the order so promptly.

(**NOT:** I appreciated *you shipping* the order so promptly.)

e. Do not confuse certain possessive pronouns with contractions and other phrases that sound like the possessive pronouns.

its (possessive)   it's (it is **OR** it has)

their (possessive)   they're (they are) **OR** there're (there are)

theirs (possessive)   there's (there is **OR** there has)

your (possessive)   you're (you are)

As a test for the correct form, try to substitute *it is, it has, they are, there are, there is, there has,* or *you are,* whichever is appropriate. If the substitution does not make sense, use the corresponding possessive form.

The firm must protect *its* assets. ("Protect it is assets" makes no sense.)

BUT: *It's* time to take stock of our achievements.

How would you go about estimating *its* worth?

BUT: How much would you say *it's* worth?

Their investing in high-tech stocks was a shrewd idea.

BUT: *They're* investing in high-tech stocks.

Their complaints have proved to be unfounded.

BUT: *There are* complaints that have proved to be unfounded.

Theirs no longer works; that's why they borrow ours.

BUT: *There's* no use expecting him to change.

(Continued on page 264.)

10

Your thinking is sound, but we lack the funds to underwrite your proposal.
BUT: *You're* thinking of applying for a transfer, I understand.

☞ *For other possessive pronouns, see also ¶¶636–637.*

1057 When a pronoun follows *than* or *as* in a comparison, determine the correct form of the pronoun by mentally supplying any missing words.

She writes better than *I*. (She writes better than *I* do.)

I like you better than *him*. (I like you better than *I like him*.)
BUT: I like you better than *he*. (I like you better than *he does*.)

Joe is not as talented as *she*. (Joes is not as talented as *she is*.)

1058 When a pronoun is used to identify a noun or another pronoun, it is either nominative or objective, depending on how the antecedent is used.

The committee has asked *us*, Ruth and *me*, to present the report. (Since *us* is objective, the identifying pronoun *me* is also objective.)

The explanation was for the *newcomers*, Marie and *me*. (Was for *me*.)

The exceptions were the *newcomers*, Marie and *I*. (Exception was *I*.)

Let's *you* and *me* schedule a brown-bag lunch. (*Let's* is a contraction for *let us*. Since *us* is the objective form, the pronouns *you* and *me* are also objective.)

NOTE: In sentences like the following, mentally omit the noun *(employees)* to determine the correct form.

The company wants *us* employees to work on Saturdays. (The company wants *us* to work on Saturdays.)

We employees need to confer. (*We* need to confer.)

1059 Some writers consistently use *we* instead of *I* to avoid a seeming overemphasis on themselves. However, it is preferable to use *we* only when you are speaking on behalf of an organization you represent and to use *I* when speaking for yourself alone.

We shall prepare the necessary forms as soon as you send *us* a signed release. (This writer is speaking on behalf of the firm.)

It is *my* opinion that this patient may be discharged at once. (This writer is speaking only for himself. Under these circumstances it would sound pompous to say, "It is *our* opinion.")

Compound Personal Pronouns

1060 The *self-* or *selves*-ending pronouns (*myself, yourself, himself, herself, itself, ourselves, yourselves, themselves*) should be used:

a. To direct the action expressed by the verb back to the subject.

She found *herself* the only one in favour of the move.

We have satisfied *ourselves* as to the wisdom of the action.

We think that *they* have insured *themselves* against a possible loss.

b. To emphasize a noun or pronoun already expressed.

The *trainees themselves* arranged the program.

I *will* write her *myself*.

I *myself* am bewildered. (**BUT NOT:** I *myself* am *personally* bewildered. Using *myself* and *personally* in the same sentence creates redundancy, not emphasis.)

NOTE: Do not use a compound personal pronoun unless the noun or pronoun to which it refers is expressed in the same sentence.

The tickets are for the Wrights and *me*. (**NOT:** myself.)

Henry and *I* can handle all the mail. (**NOT:** Henry and myself.)

Interrogative and Relative Pronouns

1061 *WHO* AND *WHOM; WHOEVER* AND *WHOMEVER*

a. These pronouns are both *interrogative* pronouns (used in asking questions) and *relative* pronouns (used to refer to a noun in the main clause).

Who is going? (Interrogative.)

Mr. Sears is the one *who* is going. (Relative, referring to *one*.)

To *whom* shall I deliver the message? (Interrogative.)

Ms. DeAngelis, *whom* I have never met, is in charge of the program. (Relative, referring to *Ms. DeAngelis*.)

b. These pronouns may be either singular or plural in meaning.

Who is talking? (Singular.)	*Whom* do you prefer for this job? (Singular.)
Who are going? (Plural.)	*Whom* do you prefer for these jobs? (Plural.)

c. *Who* (or *whoever*) is the nominative form. Use *who* whenever *he, she, they, I,* or *we* could be substituted in the *who* clause. (If in doubt, mentally rearrange the clause as is done in parentheses after each of the following examples.)

Who is arranging the teleconference? (*She* is arranging the teleconference.)

Who shall I say is calling? (I shall say *he* is calling.)

Who did they say was chosen? (They did say *she* was chosen.)

Who could it have been? (It could have been *he*.)

The matter of *who should pay* was not decided. (*He* should pay.)

Everybody wants to know *who you think should be appointed*. (You think *she* should be appointed.)

Whoever wins the nomination will win the election. (*She* wins the nomination.)

We will select *whoever meets our minimum qualifications*. (*He* meets our minimum qualifications.)

I will speak to *whoever answers the phone*. (*He* answers the phone.)

Please write at once to *whoever you think can supply the information desired*. (You think *she* can supply the information desired.)

Gloria is the one *who can best do the job*. (*She* can best do the job.)

(Continued on page 266.)

10

James is the one *who we expect will win*. (We expect *he* will win.)

Please vote for the member *who you believe has done the most for the firm*. (You believe *he* has done the most for the firm.)

We have referred your claim to our lawyer, *who we are sure will reply soon*. (We are sure *she* will reply soon.)

d. *Whom* (or *whomever*) is the objective form. Use *whom* whenever *him, her, them, me,* or *us* could be substituted as the object of the verb or as the object of a preposition in the *whom* clause.

Whom did you see today? (You did see *her* today.)

To *whom* were you talking? (You were talking to *him*.)

Whom did you say you wanted to see? (You did say you wanted to see *her*.)

It depends on *whom they mean*. (They mean *him*.)

The question of *whom we should charge* is at issue. (We should charge *her*.)

I will give the job to *whomever you think you can safely recommend*. (You think you can safely recommend *him*.)

BUT: I will give the job to *whoever you think can be safely recommended*. (You think *he* can be safely recommended.)

I need a cashier *whom I can trust*. (I can trust *her*.)

The man to *whom I was referring* is Ed Meissen. (I was referring to *him*.)

The person *whom I was thinking of* doesn't have all those qualifications. (I was thinking of *her*.)

The person *whom we invited to address the committee* cannot attend. (We invited *him* to address the committee.)

Jo Fry is the nominee *whom they plan to support*. (They plan to support *her*.)

1062 *WHO, WHICH,* AND *THAT*

a. *Who* and *that* are used when referring to persons. Select *who* when the individual person or the individuality of a group is meant and *that* when a class, species, or type is meant.

She is the only one of my managers *who* can speak Japanese fluently.

He is the kind of student *that* should take advanced math.

b. *Which* and *that* are used when referring to places, objects, and animals. *Which* is always used to introduce non-essential clauses, and *that* is ordinarily used to introduce essential clauses.

Laura's report on employee benefits, *which* I sent you last week, should be of some help. (*Which* introduces a non-essential clause.)

The report *that* I sent you last week should be of some help. (*That* introduces an essential clause.)

NOTE: Many writers now use either *which* or *that* to introduce an essential clause. Indeed, *which* is preferred to *that* (1) when there are two or more parallel essential clauses in the same sentence, (2) when *that* has already been used in the sentence, or (3) when the essential clause is introduced by an expression such as *this . . . which, that . . . which, these . . . which,* or *those . . . which.*

Vivian is taking courses *which* will earn her a higher salary rating in her current job and *which* will qualify her for a number of higher-level jobs.

That is a movie *which* you must not miss.

We need to reinforce *those* ideas *which* were presented in earlier chapters.

c. The verb in a relative clause introduced by *who, which,* or *that* should agree in number with the subject of the relative clause. In many cases the subject is clearly expressed.

The laser printer that *you have ordered* will be delivered in two weeks. (The subject of the relative clause is *you,* which requires a plural verb, *have ordered.*)

However, when the relative pronoun *who, which,* or *that* is itself the subject of the relative clause, the verb in the relative clause must agree with the antecedent of the relative pronoun.

The laser *printer* that *was ordered* on May 4 will be delivered in two weeks. (The relative pronoun *that* is the subject of the relative clause and refers to a singular antecedent, *printer.* Therefore, the verb in the relative clause—*was ordered*—must be singular.)

BUT: The laser *printers* that *were ordered . . .*

Sometimes it is difficult to determine the antecedent of the relative pronoun. In such cases mentally rearrange the wording, as is done in the following example.

Hyphenate the *elements* of a *compound adjective* that occur?/occurs? before a noun. (To determine whether the antecedent of *that* is the plural term *elements* or the singular term *compound adjective,* recast the sentence: "When a *compound adjective* occurs before a noun, hyphenate the elements." This makes it clear that in the original sentence *compound adjective* is the antecedent of *that;* thus the verb in the relative clause must be singular: *occurs.*)

Hyphenate the elements of a *compound adjective* that *occurs* before a noun.

d. *Which, that,* and *who* may be used to refer to organizations. When you are referring to the organization as a single entity (in other words, as *it*), then use *which* or *that* as indicated in ¶1062b. However, when you are thinking of the organization in terms of the individuals who make up the organization (in other words, when you think of the organization as *they*), you may use *who* or *that* as indicated in ¶1062a. (See also ¶1020.)

Whenever we run short of computer supplies, the Brown & Lebrun Company is the one *that* gives us the best service and the best prices.

We really like doing business with the people at the Brown & Lebrun Company. They are a customer-oriented group *who* give us the best service and the best prices. (*That* may also be used in this sentence in place of *who.*)

10

1063 *WHOSE* AND *WHO'S*

Do not confuse *whose* (the possessive form of *who*) with *who's* (a contraction meaning "who is" or "who has").

Whose house is it? (**NOT:** Who is house is it?)

Who's the owner of that house? (Who is the owner of that house?)

Who's had the most experience? (Who has had the most experience?)

Who's the most experienced person? (Who is the most experienced person?)

Whose experience is best? (**NOT:** Who is (has) experience is best?)

Pronouns With To Be

1064 a. If a pronoun is the subject of *to be*, use the *objective* form.

I want *her* to be successful.   I expected *them* to be late.

Whom do you consider to be the more expert driver? (You do consider *whom* to be the more expert driver?)

b. If *to be* has a subject and is followed by a pronoun, put that pronoun in the *objective* case.

They mistook the *visitors* to be *us*. (*Visitors*, the subject of *to be*, is in the objective; therefore, the predicate pronoun following *to be* is objective, *us*.)

They took *her* to be *me*.

Whom did you take *him* to be? (You did take *him* to be *whom*?)

c. If *to be* has *no* subject and is followed by a pronoun, put that pronoun in the *nominative* case.

The *caller* was thought to be *I*. (*I* agrees with the subject of the sentence, *caller*.)

The *Gaidhars* were thought to be *we*.

Who was *he* thought to be? (*He* was thought to be *who*?)

NOTE: The examples above are all grammatically correct, but they also sound quite awkward. Whenever possible, use more idiomatic wording. For example, the three sentences above could be recast as follows:

They thought I was the one who called.

The Gaidhars were mistaken for us.

Who did they think he was?

Troublesome Pronouns

☞ *See the paragraphs indicated for each of the following pronouns.*

All of	Both Alike	Most
(Section 11)	(Section 11)	(Section 11)
Anyone—Any One	Each Other—One Another	Nobody—No Body
(¶1010, note)	(Section 11)	(Section 11)
Between You and Me	Everyone—Every One	None—No One
(¶1055b)	(¶1010, note)	(Section 11)
Both—Each	Its—It's	Someone—Some One
(Section 11)	(Section 11)	(¶1010, note)

10

That—Which—Who	Whatever—What Ever	Whoever—Who Ever
(¶1062)	(Section 11)	(¶1061)
This Sort—This Kind	Who—Whom	
(Section 11)	(¶1061)	

☞ *See a style manual for greater clarity in writing.*

ADJECTIVES AND ADVERBS

For definitions of the terms *adjective* and *adverb*, see the appropriate entries in the Glossary of Grammatical Terms (Section 19).

1065 Only an adverb can modify an adjective.

> They will give you a *really* good buy on printers.
>
> (**NOT:** They will give you a *real* good buy on printers.)

1066 When a word in the predicate refers to the *action of the verb*, use an *adverb* (not an adjective).

> We guarantee *to ship* the portfolios *promptly.*
>
> They *were injured badly* in the accident.

TEST: If *in a . . . manner* can be substituted for the *ly*-ending word, choose the adverb.

> *Read* the directions *carefully* (in a careful manner).

1067 When a word in the predicate describes the *subject* of the sentence, use an *adjective* (not an adverb). Verbs of the *senses (feel, look, sound, taste, smell)* and *linking* verbs (the various forms of *be, seem, appear, become*) are followed in most cases by adjectives. A few other verbs (such as *grow, prove, get, keep, remain,* and *turn*) are sometimes followed by adjectives.

I feel *bad* (**NOT** badly).	He has grown *tall.*
She looked *happy.*	The work proved *hard.*
Your voice sounded *strong.*	I got *lucky.*
He seemed (**OR** appeared) *shy.*	Let's all keep (**OR** remain) *calm.*
They became *famous.*	The weather has turned *cold.*

TEST: If *is, are, was, were,* or some other form of *be* can be substituted for the verb, choose the adjective.

> He *looks* happy.   He *is* happy.

NOTE: In the following group of examples, verbs of the senses and linking verbs are used as verbs of action. (See ¶1066.) Since the modifier refers to the action of the verb (and does not describe the subject), the modifier must be an adverb.

> She *looked suspiciously* at the visitor in the reception room.
>
> He *felt carefully* along the ledge for the key.
>
> Our market share *has grown quickly.*
>
> He *appeared quietly* in the doorway.

10

1068 Several of the most frequently used adverbs have two forms.

close, closely	fair, fairly	loud, loudly	short, shortly
deep, deeply	hard, hardly	quick, quickly	slow, slowly
direct, directly	late, lately	right, rightly	wide, widely

a. In a number of cases the two forms have different meanings.

Ship the goods *direct*. (Meaning "straight," "without detour.")
They were *directly* responsible. (Meaning "without any intervention.")

They arrived *late*.	The truck stopped *short*.
I haven't seen her *lately*.	You will hear from us *shortly*.
You've been working too *hard*.	Turn *right* at the first traffic light.
I could *hardly* hear him.	I don't *rightly* remember.

b. In some cases the choice is largely a matter of idiom. Some verbs take the *ly* form; others take the short form.

dig deep	go slow	open wide	come close	play fair
wound deeply	proceed slowly	travel widely	watch closely	treat fairly

c. In still other cases the choice is simply one of formality. The *ly* forms are more formal.

sell cheap   **OR**   sell cheaply   talk loud   **OR**   talk loudly

1069 a. Although the *ly* ending usually signifies an adverb, a few adjectives also end in *ly*—for example, *costly, orderly, timely, motherly, fatherly, friendly, neighbourly, worldly, earthly, lively, lovely, lonely.*

Let's look for a less *costly* solution.

Her offer to help you was intended as a *friendly* gesture.

b. A few common *ly*-ending words are used both as adjectives and adverbs— for example, *early, only, daily, weekly, monthly, yearly.*

I always try to leave for work at an *early* hour. (Adjective.)
The surge in sales began *early* last month. (Adverb.)

We issue our sales reports on a *quarterly* basis. (Adjective.)
We issue our sales reports *quarterly*. (Adverb.)

We are waiting for the *first-quarter* sales report. (Compound adjective.)
NOT: We are all waiting for the *first-quarterly* sales report.

c. The words *fast, long,* and *hard* are also used both as adjectives and as adverbs.

ADJECTIVES:	a *fast* talker	a *long, hard* winter
ADVERBS:	talks *fast*	thought *long* and *hard*

1070 Words such as *up, in, out, on,* and *off*—commonly recognized as prepositions— also function as adverbs, especially in verb phrases where these words are needed to complete the meaning of the verb. (See also ¶802.)

	Used as Adverbs	**Used as Prepositions**
up:	to look *up* the definition	to jog *up the hill*
down:	to take *down* your name	to walk *down the street*

in:	to trade *in* your old car	to see *in* the dark
out:	to phase *out* operations	to look *out* the window
on:	to put *on* a performance	to act *on* the stage
off:	to write *off* our losses	to drive *off* the road

NOTE: When used in headings and titles as *adverbs*, these short words are capitalized; when used as *prepositions*, they are not. (See ¶361c–d.)

1071 PROBLEMS OF COMPARISON

a. Form the comparative degree of *one-syllable* adjectives and adverbs by adding *er* to the positive form. Form the superlative degree by adding *est*. (See ¶1071e for a few exceptions.)

thin: thinner, thinnest   soon: sooner, soonest

b. Form the comparative degree of *two-syllable* adjectives and adverbs either by adding *er* to the positive form or by inserting either *more* or *less* before the positive form. Form the superlative degree by adding *est* in some cases or by inserting *most* or *least* before the positive form. In some cases the addition of *er* and *est* will create very awkward forms. Your ear will tell you when to avoid such forms.

happy: happier, more (**OR** less) happy	more hopeful (**NOT:** hopefuller)
likely: likeliest, most (**OR** least) likely	more hostile (**NOT:** hostiler)
often: oftener, more (**OR** less) often	most complex (**NOT:** complexest)
highly: highest, most (**OR** least) highly	most troubled (**NOT:** troubledest)

☞ *See ¶825b and Section 11 for a usage note on* more.

NOTE: If the positive form ends in a consonant plus *y* (for example, *happy*, *likely*), change the *y* to *i* before adding *er* or *est*. Some *ly*-ending words drop the *ly* in the comparative and superlative (for example, *highly, higher, highest; deeply, deeper, deepest*). (See also ¶710.)

c. Form the comparative degree of adjectives and adverbs containing *three or more syllables* by inserting *more* or *less* before the positive form. Form the superlative degree by inserting *most* or *least* before the positive form.

competent: more competent	adventurous: less adventurous
acceptable: most acceptable	carefully: least carefully

d. Avoid double comparisons.

cheaper (**NOT:** more cheaper)   unkindest (**NOT:** most unkindest)

e. A few adjectives and adverbs have irregular comparisons. For example:

Positive	Comparative	Superlative
good or well (see Section 11)	better	best
bad or ill	worse	worst
far	farther, further (see Section 11)	farthest, furthest

10

(Continued on page 272.)

Positive	Comparative	Superlative
late	later, latter (see Section 11)	latest, last
little	littler, less, lesser	littlest, least
many, much	more	most

f. Some adjectives and adverbs—for example, *square, round, unique, completely, universally, correct, perfect, always, never, dead*—do not logically permit comparison. A square cannot be any *squarer*; a circle cannot be the *roundest of all circles*. Nevertheless, a number of these words may be modified by *more, less, nearly, hardly, virtually,* and similar adverbs to suggest something less than absolute perfection in each case.

Next year we hope to do a *more complete* study.

He is looking for a *more universally* acceptable solution.

Handicraft of this calibre is *virtually unique* these days.

We *almost never* increase our prices more than once a year.

g. When referring to *two* persons, places, or things, use the comparative form; when referring to *more than two*, use the superlative form.

That is the *finer* piece of linen. (Only two pieces are involved.)
This is the *finest* piece of linen I could find. (Many pieces are involved.)

Of the two positions open, you have chosen the *more* promising.
Of the three positions open, you have chosen the *most* promising.

That is the *more* efficient of the two methods.
This is the *most* efficient method that could be devised.

I like Evelyn's plan *better* than Joe's or Betty's. (Although three things are involved, they are being compared two at a time; hence the comparative.)

NOTE: In a few idiomatic expressions (such as *Put your best foot forward* and *May the best man win*), the superlative form is used, even though only two things are referred to.

h. When comparing a person or a thing *within* the group to which it belongs, use the superlative. When comparing a person or a thing with individual members of the group, use the comparative and the words *other* or *else*.

Susan is the *most* conscientious employee on the staff.
Susan is *more* conscientious than any *other* employee on the staff. (Without the word *other*, the sentence would imply that Susan is not on the staff.)

Toronto is the *largest* city in Ontario.
Toronto is *larger* than any *other* city in Ontario. (Without the word *other*, the sentence would imply that Toronto is not in Ontario.)

Bert's proposal was the *best* of all that were presented to the committee.
Bert's proposal was *better* than anyone *else's*. (**NOT:** anyone's.)

i. Be sure to compare like things. (See also Note ¶644.)

This year's output is lower than last year's. (In other words, "This year's *output* is lower than last year's *output*.")

NOT: This year's output is lower than last year. (Incorrectly compares *this year's output* with *last year*.)

10

1072 The adverbs *only, nearly, almost, ever, scarcely, merely, too,* and *also* should be placed as close as possible to the word modified—usually directly before it. Putting the adverb in the wrong position may change the entire meaning of the sentence.

> Our list of depositors numbers *almost* 50 000. (**NOT:** almost numbers.)

> *Only* the board can nominate the three new officers. (Cannot be nominated by anyone else.)
> The board can *only* nominate the three officers. (They cannot elect.)
> The board can nominate *only* the three officers. (They cannot nominate anyone else.)

> Maria and Dino Gados have been married for *not quite* two years.
> (**NOT:** Maria and Dino Gados have *not quite* been married for two years.)

1073 Do not use an adverb to express a meaning already contained in the verb.

assemble (**NOT:** assemble together)	finish (**NOT:** finish up or off)
begin (**NOT:** first begin)	follow (**NOT:** follow after)
cancel (**NOT:** cancel out)	refer (**NOT:** refer back)
continue (**NOT:** continue on)	repeat (**NOT:** repeat again)
convert (**NOT:** convert over)	return (**NOT:** return back)
co-operate (**NOT:** co-operate together)	revert (**NOT:** revert back)

Troublesome Adjectives and Adverbs

☞ *For the following adjectives and adverbs, see individual entries listed alphabetically in Section 11.*

A—An	Everyday—Every Day	More Important—
Accidentally	Ex—Former	More Importantly
All Right	Farther—Further	Only
Almost—All Most	Fewer—Less	Real—Really
Already—All Ready	First—Firstly, etc.	Said
Altogether—All	Flammable—Inflammable	Same
Together	Former—First	Scarcely
Always—All Ways	Good—Well	Someday—Some Day
Anxious—Eager	Hardly	Sometime—Some-
Anymore—Any More	Healthy—Healthful	times—Some Time
Anytime—Any Time	Hopefully	Sure—Surely
Anyway—Any Way	Incidentally	This Here
Awhile—A While	Indifferent—In Different	Unique
Bad—Badly	Indirect—In Direct	Up
Complementary—	Last—Latest	Very
Complimentary	Latter—Last	Wise
Different—Differently	Maybe—May Be	
Equally as Good	More	

NEGATIVES

1074 To express a negative idea in a simple sentence, use only one negative expression in the sentence. (A *double negative*—two negative expressions in the same sentence—gives a *positive* meaning.)

> We can sit by and do *nothing.*

> We can*not* sit by and do *nothing.* (The *not* and *nothing* create a double negative; the sentence now has a positive meaning: "We ought to do something.")

(Continued on page 274.)

10

Jim is *un*aware of the facts. (Here the negative element is the prefix *un*.)

Jim is *not un*aware of the facts. (With the double negative, the sentence means "Jim *is* aware of the facts.")

NOTE: A double negative is not wrong in itself. As the examples above indicate, a double negative may offer a more effective way of expressing a *positive thought* than a straightforward positive construction would. However, a double negative *is* wrong if the sentence is intended to have a negative meaning. Remember, two negatives make a positive.

1075 A negative expression gives a negative meaning to the *clause* in which it appears. In a simple sentence, where there is only one clause, the negative expression affects the entire sentence. (See ¶1074.) In a sentence where there are two or more clauses, a negative expression affects only the clause in which it appears. Therefore, each clause may safely contain one negative expression. A double negative results when there are two negative expressions within the *same* clause.

If Mr. Bogosian can*not* lower his price, there is *no* point in continuing the negotiations. (The *if* clause contains the negative *not*; the main clause contains the negative *no*. Each clause has its own negative meaning.)

I have *not* met Hironaka, and I have *no* desire to meet him.
OR: I have *not* met Hironaka, *nor* do I have *any* desire to meet him. (When the negative conjunction *nor* replaces *and*, the adjective *no* changes to *any* so as to avoid a double negative in the second clause.)

We have *never* permitted, *nor* will we permit, any lowering of our standards. (Here the second clause interrupts the first clause. If written out in full, the sentence would read, "We have *never* permitted any lowering of our standards, *nor* will we permit any lowering of our standards.")

NOTE: A second negative expression may be used in a clause to repeat or intensify the first negative expression. This construction is not a double negative.

No, I did *not* make that statement.

He would *never*, *never* do a thing like that.   That's a *no-no*.

1076 To preserve the *negative* meaning of a clause, follow these basic principles:

a. If the clause has a *negative verb* (a verb modified by *not* or *never*), do not use an additional negative expression, such as *nor, neither . . . nor, no, none, no one,* or *nothing*. Instead, use the corresponding positive expression, such as *or, either . . . or, any, anyone,* or *anything*.

I have *not* invited *anyone*. (**WRONG:** I have *not* invited *no one*.)

She does *not* want *any*. (**WRONG:** She does *not* want *none*.)

Mary did *not* have *anything* to do. (**WRONG:** Mary did *not* have *nothing* to do.)

I can*not* find *either* the letter *or* the envelope. (**WRONG:** I can*not* find *neither* the letter *nor* the envelope.)

He did *not* say whether he would mail the money to us *or* whether he would bring it himself. (**WRONG:** He did *not* say whether he would mail the money to us *nor* whether he would bring it himself.)

10

b. If a clause contains any one of the following expressions—*no, no one, none, nothing,* or *neither . . . nor* (this counts as one expression)—make sure that the verb and all other words are *positive.*

I see *nothing* wrong with *either* proposal. (**NOT:** neither proposal.)

Neither Martha Gutowski *nor* Yvonne Christopher *can* attend. (**NOT:** cannot.)

c. The word *nor* may be used alone as a conjunction (see the second and third examples in ¶1075) or together with *neither.* Do not use *nor* in the same clause with any other negative; use *or* instead.

There are *neither* diskettes *nor* printer cartridges in the stockroom.
BUT: There are *no* diskettes *or* printer cartridges in the stockroom.
(**NOT:** There are *no* diskettes *nor* printer cartridges.)

There are *no* clear-cut rights *or* wrongs in the situation.
(**NOT:** There are *no* clear-cut rights *nor* wrongs in the situation.)

Francine has *not* called *or* written us for some time.
(**NOT:** Francine has *not* called *nor* written us for some time.)

☞ *For* Hardly, Only, *and* Scarcely, *which have a negative meaning, see the appropriate entries in Section 11.*

PREPOSITIONS
Words Requiring Certain Prepositions

1077 Usage requires that certain words be followed by certain prepositions. Some frequently used combinations are given in the following list.

accompanied by (a person): I was *accompanied by* my instructor.

accompanied with (something): The speech was *accompanied with* gestures.

account for something or someone: I find it hard to *account for* his behaviour.

account to someone: You will have to *account to* Anne Crump for the loss.

agree on or **upon** (reach an understanding): We cannot *agree on* the price.

agree to (to accept another person's plan): Will you *agree to* their terms?

agree with (concur with a person or an idea): I *agree with* your objectives.

angry at or **about** something: He was *angry about* the disorder.

angry with someone: You have every right to be *angry with* me.

apply for a position: You ought to *apply for* the job.

apply to someone or something: You must *apply* yourself *to* the job in order to master it. I am thinking of *applying to* that company.

argue about something: We *argued about* the terms of the contract.

argue with a person: It doesn't pay to *argue with* Bremer.

beneficial to: Exercise is *beneficial to* good health.

compare to (assert a likeness): She *compared* my writing *to* W. P. Kinsella's. (She said I wrote like W. P. Kinsella.)

compare with (analyse for similarities and differences): When she *compared* my writing *with* E. B. White's, she said that I had a similar kind of humour but that my sentences lacked the easy flow of words.

(Continued on page 276.)

confer on or **upon** (give to): A medal was *conferred on* the brave soldier.

confer with (talk to): Tom *conferred with* his boss.

conform to (preferred to *with*): The drafts do not *conform to* the plans.

consists in (exists in): Happiness largely *consists in* wanting what you have, not having what you want.

consists of (is made up of): Their new formula for a wage settlement *consists of* the same old terms expressed in different language.

convenient for (suitable): What time will be most *convenient for* you?

convenient to (near at hand): Our plant is *convenient to* all facilities.

correspond to (agree with): The shipment does not *correspond to* the sample.

correspond with (exchange letters with): We must *correspond with* him today.

deal in (goods and services): The firm *deals in* heavy equipment.

deal with (a person): Judges *deal with* those who break the laws.

differ about (something): We *differed about* means but not about ends.

differ from (something else): This job *differs* very little *from* my previous one.

differ with (someone): I *differ with* you over the consequences of our plan.

different from: This product is *different from* the one I normally use.

different than: I view this matter in a *different* way *than* you do. (Although *from* is normally preferred, *than* is acceptable in order to avoid sentences like "I view the matter in a different way from the way in which you do.")

independent of (not *from*): He wants to be *independent of* his family.

interested in: We are *interested in* discussing the matter with you.

retroactive to (not *from*): This salary adjustment is *retroactive to* May 1.

speak to (tell something to): I will *speak to* him about his absence.

speak with (discuss with): It was good to *speak with* you yesterday.

Superfluous Prepositions

1078 Omit prepositions that add nothing to the meaning—as in the following examples. (See also Section 11 for a usage note on *all of*.)

Where is she [at]?	Where did that paper go [to]?
She could not help [from] laughing.	His office is opposite [to] hers.
The chair is too near [to] the table.	The strike is now over [with].
Let's meet at [**OR** about] one o'clock.	The box fell off [of] the truck.
We need to focus [in] on new ways.	He seems to be [of] about two years old.

Necessary Prepositions

1079 Conversely, do not omit essential prepositions.

I need to buy a couple *of* books. (**NOT:** I need to buy a couple books.)

We don't stock that type *of* filter. (**NOT:** We don't stock that type filter.)

He has a great interest *in*, as well as a respect *for*, fine antiques. (**NOT:** He has a great interest, as well as a respect *for*, fine antiques.)

10

She frequently appears in movies, *in* plays, and on television. (**NOT:** She frequently appears in movies, plays, and on television.)

NOTE: The preposition *of* is understood in expressions such as *what colour cloth* and *what size shoes.*

Prepositions at the End of Sentences

1080 a. Ending a sentence with a preposition is not incorrect. Whether you do so or not depends on the emphasis and effect you want to achieve. However, trying to avoid ending a sentence with a preposition may lead to awkward results.

INFORMAL: I wish I knew which magazine her article appeared *in.*
FORMAL: I wish I knew *in which* magazine her article appeared.

STILTED: It is difficult to know *about* what you are thinking.
NATURAL: It is difficult to know what you are thinking *about.*

b. Short questions frequently end with prepositions.

How many can I count *on*?	What is this good *for*?
What is this made *of*?	We need tools to work *with.*
Where did he come *from*?	That's something we must look *into.*
He has nothing to worry *about.*	There's a new computer I want to look *at.*

c. Some sentences end with words that seem to be prepositions but are really adverbs.

I'm sure another job will soon turn *up.*
After Yogita considers her alternatives, I'm sure she will come *around.*

Troublesome Prepositions

☞ *For the following prepositions, see individual entries listed alphabetically in Section 11.*

At About	From—Off	Off
Beside—Besides	In—Into—In to	On—Onto—On to
Between—Among	In Regards to	On—Upon—Up on
Due to—Because of—	Indifferent—In Different	Opposite
On Account of	Indirect—In Direct	Per—A
Except	Like—As, As if	Toward—Towards
	Of—Have	

☞ *For the treatment of words that can function as both prepositions and adverbs, see ¶1070.*

For the capitalization of such words, see ¶361c–d.

SENTENCE STRUCTURE
Parallel Structure

1081 Express parallel ideas in parallel form.

a. Adjectives should be parallelled by adjectives, nouns by nouns, infinitives by infinitives, dependent clauses by dependent clauses, and so on.

(Continued on page 278.)

WRONG: Your training program was *stimulating* and a *challenge*. (Adjective and noun.)
RIGHT: Your training program was *stimulating* and *challenging*. (Two adjectives.)

WRONG: The sales representatives have already started *using the new techniques* and *to produce higher sales*. (Participial phrase and infinitive phrase.)
RIGHT: The sales representatives have already started *using the new techniques* and *producing higher sales*. (Two participial phrases.)
RIGHT: The sales representatives have already started *to use the new techniques* and *to produce higher sales*. (Two infinitive phrases.)

WRONG: This scanner is *easy* to operate, *efficient*, and *it is relatively inexpensive*. (Two adjectives and a clause.)
RIGHT: This scanner is *easy* to operate, *efficient*, and relatively *inexpensive*. (Three adjectives.)

NOTE: Parallelism is especially important in displayed enumerations.

POOR: This article will discuss:

1. How to deal with corporate politics.
2. Coping with stressful situations.
3. What the role of the manager should be in the community.

BETTER: This article will discuss:

1. *Ways* to deal with corporate politics.
2. *Techniques* of coping with stressful situations.
3. The *role* of the manager in the community.

OR: This article will tell managers how to:

1. *Deal* with corporate politics.
2. *Cope* with stressful situations.
3. *Function* in the community.

b. Correlative conjunctions (*both . . . and, either . . . or, neither . . . nor, not only . . . but also, whether . . . or,* etc.) should be followed by elements in parallel form.

WRONG: Kevin is not only gifted as a painter but also as a sculptor.
RIGHT: Kevin is gifted not only *as a painter* but also *as a sculptor*.

WRONG: We are flying both to Toronto and Montreal.
RIGHT: We are flying to both *Toronto* and *Montreal*.
RIGHT: We are flying both *to Toronto* and *to Montreal*.

WRONG: He would neither apologize nor would he promise to reform.
RIGHT: He would neither *apologize* nor *promise to reform*.
RIGHT: He would not apologize, nor would he promise to reform.

NOTE: When using the correlative conjunction *not only . . . but also,* you do not have to place *also* immediately after *but;* in fact, *also* may be omitted altogether.

Shahpar is not only a *sensitive musician* but a *music critic* who is sensitive to the gifts of others.

Dangling Constructions

1082 When a sentence begins with a participial phrase, an infinitive phrase, a gerund phrase, or an elliptical clause (one in which essential words are missing), make sure that the phrase or clause logically agrees with the subject of the sentence;

otherwise, the construction will "dangle." To correct a dangling construction, make the subject of the sentence the doer of the action expressed by the opening phrase or clause. If that is not feasible, use an entirely different construction.

a. Participial Phrases

WRONG: Stashed away in the attic for the past hundred years, the owner of the painting has decided to auction it off. (Who was stashed in the attic: the owner of the painting?)
RIGHT: The owner of the painting that has been stashed away in the attic for the past hundred years has decided to auction it off.

WRONG: After coming out of a coma, the police officer asked the driver what caused the accident.
RIGHT: After the driver came out of a coma, the police officer asked her what caused the accident.

WRONG: Putting the issue of costs aside, the delays need to be discussed.
RIGHT: Putting the issue of costs aside, we need to discuss the delays.

NOTE: A few words ending in *ing* (such as *concerning, considering, pending,* and *regarding*) have now become established as prepositions. Therefore, when they introduce phrases at the start of a sentence, it is not essential that they refer to the subject of the sentence.

Considering how long the lawsuit has dragged on, it might have been wiser not to sue.

b. Infinitive Phrases

WRONG: To appreciate the full significance of Fox's latest letter, all the previous correspondence should be read.
RIGHT: To appreciate the full significance of Fox's latest letter, you should read all the previous correspondence.

WRONG: To obtain this free booklet, the enclosed coupon should be mailed at once.
RIGHT: To obtain this free booklet, mail the enclosed coupon at once.

c. Prepositional-Gerund Phrases

WRONG: By installing a computerized temperature control system, a substantial saving in fuel costs was achieved.
RIGHT: By installing a computerized temperature control system, we achieved a substantial saving in fuel costs.

WRONG: In analysing these specifications, several errors have been found.
RIGHT: In analysing these specifications, I have found several errors.

d. Elliptical Clauses

WRONG: If ordered before May 1, a 5 percent discount will be allowed on these goods.
RIGHT: If ordered before May 1, these goods will be allowed a 5 . . .

WRONG: When four years old, my family moved to Oshawa.
RIGHT: When I was four years old, my family moved to Oshawa.

e. Absolute Phrases

Absolute phrases (typically involving passive participles) are not considered to "dangle," even though they come at the beginning of a sentence and do not refer to the subject.

(Continued on page 280.)

Strictly speaking, what you did was not illegal—but it wasn't right.

All things considered, her plan may be the best way to proceed.

Weather permitting, the ceremonies will be held in the quadrangle.

Avoid using these phrases, however, when they produce awkward sentences.

WEAK: The speeches having been concluded, we proceeded to take a vote.

BETTER: After the speeches were concluded, we proceeded to take a vote.

1083 When verbal phrases and elliptical clauses fall elsewhere in the sentence, look out for illogical or confusing relationships. Adjust the wording as necessary.

WRONG: I saw two truck drivers get into a fistfight while jogging down the street.

RIGHT: While jogging down the street, I saw two truck drivers get into a fistfight.

1084 A prepositional phrase will dangle at the beginning of a sentence if it leads the reader to expect a certain word as the subject and then another word is used instead.

WRONG: As head of the program committee, we think you should make immediate arrangements for another speaker. (The head of the committee is *you*, not *we*.)
RIGHT: We think that as head of the program committee, you should make immediate arrangements for another speaker.

WRONG: As a young boy, the woman I was destined to marry did not appeal to me in any way. (That woman never was a "young boy.")
RIGHT: When I was a young boy, the woman I was destined to marry did not appeal to me in any way.

1085 A verbal phrase will dangle at the end of a sentence if it refers to the meaning of the main clause as a whole rather than to the doer of the action.

WRONG: Our sales have been steadily declining for the past six months, thus creating a sharp drop in profits. (As worded, the sentence makes it appear that *our sales*, by themselves, have created the drop in profits. Actually, it is *the fact* that our sales have been declining which has created the drop in profits.)

RIGHT: The steady decline in our sales for the past six months has created a sharp drop in profits.

RIGHT: Our sales have been steadily declining for the past six months. As a result, we have experienced a sharp drop in profits.

Misplaced Modifiers

1086 a. Watch for misplaced modifiers (either words or phrases) that provide the basis for unintended (and sometimes humorous) interpretations.

WRONG: I suspect that my assistant accidentally dropped the report I had been drafting in the wastebasket. (What an uncomfortable location in which to draft a report!)
RIGHT: The report I had been drafting has disappeared. I suspect that my assistant accidentally dropped it in the wastebasket.

WRONG: Here are some helpful suggestions for protecting your valuables from our hotel security staff. (Can no one be trusted?)
RIGHT: Here are some helpful suggestions from our hotel security staff for protecting your valuables.

WRONG: One of our assistant vice-presidents has been referred to a personal finance counsellor with serious credit problems. (Would you consult such a counsellor?)

RIGHT: One of our assistant vice-presidents has serious credit problems and has been referred to a personal finance counsellor.

b. Watch out for modifiers that are placed in such a way that they can be interpreted as modifying either what precedes or what follows. (See also ¶1072.)

WRONG: Travelling abroad frequently can become exhausting. (Does *frequently* modify *Travelling abroad* or *become exhausting*?)

RIGHT: *Frequently* travelling abroad (**OR** Making frequent trips abroad) can become exhausting.

RIGHT: Travelling abroad can *frequently* become exhausting.

☞ *To improve your writing skills, refer to a style manual for additional information on the topics covered in* ¶¶*1081–1086.*

See the Online Learning Centre at www.mcgrawhill.ca/college/gregg for related weblinks.

10

SECTION **ELEVEN**

Usage

A—An
A Lot—Alot—Allot
A—Of
Accidentally
Additionally
Affect—Effect
Age—Aged—At the Age of
All of
All Right
Almost—All Most
Already—All Ready
Altogether—All Together
Always—All Ways
Amount—Number
And
And Etc.
And/Or
Anxious—Eager
Anyone—Any One
Anymore—Any More
Anytime—Any Time
Anyway—Any Way
Appreciate
As
As . . . as—Not so . . . as
As Far As
As Well As
At About
Awhile—A While
Bad—Badly
Balance
Being That
Beside—Besides
Between—Among
Between You and Me
Biannual—Biennial—Semi-annual
Biweekly—Bimonthly
Both—Each
Both Alike—Equal—Together
Bring—Take

But . . . However
But What
Cannot Help But
Come—Go
Come and
Complementary—Complimentary
Comprise—Compose
Data
Dependant—Dependent
Different—Differently
Different From—Different Than
Done
Don't (Do Not)
Doubt That—Doubt Whether
Due to—Because of—On Account of
Each Other—One Another
Ensure—Insure—Assure
Enthused Over
Equally as Good
Etc.—And so on—Such as
Everyday—Every Day
Everyone—Every One
Ex—Former
Except
Farther—Further
Fewer—Less
First—Firstly, etc.
Flammable—Inflammable
Former—First
From—Off
Good—Well
Graduated—Was Graduated
Hardly
Healthy—Healthful
Help
Historic—Historical
Hopefully
If—Whether
Imply—Infer
In—Into—In to

In Regards to	Reason Is Because
Incidentally	Retroactive to
Indifferent—In Different	Said
Indirect—In Direct	Same
Individual—Party—Person—People	Scarcely
Irregardless	Serve—Service
Is Where—Is When	Set—Sit
Its—It's	Shall—Will
Kind	Should—Would
Kind of—Sort of	So—So That
Kind of a	Someday—Some Day
Last—Latest	Someone—Some One
Latter—Last	Sometime—Sometimes—Some Time
Lay—Lie	Supposed to
Learn—Teach	Sure—Surely
Leave—Let	Sure and
Like—As, As if	Than—Then
Literally	That
May—Can (Might—Could)	That—That
Maybe—May Be	That—Which—Who
Media	This Here
More	This Sort—This Kind
More Important—More Importantly	Toward—Towards
Most	Try and
Nobody—No Body	Unique
None—No One	Up
Of—Have	Used to
Off	Very
On—Onto—On to	Ways
On—Upon—Up on	Whatever—What Ever
Only	Where—That
Opposite	Who—Which—That
Per—A	Who—Whom
Percent—Percentage	Whoever—Who Ever
Plus	Wise
Raise—Rise	Would Have
Real—Really	

☞ *See ¶719 for words frequently misused because they sound alike or look alike.*

1101 The following entries will help you avoid a number of usage errors.

A—an. In choosing *a* or *an*, consider the sound (not the spelling) of the following word. Use the article *a* before all *consonant* sounds, including sounded *h*, long *u*, and *o* with the sound of *w* (as in *one*).

a day	a home	a unit	a youthful spirit	a one-week delay
a week	a house	a union	a euphoric feeling	a 60-day note
a year	a hotel	a uniform	a European trip	a CGA

(Continued on page 284.)

11

Use *an* before all *vowel* sounds except long *u* and before words beginning with silent *h*.

an asset	an EOM inventory
an essay	an f.o.b. order
an input	an HQ command
an outcome	an LRT ticket
an upsurge	an M.B.A. degree
an hour	an NSF cheque
an honour	an ROI objective
an 8-hour-day	an SRO performance
an 11 a.m. meeting	an X-ray (x-ray) reading (see ¶¶807, 815)

NOTE: In speech, both *a historic occasion* and *an historic occasion* are correct, depending on whether the *h* is sounded or left silent. In writing, *a historic occasion* is the form more commonly used.

A lot—alot—allot. The phrase *a lot* (meaning "to a considerable quantity or extent") always consists of two words. The form *alot* is never correct.

> Thanks *a lot* (**NOT** *alot*) for all your help on this year's budget.

Do not confuse this phrase with the verb *allot* (meaning "to distribute or assign a share of something").

> You will have to *allot* a portion of next year's budget to cover your expenses.

A—of. Do not use *a* in place of *of*.

> What sort *of* turnout did you have at your seminar?
> (**NOT:** What sort *a* turnout did you have at your seminar?)

> The weather has been kind *of* cool for this time of year.
> (**NOT:** The weather has been *kinda* cool for this time of year.)

☞ *See* Kind of—sort of *and* Kind of a.

A—per. See *Per—a*.

Accidentally. This word ends in *ally*. (The form *accidently* is incorrect.)

Additionally. Avoid the use of *additionally* as a transitional expression. Use *in addition, moreover, furthermore,* or *besides* instead. (See ¶138a.)

> **AWKWARD:** *Additionally,* the new packaging will reduce costs by 20 percent.

> **BETTER:** *Moreover,* the new packaging will reduce costs by 20 percent.

Affect—effect. *Affect* is normally used as a verb meaning "to influence, change, assume." *Effect* can be either a verb meaning "to bring about" or a noun meaning "result, impression."

> The court's decision in this case will not *affect* (change) the legal precedent.

> She *affects* (assumes) an unsophisticated manner.

> It is essential that we *effect* (bring about) an immediate improvement in sales.

> It will be months before we can assess the full *effect* (result) of the new law.

NOTE: In psychology, *affect* used as a noun means "emotion," and the related adjective *affective* means "emotional." Because of the limited context in which these terms are likely to be used, it should be easy to distinguish them from *effect* as a noun and the related adjective *effective*.

> We need to analyse the *effects* (results) of this new marketing strategy.
> We need to analyse the *affects* (emotions) produced by this conflict.

> Which technique is *effective* (capable of producing the desired results)?
> Let's deal with the *affective* (emotional) factors first.

Age—aged—at the age of.

> I interviewed a man *aged* 52 for the job. (NOT: a man age 52.)

> I don't plan to retire *at the age of* 65. (NOT: *at age 65.*)

NOTE: Elliptical references to age—for example, *at age 65*—should not be used except in technical writing such as human resources manuals.

> See the chart on page 6 for the schedule of retirement benefits for employees.

All of. *Of* is not necessary after *all* unless the following word is a pronoun.

> PREFERABLE: *All* the staff members belong to the softball team.
> ACCEPTABLE: *All of* the staff members belong to the softball team.

> *All of* us belong to the softball team.

All right. Like *all wrong*, the expression *all right* should be spelled as two words. (The spelling *alright* is not as yet generally accepted.)

Almost—all most. See also *Most*.

> The plane was *almost* (nearly) three hours late.

> We are *all most* pleased (all very much pleased) with the new schedule.

Already—all ready.

> The order had *already* (previously) been shipped.

> The order is *all ready* (all prepared) to be shipped.

Altogether—all together.

> He is *altogether* (entirely) too lazy to be a success.

> The papers are *all together* (all in a group) in the binder I sent you.

Always—all ways.

> She has *always* (at all times) done good work.

> We have tried in *all ways* (by all methods) to keep our employees satisfied.

Among—between. See *Between—among*.

Amount—number. Use *amount* for things in bulk, as in "a large amount of oil." Use *number* for individual items, as in "a large number of tins."

And. Retain *and* before the last item in a series, even though that last item consists of two words joined by *and*.

> We need to increase our expense budgets for advertising, staff training, *and* research and development.

> (NOT: We need to increase our expense budgets for advertising, staff training, research and development.)

(Continued on page 286.)

11

Beginning a sentence with *and* or some other co-ordinating conjunction (*but, or,* or *nor*) can be an effective means—*if not overused*—of giving special attention to the thought that follows the conjunction. No comma should follow the conjunction at the start of a new sentence unless a parenthetical element occurs at that point.

> Last Friday George promised to have the market analysis on my desk this Monday. *And* then he took off on a two-week vacation.

> Tell him to return to the office at once. *Or* else.

> **BUT:** George just called from his home to say that the report was undergoing some last-minute changes and would be on my desk at 11 a.m. *And*, to my delight, it was!

And etc. Never use *and* before *etc.* (See *Etc.*)

And/or. Try to avoid this legalistic term in ordinary writing.

Anxious—eager. Both *anxious* and *eager* mean "desirous," but *anxious* also implies fear or concern.

> I'm *anxious* to hear whether we won the bid or not.

> I'm *eager* (**NOT** anxious) to hear about your new house.

Anymore—any more.

> We used to go to the club, but we don't go there *anymore* (any longer).

> Please call me if you have *any more* (any additional) suggestions.

Anyone—any one. See ¶1010, note.

Anytime—any time.

> Come see us *anytime* you are in town. (One word meaning "whenever.")

> Did you have dealings with Crosby at *any time* in the past? (Two words after a preposition such as *at*.)

> Can you spend *any time* (any amount of time) with Jill and me next week?

Anyway—any way. The form *anyways* is never correct.

> *Anyway* (in any case), we can't spare him now.

> If we can help in *any way* (by any method), please phone.

Appreciate. When used with the meaning "to be thankful for," the verb *appreciate* requires an object.

> **NOT:** We would appreciate if you could give us your decision by May 1.

> **BUT:** We would appreciate *your* (**NOT** you) *giving us your decision by May 1.* (Noun clause as object. See ¶647b on the use of *your* before *giving*.)

> **OR:** We would appreciate *it* if you could give us . . . (Pronoun as object.)

> I will appreciate *whatever you can do for us.* (Relative clause as object.)

> We will always appreciate the *help* you gave us. (Noun as object.)

As. Do not use for *that* or *whether*.

> I do not know *whether* (**NOT** as) I can go.

Use *because, since,* or *for* rather than *as* in clauses of reason.

> I cannot attend the meeting on Friday *because* (**NOT** as) I will be away that day.

As—as if. See *Like—as, as if.*

As . . . as—not so . . . as. The term *as . . . as* is now commonly used in both positive and negative comparisons. Some writers, however, prefer to use *not so . . . as* for negative comparisons.

> Bob is every bit *as* bright *as* his older sister. (Positive comparison.)

> It is *not as* important *as* you think. **OR:** . . . *not so* important *as* you think. (Negative comparison.)

> **NOTE:** Do not replace the second *as* with *than.*

> We spend twice *as* much money on entertainment *as* we do on food.

> (**NOT:** We spend twice *as* much money on entertainment *than* we . . .)

As far as. *As far as* may be used as a preposition or as a subordinating conjunction.

> I can drive you *as far as* Salmon Arm. (Used as a preposition.)

> I would recommend this template *as far as* format is concerned. (Used as a subordinating conjunction.)

> **BUT NOT:** I would recommend this template *as far as* format. (Either create a clause following *as far as* or change *as far as* to *on the basis of* or a similar expression.)

As well as. When using *as well as,* be on guard against the possibility of misleading your reader.

> **CONFUSING:** Ms. Paglia plans to meet with Mr. Pierce and Mrs. Hamer as well as Ms. Fieno. (Is Ms. Paglia planning to meet with three people, or are Ms. Paglia and Ms. Fieno both planning to meet with two people?)

> **CLEAR:** Ms. Paglia plans to meet *with* Mr. Pierce and Mrs. Hamer as well as *with* Ms. Fieno. (Repeating the preposition *with* makes it clear that Ms. Paglia will meet with three people.)

> **CLEAR:** Ms. Paglia *as well as* Ms. *Fieno* plans to meet with Mr. Pierce and Mrs. Hamer. (Rearranging the word order makes it clear that both Ms. Paglia and Ms. Fieno will meet with two people. Note that an *as well as* phrase following the subject, *Ms. Paglia,* does not affect the number of the verb. See ¶1007.)

Assure. See *Ensure—insure—assure.*

At about. Use either *at* or *about,* but not both words together. For example, "Plan to arrive *at* ten" **OR** "Plan to arrive *about* ten." (**BUT NOT:** Plan to arrive *at about* ten.)

Awhile—a while. One word as an adverb; two words as a noun.

> You may have to wait *awhile.* (Adverb.)

> You may have to wait for *a while.* (Noun: object of the preposition *for.*)

Bad—badly. Use the adjective *bad* (not the adverb *badly*) after the verb *feel, felt,* or *look.* (See ¶1067.)

> I feel *bad* (**NOT** badly) about the mistake. **BUT:** He was hurt *badly.*

NOTE: One way you can "feel badly" is to burn your fingertips!

11

Balance. Do not use *balance* to mean "rest" or "remainder" except in a financial or accounting sense.

> I plan to use the *rest* of my vacation time next February.
>
> (**NOT:** I plan to use the *balance* of my vacation time next February.)
>
> **BUT:** The *balance* of the loan falls due at the end of this quarter.

Because. See *Reason is because.*

Because of. See *Due to—because of—on account of.*

Being that. Do not use for *since* or *because.*

> *Because* I arrived late, I could not get a seat.
>
> (**NOT:** *Being that* I arrived late, I could not get a seat.)

Beside—besides.

> I sat *beside* (next to) Mr. Parrish's father at the meeting.
>
> *Besides* (in addition), we need your support of the measure.

Between—among. Ordinarily, use *between* when referring to *two* persons or things and *among* when referring to *more than* two persons or things.

> The territory is divided evenly *between* the two sales representatives.
>
> The profits are to be evenly divided *among* the three partners.

Use *between* with more than two persons or things when they are being considered in pairs as well as in a group.

> There are distinct differences *between* Montreal, Toronto, and Halifax.
>
> In packing china, be sure to place paper *between* the plates.
>
> The memo says something different when you read *between* the lines.

Between you and me (not *I*). See ¶1055b.

Biannual—biennial—semi-annual. *Biannual* and *semi-annual* both mean "occurring twice a year." *Biennial* means "occurring every two years." Because of the possible confusion between *biannual* and *biennial*, use *semi-annual* when you want to describe something that occurs twice a year.

> **PREFERRED:** our *semi-annual* sales conference
>
> **CLEARER THAN:** our *biannual* sales conference

If you think that your reader could misconstrue *biennial*, avoid the term and use *every two years* instead.

> Each national sales conference is held semi-annually; an international sales conference is held *biennially* (**OR** *every two years*).

Biweekly—bimonthly. These two words do not mean the same thing. Moreover, *bimonthly* has two quite different meanings. Originally it meant *every two months*, but it is now more commonly used to mean *twice a month*. To avoid confusion, use *semi-monthly* or *twice a month* for one meaning and *every two months* for the other.

If you are paid *biweekly* (every two weeks), you get 26 cheques a year.

If you are paid *bimonthly* (twice a month), you get 24 cheques a year.

OR: If you are paid *bimonthly* (every two months), you get only 6 cheques a year.

Both—each. *Both* means "the two considered together." *Each* refers to the individual members of a group considered separately.

Both designs are acceptable.	The designs are *each* acceptable.
Each boy wrote about the other.	**NOT:** *Both* boys wrote about the other.

Both alike—equal—together. *Both* is unnecessary when used with *alike*, *equal*, or *together*.

These inkjet printers are *alike*. (**NOT:** both alike.)

These tape systems are *equal* in cost. (**NOT:** both equal.)

We will travel *together* to the Far East. (**NOT:** both travel together.)

Bring—take. *Bring* indicates motion toward the speaker. *Take* indicates motion away from the speaker.

Please *bring* the research data with you when you next come to the office.

Please *take* the enclosed letter to Farley when you go to see him.

You may *take* my copy with you if you will *bring* it back by Friday.

☞ *See note under* Come—go.

But . . . however. Use one or the other.

We had hoped to see the show, *but* we couldn't get tickets.

OR: We had hoped to see the show; *however*, we couldn't get tickets.

(**BUT NOT:** . . . *but* we couldn't get tickets, *however*.)

But what. Use *that*.

I do not doubt *that* (**NOT** but what) he will be elected.

Can—could. See *May—can (might—could)*.

Cannot help but. This expression is a confusion of two others, namely, *can but* and *cannot help*.

I *can but* try. (**BETTER:** I *can only* try.)

I *cannot help* feeling sorry for her. (**NOT:** cannot help but feel.)

Class. See *Kind*.

Come—go. The choice between verbs depends on the location of the speaker. *Come* indicates motion *toward*; *go*, motion *away from*. (See also *Bring—take*.)

When Bellamy *comes* back, I will *go* to the airport to meet him.

A manager speaking over the phone to an outsider: Will it be convenient for you to *come* to our office tomorrow?

(*Continued on page 290.*)

11

NOTE: When discussing your travel plans with a person at your destination, adopt that person's point of view and use *come*.

> *An outsider speaking over the phone to a manager:* Will it be convenient for me to *come* to your office tomorrow?

> *Westerner to Nova Scotian:* I am *coming* to Nova Scotia during the week of the 11th. I will *bring* the plans with me if they are ready.

However, if you are discussing your travel plans with someone who is *not* at your destination, observe the regular distinction between *come* and *go*.

> *An outsider speaking to an outsider:* I hope it will be convenient for me to *go* to their office tomorrow.

> *Westerner to Westerner:* I am *going* to Nova Scotia during the week of the 11th. I will *take* the plans with me if they are ready.

Come and. In formal writing, use *come to* instead of the colloquial *come and*.

> Come *to* see me. (NOT: Come *and* see me.)

Complementary—complimentary. *Complementary* means "serving to complete" or "mutually supplying what each other lacks." *Complimentary* means "flattering" or "given free." (For the meanings of *complement* and *compliment*, see ¶719.)

> Our executives bring *complementary* skills and expertise to their jobs.

> May I get a *complimentary* copy of your new book?

Comprise—compose. *Comprise* means "to include, contain, consist of"; *compose* means "to make up." The parts *compose* (make up) the whole; the whole *comprises* (includes) the parts; the whole *is composed of* (NOT is comprised of) the parts.

> The parent corporation *comprises* (consists of) three major divisions.

> Three major divisions *compose* (make up) the parent corporation.

> The parent corporation *is composed of* (is made up of) three major divisions.

Data. See ¶1018, note.

Dependant—dependent. These words are now interchangeable as nouns; however, most writers use *dependant* only as a noun. In both forms, *dependent* is an adjective.

> The mother lives with her son as a *dependant*. (Used as a noun; she depends upon her son for support.)

> A good harvest is *dependent* on the weather. (Used as an adjective; the harvest is influenced by the weather.)

Different—differently. When the meaning is "in a different manner," use the adverb *differently*.

> I wish we had done it *differently*.   *It came out differently* than we expected.

After linking verbs and verbs of the senses, the adjective *different* is correct. (See ¶1067.)

That music sounds completely *different.*

He seems (appears) *different* since his promotion.

Don't believe anything *different.* (Meaning "anything that is different.")

Different from—different than. See ¶1077.

Done. Do not say "I *done* it." Say "I *did* it." (See also ¶1032.)

Don't (do not). Do not use *don't* with *he, she,* or *it;* use *doesn't.*

He *doesn't* talk easily.	**BUT:** I *don't* think so.
She needs help, *doesn't* she?	They *don't* want any help.
It *doesn't* seem right to penalize them.	We *don't* understand.

Doubt that—doubt whether. Use *doubt that* in negative statements and in questions. Use *doubt whether* in all other cases. (See also *If—whether.*)

We do not *doubt that* she is capable. (Negative statement.)

Does anyone *doubt that* the cheque was mailed? (Question.)

I *doubt whether* I can go.

Due to—because of—on account of. *Due to* introduces an adjective phrase and should modify nouns. It is normally used only after some form of the verb *to be* (*is, are, was, were,* etc.).

Her success is *due to* talent and hard work. (*Due to* modifies *success.*)

Because of and *on account of* introduce adverbial phrases and should modify verbs.

He resigned *because of* ill health. (*Because of* modifies *resigned.*)

(**NOT:** He resigned *due to* ill health.)

Each—both. See *Both—each.*

Each other—one another. Use *each other* to refer to two persons or things; *one another* for more than two.

The two partners had greater respect for *each other's* abilities.

The four winners congratulated *one another.*

Eager—anxious. See *Anxious—eager.*

Effect—affect. See *Affect—effect.*

Ensure—insure—assure. *Ensure* means "to make certain." *Insure* means "to protect against loss." *Assure* means "to give someone confidence"; the object of this verb should always refer to a person.

I want to *ensure* (make certain) that nothing can go wrong tomorrow.

I want to *insure* this necklace (protect it against loss) for $5000.

I want to *assure* you (give you confidence) that nothing will go wrong.

Enthused over. Use *was* or *were enthusiastic about* instead.

The sales staff *was enthusiastic about* (**NOT** enthused over) next year's styles.

Equal. See *Both alike—equal—together.*

11

Equally as good. Use either *equally good* or *just as good*. The form *equally as good* is never correct.

> This model is newer, but that one is *equally good*. (**NOT:** equally as good.)

> Those are *just as good* as these. (**NOT:** equally as good.)

Etc.—and so on—such as. The abbreviation of *et cetera* means "and other things." Therefore, do not use *and* before it. A comma both precedes and follows *etc.* (See ¶164.) In formal writing, avoid the use of *etc.*; use a phrase such as *and the like* or *and so on.*

NOTE: Do not use *etc.* or an equivalent expression at the end of a series introduced by *such as*. The term *such as* implies that only a few selected examples will be given; therefore, it is unnecessary to add *etc.* or *and so on*, which suggests that further examples could be given.

> As part of its employee educational program, the company offers courses in report writing, business communication, grammar and style, *and so on.*

> **OR:** . . . the company offers courses *such as* report writing, business communication, and grammar and style.

> (**BUT NOT:** . . . the company offers courses *such as* report writing, business communication, grammar and style, *and so on.*)

☞ *For the use or omission of a comma before* such as, *see* ¶¶148–149.

Everyday—every day. *Everyday* is an adjective followed by a noun. *Every day* is an adjective plus a noun.

> You'll soon master the *everyday* (ordinary or daily) routine of the job.

> He has called *every day* (each day) this week.

Everyone—every one. See ¶1010, note.

Ex—former. Use *ex-* with a title to designate the person who *immediately* preceded the current titleholder in that position; use *former* with a title to designate an earlier titleholder.

> Charles Fellows is the *ex-president* of the Hamilton Chamber of Commerce. (Held office immediately before the current president.)

> **BUT:** . . . is a *former* president of the Hamilton Chamber of Commerce. (Held office sometime before the current president and that person's immediate predecessor.)

Except. When *except* is a preposition, be sure to use the objective form of a pronoun that follows. (See also ¶1055b.)

> Everyone has been notified *except* Jean and *me*. (**NOT:** except Jean and I.)

Farther—further. *Farther* refers to actual distance; *further* refers to figurative distance and means "to a greater degree" or "to a greater extent."

> The drive from the airport was *farther* (in actual distance) than we expected.

> Let's plan to discuss the proposal *further* (to a greater extent).

Fewer—less. *Fewer* refers to number and is used with *plural* nouns. *Less* refers to degree or amount and is used with *singular* nouns.

Fewer accidents (a smaller number) were reported than was expected.

Less effort (a smaller degree) was put forth by the organizers, and thus *fewer* people (a smaller number) attended.

The expression *less than* (rather than *fewer than*) precedes plural nouns referring to periods of time, amounts of money, and quantities.

less than ten years ago	**FORMAL:** fewer than 60 people
less than $1 million	**COLLOQUIAL:** less than 60 people

The expression *or less* (rather than *or fewer*) is used after a reference to a number of items.

in words of 100 or less   in groups of six people or less

First—firstly, etc. In enumerations use the forms *first, second, third* (**NOT** firstly, secondly, thirdly).

Flammable—inflammable. Both terms mean "easily ignitable, highly combustible." However, since some readers may misinterpret *inflammable* to mean "*non*flammable," *flammable* is the clearer form.

Former—ex. See *Ex—former*.

Former—first. *Former* refers to the first of two persons or things. When more than two are mentioned, use *first*. (See also *Latter—last*.)

This item is available in wool and in Dacron, but I prefer the *former*.

This item is available in wool, in Dacron, and in Orlon, but I prefer the *first*.

From—off. Use *from* (**NOT** off) with persons.

I got the answer I needed *from* Margaret. (**NOT:** off Margaret.)

Go—come. See *Come—go*.

Good—well. *Good* is an adjective. *Well* is typically used as an adverb, but it may be used as an adjective to refer to the state of someone's health.

Marie got *good* grades in school. (Adjective.)

I will do the job as *well* as I can. (Adverb.)

He admits he does not feel *well* today. (Adjective.)

The security guards look *good* in their new uniforms. (Adjective.)

NOTE: *To feel well* means "to be in good health." *To feel good* means "to be in good spirits."

Graduated—was graduated. Both forms are acceptable. However, use *from* after either expression.

My son *graduated from* UBC last year. (**NOT:** My son *graduated* UBC last year.)

Hardly. *Hardly* is negative in meaning. To preserve the negative meeting, do not use another negative with it.

You *could hardly* (**NOT** couldn't hardly) expect him to agree.

Have—of. See *Of—have*.

11

Healthy—healthful. People are *healthy;* a climate or food is *healthful.*

> You ought to move to a more *healthful* (**NOT** healthier) climate.

Help. Do not use *from* after the verb *help.* For example, "I couldn't *help* (**NOT** help from) telling her she was wrong."

Historic—historical. *Historic* means "important" or "momentous." *Historical* means "relating to the past."

> July 1, 1867, is a *historic* date in Canadian history.

> The following article provides a *historical* account of the War of 1812.

Hopefully. The use of *hopefully* at the beginning of a sentence should be avoided in formal writing. However, it is sometimes used as an independent comment functioning similarly to words such as *obviously, fortunately,* and *apparently.* (See ¶138b.) These adverbs express the writer's attitude toward what he or she is about to say.

> *Hopefully,* the worst is over and we will soon see a strong upturn in sales.

However. See *But . . . however.*

If—whether. *If* is often used colloquially for *whether* in such sentences as "He doesn't know *whether* he will be able to leave tomorrow." In written material, use *whether,* particularly in such expressions as *see whether, learn whether, know whether,* and *doubt whether.* Also use *whether* when the expression *or not* follows or is implied. See ¶719 for whether/weather.

> Find out *whether* (**NOT** if) this format is acceptable *or not.*

Imply—infer. *Imply* means "to suggest"; you imply something by *your own* words or actions.

> Verna *implied* (suggested) that we would not be invited.

Infer means "to assume, to deduce, to arrive at a conclusion"; you infer something from *another person's* words or actions.

> I *inferred* (assumed) from Verna's remarks that we would not be invited.

In—into—in to.

> The correspondence is *in* the file. (*In* implies position within.)

> He walked *into* the outer office. (*Into* implies entry or change of form.)

> All sales reports are to be sent *in to* the sales manager. (*In* is an adverb in the verb phrase *are to be sent in; to* is a simple preposition.)

> Mr. Boehme came *in to* see me. (*In* is part of the verb phrase *came in; to* is part of the infinitive *to see.*)

In regards to. Substitute *in regard to, with regard to, regarding,* or *as regards.* The form *in regards to* is never correct.

> I am writing *in regard to* (**NOT** in regards to) your letter of May 1.

Incidentally. Note that this word ends in *ally.* Never spell it *incidently.*

Indifferent—in different.

She was *indifferent* (not caring one way or the other) to the offer.

He liked our idea, but he wanted it expressed *in different* (in other) words.

Indirect—in direct.

Indirect (not direct) lighting will enhance the appearance of this room.

This order is *in direct* (the preposition *in* plus the adjective *direct*) conflict with the policy of this company.

Individual—party—person—people. Use *individual* to refer to someone whom you wish to distinguish from a larger group of people.

We wish to honour those *individuals* who had the courage to speak out at a time when popular opinion was defending the status quo.

Use *party* only to refer to someone involved in a legal proceeding.

All the *parties* to the original agreement must sign the attached amendment.

Use *person* to refer to a human being in all other contexts.

Please tell me the name of the *person* in charge of your credit department.

If reference is made to more than one person, the term *people* usually sounds more natural than the plural form *persons*. In any event, always use *people* when referring to a large group.

If you like, I can send you a list of all the *people* in our corporation who will be attending this year's national convention.

Inflammable—flammable. See *Flammable—inflammable.*

Insure. See *Ensure—insure—assure.*

Irregardless. The word *irregardless* is never correct. Use *regardless.*

Is where—is when. Do not use these phrases to introduce definitions.

A dilemma is a situation in which you have to choose between equally unsatisfactory alternatives.

(**NOT:** A dilemma *is where* you have to choose between equally unsatisfactory alternatives.)

However, these phrases may be correctly used in other situations.

The Royal York *is where* the dinner-dance will be held this year.

Two o'clock *is when* the meeting is scheduled to begin.

Its—it's. See ¶1056e.

Kind. *Kind* is singular; therefore, write *this kind, that kind, these kinds, those kinds* (**BUT NOT** *these kind, those kind*). The same distinctions hold for *class, type,* and *sort.*

Kind of—sort of. These phrases are sometimes followed by an adjective (for example, *kind of sorry, sort of baffled*). Use this kind of expression only

(Continued on page 296.)

in informal writing. In more formal situations, use *rather* or *somewhat* (*rather sorry, somewhat baffled*).

> I was *somewhat* (**NOT** kind of, sort of) surprised.
>
> She seemed *rather* (**NOT** kind of, sort of) tired.

NOTE: When *kind of* or *sort of* is followed by a noun, the expression is appropriate in all kinds of situations.

> What *sort of business* is Vern Forbes in?

Kind of a. The *a* is unnecessary. For example, "That *kind of* (**NOT** kind of a) material is very expensive."

Last—latest. *Last* means "after all others"; *latest,* "most recent."

> Mr. Lin's *last* act before leaving was to recommend Ms. Roth's promotion.
>
> Attached is the *latest* report we have received from the Southern Region.

Latter—last. *Latter* refers to the second of two persons or things mentioned. When more than two are mentioned, use *last*. (See also *Former—first.*)

> July and August are good vacation months, but the *latter* is more popular.
>
> June, July, and August are good vacation months, but the *last* is the most popular.

Lay—lie. *Lay* (principal parts: *lay, laid, laid, laying*) means "to put" or "to place." This verb requires an object to complete its meaning.

> Please *lay* the *boxes* on the pallets with extreme care.
>
> I *laid* the *message* right on your desk.
>
> I *had laid* two other *notes* there yesterday.
>
> He *is* always *laying* the *blame* on his assistants. (Putting the blame.)
>
> The dress *was laid* in the box. (A passive construction implying that someone *put* or *placed* the dress in the box.)

Lie (principal parts: *lie, lay, lain, lying*) means "to recline, rest, or stay" or "to take a position of rest." It refers to a person or thing as either assuming or being in a reclining position. This verb cannot take an object.

> Now he *lies* in bed most of the day.
>
> The mountains *lay* before us as we proceeded west.
>
> This letter *has lain* unanswered for two weeks.
>
> Today's mail *is lying* on the receptionist's desk.

TEST: In deciding whether to use *lie* or *lay* in a sentence, substitute the word *place, placed,* or *placing* (as appropriate) for the word in question. If the substitute fits, the corresponding form of *lay* is correct. If it does not, use the appropriate form of *lie*.

> I will (*lie* or *lay?*) down now. (You could not say, "I will *place* down now." Write "I will *lie* down now.")

I (*laid* or *lay?*) the pad on his desk. ("I *placed* the pad on his desk" works. Write "I *laid* the pad.")

I (*laid* or *lay?*) awake many nights. ("I *placed* awake" does not work. Write "I *lay* awake.")

These files have (*laid* or *lain?*) untouched for some time. ("These files have *placed* untouched" does not work. Write "These files have *lain* untouched.")

He has been (*laying* or *lying?*) down on the job. ("He has been *placing* down on the job" does not work. Write "He has been *lying* down.")

NOTE: When the verb *lie* means "to tell a falsehood," it has regularly formed principal parts *(lie, lied, lied, lying)* and is seldom confused with the verbs just described.

Learn—teach. *Learn* (principal parts: *learn, learned, learned, learning*) means "to acquire knowledge." *Teach* (principal parts: *teach, taught, taught, teaching*) means "to impart knowledge to others."

I *learned* from a master teacher.　　　A first-rate instructor *taught* me how.

(**NOT:** I *was learned* by a master teacher.)　　　I was *taught* by a first-rate instructor.

Leave—let. *Leave* (principal parts: *leave, left, left, leaving*) means "to move away, abandon, or depart." *Let* (principal parts: *let, let, let, letting*) means "to permit or allow." **TEST:** In deciding whether to use *let* or *leave*, substitute a suitable form of *permit*. If *permit* fits, use *let*; if not, use *leave*.

I now *leave* you to your own devices. (Abandon you.)

Mr. Morales *left* on the morning train. (Departed.)

Let me see the last page. (Permit me to see.)

Leave me alone. **OR:** *Let* me alone. (Either is acceptable.)

Less—fewer. See *Fewer—less*.

Like—as, as if. *Like* is correctly used as a preposition. Although *like* is also widely used as a conjunction in colloquial speech, use *as, as if,* or a similar expression in written material.

We need to hire another person *like* you.
Kate, *like* her predecessor, will have to cope with the problem.
As (**NOT** Like) I told you earlier, we will not reorder for six months.

It looks *like* snow.　　　　　　It looks *as if* it will snow.
(**NOT:** It looks *like* it will snow.)

Mary looks *like* her mother.　　　Mary looks *as* her mother did at the same age.
(**NOT:** Mary looks *like* her mother did at the same age.)

Literally. This adverb means "actually, truly." Do not use it in the sense of "almost" to modify a reference to an exaggerated or unreal situation.

May—can (might—could). *May* and *might* imply permission or possibility; *can* and *could*, ability or power. *Might* is the past tense of *may; could* is the past tense of *can*. In expressing possibility *might* and *could* suggest more doubt than *may* or *can*.

(Continued on page 298.)

11

You *may* send them a dozen cans of paint on trial. (Permission.)

The report *may* be true. (Possibility.)

Can he present a workable plan? (Has he the ability?)

Miss Kovacs said I *might* (permission) have the time off if I *could* (had the ability to) finish my work in time.

Call me if you think I *can* be of any help. (Emphasizes the ability to help.)

Call me if you think I *may* be of any help. (Emphasizes the possibility of helping.)

The CEO *could* change this policy if he wanted to. (Power.)

Maybe—may be. *Maybe* is an adverb; *may be* is a verb.

If we don't receive a letter from them today, *maybe* (an adverb meaning "perhaps") we should call.

Mr. Boston *may be* (a verb) out of town next week.

Media. *Media*, referring to various channels of communication and advertising, is a plural noun. *Medium* is the singular. (See ¶1018.)

More. In some sentences it may not be clear whether *more* is being used to form the comparative degree of an adjective (for example, *more experienced*) or is being used as an adjective meaning "a greater number of." In such cases reword to avoid confusion.

CONFUSING: We need to hire more experienced workers. (A greater number of experienced workers? Or workers who are more experienced than those now on staff?)

CLEAR: We need to hire a greater number of experienced workers.

CLEAR: We need to hire workers who are more experienced.

More important—more importantly. *More important* is often used as a short form for "what is more important," especially at the beginning of a sentence. *More importantly* means "in a more important manner."

More important, we need to establish a line of credit very quickly. (What is more important.)

The incident was treated *more importantly* than was necessary. (In a more important manner.)

Most. Do not use for *almost.*

Almost all the money is gone. OR: *Most* of the money is gone.

BUT NOT: *Most all* of the money is gone.

Nobody—no body.

There was *nobody* (no person) at the information desk when I arrived.

No body (no group) of employees is more co-operative than yours. (Spell *no body* as two words when it is followed by *of.* See also ¶1010.)

None—no one. See ¶1013.

Not so . . . as. See *As . . . as—not so . . . as.*

Number. See *Amount—number.*

Of—a. See *A—of.*

Of—have. Do not use *of* instead of *have* in verb forms. The correct forms are *could have, would have, should have, might have, may have, must have, ought to have,* and so forth.

> What *could have* happened? (**NOT:** What could *of* happened?)

Off. Do not use *off of* or *off from* in place of *off.* (See also ¶1078.)

> The papers fell *off* the desk. (**NOT:** off of the desk.)

Off—from. See *From—off.*

On—onto—on to.

> It's dangerous to drive *on* the highway shoulder. (*On* is a preposition that implies position or movement over.)

> He lost control of the car and drove *onto* the sidewalk. (*Onto* is a preposition that implies movement toward and then over.)

> Let's go *on to* the next problem. (*On* is an adverb in the verb phrase *go on; to* is a preposition.)

On—upon—up on.

> His statements were based *on* (**OR** *upon*) experimental data. (*On* and *upon* are interchangeable.)

> Please follow *up on* the Underhill case. (*Up* is part of the verb phrase *follow up; on* is a preposition.)

On account of. See *Due to—because of—on account of.*

One another—each other. See *Each other—one another.*

Only. The adverb *only* is negative in meaning. Therefore, do not use another negative with it unless you want a positive meaning. (See ¶1072 for the placement of *only* in a sentence.)

> I use this letterhead *only* for foreign correspondence. (I do not use this letterhead for anything else.)

> **BUT:** I do not use this letterhead *only* for foreign correspondence. (I use it for a number of other things as well.)

Opposite. When used as a noun, *opposite* is followed by *of.*

> Her opinion is the *opposite of* mine.

In other uses, *opposite* is followed by *to* or *from* or by no preposition at all.

> Her opinion is *opposite to* (**OR** *from*) mine.

> She lives *opposite* the school.

Party. See *Individual—party—person—people.*

Per—a. *Per,* a Latin word, means "by the" as in *80 kilometres per hour (80/h).* Whenever possible, substitute with *a* or *an;* for example, *$8 an hour, 75 cents*

(Continued on page 300.)

11

a dozen. Per must be retained in Latin phrases; for example, *per diem* (by the day) or *per capita* (for each person).

NOTE: Do not use *per* to mean "according to" or "in accordance with."

We are sending you samples *as you requested.* (**NOT:** per your request.)

Percent—percentage. In ordinary usage, *percent* should always be accompanied by a number; for example, *20 percent, 0.5 percent.* In a table a column of percentage figures may be headed *Percent of Total* or something comparable. In all other cases, use the term *percentage.*

A large *percentage* of the calls we got yesterday came from customers who misread our ad. (**NOT:** A large *percent* of the calls . . .)

What *percentage* of our subscribers are in the 30–49 age group? (See ¶1025.)

NOTE: In the percentage formula (base × rate = amount), the rate is called a *percent* and the amount is called a *percentage.*

Plus. This word can be correctly used as a noun, an adjective, or a preposition. However, do not use it as a conjunction (with the sense of "and").

Your presence was a real *plus* for our cause. (*Plus* used correctly as a noun.)

The decision to offer a 10 percent discount on all orders received by June 1 was a *plus* factor in the campaign. (*Plus* used correctly as an adjective.)

Your willingness to innovate *plus* your patient perspective on profits has permitted this company to grow at an astonishing rate. (*Plus* used correctly as a preposition. Note that a *plus* phrase following the subject of a sentence does not affect the number of the verb. See ¶1007.)

BUT NOT: You have always been willing to innovate, *plus* you have been patient about the profits to be derived from the innovations. (Do not use *plus* as a conjunction; use *and* instead.)

Raise—rise. *Raise* (principal parts: *raise, raised, raised, raising*) means "to cause to lift" or "to lift something." This verb requires an object to complete its meaning.

Mr. Pon *raises* a good *question.*	Farmers *have raised* the *price* of grain.
Our rent *has been raised.* (See ¶1036.)	We *are raising money* for the United Way.

Rise (principal parts: *rise, rose, risen, rising*) means "to ascend," "to move upward by itself," or "to get up." This verb cannot be used with an object.

We will have to *rise* to the occasion.	The sun *rose* at 6:25 this morning.
The river *has risen* to flood level.	The temperature *has been rising* all day.

TEST: Remember, you cannot "rise" anything.

Real—really. *Real* is an adjective; *really,* an adverb. Do not use *real* to modify another adjective; use *very* or *really.*

One taste will tell you these cookies were made with *real* butter. (Adjective.)

We were *really* expecting a lower price from you this year. (Adverb.)

BUT: It was *very* nice (**NOT:** real nice) to see you and your family again.

Reason is because. Substitute *reason is that.*

> The *reason* for such low sales is *that* (**NOT:** *because*) prices are too high.

Retroactive to. After *retroactive* use *to* (**NOT:** *from*).

> These improvements in benefits under the company dental plan will be *retroactive to* July 1. (See also ¶1077.)

Said. The use of *said* in a phrase like "the *said* document" is appropriate only in legal writing. In normal usage write "the document referred to above."

Same. Do not use *same* to refer to a previously mentioned thing.

> We are now processing your order and will have *it* ready for you Monday.
>
> (**NOT:** We are now processing your order and will have *same* ready . . .)

Scarcely. The adverb *scarcely* is negative in meaning. To preserve the negative meaning, do not use another negative with it. (See ¶1072 for the placement of *scarcely.*)

> I *scarcely* recognized (**NOT** didn't scarcely recognize) you.

Semi-annual. See *Biannual—biennial—semi-annual.*

Serve—service. Things can be *serviced,* but people are *served.*

> We take great pride in the way we *serve* (**NOT** service) our clients.
>
> For a small additional charge we will *service* the equipment for a full year.

Set—sit. *Set* (principal parts: *set, set, set, setting*) means "to place something somewhere." In this sense, *set* requires an object to complete its meaning. **REMEMBER:** You cannot "sit" anything.

> It's important to *set* down your *recollections* while they are still fresh.
>
> I must have dropped my wallet when I *set* my *suitcase* down.
>
> I *have set* my *alarm* for six in the morning.
>
> The crew *was setting* the *stage* for the evening performance.
>
> The date *was set* some time ago. (A passive construction implying that someone *set* the date.)

NOTE: *Set* has a few other meanings in which the verb does *not* require an object, but these meanings are seldom confused with *sit.*

> He *set* out on a hiking trip.   The sun *set* at 5:34 p.m. Monday.
>
> Allow an hour for the sauce to *set.*   The bracelet is *set* with diamonds.

Sit (principal parts: *sit, sat, sat, sitting*) means "to be in a position of rest" or "to be seated." This verb cannot be used with an object.

> Here we *sit,* waiting for a decision.   They *had sat* on the plane for an hour.
>
> I *sat* next to Ebrahim at the meeting.   We *will be sitting* in the top balcony.

11

Shall—will. The helping verb *shall* has largely given way to the verb *will* in all but the most formal writing and speech. The following rules reflect both ordinary and formal usage:

a. To express simple future time:

(1) In *ordinary* circumstances use *will* with all three persons.

I (**OR** *we*) *will* be glad to help you plan the program.

You will want to study these recommendations before the meeting.

He (**OR** *she, it, they*) *will* arrive tomorrow morning.

(2) In *formal* circumstances use *shall* with the first person *(I, we)* and *will* with the second and third persons *(you, he, she, it, they).*

I (**OR** *we*) *shall* be glad to answer all inquiries promptly.

You will meet the McGinnesses at the reception this evening.

They (**OR** *he, she*) *will* not find the trip too tiring.

b. To indicate *determination, promise, desire, choice,* or *threat:*

(1) In *ordinary* circumstances use *will* with all three persons.

(2) In *formal* circumstances use *will* for the first person *(I, we)* and *shall* for the second and third persons *(you, he, she, it, they).*

In spite of the risk, *I will* go where I please. (Determination.)

They shall not interfere with my department. (Determination.)

I will send my cheque by the end of the week. (Promise.)

We will report you to the authorities if this is true. (Threat.)

You shall regret your answer. (Threat.)

He shall study or *he shall* leave college. (Threat.)

c. To indicate *willingness* (to be willing, to be agreeable to) in both *ordinary* and *formal* circumstances, use *will* with all persons.

Yes, I *will* meet you at six o'clock.

Should—would. *Should* and *would* follow the same rules as *shall* and *will* in expressions of future time, determination, and willingness. The distinctions concerning ordinary and formal usage also apply here.

ORDINARY: I *would* like to hear from you.
FORMAL: I *should* like to hear from you.

ORDINARY: We *would* be glad to see her.
FORMAL: We *should* be glad to see her.

ORDINARY: I *would* be pleased to serve on that committee.
FORMAL: I *should* be pleased to serve on that committee.

a. Always use *should* in all persons to indicate "ought to."

I *should* study tonight.   He *should* pay his debts.

You *should* report his dishonesty to the manager.

b. Always use *would* in all persons to indicate customary action.

Every day I *would* swim half a mile.   They *would* only say, "No comment."

11

c. Use *should* in all three persons to express a condition in an *if* clause.

If I *should* win the prize, I will share it with you.

If you *should* miss the train, please call me collect.

d. Use *would* in all three persons to express willingness in an *if* clause.

If he *would* apply himself, he could win top honours easily.

If you *would* delay your decision, I could offer you more attractive terms.

So—so that. *So* as a conjunction means "therefore"; *so that* means "in order that."

The work is now finished, *so* you can all go home. (See also ¶179.)

Please finish what you are doing *so that* we can all go home.

Someday—some day.

Please set up a meeting with Al and Jerry *someday* (on an unspecified day) next week.

BUT: Please set up a meeting with Al and Jerry *for some day* next week. (Two words when used as the object of a preposition such as *for*.)

Someone—some one. See ¶1010, note.

Sometime—sometimes—some time.

The order will be shipped *sometime* (at some unspecified time) next week.

Sometimes (now and then) reports are misleading.

It took me *some time* (a period of time) to complete the job.

I saw him *some time* ago (a long time ago).

NOTE: Spell *some time* as two words when the term follows a preposition.

We will be happy to reconsider your proposal *at some time* in the future.

I've been thinking about retiring *for some time*.

Sort. See *Kind.*

Sort of—kind of. See *Kind of—sort of.*

Such as . . . etc. See *Etc.*

Supposed to. Be sure to spell *supposed* with a *d*.

Under the circumstances what was I *supposed to* think? (**NOT:** suppose to.)

Sure—surely. *Sure* is an adjective, *surely* an adverb.

I am *sure* that I did not make that mistake. (Adjective.)

You can *surely* count on our help. (Adverb.)

Do not use *sure* as an adverb; use *surely* or *very*.

I was *very* (**OR** *surely*) glad to be of help. (**NOT:** sure glad.)

Sure and. In formal writing use *sure to* in place of the colloquial *sure and*.

Be *sure to* give my best regards to the Nakanos.

(**NOT:** Be *sure and give* my best regards to the Nakanos.)

11

Take—bring. See *Bring—take.*

Teach—learn. See *Learn—teach.*

Than—then. *Than* is a conjunction introducing a dependent clause of comparison. *Then* is an adverb meaning "at that time" or "next."

> They *then* asserted that they could handle the account better *than* we. (See ¶1057 for the case of pronouns following *than*.)

> The compulsory retirement age is higher now *than* it was *then.*

NOTE: Remember that *then* (like *when*) refers to time.

That. As a subordinating conjunction, *that* links the dependent clause it introduces with the main clause. *That* is often omitted (but understood).

> We realize *that* our bargaining position is not a strong one.

> **OR:** We realize our bargaining position is not a strong one.

However, under certain circumstances *that* should not be omitted:

a. When the word or phrase following *that* could be misread as the object of the verb in the main clause.

> **NOT:** I heard your speech next Wednesday had to be rescheduled.

> **BUT:** I heard *that* your speech next Wednesday had to be rescheduled.

b. When *that* introduces two or more parallel clauses.

> **NOT:** Hilary said she had narrowed the applicants for the job down to three people and *that* she would announce her choice by this Friday.

> **BUT:** Hilary said *that* she had narrowed the applicants for the job down to three people and *that* she would announce her choice by this Friday.

c. When an introductory or interrupting element comes between *that* and the subject of the dependent clause.

> **NOT:** I think whenever possible, you should consult everyone involved before making your decision.

> **BUT:** I think *that* whenever possible, you should consult everyone involved before making your decision. (See ¶130d.)

NOTE: If you are in doubt, do not omit *that.*

That—that. Avoid unnecessary repetition of *that.*

> I think *that* the project should be finished.

> **NOT:** I think *that that* project should be finished.

That—where. See *Where—that.*

That—which—who. See ¶1062.

This here. Do not use for *this*; for example, "*this* (**NOT** this here) word processor."

This sort—this kind. The correct forms are *this* sort, *this* kind, these *sorts*, these *kinds*. (See Kind.)

Together. See *Both alike—equal—together.*

Toward—towards. *Toward* is more common, but both forms are correct.

Try and. In written material use *try to* rather than the colloquial *try and.* For example, "Please *try to* be here on time." (**NOT:** try and be here.)

Type. See *Kind.*

Unique. Do not use *unique* in the sense of "unusual." A unique thing is one of a kind. (See ¶1071f.)

Up. Many verbs (for example, *end, rest, lift, connect, join, hurry, settle, burn, drink, eat*) contain the idea of "up"; therefore, the adverb *up* is unnecessary. In the following sentences, *up* should be omitted.

> You need to rest (up) for a bit.   Save $50 if you join (up) now.
>
> Let's divide (up) the work load.   I will call him (up) tomorrow.

Upon—up on. See *On—upon—up on.*

Used to. Be sure to spell *used* with a *d.*

> We *used* to use Foremost as our main supplier. (**NOT:** We *use* to use . . .)

Very. This adverb can be used to modify an adjective, another adverb, a present participle, or a "descriptive" past participle.

> We are *very happy* with the outcome. (Modifying an adjective.)
>
> This finish dries *very quickly.* (Modifying an adverb.)
>
> It was a *very disappointing* showing. (Modifying a present participle.)
>
> I was *very pleased* with the pictures. (Modifying a descriptive past participle.)

When the past participle expresses action rather than description, insert an adverb like *much* after *very.*

> They are *very much opposed* to your plan. (*Opposed* is part of the complete verb *are opposed* and expresses action rather than description.)
>
> (**NOT:** They are *very opposed* to your plan.)

Ways. Do not use for *way* in referring to distance. For example, "I live a short *way* (**NOT** ways) from here."

Well—good. See *Good—well.*

Whatever—what ever.

> You may write on *whatever* (any) topic you wish.
>
> *What ever* made you think that was true? (*Ever* is an adverb here.)

Where—that. Do not use *where* in place of *that.*

> I saw in the paper *that* Robinson's had changed its mind about closing its store.
>
> (**NOT:** I saw in the paper *where* Robinson's had changed its mind about closing its store.)

Whether—if. See *If—whether.* For *whether—weather,* see ¶719.

Who—which—that. See ¶1062.

11

Who—whom. See ¶1061.

Whoever—who ever.

> *Whoever* (anyone who) made such a statement should be fired.
>
> *Who ever* made such a statement? (*Ever* is an adverb.)

Will—shall. See *Shall—will.*

Wise. Avoid the temptation to coin new words by attaching the suffix *wise* to various nouns.

> **NOT:** *Costwise*, we're already 20 percent over budget.
>
> **BUT:** We're already 20 percent over budget on costs.

Would—should. See *Should—would.*

Would have. Note that the second word in this verb phrase is *have*. (The spelling *would of* is wrong.)

> I myself *would have* (**NOT** would of) taken a different tack.

In a clause beginning with *if*, do not use *would have* in place of *had*.

> If you *had* come early, you could have talked with Dr. Faqiryar yourself.
>
> **NOT:** If you would have come early, you could have talked with Dr. Faqiryar yourself.

See the Online Learning Centre at www.mcgrawhill.ca/college/gregg for related weblinks.

P A R T

TWO

Techniques and Formats

SECTION **TWELVE**

Office Applications

Computers greatly affect the way documents are prepared today. More people not only compose and produce the final documents themselves, but they incorporate the skills of proofreading and editing as part of their overall writing process. The guidelines in this section are presented to help you achieve a higher level of quality in the documents produced.

PROOFREADING AND EDITING

The Proofreading and Editing Process

1201 a. *Proofreading* is the process by which you compare the copy that you or someone else has written and confirm that this version faithfully reproduces the original material in the intended form. It is a *mechanical* process of looking to see where the copy deviates from the original and then making the necessary corrections.

If the original material is complex, involved, or contains figures, it is wise for two people to share the proofreading function: one (the *copyholder*) reads the text aloud and indicates the intended punctuation, paragraphing, capitalization, format, and details of style, while the other person (the *proofreader*) examines the copy closely to ensure that everything appears as it should.

b. *Editing* is the process by which you look at material that you or someone else has written and evaluate it. It is an *analytical* and *judgmental* process that questions the material based on accuracy, clarity, coherence, consistency, and effectiveness. If the material is yours, you may need to revise it several times. However, if it is someone else's writing, you may solve only those problems you are able and authorized to address.

c. Most people function simultaneously as proofreaders and editors. Editing problems of substance, grammar, style, and format are first completed at the computer and printed as draft copies. If problems have gone undetected in earlier edits, the final draft needs to be read in a challenging, questioning manner that distinguishes editing from mechanical proofreading. It may take several readings, focusing each time on different things, before the final printing and proofreading.

Proofreading and Editing at the Computer

1202 Whether you are working on someone else's material or whether you are solely responsible for all phases of the writing process, proofreading and editing are necessary skills to practise and perfect.

a. The advantage the computer brings to the production of documents is the ease by which changes in copy can be made—inserting, deleting, and rearranging. Yet in this process of "cutting and pasting," new kinds of errors, such as those listed below, are inadvertently created.

- Deleting only part of an old version

- Ignoring verb number when the subject changes from singular to plural
- Inserting new copy in the wrong place
- Reading on-screen for a length of time; resulting eyestrain makes errors more difficult to find

b. Run the text through spelling and grammar checkers; scan the text again on the screen for any obvious mistakes; and make the necessary corrections. (See ¶¶1203–1204.) Further proofreading and editing, however, will still be required.

c. It is imperative that copy be proofread from the printed page. Examine it carefully for all types of errors. After correcting the copy, review the text once more on the screen and then again on the final printout. Check to see that all the corrections have been executed in the proper location and that no new errors have been introduced.

What to Look for When Proofreading

1203 When *proofreading* a document, be especially watchful for the following types of mistakes:

a. Repeated words (or parts of words), especially at the end of one line and the beginning of the next. A spell checker may highlight some of these errors, but not all of them. So proofread carefully.

What are the chances of your your coming to see us sometime this summer?	I have been awaiting some indi-indication of a willingness to compromise.
I can help you in the event in the event you have more work than you can handle.	We are looking forward to the to the reception you are planning for the Lockwoods.

b. Substitutions and omissions, especially those that change the meaning. Be alert to find these errors. Since nothing is misspelled, no spell checker will find them.

Original Material	Erroneous Copy
The courts have ruled that the contract is now legal.	The courts have ruled that the contract is not legal.
All Keng's actions reflect his upright character.	All Keng's actions reflect his uptight character.
In my opinion, there is no reason to suspect Fred.	In my opinion, there is reason to suspect Fred.
I hereby agree to pay you $87.50 in full settlement of your claim.	I hereby agree to pay you $8750 in full settlement of your claim.
I'll gladly give you the job if you'll do it in a week and if you'll reduce your price by $200.	I'll gladly give you the job if you'll reduce your price by $200.

(Continued on page 312.)

c. Errors in copying key data.

	Original Material	Erroneous Copy
NAMES:	Katharine Ann Mar	Katherine Anne Mah
TITLES:	Ms. Margaret Peiris	Mrs. Margaret A. Peiris
INSIDE ADDRESSES:	519 Magnus Avenue	591 Magnus Avenue
	Winnipeg, MB R2W 2C4	Winnipeg, MN R2W 2C4
DATES:	October 13, 2003	October 31, 2004
PHONE NOS.:	506-555-1551	306-555-1515
AMOUNTS OF MONEY:	$83 454 000 000	$38 454 000
DECIMALS:	sales fell 5.2 percent	sales fell 52 percent
CLOCK TIME:	arrive at 4:15 p.m.	arrive at 4:51 p.m.
PERIODS OF TIME:	boil for 2 minutes	boil for 20 minutes

d. Transpositions in letters, numbers, and words.

Original Material	Erroneous Copy
I'll buy two boats this May	I'll buy tow boats this May.
a process of trial and error	a process of trail and error
Let's form a committee to review our pricing policy.	Let's from a committee to review our pricing policy.
We'll need 82 binders for the seminar beginning July 12.	We'll need 28 binders for the seminar beginning July 21.
How can we thank you all for your thoughtfulness?	How can we thank you for all your thoughtfulness?

e. Errors in spacing and inconsistencies in format (for example, indenting some paragraphs but not others, leaving too little or too much space between words or after punctuation, improperly aligning, or inappropriately placing hard returns in a line).

f. As a final step in proofreading, check the appearance of the document.

- Does each page as a whole look attractive?
- Is the style consistent in all headings? displayed extracts? lists?
- Is the vertical placement consistent throughout the document?
- Are there any widows/orphans?
- If justifying, are there too many large white spaces within a line?

What to Look for When Editing

1204 When *editing* a document at any stage in the writing process, consider the material in light of the following factors.

☞ *For an explanation of the* proofreaders' marks *used to indicate the necessary corrections in the following examples, see pages 314, 315.*

a. Use the spell checker first. Because it is not infallible, still check for errors in *spelling* (see Section 7) and particularly for words accepted by the spell checker that are not in the correct form for the word in context. Give special attention to *compound words* (see Section 8) and those with *plural and possessive endings* (see Section 6). Confirm the correctness of any *word divisions* (see Section 9).

> We had a similar break down when a high=level executive failed to inform us that the corporations attorneys had advised against it's proceeding with merger negotiations.

b. Make sure that every necessary mark of *punctuation* is correctly inserted. (See Sections 1 and 2.)

> How do you account for the fact that, whenever we are about to launch a new product the company cuts our marketing dollars?

c. Inspect the material for possible errors in *capitalization, number,* and *abbreviation style.* (See Sections 3, 4, and 5.)

> Be sure to attend the Managers' meeting on june 4th at two p. m. There will be 5 or 6 announcements of special interest.

NOTE: Be aware of auto correct features that might yield unwanted capitals or symbols.

d. Correct any errors in *grammar* and *usage.* (See Sections 10 and 11.)

> Everyone of the sales representatives has made fewer calls in the past six months then they did in the previous period.

e. Be especially alert to wording that conveys a meaning you did not intend. If you are editing someone else's writing, resolve any problems that you can and refer the rest to the author.

> When I met with you, Harry Mills, and Paula Fierro on May 8, we agreed that . . . [Ed: wasn't Paula at the 5/8 meeting?] I think that as a next move you ought to fill Paula Fierro in on what happened at our May 8 meeting.

WRONG: We take pride in offering excellent food and service every day except Sunday. (Does this mean that on Sundays the food and service are perfectly dreadful?)

RIGHT: We take pride in offering excellent food and service. We are open every day except Sunday.

WRONG: To enjoy our specially priced pretheatre menu, you must be seated by 6 p.m. Remember, the early bird gets the worm. (Does the menu offer anything more appetizing?)

RIGHT: To enjoy our specially priced pretheatre menu, you must be seated by 6 p.m. Please try to come earlier if you can.

(Continued on page 314.)

12

PROOFREADERS' MARK	DRAFT	FINAL COPY
ss⌊ Single-space	ss⌈I have heard ⌊he is leaving.	I have heard he is leaving.
ds⌊ Double-space	ds⌈When will you ⌊have a decision?	When will you have a decision?
+1ℓ#→ Insert 1 line space	**Percent of Change** +1ℓ#——→16.25	**Percent of Change** 16.25
−1ℓ#→ Delete (remove) 1 line space	Northeastern −1ℓ#→ regional sales	Northeastern regional sales
⌒ Delete space	to gether	together
# Insert space	It may be	It may not be
� Move as shown	it is not true	it is true
⌒ Transpose	believable	believable
	is it so	it is so
O Spell out	②years ago	two years ago
	16 Elm St.	16 Elm Street
∧ Insert a word	How much it?	How much is it?
⌒ OR — Delete a word	it may not be true	it may be true
∧ OR ⌄ Insert a letter, space, or punctuation mark	temperature	temperature
⌒ OR ⌄ Delete a letter and close up	commitment to buy	commitment to buy
∧ OR ⌒ Add on to a word	a real good day	a really good day
⌒ OR / Change a letter	this supersedes	this supersedes
⌒ OR — Change a word	and if you won't	but if you can't
.... Stet (don't delete	I was very glad	I was very glad
/ Lowercase a letter	Federal Government	federal government
≡ Capitalize	Janet L. greyston	Janet L. Greyston

f. Look for problems in *organization* and *writing style*. Grammar, style, and usage could still be correct yet contain unclear or repetitive wording, clumsy sentences, weak organization, or a tone that is not appropriate for the occasion. By using a grammar checker, a thesaurus, a dictionary, or a style manual, you can improve the wording and structure of the document.

g. Look at the document as a whole. Is it accomplishing its *objective?* Anticipate your readers' reactions and deal with any unforeseen difficulties before a situation arises.

NOTE: If you are editing material you yourself have written, consider all the points noted in ¶1204a–g. However, if you are editing material written by someone else, the extent of your editing will depend on your experience and your relationship with the writer. If you are on your first job, determine

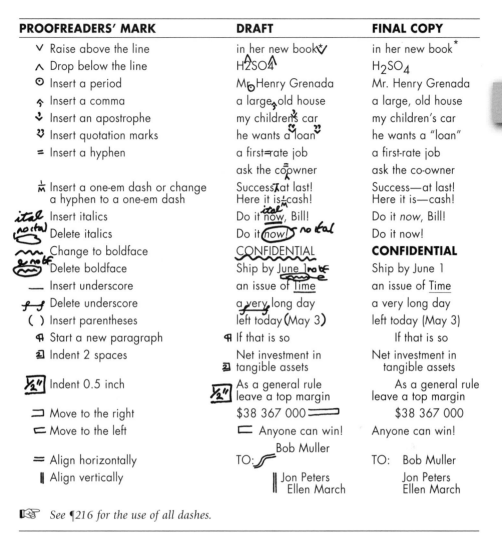

PROOFREADERS' MARK	DRAFT	FINAL COPY
∨ Raise above the line	in her new book∨	in her new book*
∧ Drop below the line	H2SO4∧	H₂SO₄
⊙ Insert a period	Mr⊙ Henry Grenada	Mr. Henry Grenada
⟨ Insert a comma	a large⟨ old house	a large, old house
⟩ Insert an apostrophe	my childrens car	my children's car
⟨⟩ Insert quotation marks	he wants a loan	he wants a "loan"
= Insert a hyphen	a first=rate job	a first-rate job
	ask the co⊙owner	ask the co-owner
⅟M Insert a one-em dash or change a hyphen to a one-em dash	Success⫪at last! Here it is⫞cash!	Success—at last! Here it is—cash!
ital Insert italics	Do it now, Bill!	Do it *now*, Bill!
no ital Delete italics	Do it now!	Do it now!
～ Change to boldface	CONFIDENTIAL	**CONFIDENTIAL**
Delete boldface	Ship by June 1	Ship by June 1
___ Insert underscore	an issue of Time	an issue of Time
Delete underscore	a very long day	a very long day
( ) Insert parentheses	left today (May 3)	left today (May 3)
¶ Start a new paragraph	¶ If that is so	If that is so
⊐ Indent 2 spaces	Net investment in ⊐ tangible assets	Net investment in tangible assets
½″ Indent 0.5 inch	As a general rule leave a top margin	As a general rule leave a top margin
⊐ Move to the right	$38 367 000	$38 367 000
⊏ Move to the left	⊏ Anyone can win!	Anyone can win!
= Align horizontally	Bob Muller TO:	TO: Bob Muller
‖ Align vertically	‖ Jon Peters Ellen March	Jon Peters Ellen March

☞ *See ¶216 for the use of all dashes.*

whether your employer has any special preferences with regard to matters of style, spelling, punctuation, etc. (What may look like an error to you could be acceptable practice that you are not familiar with.) How much your employer will appreciate your comments about the organization, writing style, and effectiveness of the material will depend on the amount of tact you use. Remember, the closer the relationship, the more tact you need to exercise.

Proofreaders' Marks

1205 Whether you are proofreading or editing, use the proofreaders' marks shown on pages 314 and 315 to indicate the corrections that need to be made. Minor variations in the way these marks are formed are unimportant as long as the marks clearly indicate what corrections have to be made.

12

DICTATING AND TRANSCRIBING

The advantage of using computers in transcribing material from recorded input cannot be understated—alterations and corrections are made easily. Both the dictator and the transcriber have roles in producing "mailable" copy. They must work co-operatively and strive constantly to perfect their skills.

The Dictating and Transcribing Process

1206 a. *Dictating* is composing and transmitting data using recording equipment. The first kind of dictation is *instructional*, providing information on how a document is to be produced—detailing the length, copies required, and enclosures. The second kind of dictation is the *delivery*.

- Speak in a conversational tone, grouping words evenly and naturally.
- Enunciate clearly, paying attention to the sounds of *p* and *b*, *m* and *n*, *f* and *v*, past tenses of verbs, and plural endings.
- Spell out proper names, technical terms, and foreign words. (Dictating capitalization, punctuation, and paragraphs is optional.)

b. *Transcribing* is placing the words of the dictator into print. Good listening skills are essential to produce good copy and to interpret the dictator's thoughts—all with minimum replays of the recording. Familiarity with the equipment and mastering the following techniques will improve these skills.

- Listen first to gain a sense of the dictation, noting any instructions.
- Listen again to recall a group of words or a phrase. Stop the recording and key the words, entering text as continuously as possible. (Voice changes and pauses are clues for punctuation and paragraphs.)
- Use the spell and grammar checkers before printing.
- Prepare draft copies, especially if the text is complicated, technical in nature, or if the dictator makes frequent changes.
- Try to correct as many errors on the screen as you possibly can, even though there is no original copy to proofread against.
- Proofread and edit all copies, both draft and final, before and after printing.
- Show your first readable transcript to the dictator for changes or approval.

RULES FOR ALPHABETIC FILING

Regardless of how a business files (manually or by computer), what system it follows (subject or geographic), or what records it saves (correspondence or cards), the goal of records management is to establish a **consistent** method of sorting and storing so that everyone can retrieve documents quickly and easily.

Filing alphabetically is based on the principles of indexing; that is, determining the name under which a document is to be filed. Indexing is breaking down a name into units, and the units are arranged in a certain sequence. After indexing is completed, the units of one document are compared to those of other documents for sorting into alphabetic order.

The basic principles of alphabetic filing by the indexing (unit-by-unit) method (see ¶¶1207–1209) and the more specific rules that follow (see ¶¶1210–1223) are those standardized by the Association of Records Managers and Administrators (ARMA). While the specific needs of your office may require some modifications to these rules, it is important that those who have access to your files know what the changes are. Consistency should always be maintained.

IMPORTANT NOTE: The following charts show names in two ways: the first column *(Name)* gives the full name in *standard format* (as it appears in the inside address of a letter); the remaining columns *(Unit 1, Unit 2,* etc.) show the name in an *indexed format* (as it is arranged unit by unit in alphabetic sequence). Note that the standard format presents the names in capital and small letters with punctuation as necessary. The indexed format presents names in all-capital letters ready for alphabetizing, ignoring the size of letters, punctuation, and in some cases, ignoring a space or hyphen between parts of a name.

If you want to use a computer (1) to print names in alphabetic order and (2) to insert names in inside addresses as well as text, you may have to create two name fields—one using standard format, the other using indexed format.

☞ *For guidelines on how to create a computerized file name, see ¶1382.*

Basic Principles
1207 ALPHABETIZING UNIT BY UNIT

a. Alphabetize names by comparing the first units letter by letter.

Name	Unit 1	Unit 2	Unit 3
Eagleton	EAGLETON		
Eaton	EATON		
Eberhardt	EBERHARDT		
Eberhart	EBERHART		
Eby Video	EBY	VIDEO	
ECO Lab Sales	ECO	LAB	SALES
Econo Holidays	ECONO	HOLIDAYS	

b. Consider second units only when the first units are identical.

Name	Unit 1	Unit 2
Foley Enterprises	FOLEY	ENTERPRISES
Foley Industries	FOLEY	INDUSTRIES

(Continued on page 318.)

12

c. Consider additional units only when the first two units are identical.

Name	Unit 1	Unit 2	Unit 3	Unit 4
Fox Hill Company	FOX	HILL	COMPANY	
Fox Hill Farm	FOX	HILL	FARM	
Fox Hill Farm Supplies	FOX	HILL	FARM	SUPPLIES

NOTE: If two names are identical, they may be distinguished on the basis of geographical location. (See ¶1220.)

1208 NOTHING COMES BEFORE SOMETHING

A single letter comes before a name that begins with the same letter. For names consisting of initial identical filing units, each part of the name is considered a separate unit. Read from left to right until a point of comparison is reached.

Name	Unit 1	Unit 2	Unit 3	Unit 4
O	O			
Oasis	OASIS			
Oberon	OBERON			
Operations	OPERATIONS			
Operations Management Consultants	OPERATIONS	MANAGEMENT	CONSULTANTS	
Operations Technologies	OPERATIONS	TECHNOLOGIES		
Opus Creek	OPUS	CREEK		
Opus Creek Home Furnishings	OPUS	CREEK	HOME	FURNISHINGS
Opus Creek Homes	OPUS	CREEK	HOMES	

1209 DECIDING WHICH NAME TO USE

ARMA advocates filing "under the most commonly used name or title." This helpful principle provides the basis for choosing which name you should use for a person or an organization when alternatives exist. Select the form most likely to be used; then provide cross-references for the alternatives. In that way anyone who is searching for material under an alternative name will be referred to the primary name being used for filing purposes. (See ¶¶1213c, 1215c, 1216a, note, and 1217a, note for specific applications of this principle.)

Personal Names

1210 RULE 1: NAMES OF PERSONS

a. Treat each part of the name of a person as a separate unit, and consider the units in this order: last name, first name or initial, and any subsequent names or initials. Ignore any punctuation following or within an abbreviation.

Name	Unit 1	Unit 2	Unit 3	Unit 4
Jacobs	JACOBS			
L. Jacobs	JACOBS	L		
L. Mitchell Jacobs	JACOBS	L	MITCHELL	
Stephen Jacobson	JACOBSON	STEPHEN		
Steven O'K Jacobson	JACOBSON	STEVEN	OK	
B. T. Jacoby	JACOBY	B	T	
Bruce Jacoby	JACOBY	BRUCE		
C. Bruce Hay Jacoby	JACOBY	C	BRUCE	HAY

b. When you cannot distinguish the last name from the first name, consider each part of the name in the order in which it is written. Whenever you can make the distinction, consider the last name first.

Name	Unit 1	Unit 2	Unit 3
Kwong Kow Ng	KWONG	KOW	NG
Ng Kwong Cheung	NG	KWONG	CHEUNG
Philip K. Ng	NG	PHILIP	K

c. In a name like *Maria López y Quintana,* the last name consists of three separate words. For purposes of alphabetizing, treat these separate words as a single unit (for example, LOPEZYQUINTANA).

1211 RULE 2: PERSONAL NAMES WITH PREFIXES

Consider a prefix as part of the name, not as a separate unit. Ignore variations in spacing, capitalization, and punctuation (including the apostrophe). Treat all prefixes (for example, *d', D', Da, de, De, Del, De la, Des, Di, Du, El, Fitz, L', La, Las, Le, Les, Lo, Los, M', Mac, Mc, Saint, San, Santa, Santo, St., Ste., Ten, Ter, Van, Van de, Van der, Von,* and *Von Der*) exactly as they are spelled.

Name	Unit 1	Unit 2	Unit 3
A. Simon De laval	DELAVAL	A	SIMON
Anna C. de Laval	DELAVAL	ANNA	C
Michael B. DeLaval	DELAVAL	MICHAEL	B
Victor P. deLaval	DELAVAL	VICTOR	P
LaVerne P. De Lay	DELAY	LAVERNE	P
Angela G. Delaye	DELAYE	ANGELA	G
Irene J. MacKay	MACKAY	IRENE	J
Roy F. Mackay	MACKAY	ROY	F
Walter G. Mac Kay	MACKAY	WALTER	G
Agnes U. M'Cauley	MCAULEY	AGNES	U
Patrick J. McKay	MCKAY	PATRICK	J
Andrew W. O'Hare	OHARE	ANDREW	W
Kyle N. Saint Clair	SAINTCLAIR	KYLE	N
Peter St. Clair	STCLAIR	PETER	
O. M. Ste. Marie	STEMARIE	O	M
D. E. van de Hoven	VANDEHOVEN	D	E
T. Van Den Hoven	VANDENHOVEN	T	

(Continued on page 320.)

NOTE: If you are using a computer, insert a hard space been the parts of a name such as De Lay, Mac Kay, or Ste. Marie. The last name will be sorted as if it were keyed without spaces, but it will appear *with spaces* in the alphabetized list of names.

1212 RULE 3: HYPHENATED PERSONAL NAMES

Treat the hyphenated elements of a name as a single unit. Ignore the hyphen.

Name	Unit 1	Unit 2	Unit 3
S. T. Kelly-O'Brien	KELLYOBRIEN	S	T
Victor Olson-Jones	OLSONJONES	VICTOR	
Jean V. Vigneau	VIGNEAU	JEAN	V
Jean-Marie Vigneau	VIGNEAU	JEANMARIE	

1213 RULE 4: ABBREVIATED PERSONAL NAMES, NICKNAMES, AND PSEUDONYMS

a. Consider any abbreviated part of a name such as *Chas.* for *Charles* as if it were written in full. Initials standing for a first or middle name are not considered abbreviations. Names such as *Tony* and *Peggy* are considered only if they are the true name or if the true name is unknown.

Name	Unit 1	Unit 2	Unit 3
Chas. E. Kassily	KASSILY	CHARLES	E
Tony Leaden	LEADEN	TONY	
Peggy Sue Marker	MARKER	PEGGY	SUE
B. J. Purcell	PURCELL	B	J

b. If a person is known by a nickname alone (without a surname) or by a pseudonym, consider each word in the nickname or pseudonym as a separate unit. If the name begins with *The,* treat *The* as the last unit.

Name	Unit 1	Unit 2	Unit 3
Big Al	BIG	AL	
The Cookie Lady	COOKIE	LADY	THE
Handy Joe Bob	HANDY	JOE	BOB
Harry the Horse	HARRY	THE	HORSE
Heavy D	HEAVY	D	

c. To file material under a person's formal name or under a nickname, pseudonym, or some abbreviated form, choose the form that best reflects how you and others are most likely to look up the name. You should also enter the person's alternative names in the appropriate alphabetic sequence and make cross-references to the primary name you have selected. (See also ¶1209.)

1214 RULE 5: PERSONAL NAMES WITH TITLES AND SUFFIXES

    a. A title (such as *Dr., Major, Mayor, Miss, Mr., Mrs.,* or *Ms.*) may be used as the *last* filing unit in order to distinguish two or more names that are otherwise identical. Treat any abbreviated titles as written.

Name	Unit 1	Unit 2	Unit 3	Unit 4
Dr. Leslie G. Mabry	MABRY	LESLIE	G	DR
Miss Leslie G. Mabry	MABRY	LESLIE	G	MISS
Mr. Leslie G. Mabry	MABRY	LESLIE	G	MR
Mrs. Leslie G. Mabry	MABRY	LESLIE	G	MRS
Ms. Leslie G. Mabry	MABRY	LESLIE	G	MS
Major Felix Novotny	NOVOTNY	FELIX	MAJOR	
Mayor Felix Novotny	NOVOTNY	FELIX	MAYOR	

    b. When a title is used with only one part of a person's name, treat it as the *first* unit. (See ¶1209.)

Name	Unit 1	Unit 2
Dr. Ruth	DR	RUTH
Grandma Moses	GRANDMA	MOSES
King Abdullah	KING	ABDULLAH
Miss Manners	MISS	MANNERS
Mother Teresa	MOTHER	TERESA
Prince Andrew	PRINCE	ANDREW
Saint Elizabeth	SAINT*	ELIZABETH

*Note that *Saint* as a title is considered a separate unit, whereas *Saint* as a prefix in a personal name is considered only part of a unit. (See ¶1211 for examples of *Saint* as a prefix.)

    c. Ordinarily, alphabetize a married woman's name on the basis of her own first name. However, consider the title *Mrs.* (as abbreviated) if a woman uses her husband's name and you do not know her first name.

Name	Unit 1	Unit 2	Unit 3	Unit 4
Mrs. June Y. Nearing	NEARING	JUNE	Y	
Mr. Peter J. Nearing	NEARING	PETER	J	
Mr. Harry L. Norton	NORTON	HARRY	L	MR
Mrs. Harry L. Norton	NORTON	HARRY	L	MRS

    d. Consider a seniority term (such as *Jr., Sr., 2nd, 3rd, II,* or *III*), a professional or academic degree (such as *CMA, M.D.,* or *Ph.D.*), or any other designation following a person's name in order to distinguish names that are otherwise identical. Numeric designations precede alphabetic designations. Moreover, Arabic numerals precede Roman numerals, and each set of numbers is sequenced in numeric order. When dealing with ordinal numbers such as *3rd* or *4th*, ignore the endings.

(Continued on page 322.)

Name	Unit 1	Unit 2	Unit 3	Unit 4
James R. Foster 2nd	FOSTER	JAMES	R	2
James R. Foster 3rd	FOSTER	JAMES	R	3
James R. Foster III	FOSTER	JAMES	R	III
James R. Foster IV	FOSTER	JAMES	R	IV
James R. Foster, D.D.	FOSTER	JAMES	R	DD
James R. Foster, M.D.	FOSTER	JAMES	R	MD
James R. Foster, Mr.	FOSTER	JAMES	R	MR
James R. Foster, Ph.D.	FOSTER	JAMES	R	PHD
James R. Foster, Sr.	FOSTER	JAMES	R	SR

NOTE: When inputting names on a computer, Arabic numerals will be sequenced in numeric order and will precede all names with a comparable unit composed of letters of the alphabet.

There is a problem, however, with Roman numerals since they are letters of the alphabet. A computer sequencing the names in the above chart would insert D.D. before the name ending with III. You will need to override the software and manually move the name with D.D. to the correct position after IV.

Organizational Names
1215 RULE 6: NAMES OF ORGANIZATIONS

a. Treat each word in the name of an organization as a separate unit, and consider the units in the same order as they are written on the company letterhead or some other authoritative document.

Name	Unit 1	Unit 2	Unit 3
Canadian Data Bank	CANADIAN	DATA	BANK
Canadian Data Express	CANADIAN	DATA	EXPRESS
I Deal Cards	I	DEAL	CARDS
Ideal Printers	IDEAL	PRINTERS	

b. When alphabetizing, ignore all punctuation—for example, periods, commas, hyphens, apostrophes, and diagonals. When words are joined by a hyphen or a diagonal, treat the phrase as a single unit.

Name	Unit 1	Unit 2	Unit 3
Baskins' Artworks	BASKINS	ARTWORKS	
Baskin's Basket Shop	BASKINS	BASKET	SHOP
Baskin-Shaw Films	BASKINSHAW	FILMS	
Baskin/Shaw Foods	BASKINSHAW	FOODS	
Curtis Imports	CURTIS	IMPORTS	
Curtis's China Gallery	CURTISS	CHINA	GALLERY
Curtiss Couriers	CURTISS	COURIERS	
Oleander's Displays!	OLEANDERS	DISPLAYS	
O'Leary's Snap Shop	OLEARYS	SNAP	SHOP
What's New?	WHATS	NEW	

c. Treat prepositions (such as *of* and *in*), conjunctions (such as *and* and *or*), and articles (*the, a,* and *an*) as separate units. When *the, a,* or *an* is the first word in a name, treat it as the last unit.

Name	Unit 1	Unit 2	Unit 3	Unit 4
In-Plant Catering	INPLANT	CATERING		
Over the Rainbow Gifts	OVER	THE	RAINBOW	GIFTS
The Pen and Pencil	PEN	AND	PENCIL	THE
Photos in a Flash	PHOTOS	IN	A	FLASH
A Touch of Glass	TOUCH	OF	GLASS	A

d. When a compound expression is written as one word or hyphenated, treat it as a single unit. If the compound expression is written with spaces, treat each element as a separate unit.

Name	Unit 1	Unit 2	Unit 3
Aero Space Systems	AERO	SPACE	SYSTEMS
Aerospace Research	AEROSPACE	RESEARCH	
Aero-Space Unlimited	AEROSPACE	UNLIMITED	
South East Condos	SOUTH	EAST	CONDOS
Southeast Chemicals	SOUTHEAST	CHEMICALS	
South-East Dental Lab	SOUTHEAST	DENTAL	LAB

e. Although organizational names are usually considered in the same order in which they are written, there are exceptions to this rule. (See ¶1209.) For instance, if the name is *Hotel Plaza, Hotel* should be the first unit; but if you are more likely to look in the *P* section of the files, choose *Plaza* as the first unit and *Hotel* as the second.

CAUTION: When introducing exceptions to the basic rule for organizational names, be sure that these exceptions are supported by cross-references.

1216 RULE 7: PERSONAL NAMES WITHIN ORGANIZATIONAL NAMES

a. When an organizational name includes a person's name, consider the parts of the personal name in the order in which they are written. Ignore any punctuation.

Name	Unit 1	Unit 2	Unit 3	Unit 4
Frank Balcom Construction Company	FRANK	BALCOM	CONSTRUCTION	COMPANY
Frank Balcom, Jr., Paving	FRANK	BALCOM	JR	PAVING
G. Ngan Optical Supplies	G	NGAN	OPTICAL	SUPPLIES
G. P. Ngan Autos	G	P	NGAN	AUTOS
Gai Ngan Interiors	GAI	NGAN	INTERIORS	
Gai P. Ngan Homes	GAI	P	NGAN	HOMES

NOTE: A more traditional rule that is still widely followed requires that a person's name within an organizational name be considered in the same

(Continued on page 324.)

way as if the person's name stood alone—namely, last name first. (See ¶1210.) On the other hand, the ARMA standard guidelines for personal names within organizational names require placing first names first. However, exceptions to the rule are inevitable. Consider the way in which the name is most likely to be used and then supply cross-references between the alternative names and the primary name that has been selected. (See also ¶1209.)

b. If a prefix is used in a personal name that is part of an organizational name, do not treat the prefix as a separate unit. (See ¶1211.)

A. de La Cruz Securities Company	A	DELACRUZ	SECURITIES	COMPANY
A. D'Elia Boat Sales	A	DELIA	BOAT	SALES
Peter Saint Clair Boatels	PETER	SAINTCLAIR	BOATELS	
Peter St. Clair Insurance Agency	PETER	STCLAIR	INSURANCE	AGENCY
R. Van Alstine Art Galleries	R	VANALSTINE	ART	GALLERIES

c. If a hyphenated personal name is part of an organizational name, treat the hyphenated elements as a single unit. (See ¶1212.)

Name	Unit 1	Unit 2	Unit 3	Unit 4
Mary Tom Packaging Consultants	MARY	TOM	PACKAGING	CONSULTANTS
Mary Tom-Katz Production Company	MARY	TOMKATZ	PRODUCTION	COMPANY

d. Consider a title in an organization's name as a separate unit in the order in which it occurs. Treat abbreviated titles as they are written and ignore punctuation.

Capt. Jack Seafood	CAPT	JACK	SEAFOOD	
Captain Ahab Tours	CAPTAIN	AHAB	TOURS	
Dr. Popper Vision Services	DR	POPPER	VISION	SERVICES
Ma Blake Food Shops	MA	BLAKE	FOOD	SHOPS
Miss Celeste Sportswear	MISS	CELESTE	SPORTSWEAR	
Mother Goose Nurseries	MOTHER	GOOSE	NURSERIES	
Mr. George Limousine Service	MR	GEORGE	LIMOUSINE	SERVICE
Mrs. Ellis Bakeries	MRS	ELLIS	BAKERIES	
Saint Margaret Thrift Shop	SAINT*	MARGARET	THRIFT	SHOP

*When *Saint* is used as a title rather than as a prefix in a personal name, it is considered a separate unit. (See ¶1214b.)

1217 RULE 8: ABBREVIATIONS, ACRONYMS, SYMBOLS, AND LETTERS IN ORGANIZATIONAL NAMES

a. Treat an abbreviation as a single unit. Consider it exactly as it is written, and ignore any punctuation.

B. C. Data Sources	B	C	DATA	SOURCES
B C Datalink	B	C	DATALINK	
B.C. Data Files	BC	DATA	FILES	
BC Data Tracers	BC	DATA	TRACERS	
CBC	CBC			
CNIB	CNIB			
Union Grain Ltd.	UNION	GRAIN	LTD	
Unisource Canada Inc.	UNISOURCE	CANADA	INC	
Urban Business Corp.	URBAN	BUSINESS	CORP	
Ursis Data Systems Co.	URSIS	DATA	SYSTEMS	CO

NOTE: When organizations are better known by their abbreviated names *(CBC, CNIB, IBM)* or acronyms *(ACTRA, CARES, CUPE)* than by their formal names, use these short forms for filing purposes and provide cross-references as necessary. (See also ¶¶520, 522.)

b. Treat acronyms and the call letters of radio and TV stations as single units.

Name	Unit 1	Unit 2	Unit 3	Unit 4
ACTRA	ACTRA			
CARES	CARES			
CFRD Radio Station	CFRD	RADIO	STATION	
CUPE	CUPE			

c. When the symbol & occurs in a name, consider it as if it were spelled out (that is, as *and*). If the symbol is freestanding (that is, with space on either side), treat it as a separate filing unit.

A & L Fabrics	A	AND	L	FABRICS
A&B Publications	AANDB	PUBLICATIONS		
Allen & Korn	ALLEN	AND	KORN	
AT&L Electrical Ltd.	ATANDL	ELECTRICAL	LTD	

d. Treat single letters as separate units. If two or more letters in a sequence are written solid or are connected by a hyphen or a diagonal, treat the sequence as a single unit.

A D S Graphics	A	D	S	GRAPHICS
AAA	AAA			
ADS Reports	ADS	REPORTS		
A/V Resources	AV	RESOURCES		
A-Z Rental Corp.	AZ	RENTAL	CORP	
Triple A Realty Trust	TRIPLE	A	REALTY	TRUST
W Z Leasing Co.	W	Z	LEASING	CO
W. Z. Yee (person)	YEE	W	Z	

1218 RULE 9: GEOGRAPHIC NAMES WITHIN ORGANIZATIONAL NAMES

a. Treat each part of a geographic name as a separate unit. However, treat hyphenated parts of a geographic name as a single unit.

Banff-Jasper Tours	BANFFJASPER	TOURS	
Golf PEI	GOLF	PEI	
Lake of the Woods Camping Store*	LAKE	OF	THE	WOODS
Niagara-on-the-Lake Tourist Centre	NIAGARAONTHELAKE	TOURIST	CENTRE
Western Canada Importing	WESTERN	CANADA	IMPORTING
Western Ontario Produce	WESTERN	ONTARIO	PRODUCE

*The words *Camping* and *Store* represent the fifth and sixth filing units in this name.

b. When a geographic name begins with a prefix followed by a space or hyphen, treat the prefix and the following word as a single unit. (See ¶1211 for a list of prefixes.)

Name	Unit 1	Unit 2	Unit 3
La Baie Cafe	LABAIE	CAFE	
Le Gardeur Hardware	LEGARDEUR	HARDWARE	
Los Angeles Film Distributors	LOSANGELES	FILM	DISTRIBUTORS
Saint John Pharmacy	SAINTJOHN	PHARMACY	
Ste-Foy Inn	STEFOY	INN	
St. John's Lumber Mart	STJOHNS	LUMBER	MART

NOTE: While a name like *St. Albert* is considered a single unit, *Sault Ste. Marie* or *Fort St. John* should be treated as three filing units (since the prefix *Ste.* or *St.* does not come at the beginning of the name).

1219 RULE 10: NUMBERS IN ORGANIZATIONAL NAMES

a. Arabic numerals *(1, 3, 5)* and Roman numerals *(IV, XIX)* are considered separate units. Treat ordinal numbers such as *1st*, *3rd*, and *5th* as if they were written *1*, *3*, and *5*.

b. The order of sequencing names with Arabic and Roman numbers and with letters of the alphabet is as follows:

1. Arabic numbers arranged in numeric order.
2. Roman numerals arranged in numeric order.
3. Letters arranged in alphabetical order.

NOTE: Computer programs will consider Arabic numerals from the left. Given the Arabic units in the following chart, a computer will place 1218 before 21 and 210. To avoid this outcome, add zeros to the left of 21 and 210 to make them the same length as 1218: 0021, 0210, 1218. The computer will then sequence these units in the correct order.

☞ *See ¶1214d, note, for an explanation in sequencing Roman numerals.*

21st Century Travel	21	CENTURY	TRAVEL
210th St. Assn.	210	St	ASSN
1218 Corp.	1218	CORP	
III Brothers Outlets	III	BROTHERS	OUTLETS
VII Hills Lodge	VII	HILLS	LODGE
CUPE Local 3501	CUPE	LOCAL	3501
CUPE Local 4255	CUPE	LOCAL	4255
Sixth Street Fashions	SIXTH	STREET	FASHIONS

c. Units containing numbers expressed in words are sequenced in alphabetic order. When a number is written with a hyphen *(Thirty-Six)*, ignore the hyphen and treat the number as a single unit *(THIRTYSIX)*.

Name	Unit 1	Unit 2	Unit 3	Unit 4
Twelve Sixteen Shoppe	TWELVE	SIXTEEN	SHOPPE	
Twentieth Century Press	TWENTIETH	CENTURY	PRESS	
Twenty-Eight Benbow Street Studios	TWENTYEIGHT	BENBOW	STREET	STUDIOS
The Warren 200 Colony	WARREN	200	COLONY	THE
Warren Sixty-Fourth Street Salon	WARREN	SIXTYFOURTH	STREET	SALON

d. When a phrase consists of a number (in figures or words) linked by a hyphen or a diagonal to a letter or word (for example, *1-A, A-1, 1-Hour, 4/Way, One-Stop*), ignore the punctuation and treat the phrase as a single unit.

e. When the phrase consists of a figure linked to another figure by means of a hyphen or a diagonal (for example, *80-20* or *50/50*), consider only the number that precedes the hyphen or diagonal.

NOTE: Most computer programs will consider the complete number and any punctuation.

f. When a phrase consists of a figure plus a letter or word (for example, *3M*) without any intervening space or punctuation, treat it as a single unit.

1-A Physical Trainers	1A	PHYSICAL	TRAINERS
3 Pro Corp.	3	PRO	CORP
3M	3M		
4X Investment Group	4X	INVESTMENT	GROUP
5-10 Household Wares	5	HOUSEHOLD	WARES
5 Star Video Arcade	5	STAR	VIDEO	ARCADE
5-Corners Pasta Dishes	5CORNERS	PASTA	DISHES
7-Eleven Food Store	7ELEVEN	FOOD	STORE
20/20 Eye Care	20	EYE	CARE
The 30-45 Singles Club	30	SINGLES	CLUB	THE
A-1 Autos Inc.	A1	AUTOS	INC
Adam's 10-Minute Pizza	ADAMS	10MINUTE	PIZZA

(Continued on page 328.)

12

g. When a symbol appears with a number, treat the two elements as a single unit only if there is no space between the symbol and the number. Consider the symbol as if it were spelled out; for example, & *(and)*, ¢ *(cent or cents)*, $ *(dollar or dollars)*, # *(number)*, % *(percent)*, and + *(plus)*. When words or numbers are placed in parentheses, for example *(Canada), (2000)*, ignore the parentheses and treat the items enclosed as separate units.

NOTE: Most computer programs will consider these symbols on the basis of where they occur in the sequence of character sets. If you convert the symbol to a spelled-out form, it will be sequenced in the correct alphabetic order.

Name	Unit 1	Unit 2	Unit 3	Unit 4
The $50 Dress Shop	50DOLLAR*	DRESS	SHOP	THE
50% Off Outlet	50PERCENT	OFF	OUTLET	
The 50+ Centre	50PLUS	CENTRE	THE	
The #1 Pizza Parlour	NUMBER1	PIZZA	PARLOUR	THE
The Original 5&10	ORIGINAL	5AND10	THE	
Plaza 5 & 10	PLAZA	5	AND	10
T&T (Canada) Inc.	TANDT	CANADA	INC	
Three-Hour Cleaners (1999) Ltd.	THREEHOUR	CLEANERS	1999	LTD

*When a $ sign precedes a number, consider the number and then the word DOLLAR (or DOLLARS) in that order.

1220 RULE 11: ALPHABETIZING BY ADDRESSES

When two organizational names are otherwise identical, alphabetize them according to address.

a. First alphabetize by city.

b. When filing units for city names are the same, consider the province. (For example, *St. Mary's, Newfoundland*, comes before *St. Marys, Ontario*.)

c. If both the city and the province are identical, alphabetize by street name.

Name	Unit 1	Unit 2	Unit 3	Unit 4
McDonald's Saint John New Brunswick	MCDONALDS	SAINTJOHN	NEW	BRUNSWICK
McDonald's St. Marys, Ontario	MCDONALDS	STMARYS	ONTARIO	
McDonald's Avenue Road Toronto, Ontario	MCDONALDS	TORONTO	AVENUE	ROAD
McDonald's 1414 Church St. Toronto, Ontario	MCDONALDS	TORONTO	CHURCH	STREET

d. If the street name is a number, treat it exactly as written. Numbered street names expressed *in figures* precede street names (numbered or otherwise) expressed *in words*. Numbered street names *in figures* are sequenced in numeric order. Numbered street names *in words* are sequenced (along with other street names in words) in alphabetic order.

e. If the street names are also the same, alphabetize by direction if it is part of the address (for example, *north, south, northeast, southwest*).

Name	Unit 1	Unit 2	Unit 3	Unit 4	Unit 5
McDonald's 2323 - 12 Ave. Toronto, Ontario	MCDONALDS	TORONTO	12	AVENUE	
McDonald's 3434 - 65 St. Toronto, Ontario	MCDONALDS	TORONTO	65	STREET	
McDonald's 4545 Fourth St. Toronto, Ontario	MCDONALDS	TORONTO	FOURTH	STREET	
McDonald's 5656 Queen St. E. Toronto, Ontario	MCDONALDS	TORONTO	QUEEN	STREET	EAST
McDonald's 6767 Queen St. W. Toronto, Ontario	MCDONALDS	TORONTO	QUEEN	STREET	WEST

f. If all the foregoing units are identical, consider the house or building numbers and sequence them in numeric order.

Name	Unit 1	Unit 2	Unit 3	Unit 4	Unit 5
McDonald's 170 Spadina Ave. Toronto, Ontario	MCDONALDS	TORONTO	SPADINA	AVENUE	170
McDonald's 2782 Spadina Ave. Toronto, Ontario	MCDONALDS	TORONTO	SPADINA	AVENUE	2782

Governmental Names
1221 RULE 12: FEDERAL GOVERNMENT NAMES

a. The first three filing units for any organization that is part of the federal government are *CANADA GOVERNMENT OF*.

b. The fourth filing unit for most departments is the name of its function— *Justice, Health, Industry*, etc. While the word *Canada* is added when referring to these departments (for instance, *Health Canada*), there is obviously no need to repeat *Canada* as it is the first filing unit. A few departments, however, use the words *Department of* in their titles. In such cases, transpose

(Continued on page 330.)

12

Department of and place at the end. (For example, treat *Department of National Defence* as four separate units: NATIONAL DEFENCE DEPARTMENT OF.)

c. Next consider the name of the office or bureau within the department. Transpose opening phrases such as *Office of* and *Bureau of* to the end. (For example, treat *Bureau of Pensions Advocates* as four separate units: PENSIONS ADVOCATES BUREAU OF.)

Name	Unit 4*	Unit 5	Unit 6	Unit 7
Canada Customs and Revenue Agency	CUSTOMS	AND	REVENUE	AGENCY
Industry Canada Competition Bureau	INDUSTRY	COMPETITION	BUREAU	
National Film Board	NATIONAL	FILM	BOARD	
Statistics Canada Consumer Services	STATISTICS	CONSUMER	SERVICES	

*The first three units are *Canada Government of.*

1222 RULE 13: PROVINCIAL AND LOCAL GOVERNMENT NAMES

a. For any organization (except an educational institution) that is part of a province, county, city, or town government, first consider the distinctive place name (for example, *New Brunswick* or *Fredericton*).

b. Then consider the name of the department, bureau, or other subdivision, transposing elements (if necessary) as was done with federal departments and bureaus in ¶1221.

Name	Unit 1	Unit 2	Unit 3	Unit 4	Unit 5
Alberta Department of Education	ALBERTA	EDUCATION	DEPARTMENT	OF	
Manitoba Public Health Department	MANITOBA	PUBLIC	HEALTH	DEPARTMENT	
County of Parkland School District	PARKLAND	COUNTY	OF	SCHOOL	DISTRICT
Police Service, City of Victoria	VICTORIA	CITY	OF	POLICE	SERVICE

1223 RULE 14: FOREIGN GOVERNMENT NAMES

a. First consider the distinctive name of the country. (For example, select the distinctive name *Egypt* from the formal name *Arab Republic of Egypt*.)

b. Next, supply the appropriate term of classification—for example, *Republic, Commonwealth, Kingdom, State*.

c. Finally, consider the name of the department, bureau, or other subdivision.

Name	Unit 1	Unit 2
Commonwealth of Australia	AUSTRALIA	COMMONWEALTH
Republic of Austria	AUSTRIA	REPUBLIC
Kingdom of Belgium	BELGIUM	KINGDOM
State of Israel	ISRAEL	STATE

See the Online Learning Centre at www.mcgrawhill.ca/college/gregg for related weblinks.

SECTION **THIRTEEN**

Letters and Memos

13

ENVELOPES (¶¶1388–1393)

MEMOS (¶¶1394–1395)

SOCIAL-BUSINESS CORRESPONDENCE (¶¶1396–1397)

LABELS (¶1398)

Section 13 provides guidelines for formatting letters and memos. These guidelines are not intended as inflexible rules. They can—and should—be modified to fit specific occasions as good sense and good taste require.

Word processing programs typically provide templates that may simplify your task of formatting documents. If the existing templates do not satisfy your needs, you can modify them to some extent or you can create your own. In the process you can include macros in the templates so as to automate repetitive tasks, such as saving and backing up files. You can also use autotext to store repetitive copy—for example, the name of a person or organization to whom you frequently write, as well as phrases, sentences, paragraphs, or the closing lines you use in letters.

Since most computer users in Canada prefer to use the default (preset) imperial measurements that are found in software programs, all formatting information in Sections 13 to 17 is presented in inches.

The following is a letter template provided by Microsoft Word for Windows, using default specifications of 10 point Times New Roman, 1.25-inch side margins, and 1-inch top and bottom margins.

[Click here and type return address]

company name here

[Date]

[Click here and type recipient's address]

Dear [Click here and type recipient's name]:

Type your letter here. For more details on customizing this letter template, double-click ⊠. To return to this letter, use the Window menu.

Sincerely,

[Click here and type your name]
[Click here and type job title]

[Type Slogan here] --

LETTERS
Parts of Letters

1301 A business letter has four parts with a variety of features:

	Standard	Optional
Heading:	Letterhead or return address (¶¶1311–1313)	Personal or confidential notation (¶1315)
	Date line (¶1314)	Reference notations (¶1316)
Opening:	Inside address (¶¶1317–1343)	Attention line (¶¶1344–1345)
	Salutation (¶¶1346–1351)	
Body:	Message (¶¶1354–1357)	Subject line (¶¶1352–1353)
Closing:	Complimentary closing (¶¶1358–1360)	Company signature (¶1361)
	Writer's name and title (¶¶1362–1369)	Enclosure notation (¶¶1373–1374)
	Reference initials (¶¶1370–1372)	Delivery notation (¶1375)
		Copy notation (¶¶1376–1380)
		Postscript (¶1381)
		File name notation (¶1382)

☞ *Each of these parts is illustrated in the model letters on pages 336–340.*

1302 A business letter is usually arranged in one of the following styles:

   a. Full-Block (Block) Style. All lines typically begin at the left margin. Nothing is indented except for displayed quotations, tables, and similar material. This is the style most commonly used. (See page 336.)

   b. Modified-Block (Semi-Block) Style—Standard Format. The date line, the complimentary closing, and the writer's identification all begin at centre. All other lines begin at the left margin. (See page 338.)

   c. Modified-Block (Semi-Block) Style—With Paragraph Indentions. This style is exactly the same as the standard format described in ¶1302b except for one additional feature; the first line of each paragraph is indented 0.25 to 0.5 inches (or more in special circumstances). This style is used most commonly in formal and in some legal correspondence. (See page 339.)

   d. Simplified Style. As in the block style, all lines begin at the left margin. However, the simplified style has these additional features: the salutation is replaced by an all-capital subject line, the complimentary closing is omitted, the writer's name and title is keyed in all-capital letters on one line, and open punctuation (see ¶1309b) is always used. (See page 340 for an illustration.)

Stationery Sizes

1303 Standard size stationery, $8\frac{1}{2}$" × 11", is the most commonly used since computer default settings and printers facilitate this size more easily. For specific or social occasions, various other sizes may be preferred.

A **Compudata Systems Inc.**

34 Algonquin Avenue
Toronto, Ontario M6R 1K7
Telephone: 416-555-4605
Fax: 416-555-4602
Web site: www.compudatasystems.com

2 inches from top of page **OR** ↓3

B December 2, 2004 ↓4–6 **HEADING**

C Ms. Susan W. Morales
2839 Carlyle Drive
London, ON N6V 4N8 ↓2 **OPENING**

D Dear Ms. Morales: ↓2

E We were pleased to receive your letter of application for a sales position with Compudata Systems. ↓2

At the moment we do not have an opening in the Lake Erie area, but we do need a field representative who is based in North Bay and can cover the northern part of the province. If you would like to be considered for this position, please complete the enclosed application and return it to me. ↓2 **BODY**

As it happens, I will be attending a convention in London next month. I would be delighted to meet with you while I'm in town and describe the job that is available. ↓2

When you return your completed application, please let me know whether you would be free to meet me at 4 p.m. on Wednesday or Thursday of the first week of January. I look forward to hearing from you. ↓2

F Sincerely yours, ↓2

G COMPUDATA SYSTEMS INC. ↓4 to 6

Kenneth R. Willmott

H Kenneth R. Willmott
National Sales Manager ↓2 **CLOSING**

I KRW/bjn
J Enclosure
K By Federal Express
L cc: Ms. A Rossi

M h:\gregg\illustration\willmotk.sp3

A Letterhead. The company's name and address, along with other information (such as a telephone number and a fax number). (See ¶¶1311–1312.)

B Date Line. The date (month, day, and year) on which the letter is keyed, starts at the margin on the third line below the letterhead or 2 inches from the top of the page, whichever is lower. (See ¶1314.)

C Inside Address (Letter Address). The name and address of the person to whom you are writing. (See ¶¶1317–1343.)

D Salutation. An opening greeting like *Dear Ms. Morales.* Do not use *Dear Susan Morales* or *Dear Ms. Susan Morales.* (See ¶¶1346–1351.)

E Message. The text of the letter; all paragraphs are keyed single-spaced with no indentions; leave 1 blank line between paragraphs. (See ¶¶1354–1357.)

F Complimentary Closing. A parting phrase like *Sincerely* or *Sincerely yours.* (See ¶¶1358–1360.)

G Company Signature. An indication that the writer is acting on behalf of the company. (See ¶1361.)

H Writer's Name and Title. The writer's identification. (See ¶¶1362–1369.)

I Reference Initials. The initials of the typist (see ¶1370a) and sometimes those of the writer as well (see ¶1370c).

J Enclosure Notation. A reminder that the letter is accompanied by an enclosure. (See ¶¶1373–1374.)

K Delivery Notation. An indication that the letter has been sent a special way. (See ¶1375 for alternative placement.)

L Copy Notation. The names of those who will receive copies of this letter. (See ¶¶1376–1380.)

M File Name Notation (Document ID). A coded notation that indicates where the document is stored in computer memory and shown here as a footer. (See ¶1382.)

The following explanations are illustrated on the following page.

N Confidential Notation. A note indicating that the letter should be read only by the person addressed. (See ¶1315.)

O International Address. The name of the country typed in all-capital letters on a line by itself. (See ¶1343.)

P Subject Line. A means of stating what the letter is about. (See ¶¶1352–1353.)

Q Displayed Extract. Copy set off from the rest of the letter for emphasis; indented 0.5 inch from the left and right margins. (See ¶1357a.)

(Continued on page 338.)

SATELLITE TRADERS INC.
1500 Balfour Street
Saskatoon, Saskatchewan S7H 4Z6
Telephone: (306) 555-6000
Fax: (306) 555-6006

John P. Gage
President

↓3 **OR** 2 inches from top of page

start at centre → October 7, 2004 ↓2–3

N **CONFIDENTIAL** ↓2–3   **HEADING**

Mr. Philip Wurlitzer Jr.
Executive Vice-President
Satellite Traders Inc.
Apartado Aero 11255   **OPENING**
Bogota, D.E.
O COLOMBIA ↓2

Dear Phil: ↓2

P **Subject: Your Request for Early Retirement** ↓2

I presented your request to the Board of Directors last Friday. They were entirely
sympathetic to your reasons for wanting to take early retirement, but they did
express concern over the timing. Al Barnes, in particular, raised the following
points in a memo he sent me today: ↓2

Q   Ask Phil to identify people in the Bogota office he considers   **BODY**
             prospective candidates for his position. Please ask him to spell out
             their present qualifications and estimate the time it would take to
             groom any one of these people for his job. ↓2

If you and I can identify at least one qualified candidate acceptable to Al and the
other directors, I know they will move quickly to honour your request. ↓2

start at centre → Sincerely, ↓4 to 6

John

John P. Gage ↓2

                                                                      CLOSING
npl
c Mr. A. J. Barnes
h:\gregg\illustration\gageconf.pw1

Modified-Block (Semi-Block) Style—With Paragraph Indentions

2 inches from top of page

R 1600 Fulton Road
Maple Ridge, BC V2X 7L4
November 25, 2004 ↓2

HEADING

S In reply to: Invoice 57389 ↓3

T Accounting Department
Byfield and Duff
Box 268
Vancouver, BC V7H 1V3 ↓2

OPENING

Dear Byfield and Duff: ↓2

U   Over two months ago I ordered a pair of hiking boots, size 5. You accepted my order, informed me that you were temporarily out of stock, and told me I could expect delivery within four weeks. ↓2

BODY

      Today I received Invoice 57389, billing me for two log carriers which I did not order and have not received. May I ask that you cancel this invoice. If the log carriers arrive, I will refuse delivery and have them shipped back to you at once. ↓2

Sincerely, ↓4 to 6

(Mrs.) Doris T. Hagerty

CLOSING

Doris T. Hagerty ↓2

V   PS: I'm still eager to have those boots. When may I expect to receive them?

R Return Address. The arrangement that is used in a *personal-business letter* when an individual writes on blank stationery. (For an alternative placement of the return address, see ¶1313; to replace the return address with professional-looking letterhead, see ¶1312.)

S Reference Notation. A filing code used by the writer or the addressee. (See ¶1316.)

T Attention Line. A means of directing the letter to a particular person or a specific department. Once positioned on a separate line below the inside address; now positioned as the first line of the inside address (without the word *Attention*) to reflect the recommended format for the mailing address. (See ¶¶1344–1345.)

U Paragraph Indentions. Customarily 0.25 to 0.5 inches. (See ¶1356a.)

V Postscript. A note for capturing the reader's attention to express a final idea or an afterthought; it is not generally used in business letters. (See ¶1381.)

(Continued on page 340.)

BTC **Business Training Consultants**

5600 Sherwood Avenue   Thunder Bay, Ontario P7B 7L4
Telephone: 807-555-6000   Web site: www.btc.ca   Fax: 807-555-6002

2 inches from top of page **OR** ↓3

W   2004 03 06 ↓4–6

HEADING

Mrs. Rita Selden
680 Forrest Road NE
Calgary, AB T3P 2Z1 ↓3

OPENING

X   THE SIMPLIFIED LETTER ↓3

You will certainly be interested to know, Mrs. Selden, that a number of years ago a fine organization called the Administrative Management Society developed a simplified letter style. This is a sample. ↓2

1. It uses the full-block style as well as open punctuation. ↓2

2. It omits the salutation and the complimentary closing. ↓2   **BODY**

3. It uses a subject line, typed in all-capital letters and preceded and followed by two blank lines. The word *Subject* is omitted. ↓2

4. It identifies the signer by an all-capital line that is preceded by four blank lines and followed by one—if further notations are used. ↓2

5. It tries to achieve a brisk but friendly tone and uses the addressee's name at least in the first sentence. ↓2

Perhaps, Mrs. Selden, you ought to give this style a trial. ↓4–6

Y *(Ms.) Helen F. Holub*

Z HELEN F. HOLUB, DIRECTOR, MANAGEMENT TRAINING ↓2

jb ↓2

CLOSING

h:\gregg\illustration\seldenr.368

W **Numeric Dating.** Shows the year, the month, and the day using 8 digits. (See ¶1314b.)

X **Subject Line.** Replaces the salutation; keyed in all-capital letters on the third line below the inside address. (See also ¶1352.)

Y **Complimentary Closing.** Omitted. (See also ¶¶1358–1360.)

Z **Writer's Name and Title.** Keyed on one line in all-capital letters. (See also ¶1363.)

Letter Placement

1304 TOP MARGIN

    a. First Page. On printed letterhead stationery, the top margin is obviously pre-set and cannot be changed. When a *letterhead* is being created or when a *return address* is being used for a personal-business letter, the top margin varies.

- A *created letterhead* may have a top margin as small as 0.5 inch (depending on how deep the letterhead is).
- A *return address* is normally positioned 1.5 to 2 inches from the top of the page.

    Any top margins that are created may be adjusted for better vertical placement if a letter is very long or very short. (See ¶¶1312–1314 for positioning guidelines.)

    b. Continuation Pages. Use the header function in a word processing program to create a continuous page header. Some computer programs default headers to a top margin of one inch, which is preferred. Always use unprinted stationery even if the first page is on printed letterhead. (See also ¶¶1383–1387.)

1305 SIDE MARGINS

    a. Word processing software includes default side margins: 1.25 inches for Word and 1 inch for WordPerfect. Generally either one of the defaults is adequate.

    b. Under certain circumstances, wider or narrower side margins may be required; for instance, the size of the stationery, the length of the document, or the size of the font.

    Two common typefaces in different sizes are displayed below to show the variation in the number of characters in an inch. Review the typeface and type size options that are available to you, and select the one that best meets your needs.

Common Type Sizes and Typefaces	Characters in 1 Inch
12 Point Times New Roman	Now is the time
10 Point Times New Roman	Now is the time for
12 Point Arial	Now is the tim
10 Point Arial	Now is the time f

    c. If it is necessary or desirable to change the default side margins, maintain equal left and right measurements or settings. Generous white space makes a page more attractive and easier to read. Therefore, minimum side margins of 1 inch are preferred.

    d. If you are using letterhead stationery with a column of printed copy running down the left side of the page, set the left margin 0.5 inch to the right of this copy and set the right margin at 1 inch from the right edge of the page.

(Continued on page 342.)

13

    e. If the printed letterhead goes across the entire page, set the right and left margins to match those of the letterhead.

1306 BOTTOM MARGIN

    a. Most word processing software defaults to a 1-inch bottom margin.

    b. If the letter requires more than one page, the bottom margin on the first page may be adjusted to as much as 2 inches or to as little as 0.5 inch to accommodate *widow/orphan* and *block-protect* functions. (See ¶1386.)

    c. If you are using letterhead stationery with a band of printed copy running across the bottom of the page, leave a minimum margin of 0.5 inch between the last line of text and the band of printed copy.

☞ *For guidelines on carrying a letter over from one page to the next, see ¶¶1383–1387.*

1307 LENGTHENING A SHORT LETTER

For a more attractive appearance of a short letter (about 8 lines of text), use any combination of the following techniques:

    a. Increase the side margins.

    b. Lower the date line by as many as 5 lines.

    c. Insert extra space above the inside address, the signature line, and the reference initials. (Do not use more than twice the recommended space in each case.)

    d. Place the writer's name and title on separate lines.

    e. Double space a 1- or 2-paragraph letter and triple space between the paragraphs.

    f. Use a modified-block style with paragraph indentions up to 1 inch.

    g. Increase the font size or select a font that yields fewer characters to an inch.

1308 SHORTENING A LONG LETTER

If only a few lines of a letter will print on a second page, it may be possible to retain readability and condense the text to fit on one page by using a software "make-it-fit" feature or by using any combination of the following techniques:

    a. Reduce the space between the date and the inside address to 2 or 3 blank lines (instead of the customary 3 to 5).

    b. Change the font size and/or the font style.

    c. Reduce the side margins and/or the top and bottom margins.

    d. In a modified style, put reference initials on the same line as the writer's identification.

    e. Avoid a letter style that has paragraph indentions.

    f. Reduce the space for the signature to a minimum of 3 blank lines.

☞ *See ¶¶1385–1386 for formatting continuation pages.*

Punctuation Styles

1309 The message in a business letter is always punctuated with normal punctuation (see Sections 1 and 2). The other parts may be punctuated according to one of the following styles.

a. Standard (Mixed, 2-point) Punctuation. A colon is used after the salutation and a comma after the complimentary closing.

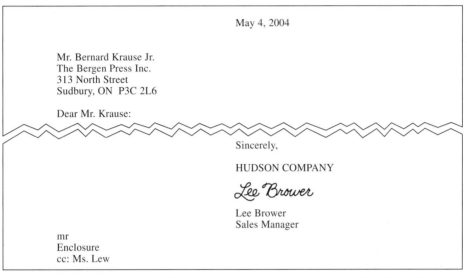

b. Open Punctuation (No Point). No punctuation is used at the end of any line outside the body of the letter unless that line ends with an abbreviation. (This is the style most commonly used.)

May 4, 2004

Mr. Bernard Krause Jr.
The Bergen Press Inc.
313 North Street
Sudbury, ON P3C 2L6

Dear Mr. Krause

Sincerely

HUDSON COMPANY

Lee Brower

Lee Brower
Sales Manager

mr
Enclosure
pc: Ms. Lew

h:\gregg\illustration\bkrause.letter1

Spacing

1310 Ordinarily, key all letters single-spaced. Use one blank line between paragraphs. (For the use of double spacing in very short letters, see ¶1307g.)

The following rules (¶¶1311–1316) deal with the *heading* of a letter. The heading may include a letterhead (¶1311–1312) or a return (letter) address (¶1313) and a date line (¶1314). It may also include a delivery (¶1375), personal or confidential (¶1315), and reference notations (¶1316). The model letters shown on pages 336–340 illustrate the position of these elements in the heading.

Letterhead or Return Address

1311 USING A PRINTED LETTERHEAD

a. The first page of a standard business letter is customarily written on stationery with a *printed letterhead* containing at least these elements: the organization's name, the street address or post office box number (or both), and the municipality, province, and postal code. Most letterheads also provide the following elements: a telephone number (with area code), a fax number, an e-mail address, a Web site URL, and a logo or some other graphic element. Some executives may have special letterheads showing their name and title. (See page 338 for an illustration.)

b. Avoid using abbreviations in a letterhead except those that are a part of an organization's legal name or that represent a provincial name. However, to achieve a more formal effect, spell out the provincial name.

c. Even if your organization uses a post office box number as its primary mailing address, show a street address as well. In that way, senders will know where to direct ordinary mail (to the post office) and where to direct express or courier mail (to the company's office). If the two addresses have different postal codes, be sure to provide this information.

COLE, STEELE & BACKUS

1880 Avenue Road   Hamilton, Ontario L9H 3V7
Telephone (416) 555-4345   www.colesteelebackus.ca
Fax (416) 555-4625   E-Mail CSB150@product.com

1312 CREATING A LETTERHEAD

In place of printed stationery, you can use templates and various fonts to create a professional-looking letterhead. The following illustrations show two such letterheads—one designed for a business and one for an individual working from home. An advantage to creating your own letterhead and printing it with the letter content enables changes to the letterhead (such as addressess, fax numbers) to be made easily and with minimum expense.

ALBERS AND PARKER INC.

250 Murray Park Road
Winnipeg, MB R3Z 4B9
Telephone: 204-444-3600

Box 3291, Station B
Winnipeg, MB R2W 3P6
Fax: 204-444-3610

13

Merle C. Forrest

SECOND WIND • BISCAY ROAD • ST. CATHARINES, ONTARIO L2M 0C7 • 416-555-9097

NOTE: Individuals who want to make themselves available to clients and customers at all hours may insert additional elements in their letterheads beyond those listed in ¶1311—for example, home and business telephone numbers, cell phone, pager, and voice-mail numbers.

1313 USING A RETURN ADDRESS

If you are using plain paper for a *personal-business letter*, key a *return address* or use your predesigned personal letterhead. (See ¶1312.)

a. As a rule, the return address appears 1.5 to 2 inches from the top of the page and shows the street address; the municipality, province, and postal code; perhaps the telephone number; and the date.

212 Westmount Drive, Apt. 2B
Cambridge, ON N1S 6J6
519-555-9097
January 24, 2004

OR Apartment 2B
212 Westmount Drive
Cambridge, ON N1S 6J6
519-555-9097
January 24, 2004

b. All lines are single spaced and each line is positioned as follows:

- Full-block (block) style letter, at the left margin
- Modified-block (semi-block) styles, at the centre of the page
- Simplified letter, at the left margin

c. An alternative style places the return address in the *closing* section of the letter, starting on the line directly below the writer's printed name. This style leaves the date line as the only element at the top of the page, and as shown in the example, each line of the return address begins at the same point as the complimentary closing and the writer's printed name.

(Continued on page 346.)

Sincerely, ↓4–6

Ms. Josephine Cardinal
Apartment 2B
212 Westmount Drive
Cambridge, ON N1S 6J6
519-555-9097

d. One-page letters may be positioned using the vertical centring feature of the word processing program or by adding additional blank space between the letter parts.

Date Line

1314 a. The preferred date line style consists of the *name of the month* (written in full—never abbreviated), the *day* (written in figures and followed by a comma), and the *complete year* (using 4 digits).

December 28, 2004 (**NOT** Dec. 28, 2004 **OR** December 28th, 2004)

NOTE: Do not use the style *12/28/04* or *'04* in the date line of a business letter.

b. A dating system used for filing chronological documents is *numeric dating*. It is a system based on the 24-hour clock and records the date by means of 8 digits arranged in descending order—the *year* first, then the *month*, and the *day*. Hours and minutes may be added if required. (See page 340.)

2004 10 08   2004-10-08   20041008   **ADD:** 2:30 p.m.: 2004 10 08 14 30

c. Some writers write the date line in this order: day, month, year. This is the style typically used in military and overseas correspondence.

28 December 2004

d. When using letterhead stationery, position the date line on the third line below the letterhead or 2 inches from the top of the page, whichever is lower. For the *full-block* and *simplified styles*, start the date at the left margin. For the *modified-block styles*, position the date in one of the following ways:

- Start at the centre of the page (preferred style).
- Position it flush right.
- Place in a position that is relative to the letterhead design.

e. When using a return address at the top of the letter, position the date as shown in ¶1313a. If the return address is placed at the bottom of the letter (as in ¶1313b), still position the date 2 inches from the top of the page.

f. If you are using the date feature of a word processing program, you can automatically insert the current day's date.

☞ *See the illustrations on pages 336–340.*

Personal or Confidential Notation

1315 If the letter is of a personal or confidential nature, provide the appropriate notation on the second or third line below the date at the *left* margin. Bold the notation, preferably using all-capital letters. For greater emphasis change the font
style and/or size.

> **PERSONAL** OR **Personal**   **CONFIDENTIAL** OR **Confidential**

Reference Notations

1316 a. Letterhead templates for law firms and large organizations sometimes contain
a line that reads *When replying, refer to:* or something similar. When using this
kind of letterhead, key the appropriate reference number or filing code after
the colon.

  b. If the guide words *When replying, refer to:* do not appear on the printed stationery but are desired, place them on the second line below the date (or
on the second line below any notation that follows the date). Position the
guide words at the same point as the date. (See page 339.)

> When replying, refer to: ALG-341

  c. When you are replying to a letter that contains a reference number or when
you want to emphasize the fact that your letter concerns an order, an
employment competition, a policy, or a similar document, follow the guidelines as mentioned in ¶1316b above.

> In reply to: G214 782   Refer to: Competition No. 3642

  d. When there are two reference notations to be given, place your own reference
notation first (as indicated below). Then key the addressee's reference notation
on the second line below. Align the notations with the date above.

> Our reference: F-17865
> Your reference: GAR-X-7

> **NOTE:** Some writers, particularly in the field of law, prefer to give the
> addressee's reference notation in a subject line. (See ¶1353d.)

  e. If you want the addressee of a letter to send a response by fax or e-mail, you
may make this request in the body of the letter or in a reference notation.

> When replying, send fax to: 780-555-9985
> When replying, send e-mail message to: grewalk@aol.com

The following rules (¶¶1317–1351) deal with the opening of a letter. The opening
typically includes two elements: the inside or letter address (¶¶1317–1343) and the
salutation (¶¶1346–1351). It may also include an attention line (¶¶1344–1345).

Inside Address

1317 LETTERS TO AN INDIVIDUAL

Most businesses use their word processing programs to format envelopes and
labels. In the case of window envelopes, the inside address of the letter and the

(Continued on page 348.)

envelope is the same. When labels or envelopes are prepared separately, the standards set by Canada Post Corporation (CPC) should be followed to ensure the most efficient delivery. (See ¶1389 for CPC address formats.) However, the traditional format for the inside address on the letter itself is preferable and more attractive than the CPC format.

The following examples show traditional styles, which are also acceptable on the mailing envelope.

a. The inside address should include the following information: (1) the name of the person to whom you are writing; (2) the apartment, unit, or suite number, the street address, the rural route number (or some other delivery indicator); and (3) the municipality, province, and postal code. The postal abbreviation for the province name is generally used, followed by 2 or 3 spaces before the postal code. Some writers prefer to spell out the province name and move the postal code to the line below.

b. Place an apartment number after the street address or, if it will not fit, on the line above.

Miss Sharon H. Mohtadi
337 Cedar Lane, Suite 23
Portage La Prairie, Manitoba
R1A 1G1

Mr. Albert W. Slifka Jr.
Apartment 1407
1533 Dufferin Avenue
Oakville, ON L9W 8H4

☞ *For the placement of the inside address, see ¶1319a.*
For the use of the postal code, see ¶1339.

c. When the address line for the municipality and province is excessively long, the postal code could be placed on the line below.

d. Use the postal abbreviations for such delivery indicators such as *RR* (rural route), *SS* (suburban service), and *MR* (mobile route). If a street name is used with a mode of delivery, it should be placed on the line above.

Mrs. Marie Allen
3864 West Columbia Road
PO Box 179, Stn Main
Lethbridge, AB T1K 6A7

Ms. Le Nham
RR1, Site 17, SS2
Riverhead Harbour Grace, NF
A0A 3PO

1318 LETTERS TO AN ORGANIZATION

a. The inside address should include the following information: (1) the name of the business or organization; (2) a street address or a post office box number; and (3) the municipality, province, and postal code. Whenever possible, address the letter to a specific person in the organization and include the person's job title and department (if known). If you do not have the name of a specific person, use a title instead (for example, *Director of Marketing* or *Advertising Manager*).

Mr. Arthur L. Quinton
National Sales Manager
Paradign Services
211 Rue Wellington
Aylmer, QC J9H 3W7

Director of Research
Stanton Chemical Company
214 Old Sackville Road Exten.
Lower Sackville, Nova Scotia
B4E 2P7

b. When a room number or a suite number is included in the inside address, the following arrangements are acceptable:

Raymond Kermain, M.D.
Suite 1205
2506 Willowdale Avenue
Montreal, QC H3T 1G2

Miss Pauline Leggett
Steele & Leggett
111 Humber Road, Suite 503
Corner Brook, NF A2H 4G1

1319 a. Whether a letter is going to an individual's home or to an organization, start the inside address 4 to 6 lines below the date. If a notation falls between the date and the inside address (see ¶¶1315–1316), start the inside address 2 to 3 lines below the notation.

☞ *See the illustrations on pages 336–340.*

NOTE: You may need to modify these guidelines if you are planning to use a window envelope. (See ¶1389k.)

b. In a social-business letter (see ¶¶1396–1397), the inside address is placed at the bottom of the letter, aligned at the left margin and starting 4 to 6 lines below the writer's name or title (whichever comes last). In a purely personal letter, no inside address is required.

c. Single-space the inside address and align each line at the left.

1320 a. If a letter is addressed to two or more people at different addresses, the individual address blocks may be placed one under the other (with 1 blank line between) or attractively positioned side by side. If the address blocks take up too much space at the opening of the letter, they may be placed at the end of the letter, starting on the second line below the final notation at the left or, if there are no notations, on the *fourth* to *sixth* line below the signature block.

b. If a letter is addressed to two or more people at the same address, list each name on a separate line. Do not show a position title for each person unless it is short and can go on the same line as the name. Moreover, omit the names of departments unless the persons are in the same department. In effect, key only those parts of the address that are common to the people named at the start. (On the respective envelopes for each individual, give the full address for that individual and omit all reference to others named in the inside address.)

Dr. Paul J. Rogers
Mr. James A. Dawes
Research Department
Sloan and Hewitt Advertising
700 North Heights Road
Toronto, ON M9B 4C2

The following rules (¶¶1321–1343) provide additional details concerning the parts of inside addresses. See also the models in Section 18 for special forms of address used for individuals, couples, organizations, professional people, education and government officials, diplomats, military personnel, and religious dignitaries.

Name of Person and Title

1321 When writing the name of a person in an inside address or elsewhere in a letter, be sure to follow that person's preferences in the spelling, capitalization, punctuation, and spacing of the name. (See ¶311.)

  a. Do not abbreviate or use initials unless the person to whom you are writing prefers that style. For example, do not write *Wm. B. Sachs* or *W. B. Sachs* if the person used *William B. Sachs* in his correspondence.

  b. When writing to a married woman, follow her preference for first and last names if you know it. She may prefer to be addressed by her original name (for example, *Ms. Joan L. Conroy*). If you do know that she is using her husband's last name, use her own first name and middle initial (for example, *Mrs. Joan L. Noonan*). The form that uses her husband's first name as well (for example, *Mrs. James W. Noonan*) is acceptable only for social purposes. It should never be used when addressing a business letter to a married woman, and it should not be used when a married woman becomes a widow unless she indicates that is her preference.

1322 In general, use a title before the name of a person in an inside address. (See ¶517 for appropriate abbreviations of such titles.)

  a. If the person has no special title (such as *Dr.*, *Professor*, or *The Honourable*), use the courtesy title *Mr.*, *Miss*, *Mrs.*, or *Ms.* (See also ¶1801.)

  b. In selecting *Miss*, *Mrs.*, or *Ms.*, always respect the individual woman's preference. If her preference is unknown, use the title *Ms.* or omit the courtesy title altogether. (See also ¶1801b–c.) Follow the same practice in the salutation. (See ¶1349.)

  c. If you do not know whether the person addressed is a man or a woman, do not use any courtesy title. (See also ¶1801d.) Follow the same practice in the salutation. (See ¶1349.)

  NOTE: People who use initials in place of their first and middle names or who have ambiguous names (like *Pat*, *Dana*, *Laurie*, and *Cory*) should always use a courtesy title when they sign their letters so that others may be spared the confusion over which title to use. (See also ¶¶1365–1366.)

  d. Address teenage girls as *Miss* or *Ms.*, and respect the individual's preference if you know it. For girls younger than 13, *Miss* or *Ms.* may be used or omitted.

  e. Address teenage boys as *Mr.* For boys younger than 13, omit the title. (*Master* is now rarely used except with the names of very young boys.)

1323 a. A letter to a husband and wife is customarily addressed in this form:

  Mr. and Mrs. Jamal S. Borhot (NOT: Mr. & Mrs.)

  b. If the husband has a special title such as *Dr.* or *Professor*, the couple is addressed as follows:

  Dr. and Mrs. Thomas P. Geiger

c. List the names of a married couple on separate lines when (1) the wife alone has a special title, (2) both spouses have special titles, or (3) each spouse has a different surname.

Dr. Amy Barber-Smith	Dean Walter O. Gafor	Ms. Peggy Noble
Mr. John Barber-Smith	Professor Ann B. Gafor	Mr. Guy Gagnon

d. Some married couples prefer a style of address that uses the first names of the spouses and omits *Mr. and Mrs.* Those who use this style typically do so because it treats both spouses as equals and does not imply that the wife can only be identified by her husband's name. Respect such preferences when you are aware of them.

Janet and Arnold Rogon (**RATHER THAN:** Mr. and Mrs. Arnold Rogon)

☞ *For other forms of address to use for couples in special circumstances, see ¶1802.*

1324 a. When *Jr., Sr.,* or a Roman numeral such as *III* is written after a name, omit the comma before this element unless you know that the person being addressed prefers the use of a comma. (See also ¶156.)

b. Do not use a title before a name if the term *Esq.* follows the name. (See also ¶¶518c, 1804a.)

Rita A. Hira, Esq. (**NOT:** Ms. Rita A. Hira, Esq.)

NOTE: A comma separates the last name from the term *Esq.*

c. As a rule, do not use an academic degree with a person's name in an inside address. However, some doctors of medicine and divinity prefer the use of the degree after their names (rather than the title *Dr.* before). (See also ¶1804b.)

NOTE: If an academic degree follows the person's name, separate it from the last name with a comma. Also omit the titles *Dr., Miss, Mr., Mrs.,* and *Ms.* before the name. Another title (for example, *Professor, The Reverend, Captain, Dean*) may be used before the name as long as it does not convey the same meaning as the degree that follows. (See ¶519c.)

Reva C. Calhoun, M.D.   The Reverend Ernest G. Wyzanski, D.D.

d. Abbreviations of religious orders, such as *S.J.* and *O.S.A.,* are keyed after names and preceded by a comma. An appropriate title should precede the name, even though the abbreviation follows the name; for example, *The Reverend John DeMaio, O.P.* (See also ¶1813.)

1325 a. A title of position, such as *Vice-President* or *Sales Manager,* may be included in an inside or letter address. Ordinarily, place it on the line following the name; if the title requires a second line, indent the turnover 2 or 3 spaces. Capitalize the first letter of every word in the title except (1) prepositions under four letters (like *of, for,* and *in*); (2) conjunctions under four letters (like *and*); and (3) the articles *the, a,* and *an* when they appear *within* the title.

Mrs. Martha Hansen   Mr. Ralph Nielsen
Executive Vice-President   Vice-President and (**NOT** &)
                                     General Manager

(Continued on page 352.)

Mr. Harry F. Nguyen	Ms. Evangeline S. Sardau
Chairman of the Board	Director of In-Service Training

NOTE: In the last example above, *In* is capitalized because it is the first element in a compound adjective (rather than a pure preposition as in *Editor-in-Chief*). By the same token, in the title *Co-ordinator of On-the-Job Training, On* is capitalized as the first element in a compound adjective but *of* and *the* are not.

b. If the title is very short, it may be placed on the same line as the person's name or the person's department in order to balance the length of the lines in the address. However, do not place a title on the same line as the name of an organization. (See ¶1327.)

Mr. J. C. Lee, President	Mrs. Lucinda Hollingsworth
National Appliance Ltd.	Manager, Support Services
	The Hathaway Group

Mr. Armand F. Aristides	**NOT:** Mr. Armand F. Aristides
Controller	Controller, Dahl, Inc.
Dahl, Inc.	

In Care of . . .

1326 Sometimes a letter cannot be sent to the addressee's home or place of business; it must be directed instead to a third person who will see that the letter reaches the addressee. In such cases use an "in care of" notation as shown below.

Professor Eleanor Marschak	**OR** Professor Eleanor Marschak
In care of Henry Wardwell, Esq.	c/o Henry Wardwell, Esq.

Name of Organization

1327 Place the organization's name on a line by itself. If the name of a division or a department is needed in the address, it should precede the name of the organization on a line by itself.

Ms. Laura J. Kidd
Assistant Vice-President
Department of Corporate Planning
Hobday, Granger Co. Ltd.

1328 When writing the name of an organization in an inside address, always follow the organization's style for spelling, punctuation, capitalization, spacing, and abbreviations. The letterhead on incoming correspondence is the best source for this information. Note the variations in style in these names.

AMJ Campbell Van Lines	Rock'n Well Servicing Inc.
Blake, Cassels & Graydon	Rosmar CADworks Inc.
Canadian 88 Energy Corp.	SAS-CAN Masonry Ltd.
Club de Hockey Canadien	Saskatchewan Mutual Insurance Co.
Fluor Daniel Canada, Inc.	Sun Life Assurance Company
Foothills Pipe Lines Ltd.	of Canada
INCO LTD	The Toronto-Dominion Bank
NASCOR Incorporated	TransCanada Pipelines Limited
Petro-Canada	Trans World Oil & Gas Ltd.
R B C Dominion Securities Inc.	Triple-A Manufacturing Co. Ltd.

NOTE: If the name is long and requires more than one line, indent any turnover or runover line 2 or 3 spaces. (See ¶1329e for examples.)

1329 If you do not have some way of determining the official form of a company name, follow these rules:

a. Spell out the word *and*. Do not use an ampersand (&).

Haber, Curtis, and Hall Inc.   Acme Lead and Tin Company

b. Write *Inc.* for *Incorporated* and *Ltd.* for *Limited*. Do not use a comma before the abbreviation.

c. As a rule, spell out *Company* or *Corporation*; if the name is extremely long, however, use the abbreviation *Co.* or *Corp.*

d. Do not use the word *the* at the beginning of a name unless you are sure it is part of the official name; for example, *The Globe and Mail* (as illustrated in *e* below).

e. Capitalize the first letter of every word except (1) prepositions under four letters (like *of, for,* and *in*); (2) conjunctions under four letters (like *and*); and (3) the articles *the, a,* and *an* when they appear *within* the organization's name.

Centre for Career Development   Once Upon a Time Travel
   and Financial Planning   (1994) Canada Inc.
10357 Crosbie Place   110 Yonge Street, Suite 478
St. John's, NF A1C 5T7   Toronto, ON M5C 1T4

NOTE: In the following example note that the article *the* is capitalized because it comes at the start of the organization's official name. Note also that the name of the newspaper is not italicized or underscored because it refers to the organization rather than to the actual newspaper. (See also ¶289e.)

The Globe and Mail
444 Front Street
Toronto, ON M5V 2S9

Building Name

1330 If the name of a building is included in the inside address, key it on a line by itself immediately above the street address. A room number or a suite number should be added as shown in the examples below.

Devonian Professional Building   Medical Arts Building
13717 - 170 Street, Room 118   5880 Garden Road, Suite 14
Edmonton, AB T5C 3E7   Halifax, NS B3H 1Y1

☞ *For additional examples, see ¶1318b.*

Street Address

1331 Always key the street address on a line by itself, immediately preceding the municipality, province, and postal code. (See ¶¶1317–1318 for examples.)

1332 Use figures for house and building numbers. Do not include the abbreviations *No.* or the symbol # before such numbers. **EXCEPTION:** For clarity, use the word *One* instead of the figure *1* in a house or building number; for example, *One Yonge Street.*

NOTE: Some house numbers contain a hyphen or a fraction; for example, *220-03 - 46th Street, 234$\frac{1}{2}$ Elm Street.*

1333 Numbers used as street names should be written as assigned by the municipality and as shown in *Canada's Postal Code Directory.* If it appears as *3rd Avenue,* use that format. If it appears as *Third Avenue,* use that format.

NOTE: Although some writers do not like it, the use of ordinals *st, nd, rd,* and *th* in street addresses is becoming more common and acceptable. Some software packages automatically print the ordinals as superscripts.

824 - 3rd Avenue   129 - 14th Street

1334 When a compass point (for example, *East, West, Southeast, Northwest*) appears *before* a street name, do not abbreviate it except in a very long street address when space is tight.

330 West Hill Street   **BUT:** 3210 N. Christie Estates Terrace

1335 When a compass point appears *after* a street name, follow these guidelines:

a. Abbreviate compound directions *(NE, NW, SE, SW)* and omit any punctuation.

817 Peachtree Street NE   2320 Palliser Drive SW

b. Spell out *North, South, East,* and *West* following a street name and omit the comma.

70 Hinton Avenue North   2049 Okanagan Avenue East

1336 Use the word *and,* not an ampersand (&), in a street address; for example, *Tenth and Market Streets.* However, avoid the use of such "intersection" addresses if a house or building number plus a single street name is available (such as *304 Tenth Street*).

1337 Avoid abbreviating such words as *Street* and *Avenue* in inside addresses. (Canada Post prefers abbreviations in envelope addresses. See ¶1389.)

☞ *For apartment and room numbers with street addresses, see ¶¶1317a, 1318b, 1330.*

Box Number

1338 a. A post office box number should be used in place of the street address when it is listed as such in *Canada's Postal Code Directory.*

b. A station name, if needed, should follow the post office box number on the same line in both the inside address and on the envelope.

Post Office Box 101, Station M   PO Box 604, Stn. Victoria
Owen Sound, ON N4K 5P1   Montreal, QC H3Z 2S4

c. Some organizations show both a street address and a post office box number in their mailing address. When you are writing to an organization with two addresses, use the post office box number for ordinary mail and the street address for courier and express mail.

Henson Supply Corp.
PO Box 181
Rothesay, NB E0G 2W6

NOT: Henson Supply Corp.
315 South Shipyard Road
PO Box 181
Rothesay, NB E0G 2W6

NOTE: Dual addressing as shown in the second example above should be avoided. Canada Post, in this case, would deliver the mail to the address immediately above the city-province-postal code line.

Municipality, Province, and Postal Code

1339 The municipality, province, and postal code must always be placed on the line following the street address, unless the name of the municipality is extremely long. (See ¶1317b.) Key the name of the municipality (followed by a comma and 1 space), the provincial postal abbreviation (followed by 2 or 3 spaces but no comma), and the postal code. The format of the alphanumeric postal code is *ANA NAN*, where *A* is an alpha character and *N* is a numeric one. There is one space between the first three and last three characters.

Edmonton, AB T5M 3N7   Vancouver, BC V6A 2T8

1340 When writing the name of a municipality (city, municipality, town, village, community, post office), use the one recognized as a valid mailing destination.

NOTE: The official name as recognized by the municipality must be used; for example, *Trois-Rivières* is correct, not *Three Rivers*.

a. Do not use an abbreviation (for example, *Mont'l* for *Montreal*, *P.A.* for *Prince Albert*, *TO* for *Toronto*).

b. Do not abbreviate the words *Fort*, *Mount*, *Point*, or *Port*. Write the name of the city or town in full; for example, *Fort McMurray*, *Mount Carmel*, *Point Edward*, *Port Elgin*.

c. Abbreviate the word *Saint* in the names of cities but only if it is the correct postal designation; for example, *St. John's, NF*; *St. Catharines, ON*; *St. Paul, AB*. **EXCEPTIONS:** *Saint John, NB*; *Saint-Laurent, QC*.

1341 a. In an inside address, it may be considered more businesslike to spell out the name of the province. However, the CPC two-letter abbreviation is also acceptable. The abbreviated format should be keyed in capital letters with no spaces or punctuation. (See page 356 for Canadian and American postal abbreviations.)

b. When giving an address in a sentence, however, insert a comma after the street address and after the city or town. Leave 1 space between the province and the postal code. Insert a comma after the postal code unless a stronger mark of punctuation is required at that point. All the usual postal abbreviations may be omitted.

My address next month will be Apt. 211, 2324 - 90th Avenue SW, Calgary, Alberta T2V 3X7, but mail sent to my office will reach me as well.

(Continued on page 356.)

13

Alberta	AB	Nova Scotia	NS
British Columbia	BC	Nunavut	NU
Manitoba	MB	Ontario	ON
New Brunswick	NB	Prince Edward Island	PE
Newfoundland and		Quebec	QC
Labrador	NF	Saskatchewan	SK
Northwest Territories	NT	Yukon	YT
Alabama	AL	Missouri	MO
Alaska	AK	Montana	MT
American Samoa	AS	Nebraska	NE
Arizona	AZ	Nevada	NV
Arkansas	AR	New Hampshire	NH
California	CA	New Jersey	NJ
Colorado	CO	New Mexico	NM
Connecticut	CT	New York	NY
Delaware	DE	North Carolina	NC
District of Columbia	DC	North Dakota	ND
Federated States		Northern Mariana Islands	MP
of Micronesia	FM	Ohio	OH
Florida	FL	Oklahoma	OK
Georgia	GA	Oregon	OR
Guam	GU	Palau	PW
Hawaii	HI	Pennsylvania	PA
Idaho	ID	Puerto Rico	PR
Illinois	IL	Rhode Island	RI
Indiana	IN	South Carolina	SC
Iowa	IA	South Dakota	SD
Kansas	KS	Tennessee	TN
Kentucky	KY	Texas	TX
Louisiana	LA	Utah	UT
Maine	ME	Vermont	VT
Marshall Islands	MH	Virgin Islands	VI
Maryland	MD	Virginia	VA
Massachusetts	MA	Washington	WA
Michigan	MI	West Virginia	WV
Minnesota	MN	Wisconsin	WI
Mississippi	MS	Wyoming	WY

1342 Omit the name of the county or area (such as *York County*) in an address. However, the name of a community, subdivision, or real estate development may be included as long as it comes before the lines containing the mail delivery address.

Ms. Janet G. Arnold
Meadowland Park
39 Owen Street
Mill Village, NS B0J 2H0

NOT: Ms. Janet G. Arnold
39 Owen Street
Meadowland Park
Mill Village, NS B0J 2H0

1343 In foreign addresses, place the name of the country on a separate line in all-capital letters. Except for the United States of America, do not abbreviate the name of the country.

134 Piccadilly
London W1V 9FJ
GREAT BRITAIN

6710 Squibb Road
Mission, KS 66202 - 3223
USA

Attention Line

1344 a. When a letter is addressed directly to an organization, an attention line may be used to route the letter to a particular person (by name or title) or to a particular department. Here is the format that has been used in the past.

Benefits & Resources Ltd.   Warham Lampton Labs
2900 Bathurst Street   1970 Briarwood Court
Toronto, ON M6B 4Z7   Scarborough, ON M1L 3T7

Attention: Mr. John Ellery   ATTENTION: SALES MANAGER

NOTE: This form of address is intended to emphasize the fact that the letter is presumed to deal with a company business matter (not a confidential or personal matter) and may be handled by others in the absence of the person named in the address. For this reason an attention line is not really needed. Moreover, placing the attention line below the inside address is not suitable if you plan to use your computer to replicate the inside or letter address on an envelope or mailing label.

b. If you use an attention line, place it on the second line below the inside address, starting at the left margin.

c. The attention line may be keyed in initial capital and small letters or in all-capital letters and may be bolded.

NOTE: Law firms often underline an attention line regardless of other formatting or additional features.

d. Do not abbreviate the word *Attention.* Use a colon after *Attention.*

☞ *For the salutation to use with an attention line, see ¶1351.*

1345 a. If you are using window envelopes or planning to generate the envelope address by repeating the inside or letter address as keyed, you should insert the attention line as the first line in the inside address—with or without the word *Attention.*

Mr. John Ellery   Attention: Sales Manager
Benefits & Resources Ltd.   Warham Lampton Labs
2900 Bathurst Street   1970 Briarwood Court
Toronto, ON M6B 4Z7   Scarborough, ON M1L 3T7

b. Once the attention line is placed on the first line of the address block, the argument for omitting the word *Attention* is further strengthened. (See the note in ¶1344.) Indeed, Canada Post Corporation considers this first line as non-address data and illustrates in the two examples above that additional information (such as a person's name, a title, or a departmental name) should be placed above the organization's name. Whether the word *Attention* is written or not is immaterial to CPC; it simply wants to have personal or departmental names or titles above the name of the organization. This is to accommodate the OCR in sorting mail easier.

NOTE: The use or omission of the word *Attention* will affect the choice of salutation. See ¶1351.

☞ *For the treatment of an attention line on an envelope, see ¶1389m.*

Salutation

1346 Start the salutation at the left margin on the second line below the inside address or on the second line below the attention line (if used). Follow the salutation with a colon unless you are using open punctuation (see ¶1308) or you are keying a social-business letter. (See ¶1397b). Omit the salutation if you are using the simplified style and replace it with a subject line. (See ¶1352.)

1347 Abbreviate only the titles *Mr., Ms., Mrs., Messrs.,* and *Dr.* All other titles, such as *Professor* and *Father*, should be spelled out. (See Section 18 for titles used by officials, dignitaries, and military personnel.)

1348 Capitalize the first word as well as any nouns and titles in the salutation; for example, *Dear Sir, Dear Mrs. Brand.*

1349 a. A list of commonly used forms of salutation begins below and continues on the next page. (See also Section 18.)

To One Person (Name, Gender, and Courtesy Title Preference Known)

Dear Mr. Smith:	Dear Ms. Simpson:
Dear Mrs. Gray:	Dear Miss Wells:

To One Person (Name Known, Gender Unknown)

Dear Lee Parker:	Dear R. V. Moore:

To One Person (Name Unknown, Gender Known)

Dear Madam: **OR**   Madam: (more formal)
Dear Sir: **OR**   Sir: (more formal)

To One Person (Name and Gender Unknown)

Dear Sir or Madam: **OR**   Sir or Madam: (more formal)
OR   Dear Madam or Sir: **OR**   Madam or Sir: (more formal)
To Whom It May Concern: (see ¶1349c)

To One Woman (Courtesy Title Preference Unknown)

Dear Ms. Malloy: **OR**   Dear Ruth Malloy: (see ¶1322b)

To Two or More Men

Dear Mr. Gelb and Mr. Harris: **OR**   Gentlemen:
OR   Dear Messrs. Gelb and Harris: (more formal)
NOT: Dear Sirs: **OR**   Dear Gentlemen:

To Two or More Women

Dear Mrs. Allen, Ms. Ott, and Miss Day:
Dear Mrs. Jordan and Mrs. Kent: (see ¶618)
OR   Dear Mesdames Jordan and Kent: (more formal)
Dear Ms. Scott and Ms. Gomez: (see ¶618)
OR   Dear Mses. (**OR** Mss.) Scott and Gomez: (more formal)
Dear Miss Winger and Miss Rossi: (see ¶618)
OR   Dear Misses Winger and Rossi: (more formal)

To a Woman and a Man

Dear Ms. Kent and Mr. Winton:	Dear Mrs. Kay and Mr. Fox:
Dear Mr. Fong and Miss Landis:	Dear Mr. and Mrs. Green:

To Several Persons

Dear Mr. Anderson, Mrs. Brodsky, Ms. Carmino,
  Mr. Dellums, and Miss Eustace:

Dear Friends (Colleagues, Members, *or some other suitable collective term*):

To an Organization Composed Entirely of Men

Gentlemen: **NOT:**   Dear Gentlemen:

To an Organization Composed Entirely of Women

Ladies: **OR**   Mesdames: **NOT:**   Dear Ladies: **OR**   Dear Mesdames:

To an Organization Composed of Men and Women (See ¶1350.)

b. Be sure that the spelling of the surname in the salutation matches the spelling in the inside address. If the person you are writing to has a hyphenated last name (for example, *Mrs. Hazel Merriman-Sparks)*, the salutation should read *Dear Mrs. Merriman-Sparks.*

c. When writing to someone you know well, use a first name or nickname in place of the more formal salutations shown above. However, once you start using an informal salutation, be sure that anyone who prepares your letters for you maintains that form of address. Otherwise, a person who is used to getting *Dear Mike* letters from you may one day receive a *Dear Mr. Romano* letter and waste a good deal of time brooding over what could have caused the sudden chill in your relationship. (See also ¶1360d.)

d. When you are preparing a letter that may be sent or shown to a number of as yet undetermined recipients, it is permissible to use *To Whom It May Concern* as a salutation. However, when you are writing to one specific person whose name and gender you do not know, use *Dear Sir or Madam* or one of the other forms shown on the preceding page.

e. In extremely formal letters, *My dear* may be used in place of *Dear.*

f. In salutations involving two or more people, use *and*, not &.

1350 For an organization composed of both men and women:

a. Use *Ladies and Gentlemen* or *Gentlemen and Ladies.* (Do not use *Gentlemen* alone.)

United Services Corporation
7505 Kennedy Road
Markham, ON L3R 6Y2

Ladies and Gentlemen: **NOT:** Dear Ladies and Gentlemen:

b. Address the letter, not to the organization as a whole, but to the head of the organization—by name and title if known, otherwise by title alone. Then the salutation would appear as shown in ¶1349.

Mr. James V. Quillan	President
President	(**OR** Chief Executive Officer)
United Services Corporation	United Services Corporation
7505 Kennedy Road	7505 Kennedy Road
Markham, ON L3R 6Y2	Markham, ON L3R 6Y2
Dear Mr. Quillan:	Dear Sir or Madam:

(Continued on page 360.)

c. In routine or informal letters when no specific information is known, as a last resort, use the name of the organization in the salutation. (See page 339 and ¶1803a.)

Dear United Services Corporation:

d. Use the simplified letter style and omit the salutation.

1351 a. When an attention line is used (see ¶1344), the letter is considered to be addressed to the organization rather than to the person named in the attention line. Therefore, use one of the organizational salutations shown in ¶¶1349 and 1350. (Whenever possible, omit the attention line and address the letter directly to an individual in the organization—either by name or by title.)

b. If the word *Attention* is dropped (as shown in ¶1345) and the letter is addressed directly to an individual in the organization either by name or title, use one of the personal salutations shown in ¶1349.

The following rules (¶¶1352–1357) deal with the *body* of a letter. The body contains the text of the letter—in other words, the message (see ¶¶1354–1357). The body may also begin with a subject line (see ¶¶1352–1353), which briefly identifies the main idea in the message.

Subject Line

1352 In the *simplified letter style:*

a. A subject line is used in place of the salutation.

b. Start the subject line on the third line below the inside address. Begin at the left margin and key the subject line in all-capital letters.

c. Do not use a term like *Subject:* to introduce the subject line. (See the illustration on page 340.)

1353 In *all other letter styles:*

a. The subject line (if used) appears between the salutation and the body of the letter, with 1 blank line above and below. (See the illustration on page 338.) The term *Subject:* usually precedes the actual subject line, except in the simplified letter style where it is omitted altogether. Do not confuse a subject line with a reference notation. (See ¶1316.)

b. Ordinarily, the subject line starts at the left margin, but it may be centred for special emphasis. In a letter with indented paragraphs, the subject line may use the same tab setting as the paragraph.

c. Key the subject line either in capital and small letters or in all-capital letters. The subject line is usually keyed without italicizing or underlining, but for special emphasis the complete subject line is often bolded.

NOTE: If the subject line is long, key it in two or more single-spaced lines of roughly equal length.

Subject: Introductory Offer to New   SUBJECT: MORAN LEASE
                Subscribers and Renewal
                Offer to Present Subscribers

d. When replying to a letter that carries a "refer to" notation, you may put the desired reference number or filing code either in a subject line or below the date line in a "refer to" line.

Subject: Policy 668485   Refer to: Policy 668485

Message

1354 a. Begin the body (message) of the letter on the second line below the salutation or the subject line, if it is used. In the *simplified letter style* begin the message on the third line below the subject line.

b. If you are writing a reply to a letter, it is sometimes helpful to refer to that letter by date in the first sentence.

Thank you for your letter of May 9, 2004. (See ¶409.)

1355 Use single spacing and leave 1 blank line between paragraphs. Very short letters may be keyed in 1.5 spacing or 2.0 (double) spacing or lengthened by means of other techniques. (See ¶1307.)

1356 a. Align each line of the message at the left margin. However, for the *modified-block (semi-block) style with indented paragraphs* and the *modified-block (semi-block) style* with the body double-spaced, indent 0.25 to 0.5 inches. For special effect, some writers indent more than 0.5 inch. (See page 339.)

b. For an attractive appearance of text, many writers choose the *full justification* setting to make full lines of text not only begin but also end at the same point. Word processing programs add extra spaces between words to give this even appearance; however, it produces unwanted and unattractive "rivers" of white space running through the text. More important, text with a *ragged* (unjustified) right margin is easier to read. Some recipients of justified letters tend to regard them as form letters and do not take them seriously.

c. If you decide on a ragged right margin, try to avoid great variations in the length of adjacent lines. (See Section 9 for guidelines on word division to keep the lines of text roughly equal in length.)

d. If a letter takes two or more pages, do not divide a two- or three-lined paragraph at the bottom of the page. In order to leave at least two lines of the paragraph at the foot of one page and carry over at least two lines to the top of the next page, use the *widow/orphan* feature of your software program. (See ¶¶1383–1387.)

e. To prevent a subheading from being separated by a page-break from the text that follows, use the *block-protect* feature of your program. Include at least two lines of paragraph text in the block that is being protected. (See Section 20.)

1357 a. Quoted Material. If a quotation will make four or more lines, key it as a single-spaced extract. Indent the extract 0.5 inches from each side margin using the word processing *double indent* feature. Leave 1 blank line above and below the extract as illustrated on page 338. If the quoted matter represents the beginning of an indented paragraph in the original, tab the first word an additional 0.25 to 0.5 inches from the left margin.

☞ *For different ways of handling a long quotation, see ¶265.*

b. Tables. When a table occurs in the text of a letter, centre it between the left and right margins. Try to indent the table at least 0.5 inches from each side margin. If the table is very wide, reduce the space between columns to a minimum of 2 spaces to prevent the table extending beyond the width of the text. Leave 1 to 3 blank lines above and below the table to set it off from the rest of the text. (See Section 16 for a full discussion on how to plan and execute tables.)

c. Items in a List. Single space a list with short lines of text and add one blank line above and below the list as a whole. Either key the list on the full width of a letter that has no paragraph indentions (see the first illustration on page 363) or use the word processing *indent* feature to indent the lines 0.5 inches from each side margin (see the illustration below). If *any* item in the list requires more than one line, align any turnovers or runovers with the first word in the line above. Leave a blank line after each item in the list to make each item clearly definable.

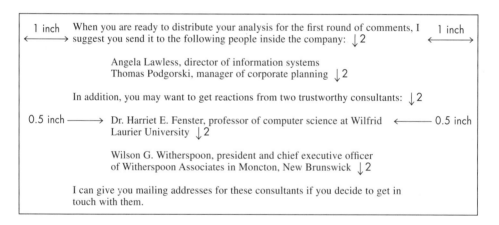

d. Enumerated Items in a List. If the items in a list each begin with a number or a letter, unless the automatic numbering feature has been turned off, the word processing program will determine how the list will be presented. Depending on the software program used and depending on the version of that software, the default settings could vary widely. The following sample text shows the preferred format.

When I review the situation as you described it in your letter of June 24, it seems to me that you have only two alternatives: ↓2

1. Agree to pay the additional amount that Henning now demands before he will start construction. ↓2

2. Drop Henning and start the search all over again to find a firm qualified to handle a project of this size and this complexity. ↓2

In the preferred format shown above, note the following features:

- The items are single-spaced with a double space **between** the numbered items.
- The number (with a period) for the item is at the left margin.
- Each line of the item is indented 0.25 inch, which is acceptable for most font sizes.
- The list itself is separated from the body of text by a double space above and below it.

Word processing software users who are familiar with their program will be able to make adjustments in the default settings to achieve the desired format. If this does not work, turn off the automatic feature and format the list manually.

NOTE: An enumerated list may be keyed to the full width of the letter, or it may be indented 0.5 inches from each side margin. However, if the first line of each text paragraph is indented, indent the enumerations as well for a better appearance. If the software default is not the same as the paragraph indentions in the text, an adjustment may be made for the same indentions to give a more uniform and attractive look.

When I review the situation as you described it in your letter of June 24, it seems to me that you have only two alternatives:

1. Agree to pay the additional amount that Henning now demands before he will start construction.

2. Drop Henning and start the search all over again to find a firm qualified to handle a project of this size and this complexity.

As painful as it may be, you may find it easier to start looking for a new contractor than to have to deal with new demands from Henning once he is a quarter of the way through the job.

NOTE: The *numbered list* feature aligns numbers and letters at the left. If your list contains 10 or more items, it is possible to adjust the numbers to align at the right, but it is a time-consuming and frustrating task to attempt when using certain word processing programs. Some writers have abandoned the preferred right alignment for numbers, letting the software dictate the style.

(Continued on page 364.)

e. **Bulleted Items in a List.** Instead of numbers or letters, you can use *bullets* before the items in a list. A variety of styles may be chosen. For example:

CIRCLES: ○ ●	TRIANGLES: ▷ ▶
SQUARES: □ ■	OTHER ASCII CHARACTERS: > → *

If you use the automatic bullet insert feature, the default position of the bullet is at 0.25 inches and the text and turnover or runover positions are at 0.5 inches.

When I review the situation as you described it in your letter of June 24, it seems to me that you have only two alternatives: ↓2

• Agree to pay the additional amount that Henning now demands before he will start construction. ↓2

• Drop Henning and start the search all over again to find a firm qualified to handle a project of this size and this complexity. ↓2

The following rules (¶¶1358–1381) deal with the *closing* of a letter. The closing typically includes a complimentary-closing phrase (¶¶1358–1360), the writer's name and title (¶¶1362–1369), and reference initials (¶¶1370–1372). It may also include a company signature line (¶1361), an enclosure notation (¶¶1373–1374), a delivery notation (¶1375), a copy notation (¶¶1376–1380), a postscript (¶1381), and a file name notation (¶1382).

Complimentary Closing

1358 Position the complimentary closing on the second line below the last line of the body of the letter. (See pages 336–339.) Placement rules include the following:

• Full-block (block) style letter, start the closing at the left margin
• Modified-block (semi-block) styles, start the closing at centre
• Simplified letter, omit the closing

NOTE: Word processing software allows you to use autotext for the complimentary closing and other elements that are frequently used in the closing of a letter.

☞ *For illustrations of complimentary closings, see pages 336–339.*

1359 Capitalize only the first word of a complimentary closing. Place a comma at the end of the line (except when open punctuation is used).

1360 a. The following complimentary closings are commonly used:

PERSONAL IN TONE:	Sincerely, Cordially,	Sincerely yours, Cordially yours,
MORE FORMAL IN TONE:	Very truly yours, Very sincerely yours,	Very cordially yours, Respectfully yours,

b. An informal closing phrase may be inserted in place of one of the more conventional closings shown above. If the wording is an adverbial phrase (one that tells *how* or *in what manner*—for example, *With all best wishes* or *With warmest regards*), follow the closing with a comma. If the wording is a complete sentence (for example, *See you in Lake Louise*), follow the closing with a period. In each case the comma or the period may be replaced with stronger punctuation as appropriate—that is, a question mark, an exclamation point, or a dash.

NOTE: If you are using open punctuation, see ¶1309b.

c. If both a complimentary closing and an informal closing phrase are used, place the complimentary closing in its regular position, and (1) key the informal phrase at the end of the last paragraph or (2) treat it as the final paragraph with the appropriate terminal punctuation.

d. Once a pattern of personal or informal closings is begun, it should not be discontinued without good reason. Otherwise, the person who receives the letter may wonder what has happened to the relationship. (See ¶1349b.)

Company Signature

1361 A company signature, which is often used in legal correspondence, may be used to emphasize the fact that a letter represents the views of the company as a whole (and not merely the individual who has written it). If included, the company signature should be in all-capital letters on the second line below the complimentary closing. Begin the company signature at the same point as the complimentary closing. (See the illustration on page 336.)

Very truly yours, ↓2

HAGGET & SMITH ↓4 to 6

John H. Smith, Q.C.

Writer's Name and Title

1362 a. Ordinarily place the writer's name on the fourth or fifth line below the complimentary closing or company signature, if used. (See the illustrations on pages 336–340.)

NOTE: Always leave at least 3 blank lines for the signature. If the letter is running short, you can leave up to 6 blank lines. (See ¶1307.)

b. Start keying at the same point as the complimentary closing.

NOTE: In the simplified letter style, position the writer's name and title on the *fifth* line below the body, in all-capital letters starting at the left margin. (See ¶1363.)

c. Although some writers prefer to give only their title and department name in the signature block, a printed signature should also be included so that the unsigned copies will clearly show who sent the letter. If the writer prefers

(Continued on page 366.)

to omit his or her name from the signature block, then it should be spelled out in the reference initials. (See ¶1370d.)

d. Top-level executives usually have special stationery with their name and title imprinted along with other elements of the letterhead. When using this type of stationery, supply a printed signature but omit the title.

1363 Arrange the writer's name, title, and department on two or more lines to achieve good visual balance. If a title takes more than one line, indent all turnovers 2 to 3 spaces from the word aligned above.

Janice Mahoney, Manager
Data Processing Division

Ernest L. Welhoelter
Head, Sales Department

Charles Saunders
Assistant Manager
Credit Department

Franklin Browning
Vice-President and
  General Manager

CHARLES SAUNDERS — ASSISTANT MANAGER, CREDIT DEPARTMENT
(simplified style)

☞ *For guidance on capitalizing in signature blocks, see ¶1325a.*

1364 For the use of a special title in a signature block, see the following guidelines:

a. A person who wants to be addressed as *Dr.* should use an appropriate academic degree after his or her name (not *Dr.* before it).

Jane Bishop, M.D.

Nancy Buckwater, Ph.D.

b. A person who wishes to be addressed by a title of academic or military rank (*Dean, Professor, Major*) should place this title *after* the name or on the next line, not before it.

Helene C. Powell
Dean of Students
(**NOT:** Dean Helene C. Powell)

Joseph F. Corey
Major, Canadian Forces
(**NOT:** Major Joseph F. Corey)

c. When a title of address cannot be placed after a surname or cannot be inferred from the initials of an academic degree, then it may precede the name.

Rev. Joseph W. Dowd

Mother Ellen Marie O'Brien

1365 Ordinarily, a man should not include *Mr.* in his signature. However, if he has a name that could also be a woman's name (*Hilary, Lee, Lynn, Morgan*) or if he uses initials in place of a first and middle name (*J. G. Eberle*), he should use *Mr.* in either his handwritten or his printed signature when writing to people who do not know him.

Sincerely,

(Mr.) Lynn Treadway

Lynn Treadway

Sincerely,

Lynn Treadway

Mr. Lynn Treadway

NOTE: If the title is given in the handwritten signature, it is enclosed in parentheses; if given in the printed signature, it appears without parentheses.

1366 a. A woman should include a courtesy title (*Ms.*, *Miss*, or *Mrs.*) or a special title in her signature. (See ¶1364.) If she gives her name without a title, someone writing to her may address her as *Ms.* or omit any title at all. If she uses initials or has a non-gender first name, she risks being addressed as *Mr.*

Sincerely,

Joan Beaudoin

Joan Beaudoin

Sincerely,

(Mrs.) Lee Ellis

Lee Ellis

b. A woman who wants to indicate her preference for *Ms.* should use this courtesy title in either her handwritten or typed signature (but not both).

Sincerely yours,

(Ms.) Constance G. Booth

Constance G. Booth

Sincerely yours,

Constance G. Booth

Ms. Constance G. Booth

c. A single woman who wants to indicate her preference for *Miss* should include this title in her handwritten or her typed signature (but not both).

Cordially,

(Miss) Margaret L. Galloway

Margaret L. Galloway

Cordially,

Margaret L. Galloway

Miss Margaret L. Galloway

d. A married woman who retains her original name for career purposes or who does not change her surname at all may use either *Ms.* or *Miss*, as illustrated in ¶1366b–c.

e. A married woman or a widow who prefers to be addressed as *Mrs.* has many variations to choose from. The following examples show some possible styles for a woman whose maiden name was Nancy O. Ross and whose husband's name is (or was) John A. Wells.

Cordially yours,

(Mrs.) Nancy O. Wells

Nancy O. Wells

Cordially yours,

Nancy Ross Wells

Mrs. Nancy Ross Wells

NOTE: Giving the husband's full name in the printed signature (as in the example below) is a style often used for social purposes. It should not be used in business, and it should not be used when a married woman becomes a widow unless she indicates that that is her preference.

Cordially yours,

Nancy O. Wells

Mrs. John A. Wells

f. A divorced woman who has resumed her maiden name may use *Ms.* or *Miss* in any of the styles shown in ¶1366b–c. If she retains her ex-husband's

(Continued on page 368.)

13

surname, she may use *Ms.* or *Mrs.* in any of the styles shown in ¶1366b and e. (**EXCEPTION:** The style that uses the husband's full name in the printed signature is not appropriate for a divorced woman.)

1367 An assistant who signs a letter at the supervisor's request usually signs the supervisor's name and adds his or her initials. However, if instructed to do so, the letter may be signed with the assistant's own name.

Sincerely yours,

Robert H. Benedict
DK

Robert H. Benedict
Production Manager

Sincerely yours,

Dorothy Kozinski

Ms. Dorothy Kozinski
Assistant to Robert H. Benedict

1368 If a person other than the assistant signs for another, either of the following forms may be used:

Sincerely yours,

(Miss) Alice R. Brentano

For Robert H. Benedict
Production Manager

Sincerely yours,

Robert H. Benedict/
ARB

Robert H. Benedict
Production Manager

1369 When two people have to sign a letter, arrange the two signature blocks side by side or one beneath the other, depending on the amount of space available.

a. If they are placed side by side, start the first signature block at the left margin and the second block at centre. The complimentary closing should also begin at the left margin and is not repeated for the second signature block. This is appropriate for all letter styles.

b. If the signature blocks are positioned one beneath the other, align the second block on the fourth line below the first block. Both signature blocks begin at the left margin in a full-block or a simplified style. Both blocks may align at a centre tab in a modified-block style. Do not repeat the complimentary closing for the second block.

Reference Initials

1370 a. When the writer's name is given in the signature block, the simplest and most unobtrusive way to provide the necessary information is to show the typist's initials alone in lower case letters. (See pages 338 and 340.)

b. Place the initials of the typist at the left margin in lower case on the second line below the writer's name and title. If the writer prefers that his or her initials also be used, they should be keyed before those of the typist.

c. The preferred format for keying two sets of initials places the writer's initials in all capitals and the typist's in lower case. Some writers prefer to use the same case for both sets of initials. In either case, use a diagonal or a colon to separate them.

TYPIST ONLY:	mhs		
WRITER AND TYPIST:	CED/mhs	**OR**	CED:mhs
	CED/MHS	**OR**	ced:mhs

d. If the writer's name is not given in the signature block, key the initials and surname before those of the typist; for example, *CEDixon/mhs.*

☞ *For the application of macros, see ¶1358.*

1371 When the letter is written by someone other than the person who signs it, this fact may be indicated by showing the writer's and the typist's initials (not the signer's and the typist's). See the illustration below.

Sincerely yours, ↓ 4 to 6

Herbert Heymann

Herbert Heymann
President ↓ 2

pbr/jbp

1372 Do not include reference initials in a personal-business letter (see the illustration on page 339) or a social-business letter (see ¶¶1396–1397 and the illustration on page 385). Moreover, omit reference initials on letters you key yourself unless you need to distinguish them from letters prepared for you by someone else. (See ¶¶1396, 1397c.)

Enclosure Notation

1373 a. If one or more items are to be included in the envelope with the letter, indicate that fact by keying the word *Enclosure* (or an appropriate alternative) at the left margin, on the line below the reference initials.

NOTE: Before sending the letter, make sure that the number of enclosures shown in the enclosure notation agrees with (1) the number cited in the body of the letter and (2) the number of items actually enclosed.

b. The following styles are commonly used:

Enclosure	2 Enclosures	Enclosures:
Enc.	2 Enc.	1. Cheque for $500
1 Enclosure	Enclosures 2	2. Invoice A37512
Cheque enclosed	Enc. 2 (see ¶503)	

c. Some writers use the term *Attachment* or *Att.* when the material is actually attached to the cover letter rather than simply enclosed.

1374 If material is to be sent separately instead of being enclosed with the letter, indicate this fact by keying *Separate cover* or *Under separate cover* on the line below the enclosure notation (if any) or on the line directly below the reference initials. The following styles may be used:

Separate cover 1	Under separate cover:
	1. Annual report
	2. Product catalogue
	3. Price list

Delivery Notation

1375 a. If a letter is to be delivered in a special way (other than ordinary mail), key an appropriate notation below the reference initials as illustrated below and on page 336. To draw attention to this notation, a *preferable* format is to capitalize the notation a double space under the date and at the left margin. Leave 2 blank lines after the notation and before the inside address. Among the notations that could be used are *By registered mail, By Priority Post, By XPRESSPOST, By Federal Express (FedEx), By Fax,* and *By courier.*

crj	HWM:FH	tpg/wwc
Enc. 2	By Federal Express	Enclosures 4
By registered mail	cc George Fox	By messenger

NOTE: If you send a letter by fax and want to record the fax number on your file copy, simply expand the delivery notation as follows: By fax (613-222-222).

b. When a letter is first faxed or e-mailed to the addressee and then a duplicate is sent by post, place a "confirmation" notation on the letter being mailed so that the addressee will realize that the document is not a new letter. Double space under the date of the letter *Confirmation of fax sent on* (or *e-mail transmitted on*) and then supply the date.

Copy Notation

1376 a. A copy notation lets the addressee know that one or more persons will also be sent a copy of a letter. The initials *cc* are still commonly used for this notation. Although the abbreviation originally stood for *carbon copies, cc* also means *circulated copies, computer copies,* or *courtesy copies.* Many e-mail and word processing memo templates continue to use the *cc* notation.

b. A more common alternative to *cc* is a single *c* or the phrase *Copies to* (or *Copy to*). Some writers prefer to use the abbreviation *pc* for *photocopies.*

c. Place the copy notation on the line directly under any previous notation (such as reference initials or an enclosure notation). If there is no previous notation, place the copy notation on the second line below the writer's name and title.

d. Type *cc* or other copy notation at the left margin. No punctuation is required, but if it is preferred, use a colon and leave 1 or 2 spaces after it.

e. If several persons are to receive copies, use the copy notation only with the first name. Align all the other names with the start of the name above. List the names according to the rank of the persons or in alphabetic order.

AMH:HT	mfn	lbw/ncy
Enclosure	Enc. 4	cc: Contract File
Registered	c Mrs. A. C. Chang	Toronto Office
cc Ms. J. Hope	Mr. R. G. Flynn	Sales Department

1377 When first names or initials are given along with last names, personal titles (*Mr., Miss, Mrs.,* and *Ms.*) may be omitted except in formal letters. Moreover, do not use personal titles if nicknames are given with last names.

c: James Dion	pc: J. Dion	cc Jim Dion
Kenneth Eustis	K. Eustis	Ken Eustis
Margaret Falmouth	M. Falmouth	Peggy Falmouth

1378 If you do not want the addressee to know that one or more persons are also being sent a copy of the letter, use a *blind copy notation*.

a. Print the original letter plus any copies on which the regular copy notation is to appear. Then print the blind copies one at a time with a blind copy notation showing the name of the designated recipient. (Under certain circumstances, you may wish to let all recipients of blind copies know who the others are.)

b. Place the blind copy notation a double space under the date line (a triple space above the inside address) at the left margin so it is noticed immediately. As an alternative, key the blind copy notation on the line below the last item in the letter.

c. The form of a blind copy notation should follow the form of the copy notation. If you have used *cc* or *c* or *Copies to*, then use *bcc* or *bc* or *Blind copies to*.

d. The file copy should show all the blind copy notations, even though the individual copies do not. Whether the file copy is stored on disk or in hardcopy form, you may need to use the file copy later to make additional copies for distribution. Be sure that no blind copy notations appear on these new copies unless you want them to.

NOTE: FOIP guidelines may change the usage of blind copies.

1379 When a letter carries both an enclosure notation and a copy notation, it is assumed that the enclosures accompany only the original letter. If a copy of the enclosures is also to accompany a copy of the letter, this fact may be indicated as follows:

cc:	Mr. D. R. Leung	(will receive only the letter)
	Ms. N. A. Warren	(will receive only the letter)
cc/enc.:	Mr. J. Bitonti	(will receive the letter and the enclosures)
	Mrs. G. Conger	(will receive the letter and the enclosures)

1380 A copy is not usually signed unless the letter is addressed to several people, and the copy is intended for one of the people named in the salutation. However, a check mark next to the name or the name highlighted indicates for whom that copy is intended.

c: Ms. A. M. Starlight ✓	c: Ms. A. M. Starlight	c: Ms. A. M. Starlight
Mr. H. W. Fried	Mr. H. W. Fried ✓	Mr. H. W. Fried
Mrs. C. Quigley	Mrs. C. Quigley	Mrs. C. Quigley ✓

NOTE: When an unsigned copy is likely to strike the recipient as cold and impersonal, it is appropriate for the writer to add a brief handwritten note at the bottom of the copy and sign or initial it.

Postscript

1381 a. A postscript can be effectively used to express an idea that has been deliberately withheld from the body of a letter; stating this idea at the very end gives
it strong emphasis. A postscript may also be used to express an afterthought;
however, if the afterthought contains something central to the meaning of
the letter, the reader may conclude that the letter was badly organized.

b. When a postscript is used:

(1) Start the postscript on the second line below the copy notation (or whatever was keyed last). If the paragraphs are indented, indent the first line
of the postscript (see page 339); otherwise, begin it at the left margin.

(2) Key *PS:* or *PS* before the first word of the postscript. Leave at least two
spaces after the postscript to permit the alignment of turnover lines with
the first word above.

(3) Use *PPS:* or *PPS* at the beginning of an additional postscript, and treat
this postscript as a separate paragraph.

PS: Instead of dashing to the airport as soon as the meeting is over, why
don't you have dinner and spend the night with us?

PPS: Better yet, why don't you plan to stay the whole weekend?

(4) An alternative format is shown below.

PS: Why don't you bring Joyce with you and plan to stay for the whole
weekend?

File Name Notation

1382 Copies of letters, memos, and reports are normally saved on computer disks
and printed as hard copies. Each document needs a unique file name so that it
can be readily identified for retrieval from storage.

a. A file name or document ID has three components: a name, a period (called
a *dot*) used as a separator, and an extension typically consisting of 1 to 3
characters. Older programs allow a name preceding the dot of no more than
8 characters. Current Windows programs allow a name preceding the dot of
up to 255 characters. Moreover, some current programs permit more than
3 characters after the dot and allow the use of more than one extension.
Users normally allow the word processing software to add its unique identifying extension automatically so documents can be found easily.

NOTE: Although 255 characters may be used in a file name, try to keep the
name as short as possible.

b. In creating a file name or document ID, choose a name that is meaningful.
Most often you can use the letters *a* to *z*, the figures *0* to *9*, spaces, and certain symbols. If an illegal symbol has been selected, a message will inform
you that the file name is not accepted and needs to be changed. Refer to your
software help file or your user's manual to confirm which symbols may or
may not be used.

c. Establish whether a numeric or alphabetic filing system is suitable for your
file names. Elements to help organize file names may include:

- an order number, a policy number, or some other specific identifying number added to the name of the recipient of the document.
- a date added to a recipient's name to identify one of several letters to the same person.
- a notation such as *draft 1, draft 2, final version* added to a file name to indicate a stage of revision.
- pre-assigned numbers added to the beginning of the file name to indicate a file folder number for documents relating to the same subject.

NOTE: Complex numbering systems to identify file folders and file names are often used by law firms.

d. Filing notations should always be included as part of the document. Place the notation a double space after the last item or line in the document. Be sure to include all paths representing the folder names (c:\greggreference-manual\chapter 13). Use a small-size font (8- or 9-point). Most word processing software programs have an automatic file name insert function that guarantees that the file name notation placed on the document will not be altered by a writer's keying error.

NOTE: Many writers prefer to place the file name notation in a footer to appear on every page or on the last page only.

Continuation Pages

1383 Use plain paper of the same quality as the letterhead (but never a letterhead) for all but the first page of a long letter.

1384 Use the same left and right margins that you used on the first page.

1385 Use the header feature to set a continuation page heading. The header should contain the name of the addressee, the page number, and the date. A top margin of 1 inch is generally preferred. Some software packages default the header to a 0.5 inch top margin and a small font size. Check your software setting and make the necessary adjustments, if desired. Either one of the following styles is acceptable, although the second illustration should only be used for the modified-block (semi-block) letter style.

↓1"
Mrs. Laura R. Austin
Page 2
September 30, 2004 ↓3

OR

↓1"
Mrs. Laura R. Austin   – 2 –   September 30, 2004 ↓3

1386 a. Most software programs default or permit only one blank line after a continuation page heading. However, if you prefer to leave two blank lines below the page heading, a hard return added at the end of the header will allow the second blank line to be inserted.

(Continued on page 374.)

b. Do not divide a short paragraph (two or three lines only) at the bottom of a page. For a paragraph of four or more lines, always leave at least two lines of text at the bottom of the page and carry over at least two lines to the continuation page. This will be done automatically by most word processing software programs if the user ensures that the *Widow/Orphan* feature is turned on. (See also ¶1356d.)

c. Never use a continuation page just for the closing section of a business letter. (The complimentary closing should always be preceded by at least two lines of the message.)

d. Try to maintain consistent bottom margins on each page.

1387 Do not divide the last word on a page.

ENVELOPES

1388 ENVELOPE SIZES

a. Since most businesses use standard stationery ($8\frac{1}{2}$" × 11"), the most common size of envelope is the No. 10 ($4\frac{1}{2}$" × $9\frac{1}{2}$"). For stationery not of standard size, envelopes of different sizes are available. Contact Canada Post Corporation toll-free at 1-800-267-1133 or visit their Web site at www.canadapost.com for clarification on size, weight, and rates of lettermail to Canada, to the United States, or to international destinations.

The maximum size, thickness, and weight of an envelope to qualify for automated processing and regular postage is

150 × 245 mm (size)   5.0 mm (thickness)   0.30 g (weight)

b. Using the envelope feature of a software program, you can select the envelope size you plan to use. The return address and the mailing address can be set with the default specifications, or you can modify them to suit your needs. Custom-size envelopes can also be accommodated (assuming your printer will support them).

1389 INSIDE-ADDRESS STYLE

You may choose from two possible formats when addressing envelopes: (1) the letter or inside-address style; and (2) the Canada Post Corporation (CPC) format, which contains all-capital letters, many abbreviations, and no punctuation (see ¶1390). The advantage of the letter style is that the computer will generate the same address information on both the letter and the envelope. Moreover, Canada Post's OCRs *(optical character readers)* are programmed to read both formats.

☞ *For the inside-address style for letters, see ¶¶1317–1343.*
For the CPC all-capital style in addressing envelopes, see ¶1390.

a. Always use single spacing and block each line at the left. Use a minimum of 3 lines. (See page 376 for an example.)

b. Follow the standard rules for capital letters in names, prepositions, and conjunctions in the address. (See ¶303.)

c. The preferred placement for the municipality, province, and postal code is the last line. If space makes it impossible for the postal code to fit on the same line, it may be keyed on the line directly below.

d. The province should be identified by the two-letter CPC abbreviation. (See ¶1341.)

e. Leave two or three spaces between the province abbreviation and the postal code.

f. The next-to-last line in the address block should contain a street address. If a municipal street address is not part of the address, include a postal service indicator such as a post office box number (PO Box), a rural route address (RR), a station designation (STN), or a general delivery notation (GD).

Mr. Christopher Scott	Mr. and Mrs. A. Collard
Colby Electronics Ltd.	Suite 202
PO Box, Stn. South	9539 Old Millcreek Road
Brandon, MB R7B 3W9	Shedden, ON N0L 2E0

g. When a room, suite, or apartment number is part of the address, insert it immediately after the street address on the same line. (See the example above and ¶1330.) If the number does not fit on the same line, place it on the line above, never on the line below.

h. If the default settings for the envelope feature of a word processing program are being used, check that the address elements will be within the OCR reading area.

i. At present the POSTNET bar code feature in Word and WordPerfect can be added only to those envelopes addressed to the United States.

j. Adjustments may need to be made for window envelopes to ensure that the address block is clearly visible.

k. Some guidelines for formatting an envelope on a typewriter are as follows:

(1) Assuming a No. 10 envelope is being used, start the address 2.25 $(2\frac{1}{4})$ inches from the top and about 0.5 $(\frac{1}{2})$ inch left of centre. This will keep the address information within the OCR reading area.

(2) If there is no printed return address on the envelope, type one in the upper left corner. Begin approximately 0.5 $(\frac{1}{2})$ inch from the top edge and 0.75 $(\frac{3}{4})$ inch from the left edge.

(3) Follow the same mailing address format. Type the following on separate lines: the name of the writer; the company name; the street address or equivalent; and the municipality, province, and postal code.

(Continued on page 376.)

No. 10 Envelope With Non-Address Data Information

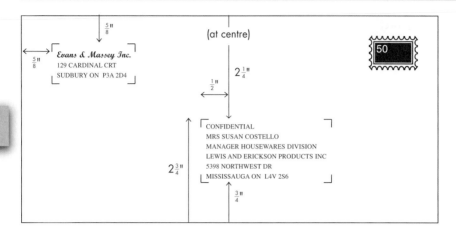

13

l. Black ink on white envelopes is best for the OCRs. If white envelopes are not being used, make sure there is good contrast between the ink colour and the paper colour. Underlining, script fonts, or italics are not suitable attributes for the OCRs to read and should not be used.

m. Notations such as *Personal*, *Attention*, and *Hold for Arrival* are considered non-address data and could be placed on the first line of the address block. (See the envelope illustration above.)

☞ *For letters being sent to two or more people at the same address, see ¶1320b.*

1390 CANADA POST STYLE

a. Key all lines blocked at the left with

- All-capital letters
- Single-spacing
- No punctuation

☞ *See the CPC Web site and the back cover of this manual for street type abbreviations.*

b. For a U.S.A. address, the POSTNET bar code may be used. If your word processing software allows the option, place the bar code on the line beneath the Zip Code.

c. For the placement of all lines in the address block, follow the same rules in ¶1389a–m.

No. 10 Envelope Showing a Mailing Label With the POSTNET Bar Code

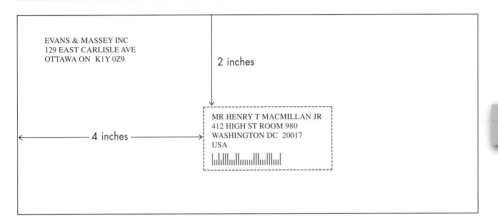

EVANS & MASSEY INC
129 EAST CARLISLE AVE
OTTAWA ON K1Y 0Z9

2 inches

MR HENRY T MACMILLAN JR
412 HIGH ST ROOM 980
WASHINGTON DC 20017
USA

← 4 inches →

13

1391 PREPARING AN ENVELOPE FOR A U.S.A. ADDRESS

a. USA (or U.S.A.) must appear alone on the last line of the address block.

b. The first part in the second last line of the address block is the full name of the municipality.

c. The two-character international state symbol follows the name of the municipality and is separated from it by a comma or one space, depending on the format used. (See the illustration below.) The use of the state symbol is preferred over the full name of the state.

d. The Zip Code is the last item in the second last line and is separated from the state symbol by two spaces. It may be either five or nine digits. If the nine-digit format is used, a hyphen will separate the fifth and sixth digits.

Inside-Address Format	CPC Format
Ms. Aileen O'Brien	MS AILEEN OBRIEN
398 North Michigan Avenue	398 N MICHIGAN AVE
Washington, DC 20019-4649	WASHINGTON DC 20019-4649
U.S.A.	USA

1392 PREPARING AN ENVELOPE FOR AN INTERNATIONAL ADDRESS

International mail as defined by CPC is mail addressed to countries other than Canada and the United States; it is sorted by country name only. Therefore, make sure the country name is correct; for example, do not use *England* for *Great Britain*.

The country name is placed alone on the last line of the address block.

MR THOMAS CLARK	KARL HAUSER GMBH
17 RUSSEL DR	LANDSTRASSE 15
LONDON W1P 6HQ	4100 DUISBURG 25
GREAT BRITAIN	GERMANY

Folding and Inserting Letters

1393 The following paragraphs describe methods for folding letters of standard size ($8\frac{1}{2}$" × 11") and inserting them into envelopes.

a. To fold a letter in thirds for a No. 10 envelope.

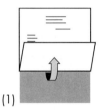 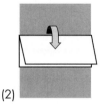 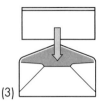

(1)   (2)   (3)

(1) Bring the bottom third of the letter up and make a crease.

(2) Fold the top of the letter down to within 0.25 inch of the crease you made in step 1. Then make the second crease.

(3) The creased edge made in step 2 goes into the envelope first.

b. To fold a letter for insertion into a window envelope.

 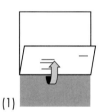 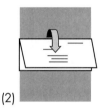 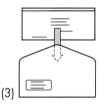

(1)   (2)   (3)

(1) Place the letter *face down* with the letterhead at the top, and fold the bottom third of the letter up.

(2) Fold the top third down so that the address shows.

(3) Insert the letter with the inside address toward the *front* of the envelope. The inside address should now be fully readable through the window. Preferably 0.25 inch white space should edge all four sides. (See ¶1389j.)

MEMOS

1394 An interoffice memo (or memorandum) is intended to expedite the flow of written communications within an organization. Depending on the circumstances, a memo may be as terse as a telegram, as impersonal as a formal announcement, or as casual as a personal note. These circumstances will help you determine whether a particular memo should contain or omit such features as a salutation or a signature line.

You can always modify a memo template that is part of your word processing software or design your own format to meet your needs and those of the organization you work for. Remember, there is no one correct format for a memo, but the following guidelines (see ¶1395) may help you in formatting your own

memos. The illustration on page 383 shows how a memo would look if executed according to these guidelines.

NOTE: Because many memos are now distributed as e-mail, see ¶¶1707–1710
for special guidelines on preparing e-mail messages.

Memo Template Provided by Word 2000

INTEROFFICE MEMORANDUM

TO:	[CLICK HERE AND TYPE NAME]
FROM:	[CLICK HERE AND TYPE NAME]
SUBJECT:	[CLICK HERE AND TYPE SUBJECT]
DATE:	TODAY'S DATE WILL AUTOMATICALLY SHOW HERE
CC:	[CLICK HERE AND TYPE NAME]

1395 If creating a memo on plain paper, observe the following guidelines. If using a
template, see ¶1395e–s.

a. Use the default or 1-inch side margins.

b. Leave a top margin of 1 inch. If the memo is very short, the top margin may
be set at 2 inches for a more attractive overall appearance on the page.

NOTE: Both top and side margins may be adjusted if it will prevent a
memo from going onto a second page.

c. Provide a document heading that includes a title and some guide words. Use
a form of the word *Memo* to create a title; for example, *Memo, Memorandum,
Interoffice Memo, Interoffice Memorandum*. Key the title at the top margin. Use
graphics and lines to enhance the appearance of the heading. Titles are commonly shown in variations of larger font size and different font styles and
may be placed at the left margin, centred, or right-aligned. Leave either 1 or
2 blank lines after the title—a large font size would need less space after it
than a smaller size font.

d. The heading of the memo should also include the following guide words—
TO:, FROM:, DATE:, and *SUBJECT:,* plus any others you wish to add. For
example, below the guide word *TO:* you could insert *COPIES TO:* or *cc:*. If
you work in a large organization and are sending memos to people you do
not know, you might insert below the guide word *FROM:* additional guide
words such as *DEPARTMENT:, FLOOR:, TELEPHONE:,* or *FAX:*.

- Start keying the guide words at the left margin. For emphasis, add any
combination of features, which could include all capital letters, bold,

(Continued on page 380.)

13

MEMORANDUM ↓2–3

TO: Bernard O'Kelly ↓2

COPIES TO: Steve Kubat, Pat Rosario

FROM: Janet R. Wiley *JRW*

DATE: April 7, 2004

SUBJECT: Test Marketing Arrangements ↓3

Dear Bernie: ↓2

Let me try to summarize the outcome of our excellent meeting last Friday, in which we discussed how your group might sell our product lines to the markets you serve. ↓2

1. Steve Kubat, chief product manager for my group, will provide you with product descriptions, catalogue sheets, ad mats, and current price lists. If you need additional information, just call Steve (or me in his absence) and we'll be glad to help in any way that we can. ↓2

2. We will pay you an 18 percent commission on all orders you generate for our products. Please forward a copy of these orders to Steve, who will arrange to have the commission credited to your account. ↓2

3. We very much appreciate your offer to give us three hours at your weeklong sales meeting next month to present our products to your field staff. We'll be there. ↓2

4. We have agreed to give this new arrangement a six-month test to see (a) how much additional sales revenue you and your people can produce with our product and (b) what effect, if any, this special marketing effort will have on your sales of other products. At the end of the test period, we will analyse the results and decide whether to continue the arrangement, modify it in some way, or abandon it altogether. ↓2

I don't think we'll be abandoning it, Bernie. In fact, I feel quite confident that this new arrangement is going to produce significant gains in sales and profits for both of us. I look forward to working with you to make it all happen. ↓2

imm

h:\marketing\okelly memo 040704

---

different size or style of font. An initial capital format, in which only the first letter is a capital letter (**Subject:**), may be used provided that another highlighted feature such as bold is applied with it.

- Follow each guide word with a colon.
- Double space between each element in the heading.

NOTE: Some writers do not include the word *Memo* or any of its variations in the title of the memorandum heading. In this case the first guide words include the words *MEMO TO:*. (See the illustration on page 383.)

e. Set a tab so that the entries following the guide words will all block at the left and will clear the longest guide word by a minimum of 2 spaces.

f. After the guide words *TO:* (or *MEMO TO:*) and *FROM:*, the names of the addressee and the writer are usually given without personal titles *(Mr., Miss, Mrs., Ms.)*. When you are doing a memo to someone within your immediate unit, the use of initials or simply a first name may suffice. In short, the way you treat these names will depend on the relative formality or informality of the occasion.

John A. Mancuso   **OR**   JAM   **OR**   Jack

g. If you want to provide additional information (such as a department name or title, a phone number, or a fax number), you can add the appropriate guide words to the heading of the memo, or you can insert the relevant information after the person's name. For example:

Cynthia Chen, Accounting Manager   **OR**   Cynthia Chen (Ext. 4782)

h. If the memo is being addressed to two or three people, try to fit all the names on the same line.

> **TO:** Hal Parker, Meryl Crawford, Mike Najar

If there are too many names to fit on the same line, then list the names in one or more single-spaced columns alongside *TO:*. Leave 1 blank line before the next guide word and fill-in entry.

> TO: Louise Letendre
>   Fred Mendoza
>   Jim Nakamura
>   Ruth O'Hare
>
> FROM: Neil Sundstrom

i. If listing all the addressees in the heading of a memo looks unattractive, key **See Distribution Below** or something similar after the guide word *TO:*. On the third line below the reference initials, the filing notation, or the enclosure notation (whichever comes last), key **Distribution:**. Use an initial capital letter and follow the word with a colon. Add italics, bold, underlining, or any combination of these for emphasis. (**REMEMBER:** Italicize and bold a

(Continued on page 382.)

colon but do not underline it.) Then leave 1 blank line, list by rank or in alphabetical order the names of those who are to receive a copy, and type them blocked at the left margin. (See the illustration on page 383.) If space is tight, arrange the names in two or more columns.

j. If the fill-in after the guide word *Subject:* is long, type it in two or more single-spaced lines of roughly equal length. Align all turnover lines with the start of the first line of the fill-in. (For an illustration, see ¶1353c.)

k. Begin typing the body of the memo on the third line below the last fill-in line in the heading.

NOTE: An interoffice memo ordinarily does not require a salutation, especially if the memo is an impersonal announcement being sent to a number of people or the staff at large. (See, for example, the illustration on page 383.) However, when a memo is directed to one person, some writers use a salutation—such as *Dear Andy:* or *Andy:* alone—to keep the memo from seeming cold or impersonal. (If a salutation is used, begin typing the body of the memo on the second line below.)

l. Use single spacing and either block the paragraphs or indent the first line of each paragraph 0.5 inch. Leave 1 blank line between paragraphs.

NOTE: If a numbered list appears within the body of a memo, the numbered items may be separated by 1 blank line for a more open look (as in the illustration on page 380). If you use the numbered list feature of your word processing program and accept all the defaults, the list will be typed single-spaced.

m. Although memos do not require a signature line, some writers prefer to end their memos in this way. If this is the case, type the writer's name or initials on the *second* line below the last line of the message as shown on page 383. If the writer plans to insert a handwritten signature or initials above the signature line, type the signature line on the *fourth* line below to allow room for the handwriting. If the writer simply inserts handwritten initials next to the typed name in the heading (as in the illustration on page 380), omit the signature line altogether.

NOTE: The position of the signature line may vary. A common placement is at the centre tab position, but it may also be placed at the left margin.

n. Key the reference initials at the left margin on the second line below the end of the message or the writer's typed name or initials, whichever comes last. (See ¶¶1370–1372.)

o. Key an enclosure notation (if needed) on the line below the reference initials. Begin at the left margin. (See ¶1373.)

p. If a copy notation is needed and is not included in the heading, key it on the line below the enclosure notation or the reference initials, whichever comes last. Use the same style for the copy notation as in a letter. (See ¶¶1376–1380.) If the addressee of the memo is not to know that a copy of the memo is being sent to other persons, use a blind copy notation. (See ¶1378.)

13

2 inches

MEMO TO: See Distribution Below ↓2

FROM: Stanley W. Venner (Ext. 3835)

DATE: May 10, 2004

SUBJECT: Car Rentals ↓3

We have just been informed that car rental rates will be increased by $1 to $2 a day effective July 1. A copy of the letter from Rentz is enclosed for your information. ↓2

This daily rate increase can be more than offset if you refill the gasoline tank before returning your rental car to the local agency. According to our latest information, the car rental companies are charging an average of 32 percent more per litre than gas stations in the same area. Therefore, you can help us achieve substantial savings and keep expenses down by remembering to fill the gas tank before returning your rental car. ↓2

SWV ↓2

jmb
Enclosure ↓2

h:\miscellaneous\car rentals 051004 ↓3

Distribution: ↓2

G. Bonard
D. Catlin
S. Folger
✓ V. Jellinek
E. Laliberte
P. Legrande
T. Pacheco
F. Sullivan
J. Trotter
W. Zysk

q. Key a file name or document ID notation as a footer or a double space below the reference initials, the enclosure notation, or the copy notation, whichever is last. (See ¶1382 and the illustrations on page 380 and above.)

r. If the message in the memo is of a confidential nature, key the word *CONFIDENTIAL* in all-capital letters, using bold, shaded background, different font style or size, or different horizontal placement on the line. (The reason

(Continued on page 384.)

for this highlighting is to draw to the attention of a reader who inadvertently receives the memo that the memo should not be read any further.)

CONFIDENTIAL (bold)
C O N F I D E N T I A L (spread—one space between each letter)
CONFIDENTIAL (shading)

s. If the memo continues beyond the first page, key a continuation heading on a fresh sheet of paper. (Use the same style as shown in ¶1385 for a letter.) Continue typing the message on the third line below the last line of the continuation-page heading. (See ¶1386 for additional details on continuing the message from one page to another.)

SOCIAL-BUSINESS CORRESPONDENCE

1396 The term *social-business correspondence* applies to the following types of letters:

a. Executive correspondence addressed to high-level executives, officials, and dignitaries. (Unlike ordinary business correspondence—which deals with sales, production, finance, advertising, and other routine commercial matters—these letters deal with such topics as corporate policy and issues of social responsibility, and they are written in a more formal style.)

b. Letters expressing praise, concern, or condolence to someone within or outside the organization. (The occasion that prompts the letter could be exceptional performance on the job or in the community, an employment anniversary, the death or serious illness of a family member, or an upcoming retirement. Such letters may be formal or informal, depending on the relationship between the writer and the person addressed.)

c. Letters to business associates within or outside the company on purely social matters.

1397 Social-business correspondence differs from ordinary business correspondence in several ways:

a. The inside address is placed at the bottom of the letter, aligned at the left margin, and keyed on the fourth to sixth line below the writer's signature or title (whichever comes last). The inside address would be typed without abbreviations for the street address and province, and a comma would be placed after the city name and before the name of the province.

b. The salutation is followed by a comma rather than a colon.

c. Reference initials and notations pertaining to enclosures, copies, and mailing are typically omitted. (It would make good sense, however, to put such notations on the file copy in case this information is needed later on.)

d. If the letter requires a *Personal* or *Confidential* notation, place the notation only on the envelope and the file copy, not on the letter itself. (For the appropriate placement of the notation on an envelope, see ¶1389m and the illustration on page 376.)

AVON ADVISORY COUNCIL

197 Avon Street Stratford, Ontario N5A 5N8

September 26, 2004 ↓6

13

Dear Annie, ↓2

You and I have worked together on the Advisory Council for nearly six years, and in that time we have gotten to know each other pretty well. So you'll understand why I was deeply pained to hear that you and your husband have sold your house and are planning to move to the North next month. ↓2

We have not always seen eye to eye (I still think you were dead wrong to vote against the parking lot expansion), but there is no one who has given as much thought and imagination and caring service to this town as you have. ↓2

All of us on the Advisory Council are going to miss you very much, both as a forceful participant and as a warm and generous friend, but we wish you and George the best of luck as you make new lives for yourselves. We envy your new neighbours, for they will be the beneficiaries of what we in Stratford have so long enjoyed—your vital presence. ↓2

We won't forget you, Annie. ↓2

Sincerely, ↓4

Harlan

Harlan W. Estabrook
Chairman ↓6

Mrs. Anne G. Wheatley
14 Avondale Avenue
Stratford, Ontario
N5A 6M4

e. Social-business correspondence also differs by being *more* formal or *less* formal than ordinary business correspondence. For example, correspondence to high-level officials and dignitaries is customarily more formal. In such cases use the word style for numbers (see ¶¶404–406) and one of the special salutations listed in Section 18. However, in letters to business associates who are

(Continued on page 386.)

also close friends, the salutation and the complimentary closing may be very informal, and the writer's printed signature and title—and even the inside address—may be omitted. Moreover, when such letters are purely personal in nature, the writer may use plain stationery and omit the return address.

LABELS

1398 If you are using the label feature of a word processing program, you can quickly prepare a wide variety of labels (for example, mailing labels, file folder labels, and cassette labels) by following these guidelines:

a. Use commercially prepared labels (packaged in rolls and sheets) that have been specifically designed for the purpose you have in mind and that are compatible with your printer.

b. Most software programs provide a menu of label types and sizes. When you select the type and size you want to use, the program automatically sets up the label windows. All you need to do is type the necessary information in each window (as illustrated on page 387).

NOTE: You can also create your own specifications for a special type of label. See your software user's manual for the procedures to follow.

c. Before you begin to key text in each label window, consider the maximum number of characters you can fit on one line and the number of lines you can fit on one label. For example, if you are preparing mailing labels, you may very well find that some mailing addresses you formatted for an inside address are too wide to fit on the labels you are planning to use. In such cases use the all-cap style designed by Canada Post. The all-cap style, with its heavy reliance on abbreviations, was specifically created to take such limitations into account. (See ¶¶1389, 1390, and the illustration on page 387.)

d. When applying a label to a No. 10 envelope or a smaller envelope, follow the placement guidelines provided in ¶1389k. (For an illustration showing the correct placement of a mailing label on a No. 10 envelope, see page 377.) On envelopes larger than No. 10, position the label so that it appears visually centred horizontally and vertically.

Screen Dump (Capture) Showing Label Feature of Word

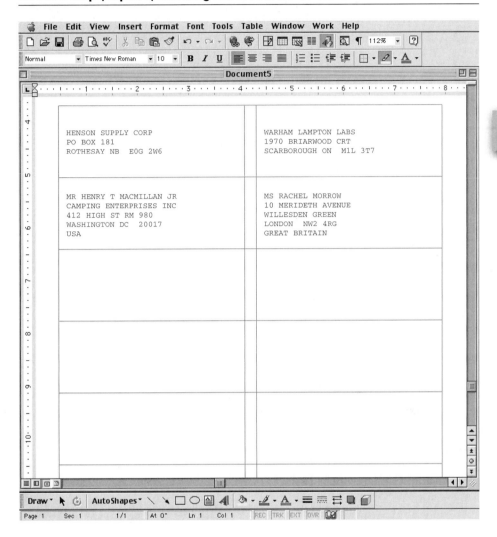

 See the Online Learning Centre at www.mcgrawhill.ca/college/gregg for related weblinks.

SECTION FOURTEEN

Reports and Manuscripts

MANUSCRIPTS (¶¶1432–1437)

Preparing Manuscript for an Article (¶¶1432–1433)
Preparing Manuscript for a Book (¶¶1434–1435)
Precautions for All Manuscripts (¶¶1436–1437)

☞ *See Section 17 for Outlines.*

REPORTS

Reports serve all kinds of purposes. Some simply communicate information—such as monthly sales figures or survey results—without any attempt to analyse or interpret the data. Others offer extensive analyses and make detailed recommendations for further action. As a result, reports come in all sizes and shapes. Some are done informally as memos or letters (depending on whether they are to be distributed inside or outside the organization). Some consist simply of fill-ins on printed or computer-generated forms. Many, however, are done in a more formal style. As you might expect, there is a wide variation to be found in what is considered acceptable—from one authority to another and from one organization to another. Regardless of which guidelines you follow, be prepared to modify them to fit a specific situation.

14

"Contemporary" Report Template Provided by Microsoft Word for Windows

FilmWatch Division Marketing Plan

Trey's Best Opportunity to Dominate Market Research for the Film Industry

How To Use This Report Template

Change the information on the cover page to contain the information you would like. For the body of your report, use styles such as Heading 1-5, Body Text, Block Quotation, List Bullet, and List Number from the Styles box on the Formatting toolbar.

How To Modify This Report

To create your own version of this template, choose File New and select this template. Be sure to indicate "template" as the document type in the bottom right corner.

Using a Template

1401 Word processing software may provide templates that you can use as is or modify to suit your preferences. Included with most report templates are a title page, table of contents, body, and some back matter such as an index or appendixes. Features like fonts, margins, and headings are preselected. Changes can be made by following the instructions provided with the templates themselves.

If you do not wish to use one of the report templates provided by your software, you can always create your own format. This section provides format guidelines for formal and informal reports. The following models show how the first page of an informal report might appear if executed according to these guidelines.

14

2 inches

NOTEBOOK COMPUTERS FOR THE FIELD SALES STAFF ↓2

A Preliminary Assessment ↓2

By Roger Khartoum ↓2

November 14, 2004 ↓3

0.25 to
0.5 inch
———→ In mid-October the Sales Managers Committee asked me to evaluate notebook ↓2

1 inch
←———→ computers now on the market. Here are my initial findings. ↓2 or 3   1 inch
←———→

SELECTION CRITERIA ↓2

Whatever models we select must meet the following specifications.

Processor. If we want to use an IBM-compatible notebook computer, it must

↓2 or 3
MODELS TO BE CONSIDERED ↓2

In identifying models that meet the foregoing criteria, we need to remember

that the market changes rapidly. Some of the models that I looked at only a month ago

have now been discontinued, and newer models—with added bells and whistles—have

1   1 inch

NOTE: In the model on page 390, boldface is used for all four lines in the heading and for side headings. To create a more open look, 2 blank lines have been inserted (a) between the heading and the text and (b) above the side headings. The next model shows the same report in a single-spaced format, which is commonly used to save space. (See ¶1425a.)

NOTEBOOK COMPUTERS FOR THE FIELD SALES STAFF ↓2

A Preliminary Assessment ↓2

By Roger Khartoum ↓2

November 14, 2004 ↓2

0.25 to
0.5 inch
⟶   In mid-October the Sales Managers Committee asked me to evaluate notebook ⟵   1 inch
1 inch   computers now on the market in light of the need to improve the productivity of our
⟵⟶   field sales staff. Here are my initial findings. ↓2

SELECTION CRITERIA ↓2

I propose the following criteria for determining which models we should evaluate before we decide which one to adopt.

Processor. The notebook computer we now use is much too slow. The models we consider must have a processor with a minimum processing speed of 1.5 gigahertz.

Memory. Since all the software is Windows-based, these models should

---

Choosing a Format

1402 If you are preparing a report at the request of someone else, always try to get some guidelines from that person on such matters as format, length, amount of detail desired, and distribution. Check the files for copies of similar reports done in the past. If guidelines or models are not provided or if you are doing the report on your own initiative, consider the following factors in choosing a format.

a. *For whom are you writing the report?* If intended for your supervisor or a colleague on staff, the report could be done simply as a memo. If intended for top management or the board of directors, the report will often require a more formal approach. By the same token, an academic term paper will require a simpler format than a thesis for an advanced degree.

b. *What outcome do you hope to achieve?* If you are merely providing information without attempting to win someone over to your point of view, the simplest and clearest presentation of the information will suffice. If you are trying to persuade the reader to adopt your viewpoint and accept your recommendations, you may need to make a detailed argument and devise a more complex structure for your report.

(Continued on page 392.)

c. *What is the existing mind-set of your reader?* You may need to develop a number of chapters, grouped by part. If you need to demonstrate that your argument is supported by much detailed research, you may have to quote from published sources and provide an elaborate set of data in the form of tables and charts. If you know that your intended reader already supports your argument or simply wants your judgment on a certain matter, a shorter and simpler document will usually suffice.

Parts of a Formal Report

1403 A *formal* report typically has three parts: front matter, body, and back matter. Each of these parts, in turn, typically contains some (if not all) of the following elements in the sequence indicated.

a. Front Matter

TITLE PAGE	*In a business report:* gives the full title, the subtitle (if any), the writer's name, title, and department, and the date of submission; may also indicate for whom the report was written. *In an academic report:* gives the name of the writer, the instructor, and the course, along with the date of submission. (See ¶1413.)
LETTER OR MEMO OF TRANSMITTAL	May be done as a letter (for distribution outside the company) or as a memo (for inside distribution); may be clipped to the front of the report (or to the binder in which the report is inserted); may be inserted in the report itself as the page preceding the title page. (See ¶1414.)
TABLE OF CONTENTS	A list of all chapters (by number and title), along with the opening page number of each chapter. If chapters are grouped by part, the titles of the parts also appear in the table of contents. Sometimes main headings within the chapters are also given under each chapter title. (See ¶¶1415–1416.)
LISTS OF TABLES AND ILLUSTRATIONS	Separate lists of tables and illustrations are included if they are numerous and likely to be frequently referred to by the reader. (See ¶¶1417–1418.)
FOREWORD	Written by someone other than the author of the report. May explain who commissioned the report, the reasons for doing so, and the qualifications of the writer to prepare the report. May also offer an evaluation of the report, and may ask those who receive copies of the report to give their assessment or take some other action after they have read the report. (See ¶1419.)
PREFACE	Written by the author of the report. Indicates for whom the report is written, the objectives and the scope of the report, and the methods used to assemble the material in the report. Acknowledgments of help received on the report are usually included here (placed at the end), but if special emphasis is desired, the acknowledgments can be treated as a separate element of the front matter, immediately following the preface. (See ¶1419.)

14

SUMMARY	Preferably limited to a one-page document (two pages at most); designed to save the reader's time by presenting conclusions and recommendations right at the outset of the report. If a preface is not provided, the summary also includes some of the material that would have gone there. (See ¶1420.)

b. Body

INTRODUCTION	Sets forth (in greater detail than the preface) the objectives, the scope, and the methods, along with any other relevant background information. In a report with several chapters, the introduction may precede the first chapter of the text or be labelled as Chapter 1. (See ¶1422.)
MAIN DISCUSSION	Sets forth all the pertinent data, evidence, analyses, and interpretations needed to fulfil the purpose of the report. May consist of one long chapter that opens with an introduction and closes with conclusions and recommendations. May consist of several chapters; these may be grouped into *parts*, with a part-title page inserted to introduce each sequence of chapters. May use different levels of headings throughout the text to indicate what the discussion covers and how it is organized. (See ¶¶1423–1427.)
CONCLUSIONS	Summarizes the key points and the recommendations that the writer hopes the reader will be persuaded to accept. In a report with several chapters, this material represents the final chapter or the final part.

c. Back Matter

APPENDIXES	A collection of tables, charts, or other data too specific or too lengthy to be included in the body of the report but provided here as supporting detail for the interested reader. (See ¶1429.)
ENDNOTES	A collection—all in one place at the end of the report—of what would otherwise appear as footnotes at the bottom of various pages in the report. (See ¶¶1501–1502, 1505–1506.)
BIBLIOGRAPHY	A list of all sources (1) that were consulted in the preparation of the report and (2) from which material was derived or directly quoted. (See ¶¶1540–1544.)
GLOSSARY	A list of terms (with definitions) that may not be readily understood when encountered in the body of the report. (See ¶1431.) May be treated as an appendix.

Parts of an Informal Report

1404 a. An *informal* report has no front matter. The information that would go on a separate title page appears at the top of the first page and is immediately followed by the body of the report. (See ¶¶1410–1412 for format guidelines.)

(Continued on page 394.)

b. An informal report typically contains no back matter except possibly a list of *endnotes* (in place of separate footnotes throughout the body of the report) and a *bibliography*. (See ¶1505 for an illustration of endnotes and ¶1543 for an illustration of a bibliography.) Tables that cannot be easily incorporated in the body of the informal report may also be placed in an appendix in the back matter.

Margins

1405 SIDE MARGINS

a. Unbound Reports. If a report is to remain unbound or will simply be stapled in the upper left corner, use 1-inch side margins. (If the overall length of the report is not a problem, you can increase the side margins equally to give the report a more open look. See ¶1305b for guidelines on increasing margins.)

b. Bound Reports. Use a 1.5-inch left margin and a 1-inch right margin. (The extra half inch at the left will provide space for the binding.)

1406 TOP AND BOTTOM MARGINS OF OPENING PAGES

The following guidelines apply to (1) the first page of each chapter, (2) the first page of each distinct element in the front matter and back matter, and (3) the first page of an informal report that consists of only one chapter (without any separate title page or other front matter). (See the illustration on page 390.)

a. On these opening pages, leave a top margin of 2 inches and a bottom margin of 1 inch. **EXCEPTION:** Title pages and part-title pages may be shown

2 inches

CHAPTER 2. ADMINISTRATIVE SERVICES ↓2 or 3

As part of an ongoing, broad-based investigation into ways of increasing ↓2

productivity and improving operating efficiency, the managers of all domestic

the-art desktop publishing software. Furthermore, it will require hiring a number

14

as centred on the page by using the software page command to centre vertically.

b. Opening pages do not require a page number. If showing a page is preferred, use the page numbering feature of the software to place the *page number only* at the bottom centre or the bottom right of the page.

NOTE: Additional pages most often show page numbers at the top of the page. (See ¶1407b.)

c. Ordinarily, nothing is keyed in the space that represents the top margin. However, in informal academic reports, certain information is often keyed in the upper right corner. (See ¶1412.)

1407 TOP AND BOTTOM MARGINS OF OTHER PAGES

a. The top and bottom margins should be set at 1 inch.

b. For pages in the *body* and *back matter* of a report, use the page numbering feature of your word processing program and position the page number at the top centre or top right position. The word *Page* may also be used in the top right position only. Leave 1 or 2 blank lines before continuing the text. If you wish to provide additional information along with the page number (for example, the report or chapter title), use the header feature of your software rather than the page numbering feature. (See ¶1411c.)

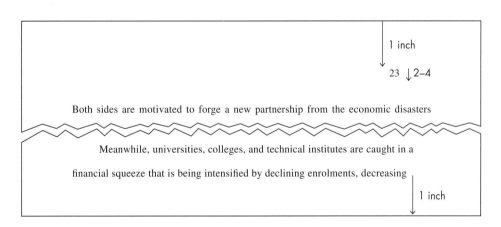

c. For pages in the *front matter* of a report, use the page numbering feature of your software to centre the page number at the bottom of the page. (See ¶1421.) Some programs include one blank line before the page number. If two blank lines are preferred before the page number line, make the necessary adjustments. If you wish to provide additional information along with the page number, use the footer feature of your software package.

(Continued on page 396.)

1 inch

Part Three will explore alternative recommendations for improving working

Part Six will analyse the advantages and disadvantages of constructing a

new, fully-automated facility for the manufacturing division as opposed to an

vii

14

1408 HANDLING PAGE BREAKS

Your word processing software can help you avoid most page-ending problems as outlined in *a–d*. There are, however, page-ending situations in which you must use your own judgment as outlined in *e* and *f*.

a. The *page numbering feature* ensures that the bottom margin will always be 1 inch (or whatever margin you have selected). When your text reaches the bottom margin, the computer automatically inserts a page break, called a *soft page break*, to begin a new page (even if part of a sentence is carried to the top of the next page). Because a *soft page break* is defined by the computer program, it cannot be adjusted. If you do not like what the computer has done, you may insert a *hard page break*. (See ¶1408b.)

   NOTE: The *preview* feature permits you to see an entire page on the screen prior to printing so that you can tell whether adjustments will be necessary. See ¶1408e–f below for page-ending situations that may require adjustments.

b. A *hard page break* permits you to end a page wherever you want and ensures that any copy that follows will appear at the top of the next page.

c. To prevent situations where a single line of a paragraph is left at the bottom of a page or is carried over to the top of a new page, use the *widow/orphan* feature of your software. This will ensure that a minimum of two lines of a paragraph will stay together at a page ending or a page beginning. The widow/orphan feature should automatically be turned on for any document that will be more than one page. In some software programs, it is on by default.

d. The *block protect* feature (or *keep lines together* or *keep with next*) ensures that a designated block of copy (such as a table, an enumerated list, or selected lines of text) will not be divided at the bottom of a page but will, if necessary, be carried over intact to the top of the next page. This feature should also be used to keep a heading with at least two lines of text together on the same page.

NOTE: If a list of items (see ¶1425d–f) has to be divided at the bottom of the page, try to **divide between items** (not within an item). Moreover, try to leave at least two items at the bottom of one page and carry over at least two items to the top of the next. If you do need to divide *within* an item, leave at least two lines at the bottom of one page and carry over at least two lines to the next.

e. Do not divide a quoted extract (see ¶1425d) unless you can leave at least two lines at the bottom of one page and carry over at least two lines to the top of the next page. Use the *widow/orphan* feature.

f. If it is not possible to start keying a table at the desired point of reference and have it all fit on the same page, then insert a parenthetical note at the appropriate point in the text (referring the reader to the next page) and continue with the text to the bottom of the page. At the top of the next page, key the complete table, leave 1 to 3 blank lines, and resume keying the text. (See Section 16 for guidelines on the typing of tables.)

NOTE: If a table is so long that it will not fit on one page even when keyed single-spaced, then look for a sensible division point in the body of the table and end the first page there. At the top of the next page, repeat the complete title of the table (with *Continued* or *Cont.* inserted in parentheses at the end); also repeat any column headings before continuing with the rest of the table. If there is any possibility that a reader could mistake the first part of the divided table as the complete table, key a continuation line (in parentheses or brackets) at the point where the table breaks off. (See ¶1636 for details.)

☞ *For a formal definition of terms such as* block protect, keep with next, *and* widow/orphan protection, *see Section 20.*

1409 SHORTENING A LONG REPORT

When the cost of photocopying and distributing a large number of copies of a long report becomes prohibitively expensive, consider the following devices for reducing the number of pages without having to cut the copy. (Note that these devices will also reduce the readability and the attractiveness of the report, so use them only in extreme circumstances.)

a. Use a smaller font size or choose a different font that yields more characters to an inch.

b. Reduce the standard top margin for all opening pages from 2 inches to 1.5 inches. (See ¶1406.)

c. Reduce side margins, top and bottom margins, or a combination of both for all other pages from 1 inch to as small as 0.5 inch.

NOTE: It may not be possible to reduce the top or bottom margin if the header, footer, or page numbering feature is placed in the margin area.

d. Single space the report (but always leave 1 blank line between paragraphs).

(Continued on page 398.)

e. If the report has only one level of heading, use paragraph headings rather than side headings. (See ¶1426.)

f. Whenever the guidelines call for 2 blank lines between elements, use only 1.5 blank lines. Wherever 1 blank line is called for, reduce it to half a line.

Informal Business Reports

These guidelines apply to business reports that consist of only one chapter and have no separate title page or other front matter.

1410 If the first page is keyed on a *blank sheet of paper* (as in the illustration below):

a. Leave a top margin of 2 inches.

b. Use single spacing while executing the title, the subtitle, the writer's name, and the date.

c. Key the title of the report centred in all-capital letters. If a subtitle is used, key it centred in capital and small letters on the second line below the main title. (If the title or subtitle is long, divide it into sensible phrases and arrange them on two or more single-spaced lines.)

NOTE: Use boldface for the title and subtitle (and for the writer's name and the date as well). The by-line and the date are optional and may be omitted.

d. If used, type *By* and the writer's name centred in capital and small letters on the second line below the title and subtitle.

e. If used, type the date on which the report is to be submitted on the second line, centred, below the writer's name.

NOTE: Additional details that appear on a title page (such as the writer's title and affiliation or the name and affiliation of the person or group for whom the report has been prepared) are omitted when the title starts on

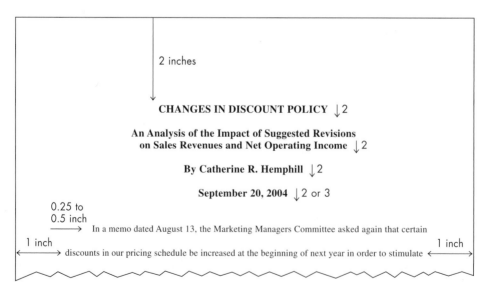

2 inches

CHANGES IN DISCOUNT POLICY ↓2

**An Analysis of the Impact of Suggested Revisions
on Sales Revenues and Net Operating Income** ↓2

By Catherine R. Hemphill ↓2

September 20, 2004 ↓2 or 3

0.25 to
0.5 inch
⟶ In a memo dated August 13, the Marketing Managers Committee asked again that certain

1 inch
⟶ discounts in our pricing schedule be increased at the beginning of next year in order to stimulate

1 inch

the same page as the body. If these elements need to be provided, you will have to prepare a separate title page. (See ¶1413.)

f. On the second or third line below the date, start the body of the report. (See ¶¶1425–1427.) At this point switch to double spacing.

NOTE: On the first page of an informal business report, a page number is not required. If the writer wishes to include a page number, it should be centred at the bottom of the page. Use the page numbering or footer feature of the software. (See ¶1408.)

g. If the report requires more than one page, use the page numbering feature to automatically insert the page number at the top right margin of each continuation page. Leave 1 or 2 blank lines below the page number, and resume the text on the following line. (See also ¶1427g.)

---

1 inch ↓

Page 2 ↓2 or 3

we are expected to produce sales increases of over 20 percent in the first quarter of next year, 18 ↓2

percent in the second quarter, 15 percent in the third quarter, and 20 percent in the fourth quarter.

---

h. If the report requires one or more elements of back matter—for example, endnotes or a bibliography—follow the style established for a formal report. (See ¶¶1501–1502, 1505–1506, 1540–1544.)

1411 If the first page of a report is prepared in *memo form*:

a. Give the report title (and subtitle, if any) as the *subject* of the memo. Supply all the other elements called for in the heading of the memo in the usual way. (See ¶¶1394–1395.)

MEMORANDUM

TO: Executive Committee ↓2

FROM: Catherine R. Hemphill ↓2

DATE: September 20, 2004 ↓2

SUBJECT: Changes in Discount Policy—An Analysis
of the Impact of Suggested Revisions on
Sales Revenues and Net Operating Income ↓2 or 3

In a memo dated August 13, the Marketing Managers Committee asked again that certain

---

(Continued on page 400.)

b. Begin keying the body of the report on the second or third line below the last fill-in line in the heading. (See ¶¶1425–1427.)

c. If the report requires more than one page, use a blank sheet of paper for each continuation page. Key the same kind of continuation heading called for in any long memo. (See also ¶1395s.) Leave 1 or 2 blank lines and resume the text on the following line.

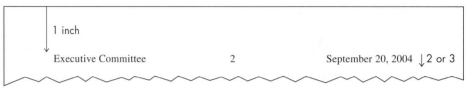

OR:

Informal Academic Reports

1412 An academic report that consists of only one chapter and has no separate title page or other front matter is keyed like an informal business report (see ¶¶1410–1411) except for the opening of the first page.

a. Leave a default top margin of 1 inch. Type the following information on four separate lines, single-spaced, in the upper left or right corner of the first page: the writer's name, the instructor's name, the course title, and the date. If placed in the right corner, all lines should align at the left with the longest line ending at the right margin.

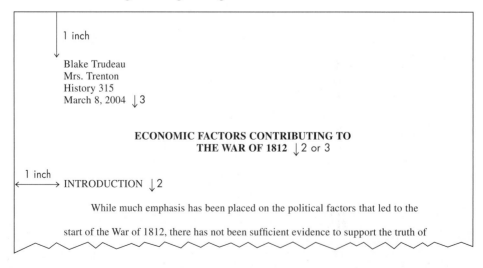

b. On the third line below the date, key the title and subtitle (if any) just as in an informal business report. (See ¶1410b.)

c. Start typing the body of the report on the second or third line below the preceding copy (the title or subtitle). At this point switch to double-spacing for the body text.

The Front Matter of Formal Reports

The following guidelines deal with the preparation of a title page, a letter or memo of transmittal, a table of contents, a list of tables, a list of illustrations, a preface or foreword, and a summary. For a formal report, only a separate title page is essential; all the other elements are optional.

1413 TITLE PAGE

There is no one correct arrangement for the elements on a title page.

- Horizontally centre each line of text leaving similar line spacing between sections.
- Double space between different parts of the same element.
- Use the centre page command to centre text vertically on the page.
  REMEMBER: Be careful not to have extra hard returns before the first line of text and after the last line of text.
- Enhance the title page with a combination of bold, italics, or a maximum of 2 different font sizes.

See the illustrations that follow for acceptable formats.

a. **Three-Block Arrangement.** Group the material into three blocks of type, and leave equal space above and below the middle block. Position the material as a whole so that it appears centred horizontally and vertically on the page. (See the illustration on page 402.)

b. **Two-Block Arrangement.** Group the material into two blocks of type, and leave at least 5 blank lines between blocks. Centre the material as a whole horizontally and vertically on the page. (See the illustration on page 402.)

NOTE: The two-block arrangement works well when the title page does not attempt to show the name of the person or group to whom the report is being submitted.

c. **Margins.** Regardless of which arrangement you use, each line should be short and blocked as attractively as possible.

d. **Title.** Key the title in all-capital letters, using boldface. If the title is long, type it on two or more lines, single-spaced; try to divide the title into meaningful phrases.

e. **Subtitle.** Key the subtitle, if any, in capital and small letters, using boldface. If the subtitle requires more than one line, type it single-spaced. Leave 1 blank line between the main title and the subtitle.

(Continued on page 402.)

3-Block (Business Report Style)

TITLE TITLE TITLE
TITLE TITLE ↓2

Subtitle Subtitle
Subtitle ↓6 to 12

Prepared by ↓2

Writer's Name
Writer's Title
Writer's Department ↓6 to 12

Submitted to ↓2

Name of Individual or Group
Organizational Affiliation ↓2

Date

2-Block (Academic Report Style)

TITLE TITLE TITLE
TITLE TITLE ↓2

Subtitle Subtitle
Subtitle ↓6 to 12

Submitted by
Student's Name ↓2

Instructor's Name
Course Title ↓2

Date

f. **Writer's Identification.** Leave 1 to 2 inches before keying the writer's identification block. The writer's name may be preceded by the word *By* on the same line or by a phrase such as *Prepared by* or *Submitted by* (or simply *By*) keyed 2 lines above. If appropriate, the writer's name may be followed by a title on the next line and by an organizational affiliation on the following line.

↓ 6 to 12

By Doris Eberle
Manager, Telemarketing
Circulation Department

↓ 6 to 12

Prepared by ↓2

Van Nguyen
Acting Director
Marketing Research Unit

g. **Reader's Identification.** It is customary (but not essential) to identify the individual or group for whom the report has been prepared. Leave 1 to 2 inches before keying *Submitted to* or *Prepared for* or a similar phrase. Then on the second line below, key the name of the individual or the group. On succeeding lines, supply a title, an organizational affiliation, or both.

```
          6 to 12                           6 to 12
      Submitted to ↓2                   Prepared for ↓2

      Robert G. Paterno              The Finance Committee
      General Manager                Davenport, Pierson,
      Corporate Graphic Arts            and Associates
```

NOTE: As an alternative, provide the reader's identification in the form of a subtitle.

```
        AN ANALYSIS OF COMPUTERIZED GRAPHICS EQUIPMENT ↓2

                A Report to Robert G. Paterno
             General Manager, Corporate Graphic Arts
```

h. Date. Supply the date (month, day, and year) on which the report is being submitted. Key it on the second line below the reader's identification block (or, if none is given, on the second line below the writer's identification). (See the illustrations on page 402.)

i. Graphic Elements. You can use special display type and add an organizational logo or some other graphic element to enhance the appearance of a title page.

1414 LETTER OR MEMO OF TRANSMITTAL

a. A formal report is often accompanied by a letter or memo of transmittal. If you are sending the report to people outside the company, use the letter format (see the illustration on page 404); if you are sending the report only to people within the company, use a memo.

b. The message typically covers the following points: (1) a brief description of what is being transmitted; (2) a brief reference to the circumstances that prompted the report; (3) if necessary, a brief indication of why the report is being sent to the addressee; and (4) a statement about what action the addressee is expected to take. (See the illustration on page 404.)

c. The letter or memo of transmittal is typically clipped to the front of the report. If the report is in a binder, the transmittal document may be clipped to the front of the binder or inserted in the binder preceding the title page.

1415 TABLE OF CONTENTS

Most word processing software has a feature that allows the creation of a table of contents. Users scroll through the text and code (according to the level of subordination) every part title, chapter title, main heading, and subheading that should appear in the table of contents. If any titles or headings are subsequently added, deleted, or changed, the table of contents will reflect these changes.

14

ATLANTIC ENTERPRISES INCORPORATED

5280 Duke Street / Halifax, Nova Scotia / B3J 1P4 / 902-555-5166 Fax: 902-555-5167

↓2 inches from top of page or ↓3

February 5, 2005 ↓4 to 6

Mr. Frank M. Eggleston
Blockhouse Hill Road
Lunenburg, NS B0J 2C0 ↓2

Dear Frank: ↓2

1 inch →   Enclosed is a copy of the report, "Acquisition of Desktop Publishing Equipment,"   ← 1 inch
which I just completed for George Pendergast. Because of your expertise in this
area, George has suggested that I send you the report with the hope that you
might offer your comments and suggestions. ↓2

Because we need to make a decision by April 1 on what equipment to buy, it
would help us greatly if we could hear from you by March 15. I know that given
your busy schedule, you may not be able to get back to us in writing that quickly.
If you would let George and me take you to lunch, we could talk about the report
then and spare you the need to put your thoughts in writing. ↓2

I'll call you early next week so that we can decide what would be the best way to
proceed. ↓2

Sincerely, ↓4 to 6

Reta Nishikawa

Reta Nishikawa
Senior Systems Analyst
Office Systems Department ↓2

ctl
Enclosure ↓2

c:\wpwin\wpdocs\atlantic\transltr.wpd

1416 If you do not like the default style for a table of contents that is provided by
your software, you may be able to modify that style or select a different style. If
you prefer to create your own format, the following guidelines may be helpful.

a. Type the table of contents on a new page. (See the illustration on page 405.)

b. Start on line 2 inches. Type *CONTENTS* or *TABLE OF CONTENTS* in all-capital letters centred on the line. Bold the title to make it stand out.

c. On the second or third line below, begin keying the table of contents double-spaced. Use the same side and bottom margins as for the text pages in
the body of the report. (See ¶¶1405–1408.)

2 inches

CONTENTS ↓2 or 3

iii

d. In keying the body of the table of contents, list every separate element that *follows* the table of contents in sequence—whether in the front matter, the body of the report, or the back matter. In the illustration above, note the following aspects of the format:

- Individual entries pertaining to *front matter* and *back matter* begin at the left margin with the title keyed in capital and small letters or in all-capital letters. Set a right leader tab to include a line of leaders and to align the page number (Roman for front matter and Arabic for back matter) at the right margin. Leave 1 or 2 blank lines *after* the front matter entries and 1 or 2 blank lines *before* the back matter entries.

(Continued on page 406.)

- Centre individual entries pertaining to *part titles* in all-capital letters. The part numbers that precede the titles may be in Arabic or Roman numerals or (for formality) may be spelled out. Leave 1 or 2 blank lines before each part title and 1 blank line after.
- Individual entries pertaining to *chapters* begin with a chapter number (Roman or Arabic), followed by a period, 1 or 2 spaces, and then the chapter title typed in capital and small letters or in all-capital letters. Set a right or decimal tab to align Roman chapter numbers at the right with the longest one positioned as close to the left margin as possible. After keying the chapter text, press the right tab key (as set in the first bulleted item above) to include the leaders before you type the page number. Leave 0 or 1 blank line after each chapter title in the listing.
- Some long titles should be keyed on two lines. Type the turnover or runover line single-spaced and aligned with the first letter of the chapter title in the first line.

e. The *main headings* within each chapter may be included in the table of contents. One acceptable arrangement is to indent each heading 2 or 3 spaces from the start of the chapter title and key it in capital and small letters. Key the list of headings for each chapter as a single-spaced block, with 1 blank line above and below it. Page numbers may be provided with the headings if desired.

1417 LIST OF TABLES OR ILLUSTRATIONS

Your word processing software may have a feature that allows the creation of a list of tables or illustrations and is similar to the feature used to create the table of contents. (See ¶1415 and ¶1416.)

1418 To create your own format, the following guidelines and illustrations may be helpful.

a. Use a new page for each list. Leave a top margin of 2 inches.

b. Centre the heading—*TABLES* (or *LIST OF TABLES*) or *ILLUSTRATIONS* (or *LIST OF ILLUSTRATIONS*)—in all-capital letters. Use boldface to make the title stand out.

c. On the second or third line below the heading, type the first entry in the list. Use the same format as for chapter titles in a table of contents. (See ¶1416.) The tables or the illustrations may be numbered consecutively throughout the report or consecutively within each chapter. The latter technique uses the chapter number as a prefix in the numbering scheme. (See the illustration below.)

2 inches

TABLES ↓2 or 3

1-1. Annual Sales, 2001–2005	6 ↓2
1-2. Projected Annual Sales, 2006–2010	10
1-3. Estimated Market Share, 2006–2010	13
2-1. Marketing Costs as a Percentage of Sales	16

14

1419 PREFACE OR FOREWORD

a. If a preface (written by the author) or a foreword (written by someone else) is to be provided, then on a new page centre the appropriate title boldfaced in all-capital letters 2 inches from the top. Note that the correct spelling is *FOREWORD* (not *FORWARD*).

NOTE: If both a preface and a foreword are to appear in the front matter, the foreword should precede the preface.

b. Leave 1 or 2 blank lines below the heading and begin keying the actual text. Use the same side and bottom margins as for the text pages in the body of the report. (See ¶¶1405–1408.) Also follow the same guidelines for spacing, indentions, and headings as in the body of the report. (See ¶¶1425–1426.)

c. The preface should cover the following points: (1) for whom the report is written, (2) what prompted the writing of the report, (3) what the report aims to accomplish, (4) what the report covers and what it does not try to deal with, (5) how the data and the conclusions were arrived at, and (6) acknowledgments of those individuals and organizations who helped the writer of the report.

NOTE: The acknowledgments may be treated as a separate element in the front matter, following the foreword and the preface (in that sequence if both are given) and using the same format.

d. The foreword typically deals with these topics: (1) who commissioned the report, (2) the reasons for doing so, (3) the writer's qualifications for undertaking the assignment, (4) an assessment of the job that the writer has done, and (5) a call for some follow-up action on the part of those who receive copies of the report.

1420 SUMMARY

    a. If a summary (frequently called an *executive summary*) is to be provided, follow the format guidelines provided for a preface in ¶1419a–b.

    b. Since this element is intended to be a time-saver, keep it short—ideally one page, at most two pages. The summary may be handled as a series of ordinary text paragraphs or as a series of paragraphs typed as items in a list. (See ¶1425e–g.)

1421 NUMBERING FRONT MATTER PAGES

    a. On all pages of front matter except the title page, use the page numbering or footer feature of the software to place the page number in the bottom margin of the document.

    b. Key the page number in small Roman numerals (*ii, iii, iv,* and so on).

    c. Consider the title page as *page i,* even though no number is keyed on that page.

The Body of Formal Reports

1422 INTRODUCTION

    a. If the body of a report contains several chapters and begins with a formal introduction, treat the introduction either as Chapter 1 or as a distinct element preceding Chapter 1.

- If you decide to treat it as Chapter 1, then consider *INTRODUCTION* to be the title of this chapter and handle it as you would any other title on a chapter-opening page. (See ¶1424.)
- If you decide to have the introduction precede Chapter 1, use a new page, leave a 2-inch top margin, and centre in all-capital letters *INTRODUCTION.* Use the boldface feature to make the heading stand out. Leave 2 blank lines before beginning the actual text.
- In either case treat the first page of the introduction as page 1 of the report. (See ¶1427.)

    ☞ *For guidelines on margins, see ¶¶1405–1408.*
    For guidelines on spacing, indentions, and headings, see ¶¶1425–1426.

    b. If a report contains only one chapter and begins with an introductory section, treat the title *INTRODUCTION* as a first-level heading (see ¶1426) and key it on the second or third line below the block of copy (title, etc.) at the top of the page.

1423 PART-TITLE PAGES

    a. If the report contains several chapters organized in parts, insert a separate part-title page directly in front of the chapter that begins each part.

PART 3 ↓2 or 3

STRATEGIES FOR
REGAINING MARKET SHARE

NOTE: If the body of the report begins with a formal introduction (see ¶1422a), then the part-title page for Part 1 should *follow* the introduction. (REASON: The introduction embraces the whole work and not simply Part 1.)

b. Key the word *PART* and the part number on one line. Underneath key the part title on one or more lines as appropriate. Use all-capital letters, boldface, and arrange the copy for maximum display effect. Centre the copy as a whole, horizontally and vertically.

1424 CHAPTER-OPENING PAGES

a. Use a new page for each opening page of a chapter. Leave a 2-inch top margin.

b. Centre and boldface the chapter number and title in all-capital letters.

2 inches

CHAPTER II. THE COMPUTER REVOLUTION ↓2 or 3

c. If the title is long, divide it into sensible phrases and arrange them on two or more single-spaced lines. Put the chapter number on a line by itself, and leave 1 blank line before starting the chapter title.

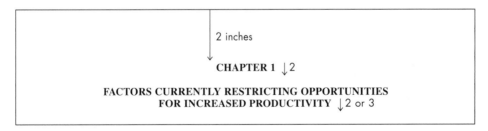

2 inches

CHAPTER 1 ↓2

**FACTORS CURRENTLY RESTRICTING OPPORTUNITIES
FOR INCREASED PRODUCTIVITY** ↓2 or 3

d. Leave 1 or 2 blank lines and begin typing the first line of text copy on the second or third line below the title.

1425 TEXT SPACING AND INDENTIONS

a. Text. Ordinarily, double-space all text matter. However, use single spacing or 1.5-line spacing in business reports when the costs of paper, photocopying, file space, and mailing are important considerations. Many writers

(Continued on page 410.)

include one blank line only before side headings when using this format. (See the illustration on page 391 and ¶1409 for a number of ways to shorten a long report.)

☞ *For guidelines on dividing words and word groups at the ends of lines and between one page and the next, see ¶¶901–920; for guidelines on the use of footnotes, endnotes, or textnotes, see Section 15; for guidelines on whether or not to justify the right margin, see ¶1356b–c.*

b. Drafts. Always double- or triple-space drafts that are to be submitted for editing or evaluation.

c. Paragraphs. Indent text paragraphs 0.25 inch to 0.5 inch. Leave 1 blank line between paragraphs, whether the text is typed in single-, double-, or 1.5-line spacing.

☞ *For guidelines on dividing short paragraphs at the bottom of a page, see ¶¶1408c.*

d. Quoted Material. If a quotation will make four or more lines, treat it as a single-spaced extract, leave 1 blank line above and below the extract, and use the word processing feature that will automatically indent *each side* margin by an additional 0.5 inch (sometimes called *double indent*). If the quoted matter represents the start of a paragraph in the original, indent the first word an additional 0.25 inch to 0.5 inch.

---

1 inch ⟶ need to consider a new phenomenon in the software market. Here is an observation ⟵ 1 inch

from Hal Pryor in a memo dated March 14: ↓2

0.5 inch ⟶ We're competing in an economy where the cost of raw technology is plummeting toward zero. This plunge will drive
0.5 inch ⟶ down prices on software products as well. The only way to survive ⟵ 0.5 inch is to establish a long-term relationship with a customer. ↓2

This is a startling idea and needs to be discussed at some length in our upcoming

session on pricing strategy.

☞ *For another illustration, see page 338.*

e. Items in a List. Key the list single-spaced with 1 blank line above and below the list as a whole. (See ¶107.) Key the list on the full width of the text (as shown in ¶1425g); or for a more attractive format (especially when paragraph indentions are in the text), use the word processing double indent feature to indent the lines 0.5 inch from *each side* margin. (See ¶1425d above and the illustration on page 411.) If any item in the list requires more than one line, leave a blank line after each item in the list.

NOTE: Sometimes a list of one-line items (with no turnovers) is keyed double-spaced to enhance the readability.

☞ *For an example, see the illustration on page 485.*

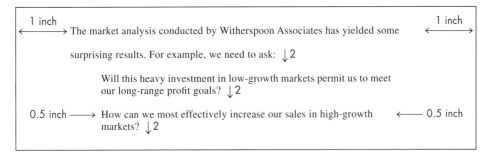

f. **Enumerated Items in a List.** If the items each begin with a number or letter, use the paragraph numbering feature. If formatting is done manually, insert a period after the number and indent 0.25 to 0.5 inch before starting the text that follows. Try to align the numbers on the period. Key the list on the full width of the text or use the double indent feature as described in ¶1425d. If an item requires more than one line, format each line as a hanging indent so turnover lines will align with the first word in the first line of text. (See ¶1425e.) Refer to your software for various ways to set this automatic function.

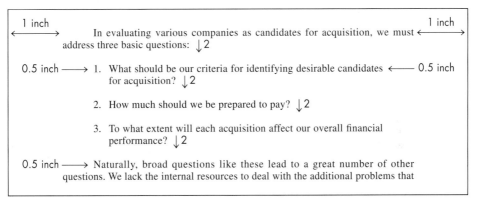

☞ See ¶1357d, note, on the formatting of enumerated items in a list.

g. **Bulleted Items in a List.** Instead of numbers or letters, you can use *bullets*, especially if there is no need to draw attention to a particular order of items. Choose from a variety of styles:

Circles: ○ ●   Triangles: ▷ ▶   Squares: □ ■   Other: > → *

Most word processing software now sets bullets to default at 0.25 inches with text and turnover (runover) lines set to 0.5 inches. If you prefer, reset the bullets to begin at the left margin and reset the text indent to 0.25 inches. (See the illustration on page 412.)

h. **Tables.** The table feature of your software should be used for the most efficient creation of tables. If tables are created manually, they may be keyed with single-, double-, or 1.5-line spacing. Establish one style of spacing for all tables within a given report.

(Continued on page 412.)

```
0.5 inch ──────→ In evaluating various companies as candidates for acquisition, we must
                address three basic questions: ↓2

                • What should be our criteria for identifying desirable candidates for acquisition? ↓2
   1 inch                                                                                    1 inch
←──────→ • How much should we be prepared to pay? ↓2

                • To what extent will each acquisition affect our overall financial per-
                  formance? ↓2

                     Naturally, broad questions like these lead to a great number of other
                questions. We lack the internal resources to deal with the additional problems that
```

☞ *See Section 16 for a full discussion on how to plan and execute tables and for numerous illustrations.*

1426 TEXT HEADINGS

Headings are the key technique for letting readers see at a glance the scope of the writer's discussion and the way in which it is organized. Therefore, make sure that the headings used throughout the report properly reflect the coverage and the structure of the material. It is also essential that the headings be keyed in a way that clearly indicates different levels of importance or subordination.

Here are several techniques for achieving these objectives:

a. Try to limit yourself to three levels of text headings (not counting the chapter title). If you use more than three levels of text headings, it will be difficult for the reader to grasp the typographical distinction between one level and another. Moreover, the use of more than three levels of text headings suggests that you may be trying to cram too much into one chapter. Consider a different organization of the material to solve this problem.

NOTE: Carefully select appropriate typefaces, type sizes, attributes (such as boldface, italics, and so on), and heading style (centred, side, or paragraph headings) that clearly distinguish one level of text heading from another and the headings from the text.

b. Before preparing the final version of the report, make an outline of the heading structure as it then stands and analyse it for:

- *Comprehensiveness.* When the headings are viewed as a whole, do they cover all aspects of the discussion, or are some topics not properly represented?
- *Balance.* Is one part of a chapter loaded with headings while a comparable part has only one or two?
- *Parallel structure.* Are the headings all worded in a similar way, or are some complete sentences and others simply phrases? (See ¶1081.)

On the basis of this analysis, revise the headings as necessary.

NOTE: Using the software outline feature of a word processing program will greatly simplify the process of reviewing and improving the wording of the headings. You can use this feature to generate a complete list of the headings as they currently appear in the report. Any changes in wording that you make in the text will automatically be reflected in a newly generated outline.

c. Headings come in three styles:

- A *centred heading* is one centred on a line by itself, with 1 to 3 blank lines above (see ¶1426g) and 1 blank line below. Use boldface and all-capital letters. If the heading is too long to fit on one line, centre the turnover on the following line. (See ¶1426e–g for illustrations.)

- A *side heading* starts flush with the left margin, on a line by itself. Ordinarily, it should have 2 blank lines above (see ¶1426g for an exception) and 1 blank line below. (See the illustrations in ¶1426d–g.) However, if a side heading comes directly below a centred heading (no intervening text), leave only 1 blank line above the side heading. (See the first illustration in ¶1426e.) Key every side heading in boldface, using all-capital letters or capitals and small letters.

- A *paragraph heading* (also called a *run-in heading*) is one that begins a paragraph and is immediately followed by text matter on the same line. Like all new paragraphs, a paragraph that begins with a run-in heading should be preceded by 1 blank line (whether the text is keyed with single-, double-, or 1.5-line spacing). Indent a paragraph heading 0.25 or 0.5 inch from the left margin. Key it in capital and small letters, using any combination of boldface or italics. The paragraph heading should be followed by a period (unless some other mark of punctuation, such as a question mark, is required). The text then begins 1 to 2 spaces after the mark of punctuation. (See the illustrations in ¶1426e–f.)

☞ *For capitalization in headings, see ¶¶360–361, 363.*

d. In a report that calls for only *one* level of heading, choose a side heading and key it in one of the styles shown below.

xxxxxxxxxxxxxxxxxxxxxxxxxxxxxxxxxxx xxxxxxxxxxxxxx. ↓2 or 3
 	
SIDE HEADING ↓2
 	
   Xxxxxxxxxxxxxxxxxxxxxxxxxxx xxxxxxxxxxxxxxxxxxxxxxxxxxxxxxxxxx
	xxxxxxxxxxxxxxxxxxxxxxxxxxxxxxxxxxx xxxxxxxxxxxxxx. ↓2 or 3
	
	Side Heading ↓2
	
	   Xxxxxxxxxxxxxxxxxxxxxxxxxxx xxxxxxxxxxxxxxxxxxxxxxxxxxxxxxxxxx

(Continued on page 414.)

e. In a report that calls for *two* levels of headings, choose one of the styles shown below.

---

xxxxxxxxxxxxxxxxxxxxxxxxxxxxxxxxxxxx
xxxxxxxxxxxxx. ↓2 or 3

        CENTRED HEADING ↓2

Side Heading ↓2

      Xxxxxxxxxxxxxxxxxxxxxxxxxxxxx
xxxxxxxxxxxxxxxxxxxxxxxxxxxxxxxxxx

---

xxxxxxxxxxxxxxxxxxxxxxxxxxxxxxxxxxxx
xxxxxxxxxxxxx. ↓2 or 3

SIDE HEADING ↓2

      Paragraph Heading. Xxxxxxxx
xxxxxxxxxxxxxxxxxxxxxxxxxxxxxxxxxx
xxxxxxxxxxxxxxxxxxxxxxxxxxxxxxxxxx
xxxxxxxxxxxxxxxxxxxxxxxxxxxxxxxxxx

14

f. In a report with *three* levels of headings, choose one of the following styles.

---

xxxxxxxxxxxxxxxxxxxxxxxxxxxxxxxxxxxx
xxxxxxxxxxxxx. ↓2 or 3

        CENTRED HEADING ↓2

      Xxxxxxxxxxxxxxxxxxxxxxxxxxxxx
xxxxxxxxxxxxxxxxxxxxxxxxxxxxxxxxxx ↓2 or 3

Side Heading ↓2

     Paragraph Heading. Xxxxxxxx
xxxxxxxxxxxxxxxxxxxxxxxxxxxxxxxxxxxx

---

xxxxxxxxxxxxxxxxxxxxxxxxxxxxxxxxxxxx
xxxxxxxxxxxxx. ↓2 or 3

        CENTRED HEADING ↓2

      Xxxxxxxxxxxxxxxxxxxxxxxxxxxxx
xxxxxxxxxxxxxxxxxxxxxxxxxxxxxxxxxx ↓2 or 3

SIDE HEADING ↓2

     Paragraph Heading. Xxxxxxxxx
xxxxxxxxxxxxxxxxxxxxxxxxxxxxxxxxxx

---

g. When showing double-spaced (body) text, the word processing software sometimes makes it difficult or awkward to leave 2 blank lines above centred and side headings. In this case, choose one of the following styles. However, be consistent in your pattern of choices.

---

xxxxxxxxxxxxxxxxxxxxxxxxxxxxxxxxxxxx
xxxxxxxxxxxxx. ↓4

        CENTRED HEADING ↓2

      Xxxxxxxxxxxxxxxxxxxxxxxxxxxxx
xxxxxxxxxxxxxxxxxxxxxxxxxxxxxxxxxx

---

xxxxxxxxxxxxxxxxxxxxxxxxxxxxxxxxxxxx
xxxxxxxxxxxxxxxxxxxxxxxxxxxxxxxxxxxx
xxxxxxxxxxxxx. ↓2

Side Heading ↓2

      Xxxxxxxxxxxxxxxxxxxxxxxxxxxxx
xxxxxxxxxxxxxxxxxxxxxxxxxxxxxxxxxx
xxxxxxxxxxxxxxxxxxxxxxxxxxxxxxxxxx

1427 NUMBERING TEXT PAGES

  a. When using the page numbering feature of your software, the appropriate page number will be properly positioned on each page in the correct sequence. If you later add or delete copy in a way that changes the overall length of the report, the page numbering will be automatically adjusted.

  NOTE: The page numbering feature will often leave only 1 blank line after a page number at the top of a page or before a page number at the bottom. However, for a better appearance, you can increase this space to 2 blank lines.

  b. When the first page contains the title of the report and the body starts on the same page, count this as page 1. Generally, no page number is required on this page; but if one is desired, it must be set at the bottom of the page, regardless of the numbering format used for successive pages.

  NOTE: With the page numbering feature, you can prevent or suppress a page number from being printed, yet still have the page counted in the overall numerical sequence.

  c. When the report begins with a formal title page and one or more additional pages of front matter, give these pages a separate numbering sequence, using small *Roman* numerals. (See ¶1421.)

  d. In a formal report, consider the first page *following* the front matter as page 1 in the *Arabic* numbering sequence.

  e. If part-title pages are included in the report (see ¶1423), consider them in the numbering sequence for the body of the report. No page number is required on this page. However, if one is preferred, it must be at the bottom of the page, regardless of the numbering format followed for successive pages.

  f. On the first page of each new element in the body or back matter of the report, use the page numbering or footer feature to centre the page number at the bottom of the page. Leave 2 blank lines above the page number.

  g. On all other pages in the body or back matter of the report, place the page number in the same position on each page. Use the page numbering or the header/footer feature of your software program. Common placements include top-centred, top right-aligned, bottom-centred, and bottom right-aligned positions. At any right-aligned position, the word *Page* may be added. Adjust the header to include a top margin of 1 inch and 2 blank lines after the header. For a bottom-page placement, leave a 1-inch margin with 2 blank lines above the page number.

  h. If the final version of a report is to be printed on both sides of the paper (as in a book), the odd-numbered pages will appear on the front side of each sheet and the even-numbered pages on the back. If the report is bound, then on a spread of two facing pages, the even-numbered pages will appear on the left and the odd-numbered pages on the right. In such cases it is more convenient for the reader if the page numbers at the top or bottom of the page appear at the outside corners, as in the following illustration.

(Continued on page 416.)

14

```
┌──────────────────────────────────────┐   ┌──────────────────────────────────────┐
│                                        │   │                                        │
│  14 ↓2 or 3                            │   │                            15 ↓2 or 3  │
│                                        │   │                                        │
│  xxxxxxxxxxxxxxxxxxxxxxxxxxxxxxxxxx     │   │     xxxxxxxxxxxxxxxxxxxxxxxxxxxxxxxxxx  │
│  xxxxxxxxxxxxxxxxxxxxxxxxxxxxxxxx       │   │     xxxxxxxxxxxxxxxxxxxxxxxxxxxxxxxx    │
│                                        │   │                                        │
└──────────────────────────────────────┘   └──────────────────────────────────────┘
```

NOTE: You can direct the page numbering feature of a word processing program to alternate the placement of these page numbers in the outside corners, depending on whether the page has an odd or even number.

i. In a long report with several chapters written by different authors under a tight deadline, it may be necessary to prepare the final version of the chapters out of order. In such cases, you may use a separate sequence of page numbers for each chapter, with the chapter number serving as a prefix. Thus, for example, the pages in Chapter 1 would be numbered 1-1, 1-2, 1-3, . . . ; those in Chapter 2 would be numbered 2-1, 2-2, 2-3, . . . ; and so on.

NOTE: If the authors submit their material on disk, it is easy to renumber the entire report at the last minute, using one continuous sequence of numbers throughout.

The Back Matter of Formal Reports

1428 Following the last page of the body of the report are those elements of back matter that may be needed: appendixes, endnotes, bibliography, and glossary. Begin each of these elements on a new page. Use the same margins as for other pages in the report (see ¶¶1405–1408), and treat the numbering of these pages as discussed in ¶1427f–i.

1429 APPENDIXES

a. If you plan to include more than one appendix, number or letter each one in sequence. (For an example of the treatment of two appendixes, see the illustration of the table of contents on page 405.)

b. On a new page, start on line 2 inches. Centre and boldface in all-capital letters the word *APPENDIX* (plus a number or letter, if appropriate).

```
┌──────────────────────────────────────────────────────────┐
│                                                            │
│                    │                                       │
│              2 inches │                                    │
│                    │                                       │
│                    ↓                                       │
│      APPENDIX A. PROFILES OF MAJOR COMPETITORS  ↓2 or 3    │
│                                                            │
└──────────────────────────────────────────────────────────┘
```

NOTE: If the title is long, key it in two or more centred lines, single-spaced. Leave 1 blank line before starting the appendix title.

---

2 inches

↓

APPENDIX A ↓2

**SIGNIFICANT CHANGES IN
FEDERAL LEGISLATION DURING
THE PAST FIVE YEARS** ↓2 or 3

---

    c. Leave 1 or 2 blank lines before keying the body of the appendix. Since this material may be a table, a chart, a list, or regular text, choose the format that displays this copy to the best effect.

1430 ENDNOTES AND BIBLIOGRAPHY

For detailed guidelines, see ¶¶1501–1502, 1505–1506, 1540–1544.

1431 GLOSSARY

If you plan a glossary, then on a new page centre *GLOSSARY* or some other heading in boldface and all-capital letters. Leave a 2-inch top margin and begin the text on the second or third line below. There are a variety of ways to set up a glossary.

    a. **Two Columns.** In the left column, list the terms in alphabetic order, using boldface or italics. In the right column, put the corresponding definition. Begin the right column at least 2 to 3 spaces to the right of the longest term in the left column. Single-space each definition, and align turnover lines flush with the left margin of the column. Leave 1 blank line between entries.

    NOTE: The table feature of your software can be used to create these columns.

Elliptical expression   A condensed expression from which key words are omitted. ↓2

Essential elements   Words, phrases, or clauses that are necessary to the completeness of the structure or the meaning of a sentence.

---

    b. **Hanging Indention.** Begin each term at the left margin, using boldface or italics. Follow with a colon, a dash, or some other device and then the definition. Key the definition single-spaced, and indent turnover lines 0.25 to 0.5 inch so that the term in the first line will stand out. Leave 1 blank line between entries. (Most software includes a hanging indent feature, which automatically indents the turnover lines.)

---

      elliptical expression: a condensed expression from which key words are
0.5 inch ⟶ omitted. ↓2

      essential elements: words, phrases, or clauses that are necessary to the completeness of the structure or the meaning of a sentence.

(Continued on page 418.)

c. Paragraph Style. Indent each term 0.25 to 0.5 inch from the left margin, using boldface or italics. Follow with a colon, a dash, or some other device and then the definition. Key the definition single-spaced, with turnover lines flush with the left margin. Leave 1 blank line between entries.

0.5 inch ⟶ **Elliptical expression**—a condensed expression from which key words are omitted. ↓2

     Essential elements—words, phrases, or clauses that are necessary to the completeness of the structure or the meaning of a sentence.

NOTE: Regardless of the format selected, the terms may be keyed with initial caps or all in small letters (except for proper nouns and adjectives). The definitions may also be styled either way; however, if they are written in sentence form, it is best to use initial caps for both the term and the definition. The use of periods at the end of definitions is optional unless, of course, the definitions are written as complete sentences. (See the illustration in ¶1431a for an example of the use of initial caps for both the term and the definition.)

MANUSCRIPTS

The preparation of manuscripts is subject to virtually the same considerations that apply to reports (¶¶1401–1431). However, manuscripts differ from reports in one fundamental way: They are written with the idea of publication in mind—a self-contained book, a magazine article, or a bulletin or newsletter item. As a result, manuscripts require special formatting.

When submitting your manuscript to a publisher, the hard copy of your manuscript should be sent with a copy of your manuscript disk. It is possible that each copy may need to be formatted differently. Since publishers' printers often prefer to format the final text themselves, the disk may be simply formatted with nothing more than double spacing and 1-inch side margins. For a better visual presentation, however, the hard copy should conform to the guidelines in ¶1433.

Preparing Manuscript for an Article

1432 If you have been invited to write an article for a specific publication, ask the editor for concrete guidelines on line length, line spacing, font style and size, paragraph indentions, heading style, preferences in capitalization and punctuation, overall length of the article, and so on.

1433 If you are writing an article only with the hope that it may be accepted by a certain publication, you will enhance your chances of favourable consideration by imitating all aspects of the publication's format and style.

 a. Select a proportional font style and size that resemble as closely as possible the typeface used by the publication.

b. Determine the appropriate line length by copying 10 to 20 lines—on a line-for-line basis—from a representative article. Observe at what point most lines end, and set your margins accordingly. From this copy try to match the line spacing used. Many publications print 7 to 8 lines per inch.

c. Since traditional standards of spacing are not used, you will need to measure the paragraph indentions. They may be 0.25 inch or even less. As well, you will need only one space after an ending punctuation mark. (See ¶298.)

d. Even if the publication puts two or more columns on a page, key only one column on a manuscript page. The wider margins will provide space for editing.

e. Key your manuscript double-spaced to allow room for editing.

f. Consistently key 25 lines of copy on a manuscript page (counting blank space above and below freestanding headings as lines of copy). In this way you and the editor can quickly calculate the total number of lines of copy.

g. Be sure to keep the overall length of your manuscript within the range of the materials typically used by the intended publication. There is little point in submitting a 2000-line manuscript to a publication that carries articles of no more than 500 lines.

NOTE: Your word processing program very likely has a feature that will provide the following information you can share with your editor: the number of characters in your manuscript, the number of words, the number of lines, the number of paragraphs, and the number of pages.

Preparing Manuscript for a Book

If you are writing a book or assisting someone who is, consider the following guidelines.

1434 If your manuscript will consist essentially of straight-text matter (with perhaps a few tables and illustrations), then in establishing a format for your manuscript, you can follow the standard guidelines for a formal report with respect to spacing, headings, page numbering, and other aspects involved in keying the front matter, the body, and the back matter. You may want to adopt the settings for a *bound* report—a 6-inch line with a left margin of 1.5 inches and a right margin of 1 inch. (See ¶1405b.) Although a book manuscript should not be bound, the left margin gives extra space for editing.

1435 If you think your manuscript, when set in type, will require a special format—for example, a larger-than-usual page size to accommodate extremely wide tables or to permit notes and small illustrations to run alongside the text or to allow for a two-column arrangement of the printed text—then the easiest way to establish a format for your manuscript page is to select a published work that has the kind of format you have in mind. Then copy a full page of representative printed text—on a line-for-line basis—to determine the manuscript equivalent of a printed page. Then, as you develop the manuscript, you can exercise some real control over the length of your material.

Precautions for All Manuscripts

1436 When sending material to a publisher, always retain a duplicate of your hard copy and disk in case the material goes astray or the publisher calls to discuss the manuscript.

1437 Your unpublished manuscript is automatically protected by copyright law. What is protected, however, is the *written* expression of ideas and facts and not the ideas and facts themselves. If you fear possible infringement of your ideas or of not receiving credit or compensation for your work, you could place a note of copyright (© your name, date) on the front page of your book. It may be necessary, too, to consult a lawyer if you think you have an original publishing idea that could be misappropriated.

For information or a copyright application, write to the Copyright Office, Canadian Intellectual Property Office (CIPO), Industry Canada, 50 Victoria Street, Place du Portage I, Hull, QC K1A 0C9, or visit CIPO on the Internet at http://cipo.gc.ca.

Some owners of copyrights belong to a collective or licensing body that collects royalties on their behalf. Such a collective is CANCOPY. It grants permission to schools, for instance, to copy your work and collects the fees. For information about photocopying of this kind, write to CANCOPY at 6 Adelaide Street East, Suite 900, Toronto, ON M5C 1H6, or refer to their Web site at www.cancopy.com.

 See the Online Learning Centre at www.mcgrawhill.ca/college/gregg for related weblinks.

SECTION **FIFTEEN**

Notes and Bibliographies

NOTES BASED ON ONLINE SOURCES (¶¶1533–1539)

BIBLIOGRAPHIES (¶¶1540–1544)

FOOTNOTES, ENDNOTES, AND TEXTNOTES
Functions of Notes

15

1501 a. In a report or manuscript, *notes* serve two functions: (1) they provide *comments* on the main text, conveying subordinate ideas that the writer feels might be distracting if incorporated within the main text; and (2) they serve as *source references*, identifying the origin of a statement quoted or cited in the text.

Comment

[1]The actual date on which Mayor Wade made this statement is uncertain, but there is no doubt that the statement is his.

Source Reference

[2]Patrick Watson, *The Canadians*, McArthur & Company, Toronto, 2000, p. 108.

b. When notes appear at the foot of a page, they are called *footnotes*. (See ¶¶1503–1504.)

---

humorous practicality of Prairie phrases, the peculiar lilt of Ottawa Valley speech,

the local words like "skookum" that sometimes brighten chat with a person from

British Columbia's Lower Mainland.[1]

_____

[1]Bill Casselman, *Casselmania: More Canadian Words and Sayings*, Little, Brown and Company (Canada) Limited, Toronto, 1996, p. 273.

☞ *For a discussion on whether to type the note number as a superscript (as shown above) or on the line, see ¶1523b.*

For a discussion of default formats provided by software, see ¶1503.

c. When notes appear all together at the end of a complete report or manuscript (or sometimes at the end of each chapter), they are called *endnotes.* (See ¶¶1505–1506.)

---

2 inches

NOTES ↓2 or 3

¹Bill Casselman, *Casselmania: More Canadian Words and Sayings*, Little, Brown and Company (Canada) Limited, Toronto, 1996, p. 273. ↓2

²Ibid., pp. 276–277.

☞ *For a discussion of default formats provided by software, see ¶1505.*

d. When source references appear parenthetically within the main text, they are called *textnotes.* (See ¶1507.)

---

how we say the word *kilometre*. Is it KIL ometre or Kil OM etre? Here's some

expert advice. ↓2

0.25 to
0.5 inch ⟶

KIL ometre. This is the word from Canada's former chief of weights and measures, Robert Bruce. The federal metric commission made the same call . . . Most of the world accents the first syllable. Britons accent the second. They also drive on the wrong side of the road. (Walter Stefaniuk, "A Few Words in Passing," *You Asked Us—About Canada*, Doubleday Canada Limited, Toronto, 1996, p. 151.)

⟵ 0.25 to
0.5 inch

---

e. Footnotes or endnotes are ordinarily keyed by an Arabic number to a word, phrase, or sentence in the text. Textnotes (which appear parenthetically at the desired point of reference right in the text itself) do not have to be keyed this way.

f. Endnotes are popular because they leave the text pages looking less cluttered and less complicated. They do present one drawback, however: the reader does not know in each instance whether the endnote will contain a comment of substance (which is typically worth reading) or simply a source reference (which is usually of interest only in special cases).

g. Textnotes are also popular for the same reason: lack of clutter. While it is possible to provide in a textnote all the information that a source reference typically contains, writers more often use the textnote to provide an abbreviated reference in the text, with the understanding that the reader who wants complete information will be able to consult a bibliography at the back of the report or manuscript. (See ¶1507 for examples of these abbreviated references.)

(Continued on page 424.)

h. To take advantage of the benefits and avoid the drawbacks of these three types of notes, some writers use a hybrid system: they treat *comments* as footnotes and *source references* as endnotes or textnotes. In this way comments of substance are conveniently at hand, whereas all or most of the information about sources is tucked out of sight but accessible when needed. (See ¶1502g.)

Text References to Footnotes or Endnotes

1502 a. To indicate the presence of a comment or a source reference at the bottom of the page or in a special section at the end of the report or manuscript, use the footnote or endnote feature to insert a superscript figure following the appropriate word, phrase, or sentence in the text. (See ¶1502b for examples.)

b. Do not leave any space between the superscript figure and the preceding word. If a punctuation mark follows the word, place the superscript immediately after the punctuation mark. (There is one exception: the superscript should precede, not follow, a dash.)

A research study published last month by a leading relocation consulting firm[1] provides the basis for the recommendations offered in Chapter 5.

The alternative approaches discussed in this report have been taken largely from an article entitled "Getting a Handle on Health Care Costs."[2]

An article entitled "Getting a Handle on Health Care Costs"[2]—written by an eminent authority in the field—was the source of the alternative approaches discussed in this report.

c. While the superscript should come as close as possible to the appropriate word or phrase, it is often better to place the superscript at the end of the sentence (if this will cause no misunderstanding) so as to avoid distracting the reader in the midst of the sentence.

PREFERABLE: Her latest article, "Automating the Small Legal Office," was published about three months ago.[1] I urge you to read it.

ACCEPTABLE: Her latest article, "Automating the Small Legal Office,"[1] was published about three months ago. I urge you to read it.

NOTE: The spacing left after a superscript should be the same spacing that normally would be left after the punctuation mark that comes before the superscript.

d. When a paragraph calls for two or more footnotes or endnotes, try to combine all the necessary information within one note if this can be done without any risk of confusing the reader. This approach will reduce the sense of irritation that large numbers of footnotes or endnotes tend to produce.

NOTE: When this approach is used, the superscript is typically placed after the last word in the sentence or paragraph, depending on how the text references are dispersed.

PREFERABLE: The following analysis draws heavily on recent studies undertaken by Andrew Bowen, Frances Kaplan, and Minetta Coleman.[1]

---

[1]Andrew Bowen, . . . ; Frances Kaplan, . . . ; and Minetta Coleman, . . .

AVOID: The following analysis draws heavily on recent studies undertaken by Andrew Bowen,[1] Frances Kaplan,[2] and Minetta Coleman.[3]

---

[1]Andrew Bowen, . . .

[2]Frances Kaplan, . . .

[3]Minetta Coleman, . . .

e. The numbering of footnotes or endnotes may run consecutively throughout or begin again with each new chapter.

f. Footnotes and endnotes are sometimes keyed by symbol rather than by number. This often occurs in tables with figures and in technical material with many formulas, where a raised figure—though intended to refer to a footnote or endnote—could be mistaken for part of the table text or the formula. When the use of symbols is appropriate, choose one of the following sequences: *, **, ***, etc.; *, †, ‡, §, ¶; or *a, b, c, d, e,* etc.

These tests confirmed that there was a reduction over time of the consumption of natural gas by at least 2.3 m^3.***

NOT: These tests confirmed that there was a reduction over time of the consumption of natural gas by at least 2.3 m^3.[3]

g. If you wish to treat *comments* as footnotes and *source references* as endnotes (as suggested in ¶1501h), use *symbols* for the notes containing comments (at the bottom of the page) and use *figures* for the notes containing source references (at the end of the report or manuscript).

Footnotes

1503 a. The footnote feature of a word processing program will automatically position your footnotes at the bottom of the page where the footnote reference appears in the text. The software will also (1) insert a horizontal line to separate the footnotes from the text above, (2) continue a footnote on the following page if it is too long to fit as a whole on the page where it started, and (3) automatically number your footnotes. If subsequent additions or deletions in the text cause the text reference to shift to another page, the related footnote will automatically shift as well. If a footnote is subsequently inserted or deleted, all the remaining footnotes (and their related text references) will be automatically renumbered from that point on.

b. The first illustration on page 426 shows how your footnotes will look if you use the footnote feature of Microsoft Word for Windows and if you accept all the defaults. Note the following default details: (1) the first line of each footnote begins at the left margin; (2) no extra space is inserted between footnotes; (3) no extra space is inserted between the horizontal rule and the first footnote; and (4) one space is inserted after the superscript.

(Continued on page 426.)

into the new century.[1] According to one source: ↓2

0.25 to
0.5 inch ⟶

The Internet is like an ocean surrounding each of these online service islands. When the Web made that ocean, a popular place to swim, some of the larger online services started offering their members visual surfboards.[2]

⟵ 0.25 to
0.5 inch

―――――――――

[1] For a more detailed analysis of these technological developments, see Chapter 2, pp. 29–38.
[2] Brad Hill, *Yahoo! for Dummies*, 2nd ed., IDG Books Worldwide Inc., Foster City, CA, 2001, p. 25.

---

into the new century.[1] According to one source: ↓2

0.25 to
0.5 inch ⟶

The Internet is like an ocean surrounding each of these online service islands. When the Web made that ocean, a popular place to swim, some of the larger online services started offering their members visual surfboards.[2]

⟵ 0.25 to
0.5 inch

―――――――――

[1] For a more detailed analysis of these technological developments, see Chapter 2, pp. 29–38.

[2] Brad Hill, *Yahoo! for Dummies*, 2nd ed., IDG Books Worldwide Inc., Foster City, CA, 2001, p. 25.

15

NOTE: Whether you are writing business or academic reports or developing a manuscript for a publisher, you will be expected in most cases to follow a definite style for footnotes. In situations where no format is prescribed but professional editorial standards must be met, follow the guidelines for the standard format shown in the second illustration above and explained below in ¶1504.

1504 To create your own format for footnotes, consider the following guidelines. (See the illustration above.) For advanced word processing software users, the format described could be used to create a new "style" for your documents.

a. The line that separates footnote material from the main text above should be about 2 inches long.

NOTE: If the text runs short on a page (for instance, the last page of a chapter), any footnotes related to that text must still be positioned at the *foot* of the page.

b. Start the first footnote a double space below the separation line. (See ¶1504a above.)

☞ *For guidelines on how to construct source reference footnotes, see ¶¶1508–1532.*

c. Single-space the text within each footnote but double-space *between* the footnotes.

d. Indent the first line of each footnote using the same paragraph tab that is used within the text material of the document, that is, 0.25 to 0.5 inch.

e. The preferred format for the footnote number is a superscript figure with no spaces after the number. An alternative format is to use a figure followed by a period placed normally on the line. The font style and size should match the font style and size of the body of the document. Leave one or two spaces after the period, and follow the same style for spacing after periods that is used in the body of the document.

Starting a Long Footnote

> and computers should not be used to write thank-you notes.[2]
>
> ---
>
> [2]Judith Martin (in *Miss Manners' Basic Training: Communications*, Crown, New York, 1998, p. 37) clearly supports this position: "Thank-you letters should be written by hand. Miss Manners . . . grants exemptions only to people with

f. In some software programs, if a footnote is considered too long to fit on the same page as the actual reference, the program will automatically split the footnote text and place part of it on the next page. If at all possible, try to avoid this situation. You may have to reset some formatting (for example, the bottom margin) to accommodate this.

Continuing a Long Footnote on the Next Page

> on which there still is a considerable difference of opinion.[3]
>
> ---
>
> specific physical disabilities that prevent them from writing. Those who claim illegible handwriting should be home practicing their penmanship instead of bragging about it." ↓2
>
> [3]Baldrige, p. 593.

NOTE: If you have a number of long notes that may not easily fit on the page where they are first referred to, you have an excellent reason for abandoning the footnote format and using endnotes instead. (See ¶¶1505–1506.)

☞ *For the treatment of footnotes that pertain to a table, see ¶¶1632–1634.*

Endnotes

1505 a. The endnote feature of a software program will automatically position all endnotes at the end of the document. If you add or delete endnotes, all the remaining endnotes (and their related text references) will be automatically renumbered from that point on.

b. The endnote feature will also automatically format the endnotes for you. Here is how your endnotes will look if you accept all the defaults of the endnote feature of Microsoft Word for Windows. Note that the endnote section begins on the same page as the conclusion of the main text, separated by a short horizontal rule starting at the left margin but with no heading (such as *NOTES*) to introduce this section. Note also that each entry begins at the left margin with superscripts in small Roman numerals and a space after the superscript. There is no blank linespace between the notes.

---

growth. Equipping your SOHO office with the right equipment is easy . . . The key is knowing which technological tools you need, what you can do without, and where to find technical support.[2]

---

[i]Lisa Kanarek, "Wired for Business," *OfficePRO*, Vol. 61, No. 4, April 2001, p. 14.
[ii]Ibid.

1506 If you want to modify the default format shown above or if you prefer to create your own format for endnotes, consider the following guidelines. (See the illustration on page 429.)

a. Endnotes should start on a new page. The title *NOTES* or *ENDNOTES* should be centred 2 inches from the top of the page and typed in all-capital letters and in boldface. Leave 1 or 2 linespaces after the title.

b. The preferred format for an endnote page is to have the first line of each endnote indented the equivalent to the tab stop that has been set for the body of the document, that is, 0.25 to 0.5 inch. Place Arabic numbers on the line, rather than using superscripts. All turnover lines should return to the left margin.

NOTE: The numbers in the endnotes may appear as superscripts, but the on-the-line style is more commonly used.

c. Leave one or two spaces after the period. Follow the same format for spacing after punctuation that is used in the body of the document.

d. Single-space the text within each endnote but double-space *between* the endnotes.

☞ *For guidelines on how to construct source reference endnotes, see ¶¶1508–1523.*

```
                        ┌─────────────────────────────────────────────┐
                        │ 2 inches                                     │
                        │    ↓                                         │
                        │ ENDNOTES ↓2 or 3                             │
0.25 to                 │                                             │
0.5 inch ──→ 1. Lisa Kanarek, "Wired for Business," OfficePRO, Vol. 61, No. 4, April
             2001, p. 14. ↓2                                          
                                                                     
                  2. Ibid.                                           
```

e. Use the same margins as for other pages in the body of the report or manuscript (see ¶¶1405–1408), and treat the numbering of these pages as shown in ¶1427f–g.

f. If the numbering of endnotes starts again with each new chapter or on each new page, insert an appropriate heading—*Chapter 1, Chapter 2*, etc., or *Page 1, Page 2*, etc.—over each sequence of endnotes in this section. Key the heading at the left margin in capital and small letters (using boldface or italics), and leave 2 blank lines above and 1 blank line below.

NOTE: If the numbering of endnotes is consecutive throughout, no headings are needed.

g. Insert this special section of endnotes in the back matter following any appendixes. If no appendix is given, the endnotes begin the back matter. (See also ¶1428.)

NOTE: When individual chapters of a report or a manuscript are prepared by different writers, it may be advantageous to have the endnotes that each author prepares inserted at the end of the respective chapter instead of redoing all the endnotes as one continuous section in the back matter. If this approach is used, expand the heading *NOTES* in each case to read *NOTES TO CHAPTER 1, NOTES TO CHAPTER 2*, and so on. The disadvantage of this approach is that the reader will have a bit more difficulty locating the notes for each chapter than is true when all the endnotes are presented in one section at the very end.

Textnotes

1507 a. In a report or manuscript with only a few source references and no bibliography at the end, the complete source data may be inserted within the text in the form of parenthetical textnotes. (See the illustration at the top of the next page.)

☞ *For guidelines on how to construct source reference textnotes, see ¶¶1508–1532.*

(Continued on page 430.)

> recommended by Canada Post. As for the abbreviations devised to hold down the
>
> length of place names in addresses, here is what one authority had to say:
>
>> And all you people with beautiful words in your addresses: Cut 'em down. There's a bright golden haze on the MDWS; a fairy dancing in your GDNS; and a safe HBR past the happy LNDG at the XING, where no hope SPGS. Environmentalists are now GRN, as in how GRN was my VLY. . . . Is the language not lessened when words like *meadow, gardens, harbor, landing, crossing, green, valley*—even *islands (ISS)*—are disemvoweled? (William Safire, *In Love With Norma Loquendi,* Random House, New York, 1994, p. 166.)

NOTE: If some of the data called for in a source reference is already provided in the main text, there is no need to repeat it in the textnote.

15

> recommended by Canada Post. As for the abbreviations devised to hold down the
>
> length of place names in addresses, here is what William Safire had to say:
>
>> And all you people with beautiful words in your addresses: Cut 'em down. There's a bright golden haze on the MDWS; a fairy dancing in your GDNS; and a safe HBR past the happy LNDG at the XING, where no hope SPGS. Environmentalists are now GRN, as in how GRN was my VLY. . . . Is the language not lessened when words like *meadow, gardens, harbor, landing, crossing, green, valley*—even *islands (ISS)*—are disemvoweled? (*In Love With Norma Loquendi,* Random House, New York, 1994, p. 166.)

b. In a report or manuscript that contains a number of source references *and* a complete bibliography, textnotes may be used as follows:

- At the appropriate point in the main text, supply the author's last name and the appropriate page number in parentheses. The reader who wants more complete information can consult the full entry in the bibliography.

  As stated in his guide book to the Internet (Kent, p. 252), people feel they know the person with whom they are communicating, but they do not.

  NOTE: Some authorities omit *p.* and *pp.* as well as the comma between the name and the page number. For example:

  . . . book on the Internet (Kent 252) . . .

- If the author's name already appears in the main text, give only the page number in parentheses.

  Peter Kent, *The Complete Idiot's Guide to the Internet* (p. 252), says that . . .

- If the bibliography lists more than one publication by the same author, then in the textnote use an abbreviated title or the year of publication to indicate which publication is being referred to.

  In his book about communicating electronically (Kent, *Idiot's Guide*, p. 252) . . .
  OR: . . . book about communicating electronically (Kent, 1998, p. 252), . . .

- If the bibliography lists publications by two or more authors with the same surname, use each author's first name or initial along with the surname.

  In his book about communicating electronically (Peter Kent, p. 252), . . .

- If the entries in the bibliography are numbered in sequence (see ¶1542c), then the textnote can simply list the appropriate "entry number" along with the page reference. Italicize or underline the entry number to distinguish it from the page number, especially if the abbreviation *p.* or *pp.* is omitted.

  In his book about . . . (*18*, p. 252), . . . **OR:** (18, p. 252), . . .

Constructing Source Reference Notes

The following guidelines for constructing source reference notes deal with the situations that most commonly occur—whether in the form of footnotes, endnotes, or the type of textnote discussed in ¶1507. There is no clear-cut agreement among authorities on how these notes should be constructed; rather, there are several schools of thought on the subject, and within each school there are variations between one reference manual and another.

Of all the well-established conventions and variations, the style best suited for business use—and the one presented here—is a style that employs the simplest punctuation and the most straightforward presentation of the necessary data without any sacrifice in clarity or completeness. However, certain professional organizations have established distinctive styles that sometimes show up in other fields. For example, the style recommended by the American Psychological Association (APA) is followed by some Canadian universities. Moreover, slightly different patterns are often used in academic materials, such as those featured in *The MLA [Modern Language Association] Style Manual* and *The Chicago Manual of Style*. If you are one of the many full-time business workers who are simultaneously taking one or more academic courses or one of the many full-time academic students who are concurrently holding down part- or full-time office jobs, you may need to familiarize yourself with more than one style. Note that along with the basic pattern for citing book titles (see ¶1508), you will find an "academic" variation that you may need to use from time to time. However, unless you are specifically directed to follow a particular style, the following "all-purpose" patterns—based on well-established conventions—should meet your needs in virtually every type of situation you encounter.

NOTE: For detailed information about specific elements within these patterns, see the following paragraphs:

☞ *Note number: see ¶1524.*   *Place of publication: see ¶1528.*
Names of authors: see ¶1525.   *Date of publication: see ¶1529.*
Title of the work: see ¶1526.   *Page numbers: see ¶1530.*
Publisher's name: see ¶1527.   *Subsequent references: see ¶¶1531–1532.*

1508 BOOK TITLE: BASIC PATTERN

a. Business Style

[1]Author, *book title*, publisher, place of publication, year of publication, page number [if reference is being made to a specific page].

[1]Laurier L. LaPierre, *Quebec: A Tale of Love*, McClelland & Stewart, Toronto, 2001, p. 387.

OR:

1. Laurier L. LaPierre, *Quebec: A Tale of Love*, McClelland & Stewart, Toronto, 2001, p. 387.

NOTE: If any of these elements have already been identified in the text (for example, the author's name and the book title), they need not be repeated in the note. Moreover, if reference is made to the book as a whole rather than to a particular page, omit the page number. In the following illustration, observe that the quoted material requires more than three lines. For that reason, it is indented 0.25 to 0.5 inch from each side margin. (See ¶1425d.)

---

in his recent book, *Quebec: A Tale of Love*, Laurier L. LaPierre reminds us of the

role of Quebec in shaping our nation.

0.25 to
0.5 inch ⟶ These people opened a continent to a civilization that has much
nobility in it, and they introduced a new language to North America. . . . ⟵ 0.25 to
0.25 to These people have great courage and a zest for life that many try to 0.5 inch
0.5 inch ⟶ emulate. They are a good people and sometimes a great people.[1]

---

[1]McClelland & Stewart, Toronto, 2001, p. 387.

---

b. Academic Style

[1]Author, *book title* (place of publication: publisher, year of publication), page number [if reference is being made to a specific page].

[1]Laurier L. LaPierre, *Quebec: A Tale of Love* (Toronto: McClelland & Stewart, 2001), p. 387.

(In endnotes, the note number is shown on the line; in academic-style footnotes, the note number is typically shown as a superscript. See ¶1524b.)

NOTE: The key distinction between the business style and the academic style lies in a slightly different sequence of elements and a slightly different form of punctuation:

BUSINESS STYLE: . . . publisher, place of publication, year of publication . . .

ACADEMIC STYLE: . . . (place of publication: publisher, year of publication) . . .

The following patterns for books (in ¶¶1509–1516) show only the business style. However, you can readily convert them to the academic style by simply changing the treatment of these three elements.

☞ *For the academic style for entries in bibliographies, see ¶1544c.*

1509 BOOK TITLE: WITH EDITION

a. Edition Number

¹Author, *book title*, edition number [if not the first edition], publisher, place, year, page number.

¹John Friesen, *When Cultures Clash: Case Studies in Multiculturalism*, 2nd ed., University of Calgary, 2000, p. 189. (Since the name of the publisher includes the place of publication, it does not need to be repeated.)

NOTE: Use an edition number only when the book is not the first edition in its country of origin. If included, the edition number follows the main title and any related elements, such as the subtitle or the volume number and title. (For an example, see ¶1516.) The following abbreviated forms are commonly used: *2nd ed., 3rd ed., 4th ed.,* and *rev. ed.* (for "revised edition").

b. Edition Notation

¹Author, *book title*, edition notation, publisher, place, year, page number.

¹Gary Dessler, Nina D. Cole, and Gini Sutherland, *Human Resources Management in Canada*, 8th Canadian Edition, Prentice Hall, Toronto, 2002, p. 91.

NOTE: Some books first published outside Canada, usually those from the United States and Great Britain, are edited for the Canadian market. The word *Canadian* is included in the title of the book or is used to note a particular edition. (See ¶¶1516, 1525.) Other descriptions, such as *International, Educational,* and *Special,* are sometimes indicated.

1510 BOOK TITLE: WITH SUBTITLE

¹Author, *book title: subtitle*, edition number [if not the first edition], publisher, place, year, page number.

¹Roberta L. Hursey, *Trucking North: On Canada's Mackenzie Highway*, Detselig Enterprises Ltd., Calgary, 1999, pp. 144–165.

²W. F. Garrett-Petts, *Writing About Literature: A Guide for the Students*, Broadview Press, Peterborough, 1999, p. 56.

NOTE: Do not give the subtitle of a book unless it is significant in identifying the book or in explaining its basic nature. If a subtitle is to be shown, separate it from the main title with a colon (unless the title page shows some other mark such as a dash). Italicize the main title and the subtitle. Capitalize the first word of the subtitle, even if it is a short preposition like *for*, a short conjunction like *or*, or an article like *the* or *a*. (See ¶361b.)

³Ila Bussidor and Üstün Bilgen-Reinart, *Night Spirits: The Story of the Relocation of the Sayisi Dene*, University of Manitoba Press, Winnipeg, 1997, p. 43.

1511 BOOK TITLE: WITH VOLUME NUMBER AND VOLUME TITLE

[1]Author, *book title*, volume number, *volume title*, edition number [if not the first edition], publisher, place, year, page number.

[1]Stephen Clarkson and Christina McCall, *Trudeau and Our Times*, Vol. 2, *The Heroic Delusion*, McClelland & Stewart, Toronto, 1997, p. 189.

NOTE: As a rule, do not show the volume title in a note unless it is significant in identifying the book. When the volume title is included, both the volume number and the volume title follow the book title (and subtitle, if any) but precede the edition number. The volume number is usually preceded by the abbreviation *Vol.* or by the word *Book* or *Part* (depending on the actual designation). The volume number may be Arabic or Roman depending on the style used in the actual book. Some writers prefer to use one style of volume number throughout the notes. (See also ¶1512.)

1512 BOOK TITLE: WITH VOLUME NUMBER ALONE

[1]Author, *book title*, edition number [if not the first edition], publisher, place, year, volume number, page number.

[1]Gary R. R. Swinton, *Swinton: An Inventory of the Family*, 7th ed., Melbourne, Australia, 2000, Vol. 2, p. 9.

NOTE: When the volume number is shown without the volume title, it follows the date of publication. When the volume number and page number occur one after the other, they may be styled as follows:

Style for Roman Volume Number
Vol. III, p. 197 **OR** III, 197

Style for Arabic Volume Number
Vol. 5, pp. 681–684 **OR** 5:681–684

[1]Gary R. R. Swinton, *Swinton: An Inventory of the Family*, 7th ed., Melbourne, Australia, 2000, 2:9.

However, the form with figures alone may be difficult to follow.

1513 BOOK TITLE: WITH CHAPTER REFERENCE

[1]Author, *book title*, publisher, place, year, chapter number, "chapter title" [if significant], page number.

[1]Thomas Paul D'Aquino and David Stewart-Patterson, *Northern Edge: How Canadians Can Triumph in the Global Economy*, Stoddart Publishing Co. Ltd., Toronto, 2001, Chap. 7, "Walking Tall Among Nations," pp. 263–312.

NOTE: When a note refers primarily to the title of a book, the chapter number and the chapter title are not usually included. If they are considered significant, however, these details can be inserted just before the page numbers. The word *chapter* is usually abbreviated as *Chap.*, the chapter number is Arabic or Roman (depending on the original), and the chapter title is enclosed in quotation marks. Some writers prefer to use one style of chapter number throughout the notes.

1514 SELECTION FROM COLLECTED WORKS OF ONE AUTHOR

[1]Author, "title of selection," *book title*, publisher, place, year, page number.

[1]Stuart McLean, "Odd Jobs," *Vinyl Cafe Unplugged*, Penguin Books Canada Ltd., Toronto, 2000, pp. 171–185.

1515 SELECTION IN ANTHOLOGY

[1]Author of selection, "title of selection," **in** editor of anthology (**ed.**), *book title*, publisher, place, year, page number.

[1]Guy Vanderhaeghe, "The Jimi Hendrix Experience," in Joan Thomas and Heidi Harms (eds.), *Turn of the Story*, House of Anansi Press Limited, Toronto, 1999, p. 57.

[2]Lorna Crozier, "Seasons," in Paul Sonntag and Grant Loewen (eds.), *Moosemilk: The Best of Moosehead From 1977 to 1999*, DC Books, Montreal, 1999, p. 17.

[3]Jeannette C. Armstrong, "History Lesson," in Daniel David Moses and Terry Goldie (eds.), *An Anthology of Canadian Native Literature in English*, 2nd ed., Oxford University Press, Toronto, 1998, pp. 226–227.

[4]Alfred W. Purdy, "Postscripts," in Sabine Campbell, Roger Ploude, and Demetres Tryphonopoulos (eds.), *Fiddlehead Gold*, Goose Lane Editions, Fredericton, 1995, p. 22.

1516 ARTICLE IN REFERENCE WORK

[1]Author [if known], "article title," *name of reference work*, edition number [if not the first edition], publisher [usually omitted], place [usually omitted], year, page number [may be omitted].

[1]Ted Landau, "What Is Fragmented Memory?" *Sad Macs, Bombs, and Other Disasters*, 4th ed., Peachpit Press, Berkeley, CA, 2000, p. 473.

[2]Bud Smith and Arthur Bebak, "Protocols," *Creating Web Pages for Dummies*, IDG Books, Foster City, CA, 2000, p. 45.

[3]*The Canadian Style: A Guide to Writing*, 2nd ed., Dundurn Press Ltd., Toronto, 1997, pp. 86–97.

NOTE: It is not necessary to give the name of the publisher or the place of publication unless there is some possibility of confusion or the reference is not well known.

[4]"Canadian English: 250 Years in the Making," *The Canadian Oxford Dictionary*, 1998, pp. ix–x.

Moreover, if you are making reference to an article or an entry that appears in alphabetic order in the main portion of the work, even the page number may be omitted. If the reference work carries the name of an editor rather than an author, the editor's name is also usually omitted.

[5]"Resource Management," *The Canadian Encyclopedia*, Hurtig Publishers, Edmonton, 1985.

[6]"Internet," *ITP Nelson Canadian Dictionary of the English Language*, 1997.

1517 ARTICLE IN NEWSPAPER

> [1]Author [if known], "article title," *name of newspaper*, date, page number, column number.

> [1]Mark Dunn, "Of Kings and Castles," *The Calgary Sun*, May 30, 2001, p. 37, col. 2.

☞ *See ¶1518, note.*

NOTE: If a particular issue of a newspaper is published in several sections and the page numbering begins anew with each section, include the section letter or number before the page number.

> [2]"The Writing Imperative," *The Ottawa Citizen*, April 22, 2001, Sec. C, p. 14, cols. 2–3.

OR: . . . April 22, 2001, p. C14, cols. 2–3.

1518 ARTICLE IN MAGAZINE OR JOURNAL

a. Article in Magazine

> [1]Author [if known], "article title," *name of magazine*, date, page number.

> [1]Robert Kuner, "My First Job," *Reader's Digest*, February 2001, pp. 14–20.

> [2]Andy Holloway, "Deconstructing Dell," *Canadian Business*, April 20, 2001, pp. 97–99.

> [3]Lucie Renaud, "Contemporary Music for All Generations," *La Scena Musicale*, February 2001, p. 16.

NOTE: Omit the comma between the article title and the name of the periodical if the article title ends with a question mark or an exclamation point.

> [4]Ray Kurzweil, "Will My PC Be Smarter Than I Am?" *Time*, June 19, 2000, pp. 52–53.

> [5]Peter Gzowski, "Paree? Oui, Oui!" *Canadian Living*, January 1998, p. 39.

b. Article in Professional Journal

> [1]Author, "article title," *title of journal* [frequently abbreviated], series number [if given], volume number, issue number [if given], date, page number.

> [1]Jack M. Balkin, "Freedom of Expression in the Digital Age," *McGill International Review*, Vol. II, No. 4, Winter 2001, p. 16.

NOTE: Titles of journals are often abbreviated in notes whenever these abbreviations are likely to be familiar to the intended readership or are clearly identified in a bibliography at the end.

> [1]Jack M. Balkin, "Freedom of Expression in the Digital Age," *MIR*, Vol. II, No. 4, Winter 2001, p. 16.

1519 BULLETIN, PAMPHLET, OR MONOGRAPH

[1]Author [if given], "article title" [if appropriate], *title of bulletin*, series title and series number [if appropriate], volume number and issue number [if appropriate], sponsoring organization, place [may be omitted], date, page number.

[1]Judith Briles, "Plant Your Money Tree," *OfficePRO*, Vol. 61, No. 5, International Association of Administrative Professionals, May 2001, p. 11. (The name of the sponsoring organization was listed separately since a reader may not have known the initials *IAAP*.)

[2]"Small Business," *Government of Canada Services: For You*, No. PF4-2, Minister of Public Works and Government Services, 2000, p. 7.

NOTE: Because the pertinent data used to identify bulletins, pamphlets, and monographs may vary widely, adapt the pattern shown above as necessary to fit each particular situation.

1520 UNPUBLISHED DISSERTATION OR THESIS

[1]Author, "title of thesis," **doctoral dissertation OR master's thesis** [identifying phrase to be inserted], name of academic institution, place, date, page number.

[1]Colin Bryce Comfort, "Evaluating the Effectiveness of Parent Training for Preschoolers: A Meta-Analytical Review," doctoral dissertation, University of Calgary, 2002, p. 144.

1521 QUOTATION FROM A SECONDARY SOURCE

[1]Author, *book title*, publisher, place, date, page number, **quoted by or cited by** author, *book title*, publisher, place, date, page number.

[1]Tom Thomson, *Masterpieces of the Group of Seven*, Rous & Mann Press Limited, Toronto, 1964, quoted by Joan Murray, *Northern Lights*, McClelland & Stewart, Toronto, 1995, p. 21.

[2]Pierre Elliott Trudeau, *Against the Current*, McClelland & Stewart, Toronto, 1944, cited by "The Ascetic in a Canoe," *Canadian Geographic*, November/December 2000, pp. 40–42.

NOTE: While it is always preferable to take the wording of a quotation from the original source, it is sometimes necessary to draw the wording from a secondary source. In such cases construct the note in two parts: in the first part, give as much information as possible about the *original* source (derived, of course, from the reference note in the secondary source); in the second part, give the necessary information about the *secondary* source (which is at hand). Bridge the two parts of the note with a phrase such as *quoted by* or *cited by*. The pattern shown above assumes that the quotation originally appeared in a book and that the secondary source for the quoted material was also a book. Naturally, if the original source or the secondary source is a work other than a book, use the pattern appropriate for that work.

1522 QUOTATION FROM A CD-ROM

[1]Author [if known], "article title" [if appropriate], *title of work* (**CD-ROM**), publisher [may be omitted], place of publication [may be omitted], year of publication, reference to location of quotation [if available].

[1]"Pronouns," *Glencoe Interactive Grammar* (CD-ROM), McGraw-Hill Companies Inc., Westerville, Ohio, 1999, Topic 4.

[2]"Sentence Structure," *Essential Business Communications* (CD-ROM), Pro One Software, Los Cruces, NM, 1996.

NOTE: When citing material taken from a CD-ROM, try to provide some specific guidance on how to access the quoted passage on the disk. For example, if the material is organized in numbered paragraphs or pages, give the appropriate paragraph or page number. If the quoted passage is taken from a work organized like an encyclopedia or a dictionary (that is, in the form of brief articles or entries organized in alphabetic sequence), provide the article title or key word used to identify the article or entry. Without such assistance, a person can usually input a key phrase (or character string) from the quoted material and use the search feature of a word processing program to locate the complete passage.

1523 OTHER REFERENCE SOURCES

Writers frequently use other sources to gather information; for example, interviews, radio or television programs, films, visual and audio recordings, musical compositions, works of art, etc. Considering all the recent advancements in communication technology, the list is never-ending. The substance of a note or bibliographic reference, therefore, should be based on the type of material it is, its use to you, and the facts needed to find or retrieve it. Following the guidelines in ¶¶1508–1522 may be of some assistance, but ultimately your aim in reporting a citation should be for clarity and completeness. Perhaps the few examples below might be of some assistance.

[1]Blaine Lee, *The Power Principle: Influence with Honor*, Simon and Schuster, New York, 1997, videocassette.

[2]William Zinsser, *How to Write a Memoir*, Produced by Rick Harris, Harper Audio, HarperCollins, New York, 1999, audiocassette.

[3]J. B. Mansbridge, "Security on the Internet," telephone conversation with ABC security specialist, October 14, 2000.

[4]Deidre McMurdy, *Prime Business*, "Replacing the CEO," Prime TV channel, Toronto, May 31, 2001.

☞ *For online sources, see ¶1533–1539.*

Elements of Source Reference Notes

1524 NOTE NUMBER

a. Make sure that the number at the start of a footnote or an endnote corresponds to the appropriate reference number in the text.

b. Indent the note number 0.25 to 0.5 inch, and key it (1) on the line (like an ordinary number), followed by a period and 1 or 2 spaces, or (2) as a superscript without any space following it. The on-the-line style is always used in endnotes. (See ¶¶1505–1506.)

1. Faye Reineberg Holt, *Sharing the Good Times*, Detselig Enterprises Ltd., Calgary, 2000, p. 134.

OR:

[1]Faye Reineberg Holt, *Sharing the Good Times*, Detselig Enterprises Ltd., Calgary, 2000, p. 134.

☞ *See ¶1502e on numbering notes; ¶1502f–g on the use of symbols in place of figures.*

1525 NAMES OF AUTHORS

a. Key an author's name (first name first) exactly as it appears on the title page of a book or in the heading of an article. (See ¶1508a, note.)

[1]Pete Sarsfield, M.D., *Running with the Caribou*, Turnstone Press, Winnipeg, 1997, p. 84.

[2]Heather-jane Robertson, *No More Teachers, No More Books*, McClelland & Stewart, Toronto, 1998, pp. 121–162.

[3]Eric W. Kierans with Walter Stewart, *Remembering*, Stoddart Publishing Co. Ltd., Toronto, 2001, p. 105.

[4]Larry Fisk and John Schellenberg, *Pattern of Conflict Paths to Peace*, Broadview Press, Peterborough, 2000, p. 67.

b. When two authors have the same surname, show the surname with each author's listing.

[5]Mary Purbhoo and Dhirajlal Purbhoo, *Teach Yourself Simply Accounting Version 8.0 for Windows*, Addison Wesley Longman, Toronto, 2001, p. 5.

c. When there are three or more authors, list only the first author's name followed by *et al.* (meaning "and others"). Do not italicize or underline *et al.*

[6]William A. Sabin et al., *The Gregg Reference Manual*, 6th Canadian Edition, McGraw-Hill Ryerson, Toronto, 2003, p. 443.

NOTE: The names of all the authors may be given, but once this style is used in a source reference note, it should be used consistently.

[7]William A. Sabin, Wilma K. Millar, Sharon L. Sine, G. Wendy Strashok, *The Gregg Reference Manual*, 6th Canadian Edition, McGraw-Hill Ryerson, Toronto, 2003, p. 443.

d. When an organization (rather than an individual) is the author of the material, show the organization's name in the author's position.

[8]The St. Patrick's Benevolent Society of Toronto, *A History*, Providence Road Press, Ottawa, 1999, p. 45.

However, if the organization is both the author and the publisher, show the organization's name only once—as the publisher.

[9]"Outright Gifts," *Tax Guide to Planned Giving*, Certified General Accountants Association of Canada, rev. ed., Vancouver, 2000, p. 9.

(Continued on page 440.)

e. When a work such as an anthology carries an editor's name rather than an author's name, list the editor's name in the author's position, followed by the abbreviation *ed.* in parentheses. (If the names of two or more editors are listed, use the abbreviation *eds.* in parentheses.)

> [10]Jeffrey M. Heath (ed.), *Profiles in Canadian Literature*, Vol. 8, Dundurn Press Limited, Toronto, 1991, p. 107.

> [11]Elisabeth Boetzkes and Wilfrid J. Waluchow (eds.), *Readings in Health Care Ethics*, Broadview Press, Peterborough, 2000, p. 86.

NOTE: If a reference work (such as an encyclopedia, a dictionary, or a directory) carries the name of an editor rather than an author, the editor's name is usually omitted. (See ¶1516, note.)

> [12]*The Oxford Companion to Canadian Literature*, 2nd ed., Oxford University Press, Toronto, 1997, pp. 239–241.

RATHER THAN:

> [12]Eugene Benson and William Toye (eds.), *The Oxford Companion to Canadian Literature*, 2nd ed., Oxford University Press, Toronto, 1997, pp. 239–241.

f. If the author of a work is unknown, begin the note with the title of the work. Do not use *Anonymous* in place of the author's name.

1526 TITLE OF THE WORK

a. In giving the title of the work, follow the title page of a book or the main heading of an article for wording, spelling, and punctuation. However, adjust the capitalization as necessary so that all titles cited in the notes conform to a standard style. For example, a book entitled *Assertiveness*, with a subtitle (*the right to be you*) shown entirely in small letters on the title page for graphic effect, would appear in a note as follows: Claire Walmsley, *Assertiveness: The Right to Be You.*

☞ *For the capitalization of titles, see ¶¶360–363.*

b. If a title and a subtitle are shown on separate lines in the original work without any intervening punctuation, use a colon to separate them in the source reference note. (See ¶1510 for an example.)

c. In general, use italics or underlining for titles of *complete* published works and quotation marks for titles that refer to *parts* of complete published works.

☞ *For the use of italics or underlining with titles, see ¶¶289, 1508a; for the use of quotation marks with titles, see ¶¶242–243.*

1527 PUBLISHER'S NAME

a. List the publisher's name as it appears on the title page (for example, *John Wiley & Sons*) or in a shortened form that is clearly recognizable (*Wiley*); use one form consistently throughout. If a division of the publishing company is also listed on the title page, it is not necessary to include this information in the footnote. Publishers, however, often do so in references to their own materials.

b. Omit the publisher's name from references to newspapers and other periodicals. The publisher's name is also usually omitted from references to dictionaries and similar works unless confusion might result or the work is not well known. (For examples, see ¶1516.)

1528 PLACE OF PUBLICATION

a. As a rule, list only the city of publication (for example, *Vancouver, Winnipeg, Toronto, New York*). If the city is not well known to your intended audience or if it is likely to be confused with another city by the same name, add the country or the abbreviation for the province or state (for example, *Cambridge, England; Cambridge, Ontario; Cambridge, Massachusetts*). If the title page lists several cities in which the publisher has offices, use only the first city named.

b. Omit the place of publication from references to periodicals and well-known reference works.

c. Incorporate the city name in the name of a newspaper that might otherwise be unrecognized. For example, *The Sun* (a common newspaper name) should be referred to in notes as *The Vancouver Sun* or *The Calgary Sun*. (See ¶1517.)

1529 DATE OF PUBLICATION

a. For books show the year of publication. (Use the most recent year shown in the copyright notice.)

b. For monthly periodicals show both the month and the year. (See ¶1518 for examples.)

c. For weekly or daily newspapers and other periodicals, show the month, day, and year. (See ¶1517 for examples.)

1530 PAGE NUMBERS

a. Page references in notes occur in the following forms:

p. 3	p. v
pp. 3–4	pp. v–vi

pp. 301 f. (meaning "page 301 and the following page")

pp. 301 ff. (meaning "page 301 and the following pages")

NOTE: Whenever possible, avoid using the indefinite abbreviations *f.* and *ff.*, and supply a specific range of page numbers instead.

b. In a range of page numbers, the second number is sometimes abbreviated; for example, *pp. 981–983* may be expressed as *pp. 981–83*. (See ¶460.)

c. There is a trend toward dropping *p.* and *pp.* when there is no risk of mistaking the numbers for anything but page numbers.

☞ *For the use of an en dash or a hyphen in a range of numbers, see ¶459a.*

15

Subsequent References

1531 a. When a note refers to a work that was fully identified in the note *immediately preceding*, it may be shortened by use of the abbreviation *ibid.* (meaning "in the same place"). *Ibid.* replaces all those elements that would otherwise be carried over intact from the previous note. Do not italicize or underline *ibid.*

> [1]Craig McKie, *Using the Web for Social Research*, McGraw-Hill Ryerson, Toronto, 1997, pp. 57–71.
>
> [2]Ibid., p. 94. (*Ibid.* represents all the elements in the previous note except the page number.)
>
> [3]Ibid. (Here *ibid.* represents everything in the preceding note, including the same page number.)

b. If you plan to use *ibid.* in a *footnote*, make sure that the footnote "immediately preceding" is no more than a few pages back. Otherwise, the interested reader will have to riffle back through the pages in order to find the "immediately preceding" footnote. To spare your reader this inconvenience, use the forms suggested in ¶1532d.

c. Do not use *ibid.* in a *textnote* unless the one "immediately preceding" is on the same page and easy to spot; otherwise, your reader will have to search through lines and lines of text to find it. To spare your reader, construct these "subsequent reference" textnotes along the same lines as "first reference" textnotes. (See ¶1507b.)

NOTE: With *endnotes*, the use of *ibid.* will cause no inconvenience, since it refers to the note directly above.

1532 a. When a note refers to a work fully identified in an earlier note but *not the one immediately preceding*, it may be shortened as follows:

> [1]Author's surname, page number.
>
> [8]McKie, p. 145. (Referring to the work fully identified in an earlier note; see the first example in ¶1531a.)

NOTE: When short forms are used for subsequent references, it is desirable to provide a complete bibliography as well, so that the interested reader can quickly find the complete reference for each work in an alphabetic listing.

b. When previous reference has been made to different authors with the same surname, the use of a surname alone in a subsequent reference would be confusing. Therefore, the basic pattern in ¶1532a must be modified in the following way:

> [1]Author's initial(s) plus surname, page number.

OR: [2]Author's full name, page number.

> [1]R. Douglas Francis et al., *Origins: Canadian History Since Confederation*, 3rd ed., Harcourt Brace Canada, Toronto, 1996, pp. 348–389.
>
> [2]Daniel Francis, *National Dreams: Myth, Memory & Canadian History*, Arsenal Pulp Press, Vancouver, 1997, p. 45.
>
> [3]R. Douglas Francis, pp. 401–455.
>
> [4]Daniel Francis, p. 67.

c. If previous reference has been made to different works by the same author, any subsequent reference should contain the title of the specific work now being referred to. This title may be shortened to a key word or phrase; the word or phrase should be sufficiently clear, however, so that the full title can be readily identified in the bibliography or in an earlier note.

> [1]Author's surname, *book title* [shortened if feasible], page number.

> [1]Don Tapscott, *Digital Capital: Harnessing the Power of Business*, McGraw-Hill, New York, 2000, p. 58.

> [2]Don Tapscott, David Ticoll, and Alex Lowy, *Blueprint to the Digital Economy*, McGraw-Hill, New York, 1998, p. 89.

> [3]Don Tapscott, *Creating Value in the Network Economy*, McGraw-Hill, New York, 1999, p. 107.

> [4]Tapscott, *Digital Capital*, p. 85.

> [5]Tapscott, *Creating Value*, p. 144.

If referring to an article in a periodical, use the periodical title rather than the article title.

> [2]Author's surname, *periodical title* [shortened if feasible], page number.

> [6]Jacqueline Thompson, "Small Business: Tech Support," *IE: Money*, June 2001, p. 31.

> [7]Arthur Siegel, . . .

> [8]Jacqueline Thompson, *IE: Money*, p. 33. (Referring to the work identified in note 6 above.)

d. A more formal style in subsequent references uses the abbreviations *loc. cit.* ("in the place cited") and *op. cit.* ("in the work cited").

> [1]Author's surname, **loc. cit.** (This pattern is used when reference is made to the *very same page* in the work previously identified.)

> [2]Author's surname, **op. cit.**, page number. (This pattern is used when reference is made to a *different page* in the work previously identified.)

> [1]Michael Alexander, *A History of Old English Literature*, Broadview Press, Peterborough, 2001, p. 102.

> [2]Stephen Cain, "The Horseshoe," *Torontology*, ECW Press, Toronto, 2001, p. 5.

> [3]Alexander, op. cit., p. 178. (Referring to a different page in *Old English Literature*.)

> [4]Cain, loc. cit. (Referring to the same page in *Torontology*.)

> [5]Ibid. (Referring to exactly the same page as shown in note 4. *Ibid.* may be used only to refer to the note immediately preceding. See ¶1531.)

NOTE: Do not italicize or underline *loc. cit., op. cit.,* or *ibid.*

NOTES BASED ON ONLINE SOURCES

Business and academic writers increasingly rely on the Internet as the source of information to be quoted, paraphrased, or summarized in the reports and manuscripts they prepare. Hence the critical need for guidelines on how to construct *online citations*—that is, footnotes, endnotes, and bibliographic entries that are based on online sources.

IMPORTANT: Users should be aware and astute as information on the Internet is not always correct. Footnotes become very important as proof of information found. (See ¶1535.) Since much online material originally appeared in print (a much more stable medium), refer whenever possible to the printed source rather than the online source.

Dealing With Online Addresses

The feature that distinguishes an online citation from one based on printed material is the inclusion of an *online address*—an element that takes the place of information about the name and location of the publisher. There are two major types of online addresses: a URL address (discussed in ¶1533) and an e-mail address (discussed in ¶1534).

1533 URL ADDRESSES

Every unit of information on the Internet has its own unique address—a Uniform Resource Locator, commonly referred to as a URL and pronounced as individual letters *(you-are-el)* or as a word *(earl)*. (See ¶501b.) A URL represents not only the storage location of a particular document on the Internet but also the means by which a document can be retrieved. If a URL is not accurately presented in an online citation, it will be impossible to locate the material being cited.

A URL consists of at least two parts: (1) the *protocol* (the name of the system to be used in linking one computer with another on the Internet) and (2) the *host name* (the name of the host computer where the desired material is stored). Here, for example, is the URL for Yahoo!, a large directory of Web pages.

Protocol Host Name
http://www.yahoo.com

a. **Protocol.** There are a number of protocols that you can use to locate material stored on another computer on the Internet.

- **HTTP (HyperText Transfer Protocol).** The most widely used of all the protocols, HTTP permits you to surf the World Wide Web—that part of the Internet that provides access not only to text material but also to photographs, drawings, animations, and video and sound clips.

- **FTP (File Transfer Protocol).** FTP permits you to transfer text material from an *ftp server* (the host computer where the desired material is stored) to your own computer.

- **Listserv.** Listserv (a short form for *mailing list server*) permits you to retrieve messages posted to a network of mailing lists and to post your own messages as well.

- **Usenet.** Usenet is a network consisting of thousands of newsgroups (discussion groups each focused on a particular topic of interest). A message posted to a particular newsgroup can be read and commented on by any interested member of that newsgroup, and those comments may prompt additional rounds of comments. The original message (known as an *article*) and the subsequent series of comments create what is known as a *thread.* Users doing research on Usenet have the option of citing only the article, one or more of the comments, or the entire thread.

When these protocols appear as the first part of a URL, they are represented as follows:

HTTP:	http://	Listserv:	listserv://
FTP:	ftp://	Usenet:	news://

The first part of a URL always ends with a colon and two forward slashes (://).

b. Host Name. The second part of a URL, the host name, consists of several elements separated by *dots* (never referred to as *periods*). Here are some representative host names as they appear in Web-based URLs:

	Protocol Host Name
eBay:	http://www.ebay.com
Gateway 2000:	http://www.gw2k.com
Intel:	http://www.intel.com
PBS Online:	http://www.pbs.org
NASA:	http://www.nasa.gov
PSINet:	http://www.psi.net

In the host names shown above, the first element—www—refers to the World Wide Web. The second and third elements—for example, *.ebay.com* (referred to as *dot-ebay-dot-com*)—represent the domain name. The second element often reflects some form of the name of the organization or country. The third element is usually a two- or three-letter unit preceded by a dot; it is called a *top-level domain* (TLD) or a *zone,* and it indicates the country or type of organization that owns the host computer. For example:

.ca	Canada	.de	Germany
.fr	France	.it	Italy
.jp	Japan	.uk	United Kingdom

.com	commercial organization	.mil	military site
.edu	educational institution	.net	network organization
.gov	government body or agency	.org	non-profit, non-commercial
.int	international organization		organization

Seven new TLDs have been proposed and may soon be adopted:

.arts	an organization dealing with arts and entertainment activities
.firm	a business or firm

(Continued on page 446.)

.info   a provider of information services

.nom   an individual or personal terminology

.rec   an organization dealing with recreation and entertainment activities

.store   a business offering goods for sale

.web   an organization dealing with activities relating to the Web

c. File Name. A URL may also provide a file name as the final element. For example, the following URL directs a Web browser to retrieve a file named *iway.html* from a host computer named *www.cc.web.com* using the HyperText Transfer Protocol.

Protocol   Host Name   File Name

http://www.cc.web.com/iway.html

NOTE: A *tilde* (~), also referred to as a *swung dash*, is sometimes used to introduce a file name. For example,

http://www.netaxs.com/~harrington

d. A URL may also include one or more elements between the host name and the file name. These elements indicate the electronic path to be taken (after the host computer is reached) in order to locate the desired file. For example,

Protocol   Host Name   Path   File Name

http://www.yahoo.com/Computers/World_Wide_Web/HTML_Editors

e. URLs are usually typed in small letters, but when capital letters appear, follow the style of the particular URL exactly as shown. Also note that spaces between words in any part of a URL have to be signified by means of an underline (as in the example in *d* above) or some other mark of punctuation such as a hyphen (as in the example below).

http://www.vpl.vancouver.bc.ca/hypertext/faq/usenet/FAQ-List.html

NOTE: The URLs shown in ¶1533b–e end with a forward slash but others do not. Always follow the style of a URL exactly as shown.

f. When Web-based URLs are given in documents and publications aimed at computer professionals, the protocol *http://* is often omitted; the fact that the host name begins with *www* makes it clear to knowledgeable readers which protocol is to be used. When constructing your own citations, consider how much your readers will know. As a general rule, it is safer to insert the protocol at the start of a URL, even if it is omitted in your source.

1534 E-MAIL ADDRESSES

An e-mail address consists of two parts separated by an *at* sign (@). The part before the @ is called the *mailbox*; the part after the @ is called the *domain*.

a. The mailbox typically consists of the user's name (the name assigned by an e-mail service provider). However, some commercial online services assign users a numerical mailbox.

Mailbox   Domain   Mailbox   Domain

jclarkson@home.com   73004.5011@aol.com

b. The domain represents the system on which the e-mail message is delivered; for example, Home and America Online as shown above. The last part of the domain, *.com*, is called the *zone*.

☞ *For guidelines on the formatting of e-mail messages, see ¶¶1707–1710.*

1535 GENERAL GUIDELINES FOR ONLINE CITATIONS

Making use of online sources can pose special problems. After you have quoted or made reference to certain online materials in your report or your manuscript, the person who originally posted the material may later decide to change it or transfer it to a new location (with a new URL or e-mail address) or remove it from the Internet altogether. If any of these things should happen, readers who try to confirm the accuracy of your citations may very well draw unfair conclusions about your competence as a researcher and as a writer. To protect yourself against these potential problems, take the following precautions.

a. Save every cited online document as hard copy and as part of your backup files. If the document is very long, save at least enough of the document to establish the full context from which the cited material was taken. Then if the need arises, you can always show that you have not taken the material out of context or distorted its intended meaning.

b. Include not only the date on which the material was posted on the Internet but also the date on which you accessed the material you plan to cite. If the material is subsequently changed or removed, you will still be able to prove the accuracy of your citation.

c. When URLs or e-mail addresses appear in footnotes, endnotes, bibliographies, or in the main text, enclose each address in angle brackets (<>). The use of angle brackets makes it possible to insert sentence punctuation before and after an online address and not have the punctuation mistaken for an integral part of the online address.

d. Always present a URL or an e-mail address exactly as it is given. Never alter the capitalization, the internal spacing, or the symbols used. Failure to provide an accurate online address will usually make it impossible to locate the desired information.

e. Try to fit a URL on one line. If it becomes necessary to divide a URL at the end of a line, observe the following:

- You may break *after* the double (//) that marks the end of a protocol (but not within the protocol itself).

Acceptable Line Ending	Next Line
<http://	www.nowonder.com>
NOT <http:	**NOT** //www.nowonder.com>

- You may break *before* (but never after) a dot (.), a single slash (/), a hyphen (-), an underscore (_), or any other mark of punctuation.

(Continued on page 448.)

Acceptable Line Ending	Next Line
<http://www	.pbs.org>
NOT <http://www.	NOT pbs.org>
<http://www/mcgraw	-hill.com>
NOT <http://www/mcgraw-	NOT hill.com>

- Never insert a hyphen within an online address to signify an end-of-line break.

f. Try to fit an e-mail address on one line. If it becomes necessary to divide it at the end of a line, observe the following:

- You may break *before* the *at* symbol (@) or *before* a dot.

Acceptable Line Ending	Next Line
<wryter6290	@aol.com>
NOT <wryter6290@	NOT aol.com>
<sines@home	.midcoast.com>
NOT <sines@home.	NOT midcoast.com>

- Never insert a hyphen within an e-mail address to signify an end-of-line-break.

Constructing Online Citations

The following guidelines provide a number of basic patterns for constructing source reference notes based on online sources. These patterns are much the same as those presented in ¶¶1508–1521 for printed works with one fundamental difference: the name and location of the publisher of a printed work are replaced in these patterns by URLs or e-mail addresses enclosed in angle brackets (< >).

The following patterns cannot cover every contingency that you may encounter when constructing online citations. Therefore, be prepared to adapt these patterns as necessary to fit each particular situation.

NOTE: These notes are appropriate for use in constructing footnotes and endnotes in business and academic documents. For examples showing how these patterns should be adjusted for use in a bibliography, see ¶1542a, c.

1536 WORLD WIDE WEB SOURCES

[1]Author's name, "title of document," *title of complete work*, date of posting, <URL beginning http://> (date of access).

[1]James Karney, "The E-Web Arrives," *Internet World*, June 15, 2001, <http://www.internetworld.com/061501/06.15.01internettech1.jsp> (June 23, 2001).

1537 E-MAIL SOURCES

[1]Author's name, <author's e-mail address>, "subject line," date of posting, type of e-mail (date of access).

[1]Erich Volk, <ErichV@mcgrawhill.ca>, "Gregg Reference Manual, Canadian Edition," June 15, 2002, webmaster communication (June 17, 2002).

NOTE: For the entry, *type of e-mail*, personal e-mail addresses should not appear in a list of references.

1538 LISTSERV SOURCES

[1]Author's name, <author's e-mail address>, "subject line," date of posting, <URL beginning listserv://> (date of access).

[1]Bo Ekvall, <bo@PARTENON.COM>, "NEW: FREE Business-Related E-Zine. FREE Ad!" November 23, 1998, <listserv://scout.cs.wisc.edu/> (March 3, 1999).

1539 USENET SOURCES

[1]Author's name, <author's e-mail address>, "subject line," date of posting, <newsgroup's URL beginning news://> (date of access).

[1]Laura Beall, <beall@azstarnet.com>, "Enterprises for Women," November 7, 1998, <news://alt.business> (May 27, 1999).

NOTE: If the date of posting cannot be determined, insert the abbreviation *n.d.* (no date).

[1]Peter Hardy, "Visiting Auyuittuq National Park," Arctic Library, n.d., <http://www.frozentoes.com/library/default.html> (June 25, 2001).

BIBLIOGRAPHIES

A bibliography at the end of a report or a manuscript typically lists all the works *consulted* in the preparation of the material as well as all the works that were actually *cited* in the notes. The format of a bibliography is also used for any list of titles, such as a list of recommended readings or a list of new publications.

1540 Word processing programs may provide templates for bibliographies. Some special word processing programs, however, will format not only footnotes and endnotes but bibliographies as well. These programs ask you to create a database (also referred to as a *reference library*) in which you enter the necessary data for each title you plan to cite. Then you select (1) one of the standard formats built into the software or (2) a format that you have modified or created. In effect, once you have developed the reference library, you can extract the data in the form of footnotes, endnotes, or entries in a bibliography.

1541 Consider the following guidelines for formatting a bibliography. (See the illustration on page 451.)

a. On a new page key *BIBLIOGRAPHY* (or some other appropriate title) in all-capital letters and in boldface. Centre this title 2 inches from the top and begin the text on the second or third line below.

b. Use the same margins as for other pages in the body of the report or manuscript (see ¶¶1405–1408), and treat the numbering of these pages as indicated in ¶1427f–g.

c. Bibliographical entries are usually not numbered. (See ¶1542c.) Use the *hanging indent* feature to start the first line of the entry at the left margin and to begin the turnover lines at the tab setting already established for the body of the document.

(Continued on page 450.)

d. Indent turnover lines 0.5 inch so that the first word in each entry will stand out.

e. Leave 1 blank line between entries (whether they are single- or double-spaced).

1542 a. List the entries alphabetically by author's last name.

b. Entries lacking an author are alphabetized by title. Disregard the word *The* or *A* at the beginning of a title in determining alphabetic sequence. (For examples, see the fifth and eleventh entries in the illustration on page 451.) Note that the fifth entry is alphabetized on the basis of *Guide* following *Guerilla* and the eleventh entry is alphabetized on the basis of *Two* following *Tapscott.*

NOTE: When a publication lacks an author and the title begins with a figure (see the next-to-last entry in the illustration on page 451), alphabetize the title on the basis of how the figure would appear if spelled out. Thus when *2000* is converted to *Two Thousand*, the title is alphabetized on the basis of *Two*, following *Tapscott.*

c. If you plan to use the style of textnotes described in ¶1507b, then the bibliographical entries should be numbered. In that case begin each entry of the bibliography with a number keyed at the left margin, followed by a period and 1 or 2 spaces. Then key the rest of the entry in the customary way, but indent any turnover lines so that they begin under the first word in the line above. (In the parenthetical textnotes, you can then make reference to different works by their bibliographic "entry number" instead of by author.)

d. In a bibliography with numbered entries, align the numbers on the period.

> 9. Hoffert, Paul, *All Together Now: Connect Communities*, Stoddart Publishers, Toronto, 2000.
> 10. Jones, David D., *A Funny Bone That Was*, Detselig Enterprises Inc., Calgary, 2000.
> 11. Newman, Peter C., *Titans: How the Canadian Establishment Seized Power*, Penguin Books, Toronto, 1999.

NOTE: If you use the numbered list feature of your software program, the turnover lines will automatically be indented. The list will also be typed single-spaced. For a more open look, insert 1 blank line between entries (as shown in the illustration above). The numbered list feature also aligns single- and double-digit numbers on the left. However, you can make an adjustment so that the numbers align at the right (as in the examples in ¶1542d). For additional details, see ¶1357d.

1543 When a bibliography contains more than one work by the same author, replace the author's name with a long dash (using 3 em dashes) in all the entries after the first. List the works alphabetically by title. (See the eighth and ninth entries in the illustration on page 451 for examples.) Note that these titles are alphabetized on the key words *Creating* and *Digital*. The tenth entry involves co-authors and therefore follows the works written by the first author alone.

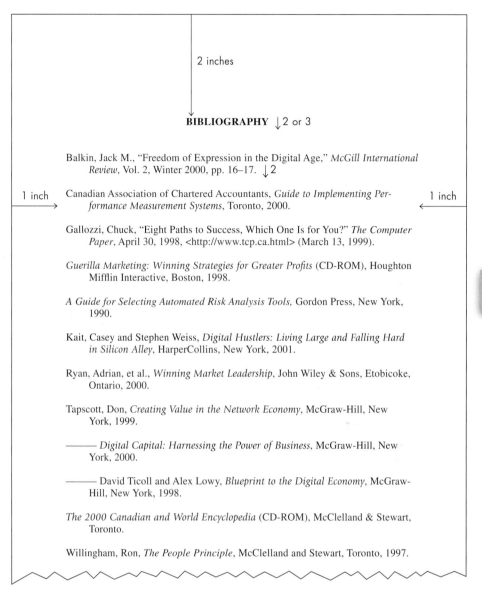

BIBLIOGRAPHY ↓2 or 3

Balkin, Jack M., "Freedom of Expression in the Digital Age," *McGill International Review*, Vol. 2, Winter 2000, pp. 16–17. ↓2

Canadian Association of Chartered Accountants, *Guide to Implementing Performance Measurement Systems*, Toronto, 2000.

Gallozzi, Chuck, "Eight Paths to Success, Which One Is for You?" *The Computer Paper*, April 30, 1998, <http://www.tcp.ca.html> (March 13, 1999).

Guerilla Marketing: Winning Strategies for Greater Profits (CD-ROM), Houghton Mifflin Interactive, Boston, 1998.

A Guide for Selecting Automated Risk Analysis Tools, Gordon Press, New York, 1990.

Kait, Casey and Stephen Weiss, *Digital Hustlers: Living Large and Falling Hard in Silicon Alley*, HarperCollins, New York, 2001.

Ryan, Adrian, et al., *Winning Market Leadership*, John Wiley & Sons, Etobicoke, Ontario, 2000.

Tapscott, Don, *Creating Value in the Network Economy*, McGraw-Hill, New York, 1999.

———— *Digital Capital: Harnessing the Power of Business*, McGraw-Hill, New York, 2000.

———— David Ticoll and Alex Lowy, *Blueprint to the Digital Economy*, McGraw-Hill, New York, 1998.

The 2000 Canadian and World Encyclopedia (CD-ROM), McClelland & Stewart, Toronto.

Willingham, Ron, *The People Principle*, McClelland and Stewart, Toronto, 1997.

NOTE: As an alternative, multiple entries pertaining to the same author may be listed according to the date of each publication.

☞ *For guidelines on three-em dashes, see ¶216c.*

1544 Entries in bibliographies contain the same elements and follow the same style as source reference notes except for two key differences.

   a. Begin each entry with the name of the author listed in inverted order (last name first). When an entry includes two or more authors' names, invert only

(Continued on page 452.)

the first author's name. When an organization is listed as the author, do not invert the name.

Deloite & Touche, *How to Reduce the Tax You Pay*, 13th ed., Key Porter Books, Toronto, 2000.

Foot, David K., with Daniel Stoffman, *Boom, Bust, and Echo*, rev. ed., MacFarlane Walter & Ross, Toronto, 2000.

Wackershauser, Larry H., *Absolutely No GST Charged Here: Tilting at Windmills*, Diggety Dank Publishers, Cochrane, Alberta, 2000.

b. Include page numbers in bibliographic entries only when the material being cited is part of a larger work. In such cases show the page number or numbers (for example, *pp. 215–232*) on which the material appears.

Janigan, Mary, "Opening the Floodgates," *Maclean's*, June 4, 2001, pp. 40–42.

☞ *For the use of an en dash or a hyphen in a range of page numbers, see ¶459a.*

c. In academic material, bibliographic entries typically follow a slightly different style. In the examples below, note that a period follows each of the three main parts of the entry (author's name, the title, and the publishing information). Also note that the parentheses that normally enclose the publishing information in an academic-style footnote or endnote are omitted in the bibliographic entry. (See ¶1508b.)

Carroll, Jim and Rick Broadhead. *Canadian Internet Handbook 2000*. Toronto: Stoddart, 1999.

Harmon, Fred. *Business 2010: Five Forces That Will Reshape Business*. Washington: Kiplinger, 2001.

Janigan, Mary. "Opening the Floodgates." *Maclean's*, June 4, 2001, p. 40. (Note that the magazine title—in this case *Maclean's*—is considered part of the publishing information. Thus a period follows the article title to mark the end of the title information in the entry.)

Rosenberg, DeAnne. "Women in Business: Gender Differences in the Professional World—Are Male and Female Managers Like Oil and Water?" *Business Credit*, November 1, 1989, <telnet://132.162.37.16> (April 9, 1999).

 See the Online Learning Centre at www.mcgrawhill.ca/college/gregg for related weblinks.

SECTION **SIXTEEN**

Tables

You can fit a good deal of material into a compact space when you present it in the form of a table—with items arranged in *rows* (to be read horizontally) and in *columns* (to be read vertically). However, in designing a table, you should aim for more than compactness. Your reader should be able to locate specific information faster—and detect significant patterns or trends in the data more quickly—than if the same information were presented in the regular text.

The table feature of word processing programs is commonly used to display data that appears in a row and column format, including such documents as résumés, agendas, itineraries, etc. Most users who create tables with many calculations will use a spreadsheet program; they may import the table into a word processing document.

The following paragraphs provide detailed guidelines for creating a table in a word processing program. Modify these guidelines as necessary to achieve results that are easy to understand, attractive to look at, and as simple as possible to execute.

Using the Software Table Feature

A table can be created with little advance planning. Corrections and format adjustments can be made with relative ease to give the appearance of a professionally typeset table.

Table A-15		
LIFE INSURANCE IN FORCE		
($000 000 Omitted)		
Year	**Ordinary**	**Group**
1910	11 783	—
1940	79 346	14 938
1950	149 116	47 793
1960	341 881	175 903
1970	734 730	551 357
1980	1 760 474	1 579 355
1990	5 366 982	3 753 506
2000	8 337 188	5 158 538

Source: *The Canadian World Almanac and Book of Facts: 2002*, p. 837.

Note that within each column the column heading and the text are centred between vertical rules. Note also the use of extra space surrounding various elements of the table, which gives it an open look, making it easier to read.

Paragraphs 1601–1606 show (1) the results you will achieve if you prepare this table with the Microsoft Word table feature, accepting all the default specifications, and (2) the steps you need to take in order to achieve the look of a professionally typeset table.

IMPORTANT NOTE: When you use the table feature to execute a table, how far you go in modifying the default specifications will depend on a number of factors. If the table is intended for your eyes alone *and* speed rather than appearance is critical, you may want to limit modifying the default specifications. On the other hand, if the table will appear in a document to be presented to higher management or to people outside the organization, you will have to invest the extra time and effort needed to create a more professional-looking table.

1601 The default format provided by the Microsoft Word table feature encloses the complete table (including any heading at the top and any notes at the bottom) in a grid of horizontal and vertical lines. Each "box" formed is called a cell.

- At the outset specify the number of columns and rows you may need to complete the table; this setting can be easily adjusted if more or less are required.

- In the absence of other instructions, the table grid will have the same width as the regular text. You may find it simplest to accept this dimension at the outset and adjust the width of the table later on.

- Tables will automatically be single-spaced.

1602 a. Begin by entering all the data for your table. Notice that everything defaults to a left alignment. For long lines of headings or titles, the text may not fit nicely into the table cell. This will be adjusted later. (See ¶¶1602c and 1603b.) Include the bold attribute for title(s) and column headings. Also include Italics for the source reference referred to at the bottom of the table.

Table A-15 **LIFE INSURANCE IN FORCE** **($000 000 Omitted)**		
Year	**Ordinary**	**Group**
1910	11 783	—
1940	79 346	14 938
1950	149 116	47 793
1960	341 881	75 903
1970	734 730	551 357
1980	1 760 474	1 579 355
1990	5 366 982	3 753 506
2000	8 337 188	5 158 538
Source: *The Canadian World Almanac and Book of Facts: 2002,* p. 837.		

(Continued on page 456.)

b. It is appropriate to use left alignment when the column text consists entirely of words or figures representing years as shown in the first column. However, when the column text consists of figures that have to be added or compared in some way, the figures should align at the right. The following illustration shows that the "align right" feature has been applied to the second and third columns.

c. In order to set up the titles and the source reference, refer to the illustration below to notice that the cells in the first row and the last row of the table have been joined (merged). To further display these elements, centre align the titles and set the tab to 0.25 inch for the word *Source*.

Table A-15 LIFE INSURANCE IN FORCE ($000 000 Omitted)		
Year	**Ordinary**	**Group**
1910	11 783	—
1940	79 346	14 938
1950	149 116	47 793
1960	341 881	75 903
1970	734 730	551 357
1980	1 760 474	1 579 355
1990	5 366 982	3 753 506
2000	8 337 188	5 158 538
Source: *The Canadian World Almanac and Book of Facts: 2002*, p. 837.		

1603 a. The table, as it now stands, has excessively wide columns. To remedy the situation, manually adjust the column widths. Click on the appropriate vertical line and drag it to the desired point. Use the ruler bar to help determine the distance where each outer column is being dragged, as each outer edge should be dragged approximately the same distance. Use the print preview feature (full page view) often to verify the most attractive horizontal position on the page.

NOTE: To centre a table exactly horizontally on a page, use the Table Properties feature to make the adjustment.

b. Once the table is sized, it will be obvious that the column headings need to be centred in each column. Use the centre align button.

Table A-15
LIFE INSURANCE IN FORCE
($000 000 Omitted)

Year	Ordinary	Group
1910	11 783	—
1940	79 346	14 938
1950	149 116	47 793
1960	341 881	75 903
1970	734 730	551 357
1980	1 760 474	1 579 355
1990	5 366 982	3 753 506
2000	8 337 188	5 158 538

Source: *The Canadian World Almanac and Book of Facts: 2002*, p. 837.

1604 To further improve the appearance of the table, consider making these adjustments.

a. Use Enter to insert 1 blank line space between the lines in the table heading and above and below the heading as a whole.

NOTE: If the table title or subtitle will not fit all on one line, break it into sensible phrases and single-space the turnover. (See ¶1620 for illustrations of the ways in which the elements in the table heading may be arranged.)

b. Use Enter to insert 1 blank line space above and below the column headings.

c. Use Enter to insert 1 blank line space above and below the notes section at the bottom of the page.

d. If the footnotes each require no more than one full line, begin each note at the left margin. However, if any one of the notes turns over to a second line, indent the first line of each note 0.25 to 0.5 inch.

e. Add shading to portions of the table as desired to give special emphasis to certain elements and make the table more attractive as a whole.

NOTE: If all of these modifications are made, the table will then look like the following illustration.

(Continued on page 458.)

Table A-15

LIFE INSURANCE IN FORCE

($000 000 Omitted)

Year	Ordinary	Group
1910	11 783	—
1940	79 346	14 938
1950	149 116	47 793
1960	341 881	175 903
1970	734 730	551 357
1980	1 760 474	1 579 355
1990	5 366 982	3 753 506
2000	8 337 188	5 158 538

Source: *The Canadian World Almanac and Book of Facts: 2002*, p. 837.

1605 a. If you want to achieve a more open look, you can remove the borders and increase the space between rows as shown in the following illustration.

Table A-15
LIFE INSURANCE IN FORCE
($000 000 Omitted)

Year	Ordinary	Group
1910	11 783	—
1940	79 346	14 938
1950	149 116	47 793
1960	341 881	175 903
1970	734 730	551 357
1980	1 760 474	1 579 355
1990	5 366 982	3 753 506
2000	8 337 188	5 158 538

Source: *The Canadian World Almanac and Book of Facts: 2002*, p. 837.

b. As an alternative, you may simply eliminate all the vertical rules in the grid.

Table A-15

LIFE INSURANCE IN FORCE

($000 000 Omitted)

Year	Ordinary	Group
1910	11 783	—
1940	79 346	14 938
1950	149 116	47 793
1960	341 881	175 903
1970	734 730	551 357
1980	1 760 474	1 579 355
1990	5 366 982	3 753 506
2000	8 337 188	5 158 538

Source: *The Canadian World Almanac and Book of Facts: 2002*, p. 837.

1606 Most word processing programs provide a number of autoformats that can enhance the appearance of your tables. The following illustration provides an example of a style offered by Microsoft Word: Elegant

TABLE A-15		
LIFE INSURANCE IN FORCE		
($000 000 OMITTED)		
Year	Ordinary	Group
1910	11 783	—
1940	79 346	14 938
1950	149 116	47 793
1960	341 881	175 903
1970	734 730	551 357
1980	1 760 474	1 579 355
1990	5 366 982	3 753 506
2000	8 337 188	5 158 538
Source: The Canadian World Almanac and Book of Facts: 2002, p. 837.		

(Continued on page 460.)

NOTE: When you create a table following the guidelines offered in ¶¶1601-1606, you will notice that the preceding illustration has "lost" the bold and italics attributes and some words in the heading have changed to all-capital letters. These changes are all attributes of the Elegant format. However, it is easy to reformat the fonts.

Locating Tables Within the Text

1607 a. Tables should be easy to refer to. Therefore, try to locate each table on the same page where the subject of the table is introduced in the text. In this way, the reader will have ready access to the table while reading the text commentary that may precede and follow.

b. Ideally, every table should fall immediately after the point in the text where it is first mentioned. However, if placing the table within a paragraph is likely to disrupt the reader's grasp of the material, then locate the table at the end of the paragraph or at the top or bottom of the page. (See ¶1609d.)

1608 a. Avoid breaking a table at the bottom of a page. If starting a table at the ideal point means that it will not all fit in the space remaining on the page, then place the complete table at the top of the next page. (At the point in the text where the table is first mentioned, insert an appropriate cross-reference in parentheses. See ¶1613.)

NOTE: Most word processing programs have a feature (*block protect* or *keep lines together*) that prevents a page break from occurring within a block of text. (See the entry on *keep lines together* in Section 20.)

b. If you have to fit a number of relatively short tables (half a page or less) in a given document, single-space the table text (Microsoft default) to maximize your chances of locating each table in the ideal place. (See ¶1623.)

☞ *For other techniques to limit the length of a table to one page, see ¶1635. For guidelines on dealing with a table too long to fit on one page, see ¶1636.*

1609 If a table is to appear on a page that also carries regular text:

a. Centre the table horizontally within the established margins.

b. Try to indent the table at least 0.5 inch from each side margin. In any case, the width of the table should not exceed the width of the text. (See ¶1638.)

c. Use blank lines to set off a table from the text above and below it as follows:

(1) Leave only 1 blank line above and below the table if horizontal rules or shading sets the table off from the text.

with prefixes indicating multiples or fractions of a unit. There are seven base units in the S1 metric system. ↓2

Quantity	Unit	Symbol
Length	metre	m
Mass	kilogram	kg
Time	second	s
Electric current	ampere	A
Thermodynamic temperature	kelvin	K
Amount of substance	mole	mol
Luminous intensity	candela	cd

↓2

In addition, there are two supplementary units, the radian and the steradian.

(2) Leave 1 blank line above and below an open table (one without horizontal rules) that has neither column headings nor a table title.

Our analysis of the latest reports indicates that sales are up by at least 10 percent in all regions: ↓2

Eastern Region	16.2%
North Central Region	11.0%
Southern Region	18.4%
Western Region	13.9%

↓2

The primary reason for this upsurge, according to the managers of these regions, is the rebuilding of inventories, which were allowed to deplete due to

NOTE: The dotted lines show the original outside gridlines of the table. In examples from (2), (3), and (4), all borders are removed for printing.

(3) Leave 2 blank lines above and below an open table that uses column headings as its first element.

(Continued on page 462.)

When designing buildings for Canadian winters, keep in mind typical outdoor temperatures. For example: ↓2

City	Temp. (°C)
Calgary, AB	−18
Fredericton, NB	−15
Saskatoon, SK	−25
Yellowknife, NT	−33

↓3

As you can see, such cold weather affects not only the design of the structure, but

NOTE: The blank line above a column heading or a title within the grid will automatically achieve the appearance of 2 blank lines above the table when you remove the grid.

(4)   Leave 2 blank lines above and below an open table that begins with a table title. (See the note in (3) above).

as shown in Table 12-5, the public debt tripled in the fifteen-year period between 1960 and 1975—from $600 million to $2 billion. ↓2

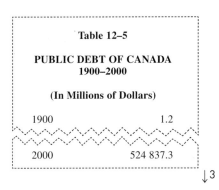

Table 12–5

PUBLIC DEBT OF CANADA
1900–2000

(In Millions of Dollars)

1900	1.2
2000	524 837.3

↓3

However, it took only five years (between 1980 and 1985) for the increase to reach

d. Use the table feature to insert the table copy at the desired location in the regular text. If you discover that the table will not all fit on the same page, you can move the table as a whole to the top or bottom of the page, make other adjustments (as noted in ¶¶1635–1637), or place the table on a page by itself (see ¶¶1610–1613). If you use the *keep lines together* feature (see ¶1608, note), the table will not be divided at the bottom of a page; instead the table as a whole will be moved to the top of the next page.

16

e. Be sure you can fit at least two full lines of regular text above or below the table. If the results look unattractive, devote the full page to the table (see ¶¶1610–1613) and resume the text on the following page.

Locating Tables on Separate Pages

1610 When a table occupies more than two-thirds of a page, it can often be difficult to fit it on the same page with regular text. In such cases type the table on a separate page and place it immediately after the text page on which the reference to the table is first made.

NOTE: Insert a hard page break before and after the table to ensure that the table will appear on a page by itself. (See ¶1637b.)

1611 If a given document contains a number of tables, most of which will each require a separate page, then all the tables (short as well as long) may be executed as an appendix or as an attachment. This arrangement—which permits the reader to keep the full set of tables alongside the regular text (except in the case of bound reports)—can be very convenient, especially if some of the tables are repeatedly cited throughout the regular text. (This arrangement also eliminates the problem of trying to fit long tables within the text.)

1612 When a table is to appear on a page by itself, centre the table horizontally and vertically within the established margins of the page.

NOTE: If no margins have been established, leave a minimum margin of 1 inch on all four sides of the table.

1613 When a table must be placed on another page, provide a cross-reference in parentheses to the appropriate page.

(See Table 4 on page 18.)   **OR**   (See Table 2–2 on page 31.)

NOTE: These parenthetical cross-references may be treated as a separate sentence (as shown above) or as part of another sentence. (See ¶220.)

☞ *For the advisability of numbering tables to simplify the matter of cross-references, see ¶1616.*

Centring Tables

1614 a. The table feature of a word processing program extends the table to the full width of the regular text. If you decide to reduce the overall width of the table, first type the table. Then *click and drag* the outside lines or use *autofit* to adjust the width of the columns. Choose the *table horizontal centre* setting to position the whole table horizontally.

  b. If a table appears on a page by itself, centre the table vertically as well. (Use the *centre page* feature of your software.)

Table Identification

1615 Identify tables by *title* unless they are not very numerous and the significance of the material in the table is clear without some descriptive label. (See ¶1618a.)

1616 Also identify tables by *number* unless they are quite short, not very numerous, and typically referred to only on the page on which they fall. The use of table numbers simplifies the matter of cross-references, an important consideration if you expect that a number of tables will not fit on the page where they are first mentioned or if you know that certain tables will be referred to repeatedly throughout the regular text.

NOTE: Tables may be numbered consecutively throughout a given document or consecutively within each chapter and each appendix. With the latter technique, the chapter number (or the appendix number or letter) is used as a prefix in the numbering scheme. For example, Table 3–2 would be the second table in Chapter 3, and Table A–5 would be the fifth table in Appendix A.

1617 The table title may be followed by a *subtitle*, which provides additional information about the significance of the table, the period of time it covers, or the manner in which the information is organized or presented. Since a subtitle should be held to one line if possible (two at the most), a lengthy comment on any of these points should be handled as a note to the table rather than as a subtitle. (See ¶¶1632–1634.)

1618 Type the elements of table identification as follows:

a. **Table Title.** Centre the table title, using all-capital letters in boldface. (See ¶1609c for spacing.)

b. **Table Number.** Type the word *Table* in capital and small letters, followed by the appropriate number. To give the table number special emphasis, centre it on the second line above the table title and use boldface. To hold down the length of the table, key the table number on the same line with the table title; in this case, insert a period after the table number and leave 1 or 2 spaces before keying the table title. (See the illustrations on page 465.)

NOTE: Within a given document, treat all table numbers the same way.

c. **Table Subtitle.** Centre the subtitle on the second line below the title, using capital and small letters in boldface. The subtitle is usually enclosed in parentheses when it simply comments on the listing of data in some special order (for example, *In Descending Order by Sales Revenue*) or on the omission of zeros from figures given in the table (for example, *In Millions* or *000 Omitted*).

☞ *For examples of subtitles enclosed in parentheses, see the tables illustrated in ¶¶1602–1606.*

NOTE: If either the title or the subtitle requires more than one line, break it into sensible phrases; then single-space and centre any turnover lines. If possible, try to hold the title and the subtitle to two lines each.

Table 5	Table 3–4. TITLE OF THE TABLE
TITLE OF THE TABLE	WITH ONE TURNOVER LINE
WITH ONE TURNOVER LINE	
	Table Subtitle
Table Subtitle	With One Turnover Line

Column Headings

1619 a. Unless a table is very simple and the significance of the material is clear without headings, provide a heading for each column. (A heading may be omitted over the first column, also known as the *stub*. See, for example, the table in ¶1630a.)

b. Whenever possible, use singular forms in the column headings. Thus, for example, over a column listing a number of cities, use the heading *City* rather than *Cities*. (See ¶1609c(3).)

c. In order to hold down the length of column headings, use abbreviations and symbols as necessary. For example:

Acct. No.	Account number
% of Total	Percent of total
FY2004	Fiscal year 2004 (also used to indicate that a company's
OR FY04	*fiscal* year does not coincide with the *calendar* year)
1Q/2005	First quarter of 2005 (also used with 2Q, 3Q, and 4Q
OR 1Q/05	to signify the other three quarters of the year)
2004A	Actual results in 2004
2005B	Budgeted results in 2005
2005E	Estimated results in 2005
2006F	Forecast of results in 2006

If your reader may not understand some of the abbreviations and symbols you use, explain the unfamiliar ones in a footnote to the table. For example:

Note: A = actual; E = estimated; F = forecast. (See ¶1621c.)

NOTE: As an alternative to the use of abbreviations, select a smaller font size for the column headings.

d. Column headings should be single-spaced and may be broken into as many as five lines. Column headings are normally centred on the column width, but under certain circumstances the lines that make up the column headings may all be blocked left or right on the column width.

e. Capitalize the first letter of each word in a column heading except articles *(a, an, the)*, conjunctions under four letters (such as *and* and *or*), and prepositions under four letters (such as *of* and *in*). See ¶¶360–361, 363 for detailed guidance on capitalizing words in column headings.

(Continued on page 466.)

  f. Type all column headings in boldface.

  g. If the column headings do not all take the same number of lines, align the column headings at the bottom. Choose the *cell bottom alignment* option for automatic alignment.

  h. Leave 1 blank line above and below the tallest column heading. (See ¶1604a and e.)

  i. When column headings are extremely long, consider using abbreviations in the column headings and explaining them (if necessary) in a table footnote. As an alternative, use a smaller font size. (See ¶1634.)

1620 a. When you use the table feature, the default alignment for all column headings is at the left. (See the illustration in ¶1602a.)

  b. If you change the alignment of the column text from left to right (for example, with a column of figures), align the column heading at the right as well. (See the illustration in ¶1602c.)

  c. When a very narrow column heading falls above a very wide column of text, the table may look more attractive if the column heading is centred over the column text.

Name	Name
A. Michael Ashworth	A. Michael Ashworth
Dwayne Gilpatrick Jr.	Dwayne Gilpatrick Jr.
Bradley M. Harrington	Bradley M. Harrington

Sales	Sales
95 517 833	95 517 833
1 039 875 742	1 039 875 742
874 320 199	874 320 199

  d. When a very wide column heading falls above a very narrow column of text, you may produce some very odd-looking tables. To avoid this problem, centre the column text as a block.

Applications Received	Applications Received
98	98
182	182
87	87

  e. All column headings should be either blocked or centred. Do not mix styles within a table.

1621 BRACED COLUMN HEADINGS

  a. Some complex tables contain *braced* column headings (headings that "embrace" two or more columns). They are also called *straddle* headings because they straddle two or more columns. (See the illustration on page 467.)

16

b. There are two ways to create a table with braced headings. You can create the table body—5 columns in the following illustration—and merge the cells that will be used for the braced headings. Or you can create a 3-column table, type the braced headings in the appropriate cells, and then split the cells below the braced headings to complete the table.

c. To achieve the best appearance, centre each braced column heading over the appropriate columns; centre the other column headings and the related column text between the vertical rules in each case.

Table With Braced Column Headings

Table 12. CABLE DIVISION SALES AND NET OPERATING INCOME From 2000 to 2005				
	Sales		Net Operating Income	
Year	Thousands of Dollars	Percent of Increase	Thousands of Dollars	Percent of Increase
2001A	1429	—	252	—
2004E	1300	(13.3)	216	(9.2)
2005F	3000	130.8	480	122.2

Note: A = actual; E = estimated; F = forecast.

1622 CROSSHEADINGS

a. Crossheadings are used to separate the data in the body of a table into different categories. (See the illustration on page 468.)

b. The first crossheading falls immediately below the column headings across the top of the table; the other crossheadings occur within the body of the table at appropriate intervals.

c. Key each crossheading in capital and small letters, centred on the full width of the table. Centre each crossheading after you join the cells in that row.

d. Each crossheading should be preceded and followed by a horizontal rule running the full width of the table. Leave 1 blank line between the rule and the crossheading.

Table Text
1623 SPACING

a. The table text may be typed with single, or one and a half, or double spacing. However, you may find it easiest to accept the default spacing provided

(Continued on page 468.)

by your software. (Microsoft Word uses single spacing.) Within the same document try to treat all tables alike.

b. Although double-spaced tables may be more readable, single-spacing reduces the overall length of a document and maximizes your chances of locating each table on the page where it is first mentioned.

NOTE: You can make single-spaced tables more readable by retaining the horizontal rules between rows and by the use of shading. (See ¶1604.) A slight increase in spaces between rows can make single-spaced tables more readable. (See ¶1605a.)

c. As a rule, type the table with the same spacing (or less) used for the regular text. If regular text is single-spaced, all the tables should also be single-spaced. If regular text is double-spaced, all tables may be typed with single- or double-spacing.

Table With Crossheadings

Table 8–4

CONTRIBUTION RATE SCHEDULE

(Percent of Covered Earnings)

Year	Total	HCD*	PD**
Employees and Employers Each			
1990	7.05	5.70	1.35
1991–1994	7.05	5.70	1.45
1995–1998	7.51	6.06	1.45
1999 and after	7.65	6.20	1.45
Self-Employed			
1990	14.10	11.40	2.70
1991–1994	14.30	11.40	2.90
1995–1998	15.02	12.12	2.90
1999 and after	15.30	12.40	2.90

Source: *The Canadian World Almanac and Book of Facts: 2002*, p. 799.

*Health care and dental.

**Professional dues.

1624 ITEMS CONSISTING OF WORDS

If the table text consists of items expressed entirely in words:

a. Capitalize only the first word of each item in the table text plus any proper nouns and proper adjectives.

NOTE: In special cases, where it may be important to show whether terms are capitalized or written with small letters, the first word in each item need not be consistently capitalized. (See, for example, the second and third columns of the table in ¶1609c.)

b. Use abbreviations and symbols as necessary to hold down the length of individual items. (See ¶1619c for examples.)

c. Align each item at the left margin of the column. If any item requires more than one line, set a tab to indent the runover line 0.25 inch. However, if a column contains both main entries and subentries, begin the main entry at the left margin of the column text, set tabs to indent the first line of subentries 0.25 inch, and indent all turnover lines 0.5 inch.

Photographs, prints, and illustrations	Total weekly broad-cast hours
Scientific or technical drawings	General programs
Commercial prints	Instructional programs
Reproductions of works of art	

NOTE: You can avoid the need to indent turnovers (but not subentries) if you use horizontal rules or extra space to separate the entries. The table feature will automatically align turnovers at the left, and the horizontal rules or extra space will help to make each entry visually distinct.

Photographs, prints, and illustrations	Total weekly broadcast hours
Scientific or technical drawings	General programs
Commercial prints	Instructional programs
Reproductions of works of art	

d. If an item in the first column requires more than one line and all the other items in the same row require only one line, align all the items in that row at the bottom.

Chemical and allied products	151	201
Petroleum refining and related products	69	73
Paper and allied products	391	364

e. Do not use a period as terminal punctuation at the end of any item except in a column where all entries are in sentence form. Some writers prefer to retain the space or comma in four-digit numbers under all circumstances.

1625 ITEMS CONSISTING OF FIGURES

   a. If a column of table text consists of items expressed entirely in figures:

     (1) Align columns of whole numbers at the right (right align).

     (2) Align columns of decimal amounts on the decimal point (decimal tab).

     (3) In a column that contains both whole numbers and decimals, add a decimal point and zeros to the whole numbers to maintain a consistent appearance.

     (4) Omit spaces or commas in four-digit whole numbers unless they appear in the same column with larger numbers containing spaces or commas.

325	325	465.2137
1	1	1250.0004
152 657	152,657	1.0000
1 489	1,489	37.9898

☞ *For the way to handle a total line in a column of figures, see ¶1627c.*

   b. If a column of table text consists entirely of "clock" times (as in a program or schedule):

     (1) Align the figures in "on the hour" expressions at the right. Add 1 or 2 spaces before a single-digit number to maintain right alignment.

                                                     11 a.m.
             12 noon
              1 p.m.
             12 midnight

     (2) Align the figures in "hour and minute" expressions on the colon. (Add two zeros to exact times to maintain a uniform appearance.)

              8:15 a.m.
            10:30 a.m.
              1:45 p.m.
           12:00 midnight

     (3) When the items in a column each consist of a starting and an ending time, either align them on the hyphen or en dash within the items or align all the items at the left.

Preferred	Acceptable	24-Hour Clock
8:30– 9:30	8:30–9:30	0830–0930
10:30–11:30	10:30–11:30	1030–1130
12:30– 1:30	12:30–1:30	1230–1330
2:30– 3:30	2:30–3:30	1430–1530
4:45– 6:00	4:45–6:00	1645–1800

NOTE: In the "24-hour" system of expressing clock time (in which midnight is 0000 and 11:59 p.m. is 2359), the alignment of clock times poses no problem since all times are expressed in four digits (with no colons and no reference to *a.m.* and *p.m.*).

1626 ITEMS CONSISTING OF FIGURES AND WORDS

   If a column consists of both figures and words (as in the second column in the following illustration), align the items at the left. Note, however, that a column consisting only of words aligns at the left (as in the first column) and a column consisting only of whole numbers aligns at the right (as in the third column).

Type of Food	Average Serving	Calorie Count
Bacon	2 strips	97
Beef, roast	4 oz	300
Broccoli	1 cup	44
Tomato, raw	Medium size	30

1627 AMOUNTS OF MONEY

a. In a column containing dollar amounts, insert a dollar sign only before the first amount at the head of the column and before the total amount.

```
$   45.50       $     165       $ 423.75
   2406.05        3 450            584.45
    783.25       98 932           1228.00
$3234.80       $102 547         $2236.20
```

b. The dollar signs at the head and foot of the column should align in the first space to the left of the longest amount in the column. If the item at the head of the column is shorter than the one at the foot, aligning the dollar signs can be troublesome. Choose one of the following approaches to deal with the problem:

(1) Avoid the problem altogether by incorporating the dollar sign in the column heading—for example *($000,000 Omitted)*. Then there is no need for dollar signs alongside the figures below.

(2) Type the dollar sign in the space before the first number. After the column is finished, insert spaces between the first dollar sign and the first digit to align the dollar signs (2 spaces for each digit, 1 space for each comma, if used).

c. Do not insert spaces or commas to set off thousands in four-digit numbers unless they appear in the same column with larger numbers. (See the examples in ¶1625a and ¶1627a.) Moreover, if all the amounts in a column are whole dollar amounts, omit the decimal and zeros (as in the second example in ¶1627a). However, if any amount in a column includes cents, use a decimal and zeros with any whole dollar amount in the same column (as in the third example in ¶1627a).

d. If the table text ends with a *total* line, a horizontal rule should separate the body of the table from the total line.

(1) If the table displays any horizontal rules that set off key sections of the table, the necessary separation will be automatically provided. To give the total amount greater emphasis in a single-spaced table (as in the following illustration), adjust the spacing so that there is 1 blank line

(Continued on page 472.)

above and below the total line; the word *Total* or *Totals* can also be typed in bold and in all-capital letters.

2003 SALES REVENUES

Region	2003B	2003A	Percent of Difference
Eastern	$ 300 000	$ 345 108	15.0
Central	450 000	467 380	3.9
Southern	260 000	291 849	12.2
Western	240 000	241 005	0.4
Totals	$1 250 000	$1 345 342	7.6

(2) In an open-style table (one with no horizontal or vertical lines), you must insert a horizontal rule that is as wide as the longest entry in the column (including the dollar sign at the left). Before typing the last amount before the total, choose the *underline appearance* option. You may have to insert spaces before the last amount above the total so that the horizontal line will be as wide as the longest entry (2 spaces for the dollar sign and each digit, 1 space for each comma, if used).

$1115.59 ↓1	$ 529 310 ↓1	$21 348.75 ↓2
803.61	1 114 310	
1027.64	1 227 620	2 294.35
528.66	↓2	
$3475.50 ↓1	$2 871 240	688.50
		↓2
		$24 331.60

NOTE: In a single-spaced table, type the total amount on the line directly below the underline (as in the first example above). To give the total amount greater emphasis, type it on the second line below the underline (as in the second example above). In a double-spaced table, type the amount on the second line below the underline (as in the third example above).

1628 PERCENTAGES

a. If all the figures in a column represent percentages, type a percent sign (%) directly after each figure unless the column heading clearly indicates that these are percentages.

b. Percentages involving decimals should align on the decimal point. If necessary, add zeros after the decimal part of the number so that each figure will align at the right. If any percentage is less than 1 percent, add one zero to the left of the decimal point.

Increase	Percent of Increase	Increase (%)
55.48%	11.63	24
0.08%	4.00	37
2.09%	24.60	120
13.00%	0.40	8

1629 SPECIAL TREATMENT OF FIGURES IN TABLES

a. Columns of long figures can be reduced in width by omitting the digits representing thousands, millions, or billions and indicating this omission in parentheses. For example:

(In Thousands)	**OR**	(000 Omitted)
(In Millions)		(000 000 Omitted)
(In Billions)		(000 000 000 Omitted)

NOTE: The word forms on the left are easier to grasp.

b. If the parenthetical comment applies to all columns of figures in the table, insert it as a subtitle to the table. However, if the comment applies only to one column of figures, insert the parenthetical comment in the column heading.

NOTE: Sometimes because of space limitations a comment such as *(000 Omitted)* is reduced to *(000)*. The latter form is permissible if you are sure your reader will understand it.

c. If the parenthetical comment applies to columns of dollar amounts, this fact can also be noted within parentheses and the dollar sign can then be omitted from the column of figures.

($000 Omitted)   **OR**   (In Thousands of Dollars)   **OR**   ($000)

d. When omitting thousands, millions, or billions from a wide column of figures, you may use rounding or a shortened decimal (or both) to reflect the portion of the number that is being omitted.

Complete Version	Shortened Versions		
Sales Revenues	Sales Revenues ($000 Omitted)	Sales Revenues (In Millions)	Sales Revenues ($000 000)
$ 5 878 044	5 878	$ 5.9	6
29 023 994	29 024	29.0	29
14 229 683	14 230	14.2	14
$49 131 721	49 132	$49.1	49

(Continued on page 474.)

e. A negative figure in a column may be designated by enclosing the figure in parentheses or by inserting a minus sign (represented by a hyphen or an en dash) directly to the left of the negative figure.

$1642.38	28.2%	Sales in 2002 ...	$264 238
-82.41	-14.5%	Sales in 2003 ...	262 305
$1559.97	6.1%	Gain/(loss)	$ (1 933)

1630 LEADERS

a. If the items in the first column vary greatly in length, use leaders (rows of periods) to lead the eye across to the adjacent item in the next column. Every line of leaders should have at least three periods.

b. To insert a row of leaders within a column, set a right leader tab as close to the right edge of the column as possible. After typing the text, press Ctrl + tab to insert the leaders; then press tab to go to the next column.

c. The *leader* feature in Microsoft Word offers the choice of solid periods, solid hyphens, or solid underscores. Other programs may allow you to specify the character to be used and the space to be left between characters.

Table With Leaders

Table 3

NATIONAL INCOME BY SELECTED INDUSTRIES

(In Billions of Dollars)

	1980	1990	2000
Agriculture, forestry, and fisheries	61.4	97.1	105.3
Construction	126.6	234.4	228.0
Finance, insurance, and real estate	279.5	679.8	816.0
Government enterprises	321.8	657.9	765.3
Manufacturing	532.1	846.9	928.2
Services	341.0	948.3	1171.0

1631 ACCOUNTING FOR OMITTED ITEMS

When there is no entry to be keyed in a given row, you can simply leave a blank at that point. However, if doing so may raise a question in the mind of your reader, consider these alternatives:

a. Key the abbreviation *NA* (meaning "not available" or "not applicable") centred on the column width.

b. Key a row of periods or hyphens. Use as few as three (centred on the column width) or key the row to the full width of the column.

23 804	23 804	23 804
16 345	16 345	16 345
....	----	NA
38 442	38 442	38 442

☞ *See page 467 for another illustration.*

NOTE: If any one of the columns in a table contains omitted items, you will not be able to use a formula to perform calculations.

Table Notes

1632 a. If a table requires any explanatory notes or an identification of the source from which the table was derived, place such material at the foot of the table. (Do not treat it as part of a sequence of notes related to the main text.)

b. A horizontal rule should separate the body of the table from the table notes.

(1) If the table displays horizontal rules, the separation will be automatically provided. (See ¶1604.)

(2) If the table has been executed in an *open* style (without horizontal and vertical rules), leave 1 blank line below the last line of the table text and type a 1-inch line of underscores. (See ¶1605a.)

c. Begin the first table note on the second line below the horizontal rule.

d. If all the notes occupy no more than one full line each, begin each note at the left margin of the table text (for the sake of appearance) and single-space the notes. However, if any of the notes turn over onto a second line, indent the first line of each note 0.25 to 0.5 inch, start all turnover lines at the left margin of the table text, and leave 1 blank line between each pair of notes.

1633 If the material in the table has been derived from another source, indicate this fact as follows:

a. Type the word *Source* with an initial cap or in all-capital letters, followed by a colon, 1 or 2 spaces, and the identifying data. (See ¶¶1508–1523 for models to follow in presenting this bibliographic data.)

b. A source note should precede any other table note. (See ¶1623.)

1634 a. If you use abbreviations or symbols that the reader may not understand, explain them in a note at the bottom of the table. This explanation should follow the source note (if any) and precede any other table note. If more than one abbreviation or symbol needs decoding, the explanation can be handled as a series of separate notes (each preceded by a superscript symbol or letter), or it may be done all in one note. (See ¶1623b.)

(Continued on page 476.)

b. Except for source notes and a single note explaining symbols and abbreviations (like the one shown on page 467), every table note should begin with a superscript symbol or letter that keys the note to the appropriate word or figure in the table text (or title or subtitle) above. Type the corresponding superscript symbol or letter immediately after the appropriate word or figure above, without any intervening space. (See ¶1634d, note.)

c. Use the following sequence of symbols: *, **, *** OR *, †, ‡, §, ¶. (See ¶1502f.)

d. Use superscript lower case letters (^{a}, ^{b}, ^{c}, etc.) in place of symbols when there are more than five footnotes for a given table.

NOTE: Avoid the use of superscript *figures* to identify table notes. They could be confusing if used in conjunction with figures in the table text. Moreover, if superscript figures are already used for notes pertaining to the main text, it is wise to use letters or symbols so as to distinguish notes that pertain to a specific table.

e. In assigning symbols or letters in sequence, go in order by row (horizontally), not by column (vertically).

16 Dealing With Long Tables

1635 To keep a table from extending beyond the page on which it starts, consider these techniques:

a. Put the table number (if any) on the same line as the table title rather than on the second line above. (See also ¶1618b.)

b. Use single spacing for the table text or group items within a cell. (See also ¶1623.)

c. Shorten the wording of the table title, subtitle, column headings, and items in the table text to reduce turnover lines. Use abbreviations and symbols to achieve this. (See also ¶1619c.) If necessary, provide a brief explanation in the table notes of any abbreviations and symbols that your reader may not immediately understand. (See also ¶1634.)

d. When there is a long item in the table text that is out of proportion to all the other items (or is to be entered in several places in the table text), try to convert the item into a table note, keyed by a symbol or letter appropriately placed in the table above.

e. If a table is both narrow and long, you can save space by repeating the same sequence of column headings on both the left and right sides of the table. The first half of the table text appears on the left side of the table, and the remaining table text appears on the right.

FIRE LOSSES FROM 1993 TO 2000

Year	Total (000 000 Omitted)	Per Capita	Year	Total (000 000 (Omitted)	Per Capita
1993	$5625	$24.50	1997	$7753	$32.47
1994	5894	25.42	1998	8488	35.21
1995	6320	26.98	1999	8634	35.44
1996	7602	32.15	2000	9626	39.12

f. Select a smaller size of font than the one you are using for other tables.

1636 If a table requires more than one page, follow this procedure:

a. At the bottom of the page where the table breaks, type a continuation line in parentheses—for example, *(Continued on page 14)*—unless it is quite obvious that the table continues on the next page. Merge the cells in the last row at the bottom of the page, then, using right alignment, type the continuation line.

TWENTIETH-CENTURY INVENTIONS

Invention	Date	Nation
Airship, rigid dirigible	1900	Germany
Washer, electric	1901	United States
Pen, ballpoint	1938	Hungary
Teflon	1938	United States
Airplane jet engine	1939	Germany
		(Continued on page 14)

b. At the top of the next page, before continuing with the table text, insert the table number (if used), title, and column headings by marking those rows as header rows. If your software will permit it, insert *Continued* in parentheses after the table number (if used) or after the table title.

(Continued on page 478.)

TWENTIETH-CENTURY INVENTIONS (Continued)

Invention	Date	Nation
CAT scan	1973	England
Microcomputer	1973	France
Disk player, compact	1979	Japan
Heart, artificial	1982	United States

If your software will not permit you to make insertions in the header rows, merge the cells in the first row beneath the column headings; then insert a continuation line in parentheses and align it at the left margin.

TWENTIETH-CENTURY INVENTIONS

Invention	Date	Nation
(Continued from page 13)		
CAT scan	1973	England
Microcomputer	1973	France
Disk player, compact	1979	Japan
Heart, artificial	1982	United States

16

    c. Ordinarily, all table notes should appear only on the page on which the table ends. However, if certain notes will help the reader interpret the data in the table (for example, notes explaining certain abbreviations or symbols), repeat these notes on each page on which the table appears. (A source note would appear only on the page where the table ends.)

1637 a. Do not start a table at the bottom of one page and continue it on the top of the next page if the entire table will fit on one page (either by itself or with regular text). In such a case start the table at the top of the next page and insert a cross-reference in the text. (See ¶1613.)

    b. If you use the *keep lines together* feature to keep a table from breaking at the bottom of a page, the table as a whole will appear at the top of the next page. However, the space previously occupied by the first part of the table will remain empty; the text that follows the table will not come forward to fill up this vacant space. If you want to avoid this result, do not use *keep lines together*. Use the following approach instead:

        (1) Let the table break naturally and continue typing the rest of the document.

(2)   When the document is completed in all other respects, select and cut the table; the text following the table will flow forward. Insert a hard page break at the bottom of the page where the table was removed, and paste the whole table at the top of the following page.

Dealing With Wide Tables

1638 To keep a wide table from extending beyond the margins established for the page, consider the following techniques:

a. Click and drag column borders to manually reduce the width of the columns or use the autofit feature.

b. Use abbreviations and symbols to hold down the length of lines in the column headings and the column text.

c. If only a few entries are disproportionately wide or are repeated in the table and make it difficult to fit the table in the space available, consider the possibility of converting these items to table footnotes. (See also ¶1635d.)

d. Select a smaller font size in order to make the table fit within the space available.

e. Whenever possible, a table should read horizontally *(portrait orientation)*, just like the regular text. However, when other alternatives do not work, create the table in *landscape orientation*, which places the table sideways on the page. This will allow two or more additional inches in width. Any other combination of the above considerations may also have to be used. If the finished document will be bound, leave a larger top margin (for instance, 1.5 inches) on a landscape table page to allow for the binding.

 See the Online Learning Centre at www.mcgrawhill.ca/college/gregg for related weblinks.

Other Business Documents

Section 17 provides models for a number of common business documents. The models reflect formats widely used, but they should not be regarded as rigid patterns. Modify these formats to fit your needs. As always, good sense and good taste should prevail.

IMPORTANT NOTE: Your software program may provide templates for many of the documents discussed in Section 17. If you decide to use a template provided by your software, you may find it helpful to examine the corresponding model in this section to see whether there are certain features or details that are worth adding to the basic template.

GENERAL FORMAT CONSIDERATIONS

Paragraphs 1701–1702 deal with the issues of formatting margins and headings and apply to all the documents discussed later in Section 17.

Margins

1701 a. Top Margin. Use a top margin of about 2 inches if you are using standard stationery. However, accept the default top margin of 1 inch in order to fit more copy on the page and avoid the need for a second page. If you are using letterhead for the first page, begin typing at least 0.5 inch below the letterhead. If the document requires more than one page, use plain paper for the continuation pages and leave a top margin of 1 inch.

b. Side Margins. Leave the default settings as is for standard stationery. In some instances, it may be appropriate to set wider margins if you want to bring columns of text closer together for easier reading or you want to achieve a more open look or a more balanced copy arrangement.

c. Bottom Margin. Leave a bottom margin of 1 inch but adjust if necessary.

NOTE: Try to maintain consistency in white space around the document.

Headings

1702 a. Main Heading. The title of the document or the name of the organization ordinarily appears centred and bolded on the first line in all-capital letters. Additional details (such as a date or a location) appear in capital and small letters on separate lines, with 1 blank line between them. The use of boldface for these lines is optional. Leave 1 or 2 blank lines between the last line of the main heading and the body of the document. (See pages 485 and 488.)

NOTE: If any item in the heading requires more than 1 line, type the turnover line single-spaced and centred on the line above.

b. Continuation Heading. If a document requires more than one page, use the header feature to create and automatically position the continuation heading. (See ¶1385 for format details.)

EXECUTIVE DOCUMENTS

The following paragraphs (¶¶1703–1706) present formats for **agendas**, **minutes**, **itineraries**, and **fax cover sheets**.

Agendas

1703 An *agenda* is a list of items to be considered or acted upon. The format of an agenda varies with the circumstances. The agenda for an informal staff meeting

(Continued on page 482.)

may be done as a simple numbered list of topics in a memo addressed to the attendees. (See page 484.) The agenda for a formal meeting (for example, of a corporate board of directors) will typically call for a more structured list of topics. (See page 485.) The agenda for a formal program (for example, for a conference or a seminar) will be structured around a timetable, with specific time slots allotted to formal presentations by speakers and topical discussions in small groups. (See page 486.)

The illustrations that follow are intended only to suggest various ways in which an agenda can be formatted. The format you decide to use should be tailored to fit the needs of the meeting or program being planned.

Minutes

1704 *Minutes* provide a record of what was discussed and decided upon at a meeting. The minutes of small committee meetings within an organization are usually done in an informal style. When the participants at a meeting come from a number of different organizations (for example, at meetings of professional associations), the minutes tend to be more formal.

Increasing government regulations and shareholders' lawsuits make it critically important that the minutes of a meeting of a corporation's board of directors be complete and accurate, since they may have to serve as legal evidence as to what the corporation's directors did or intended to do. When minutes may have to serve a legal use, they are typically done in a highly formal style.

☞ *Refer to* Robert's Rules of Order *for conducting meetings and recording minutes.*

Itineraries

1705 An itinerary should clearly set forth the travel arrangements and the appointment schedule of the person making the trip. If the itinerary is intended only for the use of the person travelling, it should be possible to eliminate certain items and abbreviate details that the person is quite familiar with. However, if the itinerary will be distributed to others (who may need to contact the person who is travelling), present the information as fully and as clearly as possible. (For an example, see the illustration on page 490.)

Fax Cover Sheets

1706 Most messages sent by fax (facsimile) equipment are accompanied by a fax cover sheet that indicates (1) the name and fax number of the person receiving the fax, (2) the name and fax number of the person sending the fax, (3) the number of pages being sent, and (4) the name and the telephone number of the person to be called in case the transmission is not satisfactorily completed. Rather than preparing your own cover sheet, commercially prepared stick-on labels and stamps are available.

There are different ways to prepare a fax cover sheet. Your software may provide a fax template that you can use as is or modify to suit your preferences. If you are designing a fax cover sheet as a form to be filled in by hand, you will need to add fill-in lines. (See page 483.)

facsimile
TRANSMITTAL

BURNHAM & FRYE INC.
226 High Ridge Road
Stratford, ON N5A 4Y2

Date/Date: **A** _____

To/A: **B** _____
                                 _____
                                 _____

Fax number/Numéro
  du télécopieur: _____

From/De: _____
                                 _____
                                 _____

Fax number/Numéro
  du télécopieur: _____

Number of pages
  including this page/
Nombre de pages
  incluant celle-ci: _____

Confirm Receipt/
Confirmer la réception: _____ Yes/Oui   _____ No/Non

Remarks/Remarques: _____
                    C ↓ _____

A Format Considerations. If you are using software to create a template for a fax cover sheet that only you will use, insert any information that will not change (such as your name and fax number) as a part of the template. However, if you are creating a form to be used by a number of people, provide blank fill-in lines to accommodate this variable information.

B Fill-in Lines. If you are designing a fax cover sheet as a form to be filled in by hand, arrange the fill-in lines so that all entries can start at a common point.

C Confidentiality Statement. You should make sure that the recipient is standing by the receiving fax machine. Some cover sheet templates (particularly legal) include at the bottom of the page a confidentiality statement such as the one shown below.

> The contents of this fax transmission are confidential. If this transmission has been directed to the wrong office, please destroy the contents of this fax immediately and notify [name] at [phone number].

A **MEMO TO:**   Marketing Managers Committee ↓2

    FROM: Dorothy Innie ↓2 *DI*

    DATE: July 10, 2004 ↓2

    SUBJECT: Agenda for July 20 Meeting ↓2 or 3

Our July 20 meeting will begin at 9:30 a.m. in the small conference room on the second floor. (The large conference room, where we normally meet, has been reserved by Mrs. Harper for an all-day meeting.) ↓2

Please come prepared to discuss the following topics: ↓2

B   1.   Sales through June for each product line. ↓2

     2.   Year-end sales forecast vs. budget for each product line.

     3.   Recommendations for changes in this year's marketing plans and requests for supplemental funding.

     4.   Proposed changes in next year's marketing strategies.

C   5.   Preliminary marketing budgets for next year. (Please put these in writing for me so that I can share them with Bill Carr, our friendly bean counter in the Finance Department.) ↓2

ma ↓2 or 3

Distribution: ↓2

G. Albers
R. Fagan
K. Garcia-Lorca
F. Li

A **Memo Format.** For the format of a memo template, see ¶1394. For the format of a memo done on plain paper (as shown here), see ¶1395.

B **Numbered List.** The numbered list feature of your software will begin with each item at the left margin, turnovers will be indented to align with the first word above, and no space will be left between items. However, an agenda requires at least 1 blank line to make the list easier to read. (See ¶1357d.)

C **End Punctuation.** The items in an agenda typically require no end punctuation. However, if any item involves the use of a complete sentence (as in item 5 in this illustration), place a period at the end of every item. For details on the use or omission of periods with items in a list, see ¶107.

Agenda—Formal Style

A

UNDERLOCK AND KEYE INC. ↓2

Agenda ↓2

Regular Meeting of Directors ↓2

Wednesday, September 23, 2004–10 a.m. ↓2

Boardroom, Fifth Floor ↓2 or 3

B
1. Call to order

2. Approval of minutes

3. Report on August operation—G. A. Horne

4. Report on corporate financial matters—A. J. McGill

5. Report on corporate development matters—L. Soaries   **C**

6. Review of international operations—W. Burgos

7. Discussion of Real Estate Committee report

8. Overview of the performance of major competitors—T. Foy

9. New business

D
10. Adjournment

A Margins. Note the use of wide (1.75") side margins for the text. This agenda has a number of very short items. If default side margin settings were used, it would look unbalanced with a relatively small left margin and a very large right margin.

B Numbered List. The numbered list feature of your software program will begin with each item at the left margin and no space will be left between items. Although single spacing is acceptable for items in a short list, an agenda requires the use of at least 1 blank line to make the list easier to read and work with during discussions. When the agenda lists ten or more items, try to align the single- and double-digit figures on the period, placing the double-digit figures at the left margin.

C End Punctuation. Note that no periods are needed at the end of the items in this illustration. (See also ¶107.)

D Formal Items. In a formal agenda it is customary to include such items as *Call to order, Approval of minutes, New business,* and *Adjournment* (or similar types of expressions).

A　　　　　　SOFTWARE APPLICATIONS SEMINAR $\downarrow$ 2

Saddle Brook Marriott $\downarrow$ 2

July 13–14, 2005 $\downarrow$ 2 or 3

B　Wednesday, July 13 $\downarrow$ 2

8:00– 9:00	Registration and Continental Breakfast	**C**	Lobby
D 9:00– 9:40	Software Applications: A State-of-the-Art Overview Speaker: Joyce Stocker-Olsen		Salons A and B
9:50–10:30	Word Processing and Communications Applications Speakers: Louis Serrano and Roy Pfaltz	**E**	Salons A and B
10:30–10:50	Coffee Break		Lobby
10:50–11:30	Desktop Publishing and Graphics Applications Speakers: Sandra Scroggins and Ed Fox		Salons A and B
11:40–12:20	Spreadsheet and Database Management Applications Speaker: Esther W. Benoit	**E**	Salons A and B
12:30– 1:45	Lunch		Ballroom
1:45– 3:15	Concurrent Sessions		
D	Session 1: Microsoft Word—Updates and Shortcuts Speaker: Tony Muzaffar		Red Oak Suite

A Headings. Include the location and date(s) of the conference or seminar in the main heading unless the program is part of a larger document that features this information prominently in some other way.

B If the program lasts more than one day, insert an appropriate side heading above each day's listing of events.

C To create this three-column format, use the table feature.

D For the alignment of "clock" times, see ¶1625b(3).

E Speaker Identification. The speakers listed on the program may be further identified by title, organization, and/or place of residence. Use commas to separate these elements of identification and, if you wish, use parentheses to enclose these elements as a whole. For example:

Gary A. Grimes, software consultant,　　　　Leola Leung, (vice-president
Kanata, Ontario　　　　　　　　　　　　Solutions Canada Ltd.,
　　　　　　　　　　　　　　　　　　Oakville, Ontario)

A MEMO TO: Marketing Managers Committee ↓2

   FROM: Paula Washington ↓2

   DATE: July 21, 2004 ↓2

B SUBJECT: Minutes of the Marketing Managers
             Committee Meeting of July 20, 2004 ↓2 or 3

C Present: Dorothy Innie (presiding), Georgia Albers, Ruth Fagan, Frank Li ↓2

   Absent: Katherine Garcia-Lorca ↓2

   Guest: Bill Carr ↓2 or 3

E

D 1. Sales through June for each product line. Each product line is behind budget
     for the first six months of the year. Bill Carr of the Finance Department
     reported that the company as a whole is running 11.2 percent behind budget.

   2. **Year-end sales forecast vs. budget for each product line.** Georgia Albers and

F The next meeting of the Marketing Managers Committee will be held on August
    24 in the *large* conference room (as usual). ↓2

    nb ↓2 or 3

    Distribution: ↓2

    G. Albers
    R. Fagan
    K. Garcia-Lorca
    D. Innie
    F. Li

17

A Memo Format. For the format of a memo (shown here), see ¶1395.

B Subject Line. For better appearance, the entry following *Subject:* has been broken
   into two lines of roughly equal length. (See ¶1353c, note.)

C Attendance Data. This block shows who was present (the person presiding listed
   first), who was absent, and who was a guest.

D Content Considerations. List topics in the order discussed. Use boldface or italics
E to highlight each topic, followed by a period. Omit the period if the comments are
   to appear below the topic, leave 1 blank line, and align the comments with the first
   word (not the number) of the topic above.

F Give the date and location of the next meeting in the last paragraph, starting at the
   left margin.

A   **UNDERLOCK AND KEYE INC.** ↓2

                                 Minutes ↓2

                Regular Meeting of Directors ↓2

                  September 23, 2004 ↓2 or 3

B   A regular meeting of the Board of Directors of Underlock and Keye Inc. was called to order at 71 Riverside Drive, Cambridge, Ontario, at 10 a.m.
C   pursuant to the notice sent to all directors in accordance with the by-laws. ↓2

D   The following directors were present, constituting all the directors: Jared C. Allison II, Kenneth L. Calderone, Deborah Georgopoulos-Keye,

D   Also present by invitation were William Burgos, Thomas Foy, Gregory A. Horne, Angela J. McGill, and Lester Soaries.

           Jared C. Allison II, Chairman, presided and David K. Rust, Assistant   I
Secretary, recorded the proceedings of the meeting.

           The minutes of the last meeting were approved.

           Mr. Allison introduced Gregory A. Horne, Executive Vice-President of   I
Operations, who reported on August operations.

E   Henry Koyama reviewed the recommendations of the Real Estate   I
Committee on the matter of building a new facility or renovating the existing facility to accommodate the Corporation's information processing needs over the next ten years.

           After further discussion, upon motion duly made and seconded, the following resolutions were unanimously adopted: ↓2

F   RESOLVED, that the Corporation is hereby authorized to under-take construction and rehabilitation activities to further the

G   The next meeting of the Board will be held on November 24 at 10 a.m.

H   There being no further business before the meeting, it was, on motion duly made and seconded, adjourned at 1:05 p.m. ↓3

                                   —————————————
                                   Assistant Secretary

17

A **Heading.** Use all-capital letters for the name of the company in the first line. Use capital and small letters for the other lines. For the date line, use the date on which the meeting was held (not the date on which the minutes were prepared). Use boldface for all the elements in the heading.

B **Format Considerations.** Use 1-inch side margins. Indent the first line of each paragraph 0.5 inch.

C **Opening Content.** Use the opening paragraph to indicate the name of the company; the time and the place where the meeting was "called to order" (the first item on the agenda shown on page 485); and whether it was a regular or special meeting.

D **Attendance and Routine Content.** Use the next paragraphs to indicate which directors were present (all were in this illustration); which were absent; which company officers and invited guests were present; who presided; and who recorded the proceedings and prepared the minutes.

E **Record of Transactions.** The body of the minutes should note in each paragraph what business was transacted and what actions were taken.

F **Format for Resolutions.** Treat resolutions as extracts, indented as a block 0.5 inch from each side margin. Type *RESOLVED* in all-capital letters followed by a comma and *that* (as illustrated). As an alternative, type *RESOLVED* followed by a colon and *That*.

G **Next Meeting.** Use the second last paragraph to indicate the date and time of the next meeting.

H **Adjournment.** Use the final paragraph to indicate the time of adjournment.

I **Capitalization Style.** Minutes done in a formal style use a formal style of capitalization. Note that short forms such as *Corporation* and *Board* are capitalized. Also note that in formal minutes such titles as *Chairman, Assistant Secretary,* and *Executive Vice-President of Operations* are capitalized when used after a person's name. (See ¶313d.)

ITINERARY ↓2

For Wallace F. Galloway ↓2

April 12–14, 2005 ↓2 or 3

A **Tuesday, April 12** ↓2

6:00 a.m.	**B** Limo to airport: Town Taxi (454-1040) ↓2	**E**
7:00 a.m.	Depart Ottawa. Air Canada Flight 113	
C 8:15 a.m.	Arrive Vancouver	

	D Limo to meeting: Arthur's Limo (604-348-5347)
	Driver will meet you at baggage carousel.
	Destination: Burnham & Frye Inc.
	  909 Burrard Street
	  Vancouver, BC
	  604-555-1216
		E

9:00 a.m.– 2:30 p.m.	Meet with Ed Burnham and Norbert Pell. They will make lunch arrangements.	**E**

2:30 p.m.	BC Ferry to Victoria: Call Arthur's Limo if 2:30 pickup
	time has to be changed.
	Hotel: Empress Hotel
	  721 Government Street
	  604-384-8111
	  Conf. No. 8941HWXQ; late arrival guaranteed	

6:30 p.m.	Dinner with Doris and Jack Cuneen; meet at restaurant (Ocean Pointe, 45 Songhees Road, 667-4677). ↓2	

A **Wednesday, April 13**

9:00 a.m.– 4:00 p.m.	Board meeting in headquarters building, 4th floor. Sam Hurley will drive you to the airport.	
5:25 p.m.	Depart Victoria. Air Canada Flight 212	
6:40 p.m.	Arrive Montreal. Dorval Airport	**E**

A Heading. If the intinerary is for two days or more, type each day as a side heading above the day's list of activities.

B Columnar Format. To create this two-column format, use the table feature.

C For the alignment of "clock" times in a column, see ¶1625b(3).

D Spacing. Leave 1 blank line between entries. Single-space any turnovers.

E **Content Considerations.** List phone numbers for all hotels, restaurants, and transportation services in case plans change. Try to provide the first names (not titles or initials) for all people whom the traveller is planning to meet. Provide the names of airports only when there is more than one serving the city (in this case, Montreal).

E-Mail

E-mail (also referred to as an electronic memo) serves to overcome the problems associated with the delivery of regular mail (postal *snail mail*) and with the frustrations that result from playing telephone tag (leaving messages but never connecting). It allows communication to be precise, screens cumbersome conversation, and expands personal contacts.

On the other hand, e-mail users have found that they are too often inundated with more messages in a day than they want to read and answer, especially when many messages are the electronic equivalent of junk mail. They have learned that their own messages should be impersonal, free of bias, and business-like and that confidential matters are better communicated by other means.

The following guidelines (¶¶1707–1710) suggest how to compose and format e-mail messages so as to make the most of what this technology offers.

1707 Keep your messages short and to the point. Long messages tend to be deleted or, at best, only scanned.

a. Organize your sentences in short, single-spaced paragraphs to make your message easier to read and understand. Use no indentions and leave a blank line between paragraphs.

b. Try to hold the overall length of the message to the number of lines that will fit on your screen. Limit each line to a maximum of 80 characters.

c. Do not use all-capital letters. This is considered the e-mail equivalent to shouting. Follow the standard rules of capitalization. (See Section 3.)

d. Type a clear and concise subject in the space provided. A subject line helps the recipient of a great many messages to scan them quickly in order to determine which require the fastest action. (See ¶1710a.)

e. Restrict each message to one subject. It is better to send separate messages than to cover all the topics in one message.

f. Consider how much background your reader needs to have in order to understand your message. It may be helpful to use the *Reply* feature in e-mail, which includes the original message as an easy and detailed point of reference for the originator.

(Continued on page 492.)

g. Watch your tone in composing the message. Before you send it, read the message from the recipient's point of view to make sure that your words and your tone are not likely to be misconstrued.

h. Do not send a *flaming* message; for example, one that is angry, outrageous, or opinionated. Moreover, if you receive *flames* (angry messages), it is wiser to ignore them than to respond.

i. Put nothing in an e-mail message that you would want anyone other than the intended recipient to see. For example, do not provide credit card numbers or other confidential information that could end up in the wrong hands.

j. Edit and proofread each message carefully, and make the necessary corrections before sending the message. Because e-mail messages are composed on the computer, it is easy to make (and overlook) mistakes in grammar, usage, spelling, and style. (See ¶¶1203–1205.)

1708 a. Keep the distribution of your e-mail messages to a minimum and make sure they are relevant only to those on your mail list. Given the ease of transmitting an e-mail message, you could be sending messages to people who don't need to see them and thus be adding to the e-mail overload.

b. Do not use e-mail to send unsolicited ads, chain letters, or other material that the recipient is likely to regard as junk mail or electronic garbage (known as *spam*). People who receive such material often take revenge by responding with flames. Some may go so far as to make use of special programs referred to as *bozo filters*. These programs automatically intercept and delete all future messages from such bozos.

c. Be sensitive to cultural differences. Remember, time zone differences and other countries' holidays could delay responses.

d. Use another means of communication, not e-mail, if you want to criticize or reprimand someone. Remember: The privacy of e-mail messages cannot be guaranteed.

e. Respect the privacy of the messages you receive. Do not pass such messages on to others unless you are sure the sender will not object.

1709 E-mail messages can be distributed through local and wide area networks, bulletin board systems, online services, and the Internet. Procedures for sending and receiving e-mail messages will therefore differ, depending on the system you use. Even the construction of mailing addresses will vary as a result.

a. An e-mail address is based on the Domain Name System (see ¶1533), which consists of a name or identifier, followed by @ (the symbol for *at*), and then followed by the domain name. Simply stated, it is *someone@somewhere*.

b. The first part of the e-mail address that precedes @ is called the *mailbox*. How this part is written will depend on the e-mail system used, the Internet vendor, or the way that names are assigned on an organization's e-mail system. Some users combine their first and last names (for example, *janiecanuck, jcanuck, canuckj*).

c. The part that follows @ is called the *domain*. It represents the mail system on which you receive your mail. The domain consists of two or more elements separated by periods (referred to as *dots*). Dots are used between elements of the domain but not at the end.

d. The final element in the domain is called the *zone*, which indicates what kind of system is being used. For example, *.com* signifies "commercial," *.gov*, "government," and *.ca*, "Canada."

☞ *For a more detailed dicussion of the zones now being used, see ¶1533.*
For notes on e-mail addresses, see ¶1534.
For guidelines on how to divide a long e-mail address at the end of a line, see ¶1535f.

1710 The format of an e-mail message is very much like that of a simplified memo with guide words. The illustration on the following page shows copies of two e-mail messages—one, the original message, requests a meeting and the other is the reply received. The bars at the top of each message show the recipient's name and e-mail address, and the date, time, and subject of the message. These bars are unique to the particular software used in these examples.

a. The most common guide words are *Date:*, *To:*, *From:*, and *Subject:*. If the message is sent to more than one person, use a comma or a semicolon to separate the entries showing each recipient's name and e-mail address. Always include a subject.

NOTE: Most e-mail programs automatically insert the sender's name and mailing address, and the date and time the message is sent.

b. Depending on the e-mail software used, you might see more guide words such as *cc:*, *bbc:*, and *attachments*.

NOTE: Some programs will display additional lines of information such as routing data to show all the relays or computer links required to forward an e-mail message.

c. An electronic signature, an important part of business e-mails, adds the name of the writer, the writer's position, department, organization, telephone and fax numbers, e-mail address, and may include the organization's address or any other relevant information. By using the insert signature feature of the e-mail software, several kinds of signatures can be created, depending upon the destination of the e-mail—within or outside the business.

(Continued on page 494.)

Original E-Mail Message with Reply

> **Wendy Strashok**
>
> **From:**   Joan Newman [joan.newman@sait.ab.ca]
> **Sent:**   Wednesday, August 01, 2003 1:44 PM
> **To:**   'Wendy Strashok'
> **Subject:** RE: Ways and Means, Meeting
>
>
>
> ATT00000.htm
>
> Unfortunately, my meeting schedule is full for Friday. Let's meet Monday at 1 p.m. in the Ninth Floor Conference Room.
>
> -----Original Message-----
>
> **From:**   **Wendy Strashok** [mailto:strashow@cadvision.com]
> **Sent:**   Wednesday, August 01, 2003 1:01 PM
> **To:**   'joan.newman@sait.ab.ca'
> **Subject:** Ways and Means, Meeting
>
> Joan,
>
> Could we get together on Friday at 2 p.m. to discuss our strategy for fund raising for the conference? We shouldn't need more than an hour. If Friday is not convenient for you, could we arrange something for Monday or Tuesday?
>
> Wendy

    d. When *replying* to a message, e-mail systems let you add the original message to serve as a reminder to the reader.

    e. Salutations and complimentary closings are optional and are often omitted in the interest of brevity. In the above illustration you will see that in the original message the name has been added to the opening and closing, but both have been omitted from the reply, which is shown first.

RÉSUMÉS
Planning a Résumé

1711 The purpose of a résumé is to get you an interview. Before writing your résumé, however, there must be careful yet creative planning in its preparation. The following guidelines should help you present your own high-quality résumé.

    a. Make a list of your achievements and other information about yourself, keeping in mind your career or job objective, the type of job you are looking for, the strengths you can bring to the job, and what you think you can accomplish for the employer's benefit.

        • Record your post-secondary education qualifications, listing the highest or most recent degree or completed program first. Indicate your academic standing or GPA (if above 3.00). Include high school education only if that is the highest level so far attained. (This is the most important area of a résumé for recent school or college graduates and should be placed before job experiences.)

- Note any job-related, continuing education courses you have taken to show that you are a person committed to learning new things.
- List both paid and non-paid experiences in reverse chronological order (the most recent item first). Focus on your achievements, capabilities, and activities rather than assigned duties. While this might appear to be a difficult task especially for new entrants to the job market, reflect upon what you have learned from your limited job experiences or other related activities that could be relevant to the job you are seeking.
- Note any special skills, community service, professional affiliations, or special interests that could be job-related; for example, computer competencies, experience with certain equipment or machinery, mastery of spoken or written foreign languages, honours or awards.

b. Review your list and consider how your background and accomplishments relate to specific areas of the job market. What can you offer to an employer with the experience you have acquired and the skills you have developed?

c. Prepare short, clear statements (not necessarily full sentences) that reflect your achievements, skills, and results. Organize and focus your strengths in light of the employer's needs. Place your strongest statement first.

- Start each statement with an active, descriptive verb; for example, *organized, initiated, implemented, maintained, supervised.*
- Use numbers whenever possible—they are impressive. *How many people did you supervise? How much money did you raise?*

d. Avoid stating your age, marital status, sex, height or weight, social insurance number, religion, ethnic origin, etc., unless such personal details are clearly required for your suitability for the job.

e. Be prepared to supply names, addresses, and telephone numbers of references at the interview. Do not include them on your résumé, nor is it always necessary to state that references are available upon request.

f. Select a résumé format that places your qualifications in an effective, attractive, and professional way. Read books and Web sites on the variety of styles used, but choose one that suits your own personal situation, keeping in mind how a specific employer will view your résumé. The most common formats are:

- **Chronological.** Education and jobs are listed by date with the most recent date first. This is the format preferred by recent graduates, others on a consistent job-related path, but more particularly by employers, because it shows career progression and job history. (See page 497.)
- **Functional.** Qualifications, skills, and achievements are emphasized in this format. Job history details may be omitted or, if included, may be listed in a separate section. This format is preferred by career-changers who want to avoid drawing attention to gaps of unemployment or who lack any direct experience. (See page 498.)

(Continued on page 496.)

- **Combination.** This format combines the best features of the two styles already mentioned. (See page 500.)

g. While traditional résumés have not been replaced, the following electronic résumés may also attract the attention of prospective employers.

- **Web Résumé.** This résumé is posted on your own personal Web site, which allows for easy transmission of the URL (via links). Your résumé then appears on numerous search engines and is readily accessible to employers.

- **Scannable Résumé.** A popular method for screening job applicants is scanning a version of your résumé by an optical character reader (OCR) into a database, where keyword searches are used to select the best résumés. The more links between the keywords in a résumé and those in a job description, the more likely the applicant will be selected for further evaluation. (See page 502.)

- **E-mail Résumé.** This is a plain text document that can be sent by e-mail, but it should still look as professional as possible.

- **Flash Résumé.** This multimedia, animated, off-the-wall résumé is suitable only if you are applying for a job in a creative field.

Formatting a Résumé

1712 To present your résumé in a professional, readable format follow these suggestions:

a. Use the table format of your software to prepare your own custom-tailored résumé.

b. Select a serif font (such as Times New Roman) that is easy to read. However, if your résumé needs to be faxed or scanned, a sans serif font (such as Arial) may provide a more readable copy. A font size of 10 to 12 points is acceptable for either font style.

c. Keep stylistic embellishments to a minimum. Use boldface for headings and bullets to separate items in the text sections. In the main body of your résumé, make consistent use of all-capitals, boldface, and italics—but use them sparingly.

d. Try to keep the résumé to one page, but no more than two pages. If a second page is used, key a proper continuation-page header.

NOTE: A one-page résumé is suitable for someone who is recently out of school and does not have much work experience. However, individuals with a great deal of work experience can also make effective use of a one-page format. In this case, the section dealing with educational achievements should *follow* the sections dealing with work experience and skills.

e. Edit continuously. Your résumé must be error-free.

f. Print your copy on best-quality paper, preferably in white, cream, or pale grey. Do not staple, paper-clip, or fold your résumé.

g. The envelope and stationery for the covering letter should be of the same quality and colour as your résumé. Place it on top of the résumé—also unstapled.

TRACY FERNANDES

A 66 Quidi Vidi Road   Telephone: 709-234-5641
St. John's, Newfoundland   E-mail: jlfernan@home.com
A1A 1C1   Fax: 709-256-2921

EDUCATION

B Sep. 2003 to   College of the North Atlantic, St. John's Campus, currently enrolled
Mar. 2004   in the Office Administration—Executive program. Will receive my
diploma, May 2004. GPA 3.7.

Sep. 2002 to   College of the North Atlantic, St. John's Campus, Office Administration
Apr. 2003   Certificate. Graduated May 2003, GPA 3.3.

Course Highlights:
Accounting, Business Law, Communications, Document Production,
Office and Special Events Management, Organizational Behaviour,
Work Exposure.

Awards and Activities:
Alumnae Keyboarding Prize for attained speed and accuracy, Graduation
Committee Treasurer, participant in college curling and hockey leagues.

EXPERIENCE

May 2003 to   **Clerical Assistant:** Beazley General Insurance Co. Ltd., St. John's
Aug. 2003   • Sorted mail, re-organized general files, answered telephone, prepared
claim forms.
• Developed self-reliance, yet appreciated the need for team work in
an office.

Jul. 2002 to   **Waitress:** Radisson Plaza Hotel Coffee Shop, St. John's
Aug. 2002   • Served breakfast and lunch to customers, prepared bills, handled
payments.
• Improved communication and organizational skills.

1997 to 2002   **Babysitter:** Cared for a number of neighbourhood children.

SKILLS

- Typing: 65 wam
- WordPerfect 9
- Telephone switchboard
- MS Word 2000
- Machine Transcription
- Reprographics
- PowerPoint
- Excel
- AccPac

A **Heading.** The heading should give all the key data an employer needs to get in touch with you.

B **Education.** Provide the estimated date of graduation if you are currently enrolled in a program.

NOTE: The use of an objective line is **optional** and should be used only by those who are seeking a job in a particular field.

ALICJA L. BEUGIN
AB Apartment 145
90 Wellesley Street East
Toronto, Ontario M4Y 1A3

Telephone: 416-555-7944
Fax: 416-555-8341
E-mail: albeugin@home.com

OBJECTIVE:

A marketing management position in which marketing and administrative experience combined with strong writing and computer skills can be used to maximize sales and profitability.

A ACHIEVEMENTS:

MARKETING EXPERIENCE

B • Participated in implementing market research studies to determine potential size of market for new product lines.
• Co-ordinated focus group sessions to determine customer attitudes.
• Analysed field sales reports and wrote summaries highlighting problem areas and commented on the feasibility of changes to product design and customer service.
• Developed detailed market plans based on rough outlines provided by the marketing manager.

A

ADMINISTRATIVE EXPERIENCE

B • Controlled budgeted expenses for advertising and promotion.
• Resolved customer complaints by taking direct action whenever possible or by routing complaint to the appropriate person.
• Established and maintained media contacts to obtain free publicity for new products.
• Supervised an assistant who handled all correspondence and clerical tasks.

A

WRITING SKILLS

B • Wrote copy for mail campaigns and catalogues.
• Wrote summaries of field sales reports adding appropriate comments.
• Wrote copy for fund-raising brochures for art museum.

A Side Headings. Note how the wording of the "objective" statement *(in which marketing and administrative experience combined with strong writing and computer skills)* leads into the wording for the side headings—*MARKETING EXPERIENCE, ADMINISTRATIVE EXPERIENCE, WRITING SKILLS,* and *COMPUTER SKILLS.* The usual side heading *EXPERIENCE* in the left column has been replaced by *ACHIEVEMENTS* because the term *experience* has been used in two of the four side headings in the right column.

B Wording of Entries. Note how the entries under the side headings emphasize the applicant's strengths in each functional area independent of the job setting in which these strengths were developed.

A COMPUTER SKILLS

B
- Initiated a software publishing program. Saved the company over $50 000 in the first year of operation.
- Designed space ads, catalogues, and fund-raising brochures.
- Created and managed a database to control budgeted expenses.
- Mastered Microsoft Word for Windows, PageMaker, PowerPoint, Excel.

C EMPLOYMENT
HISTORY:
- Administrative co-ordinator for director of marketing, Zimmer & Boyle Inc., York, Ontario, July 2000–Present.
- Administrative assistant to sales manager, Zimmer & Boyle Inc., York, Ontario, February 1998–June 2000.
- Secretary to marketing manager, Crouch and Cowar Incorporated, Toronto, Ontario, May 1996–January 1998.
- Assistant to director of public relations, the Royal Ontario Museum, Toronto, Ontario, January 1995–February 1996.

EDUCATION:

B.A. in marketing, 1994, minor in English.
University of Western Ontario, London, Ontario

- Wrote feature articles for *The Western Star* during sophomore and junior years.
- Created (with two partners) an on-campus birthday celebration service. Managed the service during junior and senior years. Tested various direct marketing techniques to solicit orders.

D CONTINUING
EDUCATION:

Courses in copywriting, telemarketing techniques, niche marketing, and computer graphics, George Brown College, Toronto, Ontario, 2000–2002.

D COMMUNITY
SERVICE:

Designed and wrote annual fund-raising brochures (since 2001) for the Toronto Shelter for Street Kids, using computer graphics.

C **Employment History.** Although this section would not appear in a purely "functional" résumé, an employment history provides prospective employers with a brief chronological listing of previous job titles, the name and location of previous employers, and employment dates. Including this section often serves to mollify employers who are more comfortable with résumés done completely in the chronological style.

D **Optional Sections.** As well as *Continuing Education* and *Community Service*, other optional job-related information provided could be *Professional Activities, Special Qualifications, Awards and Recognitions, Memberships,* and *Special Interests.*

ALICJA L. BEUGIN

AB Apartment 145
90 Wellesley Street East
Toronto, Ontario M4Y 1A3

Telephone: 416-555-7944
Fax: 416-555-8341
E-mail: albeugin@home.com

OBJECTIVE:
A marketing management position in which marketing and administrative experience combined with strong writing and computer skills can be used to maximize sales and profitability.

EXPERIENCE:

A Administrative Co-ordinator
for Director of Marketing

ZIMMER & BOYLE INC., York, Ontario,
July 2000–Present

B Created and managed a database to control budgeted expenses. Participated in implementing market research studies to determine potential size of market for new product lines. Co-ordinated focus group sessions to determine customer attitudes. Initiated a software publishing program; saved the company over $50 000 in the first year of operation.

A Administrative Assistant to
Sales Manager

ZIMMER & BOYLE INC., York, Ontario,
February 1998–June 2000

B Analysed field sales reports and wrote summaries highlighting problem areas and commented on the feasibility of changes to product design and customer service. Resolved customer complaints by taking direct

COMMUNITY
SERVICE:

Designed and wrote annual fund-raising brochures (since 2001) for the Toronto Shelter for Street Kids, using computer graphics.

A Experience. In this format, job titles (not dates) are featured in the left column. At the right the name and location of the organization plus the employment dates are given on one or two lines.

B Job Achievements. Arranging the specific achievements for each job in one paragraph is a common format, but it is not as readable as the bulleted formats found on pages 497, 498, and 499.

Planning a Scannable Résumé

1713 Compared to the traditional style of résumé writing, the scannable version is extremely plain. This is intentional because its design is to suit the needs of the OCR—not those of a human reader. Keep in mind that it is the number of keywords you write to match those of the job description in the database that is the important factor. Consider the following for maximizing the number of your keywords.

    a. Read help-wanted advertisements and job postings for the kind of job you want. Try to incorporate into your résumé as many keywords from those job descriptions as possible.

    b. Use industry jargon, current industry buzzwords, acronyms, and abbreviations, since these are likely to be the kinds of keywords that the computer database has been programmed to focus on. The first time an acronym and abbreviation is used, however, the full name should be written immediately after and placed within parentheses.

    c. Increase the total number of keywords in your résumé by using synonyms whenever possible to avoid repeating the same keywords.

    d. Change the action verbs of your traditional résumé to keyword nouns.

Formatting a Scannable Résumé

1714 To be sure that your résumé is read by the OCR, the following guidelines are recommended:

    a. For the sharpest possible image, use the best-quality white paper and a laser printer with black ink.

    b. Select a standard font (Arial or Times New Roman) with 10- to 12-point size. Use no boldface, italics, underlines, script, bullets, logos, shading, horizontal or vertical lines, or any other graphic devices. If desired, asterisks may be used to introduce individual items in a list.

    c. Begin all lines in the body of the résumé at the left margin. Columnar formats are not used.

    d. Try to limit the résumé to one page. If more than one page is required, use a paper clip (not a staple) to keep the pages together. Use a continuation heading for the second page. (See pages 502–503.)

    e. Insert your completed résumé into a plastic sleeve to keep it clean and wrinkle-free. Do not fold or crease it in any way.

Scannable Résumé

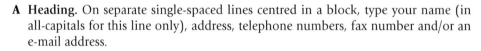

A ALICJA L. BEUGIN
Apartment 145
90 Wellesley Street East
Toronto, Ontario M4Y 1A3
Home: 416-555-7944
Fax: 416-555-8341
E-mail: albeugin@home.com

B OBJECTIVE

A marketing management position in which marketing and administrative experience combined with strong writing and computer skills can be used to maximize sales and profitability.

B MARKETING SKILLS

C Implementation of market research studies. Assessment of potential market size for new product lines. Co-ordination of focus group sessions. Assessment of customer attitudes toward product lines. Analysis of field sales reports. Prioritize problems for immediate action. Pinpoint the changes to product design and customer service. Development of detailed market plans based on input from marketing manager.

B ADMINISTRATIVE SKILLS

C Control of advertising and promotional expense budgets. Resolution of customer complaints. Contacts with newspapers, TV stations, and radio stations for free publicity. Supervised a clerical assistant.

B WRITING SKILLS

C Preparation of copy for mail campaigns and fund-raising brochures. Summaries of field sales reports.

B COMPUTER SKILLS

C Start-up of in-house software publishing program with first-year savings of $50 000. Design and layout of space ads, catalogues, and fund-raising brochures. Creation and management

A Heading. On separate single-spaced lines centred in a block, type your name (in all-capitals for this line only), address, telephone numbers, fax number and/or an e-mail address.

B Side Headings. Use all-capitals and leave 1 blank line above and below each heading. Remember: no embellishments.

C Skills. Under each side heading is one paragraph consisting of phrases, each ending with a period.

D   ALICJA L. BEUGIN   Page 2

B   EMPLOYMENT HISTORY

E   * Administrative co-ordinator for director of marketing, Zimmer and Boyle Inc., York,
Ontario, July 2000–Present.
G   * Administrative assistant to sales manager, Zimmer and Boyle Inc., York, Ontario, February
1998–June 2000.
* Secretary to marketing manager, Crouch and Cowar Incorporated, Toronto, Ontario, May
1996–January 1998.
* Assistant to director of public relations, the Royal Ontario Museum, Toronto, Ontario,
January 1995–February 1996.

B   EDUCATION

F   B.A. in marketing, 1994, minor in English, University of Western Ontario, London, Ontario

G   Wrote feature articles for The Western Star during sophomore and junior years. Created
(with two partners) an on-campus birthday celebration service. Managed the service during
junior and senior years. Tested various direct marketing techniques to solicit orders.

B   CONTINUING EDUCATION

F   Courses in copywriting, telemarketing techniques, niche marketing, and computer graphics,
George Brown College, Toronto, Ontario, 2000–2002.

B   COMMUNITY SERVICE

F   Designed and wrote annual fund-raising brochures (since 2001) for the Toronto Shelter for
Street Kids, using computer graphics.

D   Continuation Heading. Provide a heading that gives your name and the page number.

E   Employment History. Start with the most recent job. If you wish, an asterisk may introduce each job listing. But no other graphic device is scannable. There is no need to repeat the duties of each job as they have already been summarized in the Skills sections.

F   Other Sections. The same sections found in a traditional résumé would certainly be included in a scannable one.

G   Elimination of Graphic Elements. Because some OCRs cannot properly scan ampersands, note that the ampersand in *Zimmer & Boyle* has been replaced by *and*. For a similar reason, the title of the university newspaper, *The Western Star*, must appear in ordinary print and not in italics.

OTHER EMPLOYMENT DOCUMENTS

As part of the job-seeking process, you will need to write three types of letters: letters of application, follow-up letters after an interview, and a letter of acceptance. Specific guidelines are provided in ¶¶1716–1718, but a few general guidelines (¶1715) apply to all employment communications.

1715 GENERAL GUIDELINES

    a. Keep your letters short—less than one full page if possible.

    b. Resist the temptation to copy sample letters word for word. Draw on these samples for ideas, but create your own letters—letters that communicate the distinctive flavour of your personality. Thank-you cards, with or without a printed or handwritten message, are never appropriate.

    c. Edit and proofread your letters carefully. Simple typographical errors (not to mention more serious errors in grammar, style, and usage) will create a negative impression that damages your job-seeking campaign.

    d. Always try to address your letters to a specific person, using that person's full name and title. If necessary, call the specific organization to obtain this information.

    NOTE: The model letters on pages 507–509 are all written by Alicja Beugin, the fictitious person whose job qualifications are set forth in some of the résumés shown on pages 497–500. In these letters Ms. Beugin is trying to move up to a marketing management position.

    ☞ *See Section 13 for guidelines and illustrations of business letters.*

1716 APPLICATION LETTERS

Letters you write to apply for a job will vary to some extent, depending on whether you are (1) following up on an advertisement, (2) taking the initiative to find out whether any openings exist for a person with your skills and experience, or (3) following up on the suggestion of a mutual friend or acquaintance to explore job opportunities with a specific person within an organization. Yet all application letters have the same three objectives: to indicate what you have to offer the organization, to transmit your résumé, and to obtain an interview. Consider the following guidelines when you write an application letter.

    a. Before you draft your letter, try to get as much information as you can about the organization you have in mind. For example, what products or services does it offer? What special strategy or philosophy governs the way the organization operates? Such information can help you focus your letter more effectively and will let the recipient of the letter know that you have taken the initiative to learn something about the organization.

    NOTE: If you are responding to a blind advertisement (one that provides no organizational name and only a box number address), you will not be able to undertake this research. However, the advertisement will spell out the qualifications desired, something not usually available to you when you are simply exploring the possibility of job openings.

b. Begin your letter by indicating whether you are responding to an advertisement, following up on the suggestion of a mutual friend or acquaintance, or simply exploring what job opportunities currently exist.

c. Indicate what you have to offer the organization. If you are responding to an advertisement that states the qualifications desired, clearly indicate how your skills and experience relate to each of the qualifications listed. If you are simply exploring job openings, do not focus on specific tasks that you have performed in the past. Instead, highlight the things you have accomplished as a result of the way you applied your skills and experience. This approach will make it easier for someone to gauge how well you might fit the job available, even if you have not performed those exact tasks in the past.

NOTE: The recipient of your letter will probably be receiving many other application letters at the same time. It is important, therefore, that your letter and your résumé make you stand out from the others. In your letter you should aim to achieve—in much shorter form—the same things you are trying to achieve in your résumé.

d. The primary short-term objective of this letter is to arrange for an interview. Rather than wait for the recipient of your letter to call you, indicate that you will call on a specific date to determine whether an interview can take place. In stating when you will call, allow enough time for your material to be delivered and looked at. Keep in mind that the recipient may be inundated with other matters or may be travelling and thus may not look at your letter and résumé as quickly as you would like.

NOTE: Keep a record of when you promised to call so that you follow through on time. Calling a day or two later could suggest that you are not a very good manager of your time.

☞ *For a model application letter written in response to an advertised opening, see page 507.*

1717 FOLLOW-UP LETTERS

After an interview, follow up within 48 hours with a letter that covers the following points:

a. Thank the interviewer for (1) taking the time to see you, (2) giving you better insight into the available job and the organization you would be working for, and (3) considering your qualifications in light of the available job.

b. Reinforce the positive impression you tried to make during the interview, and briefly restate why you think you would be an asset to the organization.

(Continued on page 506.)

c. Offer additional information about your qualifications if they were not fully discussed during the interview. If you promised during the interview to supply additional information, do so now.

d. Address questions that arose during the interview that you were not fully prepared to answer at the time. If you know (or simply sense) that the interviewer had some doubts about your qualifications, use this opportunity to overcome such doubts if you can.

NOTE: If the interviewer made it clear at the time that you were not right for the current job opening, send a follow-up letter nonetheless. Offer thanks for having been considered for this job, and express hope that you will be considered for other jobs that may open in the future. On the other hand, if *you* decide the job is not right for you, send a follow-up letter in which you thank the interviewer and ask not to be a candidate.

☞ *For an illustration of a follow-up letter, see page 508.*

1718 ACCEPTANCE LETTERS

Of all employment communications, this is the easiest—and the most pleasant—letter to write. Use this occasion to:

a. Formally accept the job.

b. Confirm the key details of your working arrangements (including starting date) that have been previously discussed. If any of these details are not clear, ask the person who hired you to spell them out.

c. Express your pleasure in coming to work for the organization and, more specifically, for the person who has offered you the job.

☞ *For an illustration of an acceptance letter, see page 509.*

A **ALICJA L. BEUGIN**

AB Apartment 145
90 Wellesley Street East
Toronto, Ontario M4Y 1A3

Telephone: 416-555-7944
Fax: 416-555-8341
E-mail: albeugin@home.com

March 3, 2004

Mr. Oliver Digby
Director of Human Resources
Hunt and Ketcham Inc.
128 Euclid Street
Whitby, Ontario L1N 0K2

Dear Mr. Digby:

B Please consider me a candidate for the position of marketing manager that you advertised in the March 2 edition of the *Plain Dealer*.

C As you will note from my enclosed résumé, my educational qualifications in marketing and computer applications, my experience in sales and marketing, and my contacts with field sales representatives and customers come close to satisfying all your requirements.

D I would very much appreciate the opportunity to meet with you and will call your office on March 10 to arrange an interview, or you may contact me at the telephone numbers listed in the letterhead.

Sincerely,

Alicja L. Beugin

Alicja L. Beugin

Enclosure

17

A **Letterhead.** The attractive letterhead design that Alicja Beugin has created will help make her application letter stand out. It is the same letterhead she used on the first page of her résumé.
B **First Paragraph.** Alicja uses her opening paragraph to indicate how she found out about the job.
C **Second Paragraph.** Alicja refers to her résumé and shows how her qualifications compare with the job requirements stated in the advertisement.
D **Final Paragraph.** Alicja takes the initiative in saying she will call to see whether an interview can be arranged.

ALICJA L. BEUGIN

AB Apartment 145
90 Wellesley Street East
Toronto, Ontario M4Y 1A3

Telephone: 416-555-7944
Fax: 416-555-8341
E-mail: albeugin@home.com

March 24, 2004

Mr. Oliver Digby
Director of Human Resources
Hunt and Ketcham Inc.
128 Euclid Street
Whitby, Ontario L1N 0K2

Dear Mr. Digby:

A Thank you for taking the time last Friday to explain why my lack of field sales experience in the technical publishing market would prevent me from being considered for the marketing manager's position at Hunt and Ketcham.

B Thank you also for arranging an interview that same day with your director of sales. Ms. Cantrell gave me a very detailed picture of a field representative's responsibilities. She also stated that in light of all my prior experience in educational publishing, I should make the transition to technical publishing very easily. I was also encouraged to learn that after a year or two of experience in the field, I would be a strong candidate for any marketing manager's position that might open at that time.

C Ms. Cantrell has promised to let me know within the next four weeks whether she is in a position to offer me a field representative's job. If she does, I very much look forward to seeing you again. In any event, thank you very much for all the help you have given me.

Sincerely,

Alicja L. Beugin

Alicja L. Beugin

A **First Paragraph.** Alicja thanks the interviewer for clarifying the demands of the job and pointing out where her qualifications fell short.

B **Second Paragraph.** Alicja thanks the interviewer for steering her to another opportunity in the organization and for setting up an interview that same day. (Alicja should also send a follow-up letter to the second person who interviewed her.) Note that she re-affirms her hope for a marketing management job in a year or two.

C **Third Paragraph.** Alicja ends on a warm note, thanking the first interviewer for all his help.

ALICJA L. BEUGIN

AB Apartment 145
90 Wellesley Street East
Toronto, Ontario M4Y 1A3

Telephone: 416-555-7944
Fax: 416-555-8341
E-mail: albeugin@home.com

April 28, 2004

Ms. Jennifer Cantrell
Director of Sales
Hunt and Ketcham Inc.
128 Euclid Street
Whitby, Ontario L1N 0K2

Dear Jennifer:

A I am very pleased to accept the job of field sales representative with northeastern Ontario as my territory and with the opportunity to work for Hunt and Ketcham.

B The materials that Oliver Digby sent me answered all my questions about compensation arrangements and company policies. I have now completed and returned all the necessary paperwork. As I understand it, I am to start work on June 2, spending the month in Whitby for orientation and training.

C If there is anything you think I should be reading or doing in the next month, please let me know. I would welcome the opportunity to prepare myself for the job before I actually report for work on June 2.

Sincerely,

Alicja L. Beugin

Alicja L. Beugin

17

A First Paragraph. Alicja accepts the job with pleasure and acknowledges the opportunity to work for the company.
B Second Paragraph. Alicja uses this paragraph to deal with the technical details involved in starting a new job.
C Final Paragraph. Alicja shows initiative in offering to undertake advance preparation for the job before she officially starts work.

OUTLINES

1719 An outline can be used to *plan* the content and organization of any document. It identifies (1) the topics that are to be discussed and (2) the sequence in which they are to be introduced. An outline may consist of a simple list or it may contain several levels of subtopics under each main topic (as in the illustrations on the following pages).

1720 After you have finished drafting a document, you can use an outline to *review* the document in terms of content and organization. An outline of this kind typically lists key words or phrases used as headings throughout the copy to identify topics and subtopics as they are each introduced. When you use an outline for reviewing purposes, you can more easily answer questions like these:

- Have all topics been included?
- Have all topics been fully developed?
- Does the sequence of headings provide a balanced representation of all aspects of the discussion, or are some parts of the text loaded with headings while others have very few?
- Are the headings worded in a similar way, or are some complete sentences and others simply phrases?

1721 a. If you are using software with an outline feature, you can create an outline by scrolling through the text and coding (according to a level of subordination) every heading in the text. If you revise the heading structure in the document, you can use the outline feature to generate a new outline to confirm that the document is now better organized.

NOTE: The illustration on the following page shows an outline created by the outline feature (with all the default settings) of Microsoft Word for Windows. Note that the outline is single-spaced throughout. Moreover, note that the indentions established for each level of heading are based on preset tabs and do not permit the start of each new level of heading to align with the first word in the level above.

b. When you are creating an outline for your own use (say, for planning or reviewing purposes), an outline produced by the outline feature is quite acceptable. However, if the outline will be part of a formal document, you should consider using a more readable format with a more open look and a standard pattern of alignments. Because it is not easy to make adjustments to most of the outline feature's automatic settings, turn them off and set your own tabs or customize the outline numbering through the bullets and numbering feature in Microsoft Word. (See ¶1723 and the illustration on page 513.)

1722 The use of numbers and letters with the items in an outline indicates the relative importance of these items to one another. The standard outline illustration on page 513 shows six levels of headings, but many outlines do not require that many and a few may require more.

a. In the illustration of the Microsoft Word outline below, the first level of items is identified by Roman numerals, the second by capital letters, the third by Arabic numerals, the fourth by small letters, the fifth by Arabic numerals in parentheses, and the sixth by small letters in parentheses.

b. At least two items are needed for each level used in an outline. If your outline shows a Roman I at the first level, it must also show a Roman II; if you use a capital A at the second level, you must also use a capital B, and so on.

Outline Format Using the Outline Feature of Microsoft Word for Windows

---

EQUIPMENT AND SOFTWARE

Orientation for Department Staff

```
    I.  INTRODUCTION
   II.  EQUIPMENT AND SOFTWARE
        A.  Equipment
            1.  Computer
                a)  Drives
                        (1) Types
                                (a) Hard
                                (b) Floppy
                        (2) Capacity
                                (a) Hard
                                (b) Floppy
                b)  RAM
            2.  Monitor
            3.  Modem
            4.  Mouse
            5.  Printer
            6.  Scanner
        B.  Software
            1.  System
                a)  MS-DOS
                b)  MS-Windows
                c)  Other
            2.  Applications
                a)  Standalones
                        (1) Database
                        (2) Spreadsheet
                        (3) Word Processing
                        (4) Other
                b)  Suites
            3.  Registration procedure
                a)  Fax
                b)  Mail
                c)  Online
  III.  OPERATION
        A.  Startup
        B.  Start/Quit a Program
        C.  Get Help
        D.  Modifications
            1.  System Settings
            2.  New Programs
        E.  Shut Down
```

1723 If you are devising your own format for an outline, consider these guidelines and refer to the second outline illustration on page 513.

   a. Margins. Ordinarily, use side and bottom margins of 1 inch. Leave a top margin of 2 inches, but reduce it to 1 inch if doing so will prevent the outline from taking a second page. A one-page outline may also be centred vertically on the page.

   b. Heading. Key the title in all-capital letters. Use capital and small letters for the other lines. If you wish, use boldface for the complete heading of the title only. Leave 1 blank line between the lines in the heading and 1 or 2 blank lines below the last line of the heading.

   c. Enumerations. The numbers or letters that identify the items at different levels in an outline should all be followed by a period or right parenthesis [)] and 1 or 2 spaces.

   NOTE: When using Roman numerals for the first level, either set a right align tab so numbers will align on the period or accept the default left alignment for Roman numerals.

Right Alignment	Default
I.	I.
II.	II.
III.	III.

   If the right aligned format is used, the second-level items would line up at a position 1 or 2 spaces after the longest Roman numeral (for example, VIII).

   d. Capitalization. Use all-capital letters for the first-level items (those preceded by Roman numerals). Use capital and small letters for items at all lower levels.

   e. Indentions. When using Roman numerals to identify first-level items, align the second level of items (those beginning with A and B) on the first word after the Roman I. Align the third level of items (those beginnning with 1 and 2) on the first word after A in the second level; however, if there are more than nine items, align the longest number (Arabic or Roman) on the first word after the enumeration number in the previous level; then right align all the following numbers in the same level on the period.

   NOTE: Various combinations of letters and numerals can be used as level designators. The following examples show 9-level formats.

   I. A. 1. a. (1) (a) i) a) 1)
   1. a. i. (1) (a) (i) 1) a) i)

   f. Spacing Between Items. Leave 2 blank lines above and 1 blank line below each first-level item. For all other levels, use single spacing with no blank lines between items.

Standard Outline Format

EQUIPMENT AND SOFTWARE ↓2

Orientation for Department Staff ↓3

I. INTRODUCTION ↓3

II. EQUIPMENT AND SOFTWARE ↓2

    A. Equipment
       1. Computer
         a) Drives
           (1) Types
             (a) Hard
             (b) Floppy
           (2) Capacity
             (a) Hard
             (b) Floppy
         b) RAM
       2. Monitor
       3. Modem
       4. Mouse
       5. Printer
       6. Scanner
    B. Software
       1. System
         a) MS-DOS
         b) MS-Windows
         c) Other
       2. Applications
         a) Standalones
           (1) Database
           (2) Spreadsheet
           (3) Word Processing
           (4) Other
         b) Suites
       3. Registration procedure
         a) Fax
         b) Mail
         c) Online ↓3

III. OPERATION ↓2

    A. Startup
    B. Start/Quit a Program

 See the Online Learning Centre at www.mcgrawhill.ca/college/gregg for related weblinks.

P A R T

THREE

References

Forms of Address

INDIVIDUALS (¶1801)

Man With Courtesy Title (¶1801a)
Woman—Courtesy Title Preference Known (¶1801b)
Woman—Courtesy Title Preference Unknown (¶1801c)
Individual—Name Known, Gender Unknown (¶1801d)
Individual—Name Unknown, Gender Known (¶1801e)
Individual—Name Known, Gender Known (¶1801f)
Two Men (¶1801g)
Two Women (¶1801h)
Woman and Man—No Personal Relationship (¶1801i)

COUPLES (¶1802)

Married Couple With Same Surname—No Special Titles (¶1802a)
Married Couple With Same Surname—Husband Has Special Title (¶1802b)
Married Couple With Same Surname—Wife Has Special Title (¶1802c)
Married Couple With Same Surname—Both Have Special Titles (¶1802d)
Married Couple With Different Surnames (¶1802e)
Married Couple With Hyphenated Surname (¶1802f)
Unmarried Couple Living Together (¶1802g)

ORGANIZATIONS (¶1803)

Organization of Women and Men (¶1803a)
Organization of Women (¶1803b)
Organization of Men (¶1803c)

PROFESSIONALS (¶1804)

Lawyers (¶1804a)
Physicians and Others With Doctoral Degrees (¶1804b)

EDUCATION OFFICIALS (¶1805)

Chancellor of College or University (¶1805a)
President of College or University (¶1805b)
Dean of College or University (¶1805c)
Professor (¶1805d)
Superintendent of Schools (¶1805e)

Member of Board of Education (¶1805f)
Principal (¶1805g)
Teacher (¶1805h)

CANADIAN GOVERNMENT OFFICIALS (¶1806)

Governor General of Canada (¶1806a)
Prime Minister of Canada (¶1806b)
Cabinet Minister of Canada (¶1806c)
Member of the House of Commons (¶1806d)
Senator (¶1806e)
Chief Justice of Canada (¶1806f)
Judge of Federal, Provincial, County, or Territorial Court (¶1806g)
Lieutenant-Governor (¶1806h)
Premier (¶1806i)
Member, Provincial Cabinet (¶1806j)
Member, Legislative Assembly (¶1806k)
Mayor (¶1806l)
Member, Municipal Council (¶1806m)

AMERICAN GOVERNMENT OFFICIALS (¶1807)

President of the United States (¶1807a)
Cabinet Minister (¶1807b)
United States Senator (¶1807c)
United States Representative (¶1807d)
Governor (¶1807e)

THE ROYAL FAMILY (¶1808)

The Queen (¶1808a)
The Duke of Edinburgh (¶1808b)
The Prince of Wales (¶1808c)
The Duke of York (¶1808d)
The Princess Royal (¶1808e)
Prince Edward (¶1808f)

DIPLOMATS (¶1809)

Secretary-General of the United Nations (¶1809a)
Ambassador or High Commissioner of a Foreign Country to Canada (¶1809b)
Canadian Ambassador or High Commissioner Abroad (¶1809c)
American Ambassador to Canada (¶1809d)

INTERNATIONAL DIGNITARIES (¶1810)

An Emperor (¶1810a)
A King (¶1810b)
A Queen (¶1810c)
A Prince with the title *Royal* or *Serene Highness* (¶1810d)

A President of a Republic (¶1810e)
A Prime Minister (¶1810f)

MEMBERS OF THE CANADIAN ARMED FORCES (¶1811)
Officers (¶1811a)
Other Ranks (¶1811b)

NATIVE LEADERS (¶1812)
Indian Chiefs (¶1812a)
Band Councillors (¶1812b)

ROMAN CATHOLIC DIGNITARIES (¶1813)
Pope (¶1813a)
Cardinal (¶1813b)
Archbishop and Bishop (¶1813c)
Monsignor (¶1813d)
Priest (¶1813e)
Mother Superior (¶1813f)
Sister (¶1813g)
Brother (¶1813h)

PROTESTANT DIGNITARIES (¶1814)
Anglican Primate (¶1814a)
Anglican Bishop (¶1814b)
Anglican Dean (¶1814c)
Moderator, United Church (¶1814d)
Minister With Doctor's Degree (¶1814e)
Minister Without Doctor's Degree (¶1814f)

JEWISH DIGNITARIES (¶1815)
Chief Rabbi (¶1815a)
Rabbi With Doctor's Degree (¶1815b)
Rabbi Without Doctor's Degree (¶1815c)

18

The following forms are correct for addressing letters to individuals, couples, organizations, professional people, education officials, government officials, diplomats, military personnel, and religious dignitaries.

IMPORTANT NOTE: In the salutations that follow the forms of address, the most formal one is listed first. Unless otherwise indicated, the ellipsis marks in the salutation stand for the surname alone.

Because of space limitations, only the masculine forms of address have been given in some illustrations. When an office or a position is held by a woman, make the following substitutions:

For *Sir*, use *Madam*.

For *Mr.* followed by a name (for example, *Mr. Wyatt*), use *Miss, Mrs.,* or *Ms.,* whichever is appropriate.

For *His*, use *Her*.

For *Mr.* followed by a title (for example, *Mr. President, Mr. Secretary, Mr. Mayor*), use *Madam*.

Postal codes are shown on a separate line due also to lack of space.

☞ For a detailed discussion of how to construct inside addresses, see ¶¶1317–1343.
  For further information on salutations, see ¶¶1346–1351.
  For details on how to handle addresses on envelopes, see ¶¶1389–1392.

1801 INDIVIDUALS

a. Man With Courtesy Title

Mr. . . . (*full name*)
Address

Dear Mr. . . . :

b. Woman—Courtesy Title Preference Known

Ms. (**OR** Miss **OR** Mrs.) . . . (*full name*)
Address

Dear Ms. (**OR** Miss **OR** Mrs.) . . . :

NOTE: Always use the title that a woman prefers.

c. Woman—Courtesy Title Preference Unknown

Ms. . . . (*full name*)
Address

Dear Ms. . . . :

OR:

. . . (*full name with no title*)
Address

Dear . . . (*first name and surname*):

d. Individual—Name Known, Gender Unknown

. . . (*full name with no title*)
Address

Dear . . . (*first name or initials plus surname*):

e. Individual—Name Unknown, Gender Known

. . . (*title of individual*)
. . . (*name of organization*)
Address

Madam:
Dear Madam:

OR:

Sir:
Dear Sir:

f. Individual—Name Known, Gender Known

. . . (*title of individual*)
. . . (*name of organization*)
Address

Sir or Madam:
Dear Sir or Madam:

OR:

Madam or Sir:
Dear Madam or Sir:

g. Two Men

Mr. . . . (*full name*)
Mr. . . . (*full name*)
Address

Gentlemen:
Dear Messrs. . . . and . . . : (See ¶1349.)
Dear Mr. . . . and Mr. . . . :

h. Two Women

Ms. . . . (*full name*)
Ms. . . . (*full name*)
Address

Dear Mses. (**OR** Mss.) . . . and . . . :
Dear Ms. . . . and Ms. . . . :

OR:

Mrs. . . . (*full name*)
Mrs. . . . (*full name*)
Address

Dear Mesdames . . . and . . . : (See ¶1349.)
Dear Mrs. . . . and Mrs. . . . :

OR:

> Miss . . . (*full name*)
> Miss . . . (*full name*)
> Address
>
> Dear Misses . . . and . . . :
> Dear Miss . . . and Miss . . . :

OR:

> Ms. . . . (*full name*)
> Mrs. . . . (*full name*)
> Address
>
> Dear Ms. . . . and Mrs. . . . :

OR:

> Miss . . . (*full name*)
> Ms. . . . (*full name*)
> Address
>
> Dear Miss . . . and Ms. . . . :

OR:

> Mrs. . . . (*full name*)
> Miss . . . (*full name*)
> Address
>
> Dear Mrs. . . . and Miss . . . :

i. Woman and Man—No Personal Relationship

> Ms. (**OR** Mrs. **OR** Miss) . . . (*full name*)
> Mr. . . . (*full name*)
> Address
>
> Dear Ms. (**OR** Mrs. **OR** Miss) . . .
> and Mr. . . . :

OR:

> Mr. . . . (*full name*)
> Ms. (**OR** Mrs. **OR** Miss) . . . (*full name*)
> Address
>
> Dear Mr. . . . and Ms. (**OR** Mrs.
> **OR** Miss) . . . :

☞ *For forms of address for teenagers and younger children, see ¶1322d–e.*

1802 COUPLES

a. Married Couple With Same Surname—No Special Titles

> Mr. and Mrs. . . . (*husband's full name*)
> (See ¶1323d.)
> Address
>
> Dear Mr. and Mrs. . . . (*husband's surname*):

b. Married Couple With Same Surname—Husband Has Special Title

> Dr. and Mrs. . . . (*husband's full name*)
> Address
>
> Dear Dr. and Mrs. . . . (*husband's surname*):

c. Married Couple With Same Surname—Wife Has Special Title

> Professor . . . (*wife's full name*)
> Mr. . . . (*husband's full name*)
> Address
>
> Dear Professor and Mr. . . . (*husband's surname*):

d. Married Couple With Same Surname—Both Have Special Titles

> Dr. . . . (*wife's full name*)
> Dr. . . . (*husband's full name*)
> Address
>
> Dear Drs. . . . (*husband's surname*):

OR:

> Captain . . . (*husband's full name*)
> Professor . . . (*wife's full name*)
> Address
>
> Dear Captain and Professor . . .
> (*husband's surname*):

e. Married Couple With Different Surnames

> Ms. (**OR** Miss) . . . (*wife's full name*)
> Mr. . . . (*husband's full name*)
> Address
>
> Dear Ms. (**OR** Miss) . . . (*wife's surname*)
> and Mr. . . . (*husband's surname*):

OR:

> Mr. . . . (*husband's full name*)
> Ms. (**OR** Miss) . . . (*wife's full name*)
> Address
>
> Dear Mr. . . . (*husband's surname*) and
> Ms. (**OR** Miss) . . . (*wife's surname*):

NOTE: If either spouse has a special title (like those shown in ¶1802b–d), use that special title here as well.

(Continued on page 522.)

f. Married Couple With Hyphenated Surname

Mr. and Mrs. . . . (*husband's first name and middle initial, plus wife's original surname followed by hyphen and husband's surname*)
Address

Dear Mr. and Mrs. . . . (*wife's original surname followed by hyphen and husband's surname*):

g. Unmarried Couple Living Together

Ms. (**OR** Miss) . . . (*full name*)
Mr. . . . (*full name*)
Address

Dear Ms. (**OR** Miss) . . . and Mr. . . . :

OR:

Mr. . . . (*full name*)
Ms. (**OR** Miss) . . . (*full name*)
Address

Dear Mr. . . . and Ms. (**OR** Miss) . . . :

1803 ORGANIZATIONS

a. Organization of Women and Men

. . . (*name of organization*)
Address

Ladies and Gentlemen:
Gentlemen and Ladies:
Dear . . . (*name of organization*):
   (See ¶1350c.)

OR:

Mr. . . . (*name or organization head*)*
President (*or other appropriate title*)
. . . (*name of organization*)
Address

Dear Mr. . . . :*

OR:

Chief Executive Officer (*or other appropriate title*)
. . . (*name of organization*)
Address

Sir or Madam:
Madam or Sir:
Dear Sir or Madam:
Dear Madam or Sir:

*See the note on pages 519–520.

b. Organization of Women

. . . (*name of organization*)
Address

Mesdames:
Ladies:

c. Organization of Men

. . . (*name of organization*)
Address

Gentlemen:

1804 PROFESSIONALS

a. Lawyers

Mr. . . . (*full name*)*
Barrister and Solicitor
Address

OR:

. . . (*full name*), Esq.
Address

Dear Mr. . . . :*

b. Physicians and Others With Doctoral Degrees

Dr. . . . (*full name*)
Address

OR:

. . . (*full name*), M.D.
Address

Dear Dr. . . . :

NOTE: When an abbreviation such as *Esq.*, *M.D.*, or *Ph.D.* follows a name, do not use a courtesy title such as *Mr.* or *Dr.* before the name. (See also ¶¶518c, 519c.)

1805 EDUCATION OFFICIALS

a. Chancellor of College or University

. . . (*full name, followed by comma and highest degree*)
Chancellor, . . . (*name of college*)
Address

OR:

Dr. . . . (*full name*)
Chancellor, . . . (*name of college*)
Address

Dear Chancellor . . . :
Dear Dr. . . . :

b. President of College or University

. . . (*full name, followed by comma and highest degree*)
President, . . . (*name of college*)

OR:

Dr. . . . (*full name*)
President, . . . (*name of college*)

OR:

President, . . . (*full name*)
. . . (*name of college*)
Address

Dear President . . . :
Dear Dr. . . . :

c. Dean of College or University

. . . (*full name, followed by comma and highest degree*)

OR:

Dr. . . . (*full name*)
Dean, . . . (*name of school or division*)
. . . (*name of college*)

OR:

Dean . . . (*full name*)
. . . (*name of school or division*)
. . . (*name of college*)
Address

Dear Dean . . . :
Dear Dr. . . . :

d. Professor

Professor . . . (*full name*)
Department of . . . (*subject*)
. . . (*name of college*)

OR:

. . . (*full name, followed by comma and highest degree*)

OR:

*See the note on pages 519–520.

Dr. . . . (*full name*)
Department of (**OR** Professor of) . . .
(*subject*)
. . . (*name of college*)
Address

Dear Professor (**OR** Dr.) . . . :
Dear Mr. . . . :*

e. Superintendent of Schools

Mr. (**OR** Dr.) . . . (*full name*)*
Superintendent, . . . (*name of city*) Board of Education
Address

Dear Mr. (**OR** Dr.) . . . :*

f. Member of Board of Education

Mr. . . . (*full name*)*
Member, . . . (*name of city*) Board of Education
Address

Dear Mr. . . . :*

g. Principal

Mr. (**OR** Dr.) . . . (*full name*)*
Principal, . . . (*name of school*)
Address

Dear Mr. (**OR** Dr.) . . . :*

h. Teacher

Mr. (**OR** Dr.) . . . (*full name*)*
. . . (*name of school*)
Address

Dear Mr. (**OR** Dr.) . . . :*

1806 CANADIAN GOVERNMENT OFFICIALS

a. Governor General of Canada

His Excellency the Right Honourable
(*full name*)* (Orders, decorations)
Governor General of Canada
Rideau Hall
One Sussex Drive
Ottawa, Ontario K1A 0A1

Excellency:

(Continued on page 524.)

b. Prime Minister of Canada

The Right Honourable . . . (*full name*),
   P.C., M.P.
Prime Minister of Canada
Langevin Block
Ottawa, Ontario K1A 0A2

Dear Prime Minister:

c. Cabinet Minister of Canada

The Honourable . . . (*full name*), P.C., M.P.
Minister of . . .
House of Commons
Ottawa, Ontario K1A 0A6

Dear Minister:

NOTE: The initials *P.C.* are for
members of the Queen's Privy
Council for Canada. *Honourable* is
a life-time title.

d. Member of the House of Commons

Mr. . . . (*full name*), M.P.*
OR:
The Honourable . . . (*full name*),
   P.C., M.P.
House of Commons
Ottawa, Ontario K1A 0A6

Dear Mr. . . . (*surname*):*

NOTE: The initials *M.P.* follow the
name of a Member of Parliament.

e. Senator

The Honourable . . . (*full name*), Senator
The Senate
Ottawa, Ontario K1A 0A1

Dear Senator . . . (*surname*):

f. Chief Justice of Canada

The Right Honourable . . . (*full name*),
   P.C.
Chief Justice of Canada
Supreme Court of Canada
Ottawa, Ontario K1A 0J1

Dear Chief Justice:

**g. Judge of Federal, Provincial,
County, or Territorial Court**

*See the note on pages 519–520.

The Honourable . . . (*full name*)
Judge of the . . . (*name of court*)
Address

Dear Mr. Justice . . . (*surname*):*

For Judges of Provincial or Territorial
   Courts:

Dear Chief Judge:
Dear Judge . . . (*surname*):

h. Lieutenant-Governor

His Honour the Honourable . . . (*full
   name*)*
Lieutenant-Governor of (*Province*)
Provincial Capital, Province
Postal Code

Your Honour:
My dear Lieutenant-Governor:

i. Premier

The Honourable . . . (*full name*)
Premier of (*Province*)
Provincial Capital, Province
Postal Code

Dear Premier:

j. Member, Provincial Cabinet

The Honourable . . . (*full name*), M.L.A.
   OR M.P.P. **OR** M.N.A. **OR** M.H.A.
Minister of . . .
Provincial Capital, Province
Postal Code

Dear Minister:

NOTE: In the two positions above, the
title *Honourable* is only used while in
office.

k. Member, Legislative Assembly

Mr. . . . (*full name*),* M.L.A. **OR** M.P.P.
   OR M.N.A. **OR** M.H.A.
Provincial Capital, Province
Postal Code

Dear Mr. . . . (*surname*):*

NOTE: M.L.A. is used by all provinces
and territories, except Ontario,
which uses *M.P.P.*; Quebec, *M.N.A.*;
Newfoundland, *M.H.A.*

18

l. Mayor

His Worship . . . *(full name)**
Mayor of . . . *(city or municipality)*
City *(or* Municipality) Hall
Municipality, Province
Postal Code

Dear Sir:*
Dear Mr. Mayor:*

m. Member, Municipal Council

Councillor . . . *(full name)*
OR:
Alderman . . . *(full name)*
City *(or* Municipality) Hall
Municipality, Province
Postal Code

Dear Councillor . . . *(surname)*:
Dear Alderman . . . *(surname)*:*

1807 AMERICAN GOVERNMENT OFFICIALS

a. President of the United States

The Honourable . . . *(full name)*
President of the United States
The White House
Washington, DC 20500

Mr. President:*
Dear Mr. President:*

b. Cabinet Minister

The Honourable . . . *(full name)*
Secretary of . . . *(department)*
Washington, DC Zip Code
U.S.A.

Dear Mr. Secretary:*

c. United States Senator

The Honourable . . . *(full name)*
United States Senate
Washington, DC 20510

Dear Senator:

d. United States Representative

The Honourable . . . *(full name)*
House of Representatives
Washington, DC 20515

Dear Representative . . . :
Dear Mr. . . . . :*

*See the note on pages 519–520.

e. Governor

The Honourable . . . *(full name)*
Governor of . . . (state)
State Capital, State Zip Code

Dear Governor . . . :

1808 THE ROYAL FAMILY

a. The Queen

Her Majesty The Queen
Buckingham Palace
London SW1A 1AA
United Kingdom

Your Majesty:

b. The Duke of Edinburgh

His Royal Highness The Prince Philip,
    Duke of Edinburgh
Buckingham Palace
London SW1A 1AA
United Kingdom

Your Royal Highness:

c. The Prince of Wales

His Royal Highness The Prince of Wales
St. James's Palace
London SW1A 1BS
United Kingdom

Your Royal Highness:

d. The Duke of York

His Royal Highness The Duke of York
Buckingham Palace
(see address above)

Your Royal Highness:

e. The Princess Royal

Her Royal Highness The Princess Royal
Buckingham Palace
(see address above)

Your Royal Highness:

f. Prince Edward

His Royal Highness The Prince Edward
Buckingham Palace
(see address above)

Your Royal Highness:

18

1809 DIPLOMATS

a. Secretary-General of the United Nations

His Excellency . . . (*full name*)*
Secretary-General of the United Nations
United Nations Plaza
New York, NY 10017

Excellency:
Dear Mr. Secretary-General:*
Dear Mr. . . . :*

b. Ambassador or High Commissioner of a Foreign Country to Canada

His Excellency . . . (*full name*)*
Ambassador of . . . (*country*)
OR:
High Commissioner for . . . (*country*)
Address

Dear Ambassador:
High Commissioner:

EXCEPTION: Address the British High Commissioner, not the High Commissioner for Britain.

c. Canadian Ambassador or High Commissioner Abroad

Mr. . . . (*full name*)*
Ambassador of Canada to . . . (*country*)
OR:
High Commissioner for Canada to . . .
   (*country*)
Address

Dear Ambassador:
High Commissioner:

d. American Ambassador to Canada

The Honourable . . . (*full name*)
American Ambassador
(**OR** The Ambassador of the United
   States of America)
490 Sussex Drive
Ottawa, ON K1N 1G8

Sir:*
Dear Mr. Ambassador:*

1810 INTERNATIONAL DIGNITARIES

a. An Emperor

His Imperial Majesty . . . (*name*)*
Emperor of (*country*)
Address

Your dignified Majesty:

b. A King

His Majesty . . . (*name*)
King of . . . (*country*)
Address

Your Majesty:
Sire:

c. A Queen

Her Majesty Queen . . . (*name*)
Queen of . . . (*country*)
Address

Your Majesty:
Madame:

d. A Prince* with title *Royal* or *Serene Highness*

His Royal Highness*
OR:
His Serene Highness*
The Prince of . . . (*country*)
Address

Your Royal Highness:
OR
Your Serene Highness:

e. A President of a Republic

His Excellency . . . (*full name*)*
President of the Republic of . . .
   (*country*)
Address

Excellency:

f. A Prime Minister

His Excellency . . . (*full name*)*
Prime Minister of . . . (*country*)
Address

Dear Prime Minister:

*See the note on pages 519–520.

1811 MEMBERS OF THE CANADIAN ARMED FORCES

The addresses of both officers and other ranks should include full rank, initials, last name, decorations, position title, and address. Honours and decorations, listed in sequence, are always included in the address. Below are two specific examples with appropriate salutations.

a. Officers

Brigadier-General (*initials, last name*),
   OMM, CD, Commandant
Address

Dear General:

NOTE: Use the salutation *Dear General*, whether the officer is a full general or only a lieutenant-general, a major-general, or a brigadier-general. Similarly, use *Dear Colonel* for a lieutenant-colonel and *Dear Lieutenant* for a 2nd Lieutenant. In the Maritime Command, use *Dear Admiral* for a vice admiral or a rear-admiral; *Dear Commander* for a lieutenant-commander; and *Dear Lieutenant* for a sub lieutenant.

b. Other Ranks

Sergeant (*full name*), CD
Address

Dear Sergeant . . . :

OR:

Private . . . (*full name*)
Address

Dear Private (*surname*):

1812 NATIVE LEADERS

a. Indian Chiefs

Chief . . . (*full name*)
Chief of . . . (*name*)
Address

Dear Chief . . . (*surname*):

*See the note on pages 519–520.

b. Band Councillors

Mr. . . . (*full name*)*
Address

Dear Mr. . . . (*surname*):*

1813 ROMAN CATHOLIC DIGNITARIES

a. Pope

His Holiness the Pope

OR:

His Holiness Pope . . . (*given name*)
Vatican City
00187 Rome
ITALY

Your Holiness:
Most Holy Father:

b. Cardinal

His Eminence . . . (*given name*) Cardinal
   . . . (*surname*)
Archbishop of . . . (*place*)
Address

Your Eminence:
Dear Cardinal . . . :

c. Archbishop and Bishop

The Right Reverend . . . (*full name*)
Archbishop (**OR** Bishop) of . . . (*place*)
Address

Your Excellency:
Dear Archbishop (**OR** Bishop) . . . :

d. Monsignor

The Right Reverend Monsignor . . . (*full name*)
Address

Right Reverend Monsignor:
Dear Monsignor . . . :

e. Priest

The Reverend . . . (*full name, followed by comma and initials of order*)
Address

Reverend Father:
Dear Father . . . :
Dear Father:

(Continued on page 528.)

f. Mother Superior

The Reverend Mother Superior
Address

OR:

Reverend Mother . . . (*name, followed by comma and initials of order*)
Address

Reverend Mother:
Dear Reverend Mother:
Dear Mother . . . :

g. Sister

Sister . . . (*name, followed by comma and initials of order*)
Address

Dear Sister . . . :
Dear Sister:

h. Brother

Brother . . . (*name, followed by comma and initials of order*)
Address

Dear Brother . . . :
Dear Brother:

1814 PROTESTANT DIGNITARIES

a. Anglican Primate

The Most Reverend . . . (*full name*)
Address

Your Grace:

b. Anglican Bishop

The Right Reverend . . . (*full name*)
Bishop of . . . (*place*)
Address

Right Reverend Sir:*
Dear Bishop:

c. Anglican Dean

The Very Reverend . . . (*full name*)
Dean of . . . (*place*)
Address

*See the note on pages 519–520.

Very Reverend Sir:*
Dear Dean:

d. Moderator, United Church

The Right Reverend . . . (*full name*)
Moderator of the United Church of Canada
Address

Right Reverend Sir:*
Dear Moderator:

e. Minister With Doctor's Degree

The Reverend Dr. . . . (*full name*)
Address

OR:

The Reverend . . . (*full name*), D.D.
Address

Reverend Sir:*
Dear Dr. . . . :

f. Minister Without Doctor's Degree

The Reverend . . . (*full name*)
Address

Reverend Sir:*
Dear Mr. . . . :*

1815 JEWISH DIGNITARIES

a. Chief Rabbi

The Very Reverend . . . (*full name*)
Chief Rabbi
Address

Dear Sir **OR** Rabbi:

b. Rabbi With Doctor's Degree

The Reverend Rabbi . . . (*full name*),
D.D.
Address

Dear Rabbi **OR** Dr. . . . (*full name*):

c. Rabbi Without Doctor's Degree

Rabbi . . . (*full name*)
Address

Dear Rabbi . . . :

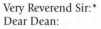 See the Online Learning Centre at www.mcgrawhill.ca/college/gregg for related weblinks.

Glossary of
Grammatical Terms

Active verb. See *Voice, active.*

Adjective. A word that answers the question *what kind* (*excellent* results), *how many* (*four* laptops), or *which one* (the *latest* data). An adjective may be a single word (a *wealthy* man), a phrase (a man of *great wealth*), or a clause (a man *who possesses great wealth*). An adjective modifies the meaning of a noun (*big* brother) or a pronoun (*unlucky* me, I was *wrong*).

Adverb. A word that answers the question *when, where, why, how, in what manner*, or *to what extent*. An adverb may be a single word (speak *clearly*), a phrase (speak *in a clear voice*), or a clause (speak *as clearly as you can*). An adverb modifies the meaning of a verb, an adjective, or another adverb. (See also *Adverbial clause.*)

> We closed the deal *quickly.* (Modifies the verb *closed.*)
> Caroline seemed *genuinely* pleased. (Modifies the adjective *pleased.*)
> My presentation went *surprisingly* well. (Modifies the adverb *well.*)

Adverbial conjunction (or **connective**). An adverb that connects the main clauses of a compound sentence; for example, *however, therefore, nevertheless, hence, moreover, otherwise, consequently.* Also referred to as a *conjunctive adverb* or a *transitional expression.* (See also ¶¶138a, 178.)

Antecedent. A noun or a noun phrase to which a pronoun refers.

> She is the *person who* wrote the letter. (*Person* is the antecedent of *who.*)
> *Owning a home* has *its* advantages. (*Owning a home* is the antecedent of *its.*)

Appositive. A noun or a noun phrase that identifies another noun or pronoun that immediately precedes it. (See ¶¶148–153.)

> Mr. Mancuso, *our chief financial officer,* would like to meet you.

Article. Considered an adjective. The *definite* article is *the;* the *indefinite, a* or *an.* (See *a—an* in Section 11 for a usage note.)

Case. The form of a noun or of a pronoun that indicates its relation to other words in the sentence. There are three cases: nominative, objective, and possessive. *Nouns* have the same form in the nominative and objective cases but a special ending for the possessive. The forms for *pronouns* are:

Nominative	Objective	Possessive
I	me	my, mine
you	you	your, yours

(Continued on page 530.)

Nominative	Objective	Possessive
he, she, it	him, her, it	his, hers, its
we	us	our, ours
they	them	their, theirs
who	whom	whose

Nominative case. Used for the subject or the complement of a verb.

> *She* publishes a newsletter. (Subject.)

> The person who called you was *I*. (Complement.)

Objective case. Used for (1) the object of a verb, (2) the object of a preposition, (3) the subject of an infinitive, (4) the object of an infinitive, or (5) the complement of the infinitive *to be*.

> Can you help *us* this weekend? (Object of the verb *help*.)

> Brenda has not written to *me*. (Object of the preposition *to*.)

> I encouraged *her* to enter the biathlon. (Subject of the infinitive *to enter*.)

> William promised to call *me* but he didn't. (Object of the infinitive *to call*.)

> They believed me to be *her*. (Complement of the infinitive *to be*.)

Possessive case. Used to show ownership and other relationships. (See ¶¶627–651, especially the examples in ¶627.)

> *Your* copy of the report contains a statistical analysis. *Mine* doesn't.

Clause. A group of related words containing a subject and a predicate. An *independent* clause (also known as a *main clause* or *principal clause*) expresses a complete thought and can stand alone as a sentence. A *dependent* clause (also known as a *subordinate clause*) does not express a complete thought and cannot stand alone as a sentence.

> I will go (independent clause) if I am invited (dependent clause).

Adjective clause. A dependent clause that modifies a noun or a pronoun in the main clause. Adjective clauses are joined to the main clause by relative pronouns *(which, that, who, whose, whom)*.

> Their bill, *which includes servicing*, seems reasonable. (Modifies *bill*.)

Adverbial clause. A dependent clause that functions as an adverb in its relation to the main clause. Adverbial clauses indicate time, place, manner, cause, purpose, condition, result, reason, or contrast.

> These orders can be filled *as soon as stock is received*. (Time.)

> I was advised to live *where the climate is dry*. (Place.)

> She worked *as though her life depended on it*. (Manner.)

> Please write me at once *if you have any suggestions*. (Condition.)

> *Because our plant is closed in August*, we cannot fill your order now. (Reason.)

Co-ordinate clauses. Clauses of the same rank—independent or dependent.

> *Carl will oversee the day-to-day operations*, and *Sheila will be responsible for the finances*. (Co-ordinate independent clauses.)

> *When you have read the user's manual* and *you have mastered all the basic operations*, try to deal with these special applications. (Co-ordinate dependent clauses.)

19

Elliptical clause. A clause from which key words have been omitted. (See ¶¶102, 111, 119, 130b, 1082d.)

> *Now, for the next topic.*   *Really?*   *If possible,* arrive at one.

Essential (restrictive) clause. A dependent clause that cannot be omitted without changing the meaning of the main (independent) clause. Essential clauses are *not* set off by commas.

> The magazine *that came yesterday* contains an evaluation of new software.

Non-essential (non-restrictive) clause. A dependent clause that adds descriptive information but could be omitted without changing the meaning of the main (independent) clause. Such clauses are separated or set off from the main clause by commas.

> Her latest book, *which deals with corporate finance,* has sold quite well.
>
> She has had a lot of success with her latest book, *which deals with finance.*

Noun clause. A dependent clause that functions as a noun in the main clause.

> *Whether the proposal will be accepted* remains to be seen. (Noun clause as subject.)
>
> They thought *that the plan was a failure.* (Noun clause as object.)
>
> Then he said, *"Who gave you that information?"* (Noun clause as object.)

Comparison. The forms of an adjective or adverb that indicate degrees in quality, quantity, or manner. The degrees are positive, comparative, and superlative. (See ¶1071.)

Positive. The simple form; for example, *new, efficient* (adjectives); *soon, quietly* (adverbs).

Comparative. Indicates a higher or lower degree of quality or manner than is expressed by the positive degree. The comparative is used when two things are compared and is regularly formed by adding *er* to the positive degree *(newer, sooner)*. In longer words the comparative is formed by adding *more* or *less* to the positive *(more efficient, less efficient; more quietly, less quietly)*.

Superlative. Denotes the highest or lowest degree of quality or manner and is used when more than two things are compared. The superlative is regularly formed by adding *est* to the positive degree *(newest, soonest)*. In longer words the superlative is formed by adding *most* or *least (most efficient, least efficient; most quietly, least quietly)*.

Complement. A word or phrase that completes the sense of the verb. It may be an object, a predicate noun, a predicate pronoun, or a predicate adjective.

Object. Follows a transitive verb. (See *Verb.*)

> I have already drafted the *contract.*

Predicate noun or pronoun. Follows a linking verb (such as *is, am, are, was, were, will be, has been, could be*). It explains the subject and is identical with it. (Also called a *predicate complement, subject complement,* and *predicate nominative.*)

> Miss Kwong is our new *accountant.* (*Accountant* refers to *Miss Kwong.*)
>
> The person responsible for the decision was *I.* (The pronoun *I* refers to *person.*)

(Continued on page 532.)

19

Predicate adjective. Completes the sense of a linking verb. (Also called a *predicate complement*.)

> These charges are *excessive*. (The adjective *excessive* refers to *charges*.)

Compound modifier. A phrase or clause that qualifies, limits, or restricts the meaning of a word. Also referred to as a *compound adjective*. (See also ¶¶813–832.)

Conjunction. A word or phrase that connects words, phrases, or clauses.

Co-ordinating conjunction. Connects words, phrases, or clauses of equal rank. The co-ordinating conjunctions are *and, but, or,* and *nor* (sometimes *for, yet,* and *so*).

Correlative conjunctions. Conjunctions consisting of two elements used in pairs; for example, *both . . . and, not only . . . but (also), either . . . or, neither . . . nor.*

Subordinating conjunction. Used to join dependent clauses to main (independent) clauses; for example, *when, where, after, before, if.* (See ¶132.)

Connective. A word that joins words, phrases, or clauses. The chief types of connectives are conjunctions, adverbial conjunctives, prepositions, and relative pronouns.

Consonants. The letters *b, c, d, f, g, h, j, k, l, m, n, p, q, r, s, t, v, w, x, y, z.* The letter *y* sometimes serves as a vowel (as in *rhyme*).

Contraction. A shortened form of a word or phrase in which an apostrophe indicates the omitted letters or words; for example, *don't* for *do not.* (See ¶505b–e.)

Dangling modifier. A modifier that is attached either to no word in a sentence or to the wrong word. (See ¶1082–1086.)

Direct address. A construction in which a speaker or a writer addresses another person directly; for example, "What do you think, Sylvia?"

Elliptical expressions. Condensed expressions from which key words have been omitted; for example, *if necessary* (for *if it is necessary*). (See ¶¶102, 111, 119a; see also *Clause; Sentence.*)

Essential elements. Words, phrases, or clauses needed to complete the structure or meaning of a sentence. (See also *Clause; Phrase.*)

Gender. The characteristic of nouns and pronouns that indicates whether the thing named is *masculine (man, boy, he), feminine (woman, girl, she),* or *neuter (book, concept, it).* Nouns that refer to either males or females have *common* gender *(person, child).*

Gerund. A verb form ending in *ing* and used as a *noun.*

> *Selling* requires special skills. (Subject.)
>
> I enjoy *selling.* (Direct object of *enjoy.*)
>
> She is experienced in *selling.* (Object of preposition *in.*)

Dangling gerund. A prepositional-gerund phrase that is attached either to no word in a sentence or to the wrong word. (See ¶1082c.)

Imperative. See *Mood.*

Indicative. See *Mood.*

19

Infinitive. The form of the verb usually introduced by *to* (see ¶¶1044–1046). An infinitive may be used as a noun, an adjective, or an adverb. (See *Phrase.*)

NOUN: *To find affordable housing* these days is not easy. (Subject.)
           She is trying *to do a hatchet job on my proposal.* (Object.)

ADJECTIVE: I still have two more contracts *to draft.* (Modifies *contracts.*)

ADVERB: He resigned *to take another position.* (Modifies *resigned.*)

Interjection. A word that shows emotion; usually without grammatical connection to other parts of a sentence.

Oh, so that's what he meant.   *Wow!* What a weekend!

Modifier. A word, phrase, or clause that qualifies, limits, or restricts the meaning of a word. (See *Adjective; Adverb; Dangling modifier.*)

Mood (mode). The form of the verb that shows the manner of the action. There are three moods: indicative, imperative, and subjunctive.

Indicative. States a fact or asks a question.

Our lease has expired.   When does our lease expire?

Imperative. Expresses a command or makes a request.

Call me next week.   Please send me your latest catalogue.

Subjunctive. Used in dependent clauses following main (independent) clauses expressing necessity, demand, or wishing (see ¶¶1038–1039); also used in *if, as if,* and *as though* clauses that state conditions which are improbable, doubtful, or contrary to fact (see ¶¶1040–1043).

I demand that we *be* heard.   It is imperative that he *be* notified.

We urge that she *be* elected.   If he *were* appointed, I would quit.

I wish I *were* going.   If she *had* known, she would have come.

Nominative case. See *Case, nominative.*

Non-essential elements. Words, phrases, or clauses that are not needed to complete the structure or meaning of a sentence. (See also *Clause; Phrase.*)

Noun. The name of a person, place, object, idea, quality, or activity.

Abstract noun. The name of a quality or a general idea; for example, *courage, freedom.*

Collective noun. A noun that represents a group of persons, animals, or things; for example, *audience, company, flock.* (See ¶1019.)

Common noun. The name of a class of persons, places, or things; for example, *child, house.* (See ¶¶307–310.)

Predicate noun. See *Complement.*

Proper noun. The official name of a particular person, place, or thing; for example, *Ellen, Saskatoon, Wednesday.* Proper nouns are capitalized. (See ¶¶303–306.)

19

Number. The characteristic of a noun, pronoun, or verb that indicates whether one person or thing (singular) or more than one (plural) is meant.

> NOUN: beeper, beepers   PRONOUN: she, they   VERB: (she) works, (they) work

Object. The person or thing that receives the action of a transitive verb. An object may be a word, a phrase, or a clause. (See *Case, objective.*)

> I need a new laptop *computer.* (Word.)
>
> She prefers *to work with hard copy.* (Infinitive phrase.)
>
> We did not realize *that your deadline was so tight.* (Clause.)

Direct object. The person or thing that is directly affected by the action of the verb. (The object in each of the three sentences above is a *direct* object.)

Indirect object. The person or thing indirectly affected by the action of the verb. The indirect object can be made the object of the preposition *to* or *for.*

> Molly gave (to) *me* a hard time about my sales performance this quarter.

Ordinal number. The form of a number that indicates order or succession; for example, *first, second, twelfth* or *1st, 2nd, 12th.* (See ¶¶424–426.)

Parenthetical elements. Words, phrases, or clauses that are not necessary to the completeness of the structure or the meaning of a sentence.

> Gina Sala, *my wife's older sister,* is my accountant.

Participle. A word that may stand alone as an adjective or may be combined with helping (auxiliary) verbs to form different tenses (see ¶¶1033–1034). There are three forms: present, past, and perfect.

Present participle. Ends in *ing*; for example, *making, advertising.*

Past participle. Regularly ends in *ed* (as in *asked* or *filed*) but may be irregularly formed (as in *lost, seen,* and *written*). (See ¶1030a–b.)

Perfect participle. Consists of *having* plus the past participle; for example, *having asked, having lost.*

When a participle functions as an *adjective*, it modifies a noun or a pronoun.

> The *coming* year poses some new challenges. (Modifies *year.*)
>
> *Having retired* last year, I now do volunteer work. (Modifies *I.*)

Because a participle has many of the characteristics of a verb, it may take an object and be modified by an adverb. The participle and its object and modifiers make up a *participial phrase.*

> *Seizing the opportunity,* Orzo offered to buy the business. (*Opportunity* is the object of *seizing.*)
>
> *Moving aggressively,* we can control the market. (*Aggressively* modifies *moving.*)

Dangling participle. A participial phrase attached either to no word in a sentence or to the wrong word. (See *Phrase* and ¶1082a.)

Parts of speech. The eight classes into which words are grouped according to their uses in a sentence: verb, noun, pronoun, adjective, adverb, conjunction, preposition, and interjection.

Passive verb. See *Voice, passive.*

Person. The characteristic of a word that indicates whether a person is speaking *(first person)*, is spoken to *(second person)*, or is spoken about *(third person)*. Only personal pronouns and verbs change their forms to show person. All nouns are considered third person.

	Singular	Plural
FIRST PERSON:	*I* like this book.	*We* like this book.
SECOND PERSON:	*You* like this book.	*You* like this book.
THIRD PERSON:	*She* likes this book.	*They* like this book.

Phrase. A group of two or more words without a subject and a predicate; used as a noun, an adjective, or an adverb. (See *Predicate.*)

Noun phrase. A phrase that functions as a noun (such as a gerund phrase, an infinitive phrase, or a prepositional phrase.)

I like *running my own business.* (Gerund phrase as object.)

To provide the best possible service is our goal. (Infinitive phrase as subject.)

Before 9 a.m. is the best time to call me. (Prepositional phrase as subject.)

Adjective phrase. A phrase that functions as an adjective (such as an infinitive phrase, a participial phrase, or a prepositional phrase).

The time *to act* is now! (Infinitive phrase indicating what kind of time.)

Adverbial phrase. A phrase that functions as an adverb (such as an infinitive phrase or a prepositional phrase).

Let's plan to meet *after lunch.* (Prepositional phrase indicating when to meet.)

Gerund phrase. A gerund plus its object and modifiers; used as a noun.

Delaying payments to your suppliers will prove costly. (Gerund phrase as subject.)

Infinitive phrase. An infinitive plus its object and modifiers; may be used as a noun, an adjective, or an adverb. An infinitive phrase that is attached to either no word in a sentence or to the wrong word is called a *dangling* infinitive (see ¶1082b).

To get TF's okay on this purchase order took some doing. (As a noun; serves as subject of the verb *took.*)

The decision *to close the Belleville plant* was not made easily. (As an adjective; tells what kind of decision.)

Janice resigned *to open her own business.* (As an adverb; tells why Janice resigned.)

NOTE: An infinitive phrase, unlike other phrases, may sometimes have a subject. This subject precedes the infinitive and is in the objective case.

I have asked *her to review this draft for accuracy.* (*Her* is the subject of *to review.*)

Participial phrase. A participle and its object and modifiers; used as an adjective.

The committee *considering your proposal* should come to a decision this week.

I prefer the cover sample *printed in blue and yellow.*

(Continued on page 536.)

19

Prepositional phrase. A preposition and its object and modifiers; may be used as a noun, an adjective, or an adverb.

From Halifax to Tofino is about 6500 km. (As a noun; serves as subject of *is.*)

Profits *in the automobile industry* are up sharply this quarter. (As an adjective; indicates which type of profits.)

You handled Dr. Wenzlawe's objections *with great skill.* (As an adverb; indicates the manner in which the objections were handled.)

Prepositional-gerund phrase. A phrase that begins with a preposition and has a gerund as the object. (See *Gerund* and ¶1082c.)

By rechecking the material before it is set in type, you avoid expensive corrections later on. (*By* is the preposition; *rechecking,* a gerund, is the object of *by.*)

Essential (restrictive) phrase. A phrase that limits, defines, or identifies; cannot be omitted without changing the meaning of the sentence.

The study *analysing our competitors' promotion activities* will be finished next week.

Non-essential (non-restrictive) phrase. A phrase that can be omitted without changing the meaning of the sentence.

Investors Group, *one of the country's largest financial organizations,* is expanding its Internet on the World Wide Web.

Verb phrase. This term is often used to indicate the individual words that make up the verb in a sentence. Sometimes the verb phrase includes an adverb. A verb phrase can function only as a verb.

You *should work together* with Nora on the report. (The verb phrase consists of the verb form *should work* plus the adverb *together.*)

Positive degree. See *Comparison.*

Possessive case. See *Case, possessive.*

Predicate. That part of a sentence which tells what the subject does or what is done to the subject or what state of being the subject is in. (See also *Verb.*)

Complete predicate. The complete predicate consists of a verb and its complement or object along with any modifiers.

Barbara *has handled the job well.*

Simple predicate. The simple predicate is the verb alone, without regard for any complement, object, or modifiers that may accompany it.

Barbara *has handled* the job well.

Compound predicate. A predicate consisting of two or more predicates joined by conjunctions.

Barbara *has handled the job well* and *deserves a good deal of praise.*

Predicate adjective. See *Complement.*

Predicate nominative. See *Complement.*

Prefix. A letter, syllable, or word added to the beginning of a word to change its meaning; for example, *afloat, immaterial, undernourished.*

Preposition. A connective (such as *from, to, in, on, at, by, for, with*) that shows the relationship between a noun or pronoun and some other word in the sentence. The noun or pronoun following a preposition is in the objective case. (See ¶¶1077–1080.)

> Martin's work was reviewed *by Hedley and me.*

Principal parts. The forms of a verb from which all other forms are derived: the *present,* the *past,* the *past participle,* and the *present participle.* (See ¶¶1030–1035.)

Pronoun. A word used in place of a noun. (See ¶¶1049–1064.)

DEMONSTRATIVE:	*this, that, these, those*
INDEFINITE:	*each, either, any, anyone, someone, everyone, few, all,* etc.
INTENSIVE:	*myself, yourself, himself, herself, ourselves, themselves,* etc.
INTERROGATIVE:	*who, which, what,* etc.
PERSONAL:	*I, you, he, she, it, we, they,* etc.
RELATIVE:	*who, whose, whom, which, that,* and compounds such as *whoever*

Punctuation. Marks used to indicate relationships between words, phrases, and clauses.

> **Terminal (end) punctuation.** The period, the question mark, and the exclamation point—the three marks that may indicate the end of a sentence.
>
> NOTE: When a sentence breaks off abruptly, a dash may be used to mark the end of the sentence (see ¶207). When a sentence trails off without really ending, ellipses (three spaced periods) are used to mark the end of the sentence. (See ¶292a.)
>
> **Internal punctuation.** *Commas, semicolons, colons, dashes, parentheses, quotation marks, apostrophes, ellipses, asterisks, diagonals,* and *brackets* are the most common marks of internal punctuation.

Question.

> **Direct question.** A question in its original form, as spoken or written.
>
> > He then asked me, "What is your opinion?"
>
> **Indirect question.** A restatement of a question without the use of the exact words of the speaker.
>
> > He then asked me what my opinion was.
>
> **Independent question.** A question that represents a complete sentence but is incorporated in a larger sentence.
>
> > The main question is, Who will translate this idea into a clear plan of action?

Quotation.

> **Direct quotation.** A quotation of words exactly as spoken or written.
>
> > I myself heard Ed say, "I will arrive in Brandon on Tuesday."
>
> **Indirect quotation.** A restatement of a quotation without the use of the exact words of the speaker.
>
> > I myself heard Ed say that he would arrive in Brandon on Tuesday.

19

Sentence. A group of words representing a complete thought and containing a subject and a predicate (a verb along with any complements and modifiers).

Simple sentence. A sentence consisting of one independent clause.

> I have no recollection of the meeting.

Compound sentence. A sentence consisting of two or more independent clauses.

> Our Regina office will be closed, and our Windsor office will be relocated.

Complex sentence. A sentence consisting of one independent clause (also called the *main clause*) and one or more dependent clauses.

> We will make an exception to the policy if circumstances warrant.

Compound-complex sentence. A sentence consisting of two independent clauses and one or more dependent clauses.

> I tried to handle the monthly report alone, but when I began to analyse the data, I realized that I needed your help.

Elliptical sentence. A word or phrase treated as a complete sentence, even though the subject and verb are understood but not expressed.

> Enough on that subject.   Why not?

Declarative sentence. A sentence that makes a statement.

> Our company is continually testing cutting-edge technologies.

Interrogative sentence. A sentence that asks a question.

> When will the conference begin?

Exclamatory sentence. A sentence that expresses strong feeling.

> Don't even think of smoking here!

Imperative sentence. A sentence that expresses a command or a request. (The subject *you* is understood if it is not expressed.)

> Send a cheque at once.   Please let us hear from you.

Sentence fragment. A phrase or clause that is incorrectly treated as a sentence. (See ¶102, note.)

Statement. A sentence that asserts a fact. (See also *Sentence*.)

Subject. A word, phrase, or clause that names the person, place, or thing about which something is said. (See *Case, nominative*.)

> *The law firm with the best reputation in town* is Barringer and Doyle.
> *Whoever applies for the job from within the department* will get special consideration.

Compound subject. Two or more subjects joined by a conjunction.

> *My wife and my three sons* are off on a white-water rafting trip.

Subjunctive. See *Mood*.

Suffix. A letter, syllable, or word added to the end of a word to modify its meaning; for example, trend*y*, friend*ly*, count*less*, receiver*ship*, lone*some*. (See ¶833a.)

Superlative degree. See *Comparison.*

Syllable. One or more letters that represent one sound.

Tense. The property of a verb that expresses *time*. (See ¶¶1031–1035.) The three *primary* tenses correspond to the three time divisions:

PRESENT:	they think
PAST:	they thought
FUTURE:	they will think

There are three *perfect* tenses, corresponding to the primary tenses:

PRESENT PERFECT:	they have thought
PAST PERFECT:	they had thought
FUTURE PERFECT:	they will have thought

There are six *progressive* tenses, corresponding to each of the primary and perfect tenses:

PRESENT PROGRESSIVE:	they are thinking
PAST PROGRESSIVE:	they were thinking
FUTURE PROGRESSIVE:	they will be thinking
PRESENT PERFECT PROGRESSIVE:	they have been thinking
PAST PERFECT PROGRESSIVE:	they had been thinking
FUTURE PERFECT PROGRESSIVE:	they will have been thinking

There are two *emphatic* tenses:

PRESENT EMPHATIC:	they do think
PAST EMPHATIC:	they did think

☞ *For an illustration of how these tenses are formed, see pages 248–249.*

Transitional expressions. Expressions that link independent clauses or sentences; for example, *as a result, therefore, on the other hand, nevertheless.* (See also ¶138a; *Adverbial conjunction.*)

Verb. A word or phrase used to express action or state of being. (See also *Mood.*)

Enniston *has boosted* its sales goals for the year. (Action.)

My son-in-law *was* originally a lawyer, but he *has* now *become* a computer-game designer. (State of being.)

Helping (auxiliary) verb. A verb that helps in the formation of another verb. (See ¶¶1030c, 1033–1034.) The chief helping verbs are *be, can, could, do, have, may, might, must, ought, shall, should, will, would.*

Transitive verb. A verb that requires an object to complete its meaning. (See also *Object.*)

Fusilli *has rejected* all offers to purchase his business.

(Continued on page 540.)

Intransitive verb. A verb that does not require an object to complete its meaning.

> As market growth *occurs* and customer interest *builds,* our sales expectations *are rising* and top management's excitement *has increased.*

Linking verb. A verb that connects a subject with a predicate adjective, noun, or pronoun. The various forms of *to be* are the most commonly used linking verbs. *Become, look, seem, appear,* and *grow* are also used as linking verbs. (See *Complement* and ¶1067.)

> Laura *seemed* willing to compromise, but Frank *became* obstinate in his demands.

> Was he afraid that any concession might make him *appear* a fool?

Principal parts of verbs. See *Principal parts.*

Verbal. A word that is derived from a verb but functions in some other way. (See *Gerund; Infinitive; Participle.*)

Voice. The property of a verb that indicates whether the subject acts or is acted upon.

Active voice. A verb is in the active voice when its subject is the doer of the action.

> About a dozen people *reviewed* the report in draft form.

Passive voice. A verb is in the passive voice when its subject is acted upon.

> The report *was reviewed* in draft form by about a dozen people.

Vowels. The letters *a, e, i, o,* and *u.* The letter *y* sometimes acts like a vowel (as in *cry*). (See also *Consonants.*)

 See the Online Learning Centre at www.mcgrawhill.ca/college/gregg for related weblinks.

SECTION **TWENTY**

Glossary of Computer and Internet Terms

The following glossary provides brief and simple definitions of some key terms and concepts of computer and Internet terms. It should be noted that imperial measurements, not metric, are used with computer configurations and formats.*

NOTE: When boldface type is used to highlight a word or phrase within a definition, it signifies that the highlighted word or phrase is defined elsewhere in this glossary.

☞ *See ¶544 for a list of common computer abbreviations and acronyms.*

Access. To call up information out of **storage**.

Active matrix display. A type of **monitor** typically used on **laptop** or portable **computers**; provides a brighter, more readable display than older **LCD** equipment.

Algorithm. A step-by-step procedure designed to solve a problem or achieve an objective.

Alphanumeric. Consisting of letters, numbers, and symbols.

Antivirus software. A **program** designed to look for and destroy a **virus** that may have infected a **computer's memory** or **files**.

Application (also called *app*). A **program** designed to perform **information processing** tasks for a specific purpose or activity (for example, **desktop publishing** and **database management**).

Archie. A tool for finding a **file transfer protocol (FTP)** server.

Archive. A **file** compressed for more efficient use of storage space. The compression of files may be accomplished by means of such **programs** as WinZip.

Ascending sort. Sorting records from A to Z or 0 to 9. (See *Descending sort.*)

ASCII (pronounced *as-kee*). An acronym derived from American Standard Code for Information Interchange. ASCII is a standard **8-bit** code that represents 256 **characters**. The use of this standard code permits **computers** made by different manufacturers to communicate with one another.

---

*The following works were consulted in preparing this glossary: *Webster's New World Dictionary of Computer Terms*, 7th ed., Macmillan, New York, 1999; *Peter Norton's Introduction to Computers*, 3rd ed., Glencoe, Westerville, OH, 1999; *Microsoft Press Computer Dictionary*, 3rd ed., Redmond, WA, 1997; *The New Hacker's Dictionary*, 3rd ed., MIT Press, Cambridge, MA, 1996; *Wired Style: Principles of English Usage in the Digital Age*, Hardwired, San Francisco, 1996; and www.webopedia.com.

Background printing. The ability of a **computer** to print a **document** while other work is being done on the **keyboard** and the **display screen** at the same time.

Backup. Storage of duplicate **files** on **disks**, diskettes, or some other form of magnetic medium (such as tapes) as a safety measure in case the original medium is damaged or lost. (One word as a noun or an adjective: *backup* procedures; two words as a verb: *back up* your hard disk.)

Bandwidth. The volume of information that a **network** can handle (usually expressed in bits per second). The greater the bandwidth, the more quickly **data** can move from a **network** to a user's **computer**.

Baud rate. The rate of **data** transmission between two **computers** or other equipment.

Binary numbering system. A numbering system in which all numbers are represented by various combinations of the digits 0 and 1.

BIOS (basic input/output system). A set of **programs** stored in **read-only memory** (**ROM**) on IBM-compatible **computers**. These programs control the **disk drives**, the keyboard, and the **display screen**; and they handle start-up operations.

Bit. An acronym derived from b̲inary digi̲t. The smallest unit of information that can be recognized by a **computer**. Bits are combined to represent **characters**. (See also *Byte*.)

Bitmap. A method of storing a graphic image as a set of **bits** in a computer's **memory**. To display the image on the screen, the **computer** converts the bits into **pixels**.

Bits per second (bps). A measurement that describes the speed of **data** transmission between two pieces of equipment. (See *Baud rate*.)

Block. A segment of **text** that is selected so that it can be moved or copied to another location or processed in some other way. (See *Copy; Delete; Cut and paste*.)

Block protect. A **command** to prevent a **page break** from occurring within a block of **text**. (See also *Keep lines together; Keep with next; Widow/orphan protection*.)

Boilerplate. Standard wording (for example, sentences or paragraphs in form letters or clauses) that is held in **storage**. When needed, it can be used as is, with minor modification, or in combination with new material to produce tailor-made documents. (See *Style sheet* and *Templates*.)

Bookmark list. A customized list of a user's favourite Web sites (also referred to as a *hot list*). A bookmark list permits the user to access a particular Web site with a single **command**.

Boot (short for *bootstrap*). To start a **computer** and load the **operating system** to prepare the computer to **execute** an **application**.

Bozo filter. A **program** that screens out unwanted **e-mail** or other messages from individuals or organizations you no longer want to hear from.

bps. See *Bits per second*.

Browser. See *Web browser*.

Buffer. A holding area in **memory** that stores information temporarily. Also called *cache*.

Bug. A defect in the **software** or **hardware** that causes the **computer** to malfunction or cease to operate. (See also *Debugging; Glitch.*)

Bulletin board system (BBS). An electronic message centre serving specific interest **newsgroups**.

Bundled software. Software that is sold along with a **computer** system; several software **programs** packaged together (also called *software suites*).

Bus. An internal pathway along which electronic signals travel between the components of a **computer** system.

Button bar. An on-screen element that offers a user instant **access** to commonly used **commands**. The commands are represented by **icons** on a row of buttons shown at the top of the screen. Also called a *tool bar*.

Byte. The sequence of **bits** that represents a **character**. Each byte has 8 bits.

Cache. See *Buffer.*

Cancelbot (from *cancel robot*). A **program** that detects **spamming** and automatically issues a cancel command.

Card. See *Circuit board.*

Carpal tunnel syndrome. A wrist or hand injury caused by using a keyboard or **mouse** for long periods of time. A type of repetitive strain injury (RSI). (See also *Mouse elbow*).

CD-ROM. An acronym derived from compact disk—read-only memory. A form of optical **storage**. One compact **disk** can hold up to 250 000 **text** pages; it can also be used to store **graphics**, sound, and video. (See *DVD*.)

Cell. A box or rectangle within a table or **spreadsheet** where a **column** and a **row** intersect; an area in which information can be entered in the form of **text** or figures.

Central processing unit (CPU). The brains of an **information processing** system; the processing component that controls the interpretation and execution of instructions. (See *Motherboard*.)

Character. A single letter, figure, punctuation mark, or symbol produced by a **keystroke** on a **computer**. Each character is represented by a **byte**.

Character set. The complete set of **characters**—alphabetic, numeric, and symbolic—displayed on a **computer**. (See *ASCII*.)

Character string. A specified sequence of keyed **characters**, usually representing a word or phrase. A character string is often used to locate a particular word or phrase wherever it appears in a **document** so that it can be automatically replaced with another word or phrase. If a person's name has been consistently misspelled or a date appears incorrectly in several places, the error can be easily corrected. (See also *Find and replace*.)

Characters per inch (cpi). The number of characters in a **monospace font** that will fit within 1 inch; for example, Courier style.

Characters per second (cps). The number of **characters** printed in 1 second; a measurement frequently used to describe the speed of a **printer**.

Chatline. See *Newsgroup.*

Check box. A small square box that appears on screen alongside each option displayed in a **dialog box**. When one or more options are selected, an X or a check mark appears inside the box. (See also *Radio button*.)

Chip. An **integrated circuit** used in **computers**.

Circuit board. A board or card that carries the necessary electronic components for a particular **computer** function (for example, **memory**). The circuit boards that come with the original equipment perform the standard functions identified with that type of equipment. Additional circuit boards expand the kinds of functions that the equipment can perform. (Also called a *board*, a *card*, or an *expansion board*.)

Client/server computing. A **network** of **computers** that consists of a **file server** (a computer that runs a **database management system**) and individual clients (computers that request and process **data** obtained from the file server).

Clipboard. A holding area in **memory** where information that has been copied or **cut** (**text**, **graphics**, sound, or video) can be stored until the information is inserted elsewhere. (See *Copy; Cut; Cut and paste*.)

Coded space. See *Hard space*.

Column. A vertical block of **cells** in a table or **spreadsheet**. (See also *Row*.)

Command. An instruction that causes a **program** or **computer** to perform a function. A command may be given by means of a special **keystroke** (or series of keystrokes), or the command may be chosen from a **menu**.

Compatibility. The ability of one type of **computer** to share information or to communicate with another computer. (See also *ASCII*.)

Computer. An electronic device that is capable of (1) accepting, storing, and logically manipulating **data** or **text** that is **input** and (2) processing and producing **output** (results or decisions) on the basis of stored **programs** of instructions. Some are also capable of processing **graphics**, video, and voice input. Computers include a **keyboard** for **text entry**, a **central processing unit**, one or more **disk drives**, a **display screen**, and a **printer**—components referred to as **hardware**.

Control menu. An on-screen Windows element that appears in a box in the upper right corner of a window. The control menu allows the user the option of adjusting the size of the window, closing or reopening the window, or switching to another window.

Cookie. A device that permits a **Web site** to identify and collect information about every user who visits that site.

Copy. To reproduce information elsewhere. The original information remains in place. (See *Cut*.)

cpi. See *Characters per inch*.

cps. See *Characters per second*.

CPU. See *Central processing unit*.

Crash. A malfunction in **hardware** or **software** that keeps a **computer** from functioning. (See also *Bug; Glitch*.)

Cursor. A special **character** (usually a blinking underline, dot, or vertical line) that indicates where the next keyed character will appear on the **display screen**. Also refers to the **I-beam pointer** or **mouse** pointer (arrow). Microsoft Word refers to the cursor as the *insertion point*. (See also *Prompt*.)

Cursor positioning. The movement of the **cursor** or **I-beam pointer** on the display screen. Most computers have four keys to control up, down, left, and right movement. The **mouse** is also used to position the **cursor**.

Cut. To remove **text** from its original location and place it on a **clipboard**. (See *Paste; Copy.*)

Cut and paste. To move a **block** of **text** from one place to another.

Cyberspace. A realistic simulation of a three-dimensional world created by a **computer** system. Also referred to as *virtual reality.* Now commonly used to refer to the world of the **Internet** as a whole.

Data. Information consisting of letters, numbers, symbols, sounds, or images—in a form that can be processed by a **computer.**

Data compression. A procedure for reducing the volume of **data** so as to shorten the time needed to transfer the data.

Database. A stored collection of information.

Database management system (DBMS). The **software** needed to establish and maintain a **database** and manage the stored information.

Debugging. Locating and eliminating defects in a **program.** (See also *Bug.*)

Decimal tab. A type of tab that aligns **columns** of figures on the decimal point.

Default settings. The pre-established settings (for margins, **font**, type size, tab stops, and so on) that a **program** will follow unless the user changes them.

Delete. A **command** to erase information in **storage.**

Descending sort. Sorting records from Z to A or 9 to 0. (See *Ascending sort.*)

Desktop. The electronic work area on a **display screen.**

Desktop publishing (DTP). A system that processes **text** and **graphics** and, by means of page layout **software** and a **laser printer**, produces high-quality pages suitable for printing or in-house reproduction.

Dialog box. A message box on the screen that supplies information to—or requests information from—the user.

Dictionary. A **program** used to check the spelling of each word entered in the **computer.**

Directory. A list of **files** (**DOS** Application) stored on a **disk**. (See also *Folder.*)

Disk. A random-**access**, magnetically coated storage medium used to store and **retrieve** information. (See also *CD-ROM.*)

Disk drive. The component of a **computer** into which a **disk** is inserted so that it can be read or written on.

Display screen. A device similar to a television screen and used on a **computer** to display **text** and **graphics**. Also called a *cathode-ray tube (CRT)*, a *video display terminal (VDT)*, or a *monitor.*

Distributed processing system. A form of a **local area network** in which each user has a fully functional **computer** but all users can share **data** and **application software**. The data and **software** are distributed among the linked computers and are not stored in one central computer.

20

Document. Any printed business communication—for example, a letter, memo, report, table, or form. (See *File*.)

Domain. Typically, a three-letter element in a Web address or an **e-mail** address. The domain (commonly referred to as the *zone*) indicates the type of organization that owns the **computer** being identified in the address.

Domain name. The second part of an **e-mail** address—what follows the @ symbol. The name of the **computer** intended to receive an e-mail message. In Web addresses **(URLs)** this element is referred to as the **host** name.

DOS (disk operating system). See *MS-DOS*.

Dot. The period symbol used in **e-mail** addresses. Always referred to as a *dot* (never as a period).

Download. To transfer information to the user's **computer** from another computer.

Downtime. The period when equipment is unusable because of a malfunction.

Drag-and-drop editing. A **software** feature that allows the user to (1) highlight **text** to be moved and (2) use a **mouse** to drag the text to a new location.

DVD (digital video disk). A new type of **CD-ROM** that holds a minimum of 4.7 GB *(gigabytes)*, enough for a full-length movie.

Easter egg. An unexpected image or message that pops up on the **display screen** when the user innocently enters a secret combination of **keystrokes**. Programmers playfully code Easter eggs into **software** and **operating systems** as a way of surprising and amusing users engaged in more serious tasks.

Editing. The process of changing information by inserting, deleting, replacing, rearranging, and reformatting. Also known as *changing* or *customizing*.

E-mail (electronic mail). The transfer of messages or **documents** between users connected by an electronic **network**.

Emoticon. An acronym for *emotion icon*, a small **icon** composed of punctuation characters that indicates how an **e-mail** message should be interpreted (that is, the writer's mood). For example, a :-) emoticon indicates that the message should not be taken seriously. Although some emoticons are quite witty, many people find them excessively cute. Therefore, do not use them unless you are sure they will be appreciated. An emoticon is also called a *smiley*.

Encryption. Coding confidential **data** so that only a user with the necessary **password** can read the data.

Enter. To **input data** into **memory**. (See *Type*.)

Ergonomics. The science of adopting working conditions and equipment to meet the physical needs of workers.

Escape key. A key that permits the user to leave one segment of a **program** and move to another.

Execute. To perform an action specified by the user of the **program**.

Export. To save information in a **format** that another program can read.

Extranet. A technology that permits users of one organization's **intranet** to enter portions of another organization's intranet in order to conduct business transactions or collaborate on joint projects.

E-zine. A magazine published in electronic format. Also called *Webzine*.

FAQ. Frequently asked questions. Pronounced as a word (to rhyme with *pack*) or as separate letters.

Fax. A shortened form of the word *facsimile*. A copy of a **document** transmitted electronically from one machine to another.

Fax modem. A device built into or attached to a **computer** that serves as a facsimile machine and a **modem**.

Field. A group of related **characters** treated as a unit (such as a name); also the area reserved for the entry of a specified piece of information.

File. A collection of information stored electronically and treated as a unit by a **computer**. Every file must have its own distinctive name.

File server. **Hardware** and **software** that together provide the handling of **files** and **storage** functions for multiple users on a **local area network**.

File transfer protocol (FTP). A set of guidelines or standards that establish the **format** in which **files** can be transmitted from one **computer** to another.

Find and replace. A **command** that directs the **program** to locate a **character string** or information (**text**, numbers, or symbols) wherever it occurs in a **document** and replace this material with new information.

Firewall. Software that prevents unauthorized persons from accessing certain parts of a **program**, **database**, or **network**.

Flame. A hostile message, often sent through e-mail or posted in a **newsgroup**, from an **Internet** user in reaction to a breach of **netiquette**.

Floppy disk. See *Disk*.

Folder. A storage area (**Windows** application) on a **disk** used to organize files. (See also *Directory*.)

Font. A **typeface** of a certain size and style. Includes all letters of the alphabet, figures, symbols, and punctuation marks. (See *Monospace font; Proportional font*.)

Footer. Repetitive information that appears at the bottom (the foot) of every page of a **document**. A page number is a common footer. (See also *Header*.)

Footnote feature. The ability of a **program** to automatically position footnotes on the same page as the **text** they refer to. If the text is moved to another page, any related footnotes will also be transferred to that page.

Format. The physical specifications that affect the appearance and arrangement of a **document**—for example, margins, spacing, and **font**.

Forum. See *Newsgroup*.

Freenet. A local **network** that offers free (or low-cost) **access** to **host computers** located in libraries and to other public-interest groups in the community.

Freeware. Copyrighted **software** that is available for use without charge. (See also *Shareware*.)

Function keys. Keys on a **keyboard** (for example, F2) that give special **commands** to the **computer**—for example, to set margins or tabs.

Gateway. A machine that links two **networks** using different **protocols**.

20

Gigabyte. One gigabyte is equal to 1024 **megabytes**. Gigabyte is often abbreviated as *G* or *GB*.

Glitch. A **hardware** problem that causes a **computer** to malfunction or **crash**. (See *Bug*.)

Global. Describing any function that can be performed on an entire **document** without requiring individual **commands** for each use.

Graphics. Pictures or images presented or stored using a **computer**.

GUI (graphical user interface). (Pronounced *goo-ee*.) A **software** feature that permits the user to click on **icons** or select options from a **menu**.

Hacker. A dedicated **computer** programmer. This term should not be confused with the term for a computer criminal, a *cracker*, who penetrates and damages a computer program.

Handheld computer. A portable computer smaller than a **notebook computer**. Also called a **palmtop computer**.

Hard copy. **Text** or **graphics** printed on paper; also called a **printout**. (See also *Soft copy*.)

Hard disk. A rigid type of magnetic medium that can store large amounts of information.

Hard hyphen. A hyphen that is a permanent **character** in a word. A word that contains a hard hyphen will not be divided at this point if the word comes at the end of a line. (See also *Soft hyphen*.)

Hard page break. A page-ending code or **command** inserted by the user that must be changed by the user. A hard page break is often used (1) to prevent a table from being divided between two pages and (2) to signify that a particular section of a **document** has ended and the following **text** should start on a new page. (See also *Soft page break*.)

Hard return. A **command** used to end a paragraph, end a short line of **text**, or insert a blank line in the text. (See also *Soft return*.)

Hard space (coded space). A space inserted between words in a phrase that should remain together (for example, the word *page* and the number, month and day, number and unit of measure). The hard space ensures that the phrase will not be broken at the end of a line.

Hardware. The physical components of a **computer**: the **central processing unit**, the **display screen**, the **keyboard**, the **disk drive**, and the **printer**. (See also *Software*.)

Hardwired. Describing any **computer** function that cannot be easily modified.

Header. Repetitive information that appears at the top (the head) of every page of a **document**. A page number is a common header. (See also *Footer*.)

Hit. A single request for information made by a client computer from a Web server. The popularity of a given **Web site** is measured by the number of hits it receives.

Home. The upper left corner of the **display screen**; the starting position of a page or **document**.

Home page. The main page for a **Web site** established by an organization or an individual; it usually serves as the entrance for a series of related pages.

Host computer. A computer that provides information or a service to other computers on the **Internet**. Every host computer has its own unique host name.

Hot key. A **keyboard** shortcut that allows quick access to a **command** or **menu** option.

HTML (hypertext markup language). The formatting language used to establish the appearance of a Web page.

HTTP (hypertext transfer protocol). The **protocol** used on the **World Wide Web** that permits Web clients (**Web browsers**) to communicate with Web servers. This protocol allows programmers to embed **hyperlinks** to Web documents, using **hypertext markup language**.

Hyperlink. A highlighted word or image on a Web page. When a user clicks on a word or image, the user is connected with another related Web page.

Hypermedia. An extension of **hypertext** that integrates audio, video, and **graphics** with **text**.

Hypertext. A technology that links **text** in one part of a **document** with related text in another part of the document or in other documents. A user can quickly find the related text by clicking on the appropriate keyword, key phrase, **icon**, or button.

Hyphenation. The ability of a **program** to automatically hyphenate and divide words that do not fit at the end of a line. If the **text** is later revised so that the divided word no longer begins at the right margin, the hyphen is automatically removed and the word prints solid. (See also *Soft hyphen*.)

I-beam pointer. A **mouse**-controlled **cursor** that looks like a capital *I*.

Icon. A symbol (such as a picture of a trash can or a file folder) that represents a certain function. When the user **clicks** on the icon, the appropriate function is **executed**.

Import. To **retrieve** any **text** or other information created by one **program** (for example, images created by a **graphics** program) and transfer it to another program (for example, a **spreadsheet** program).

Indexing. The ability of a **program** to accumulate a list of key words or phrases that appear in a **document** or a **database** and to print or display the list in a selected order.

Information processing. The co-ordination of people, equipment, and procedures to handle information, including the **storage**, **retrieval**, distribution, and communication of information. The term *information processing* embraces the entire field of processing words, figures, **graphics**, video, and voice **input** by electronic means.

Ink-jet printer. A non-impact printer that forms **characters** by spraying tiny, electrically charged ink droplets on paper.

Input. To **enter** information into the **computer**.

Insert. To add information to a **file**.

Insertion point. See *Cursor*.

Integrated circuit. Multiple electronic components combined on a tiny silicon **chip**. (See *Microprocessor*.)

Interface. The electrical connection that links two pieces of equipment so that they can communicate with each other. Also, the **software** that controls the interaction between the **hardware** and the user.

20

Internet (or Net). A system that links existing **computer networks** into a world-wide network. The Internet may be accessed by means of commercial online services and **Internet service providers**.

Internet service provider (ISP). An organization that provides access to the **Internet** for a fee. These organizations may provide other services in addition to **Internet** access—for example, news, travel services, and financial and shopping information.

Intranet. A private **network** established by an organization for the exclusive use of its employees. **Firewalls** protect outsiders from gaining **access** to an organization's intranet. (See also *Extranet.*)

Justification. Aligning lines of **text** at the left margin, the right margin, both margins, or the centre. Text aligned at both margins is considered *fully justified.* Text aligned only at the left margin is said to have a *ragged right margin.*

Keep lines together. A Microsoft Word feature that prevents a page break within a paragraph. (See *Block protect.*)

Keep with next. A Microsoft Word feature that prevents a page break between the selected paragraph and the following paragraph. (See *Block protect.*)

Kern. To make fine adjustments in the space between any two **characters**.

Key. To **enter characters** into the memory of a **computer**. (*Key* is being replaced by the word *type*. See *Type.*)

Kilobyte. A measurement of a **storage** capacity of a **computer**. A single kilobyte represents 1024 **bytes**. *Kilobyte* may be abbreviated *K* or *KB*; however, *KB* is the clearer abbreviation since *K* also stands for the metric prefix *kilo* (meaning 1000).

LAN. See *Network, Local area networks.*

Landscape orientation. The positioning of a page so that information is printed across the long dimension of the paper. (See *Portrait orientation.*)

Language. The **characters** and procedures used to write **programs** that a **computer** is designed to understand.

Laptop computer. A small portable **computer**; now more commonly called a **notebook** computer.

Laser printer. A non-impact high-resolution printer that uses a rotating **disk** to reflect laser beams onto the paper. (See also *ink-jet printer.*)

LCD (liquid crystal display). A type of **monitor** typically used on **laptop computers** or portable **computers**. (See also *Active matrix display.*)

Line numbering. The ability of a **program** to automatically number each line sequentially in a **document**. The line numbers can be deleted before the preparation of the final **printout**.

Line spacing. The ability of a **program** to automatically change vertical line spacing (for example, from double to single to double again.)

Listserv. Any **software** that manages a **mailing list**.

Load. To transfer information or **program** instructions into a **computer's memory**.

Log off. To exit or leave a **computer** system.

Log on. To **access** a **computer** system.

Macro. A time-saving feature (like telephone speed dialling) that allows the user to store in **memory** a set of keystrokes or **commands** that will accomplish a certain repetitious task.

Mail merge. The process of taking information from a **database** and inserting it into a form letter or other **document** in order to customize the document for an individual recipient. For example, mail merge can be used to create the inside address and the salutation for a form letter.

Mainframe. A large **computer** system.

Megabyte. A measurement of the **storage** capacity of a **computer**. One megabyte represents more than 1 million **bytes**. *Megabyte* may be abbreviated *M* or *MB*; however, *MB* is clearer since *M* also stands for the metric prefix *mega* (meaning 1 million. See also *Gigabyte*.)

Megahertz. A measurement used to identify the speed of the **central processing unit**. One megahertz is equal to 1 million cycles per second.

Memory. The part of a **computer** that stores information. (See also *Storage*.)

> **Random-access memory (RAM).** The temporary memory that allows information to be stored randomly and accessed quickly and directly (without the need to go through intervening **data**).

> **Read-only memory (ROM).** The permanent **memory** of a **computer**; a set of instructions that has been built into the computer by the manufacturer and cannot be accessed or changed by the user.

Menu. A list of choices shown on the **display screen**. For example, a **format** menu would include such options as the type style and the type size to be selected. A menu is often referred to as a *pull-down menu* or a *pop-up menu* because it appears on screen after the user **clicks** on the **menu bar** or on some other item on the screen.

Menu bar. The bar across the top of the screen or window that displays the names of available **menus**.

Merge. A **command** to create one **file** by combining information that is stored in two different locations. For example, a **computer** can merge the **text** in a form letter with a mailing list to produce a batch of letters with a different name, address, and salutation on each letter. (See also *Mail merge*.)

Microcomputer. A small and relatively inexpensive **computer**, commonly consisting of a **display screen**, a **keyboard**, a **central processing unit**, one or more **disk drives**, and a **printer**, with limited **storage** based upon a **microprocessor**. Also referred to as a **laptop computer**.

Microprocessor. An **integrated circuit** on a silicon **chip** that serves as the **central processing unit** of a **computer**.

MIPS. An acronym derived from millions of instructions per second. Used to measure the speed of a **computer**.

Modem. An acronym derived from modulator/demodulator. A device that (1) converts digital signals into tones for transmission over telephone lines and (2) converts the tones back into digital signals at the receiving end.

Monitor. The **display screen** of a **computer**.

Monospace font. A **typeface** such as Courier in which each **character** has exactly the same width; commonly referred to as the *typewriter font*.

20

Motherboard. The **computer's** main **circuit board**, which contains the **central processing unit**, the **memory**, and expansion slots for additional circuit boards (called *cards*).

Mouse. A hand-operated electronic device used to move a **cursor** or pointer on the **display screen**. Mostly used with **microcomputers**.

Mouse elbow. A repetitive strain injury (similar to tennis elbow) that is caused by repeatedly using a **mouse**. (See also *Carpal tunnel syndrome*.)

MS-DOS (pronounced *em-ess-doss*). Derived from Microsoft disk operating system used by IBM-compatible **microcomputers**. Newer operating systems do not rely on **DOS** to the same extent, and it is predicted by some sources that DOS will eventually disappear.

Multimedia. The use of several types of media (such as **text**, **graphics**, animation, sound, and video) in a **document** or an **application**.

Multitasking. The ability of a **computer** to **execute** more than one **program** at a time.

Net. See *Internet*.

Netiquette. A set of guidelines for formatting and composing **e-mail** messages.

Network. A system of interconnected computers.

> **Local area networks (LANs)** use cable to connect a number of **computers** within the same location or at most a 2-mile radius.

> **Wide area networks (WANs)** use telephone lines or other **telecommunication** devices to link **computers** in widely separated locations.

> **Internet** is a system that links existing networks into a worldwide network.

Newsgroup (also called a *chat line* or a *forum*). An electronic discussion group tied into a **bulletin board system**. Each newsgroup is typically organized around a specific interest or matter of concern.

Notebook computer. A portable **computer** slightly smaller than the original **laptop computer** and slightly larger than a **palmtop** computer.

Number crunching. Processing large amounts of numerical **data**.

Object linking and embedding (OLE). A process that permits the user to take material (referred to as an *object*) from one source and **insert** *(embed)* it in another **document**. If the user subsequently makes changes in the original material, those changes will be automatically transferred to the second document as a result of the OLE linking process.

OCR (optical character reader). A device that can scan **text** from **hard copy** and **enter** it automatically into a **computer** for **storage** or **editing**. Also called an *optical scanner*.

Off-line. Referring to the state in which a **computer** is temporarily or permanently unable to communicate with another computer (although it is turned on and capable of performing other functions).

Online. Referring to the state in which a **computer** is turned on and ready to communicate with other computers.

Open. To transfer a **file** from a **disk** into a **computer's memory**.

Operating system (OS). **Software** that manages the internal functions and controls the operations of a **computer**.

Orphan protection. See *Widow/orphan protection*.

Output. The results of a **computer** operation.

Overwriting. Recording and storing information in a specific location on a **storage medium** that destroys whatever had been stored there previously.

Page break. A **command** that tells the **printer** where to end one page and begin the next. (See *Hard page break; Soft page break*.)

Page numbering. The ability of a **program** to automatically print page numbers on the pages that make up an entire **document**. If the document is revised and the total number of pages changes, the page numbering is automatically adjusted.

Pagination. The ability of a **program** to take information and automatically divide it into pages with a specified number of lines per page. If the information is changed because of the addition, deletion, or rearrangement of copy, the material will be automatically repaged to maintain the proper page length. (See also *Soft page break*.)

Palmtop computer. A portable **computer** smaller than a **notebook computer**. Also called a **handheld computer** or a *personal digital assistant (PDA)*.

Password. A user's secret identification code, required to **access** stored material. A procedure intended to prevent information from being accessed by unauthorized persons.

Paste. A **command** that transfers information from a **clipboard** and inserts it in another location. (See *Cut and paste*.)

Patch. A small program that improves an existing piece of **software** or corrects an error in it.

PC (personal computer). A **microcomputer** for personal and office use.

Peripheral. A device that extends the capabilities of a **computer** (for example, a **printer**).

Pixel. An acronym derived from <u>pic</u>ture <u>el</u>ement. The smallest element (a dot) on a **display screen**. Pixels are used to construct images on the screen.

Plug-and-play. The ability to plug in a **peripheral** and have it work without difficulty.

Point. A measurement used to indicate the size of a **font**; 72 points equals 1 inch.

Pop-up menu. A menu that appears in a **dialog box**; often activated by a click of the right-**mouse** button.

Port. A socket on a **computer** into which an external device (such as a printer cable) can be plugged.

Portrait orientation. Positioning paper so that information is printed across the short dimension of the paper. (See *Landscape orientation*.)

Posting. An article sent to a **Usenet** newsgroup.

Print preview. A **software** feature that reduces the pages of a **document** so that a full page, two facing pages, or several pages can be seen on the screen before printing. This feature permits the user to spot and correct problems in **format** and **page breaks**.

Printers. Output devices of various types that produce copy on paper. (See *Ink-jet printer; Laser printer.*)

Program. An established sequence of instructions that tells a **computer** what to do. The term *program* means the same as **software**.

Prompt. An on-screen symbol (for example, a **cursor**) that indicates where to **type** a **command**; a message that indicates what action is to be taken.

Proportional font. A **typeface** in which the width of each **character** varies (as in this sentence), so that the letter *I* takes much less space than the letter *M*. (See *Font.*)

Protocol. A set of standards for exchanging information between **computers**.

Radio button. An on-screen element that allows a user to select one option from a group of items. An empty circle precedes each option not selected. A dot appears in a circle to signify that the user has selected that option.

RAM. See *Memory, random-access.*

Read. To transfer information from an external storage medium into internal storage. (See also *Storage, external* and *internal.*)

Record (n.). A collection of all the information **fields** pertaining to a particular subject.

Redline. A red line through **text** on a draft **document** shows material that may be deleted on a final copy of the document. In some legal applications, the redlining stays on the **file** document so all readers are made aware of the changes in wording. **Printers** that do not support this display will print the material in a shaded panel or in some other manner.

ROM. See *Memory, read-only.*

Row. A horizontal block of **cells** in a table or **spreadsheet**. (See also *Column.*)

RSI. Repetitive strain injury. (See also *Carpal tunnel syndrome; Mouse elbow.*)

Ruler. A bar (displayed on the screen) that shows the width of the page, the margin settings, the paragraph indentions, and the tab stops.

Save. To store a **program** or **data** on a **storage** device such as a **disk**.

Scanner. An **input** device that can copy a printed page into a **computer's memory**, thus doing away with the need to **type** the copy. A scanner can also convert artwork and photographs into a digital **format** and **store** these in memory.

Screen dump (screen capture). A **printout** of what is displayed on the screen, created with the screen print function. (See ¶1398 for an illustration.)

Screen saver. A program that changes the screen display with a moving image. Without the use of a screen saver, a screen image that remains on display for any length of time can damage the screen.

Scroll. To move information horizontally or vertically on a **display screen** so that one can see parts of a **document** that is too wide or too deep to fit entirely on one screen.

Scroll bar. An on-screen element that allows a user to **scroll** by using a **mouse**.

Search engine. A free program that helps Web users locate **data** by means of a key word or concept. Among the most popular search engines are Yahoo!, Excite, WebCrawler, Google, and AltaVista.

Server. A **computer** that delivers **data** to other computers (clients) linked on the same **network**.

Shareware. Software that usually may be **downloaded** and used initially without charge; the author may subsequently ask for some payment. (Compare with *Freeware*.)

Shouting. The use of all-capital letters in **e-mail**; considered a violation of **netiquette**.

Sig block. The signature block that automatically appears at the end of every out-going **e-mail** message. Also referred to as a *.sigfile*.

Smiley. See *Emoticon*.

Soft copy. Information shown on the **display screen**. (See also *Hard copy*.)

Soft hyphen. A hyphen that divides a word at the end of a line; considered soft (non-permanent) because the hyphen will automatically be deleted if the word moves to another position as a result of a change in the **text**. (See *Hard hyphen; Hyphenation*.)

Soft page break. A line inserted by the **program** to show where a page will end. If copy is added or deleted, the original **page break** will be replaced with a new soft page break at the appropriate place. (By contrast, a **hard page break** will remain fixed, no matter what changes are made in the copy.) (See also *Pagination*.)

Soft return. A **software** feature that automatically breaks **text** between words at the right margin. The line ending is considered soft (non-permanent) because the line ending will change if the user adds or deletes **text**. (See *Hard return; Wordwrap*.)

Software. The instructions that a **computer** needs to perform various functions. The term *software* means the same as **program**. (See also *Hardware*.)

Sort. To arrange **fields**, **records**, or **files** in a predetermined sequence.

Spam. The electronic equivalent of junk mail; also called <u>u</u>nsolicited <u>c</u>ommercial <u>e</u>-mail (UCE).

Split screen. The ability of some **programs** to display information in two or more different areas on the screen at the same time. (See also *Windowing*.)

Spreadsheet. A **program** that provides a worksheet with **rows** and **columns** to be used for calculations and the preparation of reports.

Status line. A line of information on the **display screen** that indicates the position of the **cursor**, the page number, the **file** name, and any toggle keys in use (bold, typeover, capitals, etc.).

Storage. The **memory** of a **computer**.

> **External storage.** A **magnetic medium** such as a **disk**, diskette, or tape used to store information; can be removed from the **computer**.

> **Internal storage.** An integral component of a **computer**; cannot be removed.

Store. To place information in **memory** for later use.

Style sheet. A collection of the user's formatting decisions regarding **typeface**, font size, margins, **justification**, paragraph indentions, and the like.

Surfing the net. Browsing through various **Web sites** on the **Internet** in search of interesting things.

TCP/IP (transmission control protocol/Internet protocol). A collection of over 100 **protocols** that are used to connect **computers** and **networks**.

Telecommunications. The process of sending and receiving information by means of telephones, satellites, and other devices.

Telecommuter. An employee who works away from the office (usually at home) and uses a **computer** (1) to **access** needed information on the organization's **intranet** and the **Internet** and (2) to communicate with other employees, suppliers, and customers or clients.

Teleconferencing. Conducting a conference by using **computers**, video, and **telecommunications** to share sound and images with others at remote sites.

Template. A pre-established **format** for a **document**, stored in a **computer**. The template determines the margins, the type style and size to be used for the **text**, placement instructions for various elements (such as the date line), and design specifications for certain items (such as a letterhead). A user can simply call up the appropriate template, **insert text** where needed, and then print a final document. The user can modify the original template or create a new template to satisfy personal preferences.

Terminal. Any device that can transmit or receive electronic information.

Text. The written material to be displayed on a screen or printed on paper.

Tool bar. See *Button bar*.

Touchpad. The device on a laptop computer that takes the place of a **mouse**.

Touchscreen technology. The technology that permits a user to perform a function simply by touching the screen in an appropriate spot.

Type. To enter **characters** into the **memory** of a **computer**. For a number of years, the verb *type* began to be replaced by the verb *key* as a way of emphasizing the difference between a **computer** and a typewriter. However, the simpler verb *type* has made a comeback in computer terminology and is now the word commonly seen in users' manuals and on **display screens**.

Typeover. See *Overwriting*.

Upload. To transfer information from a **client computer** to a **host** computer.

URL (uniform resource locator). The specific Web address for an individual or organization. (See ¶1537.)

Usenet (from Users' Network). A **bulletin board system** that hosts thousands of **newsgroups**.

User-friendly. A description for equipment or **application software** that is easy to use.

Userid (pronounced *user-eye-dee*). The name a person must use, along with a **password**, to gain **access** to restricted areas on a **network**.

Variable. Information in a standard **document** that changes each time the document is produced (for example, the name and address in a form letter).

Virtual reality. See *Cyberspace*.

Virus. A **program** designed as a prank or as a malicious act. When a virus invades another program, it can cause serious damage to **memory** or **disks**. (See *Antivirus software*.)

WAN. See *Network, Wide area networks*.

Web browser. Software that permits a user—with the click of a **mouse**—to locate, display, and download **text**, video, audio, and **graphics** stored in a **host computer** on the Web. Common Web browsers are Netscape Navigator and Microsoft Explorer.

Webcaster. An **application** that can be custom-tailored to satisfy each user's need for constantly updated information in specific areas and will automatically deliver the needed information to the user's **computer**.

Webmaster. The person who maintains a specific **Web site** and is responsible for what appears there.

Web site. One or more related pages created by an individual or organization and posted on the **World Wide Web**. (See *Home page*.)

Widow/orphan protection. The ability of a **program** to avoid printing the first line of a paragraph as the last line of a page and to avoid printing the last line of a paragraph as the first line of the following page.

Windowing. The ability of a **program** to split its **display screen** into two or more segments so that the user can view several different **documents** or perform several different functions simultaneously. (See also *Split screen*.)

Wizard. A feature of Microsoft Word **software** that helps a user create a customized **document**; it asks the user questions about formatting and content options and uses the answers to create the document. (In WordPerfect this feature is called an *expert*.)

Word processing. The electronic process of creating, formatting, **editing**, proof-reading, and printing **documents**. (See *Information processing*.)

Wordwrap. A **software** feature that detects when a word will extend beyond the right margin and automatically transfers it to the beginning of the next line.

World Wide Web. The component of the **Internet** that combines audio, video, and **graphics** with **text**. Also called the *Web* or *WWW*.

 See the Online Learning Centre at www.mcgrawhill.ca/college/gregg for related weblinks.

INDEX

This index contains many entries for individual words. If you are looking for a specific word that is not listed, refer to ¶719, which contains a 12-page guide to words that are frequently confused because they sound alike (for example, *capital-capitol-Capitol* or *stationary-stationery*).

NOTE: The **boldface** numbers in this index refer to paragraph numbers; the lightface numbers refer to page numbers.

dialogues, quoted, **269–270**
dictation, **1206**
dictionaries, 545
  abbreviations in, **503**
  American usage, **721**
  British usage, **721**
  Canadian usage, **721**
  irregular verbs, **1030**
  in word processing software, 177
differ about-differ from-differ with, **1077**
different, **1067**
different-differently, 290–291
different from-different than, **1077**
dimensions, **432, 535**
diplomats, **1809**
direct address
  commas, **145**
  defined, 532
  titles in, **315**
direct object, 534
direct questions, **110–113, 229,** 537
direct quotation, **227–234,** 537
directory, 545
disk, 545
disk drive, 545
display screen, 545
dissertation, unpublished, **1520**
distributed processing system, 545
doctoral degrees (form of address), **1804b**
document, 546
domain, 546
domain name, 546
done, 291
don't (do not), 291
DOS. *See* MS-DOS
dot, 546
double negatives, **1074**
doubt (expression of), **118**
doubt that-doubt whether, 291
download, 546
downtime, 546
Dr. with degrees, **519c**
drag-and-drop editing, 546
due to-because of-on account of, 291
Duke of Edinburgh, **1808b**
Duke of York, **1808d**
DVD (digital video disk), 546

E

e, words ending in (silent), **707–709**
e-business/e-commerce, **903**
e-mail
  addresses, **1534, 1709**
  bozo filter, **1708b**
  definition, 546
  distribution, **1708–1709**

e-mail *(continued)*
  flame, **1707h**
  format, **1710**
  guidelines, **1707–1710**
  résumés, **1711g**
  short *vs.* long messages, **1707**
  sources, **1537**
  spam, **1708b**
e-zine, 547
each, 289, **1009**
each other-one another, 291
eager-anxious, 286
easter egg, 546
editing, 546
  abbreviation style, **1204c**
  capitalization errors, **1204c**
  at the computer, **1202**
  grammar errors, **1204d**
  meaning, **1204e**
  numbers, errors in, **1204c**
  objective of document, **1204g**
  organization problems, **1204f**
  process, **1201**
  punctuation marks, **1204b**
  spell checker, **1204a**
  usage errors, **1204d**
  writing style, **1204f**
education officials (forms of address), **1805**
effect-affect, 284–285
ei in words, **712**
either, **1009**
either...or, **1003–1005**
electronic mail. *See* e-mail
ellipsis marks, **274–280,** 292, **920g**
elliptical clauses, 531, **1082d, 1083**
elliptical expressions, 532
elliptical question, **111**
elliptical sentences, 538
emoticon, 546
emperors, **1810a**
en-dash, **216d**
enclosure notations, **1373–1374, 1395o**
encryption, 546
endnote feature, **1505**
endnotes (*see also* source reference notes)
  definition, **1501c**
  format, **1505–1506**
  keying in, **1501e**
  popularity of, **1501e**
  reports, **1403c, 1404b, 1430**
  text references to, **1502**
ensure-insure-assure, 291
enter, 546
enthused over, 291
enumerations
  breaks within, **920f**
  colons before, **188–191**

enumerations *(continued)*
  formal report, **1425f**
  in letter, **1357d**
  outlines, **1723c**
  parentheses with, **222–223**
envelopes, **1388–1393**
  attention line, **1389m**
  Canada Post style, **1390**
  folding letters, **1393**
  inserting letters, **1393**
  inside-address style, **1389**
  international addresses, **1392**
  sizes, **1388**
  typewriter formatting, **1389k**
  for U.S. address, **1391**
  window, and attention line, **1345**
equal-together-both alike, 289
equally as good, 292
ergonomics, 546
escape key, 546
Esq., **157, 518, 1324**
essential clauses, 531
essential elements, 532
essential expressions, **149–150, 260, 261c**
essential phrases, 536
etc., **164,** 286, 292
ever, **1072**
every, **1009**
every day-everyday, 292
every one-everyone, **1010**
ex-former, 292
except, 292, **1055b**
exclamation point, **119–121**
  and *O,* **121**
  with *oh,* **121**
  within parentheses, **119c**
  parentheses around, **119c**
  in place of question mark, **119b**
  with quotation mark, **249**
  strong feeling (expression of), **119–120**
exclamations, interruption of, **208**
exclamatory sentences, 538
execute, 546
executive documents
  agendas, 484, 485, 486, **1703**
  fax cover sheets, **1706**
  itineraries, 490–491, **1705**
  minutes, 487, 488–489, **1704**
explanatory expressions, **148–152**
export, 546
external storage, 555
extranet, 546

F

family titles, **318–319**
FAQ, 547
farther-further, 292
fax, 547

COMMON CANADA POST STREET TYPE ABBREVIATIONS

Street Type	Symbol	Street Type	Symbol	Street Type	Symbol
Avenue	AVE	Heights	HTS	Plaza	PLAZA
Bay	BAY	Highway	HWY	Point	PT
Boulevard	BLVD	Key	KEY	Range	RG
Centre	CTR	Lane	LANE	Ridge	RIDGE
Circle	CIR	Loop	LOOP	Rise	RISE
Close	CLOSE	Mall	MALL	Road	RD
Court	CRT	Meadow	MEADOW	Route	RTE
Cove	COVE	Mews	MEWS	Square	SQ
Crescent	CRES	Mount	MT	Street	ST
Drive	DR	Mountain	MTN	Terrace	TERR
Estates	EST	Orchard	ORCH	Trail	TRAIL
Freeway	FWY	Park	PK	View	VIEW
Gate	GATE	Parkway	PKY	Village	VILLGE
Green	GREEN	Place	PL	Way	WAY

AROUND THE WORLD TIME DIFFERENCES

Country(ies)	Time Differences*				Country(ies)	Time Differences*			
	PST	MST	CST	EST		PST	MST	CST	EST
American Samoa	–6	–5	–4	–3	Bahrain, Commonwealth of Ind. States/ Russia, Iraq, Kenya, Kuwait, Saudi Arabia, Turkey	11	10	9	8
Tahiti	–5	–4	–3	–2					
Belize, El Salvador Guatemala, Mexico	2	1	0	–1	Iran	11.5	10.5	9.5	8.5
Colombia, Ecuador, Haiti, Panama, Peru	3	2	1	0	United Arab Emirates	12	11	10	9
Bolivia, Chile, Paraguay Venezuela	4	3	2	1	Pakistan	13	12	11	10
Argentina, Brazil Guyana	5	4	3	2	India, Sri Lanka	13.5	12.5	11.5	10.5
United Kingdom	8	7	6	5	Indonesia, Thailand	15	14	13	12
Austria, Belgium, Denmark, France, Germany, Italy, Luxembourg, Netherlands, Nigeria, Norway, Poland, Spain, Sweden, Switzerland, Tunisia	9	8	7	6	Hong Kong, Malaysia, Philippines, Singapore, Taiwan	16	15	14	13
					Japan, Korea	17	16	15	14
Cyprus, Egypt, Finland, Greece, Israel, Libya, Romania, S. Africa	10	9	8	7	Australia, Guam, New Guinea	18	17	16	15
					New Zealand	20	19	18	17

*See ¶534 for explanation of all Canadian time zones.